Women in Early Medieval Europe is not j.... .... or women, but a history of the early European Middle Ages through the eyes of women. Most books about medieval women focus on such gendered topics as family and marriage, women's work, queenship, or women's status. This book combines the rich literature of women's history with original research in the context of mainstream history and traditional chronology.

It begins at the end of the Roman empire and ends at the start of the twelfth century, when women and men set out to test the old frontiers of Europe. The book recreates the lives of ordinary women but also tells personal stories of individuals. Each chapter also questions an assumption of medieval historiography, paraphrasing the famous query posed by the historian Joan Kelly-Gadol, "Did women have a renaissance?" Did women have an invasion? A Christianization? A war? An intellectual life? An economic expansion? A dream of political power? *Women in Early Medieval Europe* uses the few documents produced by women themselves, along with archaeological evidence, art, and the written records of medieval men, to tell of women, their experiences and ideas, and their relations with men. It covers the Continent and its exotic edges, such as Iceland, Ireland, and Iberia; and it treats both Christian and non-Christian women.

LISA M. BITEL is Professor of History, University of Southern California. She studied at Harvard University, the National University of Ireland, and the Dublin Institute for Advanced Studies. Her books include *Isle of the Saints: Christian Settlement and Monastic Community in Early Ireland* (1990), and *Land of Women: Tales of Sex and Gender from Early Ireland* (1996) – winner of the Byron Caldwell Prize and the James Donnelly Prize.

Cambridge Medieval Textbooks

This is a series of specially commissioned textbooks for teachers and students, designed to complement the monograph series Cambridge Studies in Medieval Life and Thought by providing introductions to a range of topics in medieval history. This series combines both chronological and thematic approaches, and will deal with British and European topics. All volumes in the series will be published in hard covers and in paperback.

For a list of titles in the series, see end of book.

WOMEN IN EARLY MEDIEVAL EUROPE, 400—1100

LISA M. BITEL

CAMBRIDGE
UNIVERSITY PRESS

PUBLISHED BY THE PRESS SYNDICATE OF THE UNIVERSITY OF CAMBRIDGE
The Pitt Building, Trumpington Street, Cambridge, United Kingdom

CAMBRIDGE UNIVERSITY PRESS
The Edinburgh Building, Cambridge CB2 2RU, UK
40 West 20th Street, New York, NY 10011-4211, USA
10 Stamford Road, Oakleigh, VIC 3166, Australia
Ruiz de Alarcón 13, 28014 Madrid, Spain
Dock House, The Waterfront, Cape Town 8001, South Africa

http://www.cambridge.org

© Lisa M. Bitel, 2002

This book is in copyright. Subject to statutory exception
and to the provisions of relevant collective licensing agreements,
no reproduction of any part may take place without
the written permission of Cambridge University Press.

First published 2002

Printed in the United Kingdom at the University Press, Cambridge

Typeface Bembo 10.75/12.5 pt   *System* LATEX 2$_\varepsilon$ [TB]

A catalogue record for this book is available from the British Library

Library of Congress Cataloguing in Publication data

ISBN 0 521 59207 0 hardback
ISBN 0 521 59773 0 paperback

Frontispiece. Ende, Beatus of Gerona, *c.* 975, "The whore of Babylon"

To Mary Cameron Bitel
and in memory of
Mary McCorrison Rosenbloom

CONTENTS

——————— • ———————

ILLUSTRATIONS

———— • ————

MAPS

ACKNOWLEDGMENTS

— • —

This book exemplifies the feminist commitment to collective action. The flaws in it are mine but many of the insights come directly from the generous contributions of friends and colleagues. Many scholars read and criticized drafts of chapters, thus inspiring and correcting me. I especially want to thank Judith Baskin, Jenny Jochens, and Lynda Coon, who participated with me in an inspiring conference panel; the anonymous reader from Cambridge University Press, who made substantive and improving suggestions; Jason Glenn, Willis Johnson, Jo Ann McNamara, David Duncan, and the many other participants in the *medfem-l* discussion list who contributed bibliographic suggestions. Members of the History Departments at the University of Canterbury and the University of Southern California supplied much useful criticism of Chapter Two. At the University of Kansas, I must thank Luis Corteguera, Marta Vicente, Richard Ring, Carolyn Nelson, Jasonne O'Brien, Joanne Nagel, and all others who regularly attended the Hall Center for the Humanities faculty seminars where I presented papers. Funding from the Hall Center as well as the Keeler Family Intra-University Faculty Fellowship allowed me to spend a year researching and writing and also learning how to interpret visual evidence. Marilyn Stokstad has been my mentor in the history of art. Summer grants from the General Research Fund at the University of Kansas sent me to archives and museums. Rosemary Williams was my thorough and cheerful copy editor. Research assistants Marie Kelleher, June Mecham, and Jennifer Thibodeaux helped with notes and bibliography.

I owe the most to Peter Mancall, who has read every word of this book too many times, made suggestions for improvement too numerous to list (and too rude to reprint), and provided endless support of all kinds. In thanks I can only renew my vow to love, honor, and edit.

ABBREVIATIONS

———— · ————

Cod. Theo.	*Codex Theodosianus*, ed. P. Krüger and T. Mommsen, 3 vols. (Berlin: Weidmann, 1905)
McNeill and Gamer	*Medieval Handbooks of Penance*, ed. and trans. John T. McNeill and Helena M. Gamer (New York: Columbia University Press, 1936, repr. New York: Octagon Books, 1965)
Mansi	*Sacrorum Conciliorum Nova et Amplissima Collectio*, ed. Giovanni Domenico Mansi, 60 vols. (Paris: Hubert Welter, 1901–27)
MGH	*Monumenta Germaniae Historica*
AA	*Auctores Antiquissimi* (Berlin: Weidmann, 1877–1919)
Cap.	*Capitularia Regum Francorum* (*Legum Sectio* II), ed. Alfred Boretius and Viktor Krause (Hanover: Hahn, 1883–97)
Concilia 1	*Concilia Aevi Merovingici* (*Legum Sectio* III), ed. Friedrich Maassen (Hanover: Hahn, 1893)
Concilia 2	*Concilia Aevi Karolini* (*Legum Sectio* III), ed. Albert Werminghoff (Hanover: Hahn, 1906–8)
Epistolae	*Epistolae* (Berlin: 1887–)
Leges	*Leges Nationum Germanicarum* (Hanover: Hahn, 1892–)
SSRG	*Scriptores Rerum Germanicarum in Usum Scholarum* (Hanover: Hahn, 1871–)

SSRL	*Scriptores Rerum Langobardicarum et Italicarum,* (Hanover: Hahn, 1885–1951)
SSRM	*Scriptores Rerum Merowingicarum,* ed. B. Krusch and W. Levison (Hanover: Hahn, 1885–1951)
SS	*Scriptores* (Hannover: Hahn, 1826–1934)
PL	*Patrologiae Cursus Completus . . . series Latina,* ed. J.-P. Migne, 221 vols. (Paris: Garnier, 1844–64)
WASW	*Anglo-Saxon Wills,* ed. Dorothy Whitelock (Cambridge University Press, 1930)
WEHD 1	*English Historical Documents,* ed. Dorothy Whitelock, vol. 1, *c. 500–1042,* 2nd edn (London: Routledge, 1979)

INTRODUCTION

———————— • ————————

This book has many queens, saints, and troublemaking females in it, but it is mostly about the generations of ordinary women who inhabited Europe over seven centuries, from about 400 to 1100. We will never know most of them by name. No one wrote stories about these women, so far as we can tell, nor even remembered them after they died. Only stray manuscript references confirm that they did, indeed, exist. "And then a certain woman came to the saint," a hagiographer declared carelessly, dismissing all the woman's days in a casual few words before turning back to his real concern, a holy man. "The king's son" who had many adventures in a saga or epic poem provides the only hint that his mother once existed, married, had a child, had a life. Women rise from medieval documents as shadows marked only by affiliation to individual men fully lit by the gaze of scribes: the wife who stood by her husband when he donated a piece of property to a church or the king's daughter who passed through a written chronicle when she left her father's house to marry another man. Other women come to us not from medieval books and scrolls but from the dirt and rubbish of the past: shards of cookpots or bits of spinning gear at an archeological dig lead us to the hidden place of women.

This book is also about men. More men than women were literate in medieval Europe, hence men wrote most of what we know about medieval women. They decided who should enter the historical documents, who should have a name in the written records of memory, and who was lost forever. They wrote stories and expressed opinions

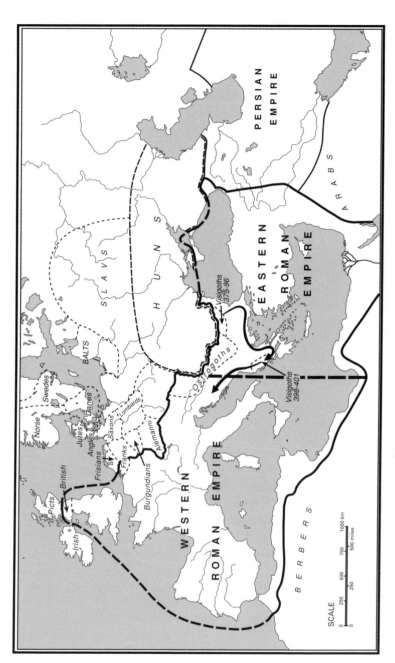

Map 1 Europe c. 400, showing Frankish and other tribes

about women, generated rules for how women should behave, and decided what was to happen when a woman erred. They were also the lords, warriors, and ecclesiastics who governed medieval societies and their religions. They owned most of the property and conducted most of the business. Still, women lurk in men's stories and in stories of men; female voices come to us sometimes in documents composed by the rare literate woman herself, but more often, faintly, through the tales and rules of men. Women colluded in the ideals that men recorded. They supported or disobeyed men's rules, but either way they lived in the communities and kingdoms supposedly guided and guarded by men. They lived and worked with, loved and hated men every day. Some women did own property, even a lot of property, and they bought from, sold to, and traded with men and with each other. But men were officially in charge of everything, both deeds and written records of them.

Today, both women and men who are professional historians take what evidence is left of medieval women and shape our memory of the distant European past. Nineteenth-century work on famous women, women's legal status, and religious activities of women has given way, in the past couple of decades, to anthropological and literary studies that let us rediscover normal women and the workings of everyday life. Scholars of literature have enlarged the medieval canon by adding newly discovered works by women. Along with historians, they have reinserted women into the written past. Although historians of women have spent a good deal of time arguing over whether women of the past were authors or objects, victims or agents, they have, at least, come to see and hear women in the documents and material evidence.[1]

And yet, despite such recoveries revealed in articles, monographs, conference papers, movies, and websites, men's memory and men's history remain the norm in which female actors participate, while women's history exists on a discrete timeline. Teachers still build their history classes upon a base of imperial decline and fall. Kingdoms still flourish, late medieval degeneracy flowers into the Renaissance. Students still learn traditional history first, only to revise its chronologies, contents, and focuses when they study women's past. Many

[1] Susan Mosher Stuard and Margaret Schaus, "Citizens of No Mean City: Medieval Women's History," *Journal of Women's History* 6:3 (1994), 170–98; Judith M. Bennett, "Medievalism and Feminism," in *Studying Medieval Women: Sex, Gender, Feminism*, ed. Nancy Partner (Cambridge, MA: Medieval Academy of America, 1993), 7–29.

authors of textbooks simply insert new female characters into the old historical pictures dependent upon the documents of men interpreted in light of male-focused history. They might add wives and mothers to a discussion of society, include some queens in political histories, write a new section on mystics and other practitioners of women's spirituality. Scholars arrange historical events, as well as art and literature, into a teleology conceived by men for male thinkers and artists. As a result, women's experience must be fitted into men's categories. For modern writers and readers, women participated in our collective past but they did not shape its pedagogical contours.

The history of medieval women remains a specialized topic. Can a general history of the early European Middle Ages be written without Charlemagne and the kingdom of the Franks? Can historians ignore the creation of the papacy, the voyages of the Vikings, or the introduction of the heavy plough and substitute a discussion of spinning and the making of clothes? Most historians and teachers would find such suggestions preposterous. But can a book be written about the early Middle Ages without reference to the legal disenfranchisement of women everywhere, the contributions of women to normative religious practice, shifts in female mortality, or any discussion of mothering? Though not every book about the Middle Ages has to treat women and their activities, we must not ignore what we have learned about our collective past from the memory of men's lives alone. Books that treat mainly men, or treat the past from the perspective of men, must be recognized as such. The shape of the Middle Ages, its periodization, ideas about historical change, and even the very concept of the Middle Ages come from the minds of men.

I am certainly not the first to suggest a challenge to the gendered position of previous histories.[2] "By God," exclaimed the Wife of Bath, a character created by a fourteenth-century man named Geoffrey Chaucer,

> if wommen hadde writen stories
> As clerkes han withinne hire oratories,
> They wolde han writen of men moore wikkednesse
> Than al the mark of Adam may redresse.[3]

---

[2] Kathleen Biddick, "Genders, Bodies, Borders: Technologies of the Visible," in Partner, *Studying Medieval Women*, 87–116.

[3] Geoffrey Chaucer, *Wife of Bath's Prologue*, ll. 693–96; in *Canterbury Tales*, trans. and ed. David Wright (Oxford University Press, 1985).

Putatively new questions and new approaches constantly inspire those who study medieval women.[4] Many recent studies on topics as varied as burial, serfdom, romance literature, private life, and romanesque architecture have begun to open the eyes of readers and colleagues to the acts of interpretation that contribute to the written history of both men and women. In this book I build on previous works of history, literary criticism, and art history, as well as the work of feminist theorists and social scientists. I steal what I can from historians of men. I also examine the medieval texts, art, and material evidence already used by others.

Men move through these chapters freely, although this study favors women. While I use this book to tell the history of seemingly unimportant women, I also aim to analyze what we already know from a woman-focused perspective. Hence, I rehearse here the history of well-known political, economic, social, and cultural developments of the period between the traditional bookends of medieval history. I treat some of the famous women who have already barged into mainstream history. I treat a period, which I call the early Middle Ages, defined by population movements and political change and marked for convenience with the years 400 to 1100. I begin with the migrations of Germanic tribes and Christian missionaries, and the creation of kingdoms; I finish with the travels of Europeans to the frontiers of their inward-looking continent. I chart familiar events and changes such as the Christianization of northern Europe, the expansion of literate cultures, the practice of agriculture, the structure of kinship and kingship, Viking incursions, influences of the Carolingian empire and its disintegration, economic developments of the tenth and later centuries. The book ends with the eleventh century not because that century was the most significant of the Middle Ages, but because changes of that period were particularly transformative for European

---

[4] Eileen Power (d. 1940), wrote *Medieval Women* (Cambridge University Press, 1975, repr. 1994) in order to provide a study of women "fuller and better grounded in evidence than any of the existing books on the subject," according to her husband and posthumous editor, M. M. Postan (see p. 7). The book originated in radio lectures given shortly before her death, when she was best known for her many years of teaching at the London School of Economics, and for her pioneering work in comparative economic and social history. Postan assembled the lectures that became Power's book, corrected the facts "at variance with results of more recent researches," and wrote the notes and the bibliography (8). For "new" histories of medieval women see also Nancy Partner, *Studying Medieval Women*, Introduction, esp. 24–27.

women and gender systems. Throughout the book, I also challenge the traditional events and structures of early medieval historiography as central to our understanding of medieval Europe and its women.[5] By casting familiar history from a differently gendered angle of enquiry, I transform some historical developments into footnotes, while the dim parentheses and sidebars of other surveys become illuminated as whole chapters in this book.

EVIDENCE

The making of a good marriage, the practice of housewifery, the spinning and weaving of cloth, the production and nurturing of children, and the individual personalities of unremarkable women good and bad all went unrecorded in official documents of memory. But the lives of women in the perilous pre-millennial period are not completely lost. We can use the texts to detect women's experience, their business, and sometimes even their thoughts. Codes of written laws exist from almost every major early medieval kingdom. Councils of Christian leaders met constantly all over Europe to generate idealistic rules for the management of churches and behavioral norms for typical Christians, which they wrote down as penitentials, canons, and decrees. Intellectuals and scholars – a few of them women – meditated upon life, God, and the cosmos and in the process often discussed the nature of Woman, the organization of the family, or the purpose and conduct of gender relations. Preachers urged women and men to lead better lives, incidentally describing their actual behavior. Charters, contracts, and wills tell of economic transactions, property rights, and social interaction. The lives of saints, written by clerics, contrast the ideal of holy conduct with the acts of other, normal people. Poems, sagas, and epics reveal heroines, villainesses, goddesses, and women warriors, as well as lovers, mothers, and an assortment of fictional but historically useful females. Carvings, frescoes, and manuscripts depict women real and ideal. We even have histories written on the spot by men who

---

[5] On change and continuity in women's history, see the review article by Catherine Peyroux, "Lands of Women? Writing the History of Early Medieval Women in Ireland and Europe," *Early Medieval Europe* 7 (1998), 217–27; Judith Bennett, "History that Stands Still: Women's Work in the European Past," *Feminist Studies* 14 (1988), 269–83; Bridget Hill, "Women's History: A Study in Change, Continuity, or Standing Still?" *Women's History Review* 2 (1993), 5–22.

watched the actions of real women and, occasionally, noted them down.

A very few women wrote. Radegund, saint and queen of Francia in the sixth century, composed, or at least inspired, a lengthy poem about her tragic childhood abduction and the destruction of her family. "I, the barbarian woman, seek not to count these tears," she wrote, "Nor to keep afloat in the melancholy lake of all those drops. Each one had her own tears; I alone have them all. Anguish is private and public both to me."[6] Whatever she revealed about her personal devastation many years before she wrote, Radegund gave a feminine account of the devastations of war meant for an audience. A few others wrote epistles, too: the ninth-century noblewoman Dhuoda sent desperate advice to her son, various queens responded to bishops' pleas, abbesses confided in colleagues. Some women scholars described other women; Baudonivia, a nun in the house of Radegund, wrote a life of her abbess and surrogate mother. Hrotsvit, another nun (d. 975) inscribed poetry, plays, and history. But the great flowering of women's writing did not occur until the end of the early Middle Ages. In the twelfth century, and in my last chapter, the reluctant abbess Heloise engages in theology while Hildegard, the scholar and mystic, puts her migrainous mind to work in a multitude of written genres, and Marie de France writes romance. Before that, though, documents held more female characters and types than authentic female voices. The eloping lover, the wicked queen, the lowly peasant wife, the humble nun may have influenced their literary existence in the sources, but did not write for themselves.

All of these documentary bits and pieces, as well as images and archaeological remains, combine to revive our memory of wives, mothers, and women workers struggling to make families, make ends meet, make order in an often violent world. Most of the women in any particular place at any given time aimed, the diverse evidence suggests, simply to live as well as possible and to help their loved ones to do likewise. Their most useful strategy was participation in the basic institutions and functions of patriarchally organized life: marriage, pregnancy, and mothering, and all the tasks that supported their prescribed social and biological roles. Who is to say that women did not choose, and enjoy choosing, such officially described social

---

[6] Jo Ann McNamara and John E. Halborg, ed. and trans., *Sainted Women of the Dark Ages* (Durham, NC: Duke University Press, 1992), 66. See also 65, n. 22.

spaces? Yet for such common ambitions individual women were never remembered. While a man who achieved peace by his deeds of war entered poetry and the hearts of later generations, anonymity was the only reward for a woman who accomplished the mundane goals that enabled communities to continue and flourish.

Hence, the rulebreakers loom largest in both the medieval evidence and in our own collective, historical memory of the early Middle Ages. Queens and noblewomen who seemed to medieval observers to achieve masculine political power were far more interesting than anonymous women. The criminals who broke men's rules, the women who defied gendered custom and social expectations to achieve the unexpected, dominate medieval history. Some anomalous women were admirable in the eyes of their medieval storytellers, but more were bad: negligent mothers, cutthroat queens, amorous nuns, amazons and valkyries, demented women, whores. Their behavior contributed to the larger ideology of Woman that, in turn, justified the subjugation of all women in the names of philosophy, religion, and nature. There were not enough atypical women to threaten longterm social change though, which made it safe for the literati of early medieval Europe to express fascination with them in the documents.

Since even the most innovative methods cannot recover all the lost women of early medieval Europe, the rulebreakers dominate this book's story of women, too. Queens, woman scholars, religious leaders, and evil women move through this book as representatives of other women's experience. St. Genovefa of Paris showed medieval readers and writers what it was like for women to cross the earliest medieval landscapes of the continent. Brynhild, the valkyrie, typified for medieval people the Germanic queen of legend, while Clothild, wife of the first king of the united Franks, represented the Christianizing women of tribal histories and saints' lives. St. Brigit of Ireland and Queen Radegund of the Franks were likewise paradigmatic Christians. Dhuoda, a Frankish noblewoman of the ninth century, was a good mother. Unnr, a pioneer who sailed to Iceland, was a settler of Europe's edge. Heloise was a famous scholar, Hildegard a famous visionary, and Emma of England a powerful ruler. But although these female figures shared some aspects of gendered existence with ordinary women, other aspects of their experience prevent them from being genuinely representative of the rest who lived between 400 and 1100 CE. They were all born of men's expectations and men's pens rather than of women; even those among them who were verifiably real took on fictional aspects in the documents. I may seem to use them as typical but you, the reader, must never forget that they are merely emissaries from the past: they speak in diplomatic voices that are not necessarily their own. Their native tongues and customs are far more exotic than first impressions suggest.

THE NATURE OF THIS BOOK

How have other historians begun their histories of medieval Europe? Mostly with the fall of Rome, the depopulation of the continent, the onslaught of the barbarians, and the penetration of Christianity – all interpreted, generally, as the failures and successes of men on the map of Europe. But the theatre for these trends and events was the land itself. Men and women dwelt upon it and moved over it before, during, and after it was called Roman, and later by the many names of medieval peoples and kings. Hence this book begins with the earth and the bodies that lived upon it at the dawn of the Middle Ages, when the literate still divided the world into more or less Roman regions.

With so many medieval landscapes to choose from, it is simplest to begin Chapter One at the beginning of the Middle Ages. Investigations of problems related to environment, such as questions posed by demographic data (how many women did the land support, for how long?), evidence for settlement (where did they live and with whom?), and movement upon the land (where did they go and when?) can direct our survey of the gendered landscape. When we come to understand medieval women's own thoughts about their various environments, and the role of women in others' thoughts about the natural and supernatural worlds, we may well clear a new path through the brambles of historiography to the Middle Ages of women.

The following chapters chart women's participation in the major historical developments of early Europe, such as the so-called barbarian invasions or migrations. Since Edward Gibbon finished his *Decline and Fall of the Roman Empire* in 1788, medieval historians have understood the period between about 300 and 900 CE as a time of mass movements: men from the east and north and south battering down the vestiges of the civilized Roman empire, sweeping into what are now France, Italy, Spain, and Britain to create a new Europe.

According to this stirring story, the origins of the Middle Ages lay not in the landscape or in the *romanitas* that once saturated it, nor even in resident populations, but in the hardy warriors who took the land by force. Those on the move overcame those in place. But women did not participate in this traditional picture since women of all stations and origins could not move as freely as men – not legitimately, not as often, not without the permission of men.

There were exceptions. St. Genovefa, the fifth-century patron of Paris who was exceptional in so many ways, roamed her province, preaching and healing. She coasted the Seine with more bravado than any of her male sailors, and marched off to far cities without a second thought. Other noble holy women, such as the Anglo-Saxon abbesses, did the same. Still, all these Christian ladies were rooted to particular churches and monasteries. Rather than rambling like missionaries, they always returned to their sanctuaries. Other kinds of heroines rampaged across the landscapes of the sagas and poetry of the invasion period. But these shield-maidens and killer-queens were fictional figments. Real queens and princesses occasionally ran away, either to seek new mates or to find God; either way, they were running to another place where they would, presumably, stay put. The few extraordinary females who were mobile and prominent in the early medieval period were women of the highest birth whose major journey was the move from one royal household to another. Medieval writers used such ambiguous figures as paradigms of extraordinarily good or bad political behavior during the period when the Germanic tribes were building their kingdoms. The earliest years of the Middle Ages, then, belonged as much to women who stayed put as to men who wandered.

In the practice of religion, women may have escaped some of the physical and legal restrictions that men laid upon them, as Chapter Three shows. Women in the early Middle Ages practiced Christianities as various as the modern versions. The diversity of beliefs and practices that constituted Christianity, and the multitude of cultures that hosted the religion, meant that the religious life of a woman at one end of Europe could vary vastly from that of her sister at the other end. Their opportunities for religious practice fluctuated from place to place as well as decade to decade. One condition shared by Christian women everywhere in Europe, whether vowed celibate or penitent sinner, noble or slave, was the suspicion of theologians and rulemakers. Yet the flexible limits and often contradictory theologies of Christianity allowed women the room to maneuver and to define meaningful religious experiences within an orthodox framework. Religious institutions even accorded women some influence as Christian professionals, despite the boundaries set by male leaders and thinkers. And although their choices and cultures were different, Muslim, Jewish, and pagan women may also have found spiritual space, negotiating between the patriarchal communities they inhabited, the misogyny that pervaded their religions, and their personal needs. For we know from the frustrating hints of the evidence – from women's attempts to participate, donate, and infiltrate men's churches, synagogues, mosques, shrines, and other holy places – that women strove to fill personal religious needs then, as now.

Chapter Four treats women's attempts to create families and communities in the midst of perilous politics, constant warfare, poor harvests, and unstinting attacks by disease. Daily survival was never a sure thing for any woman in medieval Europe, whatever her age or station. Appalling mortality rates, low life expectancies, and unbalanced sex ratios from the early Middle Ages make grimly clear how dangerous it was to be born in earlier Europe. A bad harvest, a small war, meant that dozens, hundreds, or more perished. Varied political conditions in the dissolving Carolingian empire, the new English kingdom, the emerging France, the Italian territory harassed by Muslim pirates, as well as women's personal wealth and social status, all affected how well women were able to respond to the challenge of survival. To replenish the imperiled population was so sacred and saintly a task that the greatest heroine of Christendom, the Blessed Virgin, was accorded ever-increasing devotion primarily for her motherhood of a child destined to die.

Chapter Five analyzes women's opportunities and the gendered division of labor at the point of great changes in the economy of Europe. On the physical and demographic frontiers of an expanding and centralizing Christendom, women managed to acquire property and make profits. In the Christian kingdoms of the Iberian peninsula, they shared inheritance with their brothers. On the estates of crusaders, they acted as lords and managers. In Iceland they claimed homesteads. In Ireland they married their conquerors and became mistresses of castles. And in the new towns of post-1000 Europe, they took jobs as servants and assistants. Yet this progress was not permanent. Frontiers never remain frontiers for long, and there never was a Golden Age of women's work. Some historical continuties do trump class, and in the early Middle Ages, gender ideology and the legal disenfranchisement of women were among them. Women and men brought with them to the frontiers all the gendered cultural baggage that had put women to reproductive and domestic tasks for the past millennia. When the institutions of the hinterlands became as rigid as those of the homeland, women returned to the domestic milieu and its traditional economic possibilities.

Although change constantly affected the experience of European women, the end of the early Middle Ages brought more profound and pervasive transformation to women's lives. Although men directed most of the changes, women could not help but be affected. The early Middle Ages ended for women when their vistas opened up to include the world outside their rural interiors, and when they began to move over familiar landscapes to new places. New trends in formal philosophy, theology, and law led Europeans to revise their gender ideologies and readjust the status of women after 1100. At the same time, more women began to participate in formal culture and to remember their experiences in writing. The book begins with women as nameless statistics and finishes with a study of the newly prominent voices of famous women in the texts of the central Middle Ages. By the end of this book, more individuals have begun to step out from the undifferentiated mass of silent, anonymous women.

This book is not just a history of women, but a history of the early European Middle Ages through the eyes of women. It begins at a point made familiar by traditional histories, the end of the Roman emperors' rule, but it ends with an ill-defined chronological boundary of a long eleventh century, and with the new mobility of women travelling beyond the old imperial limits. Every chapter questions an assumption of current historiography, paraphrasing repeatedly the famous question posed by the historian Joan Kelly-Gadol, "Did women have a renaissance?": Did women have an invasion? A Christianization? A war? An intellectual life? An economic expansion? A dream of political power?[7] I use the written memories of men not as they intended, to commemorate themselves, but to tell of women, women's experience, women's relations with men, and women's participation in what we call history. Sometimes women sneak in the back door of these chapters, under cover of men's history and men's evidence, but they always have the last word in this book.

[7] Joan Kelly-Gadol, "The Social Relation of the Sexes," *Signs: Journal of Women in Culture and Society* 1 (1976), 809–23; Julia H. Smith, "Did Women Have a Transformation of the Roman World?," *Gender and History* 12 (2000), 552–71.

—— I ——

GENDER AND LANDSCAPES

———— · ————

The physical world of the fourth, fifth, and sixth centuries was the same, with minor climatic variation, for all the inhabitants of Europe. The same rains fell upon Germans, Celts, Huns, and Romans, pagans and Christians, men and women. They were frozen by the same icy winds and warmed by the very same sunshine. In the fourth century, when the prevailing weather patterns in Europe changed for the worse, people of the south may have noticed the increasing aridity of the land, while up north they suffered more rains and snowier winters. Indeed, some archeologists believe that the bad weather was largely responsible for initiating population decline at the start of the Middle Ages.[1] Either way, suffering the dusty winds of southern Gaul or the endless wet of the British midlands, men and women dwelt together in houses on the same land, working to make it feed them. Women looked out of their doors at the same woods and fields in which their men toiled.

LANDSCAPES AND POPULATIONS AT THE END OF ANTIQUITY

Europe at the beginning of the Middle Ages was composed of landscapes far different from those of modern Europe with its metropolises and many millions of people. There were fewer people in the sixth century than there are now. There were also far fewer

[1] H. Lamb, "Climate from 1000 B.C. to 1000 A.D.," in *The Environment of Man*, ed. J. Jones and G. Dimbleby (Oxford: British Archaeological Reports, 1981), 53–65.

souls than there had been in the second or third century. In 200 CE, the population of the continent was probably around 35 million. By 500 it had sunk to 27.5 million. In 650, after a devastating pandemic of bubonic plague, along with other disasters, it plummeted to 18 million.[2] The third-century imperial city of Rome, heart of the known world, had a population of about half a million, an enormous metropolis by pre-modern standards. Rebuilt and walled by Emperor Aurelian in 271, it enclosed more than 3000 acres. Even in the fifth century, the city still may have contained close to 400,000 women, men, and children.[3] By 700 or so, neither Rome nor Paris nor any other population center in western Europe had more than 20,000 people in it, and those numbers were rare.[4]

The causes of Rome's fall concern us here as little as they probably bothered most women in the early fifth century. Political fractures within the ruling class, withdrawal of western legions to eastern frontiers, decadence among the senatorial nobility, economic disaster, the emasculating effects of pacifist Christians, lead poisoning, bad weather, malaria – none of this mattered much to a woman living from day to day in Aix or Trier or Colchester. But in rural reaches of the old empire, people must have remembered earlier times of bustle and plenty while anxiously eyeing the spread of empty estates and bemoaning the decline of neighborhoods. By 400, a sixth to a third of land cultivated at height of empire was lost to young trees and desert fields.[5] People may not actually have disappeared in significant numbers, but simply shifted locally. They abandoned houses but not the fields that had been worked for generations. What sensible farmer would leave the best arable, handed down in his or her family since before anyone could remember? Population groups constantly moved within their own agricultural regions, but did not suddenly

---

[2] Josiah Cox Russell, *Medieval Demography: Essays* (New York: AMS Press, 1987), 99–111; idem, "Population in Europe," in *The Fontana Economic History of Europe: The Emergence of Industrial Societies* (London: Collins, 1973), 25–41.

[3] David Whitehouse, "Rome and Naples: Survival and Revival in Central and Southern Italy," in *The Rebirth of Towns in the West A.D. 700–1050*, ed. Richard Hodges and Brian Hobley (London: Council for British Archeology, 1988), 23–81.

[4] David Herlihy, "Ecological Conditions and Demographic Change," in *One Thousand Years: Western Europe in the Middle Ages*, ed. Richard DeMolen (Boston: Houghton Mifflin, 1974), 4.

[5] N. J. G. Pounds, *An Historical Geography of Europe: 450 B.C. – A.D. 1330* (Cambridge University Press, 1973), 84–89; Herlihy, "Ecological Conditions," 5.

leave an area or drastically dwindle in total numbers, until the arrival of plagues, great climactic changes, or groups of immigrants.

The empire lasted longest in Italy and was even briefly reimposed by the emperors between Ostrogothic and Lombard invasions, yet even there the number of known settlements declined moderately. Most of the peninsula remained organized into villages throughout the subsequent period of barbarian invasions. In the northern plains of the Po, about three-quarters of the imperial *municipia* survived to 1000 – even if only as hut clusters – and still do (thirty-five out of fifty provincial capitals in the area were Roman cities.)[6] In some areas, peasants simply moved house, not arable. They put their homes on defensible hilltops but went out each day to farm the same fields in the same valleys.[7] Yet the Italians had always had uninhabited patches of forest and mountain between their cities; writers of Antiquity had simply failed to mention them because they rarely visited the arcadia they praised in poetry and essay.[8] In the Piedmont region of Italy, south of the Po but north of Rome, neither Hunnish raids nor epidemics increased the wilderness or reduced the population; it simply could not sustain the intense colonization of the late imperial period. The cities of Augustus and his second-century successors dwindled to ruins while the shrinking farm families relocated their small settlements to more practical places.[9] By comparison, in Britain, the total arable hardly diminished, but people left the marginal lands along hillsides and in the fens that they had used for non-agricultural purposes at the height of Roman prosperity. They also moved out of cities back to farms, although most of the Roman cities were never completely lost as recognizable sites.[10]

Even if the effects of depopulation were regionally determined, though, they were everywhere: swamps and forests grew, marshes spread, people frequented safer highlands or more cultivable lowlands, and ports once on the coast are today miles from the sea because

---

[6] Chris Wickham, *Early Medieval Italy: Central Power and Local Society, 400–1000* (London: Macmillan, 1989), 80–99, esp. 80, 98.

[7] J. Ward-Perkins, "Etruscan Towns, Roman Roads and Medieval Villages: The Historical Geography of Southern Etruria," *Geographical Journal* 128 (1952), 389–405.

[8] Wickham, *Early Medieval Italy,* 9–10.

[9] Christina La Rocca, "Using the Roman Past: Abandoned Towns and Local Power in Eleventh-Century Piemonte," *Early Medieval Europe* 5 (1996), 45–69.

[10] Nicholas Higham, *Rome, Britain, and the Anglo-Saxons* (London: Seaby, 1992), 70–79.

marshes silted up the estuaries in the late antique and very early medieval period.[11] As the number of people decreased, they realized that the wilderness, which had always divided areas of settlement, had become a growing hindrance to long-distance travel. Devout Christians of the late antique period, such as the former soldier Martin (later patron saint of Tours), could flee civilization to live alone in monastic caves only because the bush flourished so near the dwindling towns of the empire. The last emperors had tried to halt the deterioration of the human landscape by ordering soldiers to settle on abandoned acreage, or decreeing that semi-free farmers were bound by law to remain on farms.[12] But nothing worked. No one could repeople the cities, rebuild the population, or force peasants to permanently move their homes and fields. The desert seemed to spread across the land and minds of Europe's peoples.

Cities of the Roman north dwindled, along with their urban markets, the economic exchange between city and countryside, urban industries, and specifically urban professional classes of men – lawyers, teachers, the great thinkers of Antiquity.[13] With its cities losing strength, the empire's military and political influence was diverted and waned, and so the empire's greatest accomplishment – its roads – lay untended. Travel became dangerous, money rare. Economies throughout the continent became subsistence ventures marked by sporadic local trade. The woman who had made her living by running a laundry or a wineshop no longer had products, customers, or even a venue in which to do business. Prostitution, defined as sex for cash in a brothel, became practically unknown in Europe. If a woman wished to trade upon her sex, she had to accept other commodities besides cash in exchange and carry our her transactions, as the early Irish laws put it literally, "in the bush."

Pockets of imperial living continued to dot the European landscape on the eve of the Middle Ages. Not every city north of Tuscany crumbled and blew away on the new winds of the medieval climate. In the fifth century, in sizeable population centers throughout the old empire, citizens still lived in architecturally complex spaces composed of government buildings, basilicas, baths, theatres, racecourses,

---

[11] Herlihy, "Ecological Conditions," 5.
[12] *Cod. Theo.* v.17.1; vii.20.3; see also A. H. M. Jones, ed., *A History of Rome through the Fifth Century* (New York: Harper & Row, 1970), 312–15.
[13] M. I. Finley, *The Ancient Economy* (rev. edn. Berkeley: University of California Press, 1999), 123–76; Herlihy, "Ecological Conditions," 5–6.

and arenas. Vestiges of *romanitas* lingered along the Po Valley, in
Ravenna, in Rome itself. In southern France and Italy, noblewomen
and men continued to occupy villas into the sixth century, hiding
out, dining elegantly, and writing elaborate poetry or maybe gathering like-minded Christians to make a monastic life among the
fountains and courtyards. The cities of Gaul hosted Roman imperial courts in the fourth and fifth centuries, along with all their
hangers-on: poets, visiting foreign officials, provincial noblewomen
and men, military leaders, churchmen. Increasingly during the fifth
century, cultivated nobles with enough wealth withdrew to their
country estates where they survived by the labor of slaves as long
as they could, deluding themselves about the endurance of Roman
culture and dreaming of philosophical and poetic glories. Yet even
when the Gothic wars of the sixth century brought destruction and
famine to Rome and when rebellions and shifts in leadership plagued
northern Gaul, provincial landowners continued to journey regularly to towns for Christian rituals, markets, judicial matters. Those
civitates and *municipia*, which had once been thriving market towns
and administrative centers, lingered inside their patched walls.

In northern Gaul, at the edges of Germany, in Spain, and in Britain,
people began a less Roman way of life, not always forsaking the old
towns and forts, but redefining them for new uses. The baths and
forum of Paris continued in use, along with its new churches, at least
until the time of St. Genovefa, its fifth-century patron. Merovingian
invaders occupied these Roman buildings in the sixth century, turning the town into the capital of a new, Christianizing tribal kingdom.
By the sixth century, when Gregory of Tours was writing, the cities of
northern Gaul presented an "anarchic juxtaposition of ancient stone
edifices and thatch-covered mud huts," according to one archeologist.[14] Gregory saw ancient basilicas and baptistries, paved avenues
and public spaces. His Frankish neighbors concentrated on the courts
where they displayed their Roman-style authority, the new funerary
chapels where they buried their royal dead, and the fields of battle
where they proved their rights to rule.

Out in the countryside of Gaul, occupants of a villa might leave the
house but continue planting the cleared fields attached to it, a pattern
observable throughout northern, once-Romanized Europe. Some

---

[14] Nancy Gauthier, "Le paysage urbain en Gaule au Ve siècle," in *Grégoire de Tours et
l'espace gaulois*, ed. N. Gauthier and H. Galinié (Tours: Revue Archéologique du
Centre de la France, 1997), 55.

fancied themselves Roman citizens and kept houses in the cities while maintaining villas, or at least houses with identifiable Roman-style features, in the country. Approximately one-quarter of all settlements in late antique Gaul had been such villas, but most of these existed south of the Loire where a senatorial class lingered. But housebuilders of the late antique period did not obligingly abide by the duality of native-versus-Roman, tending instead to adapt some architectural suggestions from merchants, soldiers, and government officials of the Mediterranean region. Some Gaulish landowners chose to decorate their walls with paintings or to use hypocausts (hot air ducts) to heat their feet and prove their good taste. Even in *Belgica Secunda*, up north where Roman rule had never been secure, farmers had imitated villa architecture in wood.[15] Not only the architecture but the spatial organization of houses and farmyards changed with the new politics of the fifth and sixth centuries, giving way to other principles besides Roman divisions of space. When countryfolk rebuilt dilapidated villas in more traditional native styles, or used the stones of villas to fix barns instead of hypocausts, or switched to the Germanic housing style of post-built houses, they were practicing a form of architectural conversion to the new Germanic regime, just as previous generations had selected the signifiers of their Romanization.[16]

Instead of the self-sufficient villa idealized by rural Romans, with its ties to urban centers elsewhere, the farmyards and hamlets of the very early Middle Ages merged into population islands distinct from cities. The roadside villages of late Antiquity became ritual centers with a single sacral focal point, such as a church or cemetery, which allowed residents from surrounding farms to consider themselves a single community. Nonetheless, the settlement system that Romans had encouraged during their tenure of Gaul continued, along with the traditional system that had preceded invasion. *Villae* sat on open agricultural plains amidst organized fields of cereals, whereas typical Celtic or Germanic settlement tended toward hillsides, pastures, and forest edges. Throughout the political changes of the period, settlement remained stable and farms continued producing regularly. The total number of inhabited sites dipped in the third century but

---

[15] Nico Roymans, *From the Sword to the Plough: Three Studies on the Earliest Romanisation of Northern Gaul* (Amsterdam University Press, 1996), 52–55.

[16] Guy Halsall, "Social Identities," in *Leadership and Community*, ed. Raymond Van Dam (Berkeley: University of California Press, 1985), 147–49.

revived in the fourth.[17] Similarly woodland, which had decreased slightly when the Romans arrived in the first century with their quarries and limekilns for building, declined a little more after the fourth century, but not enough to suggest a major resurgence of forest or drastic depopulation.[18] Markets continued to exist locally and regionally; hagiographers of the period mentioned the quays of Paris where merchants came and went with goods from the countryside – someone had to feed the towns. For Christian writers, only proper cities (*civitates*) remained meaningful points of lasting Romanization whereas markers of *romanitas* began to vanish from the countryside

Further from the heart of old empires and Frankish capitals, in Verulamium in England, *romanitas* had always been more superficial upon the landscape, so its markers disappeared even more speedily when government control and investment lapsed. A public building brand-new in 380 had become a barn within fifty years; its public function no longer necessary, it housed corn-drying kilns for preserving the harvest from damp winters. Elsewhere on the same island, locals carted stones from useless public edifices to make their own barns and houses. In Wroxeter, for instance, farmers busted up the roads that once led into town to use in crude, mortar-less buildings. Unlike Gaul, where new rulers of former Roman provinces were eager to take up Christianity and its buildings, no Christian basilicas survived the departure of the Romans from England. Native Britons retreated to their farms, ignoring the decaying villas that once served as houses of their lords, and reused the hillforts of their ancestors as tribal and sacral centers. The cities of the old empire later became the markets and cemeteries of Anglo-Saxon invaders.[19] Even farther from Rome, in Ireland and Scandinavia, change was less architecturally obvious: no aqueducts, towns, roads, or Latin language had ever infiltrated the local culture. But the basic conditions of life, and

---

[17] Patrick Geary, *Before France and Germany: The Creation and Transformation of the Merovingian World* (New York: Oxford University Press, 1988), 108–09: Georges Duby, *Early Growth of the European Economy: Warriors and Peasants from the Seventh to the Twelfth Century* (Ithaca: Cornell University Press, 1974), 17–30.

[18] Willy Groenman-Van Waateringe, "Wasteland: Buffer in the Medieval Economy," in M. Colardelle, ed., *L'Homme et la nature au Moyen Age: paléoenvironnement des sociétés occidentales : actes du Ve Congrès international d'archéologie médiévale tenu à Grenoble (France), 6–9 octobre 1992 (Société d'archéologie médiévale)* (Paris: Editions Errance, 1996), 113–17.

[19] Higham, *Rome, Britain and the Anglo-Saxons,* 82–104.

the facts of a dwindling population in an untrustworthy landscape, were the same everywhere, no matter what the linguistic or architectural trimmings.

Especially in the more distant ends of empire, then, men and women in villages or on farmsteads slowly came to depend upon themselves and the occasional traveler for all kinds of sustenance, material, intellectual, and spiritual. Increasingly, settlement consisted primarily of small thatched huts of mud and wood, often hidden by wooden palisades and facing fearfully inward. Such huts had always existed and even formed the majority of built structures, but now they were almost the only structures littering the landscape. Domestic animals such as lambs or calves lived in pens within the farmyard and even shared people's houses. Mature animals roamed the pastureland; pigs rooted in the forest's edge. Men tramped out to the fields dragging their light ploughs, scraping and scraping again to make a living out of the soil. Women minded the animals, grew vegetables – although not the exotic garden varieties of Roman taste – and took the sheep's wool to spin and weave into clothing for the whole household.

Women and men clustered in related, enclosed farmsteads or in small villages, separated from other islands of life by unpeopled land. The nature of these population islands and their inter-relations varied by region. The Celts of Gaul, Britain, and Ireland preferred small hamlets and isolated, fortified homesteads sheltering five to, at most, fifty people. In Spain, natives lived in large, walled villages of up to several hundred occupants.[20] Everywhere in the north, within these rural fortresses, the population pushed to its boundaries. People never spread themselves over the landscape because they could not – or feared that they could not – survive. As late as about 800, during the reign of the Frankish emperor Charlemagne, the monastery of St-Germain des Près in what is now Paris drew up a list of servile holdings and workers on its twenty nearby estates. The lists show that about 10,000 souls lived there, with a relatively high density of 26 to 29 people per square kilometer (modern Paris, by comparison, has a density of over 20,000 per square kilometer.)[21]

But not all the countryside was so thickly settled. Throughout the early Middle Ages, until the great reordering of the environment in the tenth and later centuries, only certain spots on the otherwise disorderly landscape were organized and peopled. In between

[20] Russell, "Population in Europe," 30.   [21] Herlihy, "Ecological Conditions," 14.

settlements, the land was not only untidy and inhospitable, home to beasts and invaders, but also the source of fears that bound people to their cultivated islands. Everyone dreaded what was out in the woods, as both medieval romances and modern fairy-tales remind us, with their trolls and witches and giants. The earliest medieval poets and hagiographers imagined the dangers as pagans, devils, rushing rivers, and impenetrable woods where a wandering saint could get lost forever. Once, ladies of the north had traveled the roads with their husbands to visit Rome or even more distant lights of the empire, such as Constantinople and Jerusalem; they had brought back the latest hairstyles, poems composed by monks, robes and perfumes and wines. Now it took a saint armed with powers of Genovefa of Paris to move safely over the grassy tracks. A less holy but wise person needed to join a larger party to range the landscape without the protection once provided by an imperial army. When, in the 580s, the Merovingian princess Rigunth marched off to marry a Visigoth, accompanied by fifty cartloads of gold and silver and a horde of at least four thousand Frankish soldiers, she barely got out of Paris before her own escort plundered her dowry. She never made it to Spain, but was fetched home by her mother's men.[22]

Over the last centuries of the Roman empire, local officials of the imperial government transformed themselves into, or were replaced by, men whose authority derived from wealth, local lineage, and religious office. St. Genovefa was unusual, according to her sixth-century *vita*, when she imitated male bishops in Gaulish territory, but she was even more exotic for playing the tribune and tax-collecting landlord. Once in time of famine, her hagiographer wrote, the saint aided the starving of Paris by boating up the river to Arcis to collect dues on behalf of her city.[23] More often, it was men of standing in the neighborhood, such as Genovefa's father, who filled such jobs after the Roman officials left.[24] After the imperial retreat, the functions of government fell to whatever local man had the most authority or

[22] Gregory of Tours, *Historia*, ed. Wilhelm Arndt and Bruno Krusch, *MGH SSRM* 2 (1884), VI.45, VII.39; trans. Lewis Thorpe as *History of the Franks* (Harmondsworth: Penguin, 1974).

[23] Jo Ann McNamara and John E. Halborg with E. Gordon Whatley, *Sainted Women of the Dark Ages* (Durham: Duke University Press, 1992), 30–31; *Vita Genovefae Virginis Parisiensis*, in *Passiones Vitaeque Sanctorum Aevi Merovingici*, ed. Bruno Krusch and Wilhelm Levison, *MGH SSRM* 3 (1902), 204–38.

[24] Ian Wood, *The Merovingian Kingdoms, 450–751* (London: Longman, 1994), 61–63.

most armed men at his command. In Britain and Germany, he was the father-figure of the most influential kin-group in the region, ruler of the local chiefdom; in Gaul he might be a bishop or the descendant of a Romanized family, like Genovefa, or a Frank. Women were normally excluded from such business and the public places where it occurred, and left to exploit their influence in different ways, as we shall see.

Both women and men stayed close to home, no matter how many crammed into their huts to sleep at night. Only for important purposes – such as war, migration, missionary work, revenue-collecting, or pilgrimage, almost all of which were men's activities – did anyone venture beyond the pastures of the village. Occasionally, the men of several hut-clusters gathered to fight off a common enemy, such as the Huns who threatened Genovefa's Paris; although it was the saint herself who turned the invaders back, merely by praying with the matrons of the old city.[25] When men met to discuss such political and legal matters, they debated feuds, hammered out lawsuits, or complained about taxes together in the public clearing of their village, or in the chief's large house. Maybe one of the landowners from a good family counted himself a local official, still using a Roman title, and tried to collect taxes or rents as Saint Genovefa did in Arcis.

Even while emperors still claimed to rule Europe, communications across the continent became increasingly sporadic and unreliable. Not only was travel completely different for men and women in the early Middle Ages from what it had been earlier, or would be later, but it took unimaginably long. Even in the sixteenth century, a hard-riding messenger spent weeks racing from southern to northern Europe, and was probably better off going by boat, if possible.[26] In the very early Middle Ages, with few good roads and dangerous rivers as their routes, people found things much worse. Christian saints were forever using miracles to calm the seas and clear the roadways. It took most mobs and armies of Germanic immigrants and invaders several centuries to drift through the continent and England. Christian leaders sprinkled across the continent spent decades or even longer resolving theological disputes, just because it was so hard to find out what everyone from Constantinople to Canterbury actually believed.

[25] McNamara, *Sainted Women*, 23.
[26] Fernand Braudel, *The Mediterranean and the Mediterranean World in the Age of Philip the Second*, trans. Sian Reynolds, 2 vols. (London: Collins, 1972), vol. I, 355–74.

Very few long-distance pilgrims were women, only the occasional adventurous, high-status, wealthy, Romanized matron like Paula of Rome or Egeria of Iberia. Foreign messengers and local entertainers were welcomed everywhere and protected by custom because their product was so rare and valuable.

Commodities moved only when they were too temptingly profitable to resist. When folks first became Christian, they needed liturgical items such as wine, which could not be produced in the north; salt and iron also had to go from one place to another. Sometimes people relied on middlemen who could move easily from kingdom to kingdom, and from barbarian territory to the eastern empire. Gregory of Tours, the sixth-century bishop-historian, mentioned Priscus the Jew who had "acted as agent for some of the purchases" of the Frankish King Chilperic.[27] Christian relics also moved from one end of the known world to the other, although more frequently after about 800 CE. In the sixth century, St. Radegund corresponded with kings and emperors, and sent plenty of shrewd emissaries across the continent to bargain as part of her relic-collecting endeavors.[28] Trade never really stopped, but bulky commodities such as grain did not travel far until much later in the Middle Ages. After the great age of the Roman grainfleet to Africa ended, people went hungry when the harvest failed because they could neither move nor store ordinary, necessary supplies. They were unable to bring food over non-existent roads, via non-existent merchants, from distant territories that people no longer visited. No one had money enough to spare as a medium of regular exchange. In Britain and elsewhere, specie was so precious that people started using it for jewelry. When Genovefa was a girl, the missionary St. Germanus visited her village on his way to clear up some heresy in England. When he met the girl at an inn, he plucked up a Roman coin fortuitously fallen to the dust and instructed her to wear it around her neck always, to remind herself of the vanity of carnal life and the uselessness of wealth.[29] But Genovefa was not the only girl to pierce a useless Roman coin for a necklace. Women and men of Nanterre and other communities tried to be self-sufficient, meeting needs through local production and exchange. They grew

---

[27] Gregory of Tours, *Historia*, VI.5.
[28] McNamara, *Sainted Women*, "Life of Radegund," 96–98; *MGH SSRM* 2, 364–77; Patrick Geary, *Furta Sacra: Thefts of Relics in the Central Middle Ages* (Princeton University Press, 1978), esp. 49–50.
[29] McNamara, *Sainted Women*, 21.

their own food, raised animals, and got their fuel, building material, and extra rations in the woods, and caught fish in their waters. Less lucky or resourceful people starved and died.

WOMEN'S LIVES AT THE EDGE OF *ROMANITAS*

Genovefa's life-story hints at what life was like for women in one of these little outposts in the fifth and early sixth centuries, and suggests the demographic trends of the period. Although she and her parents were landowners, women in her family were farmwives, drawing their own water from the well. When famine struck her territory, it afflicted owners and workers alike.[30] Gender, more than aristocratic birth, Roman culture, or wealth, determined the contours of Genovefa's daily life, in particular affecting her life expectancy in the context of the declining empire and its economy. Although men and women shared their farmsteads, their leaders, their weather, even their starvation, they faced natural and demographic environments under different circumstances. This was the case throughout the Middle Ages. At birth, the sex ratio of every human population is normally 105 boys to 100 girls (105:100). Scanty cemetery evidence from the sixth century demonstrates a worrisomely high ratio in some parts of Europe of 120–130:100 (total cemetery population, not at birth.)[31] Historians have argued over whether these data reflect inept census techniques, local immigration patterns which altered the ratio, the effects of slavery by capture and breeding, or female neglect and infanticide.[32] Even if medieval people did not intentionally sacrifice their female children, the sex ratio of early Europe seems to have remained

---

[30] Ibid., 32.

[31] Josiah Cox Russell, *The Control of Late Ancient and Medieval Population* (Philadelphia: American Philosophical Society, 1985), 139–76; idem, "Medieval Cemetery Patterns," in *Medieval Demography: Essays* (New York: AMS Press, 1987), 150; but see Emily R. Coleman, "Medieval Marriage Characteristics: A Neglected Factor in the History of Medieval Serfdom," *Journal of Interdisciplinary History* 2 (1971), 205–21; also Charlotte Roberts and Keith Manchester, *The Archeology of Disease* (2nd edn., Ithaca: Cornell University Press, 1995), 20–29.

[32] David Herlihy, "Life Expectancies for Women in Medieval Society," in *The Role of Woman in the Middle Ages*, ed. R. T. Morewedge (Albany: State University of New York Press, 1975), 1–22; Carol Clover, "The Politics of Scarcity: Notes on the Sex Ratio in Early Scandinavia," in *New Readings on Women in Old English Literature*, ed. Helen Damico and Alexandra H. Olsen (Bloomington: Indiana University Press, 1990), 100–34; Richard Ring, "Early Medieval Peasant Households in Central Italy," *Journal of Family History* 4 (1979), 2–25; Jean-Pierre Devroey, "Men and

skewed. For the population aged 18 to 42 the ratio rose even higher, with more men surviving the crucial adolescent and early adult years than women. Pregnancy and childbirth were killers of mothers and babies alike. Complications from delivery may have claimed ten to fifteen per cent of women.[33] When disease or violence added to their troubles, women were eating less, thus becoming malnourished, and dying earlier from both pregnancies and other complications. They also shrank in average height by a greater percentage than men during tough times, a sign of chronic malnourishment.[34] No matter whether a prospective mother was queen or migrant peasant, she was in danger.

Men died early, too, but from different causes – accidents in the field, the violence of warfare – along with the some of the same illnesses that afflicted women. Life expectancy for those of both sexes who survived birth averaged about 30–35 years. However, if a Gaulish boy made it past age 20, he might expect to live twenty-five more years while a woman at age 20 could normally expect about seventeen years. And anyone who survived till 40 had a good chance at another fifteen to twenty years.[35] These were the parameters of longevity throughout the early Middle Ages.[36] Hence, although people may not have moved as easily away from home to new communities on the perilous landscapes of early Europe, they still disappeared easily, regularly.

As a result, families constantly changed in size and number. Family presents a complicated problem for historians because it meant so many things at once to medieval peoples. As we shall see in later chapters, kinship remained the basic organizing principle of early European societies until at least the end of the Middle Ages. The Romans had reckoned both mother's and father's families as part of a large social, political, and legal group they called the *cognatio*, which stretched to seven degrees of kinship.[37] That did not even

Women in Early Medieval Serfdom: The Ninth-Century North Frankish Evidence," *Past and Present* 166 (2000), 3–30, esp. 19–23.

[33] Russell, *Control of Late Ancient and Medieval Population*, 153, tab. 38.

[34] Joel Blondiaux, "La femme et son corps au haut moyen-âge vus par l'anthropologue et le paléopathologiste," in *La Femme au Moyen-âge*, ed. Michele Rouche and Jean Heuclin (Maubeuge, France: Ville de Maubeuge, 1990), 115–38.

[35] Russell, *Control of Late Ancient and Medieval Population*, 168; André Pelletier, *La femme dans la société gallo-romaine* (Paris: Picard, 1984), 33–37.

[36] Herlihy, "Life Expectancies for Women," 1–22.

[37] David Herlihy, *Medieval Households* (Cambridge, MA: Harvard University Press, 1985), 6–7.

include in-laws (affines) or pseudo-family such as adopted children or foster-relations, which Romans had in plenty. Among the other peoples of Europe, cognatic kinship also offered an organizational framework for government and society. When Goths moved across the south of Europe to colonize Spain, they at least believed they did so in units related theoretically by blood; when the Celts of Ireland, the Saxons of England, and the Franks of Gaul formed kingdoms, they built them of confederations of supposed family groups headed by men. In reality, native and incoming populations amalgamated while Roman ideas blended with native concepts to form the families of the Middle Ages. When Genovefa's parents took Roman names – Gerontia and Severus – it did not necessarily mean that they were of Gallo-Roman stock but that they had absorbed some idea of Roman family organization. In both Roman and barbarian societies, actual kinsfolk supplied important legal, social, and political support to individuals; they also offered distinct kinds of support to men and women.

Hence, a woman's household was not identical to her family, and her family was not the same as that of her husband or mate. Among Romanized aristocrats of third- or fourth-century southern Gaul, whose houses were large and many-roomed, people had space for large families, servants, and slaves on their property. But in the wood or wattled huts of most of Europe, ordinary people shared space with four or five others, usually blood relations, sometimes a servant or another familiar person. We have no reliable censuses or other documents describing the exact nature of households in Genovefa's time, but the ruins of houses tell us that a woman and her cohabitants might have dwelt in one or two rooms with a hearth in the middle. In northern Gaul their houses were often rectangular, in Ireland round, but they were small throughout Europe.

A woman and her husband might live with their children in a comfy, dark, smelly house, or with the offspring of his or her previous marriage. There might be an aunt, a pair of aging parents, a servant, or a foster-relation, and maybe a distant kinsman or woman occupying the same small space. In some regions, a woman's house and another small hut might be adjacent or within the same farmstead, increasing the number of familiar faces she encountered every day. The seventh- or eighth-century farm dug up at Warendorf in Germany had separate buildings for its residents, its servants, its provisions, its kitchen, and other activities. Inhabitants of the site moved among the buildings during a day's work, going from sleeping place to work site to the security of hearth at night. A woman who lived in such a place was probably just as well acquainted with the goats or lambs or dogs she kept as with her human colleagues. All of these comprised her daily companions and labor mates, since women spent most of their hours at home. And yet any member of this group of familiars was liable to leave the household abruptly and be replaced; her children or spouse might die, her slave be sold, her lambs move out to pasture as mature sheep.

Left behind on the days when men went to work or market or war, a woman saw a limited number of neighbors and strangers. She gathered with other women, or sometimes with folk of both sexes, for entertainment at one house or another. Women convened with the entire community for major festivals or to hear an itinerant preacher. They may not have understood a foreigner mouthing the word of God if he did not speak the local Germanic or Celtic dialect; in parts of Gaul, perhaps a Latin speaker would have made himself clear, but fewer in the village learned their Latin once it was no longer the tongue of trade or government, and only noblewomen and men, military leaders, and missionaries were normally multilingual. The arrival of bishops in a small village, as when Germanus and his friend Lupus came to Genovefa's Nanterre, was a cause for assembly and celebration, although Nanterre may have been unusual, in that it held enough Christians for a crowd to gather at short notice to hear the men preach. Visitors passing by, especially the rare female, depended upon locals for hospitality. A famous man in a sophisticated village like Nanterre lodged, as Germanus did, at an inn but few, if any, women could avail themselves of such opportunities. Genovefa, when she traveled from one community of believers to another, stayed with other kind Christian women. Most likely when ordinary women escaped the security of their homes for extraordinary ventures, such as the trip to a saint's shrine, they looked to distant relations or friends of friends for a place to stay.

More often women left their houses for the village green, enclosure, or *platea* for specific reasons. A mother went to a well for water, or sent her daughter for it. Lots of medieval saints' lives refer to women gathering at a spring or river to do the wash, get a pail-full, or bathe; there they could socialize with other women. They also went to church. This meant that they lived close enough to the village center to walk to it (although not necessarily weekly; neither women nor men attended Christian rituals on a regular basis). Women in remote areas had to be content with visiting a sacred space for occasional ceremonies, such as baptisms and funerals. In the few surviving big towns or in the settled tribal capitals of barbarian Europe, women may have had more opportunities for going into public and thus constructing larger circles of acquaintances and allies. Saints' festivals and translations of holy relics, for instance, attracted a mixed-sex crowd, as did the ritual entree of kings or bishops. Genovefa herself knew the matrons of Paris, probably meaning women of influence,

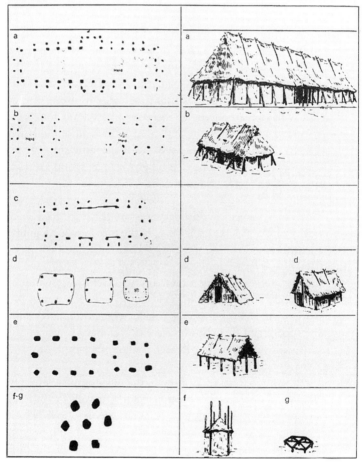

1 Buildings in Wahrendorf, seventh/eighth centuries, showing the variety of shapes and layouts for dwellings and outbuildings; chart indicates diverse names and uses for buildings.

whom she summoned to prayer when the Huns attacked. The saint also lived with other Christian women under vows and attracted girls from other villages to her house in the big city. Genovefa had contacts in a wide-reaching ecclesiastical network, which even touched St. Simeon the Stylite in Syria. Perched on his lofty pillar, the famous ascetic demanded news of the Gaulish virgin.[38] Genovefa was not unusual among noble and royal medieval nuns, who often maintained networks criss-crossing the churches of Europe, but as a member of

Legal codes

Allemans	Bavarians	Salian Franks	Ripuarian Franks	Saxons	Anglo-Saxons
– domus lib. – casa } hus – sala	– domus lib. – casa dom. – seli, casa, hus	– domus lib. } hus – casa – salina	– domus – hus – casa	– domus – casa	– hus – aern } domus – healle – seli
– scuria lib. u.a. – armenta equarum et vaccarum	– scuria lib. conclusa parietibus et pessulis cum clave munita	– scuria cum animalibus			– scipena – bern (horreum)
– granicia – cellaria – domus servi	– domus servi	– sutes cum porcis – cellarium	– sotes paricus	– stabulum – horreum	– styllan = stallbauen – fald – lochyrdl = Hürdebauen
– genicia – stuba spicaria – servi, ovile pocaricia	– coquina – balnearius – pistoria – mita – mita minoria = scopar	– genicium – screona	– ovile – appearius	– screona (alvearium)	– cylne
– spicaria dom. – scuria servi	– scuria absque parietibus = scof	– spicarium aut horreum cum tecto		– spyker	
—	– granarium = parc – fenile	– machalum = horreum sine tecto fenile		– granarium	– hreac = machalum

2 (*cont.*)

---

[38] McNamara, *Sainted Women*, 28.

the religious elite she was nonetheless unusual among women. Only exceptional women of influence, such as saints and queens, encountered many different people from exotic places.

Ultimately, a woman's social contacts and her household both depended not only on her background and wealth, but also on her chosen occupation, the identity of her sexual partner (if she had one), the location of her home, and the landscape of her life. The average woman was no Latinized aristocrat, Frankish queen, or educated nun. If she had not been called by God or recognized by Germanus of Auxerre, Genovefa might never have left her mother's house and saved Paris. She would have remained one of those lost to history, who eked out a few years on lands just barely under human management, fearing death by childbirth, totting up the babies that succumbed, and nurturing the ones who survived, hoping each day that her mate would return home safely that night. Normally, the walls of a woman's home and farmstead, and the boundaries of her family and community, surrounded her all the days of her brief life.

SACRED PLACES

When a woman of Genovefa's time looked out from her doorway to her village and the woods beyond, she saw several landscapes simultaneously. One was the map of her daily labors, focused squarely upon the house where she stood, and extending past the farmyard to the well at the end of the settlement and the edge of the forest. She might remember the road through the woods to another town, where she once trudged overnight to a shrine or a major festival. Then there was her social landscape of housemates, neighbors, servants, and friends, their houses, and the spaces where she met them. Third was the political landscape that she shared with this smaller group of allies and other such groups. She was simultaneously part of a tribal kingdom, a sub-Roman local government, a diocese, a monastic territory, or even a migratory group of families on their way to a better life. Her map might include the sites of all these political structures and more. The varied geographies of women's lives fill the following chapters of this book.

But, in addition, a woman watched the land and sky for clues to a fourth landscape infused by the sacred. She knew that certain places were inherently holy and alive with the numinous. Specific clues marked entries to otherworlds below, above, or within the physical world she saw everyday. No matter who she was, she was aware of a cosmos that enveloped all her landscapes, her visible world, and herself. From southern Gaul to Scandinavia, the land inhabited by women was dynamic with complex powers, which it was best to propitiate, venerate, or avoid.

For classical thinkers, the edges of the earth itself melted into Ocean, the great foggy stream that surrounded the entire land surface, whose waters contained all manner of monsters and spirits. More locally, citizens of the Roman empire were animist, finding gods and goddesses in bits of the landscape – trees, rocks, springs, households – just as their abstracted manifestations were resident in classical mythology.[39] In written myth, Jupiter frolicked with his divine family atop a Cretan mountain that everyone knew to be Olympus. Aeneas, like the Greeks before him, found and entered the underworld via a particular cave and a river. Ordinary folk met the gods at wells and shrines along the road. When Roman beliefs went north and westward into barbarian territory, they settled atop existing landscapes of the sacred like dust over a tabletop. No soldier or merchant in foreign parts was ready to dispute with the natives about this or that grove and its spirits. Although Romans may not have appreciated the ways of barbarian worship, or may have feared them as an impetus to rebellion, they were usually ready to rename and venerate any place with a resident spirit.

Only the Christians among them were finicky about the exclusiveness of their holy sites, although they, too, perceived a landscape alive with supernatural powers. As fierce monotheists, they rejected the idea that gods and goddesses dwelt in particular places. But they had their sacred spots, nonetheless: basilicas, where they worshiped; geographies of Jesus and his disciples, focused on the omphalos of the world, Jerusalem, and later on Rome; and, especially, resting places of the most holy dead.[40] Both Roman and Jewish traditions had prepared Christians to venerate places where dead saints lay, which Christians perceived as gateways to a more spiritual realm. The shrines of saints drew pilgrims who came for a glimpse up into heaven. Such places also attracted demons, angels, and all sorts of

---

[39] Alice K. Turner, *The History of Hell* (New York: Harcourt Brace, 1993), 35.
[40] Peter Brown, *The Cult of the Saints: Its Rise and Function in Latin Christianity* (Chicago University Press, 1981), esp. 86–105.

unearthly creatures. Wherever Christianity spread, it created saints, and wherever the saints expired and were entombed, they enhanced the spiritual landscape. Not coincidentally, Christian landscapes also overlapped with Roman and native maps of the numinous. Roman temples were converted to Christian usage. Saints tore down sacred groves to build churches, which they enhanced with bits and pieces of long-gone holy men and women. Even when avoiding old sacred places, such as the graveyards beyond the walls of old Roman towns, to build churches and dig cemeteries elsewhere, Christians remained respectful of these sites.[41]

Each barbarian people had its own local vision of an intimate landscape which, by the time Genovefa roamed Gaul, was a mix of traditional Germanic, Celtic, Latinized, and Christian-colored geographies. Yet all these traditions supported the mutual permeability of physical and invisible landscapes. The natives of northern Europe found the otherworld of spirits and the dead in dreams, in waking visions, and by accidentally wandering out on the wrong night.[42] Celtic tales told of heroes who foolishly left the house at Samain (our Hallowe'en and the Catholic feast of All Saints), the autumn festival, and found themselves in the otherworld where hanged men spoke and fairy-troops attacked the living. In other stories, men hopped in boats headed for adventure on the seas, only to end up on paradisaical islands inhabited by sexually willing beauties. Scandinavian and Germanic legends told a darker version of similar accidents, where heroes like Beowulf could dive into a pool and find a monster's hall dry as a bone, or creep into a cave and discover an immortal dragon puffing smoke atop a pile of gold.

As in Roman and Mediterranean Christian cultures, legends of the spiritual map coincided with people's vision of the natural landscape. Germanic and Celtic peoples of northern Europe carved the land into territories sacred to particular deities, which were decorated with places dedicated to them. For instance, in ancient Germany, Gaul, Britain, and Ireland, devotees marked a place sacred to the local spirit with trees. Tacitus, Lucan, and Dio Cassius complained about druids

[41] Bailey K. Young, "The Myth of the Pagan Cemetery," in *Spaces of the Living and the Dead: An Archaeological Dialogue*, ed. Catherine E. Karkov *et al.*, American Early Medieval Studies 3 (Oxford: Oxbow Books, 1999), 61–86.

[42] Lisa M. Bitel, "*In Visu Noctis*: Dreams in Early Medieval Hagiography and Histories, 500–900," *History of Religions* 31 (1991), 39–59.

and Germanic priests worshiping in groves.[43] Irish laws of the seventh and later centuries – a period when Ireland was still undergoing the long, slow process of conversion – referred to something called a *bile*, a sacred tree that marked a royal inaugural site, or even a Christian church. When a king wanted to insult another king, he rounded up his men and rode off to the other's fort, where he either abducted his enemy's women or struck down his *bile*, or both. The notion of a sacred tree lingered into the Christian era. The sixth-century monk-saint Finnian established his church as a place called Mo-bile, "my sacred tree."[44]

All the same religious traditions that blended spiritual and material landscapes also gendered them. In the documents of the early Middle Ages, produced by Christians, places significant upon the pre-Christian landscape took on female connotations. *Bili* might seem a specifically male symbol upon a male politico-sacral landscape, given this evidence of royal and ecclesiastical markers of territory, were it not for the premier female saint of Ireland, St. Brigit. Brigit chose to put her main church at Cill Dara (Kildare), which means the "church of the oak-tree." Yet before Brigit got there, the site was already sacred, probably to a neighborhood spirit. As late as the twelfth century, Cill Dara boasted an ever-burning fire tended by the ghostly saint herself, and an enclosure which men dared enter only at peril of their sanity and even their lives.[45]

In fact, when *bili* and other typically pagan places endured the transition to a Christian landscape, it may have been because they were tinged with femininity. Wells and springs were typically Celtic and Germanic healing sites; they were also places where rural women gathered. Aquae Sulis, for instance, was a mineral spring in western

---

[43] Tacitus, *Annales*, xiv.28–30; *Germania*, 9, 39, 40; trans. A. J. Church and W. J. Brodribb, *The Complete Works of Tacitus* (New York: The Modern Library, 1942); Lucan, *The Civil War (Pharsalia)*, trans. S. H. Braund (Oxford University Press, 1992) III.399–452; Dio Cassius, *Historia Romana*, LXII.2, ed. and trans. E. Cary as *Dio's Roman History* (New York: MacMillan, 1914–27). See also Miranda Green, *Symbol and Image in Celtic Religious Art* (London: Routledge, 1989), 151–55.

[44] A. T. Lucas, "The Sacred Trees of Ireland," *Journal of the Cork Historical and Archaeological Society* 68 (1963), 16–54; Lisa M. Bitel, *Isle of the Saints: Monastic Settlement and Christian Community in Early Ireland* (Ithaca: Cornell University Press, 1990), 44–45.

[45] Gerald of Wales, *Topographia Hibernica*, ed. J. F. Dimock, Rolls Series, vol. 5 (London: Longman 1867); trans. John J. O'Meara as *History and Topography of Ireland* (New York: Penguin, 1982), 60–61, 66.

England at a place now called Bath. Native Britons had long been
visiting a goddess Sul of the springs before Romans rededicated the
place to Minerva and built elegant public baths there. Even after
they took Roman names and allowed their goddess to take one, too,
locals threw lumps of lead inscribed with petitions for good health
into the goddess's waters. Like a good mother, Sul Minverva was to
listen to the pleas of her ailing children, nurse them, and provide
for them from her bountiful gardens. Archeologists have found at
least eighty-nine such wells in Gaul, twenty of which were used by
sick patients seeking cures from the gods and goddesses.[46] Suppliants
tossed hoards of coins into the wells to propitiate the spirits there.
People also carved, or had carved, little statues of afflicted joints and
organs: deformed and ulcerated hands, arms, legs, blind faces, goiters,
hernia trusses, lungs, hearts, and kidneys. They pitched these statues
into the waters, hoping that the goddess might get the message and
send a cure. The carvings suggest that sufferers had not borne acute or
deathly illnesses – they would never had made it to the shrine, if so –
but chronic, incurable, common afflictions, such as lameness, blindness, and gastrointestinal problems. These were things that people
were born with, or acquired from long hard work in an unforgiving
environment. And although the Romans had built imposing urban
shrines to the god Aesculapius and other healer divinities back in the
eastern cities of the empire, northern custom located healers nearby, at
places regularly visited by the women of their homesteads and villages.
One writer mentioned the spells practiced at the shrines, which combined classical Galenic medicine and local witchery in a Celtic dialect.
Marcellus, working in Gaul in the late fourth century, recorded in-
cantations and ceremonies involving crushed lizards and doves' blood,
ritual washings, special amulets with blessings carved on them, and
other invocations of pagan deities such as the *Matres* or divine mothers
popular throughout the Roman provinces of the north.[47]

Most sacred wells in Gaul seem to have gone out of use as shrines
by the second half of the fourth century, about a hundred years before
Genovefa was born. Perhaps the waters lost their supernatural force,

---

[46] Aline Rousselle, "Du sanctuaire au thaumaturge: La guérison en Gaule au IVᵉ
siècle," *Annales ESC* 31 (1976), 1085–107; Green, *Symbol and Image*, 155–64;
Miranda Green, *Celtic Goddesses: Warriors, Virgins, and Mothers* (New York:
Braziller, 1996), 93–99.

[47] Marcellus, *De Medicamentis Liber*, x.35, in *Corpus Medicorum Latinorum* (Berlin: in
Aedibus Academiae Scientiarum, 1916), vol. 5.

or the goddesses fled the invasion of Christian priests. But some shrines continued to attract pilgrims into the fifth century and later, and were even converted to Christianity and thus masculinized in the process. Tours, bastion of the fierce missionary St. Martin, had been a Celtic healing shrine, similar to Aquae Sulis. Tablets tossed in the water there requested favor from the goddess Sequana, spirit of the Seine. The historian Aline Rouselle has even argued that Martin himself used the healing spring to help bring locals to Christianity. He usurped the functions of the local goddess and himself cured people of chronic illnesses like paralysis, blindness, dumbness, leprosy, and possession – all the classic problems for which people sought the spirits of the wells.[48]

But in 585, the Christian council of bishops gathered at Auxerre, not far from Tours, and took back the wells from women and worshipers. They forbade veneration of the springs, specifically the practice of carving in wood human feet or faces to leave as offerings to the local deity. In the minds of the people of Tours, the rivers and springs gained new male patrons to supersede the goddesses.[49] It was no coincidence that clerics targeted places where women gathered and worked, which they believed to host the powers of female deities. Early medieval writers argued that women, more than men, stubbornly clung to the pagan landscape. Ecclesiastical officials blamed women often enough for continuing the old practices, locating their insidious activities out upon the land, not inside a church like normal Christians. Regino of Prüm complained in the ninth century of women riding on the backs of beasts through the night to indulge in Dianic rites in the woods and fields.[50] Ninth-century church leaders were more concerned with women's behavior at harvest festivals (rogation days) when they danced and sang "like pagans."[51] In the local history made famous by the twelfth-century inquisitor Stephen of Bourbon, it was the women of a small French town who continued to visit a forest-witch and to conduct woodland ceremonies

---

[48] Rousselle, "Du sanctuaire au thaumaturge."

[49] Perhaps not in Ireland, though. See Walter J. Brenneman, Jr. and Mary G. Brenneman, *Crossing the Circle at the Holy Wells of Ireland* (Charlottesville: University Press of Virginia, 1995).

[50] Regino of Prüm, *De Synodalibus Causis et Disciplinis Ecclesiasticis*, II.264; PL 132: 354.

[51] Pamela C. Berger, *The Goddess Obscured: Transformation of the Grain Protectress from Goddess to Saint* (Boston: Beacon Press, 1985), 78.

in honor of a dog-deity-saint in order to protect their newborn babies.[52]

Despite the willingness of ecclesiastics to blame women for continuing to see the landscape with pagan eyes, plenty of men committed the sin of believing the land and its powers to be divine, too, especially in the early days of northern Christianity. Both St. Martin and his successor, Gregory of Tours, living in Gaul between the mid-fourth and late sixth centuries, contended with processions of pagans toting idols around the fields in order to encourage the spirits of the land to produce abundant harvests. In fact, both these bishops spent their lives battling classical and Germano-Celtic beliefs in all their pervasive varieties, practiced by men and women, rural peasants and urban dwellers, literate and illiterate. Since what we term the "paganism" of the late antique and early medieval European landscape was no coherent doctrine but consisted of everything Christian leaders found offensive, it was hard for them to find it, define it, or eliminate it.

We know, for example, that Celts and Germanic peoples observed a seasonal religious calendar, and associated a fertility or earth goddess with some of its major festivals. Tacitus, the first-century Roman ethnographer and historian, discussed the feast of the "earth-mother" Nerthus, claiming that her worshipers believed that she "intervenes in human affairs." They supposedly honored her with a ritual ride in a chariot, a purifying bath in a secret lake, a moratorium on internal feuding, a temple, and human sacrifice.[53] Since everyone knew that survival depended upon the harvest, it made sense to venerate the powers that promoted a bounty, especially if the spirits were resident in trees and wells and fields. Celtic peoples in France, Britain, and Germany worshiped goddesses associated with the harvest and fertility whom they called, in Latin, *Matrones* or *Matres* – mothers or mother-patronesses. They may once have named the deities locally, associating goddesses with particular landmarks or tribal territories. In shrines throughout Germanic Europe, sculptors proudly recreated these mothers, sometimes carved in groups of three, in pairs, or individually. The goddesses carried baskets of fruit, cornucopias discharging an abundance, or babies, all clear symbols of their connection to the earth and its fertility. Some statuettes and friezes of *Matres* from Late Antique Gaul and Britain retained non-Roman names along

[52] Jean-Claude Schmitt, *The Holy Greyhound: Guinefort, Healer of Children Since the Thirteenth Century* (Cambridge University Press, 1983).
[53] Tacitus, *Germania*, 40; Berger, *Goddess Obscured*, 25–28.

2 *Matronae* with fruit. Small clay sculpture from the first or second century CE. The figures hold either fruit or coins, indicating their potential fertility and ability to nurture and bestow good fortune.

with their Latin titles. The little mothers found in Germany, with their bouffant hair-dos, naive expressions, and bunches of grapes clutched in their hands, represented well the expectations of both Roman and Germanic worshipers of mother-protectors. The goddesses inherent in the statuettes reflected the process of religious assimilation constantly taking place in the provinces, where the Roman pantheon hospitably expanded to include local deities. The goddesses also marked the assimilation of landscapes of the Iron Age and early Middle Ages, where Roman occupation met earlier traditions.

But the goddesses, when they turned up in written accounts and in the revised architecture of Christianity, also marked the conversion of the landscape from an old imperial Roman map to a new network of Christian regions. In the early medieval literature of Celtic cultures, especially Ireland, mother-goddesses had names that resonated with the soil and the people upon it. Emain Macha, the ancient capital of northern Ireland, was called after the goddess Macha, who turns up in three separate legends in the literature. Bóann was the name of another goddess-figure, as well as of the river that runs through the modern Boyne valley; she was the protectress of the ancient territory still called Bruig na Bóinne, the womb of Bóann, where pre-Celtic and later Celtic settlers built their magnificent necropolises. Brig, who lent her name to the Brigantes in England and to Bregenz in Austria, also appeared in Irish legendary histories as the daughter (sometimes three daughters) of the Dagda, the all-good, all-powerful god. Her namesake became the most famous of Irish women saints, Brigit, the one with a *bile*-marked church and eternal flame.

Yet these Irish tales of goddess-queens date in their earliest form to the seventh, eighth, or ninth century, and were written by Christian-educated men. Scholars have long debated whether these medieval tales actually reflect accurately a time before Christianity came to Celtic culture.[54] Did scholarly monks mindlessly copy down pagan myths in contradiction to Christian teachings? Or were they mindfully but uncreatively preserving an oral, pre-Christian culture that had once covered northern Europe? Or were they artfully authoring gorgeous stories of a long-lost, heroic time where people behaved in barbarous, peculiar ways? In the literatures of early medieval Europe, paganism was resolutely female. The past of the landscape, associated with earlier forms of worship, had a womanly glamor, too. A man on the scene of perceived paganism in the fourth century, such as St. Martin, actively involved in combating wrong belief on behalf of Christian missionaries, had to adapt the old sacred places and ways to suit his purposes. But later writers of the eighth and ninth centuries could safely condemn paganism from a safe distance and could add to its bad reputation by gendering it as female. Hence, Irish writers sketched a gendered landscape, replete with feminine influences, that lingered well into the Middle Ages. Echoes of this same landscape turned up in later medieval stories, such as the Welsh *Mabinogion*, the Scandinavian sagas, and the chivalric romances of the continent, where fairy mistresses came from mounds and woods to tempt valorous knights.

[54] Among the most recent entries in the debate over dating and Christianity of Irish texts: Seán Ó Coileáin, "Oral or Literary: Some Strands of the Argument," *Studia Hibernica* 17–18 (1977–78), 7–35; Edgar Slotkin, "Medieval Irish Scribes and Fixed Texts," *Éigse* 17 (1978–79), 437–50; Kim McCone, *Pagan Past and Christian Present in Early Irish Literature* (Maynooth: An Sagart, 1990); Joseph Falaky Nagy, *Conversing with Angels and Ancients: Literary Myths of Medieval Ireland* (Ithaca: Cornell University Press, 1997).

The female landscape embodied all the ancient dualisms associated by classical, Christian, and native European cultures with women. Writers who wrote of the fruitful goddess of the land employed a different kind of relationship to represent the deities as protectors of territories. Greek and Roman writers, as well as native Christian intellectuals, dressed their stories of European goddesses in the armor of warrior-women. Justin, Roman author of the *Philippic Histories*, wrote about a siege in 390 BCE by Catumandus, king of the Gauls, of the Greek city of Massilia, where he was terrified by a vision of the war-goddess warning him to end his siege; she was protecting the beleaguered town against the invader.[55] Other classical writers insisted that Celtic and Germanic women actually went into battle with their men in imitation of the war-goddesses, taking time off from child-bearing and rearing to wield their spears – or, at least, urging men warriors on, shrieking from the sidelines.[56] Romans reported occasional female barbarian war-leaders, such as the fearsome, red-haired queen of the Iceni, Boudicca, who led a revolt against Roman occupation in Britain.[57] But Greek and Roman writers always liked to think of barbarians as living in a cockamamy, backwards world where gender reversals simply proved the incivility of the locals. Little evidence exists, before or after Roman occupation, to demonstrate that warrior-women existed, outside the rare exceptions like Boudicca. Furthermore, classical writers did not always accurately observe the natives of the north. Even less physical evidence remains to link women with the actual worship of the sexy warrior goddesses that thrilled classical writers. Some of the *Matrones'* effigies appeared with elements that might signal their relation to death as well as birth and fertility; the mother-goddess of the late Iron Age sometimes supported a carrion-bird on her shoulder, for example. But no one left a description of women actually visiting a shrine to worship a protector who dealt in war as well as babies and harvest; we have no contemporary carvings or tablets offered to the warrior deities.[58]

[55] Justinus, *Philippic Histories*, 43.5; trans. J. C. Yardley as *Epitome of the Philippic History of Pompeius Trogus* (Oxford: Clarendon, 1997).

[56] J. J. Tierney, "The Celtic Ethnography of Posidonius," *Proceedings of the Royal Irish Academy* 60 C (1959–60), 189–275.

[57] Dio Cassius, *Roman History*, 62; Tacitus, *Annales* XIV.

[58] Only one inscription from early Gaul resonates with early medieval literature on the subject: CATHVBODVA, a cryptic name on a pillar in Savoy. It means little until

GENDERED LANDSCAPES

So the Europeans of late Antiquity and the early Middle Ages told tales of goddesses who ruled groves, healing shrines, and rivers; who guarded territories and made them prosperous; who maintained political order in violent chaos. Later writers recorded and revised these myths, giving them a Christian flavor by assigning the land's powers to Christian saints or to devilishly feminine paganism. It seems clear that the sacral landscape was gendered in European mythologies, including Christian mythologies, and that the gender was usually female. Cults organized around the numinous powers of the natural environment – perceived as female – permeated premodern Europe. Worshipers sought the aid of the landscape and its spirits in healing personal illness, in creating general prosperity, and in preserving peace. The locus of such worship – wells and springs where women worked and groves beyond built Christian space – suggests that its practice, too, belonged to women.

Yet Latinized and Christianized Europeans of the early Middle Ages consciously used a language of dual-natured female powers, inherited from earlier religions, when describing what we moderns call nature and its effects. The psychologist Karl Jung, the renowned folklorist Robert Graves, and plenty of twentieth-century goddess worshipers would have us believe that all these manifestations of goddesses, from across the vast extent of pre-modern Europe, derive from a coherent idea about the feminine principle of the landscape – maybe some great Mother Goddess.[59] Others have suggested that since survival by harvest was and is crucial to pre-technologized peoples, and since primitive peoples tended to associate human birth with the birth of crops, it makes sense for the same religious ideas to appear in cultures dispersed across the world, from India to Scandinavia. Such beliefs crossed time, as well; to romantic anthropologists and philologists, goddess worship endured for eons because primitives, by their nature, defied the constraints of time. It is predictable, too,

---

we remember that in early medieval Irish tales, a figure called *badb* or *badbcatha* – "scald-crow of battle" – was the shapeshifting goddess of battle, who shrieked in the fray to curdle the blood of warriors. William Hennessy, "The Ancient Irish Goddess of War," *Revue Celtique* 1 (1870–72), 32–55; see also Lisa Bitel, *The Land of Women: Tales of Sex and Gender from Early Ireland* (Ithaca: Cornell University Press, 1996), 204–34.

[59] Robert Graves, *The White Goddess: A Historical Grammar of Poetic Myth* (London: Faber and Faber, 1948).

that the Christian writers of the early and later Middle Ages would take a prominent trope in non-Christian thinking and react to it in two ways: with criticism, as clerics from the fifth century on, and by incorporating it into the popular legends they so loved to write. In Christian cosmological schemes, always organized hierarchically, where every plus had a negative, the land had to be female *Terra* if the purely spiritual heaven was governed by a securely male One God.[60] In popular literature, as the French historian Jacques LeGoff has shown, the ancient tale of the dragon-woman Melusine popped up in foundation legends of twelfth-century French noble dynasties, signifying the domestication of the wilderness under the new, central medieval nobility.[61] The idea of two-sided nature fit perfectly with people's notions of fickle political power and even fickler females. It meshed very well, too, with traditional Graeco-Roman and Christian constructs of the physical female and spiritual male.

Such dualisms help explain why people worshiping warrior-mothers would still deny women full participation in culture and society. Most of what we know about the worship of fertility and healing goddesses reaches us through texts composed by consciously civilized men, who tended to write truculently of paganism and barbarism. When they described a native Celtic deity, Roman writers employed a feminine vocabulary that invoked bizarre and little-understood forces, but also all the connotations of lowliness inherent in being a woman in the empire. When early medieval clerics disdained pagan rituals, they portrayed deities and sacred pagan principles as feminine. None of the bishops of Tours, or any other Christian bishops, could completely exterminate the idea that the potential lurking in the land was distinctly female. In fact, a surprising number of pre-modern cultures, from Vedic India to classical Athens, from early Roman Christians to late medieval Icelanders, called the earth their mother and worshiped her as a goddess. But if this was the case, why did all of these same cultures disenfranchise and even oppress most women? Moderns posit the connection between a primitive observation of human birth and the belief in a great earth that produces all life with simplistic, Freudian ease. Yet the potentially tense

---

[60] Winthrop Wetherbee, "Some Implications of Nature's Femininity in Medieval Poetry," in *Approaches to Nature in the Middle Ages*, ed. Lawrence D. Roberts (Binghamton: Centre for Early Medieval and Renaissance Studies, 1982), 47–62.

[61] Jacques LeGoff, "Melusina, Mother and Pioneer," in *Time, Work, and Culture in the Middle Ages* (Chicago: University of Chicago Press, 1980), 205–24.

relation between this metaphorical belief in a sustaining mother-world and early people's oppression of women should perplex more scholars than it does.[62] How could the philosophizing Greeks worship Demeter and Ceres, and yet imprison free women in the dark, private rooms of their houses, bereft of education and legal status? How could Iron Age Celts worship a goddess of fertility and war and, at the same time, limit women to household chores and childbearing? How could the Franks pray at the tombs of their many abbess-saints for help with harvests and illnesses, yet refuse women full participation in ecclesiastical and political hierarchies?

It is not true, as nineteenth-century sociologists assumed, that those societies which held the land precious and generative must have degenerated or that previously they entrusted real women with the same powers to influence and even control men that they accorded their goddesses.[63] To think so would be anachronistic, and more representative of our own era than the fourth or fifth century. On the contrary, just because people at the brink of the Middle Ages experienced the land as a supernatural entity and called her "mother" does not mean either that the men or women of pre-modern Europe believed the earth was a woman, or that women possessed any exclusive ties to the landscape. The nexus of religious metaphors employed by Germanic, Celtic, and Latinized peoples from Italy to Britain linked all sorts of ideas haphazardly in a familiar vocabulary: harvest, fertility, birth, death, and sovereignty. This mythological language is still familiar to modern Westerners, but the goddesses have gone and the landscape is a new woman. The construct of the mother-goddess, in all its manifestations, was for pre-modern European people a way of thinking about their place within physical and spiritual landscapes. There was probably no enduring, highly organized, feminine-centric religion born in the matriarchal paleolithic, forced underground with the triumph of patriarchal faiths and sword-wielding Indo-European invaders.[64] Just as modern historians have used the conceit of a

---

[62] Carolyn Merchant, *Death of Nature: Women, Ecology, and the Scientific Revolution: A Feminist Reappraisal of the Scientific Revolution* (San Francisco: Harper & Row, 1980).

[63] J. J. Bachofen, *Das Mutterecht* (2nd edn., Basel: Schwabe, 1897); Friedrich Engels, *Origins of the Family, Private Property, and the State* (Chicago Kerr, 1902; repr. New York: Pathfinder, 1972); more recently, this argument has been taken up by overtly feminist writers, e.g., Berger, *The Goddess Obscured*, among many.

[64] Marija Gimbutas, *The Goddesses and Gods of Old Europe 6500–3500 B.C.: Myths and Cult Images* (Berkeley: University of California Press, 1982); R. Eisler, *The Chalice and the Blade: Our History, Our Future* (Cambridge, MA: Harper & Row, 1987);

feminine landscape to describe history's relation to the land, so men and women of the fifth and sixth centuries – and in earlier Europe, as well as much later in the Middle Ages, too – sometimes used a gendered vocabulary to understand the arrangement of land, heavens, and larger cosmos. In practice and mythology, they invested sacred places upon the landscape with powers that were distinctly female, sexual, or motherly. They articulated their springs, rivers, and the land itself as woman. But they distinguished between myth and everyday life, just as we do.

Women's experience of their material environment was gendered. But so far as we know – and the documents do not say much about it – women did not necessarily see themselves as especially identified with the land, its trees, its rivers, and its wild, ungovernable nature. Nature was *not* to culture, in the earliest Europe, as woman is to man.[65] These are the cultural equations of a post-Rousseauan world. Genovefa earned her sanctity by fleeing to a dwindling city of the empire, Paris, rather than taking up residence in a forest glade. No one, saint or pagan, could be particularly comfortable with an environment that threatened to starve or freeze or otherwise master or ridicule its people at any given season (although even the most learned men were often perfectly willing to imagine such a harsh nature as a woman.)[66] Nor did all men envision women as attuned to nature, howling at the moon when menstruation or sexual frenzy overcame their man-civilized personae. Not everyone conceived of women, in the manner of American pioneer wives, as a domesticating force, although, as we shall see, the presence of women on the later medieval frontiers of Spain and Iceland did alter the internal workings of communities and enhance women's economic opportunities. But nothing indicates that the men or women of Europe at the dawning of the Middle Ages organized their views of the larger natural and supernatural worlds around such a conceptual link between real women and a feminine landscape. Nonetheless, a gendered

Mary Condren, *The Serpent and the Goddess: Women, Religion and Power in Celtic Ireland* (New York: Harper & Row, 1989). But for a critical review of the literature on goddess worship and matriarchy, see Cynthia Eller, *The Myth of Matriarchal Prehistory: Why an Invented Past Won't Give Women a Future* (Boston: Beacon Press, 2000).

[65] Sherry Ortner, "Is Female to Male as Nature Is to Culture?" *Feminist Studies* 1 (1972), 5–31.

[66] George D. Economou, *The Goddess Natura in Medieval Literature* (Cambridge, MA: Harvard University Press, 1972).

vocabulary of nature and the supernatural may well have affected women in other ways, particularly women's ideas about themselves and their notions of identity as a social group. We have seen already that women weathered the land, their spaces, settlement, and even time and life-span in their own ways. They may have perceived and certainly used nature and the supernatural in female-specific ways, too, especially since cultural authorities continually urged them to do so. How, though, would a woman in Gaul, or early medieval Ireland, or twelfth-century France, have reacted to the presentation of a river-goddess in a story? Such a figure had little to do with her audience's everyday realities of heavy rainfalls, difficult labors, dirty houses, and the knowledge that death often came too quickly.

And yet, the consciousness that the world might have a female spirit may well have saved an occasional woman. Taken together, the reports of classical writers, legends of Celtic and Germanic kings, material evidence at healing shrines, and hundreds of other stories about the sacral landscape suggest that people in early European cultures venerated supernatural female figures associated with the land, and honored the land as female. Even if men and women did not necessarily associate female worshipers with female deities and a feminine landscape, they did appeal to feminine spirits and saints at particular places. We also know that people venerated traditional landmarks throughout generations and even centuries. Both of these religious principles – the permeation of the physical with the sacred, and the gendering of the landscapes – seem to have lasted through the long process of Christianization, influencing the practice of Christianity just as they had affected the practice of Roman religion. By the time that Genovefa's hagiographer was commemorating her life, the female principle of the landscape appealed to him as a motif for Christianization and order in a violent territory. Genovefa represented peace and prosperity, as had the old goddesses, but only through the lasting influence of *romanitas* in its Christian form, under the rule of newly converted Franks – the least barbarian of the barbarians. As protectress of Paris and patroness of the Frankish kings, Genovefa mothered all the inhabitants of Gaul who venerated her. Unlike the old pagan goddesses, she also provided a role model for other women.

So, perhaps the female within the landscape subtly influenced the position of women, especially prominent or holy women, in European societies, just as Christianity's doctrine of the equality of souls has preserved a kernel of gender equality within that religion.

The fact that the harvest depended upon a mother-goddess, just as the production of the next generation depended upon a man's willing and able wife, may have persuaded some men to think kindly of women. Yet Christianity has not prevented the oppression of women, so there is no reason to conclude that Germanic and Celtic conceptions of a feminine landscape did so either. To associate women with a healing spring was beneficial to women and all things female; to link barren women with a land that failed to produce, starving whole villages, was not.

Ultimately, the language of sacred landscapes had little to do with the length and quality of women's lives at the beginning of the Middle Ages. But it may have helped women understand themselves and their place in related landscapes – the material, demographic, social, and political landscapes. If we do not walk the land with the women of early Europe, we will never come to know the meaning of a virgin's journey from her family home into a nunnery, through the dread wilderness with its barbarians, spirits, and monsters. We will not comprehend a girl's choice of a new husband and a new home, nor the distance she went and the boundaries she crossed, nor the way she searched the woods for perils and the springs for sacred signs of her progress. We will never appreciate the politics of queens if we cannot believe in the importance of fertility and the immense difficulty of successfully bringing healthy children into a hostile world. To modern observers, these may seem at first like small revelations. But even a tourist's acquaintance with the constantly changing but always gendered environment of the early Middle Ages may help us to follow medieval women through the landscapes of the next chapters.

2

INVASIONS, MIGRATIONS, AND BARBARIAN QUEENS

One of the fundamental differences among the medieval population – every bit as important as the divide between Christian and pagan, clergy and laity, free and servile, hungry and sated, sword-wielding and unarmed – was the difference between the mobile and the homebound. Since Edward Gibbon finished his *Decline and Fall of the Roman Empire* in 1788, medieval historians have understood the period between about 300 and 900 CE as a time when some men perpetrated mass movements. Barbarian hordes swept from the forest wildernesses or the windblown steppes into what is now France, Italy, Spain, and Britain to batter down the vestiges of the civilized Roman empire and create a new Europe. Hardy warriors in motion overcame civilized natives in place. The division between the highly and less mobile was based on ethnic origins (Germanic versus Gallo-Roman, Viking versus Celt), status (semi-nomadic, arms-bearing warriors versus land-bound peasants), and gender.

But if women lacked mobility, what were they doing while the Ostrogoths were marching into Italy, followed by the Lombards? Or when the Visigoths took Iberia, the Franks spread into Gaul, or the Angles, Saxons, and Jutes sailed to Britain? Apparently, either staying at home or creeping invisibly after the armies. According to some of the earliest historians of medieval Europe, the chroniclers of the barbarian kingdoms, women neither migrated nor invaded. Early medieval tribal histories forgot women when telling of campaigns and battles, just as Germanic lawcodes denied them the franchise and full legal status that would have allowed them mobility. In the histories of Enlightenment men such as Gibbon – and of medieval churchmen – women were simply not part of the picture of war and invasion that marks the beginning of the Middle Ages.

Recently historians have begun to deconstruct the invasions, instead explaining Rome's fall and medieval Europe's Germanic origins as a process of political infiltration and cultural diffusion. Rather than envision primitive hordes burning through fields like locusts eating their way across the prairies, scholars speak of "motley collections of soldiers under the military leadership of a king" freely installed by Romans as rulers of Romanized territories.[1] Yet this historical model, too, eliminates women from the period by reducing invasions but focusing on the few men who did move from place to place, from one kind of power to another.[2] Even if the famous Vandals, Alamanni, Suevi, and Goths of historical textbooks were only coalitions of armed, mobile men numbering in the several thousands, they were still, in this view, the invading men who made barbarian history.

What if we focus, instead, on women's relative immobility? Modern historians, ancient historians, and other kinds of sources agree that most European women were never bona fide, spearchucking invaders. By the very fact that they were rarely allowed to wield weapons or move freely, they were not the masters who captured European kingdoms, and who have secured the attention of European historians, medieval and modern. A few were immigrants, while many more women – and men as well, of course – were natives of invaded places. They waited at home in their tents and huts while men took over territory and government, or they dwelt on farms coveted by newcomers both violent and peaceful. They either resisted or they colluded with their conquerors. They died or became the slaves of new masters. Or else they married them, paid taxes to them, learned their languages, and were buried wearing their fashions. Although women did not lead the charge out of the Germanic forests into the old cities of the empire, female collaborators and resisters alike participated thoroughly in the founding and maintenance of the new European polities. Even the tribal historians admitted, in stories of barbarian

---

[1] Patrick Amory, "The Meaning and Purpose of Ethnic Terminology in the Burgundian Laws," *Early Medieval Europe* 2 (1993), 1.

[2] On new interpretations of invasions, or lack of invasions: Lawrence Nees, "Introduction," *Speculum* 72 (1997), 959–969; Geary, *Before France and Germany*, esp. 73–75; Wickham, *Early Medieval Italy*, 64–74. For a recent feminist critique: Smith, "Did Women Have a Transformation?," 552–71.

ruling dynasties, that women were necessary to complete the assimilation of cultures and ethnic groups that created feasible kingdoms.
The history of women in the fifth and sixth centuries helps us
discard the very concept of invasion which for so long defined the
period. Change during these centuries cannot be measured in terms
of invaders and invaded, as in the early medieval sources, nor in
the male-defined sly politics and ethnic identities of more modern
analyses. Instead, women's and men's stories during the very early
Middle Ages must be told in a different vocabulary of those who
remained at home. Women's history can be found in legal codes
outlining the status and rights that they held or lacked, but which
never measured up to those of men; in their alliances, especially
sexual and reproductive, with men; in their cultural mediation among
natives and newcomers; and in stories of the special gendered politics
that dynamic royal women played in the new kingdoms. Although
women were never as mobile as men, they migrated into the Middle
Ages more by assimilation and epic imagination than by roaming over
the landscape. And their style of migration can help us understand the
effects of male invaders and immigrants, resettlement, cultural change,
and the rise of barbarian kingdoms in a newly medieval Europe.

ETHNOGENESIS AND ETHNIC DISCOURSE

It must have come as a surprise to the conventional aristocrats and
Christian clerics of Italy, Gaul, Iberia, and Britain that outsiders
from beyond their borders, who had been in the employ of the
Roman army for generations, had become their lords. Franks, Goths,
Alamanni, and Burgundians were all on the Roman horizon in the
third century, but the warriors who made up these entities and
their families had been drifting through the empire in bands and
bunches for centuries, under more specific tribal names. In subsequent decades, their membership continued to shift. The Salians,
who became the leading tribe among the Franks, did not join them
until the fourth century, and the Goths split into eastern and western groups (Ostrogoths and Visigoths) just before 300, while the
Lombards defined themselves in the 480s in opposition to a group
of which they had been a part, the Vandals.[3] Barbarians continued

[3] Herwig Wolfram, *The Roman Empire and Its Germanic Peoples* (Berkeley: University
  of California Press, 1997), esp. xi–xx, 14–50.

to define themselves and their territories in conflict with each other, with the Roman emperors and their provincial administrators and, after 375, with the invading Huns until the fifth century. Sometimes armies took territory under the supposed control of the eastern and western emperors of what was left of Rome, as when Alaric and the Visigoths captured Rome in 410. Alaric had spent a good deal of his career leading the Goths as part of the western Roman armies, fighting on behalf of the western leader, Stilicho. Stilicho, himself the son of a Vandal cavalry officer in the Roman army and a Roman mother, married Serena, the niece of Theodosius the Great. Leader at times of both eastern and western Roman armies, protector of the boy emperors, consul, both commander and opponent of Alaric, Stilicho was pushing through a plan to pay Alaric not to invade Rome when he was defeated and executed in 408. The politics of these two leaders illustrate well the complexities of high-ranking Germanic leaders and the multifarious paths which their armies took in and out of imperial control. Leaders of Germanic fighters established themselves first as officers of the empire and rulers of their own fighters on Roman soil, or as leaders of combined federations of tribal groups sometimes in the employ of the emperors, or even as kings of whole peoples and territories. Sometimes, seemingly suddenly, their politics could cause them to attack cities that they had recently defended, as when Alaric pushed into Rome. Just as suddenly, aristocratic citizens who complained about the violence, or just the dress, smell, and poor Latin, of Goths and Franks were haunting the newcomers' courts, hoping for salaried positions as political functionaries.[4]

After a generation or two in power, recognized by their own people, the inhabitants of the territory they occupied, and whatever leaders of the empire were left, barbarian rulers demanded written tributes to their domination of the civilized world. They wanted ethnogeneses: histories of their tribes' origins that legitimated their power with literary statements about a political past.[5] They needed histories that bound diverse tribes together into single ethnic entities as, say, Visigoths or Franks or Lombards. They wanted stories

---

[4] Sidonius Apollinaris, *Epistolae*, 4.17.48, ed. and trans. W. B. Anderson in *Letters and Poems* (Cambridge, MA: Harvard University Press, 1936–65).

[5] Wolfram, *Roman Empire*, esp. 31–34, 204–06; Geary, *Before France and Germany*, 77–80; Walter Goffart, *The Narrators of Barbarian History (A.D. 550–800): Jordanes, Gregory of Tours, Bede and Paul the Deacon* (Princeton University Press, 1988), esp. 15–19.

of their many smashing victories and occasional valiant defeats, and about the clever ways in which they had disposed of enemies. They fancied praise of their ancestors' military maneuvers, their own brilliant treaties and alliances, the organization of their kingdoms, their conversions to Christianity, and their generous patronage of the learned classes. All of these stories were meant to teach lessons about the tribal past to the diverse inhabitants of the newly consolidated kingdoms. Monks and priests hurried to comply, producing historical narratives of early medieval Europe. These histories supply the best barbarian-centric evidence for the organization of medieval Western societies and polities. Of course, these histories of kings, warriors, battles, and politics only selectively treat women insofar as women were important to kingdom-making and identity politics.

When Gregory, sixth-century saint and bishop of Tours, wrote his famous history of the Franks, women played no part in the group's origin legend. Since Gregory remains the outstanding source for information about the creation of the Merovingian kingdoms, his silence about the wives and daughters of the barbarians is portentous. "The Franks came originally from Pannonia and first colonized the banks of the Rhine," he wrote, "then they crossed the river, marched through Thuringia, and set up in each country district and each city long-haired kings chosen from the foremost and most noble family of their race."[6] For Gregory, as for most writers of the period, "Franks" only tangentially included females. *Franci* were "the hardy," "the brave," "the free," none of which terms normally applied to women. The name itself referred to full membership in the coalition of fighters that composed the tribal elite, whereas the tribal kingdoms of the sixth century were polyethnic groups of a particular territory.[7] Women could only be players in the political memory of the tribal elite if they were already members or attached to members. Because the women of Gregory's day were neither mobile nor armed, and because most were not married to or descended from tribal leaders, they could never be full members of any fighting elite.[8]

---

[6] Gregory of Tours, *Historia*, II.9

[7] Geary, *Before France and Germany*, 78; Walter Pohl, "Introduction: Strategies of Distinction," in *Strategies of Distinction: The Constitution of Ethnic Communities, 300–800*, ed. Walter Pohl and Helmut Reimitz (Leiden and Boston: Brill, 1998), 4.

[8] Patrick Geary, *Phantoms of Remembrance: Memory and Oblivion at the End of the First Millennium* (Princeton University Press, 1994), 68: "Women are capable of being the persons responsible for family memory only if they are part of the family."

Unlike Gregory of Tours, other tribal historians included women in their accounts of actual invasions, but only as symbolic or bit players. Fredegar, a Frankish churchman writing his *Chronica* a century after Gregory, recalled that the Franks occupied the Rhine area "after crossing Europe with their wives and children." The mother of the eponym of the greatest Frankish family, Merovech, entered Fredegar's story when she met a Quinotaur in the Third Book of his history; apparently, the encounter with the sea monster resulted in her pregnancy with the future king and the creation of his line.[9] Fredegar was working with Vergil's *Aeneid* as a model. When Aeneas left the ruined Troy to found Rome, he brought the family (at least, his son and father) so Fredegar's Franks, whom Fredegar cast as Trojans, brought them too.[10] Indeed, in the anonymous *Liber Historia Francorum*, written about 727, the Franks actually came from Troy to the Maeotian swamps before drifting southwestward.[11] But, like the *Aeneid*, the invaders' story focused elsewhere, on the building of a new empire. The *Chronica* had no place for woman warriors but only for the bearers of royal children. Hence Fredegar left the other women on the riverbanks. Once the Franks made it to Gaul, women rarely contributed to the process of conquest. As a reimagining of ancient barbarian migrations, then, Fredegar's history presented the Franks moving as a people, not just as an army of men, but with men in the vanguard. Either there were not enough women to matter in Fredegar's story of invasion, or they did not advance with their men into Gaul, or in the author's mind women held no historical importance in the tribe's political origins. By the time Fredegar composed his *Chronica*, so many years after Gregory's first version, powerful royal women were playing a complex game of Merovingian politics which influenced Fredegar (sometimes for the misogynist worse) and may thus have allowed them this limited entree into his account.

Other tribal historians also employed a classical framework for the legends of their people's origins, for every christianized tribe needed to fit itself into the great religious history of the world that began with creation and the age of myth. Jordanes, the sixth-century Byzantinized Goth and bishop, employed the outsider's ethnography

---

[9] Fredegarius Scholasticus [Fredegar], *Fredegarii et Aliorum Chronica,* ed. Bruno Krusch, *MGH SSRM* 2 (1888), III.9; Wood, *Merovingian Kingdoms,* 35–37.

[10] Fredegar, *Chronica,* III.2.

[11] *Liber Historia Francorum,* ed. Bernard Bachrach (Lawrence: Coronado Press, 1973), secs. 1–2.

that writers of antiquity had applied to barbarians. Jordanes remembered that women had accompanied their men from an inhospitable, marshy womb of nations in the north to Vandal territory and thence to Scythia. They had settled among the Vandals, but "the number of the people increased greatly," by which Jordanes implied, presumably, that the Goths had women among them. Otherwise, sexy Gothic fighters were seducing hapless Vandal girls, but it seems unlikely that Vandals could so quickly become part of "the people." Eventually the "army of Goths with their families" decided to move on.[12] Beyond these few references, Jordanes wrote of battles, not families. He did admit to some Amazons in the ancient family of Goths. It seems that when the Goths got soft, they let women run the tribe and even conduct their wars. But once the Goths settled down under virile Roman influence, they recovered control over their women. When Jordanes repeated the genealogy of Gothic kings, he made clear who deserved pre-eminence among the ancestors and ancestresses of the Goths. The biblical-style "begats" mostly excluded mothers: Gapt who begat Hulmul who begat Augis who begat Amal....[13]

The only barbarian historian to use women as a tool for defining ethnic identity in his chapters on invasion was Paul the Deacon, the eighth-century chronicler of the Lombard invaders of Italy. For Paul, the origins of the kingdom lay in a familiar tale of the over-population of Germanic territories, which led the tribe to cast lots among its three branches in order to decide who had to leave. The lucky winners were the brothers Ibor and Aio, and their mother Gambara, who journeyed with their people southward in search of new territory. Paul told a historical anecdote about how Gambara colluded with the women of the tribe and the goddess Freya to secure a victory for the Lombards over the Wandals. The women presented themselves to the god Wotan with their long hair tied around their chins, thus disguised as warriors, and Wotan granted the battle to the invading Lombards, whose name translates to "longbeards."[14] But

[12] Jordanes, *Romana et Getica*, ed. Theodor Mommsen, *MGH AA*, 5: 1 (1882), IV; trans. C. C. Mierow as *The Gothic History of Jordanes* (New York: Barnes & Noble, 1960).

[13] Jordanes, *Getica*, XIV; Walter Pohl, "Telling the Difference: Signs of Ethnic Identity," in Pohl and Reimitz, *Strategies of Distinction*, 17–69, esp. 66–67.

[14] Paul the Deacon, *Historia Langobardorum*, ed. Ludwig Bethmann and Georg Waitz, *MGH SSRG* (1878), 1: 2–3, 7–8; trans. W. D. Foulke and ed. Edward Peters as *History of the Lombards* (Philadelphia: University of Pennsylvania Press, 1974); Wolfram, *Roman Empire*, 30–31. Cf. Gregory of Tours, *Historia*, IV.41, where he describes Lombards emigrating to Italy with their wives and children.

within this eponymous, intentionally comic appearance of women non-warriors lay two lessons. First, Paul reminded readers of the Lombards' shift to a patrilinear society, which was to him a more civilized form of social organization. Whereas once the Lombard people had been dominated by its mothers, now it organized around men, their property, and their offspring. Women entered his narrative for dramatic value, not in a historical record of their participation in invasion. As in classical ethnohistories, such as that of Tacitus, the bearded women instructed readers about the topsy-turvy world of previously uncivilized Lombards. Similarly, Jordanes' Gothic Amazons upset the gender balance of the barbarian tribe, which had to be corrected by benign Roman order. If Germanic women dressed as warriors in Paul's text, it just showed how outlandish pagan Germanic society had been in both gender relations and the practice of war. Paul's second lesson was about the distinctive identity of the Lombards as a people. The story of the women explained the source of the name that identified the Lombards, and also sacralized that origin by linking the people with the god Wotan Longbeard. All this constituted a particular symbolic strategy linking a recreated memory of the Lombard people and their origins with their current political situation. Elsewhere, Paul's chronicle was essentially one of genuine warriors and their kings.[15]

As for the English, the eighth-century historian Bede reduced the Anglo-Saxon invasions to an odyssey every bit as manly as the legendary Beowulf's seaborne adventure. In 449, according to Bede's *History of the English Church and People*, invaders came to Britain in three boats (just as the Goths had long ago left their own Scandinavian homeland in three boats):[16]

the Angles or Saxons came to Britain at the invitation of King Vortigern in three long-ships and were granted lands in the eastern part of the island on condition that they protected the country; nevertheless, their real intention was to subdue it. They engaged the enemy advancing from the north and having defeated them, sent back news of their success to their homeland, adding that the country was fertile and the Britons cowardly. Whereupon a larger fleet quickly came over with a great body of warriors which, when joined to the original forces, constituted an invincible army. These also received from the Britons grants of land where they could settle among them on condition that they maintained the peace and security of the island against all enemies in return for regular pay . . . These newcomers were from the three most formidable races of Germany, the Saxons, Angles, and Jutes.

[15] Pohl, "Telling the Difference," 57–58.　　[16] Wolfram, *Roman Empire*, 28.

From the Jutes, added Bede, came the people of Kent and the Isle of Wight; from the Saxons, the people of East, South, and West Saxons; and from the Angles came the East and Middle Angles, the Mercians, Northumbrians, and everybody else. By the eighth century, the entire recognizable, political map of lowland England derived from these three original boat-loads of men. Once these awful warriors had arrived and then invited their fighting cousins over, he added, "it was not long before such hordes of these alien peoples vied together to crowd into the island that the natives who had invited them began to live in terror."[17] Bede assumed either that the boats brought women or that the invaders took women with their new lands or both. He never bothered to say.

Leaving aside for the moment the political and social reasons why women lurked in the margins of tribal memories of invasions – and why they turned up again in accounts of the establishment of early medieval kingdoms – the tribal historians' choice of models for the process of peopling came of well-known literary precedents. Bede, like Fredegar and Paul the Deacon, consulted earlier records of migrants for his account. He had a homegrown source, written by the British churchman Gildas in the sixth century, during the respite between Germanic incursions. Gildas, who considered himself a beacon of classical learning in a benighted land, transmitted his dislike of the Angles and Saxons to Bede. The arrival of Germanic mercenaries on the island was catastrophic in his eyes, although only slightly more awful than the lazy corruption and military ineffectiveness of native British princes.[18] But Gildas' eye-witness account of the end of Roman Britain depicted three boats full of savage raiders, not settlement-minded Germanic families, arriving along the southern shore of Britain. As in other historical sources of the period, Gildas' real concern was not the arrival of Germans but the fall of Rome and its civilized provinces. Bede and other tribal historians also knew of classical histories and ethnographies, such as the works of Tacitus, and of late antique church histories such as Orosius' *Seven Books of History Against the Pagans*, the chronicle of Eusebius and Jerome, as

---

[17] Bede, *Historia Ecclesiastica Gentis Anglorum*, ed. Charles Plummer (Oxford: Clarendon, 1956), trans. J. E. King in *Baedae Opera Historica*, 2 vols. (New York: Putnam, 1930), I.15.

[18] Gildas, *De Excidio Britanniae*, ed. Joseph Stevenson (London, 1964), XIX–XX; trans. Michael Winterbottom in *The Ruin of Britain and Other Works* (London: Rowan and Littlefield, 1978), 23–24.

well as the work of the Jewish chronicler Josephus.[19] In such histories, the barbarians were always savage, always fighters, and always male, whereas the conquered were soft, decadent, feminine.

Of course, tribal historians relied on the Bible, too, whose Old Testament is one long tribal history of an invading people determined to keep its bloodlines pure.[20] According to scripture, the Israelites migrated as a people around the ancient Middle East. The Jews always brought their women and children along, so that plenty of heroines and their children stood out in the biblical narratives. Rebecca, Miriam, Deborah, and Judith are just a few mothers and leaders among many. But for medieval writers there were as many negative female figures, such as Lilith, whores of Sodom, Delilah, or Jezebel, as there were heroines in the Old Testament. What is more, women as a group often seemed to disappear at crucial moments in biblical history, something barbarian historians could not have failed to notice. At Sinai, the climax of the Torah's historical narrative, when Moses and the people gained the covenant that identified them as chosen by God, women were invisible.[21] Most biblical scholars and modern Jews assume that women were there. But as a historical model for the movement of peoples, the Bible lacked gender symmetry, to say the least. Historians and other medieval thinkers found many more women in the laws of Leviticus (which have much to say about marriage, purity, and normative social roles) than in the deeds of the ancestors of the Jews.

Several other sources informed historians' accounts of invasions. Early chroniclers such as Prosper of Aquitaine offered the first drastic notice of invasions. According to Prosper, disaster struck in 406, when Vandals, Alans, and Suevi crossed the Rhine, and the trouble did not cease for half a century, at least.[22] Letters and poems from the period countered tales of disruption and violence with the continuity of life within a Romanized province.[23] Saints' lives, such as that of Genovefa and others who actually lived during the invasions, contained useful details. But since the heroes and heroines of these texts were Christians, not pagan barbarians, women entered the *vitae* more

[19] Wolfram, *Roman Empire*, 8.   [20] Nees, "Introduction," 964.

[21] Judith Plaskow, *Standing Again at Sinai: Judaism from a Feminist Perspective* (San Francisco: Harper & Row, 1990), 25–28.

[22] Prosper, *Chronicle*, in *Chronica Minora saec. IV. V. VI. VII.*, ed. Theodor Mommsen, *MGH AA* 9 (1892–98), 1230, cited in Wood, *Merovingian Kingdoms*, 6.

[23] Ibid., 20–27.

often as resisters of paganism than as indomitable invaders. Some, like Genovefa, played the important role of negotiator between the Romanized and Germanicized, or converted new rulers. The early historians may also have relied on oral traditions, passed down among the barbarians themselves, about the origins and the deeds of their fathers. Some of these legends emerged later in the Middle Ages as written sagas, a few of which featured dynamic female protagonists; but the legends of Brunhild, Kudrun, and Medb yield little reliable data about women among the Germanic and Celtic invaders. Such tales are more informative about social roles and politics in barbarian kingdoms. Finally, some of the early medieval chroniclers took the testimony of witnesses or those who personally knew participants in the bloody deeds of the past. Another reason why Gregory of Tours's history is so crucial is that he could draw on his own personal contact with historical figures, including Queen Brunhild and many who knew her, when describing the queen's political and sexual adventures.

As for motives, none of the historians aimed purposely to exclude women from the story of invasions. Each historian employed a different discourse with a different agenda, although they all aimed to compose a history of origins. Bede was writing history with a plot, but the plot concerned the establishment of Christian kingdoms and only incidentally included females and non-royals, usually as exemplars of good Christian behavior. Gregory of Tours was telling a moral tale with identifiable villains and heroes. He gave fewer pages to heroic women than to villainesses whose political and sexual antics subverted the Christian organization of barbarian rule. What these men produced was fiction meant to identify a people and its kingdom(s), and to justify the rule of its kings.[24] Part of that predictable fiction was that women and things female were more important as tropes for other figures, events, and concepts than as historical actors in the invasions. Since women were supposed to remain in the background of tribal politics they could not have participated significantly in the initial political changes and settlement shifts of the earliest Middle Ages.

Thus, both historical models and ethnic and artistic agendas conspired to keep women out of the documentary account of barbarian

---

[24] Goffart, *Narrators of Barbarian History*, esp. 17–18; Hayden White, *The Content of the Form: Narrative Discourse and Historical Representation* (Baltimore: Johns Hopkins University Press, 1987).

invasions. By comparison, twelfth-century Icelanders and Irish managed to produce national memories that included women, as we shall see in Chapter Five. But these tales were born of completely different political aims and literary sensibilities from those which produced earlier works. The presence of women in the later national histories and their absence from earlier tribal histories can suggest much (although from silence) about women's participation in the migrations and settlements of early Europe. But the texts also outlined the great shift in world views and social organization between the fifth century and the twelfth. Gregory and the others wrote violent histories and could not envision women bearing arms. They did not imagine women crashing the gates of old Roman *civitates* or sacking villages. No people of their own could have been that barbarous, even when taking new lands by force. Women might parade as men for symbolic purposes and comic relief, but in real war and accurate histories, women only died by weapons, they never killed with them. Whether tribal historians wrote in Romanized voices, the tones of non-Christian myth, biblical tropes, or some fabulous combination of all three, they told a story of men moving violently into new territory, men ruthlessly setting up kingdoms, and men building dynasties. The birth process may necessarily have included women but the memory of tribal ethnogenesis did not.

MATERIAL EVIDENCE FOR BARBARIAN WOMEN

Medieval people could not or would not remember women as invaders, but this does not mean that women did not participate in the creation of barbarian kingdoms. The tribal histories agree that once the newcomers settled into the initial business of learning how to rule, their own women were with them. Merovingian monarchs tended to marry women from their own or other Germanic tribes, not local Gallo-Roman or Celtic women. Goths did the opposite, achieving assimilation with the eastern Roman empire, but extinction as a viable dynastic group, by marrying their princesses to offspring of the emperors. The non-royal natives of Gaul, northern Italy, Aquitaine, Iberia, and Britain freely mixed family lines and names with newcomers.[25] But even when the early historians admitted elite

---

[25] For the precise chronology of Visigothic intermarriage and hindrances to it, see Hagith Sivan, "'Roman–Barbarian' Marriage in Visigothic Gaul and Spain," in Pohl and Reimitz, *Strategies of Distinction*, 189–204.

women into their exclusive schemes of conquest and rule, women
arrived in the written histories only after men had breached the
defenses of the old empire, and after barbarian leaders were ready
to negotiate, expropriate, settle, and establish government. Then
women did what women were supposed to do: they married and
produced generations of Frankish, Burgundian, Lombard, Visigothic,
and English rulers. Women, as well as their husbands and sons, consumed and redistributed the revenues that Romans had once taken
from the natives. They played new politics with the various ethnic
and religious groups inhabiting their territories. In Lombard Italy,
queens rampaged in factional disputes across Paul the Deacon's history as fiercely as their husbands and sons. And in every history, they
helped introduce and organize Christianity (as Chapter Three will
show in detail). Once Childeric settled down to politics, his would-
be wife Basina came into the picture. Once Clovis had taken Gaul, his
wife Clothild entered Gregory's narrative as a major character. When
the kings of Kent and Northumbria began to consider Christianity
as a useful tool for kingdom-building, their wives and daughters appeared on the pages of Bede. In other words, once barbarian conquests were reborn as Christian kingdoms, elite women reappeared
in their written records to produce and mother sons of the new
elites.

Although early medieval historians refused to reveal women among
either invaders or invaded, the bits and pieces of material life in the
fifth and sixth centuries are more forthcoming. Modern archeologists and a few historians have spent long hours and many chapters
debating not only the number of barbarians that took new territories
and their methods of triumph, but also the proportion of women
among them. Yet the evidence dug from the mud suggests that even
if women were present among the new ruling class, the nature of
their part in the migrations remains guesswork.

Continental archeologists estimate, for example, that only about
two or three per cent of the sixth-century population of Gaul was
Frankish, maybe 150,000–200,000 putative invaders among six or
seven million natives, with Germanic peoples concentrated above the
Loire. Lombards in Italy comprised, at most, five to eight per cent of
the population.[26] In Visigothic Spain, burial evidence suggests approximately 130,000 Visigoths in the late fifth and early sixth centuries,

---

[26] Wickham, *Early Medieval Italy*, 65.

among at least seven million others.[27] These numbers contradict the gory picture described by early medieval narrators, who depicted barbarian hordes ruthlessly attacking civilized Europe. More likely, mercenaries with training in Roman armies and administration, heavily influenced by Roman politicking and sensitive to local opportunities for advancement, assumed control over territories they might have been expected to protect on the empire's behalf. Roman rulers had long employed the tribes as border soldiers. By the third or fourth century, whole legions of non-Romans were being sent to the hinterland to fight other non-Romans. It could not have been easier for men of Germanic descent who had grown up in a Roman military or administrator's family to move into (or stay in) formerly imperial territory and use their own loyal troops to take over the defense and policing of towns and farms. Clovis was a good example of the process, for he ruled the Roman province of Belgica Secunda as a representative of empire, just as his father had after taking over from a Roman general.[28] Clovis secured his position by defeating a son of Roman aristocrats, Syagrius, who ruled as a barbarian-style "king" of Rome. He campaigned against other Germanic groups such as the Visigoths and Burgundians who bordered his desired domain. Yet during all this conflict, the continued vitality of Gaulish *civitates* under Merovingian, Burgundian, and Gothic rule shows their usefulness to their new rulers as centers of administration, religion, and culture. Apparently, native Gauls became Germanicized as rapidly as their conquerors absorbed the estates, language, and customs of the locals.[29]

But the new model of barbarian take-over suggested by demography and historians such as Patrick Geary and Ian Wood is no more inclusive of women than the old model of the early medieval historians. The story remains one of clever men taking territory that belonged to other men by craft rather than force. Although in the modern version of early medieval origins barbarian leaders were not

---

[27] Gisela Ripoll López, "The Arrival of the Visigoths in Hispania: Population Problems and the Process of Acculturation," in Pohl and Reimitz, *Strategies of Distinction*, 151–87, esp. 163.

[28] See the famous letter of Bishop Remigius to Clovis in 481 or 486: *Epistulae Austrasiacae*, ed. W. Gundlach in *MGH Epistolae 3, Epistolae Merowingici et Karolini Aevi* (Berlin, 1892), 1, 2.

[29] Patrick Périn, "A propos de publications récentes concernant le peuplement en Gaule à l'époque mérovingienne: la 'question franque'," *Archéologie Médiévale* 11 (1981), 125–45; Geary, *Before France and Germany*, 114–15.

so barbarian, and were more interested in fighting with each other
for control over territory than in wiping out natives of conquered
lands, the historians' gaze remains fixed on the number of barbarian
fighters in any group, the interrelations of different groups, and the
degree of Romanization among their male leaders. If so few Franks
took Gaul, and if they came as soldiers and administrators, then only
a tiny number of women must actually have participated in political-
style Frankish invasions (on the invaders' side, at least) and women
remain peripheral to the question of barbarian ethnic identity and
the creation of the new kingdoms.[30]

Yet, in fact, women were intimately involved in the reconstruction
of the European map, the revision of ethnic identities, and the re-
structuing of communities and kin-groups. Archeological evidence
from burials shows that from the earliest barbarian drift into the
Romanized regions of Europe, women accompanied immigrants and
invaders and were among barbarians laid to rest. Not much evidence
exists to place women on the scene of battle when Stilicho was trying
to hold the Rhine, or Alaric was burning Rome, or Clovis was am-
bushing Syagrius. Yet the evidence of women's bodies provides some
of the best evidence for a revised view of the whole process of invasion
and immigration. Together, burial remains from the Continent and its
related islands suggests that "invasion" may be a less accurate word for
what happened in Europe during the fourth, fifth, and sixth centuries
than vaguer terms like "drift," "acculturation," or "migration," even
"two-way migration." In other words, the movement of peoples in
and around the fifth century did not occur suddenly, as a single event,
and in a single direction. It was a long process of migrations that involved travel out of and into non-Germanic territories, and the constant redistributing of territory within western Europe.[31] It was also
a process that included the political assimilation and ethnic reidenti-
fication of native women and men as much as the arrival of outsiders.

In Italy, for instance, where groups of warriors did actually sweep
across the countryside during the sixth-century Gothic wars, the

[30] As in Peter Heather, "Disappearing and Reappearing Tribes," in Pohl and Reimitz,
Strategies of Distinction, 95–116.

[31] In a related scholarly development, some archeologists have decided that Celts did
not necessarily invade and dominate Europe in the Bronze and Iron ages, but that
their culture did, indeed, spread everywhere: Barry Raftery, review of *The Ancient
Celts*, by Simon James, *The Times Literary Supplement* 4967 (June 12, 1998), 9. See
also Simon James, *The Atlantic Celts: Ancient People or Modern Invention?* (Madison:
University of Wisconsin Press, 1999), 43–66.

same burial evidence once used to prove the existence of southward-migrating barbarian hordes now suggests quite the opposite. Small groups of warriors settled and very quickly assimilated into the local population. Burials in northern Italy commonly reveal both Lombard metalwork and Roman-style pottery vessels. Whether Lombard-influenced Roman hands produced the pots or Romanized Lombard craftspeople made them, mutual influence is indisputable. Lombards picked up the Latin language and Roman ways of dress. Romans used Lombard principles in their ancient legal codes. Both groups mixed names. If the Lombard invasions were violent it was because the Lombards were not very organized; they overcame each region differently with local effects. No material evidence supports a story of cities destroyed or population dispersed and massacred. Settlement and social structure remained largely the same, and those who had lived upon and worked the land for their landlords continued to do so.[32] Together, conquerors and conquered, women and men, created the kingdom of the Lombards and the infrastructure that supported it.

In England, archeologists have dug up many kinds of physical evidence for the lives of women during the invasion period, although most of the bits and pieces remain difficult to interpret. Settlement sites of the newcomers are hard for archeologists to find because the shape and arrangement of fields did not really change until much later in the Saxon period, after about 800. In other words, the Angles and Saxons did not arrive in Britain and immediately redefine the landscape according to their own customs, forcing natives off their farms. Rural communities of Britons were not completely displaced by newcomers. Housewives kept the same houses or had new ones built very near by, while farmers kept on planting and pasturing animals where they always had. Even field boundaries and the tracks between them remained much the same in much of Britain.[33] Changes in language also suggest assimilation rather than massive migration and conquest. Many place names in England contain elements of the original language of the Britons, suggesting the melding of Germanic and Brythonic languages and peoples in the fifth and sixth centuries. Communities may have chosen to become "English" by taking on the language and customs of a few powerful newcomers to their territory. Further, genetic evidence shows that the few boat-loads of Germanic invaders described by Bede were more likely than the

---

[32] Wickham, *Early Medieval Italy*, 68–71.
[33] Higham, *Rome, Britain, and the Anglo-Saxons*, 131–36.

arrival of large armies that displaced the native population. Genetic variants common in Frisia and Schleswig, homelands of the invading tribes, turn out to be rare in modern Britain, even in the southeast, where historical, archeological, and linguistic evidence suggests the greatest displacement of the natives. DNA evidence from Cheddar, in the southwest of England, hints that the same families may have lived in the area from the Paleolithic.[34] So, Bede's report of invasions was accurate insofar as only small numbers of Germanic newcomers actually migrated to Britain, followed by major assimilation among Germanic and British inhabitants of the island. If women came along in Bede's boats, they cannot have been many, although female and male kinfolk probably followed the initial invaders. Given material, linguistic, and biological evidence, far more important to the creation of England was the contribution of women already in Britain.

The process of immigration and invasions was quick and violent at times, but slow and more peaceful at others. In England, as in northern Italy, the pace of architectural change in combination with the literary record provides slight clues to regional variations. When Gildas, writing in a lull between invasions, lamented the political chaos among British kingdoms, he must have known that Britons had already begun to abandon Roman public buildings and spaces. Depopulation and bad weather were a more likely cause than warriors from Denmark and Sweden. Similar trends also appeared in northern Gaul in the fourth and fifth centuries, where residents of villas let them crumble and Roman towns shrank within their walls.[35] Pottery, which has always attracted archeologists as a way of charting population movements or detecting the diffusion of foreign influences, shows that both invaders and previous inhabitants of Britain sought out new places to live within already established landscapes. What is more, shards from British pots, Roman-influenced British pots, Germanic pots, Roman-influenced Germanic pots, Germanic-influenced British pots, and all the rest are very difficult to tell apart,

---

[34] Martin Evison, "Lo the Conquering Hero Comes (or Not)," *British Archaeology* 23 (Apr. 1997), http://www.britarch.ac.uk/ba/ba23/ba23feat.html; Colin Renfrew and Katie Boyle, eds., *Archaeogenetics: DNA and the Population Prehistory of Europe* (Cambridge: McDonald Institute for Archaeological Research, 2000).

[35] For the shrinking of Paris in the late fourth century: Michel Provost, ed., *Carte archéologique de la Gaule* (Paris, 1988–), vol. 75, *Paris*, 76–77, 161–62; for the increase in woodland in post-Roman Gaul: Groenman-Van Waateringe, "Wasteland: Buffer in the Medieval Economy."

thus yielding more proof of quick assimilation. As with the Romano-Lombard pots of Italy, the Anglo-Romano-British pots of England could have been made by anyone living in ethnically mixed communities. Place names and burial sites likewise suggest cultural mixing rather than drastic violence or expropriation and resettlement.

Although all the evidence taken from the ground points to minimal population changes with great cultural and political effects, none of it reveals much about the specific involvement of women. But dead women tell a different story, helping to refocus the question of invasion by men to one of cultural change among both women and men. Burial evidence and the arrangement of cemeteries have long formed the basis of nationalistic arguments about the origins of barbarian kingdoms. German scholars have pointed to the spread of Frankish custom as evidence of Germanic conquest, while proponents of native Celtic peoples or Roman sympathizers have interpreted the same evidence as local rather than Germanic, Christian rather than pagan, Romanized rather than barbarian.[36] Few dispute that immigrants brought with them their own funeral rituals and styles of burial, as well as artifacts that they buried with bodies. Yet the testimony of graves does not reveal the extent of Germanic influence in fifth-century Gaul or Iberia or Britain so clearly as it reveals the role of women as cultural negotiators.

In Britain, for instance, fifth-century Germanic families liked to cremate their bodies and deposit the ashes in urns, whereas previously native Britons buried their corpses. As early as 420, Saxons were dumping their urns along the eastern coast of Britain. A little later, they moved inland and placed their urns near old Roman settlements, signaling their recognition and mastery of these cultural, political, and agricultural foci upon the landscape. Within a few decades, though, the newcomers had switched to inhumations like everyone else, although they preferred to leave the dead with personal symbols of past status. In particular, they liked to bury the elite wearing jewelry and carrying weapons. Already, in the first half of the century, women's brooches crafted in northern Germanic styles were going into the ground in the southeast of Britain. By the middle of the fifth century, burials from York to Dorchester included brooches in typically Anglian, Saxon, and Jutish styles.[37] At first, this seems good

---

[36] Périn, "A propos de publications récentes"; Bailey K. Young, "The Myth of the Pagan Cemetery," in Karkov *et al.*, *Spaces of the Living and the Dead*, 61–86.

[37] Higham, *Rome, Britain, and the Anglo-Saxons*, 162–81.

evidence that women were in the first or second landings of invaders. They died with their men, and were buried with their brooches on. If so, then the increase in brooches in the later fifth century signals that women came in growing numbers after the initial incursions.

But burial evidence in southeast Britain does not really demonstrate that either women or men invaded. Artifacts prove the spread of Germanic custom via females, but not necessarily the spread of Germans. First, however, who is to say that only ladies wore what archeologists have called "ladies'" brooches? The sexing of burials and artifacts has proceeded along suspiciously Victorian lines of thinking. When the bones themselves are insufficient to determine the sex of the body, archaeologists sex the burial by artifacts. That is, if they think that women should have worn brooches, then burials including brooches become women's burials. Burials with weapons become men's burials. One archeologist divided the finds of Yorkshire burials from two cemeteries into four groups: burials with jewelry; burials with weapons; burials with other goods; and burials with no artifacts. Approximately half the burials had neither jewelry nor weapons; about twelve per cent at one site seemed to be women buried with weapons; about fifteen per cent at one site included men buried with jewelry.[38] In other words, brooches might not indicate burials of women. Or only certain kinds of women may have worn brooches to the grave, as in sixth-century northern Gaul where older women were buried with only an occasional necklace, while nubile females went into the ground with a full array of ornaments and the odd weapon. The Merovingians structured a "grammar of display" in their burials according to sex, age, and status.[39]

The burial of female skeletons with Germanic items implicates women in the spread of Germanic custom. However, the burial of what might be women with what might be Germanic brooches does not necessarily indicate the presence of Germanic women. Brooches or jewelry styles might have immigrated instead of, or along with, Germans themselves. Jewelry and burial styles also reached England

---

[38] Sam Lucy, "Housewives, Warriors and Slaves? Sex and Gender in Anglo-Saxon Burials," in *Invisible People and Processes: Writing Gender and Childhood into European Archaeology*, ed. Jenny Moore and Eleanor Scott (London: Leicester University Press, 1997), 150–68.

[39] Guy Halsall, "Female Status and Power in Early Merovingian Central Austrasia: The Burial Evidence," *Early Medieval Europe* 5 (1996), 1–24. Halsall argues that sexing burials by gender-appropriate finds is valid.

via trade or other cultural contact. Or Germanic style may have caught on among indigenous women soon after the early invasions. Women may have helped accommodate Germanic arrivals by trading with Angles, Saxons, and Jutes for Germanic-style items, or by encouraging the local manufacture of newly fashionable objects, or just by mating with Germanic newcomers and accepting gifts of brooches. Graves are rarely obviously native or Germanic, pagan or Christian, in Britain or elsewhere, no matter what nationalist interpreters have said in the past. A body wearing a typically British cloak fastened with a Germanic brooch, oriented to the east in Christian fashion but buried far from a church, presents an alarming puzzle for archeologists.

As best we can guess, then, the material evidence for the peopling of Britain points to a small invasion mostly by male warriors followed by quick acculturation there, as in Gaul, Iberia, and Italy. The continuity of field systems, the small amount of resettlement, the mixed burials, minor genetic change measured in the DNA of bodily remains, along with the quick adoption of English language and place names, all suggest that groups of Anglo-Saxon men came to settle as lords of the British landscape and its population. Indeed, by the early seventh century, the land had been carved into recognizable kingdoms, each with its Germanic ruling dynasty, yet based on older provincial and tribal boundaries upon the landscape. Already by the early seventh century, the king of Kent had issued a formal, written, Roman-style legal code of Germanic custom to guide the interactions of all his subjects, of all ethnic origins.

Everywhere in Europe, military men established new kingdoms by a combination of means. Some mercenary troops raided territory and seized local rule, whereas elsewhere men with Roman sensibilities practiced gradual political infiltrations. In some areas, new rulers encouraged the cultural assimilation of diverse peoples, not population replacement or large-scale expropriation of property. The pace of change varied by region and period. In Gaul, groups of Germanic warriors had long been harrying the borders of the Roman provinces before Clovis finally unified the Frankish tribes in the middle of the fifth century, fought back the Burgundians and Alamanni, and declared himself king. The Visigoths moved more efficiently as a large group of mercenaries through Toulouse and into Iberia and settled rather quickly as rulers until the Arab invasions of the early eighth century. In Britain, mercenaries from the mainland, initially allied with native lords, subdued their allies and assumed rule beginning in the southeast in the middle of the fifth century, and gradually spread in armed groups throughout the island as far as Hadrian's wall. Everywhere, the invaders and immigrants met a different combination of resistance and compliance, a different degree of ethnic exclusivity or fluidity, and a variety of military and cultural tactics for accommodation. None of these kingdoms grew in isolation. Trade, warfare, pilgrimage, and inter-marriage among the ruling elite continued throughout the continent in the fifth, sixth, and seventh centuries.

Nowhere were women allowed to wield weapons in the process. Nowhere did historians recall women accompanying or openly resisting the men who initially came to power. Yet everywhere women assimilated and acculturated with the best of men. In fact, their role as mediators among cultures and classes of men is well established in the historiography. The period was not without women, despite the barbarian chroniclers, traditional historians, or forward-thinking archeologists. Only men's histories of men are without women. Gregory and the others may not have noticed them, but a few women probably did accompany groups of marauders and mercenary armies as wives and kinswomen of leaders, slaves, or hangers-on. They probably followed after, too. But the most important deed of the majority of women and men in this period of transitions was to remain and wait. Women who became subjects of the new lords of Europe were already waiting in Britain, Gaul, and throughout Europe when alien men arrived. To return women to the history of the period, and indeed to rethink our whole notion of the period of "invasions," we must turn our eyes away from the tiny percentage of charging barbarians and their faithful chroniclers, away from the newer histories of barbarian identities, and even from archeological arguments over the ethnicity of material finds, to discover what the larger population was doing during and after the warfare. If we cannot find women on the move, we can certainly find them standing still.

THE STATUS OF WOMEN IN THE NEW KINGDOMS

What were women doing while warriors went off to fight other warriors, while newly established rulers tried to expand their frontiers, while dynasties fell and rose? They followed stoically. They cowered at home in fear. They complained and tried to get on with the business of raising children and managing the farm, depending on their status and relation to the men in control. Like it or not, waiting and following were enduring conditions of life for virtually all females and many men in pre-modern Europe. It does not mean that women never traveled, just that most traveled locally and incidentally. Nor does it signal that women were passive, rather than active, powerful, and influential among ruling men. It does mean, however, that women's participation in the visible politics of early medieval history depended upon their legal and social ties to the armed, enfranchised, visible citizens of the pre-modern world. Their family and ethnic origins mattered only if these issues deterred men from marrying them. Their legal status affected their assimilation if they were slaves. Both of these factors operated differently for men than for women in the slow melding of population groups and cultures.

Laws of status, assault, property and inheritance, and betrothal and marriage tell us more about the history of most women during and after the period of "invasions" than narrative histories. Legal evidence from the early Middle Ages is notoriously difficult to interpret for many annoying reasons. Different combinations of Roman law and oral heritage influenced the content of legal codes, but specific political circumstance sometimes inspired particular kings to issue or reissue older versions of laws.[40] Kings used the proclamation of revised codes to announce their authority to those they ruled or wanted to rule; laws were also useful tools for defining the ethnic identity of the inhabitants of their territories, or for molding diverse ethnic groups into confederations. However, laws themselves cannot tell us whether legal practice followed the pronouncement of king's law. For one thing, local warleaders and aristocrats were more likely to have been responsible for the execution of justice than were kings at a distance.[41] For another, even law-abiding citizens do not always interpret law as their rulers do. What is more, the process of making and preserving law, as well as enforcing laws, was not the same throughout barbarian Europe, although many of the codes seem much the same in content. Despite the difficulties of reading the early medieval laws, however, certain themes and assumptions in the texts help explain

---

[40] P. S. Barnwell, "Emperors, Jurists and Kings: Law and Custom in the Late Roman and Early Medieval West," *Speculum* 168 (2000), 6–29.

[41] Patrick Wormald, "*Lex Scripta* and *Verbum Regis*: Legislation and Germanic Kingship from Euric to Cnut," in Wormald, *Legal Culture in the Early Medieval West: Law as Text, Image, and Experience* (London: Hambledon Press, 1999), 1–44.

why some women were able to participate in the organization of the new societies, even at their highest levels. The laws also suggest why early medieval writers finally got around to remembering women once the new Christian kingdoms came into existence. As those who codified the laws at the command of kings knew well, women's well-defined social roles and functions were crucial to the formation of new states.

Once barbarian polities became territorial kingdoms, kings began to demand codifications of laws just as they ordered up tribal histories. Like the Roman officials they admired, kings wished to create, collect, and record rules for governance. Euric, king of the Visigoths, was the first to set down laws in the 480s. Gundobad committed Burgundian laws to writing before his death in 516, and Clovis ordered his literate, Roman jurists to record Frankish law around the same time. The codes of other Franks, such as the Bavarians and the Alamanni, followed. The Kentish king Æðelbehrt ordered the first Anglo-Saxon code into writing around 602, and the Lombards recorded their rules in the middle of the seventh century. The Irish and Welsh were among the last to record their laws, although Celticists argue that the laws themselves derived from much older, orally transmitted legal maxims. Irish laws were unique in that they contained little in the way of Roman material (except references to Romanized Christian rulings) and belonged to no particular king, but were kept by a class of professional jurists or legal teachers.[42] All of the codes continued to be revised and updated by later kings of the early Middle Ages and their literate legal experts.[43]

Germanic rulers relied on Roman legal precedents combined with what they believed to be their own people's legal traditions to govern their diverse subjects. As early as 319 an imperial Roman enactment decreed that customary law supplied a valid precedent for legal rulings among inhabitants of the West; likewise, barbarian rulers in their codes sometimes quoted the Theodosian code verbatim or barely revised its provisions.[44] The earliest codes maintained the concept of personal law, in which a person was judged according to the rules

---

[42] Fergus Kelly, *A Guide to Early Irish Law* (Dublin Institute for Advanced Studies, 1988), 231–33.

[43] Rudolf Buchner, *Die Rechtsquellen*, vol. 3 of Wilhelm Wattenbach and Wilhelm Levison, *Deutschlands Geschichtsquellen im Mittelalter: Vorzeit und Karolinger* (Berlin: Hertz, 1952–57).

[44] Barnwell, "Emperors, Jurists and Kings," 15.

of his or her people, not territory. Yet even such crucial concepts among the remembered customs of the barbarians were, like the cultures which produced them, odd exchanges and amalgams of Roman learning and barbarian tradition. The Lombards, for instance, institutionalized customary tribute for their armies paid by Roman nobles in the form of *hospitalitas* (material support), which they wrote down in imperially inspired Latin codes.[45] The Visigoths revised Roman rules forbidding the intermarriage of citizens with rebellious provincials into rules against the marriage of their own subjects to Franks.[46] Neither Roman ideals nor Germanic custom could endure unmodified in territories where families of mixed ethnic descent married new immigrants and produced offspring with their own ideas about identity and community. Since Roman law and Germanic custom treated women differently, the varying mix of rulings directly affected the lives of women, particularly in their estimation of the legal (dis)enfranchisement of women.

From Ireland and England south to Lombard Italy, the laws were based on a few fundamental concepts.[47] First, everyone had a legal value, called in Germanic codes *wergeld*, calculated in material goods. This was the fine to be paid to the kin-group for the murder or harm of one of its individuals. A portion of the *wergeld* was also due if he or she committed legal offenses, such as theft or adultery. A person thus might be worth a certain number of coins or cows. Not everyone was worth the same number of cows or coins, however. Worth depended upon class, age, and gender. The legal standard in every lawcode was the arms-bearing free man, whose dependants were calculated in relation to him. Kings, the ultra-free and mightily arms-bearing, were worth far more than ordinary warriors and farmers. Women, children, slaves, and outsiders were usually worth some fraction of an arms-bearing man. However, the *wergeld* of women varied by region. In some codes, pre-menopausal women's *wergeld* was double that of men of similar status, reflecting women's worth as

---

[45] Paul the Deacon, *Historia Langobardorum*, II.31–32, III.16; *The Lombard Laws* [*Leges Langobardorum*], trans. Katherine Fisher Drew (Philadelphia: University of Pennsylvania Press, 1973).

[46] Hagith Sivan, "Why Not Marry a Barbarian? Marital Frontiers in Late Antiquity (The Example of *CTH* 3.14.1)," in *Shifting Frontiers in Late Antiquity*, ed. Hagith Sivan and Ralph Mathiesen (Aldershot: Variorum, 1996), 136–45.

[47] Lisa M. Bitel, "Women in Early Medieval Northern Europe," in *Becoming Visible: Women in European History*, ed. Renate Bridenthal and Susan Mosher Stuard (3rd edn., Boston: Houghton Mifflin, 1997), 109–12.

child-bearers.[48] Frankish–Salian law, around 500, distinguished between the value of women according to their age and potential for child-bearing:

Concerning the killing of little children and women

3. If any one has hit a free woman who is pregnant, and she dies, he shall be sentenced to 28000 denars, which makes 700 shillings.
6. If any one has killed a free woman after she has begun bearing children, he shall be sentenced to 24000 denars, which makes 600 shillings.
7. After she can have no more children, he who kills her shall be sentenced to 8000 denars, which makes 200 shillings.[49]

A pregnant woman was worth more than a potentially fertile woman, who was far more valuable than a post-menopausal female. Most legal codes followed this system of valuation, although in Irish law a woman's *lóg n-enech* or *dire* was always worth only half that of her guardian.[50] Hence, jurists built inequalities based on gender, usually favorable to men but sometimes to child-bearing women, into early medieval societies as an acceptable legal principle.

Other assumptions of the laws emphasized the importance of family and the negotiated nature of laws, at the expense of women's public participation. Family was the premier property-owning, oath-swearing and decision-making unit, and the group that prosecuted both legal suits and bloody feuds. All laws were essentially contracts and all legal offenses were primarily civil offenses negotiated among families. Perpetrators paid fines to those whom they injured or to the victim's family and, sometimes, to the king or lord of a territory. No police force brought about justice. No central government tried or punished offenders, although kings continuously tried to acquire such prerogatives. Lawyers and jurists negotiated among conflicting parties, but were powerless to enforce their decisions; only the community itself could make the law work, by witnessing and swearing to events, by abiding by the decisions of judges, and by punishing offenders. When criminals refused guilt, the result could be outlawry by the community or retribution by the injured.

---

[48] *Lex Ribuaria,* ed. F. Beyerle and R. Buchner, *MGH Leges* 3, 2 (1954), 78–79.

[49] *Pactus Legis Salicae,* ed. Karl A. Eckhardt, *MGH Leges* 4, 1 (1962), 92 (24.8–9); see also Suzanne Wemple, *Women in Frankish Society: Marriage and the Cloister, 500 to 900* (Philadelphia: University of Pennsylvania Press, 1981), 28–29.

[50] D. A. Binchy, ed., *Corpus Iuris Hibernici* (Dublin Institute for Advanced Studies, 1978), 519, 779; Kelly, *Guide,* 79; Bitel, *Land of Women,* 20–23.

Every legal code disenfranchised women to some extent. Laws required male representatives for both civil and criminal actions (although medieval lawmakers did not distinguish between civil and criminal law as we do.) Their legal protection was institutionalized in the *mundium* that a woman's legal guardian retained, similar in principle to the *patria potestas* of Roman law. A father or other kinsman would transfer his daughter's *mundium* to her husband at betrothal. Women were rarely family leaders or heads of households, responsible for prosecuting feuds or preserving family interests. They were not able to participate in the contracts and oaths that governed and organized their societies. They could perform no legal acts without the permission and guidance of male guardians – no contracts, no sales, no marriages, no refusal of marriage, no inheritance, no gifts, and no other public, rule-abiding actions. The Irish laws put it succinctly in an eighth-century tract that reflects much older ideas:

Her father watches over her when she is a girl; her *cétmuinter* watches over her when she is the wife of a *cétmuinter*; her sons watch over her when she is a woman with children; her kin watch over her when she is a woman of the kin [i.e. with no other natural guardian, father husband, or son]; the Church watches over her when she is a woman of the Church. She is not capable of sale or purchase or contract or transaction without one of her heads, save a proper gift to one of her heads, with agreement and without neglect.[51]

In fact, the earliest Irish laws often equated Irish women with children, outlaws, and the *baeth*, the senseless fool who cannot make any legal decisions, in their total legal incapacity. Yet in societies with charters, unlike Ireland, royal women and abbesses (often the same) were able to add their names to the list of witnesses who guaranteed property transactions, especially toward the end of the early Middle Ages, and co-signed their names on charters issued by their husbands.

In general, women entered the legal theory expressed by lawcodes as marriageable, married, or no-longer-married individuals, rather than as buyers, owners, claimants, or offenders. They were dependents, even property. Much of the legal material regarding women concerned sexual unions and their offspring, limitations on rights to inheritance and property, and harm done to women. Anglo-Saxon laws from the early seventh century assumed women's utter passivity

---

[51] Binchy, *Corpus*, 443–44; Rudolf Thurneysen, *Irisches Recht*, Abhandlungen der Preussischen Akademie der Wissenschaften, Phil.-Hist. Klasse. 2 (Berlin: Verlag der Akademie der Wissenschaften, 1931), 35–37.

before the law. King Æðelbehrt of Kent, for instance, was concerned with women as objects of exchange; he regulated men in the process of "buying" a wife, and penalized the cad who abducted a widow "who does not belong to him."[52] The language of possession infiltrated all barbarian legal codes, early and late, especially in rules of betrothal, marriage, abduction, and rape.

But sensible people knew that women were properly human, and such folk found ways to get around laws when they wanted. Few parents were willing to see their daughters sink into poverty just because society formally favored male heirs. Lombard laws were among the most conservative regarding the status and rights of women, but over two centuries the people of Salerno came to interpret restrictions against women's property differently than they had when Rothair issued his code in 643. By the ninth century Salernian widows could expect their *Morgengabe* (gift to the wife from husband at marriage), or a quarter-share of their husband's property, as well as the income from a good deal more of it.[53] Carolingian Franks willed property to their daughters, and both tenth-century English charters and eighth-century Irish law show that women received premortem inheritances from fond fathers, or inherited property after the deaths of husbands and kinsmen. Elites such as the *maiores* (nobles) of northern Italy or the Anglo-Saxon kings could will property to wives and daughters because they had enough to spare. Among the Anglo-Saxon charters, about eighty recorded transactions included lay women, mostly the wives or widows of kings and high nobles, and about forty listed religious women, out of about two thousand total such documents. Almost forty wills of Anglo-Saxon women from after the middle of the tenth century also survive, attesting to the property rights of a tiny percentage of England's elite women.[54] Whether or not ordinary farmers made sure to provide for their widows, or to divide up their goods equitably among all their children is another matter.

Despite a sensible concern for the wellbeing of women, Europeans upheld patriarchal legal principles throughout the Middle Ages

[52] *WEHD* 1, 393 (*c*. 76–84).

[53] Barbara Kreutz, "The Twilight of *Morgengabe*," in *Portraits of Medieval and Renaissance Living*, ed. Samuel Cohn and Steven Epstein (Ann Arbor: University of Michigan Press, 1996), 131–47.

[54] Helen Jewell, *Women in Medieval England* (Manchester University Press, 1996), 28–29.

(and well beyond). Composers of laws and their sponsoring kings were most concerned about women not as thinking participants in society, but as wives, mothers, heiresses, and victims whose legal acts affected their men. Those who organized early medieval kingdoms wanted women to move smoothly from natal kin to husband's family, settle down to keeping house and producing babies, and act as supports and helpmates to their men. The first function of slave and servant women was to labor for their masters. If free or unfree women were injured or bothered in any illegitimate way, lawmen sought to protect them. When women aged past their usefulness as reproducers, kinfolk tried to provide for them with dowries or widow's portions. The legal standard remained the free adult male, for whom women existed in relation and by comparison. Adult freemen were the actors in public life, moving through public places, with powers over persons to negotiate, bargain, make transactions, sue, and right legal wrongs by negotiation or violence. Females were to be protected, secured, bartered, and exchanged.

SUBVERSIVE WOMEN, WARRIOR WOMEN

Women and men probably abided by these laws much of the time but, of course, people also broke the rules. Disenfranchised women were to stay at home, according to the laws, but a few got out, moved around, and made trouble. Early medieval legal texts tell us what women were supposed to do and to be, but they also hint at the subversions women practiced – the contracts they made when they were not really supposed to, the sexual unions they formed against the will of their guardians, the property they controlled and allocated. The laws' insistence that women could never gain any formal authority within the new kingdoms of the early medieval West were more a legalist's dream than reality, at least if the stories of Gregory of Tours and other writers are any indication.

To a certain extent, archeology backs up the laws. The hundreds of hut-sites dug up by archeologists throughout Europe attest to the continuation of rural life during the period when barbarians were invading, settling, organizing, and writing down their laws. While Clovis was attacking and hacking his enemies, women were marrying and having babies. When Rothair issued his code to the Lombards, women were tending the vines and minding the pigs. While English kings feuded over their domination of the southern half of the island, women spun, wove, and clothed their husbands and children. All the time that Germanic warriors were moving into the neighborhood, expropriating estates or merely settling on unoccupied lands, taking over governmental positions and imposing new lordships, life went on for most women in much the same way it always had – at least, between waves of local or invasive warfare. Maybe some women were taken as slaves by newcomers, and maybe some married the foreigners who settled nearby. The earliest legal codes, with their separate rules for Romans and Germanic peoples, indicate some intermarriage or, at least, sexual intercourse of both the consensual and non-consensual kind among the two groups. Salic law, for instance, frowned upon the case of a freewoman – without specifying whether she was native or Frankish – who slept with a slave, presumably a native; also a freeborn man who carried on with an alien – which meant native bondswoman.[55] By and large, the legal codes aimed, at least in principle, to promote rather than prevent the integration of old and new cultures.

Yet just as the rules against abduction and inter-class sexual unions also revealed a community's anxiety about women who refused to cooperate with marriage laws, so the rules about women's other legal transactions existed as ideals, followed in the main but broken by exceptional women. And no women were more exceptional, more vibrant, more fabulous than the women of tribal histories. The same historians who kept silent about women in the invasion period opened their pages to the wild, fierce clamor of queens, lovers, saints, and witches. Such forceful females stormed through the post-invasion chapters of tribal histories, as well as the sagas, epics, and chronicles of the barbarian period, working their will upon kings and armies, bishops and peasants. Some of the wildest women remain to us only as figures from later medieval fiction: the warrior women and goddesses of sagas, myths, and *Edda* who supposedly rampaged the earth during the migration period. But powerful rulebreakers also appeared in the tribal histories as the authentically historical queens and ladies of the post-invasion period. Just as the works of Gregory of Tours, Paul the Deacon, Bede, and other storytellers proposed a fiction of ethnic origins, so they concocted symbolic narratives of women's roles in early medieval kingdoms.

Neither taletellers nor historians treated all these figures equally. Each genre had its literary demands, and the oral sources of some

---

[55] *Pactus Legis Salicae*, XIII.8–9.

of this material helped to determine the characters' actions. Some female figures were evil women who were punished for their presumption. Others more successfully worked their wiles through the traditional, legal roles of wife, concubine, mother, or daughter. And still others – the women most praised by early medieval writers, as we shall see in the next chapter – did so as professional holy women. But a nagging admiration for all formidable women, no matter how devious or furious, how decadent or oblivious of men's laws, pervaded all the narrative texts of the early Middle Ages. Modeled after Roman matrons, biblical heroines, and the fighting women of Germanic lore, the women of early medieval historical fiction sent messages not just about women-as-a-species but about the nature of barbarian polities and peoples.

The greatest puzzle in early medieval literature was a powerful woman. This was an age when kings declared laws in order to regulate every important aspect of gender relations, divide labor by gender, relegate women to private spaces, and control every step of their sexual careers; when Christian ideals, which also subordinated wives to husbands and female religious to their male superiors, but aimed to prevent the sexual use of female slaves, had begun to infiltrate the cultures of the European Continent. Vestiges of urbane but sexist Roman law influenced equally sexist barbarian customs, especially in the areas of family and marriage. Yet killer queens crashed through the stories of every early medieval culture. Goddesses flew above battlefields, bringing battalions down to carnage. Territorial mothers seduced and abandoned the very kings who had conquered whole islands.

Some historians and literary scholars make sense of these fearsome females by deducing a genuine authority for women in real life. Others differentiate sharply between "images" of women in medieval literature and "real" women.[56] Yet the difference that we perceive between the women of literature and those of laws may not

---

[56] For literary discussions of the symbolic importance of heroines: J. P. Mallory, ed., *Aspects of the Táin* (Belfast: December Publications, 1992); Patricia Lysaught, *The Banshee: The Irish Supernatural Death-Messenger* (Dublin: O'Brien Press, 1986); Jenny Jochens, *Old Norse Images of Women* (Philadelphia: University of Pennsylvania Press, 1996); Jane Chance, *Woman as Hero in Old English Literature* (Syracuse University Press, 1986); Damico and Olsen, *New Readings on Women in Old English Literature*; see also Fatima Mernissi, *The Forgotten Queens of Islam* (Minneapolis: University of Minnesota Press, 1993), esp. 45–49; Carol Clover, "Maiden Warriors and Other Sons," *Journal of English and Germanic Philology* 85 (1986), 35–49.

have seemed irreconcilable to early medieval Europeans, who never looked to their literature as a mirror of life – although, given that they had only the distorting mirrors of polished silver and rippled waters, perhaps they might as well have. Whatever connection medieval people themselves made between the ladies of literature and those of real life, it is true that while lawmakers sought to bind women's every step, storytellers and their audiences were ensnared by women beyond control. The very men who wrote the laws probably went home at night to read of, or hear a bard singing of, the woman who raised or devastated kingdoms. The idea of a mighty woman was familiar and fascinating to all, both those who promoted and those who demeaned women. Hence, early medieval stories of subversive women can alert us to the possibility that not all women and men lived according to the repressive legal codes of the barbarians, even if people accepted the legal principle of female subordination enshrined within the laws.

As they moved across Europe, the barbarians had generated stories, kept orally, of violent women to fit their brutal times. Some of the oldest vernacular accounts of ferocious women probably did come from the Germanic warrior elite, who eventually passed on the reworked stories to their Scandinavian cousins. History was not the appropriate format for Germanic tales of the warrior woman but poetry, it seems, was a good place. To take just one example, the greatest heroine of ancient Germanic tradition had many names in her later incarnations: Sigrdrífa, Brynhildr, Brynhild, Brunhild, Brunhilde. She was the princess of the thirteenth-century *Nibelungenlied* and the Valkyrie of Wagner's nineteenth-century *Ring* cycle. She was also the tragic shield-maiden of *Volsunga saga* and the early medieval Icelandic *Edda*, poetry that encapsulated traditional remnants from as long ago as the fourth-century Hunnic invasions.[57]

The early medieval tragedy of Brynhildr, which supposedly occurred in the fifth century, illustrated the typical disasters that female invaders and fighters could cause. Brynhildr was a shield-maiden, a Valkyrie, whom the god Óðinn had cast into a death-like sleep as punishment for disobeying him in battle. Shield-maidens were supposed to retrieve fallen warriors and escort them to Valhalla, the hall of dead heroes, but Brynhildr had engaged directly in the fight and slain a

---

[57] Jochens, *Old Norse Images of Women*, 89–95.

king to whom Ódinn had promised victory. She also refused to marry anyone who showed fear (presumably, of her). Ódinn sentenced her to slumber and decreed that she would never win a battle again but would, indeed, marry. Her reputation as a warrior and her mysterious wisdom attracted the attentions of the hero and dragon-slayer Sigurdr. Killing the dragon Fáfnir had enabled Sigurdr to understand bird-talk, which sent him to a mountain where he found the shieldmaiden hibernating behind a flaming shield wall. Brynhildr slept in her armor, which bound her so tightly that the hero began to slice it off her with his sword, thus awakening her. Sigurdr was the only man able to breach the flames, shields, and Brynhildr's resistance, signifying simultaneously the conquest of men over women, obedient warrior over the uncontrollable outsider, socialized man over savagery and uncivilized knowledge, human hero over supernatural forces, and multiple other conquerables, depending upon the version of the tale told and the sympathies of the teller.

Byrnhildr and Sigurdr felt immediate attraction but had a problem. Sigurdr was already promised to Gudrun, the sister of his friend Gunnar, and daughter of a Burgundian king. Meanwhile, Gunnar himself asked Sigurdr to woo Brynhildr for him. They rode together to the court of Brynhildr's brother, where she was won by deceit, for she thought she was getting Sigurdr as husband. In fulfillment of Ódinn's decree, then, she fought no more battles and found herself unhappily married. In revenge, she provoked Gunnar into bringing about the death of his comrade Sigurdr, which initiated an entire cycle of killing and counter-killing so familiar to early medieval societies. Brynhildr's enemies not only had to contend with her but also with her avenging brother Atli, a.k.a. Attila the Hun. Eventually, Brynhildr ran herself through with a sword, but not before she hacked up enough serving-women to accompany her to the next life, decked herself appropriately in gold and rich clothing, and sang a series of predictions about her family's future. Brynhildr's storyteller never mourned her femaleness until it became a liability to the heroine. Her earlier identity was that of a Germanic warrior who enjoyed wearing armor, mustering troops, and using her sword. Her story remained popular, appearing in bits and pieces of the Icelandic *Edda*, as the subject of several sagas, and in later medieval literature.

Brynhildr was not the only shield-maiden or warrior woman in Scandinavian tradition, but was just one of Ódinn's shield-maidens.

Other Valkyries and mortal warrior women shared both her prowess and her shortcomings. Sigrún, one of these maidens, wiped out all but one of her kinsmen while supporting her lover, Helgi, in a fight against her would-be suitor, Hodbroddr. Hervor, who appeared in another saga, was the daughter of a fourth-century Gothic king and a Russian princess. Her job was to protect the Gothic border against invading Huns, until she fell in battle.[58] Like Brynhildr, her martial sisters of traditional fiction made some serious mistakes, however. Sigrún wiped out her family. Hervor, who was loyal and heroic, died. None of these ladies was a perfect warrior. Valkyries and other female fighters were attractive saga-fodder for men and women both: women liked hearing about their sisters getting an occasional upper hand, while men could fantasize about cutting Brynhildr out of her armor without being threatened.[59]

By the time they entered barbarian saga and epic, fighting women were aggressive symbols of an uncivilized if heroic past, left behind for an era of kingdom-building. The medieval Danish historian Saxo Grammaticus, writing about 1200, scoffed at the fighting women of the earlier, barbarous Danes:

> There were once women in Denmark who dressed themselves to look like men and spent almost every minute cultivating soldiers' skills; they did not want the sinews of their valor to lose tautness and be infected by self-indulgence. Loathing a dainty style of living they would harden body and mind with toil and endurance, rejecting the fickle pliancy of girls and compelling their womanish spirits to act with a virile ruthlessness. They courted military celebrity so earnestly that one might have guessed they had unsexed themselves. Those especially who had forceful personalities or were tall and elegant embarked on their way of life. As if they were forgetful of their true selves they put toughness before allure, aimed at conflicts instead of kisses, tasted blood, not lips, sought the clash of arms rather than the arm's embrace, fitted to weapons hands which should have been weaving, desired not the couch but the kill, and those they could have appeased with looks they attacked with lances.[60]

Saxo believed that such women had actually existed, but that did not raise his opinion of them, which suggests that not all readers appreciated the heroism of women warriors. They may have been

[58] Ibid., 95–97.   [59] Ibid., 105–07.

[60] Saxo Grammaticus, *Gesta Danorum,* ed. Jorgen Olrik and Hans Raeder (Copenhagen: Levin & Munksgaard, 1931), VII.192; trans. Peter Fisher and ed. Hilda Davidson as *The History of the Danes,* 2 vols. (Cambridge: D. S. Brewer, 1979), vol. 1, 212.

good with swords, but ultimately they failed at men's wars, or they were domesticated, or both. They did not make good wives, either, if Brynhildr was typical (and she was). Either way, they ended up miserable or died young, rendering a double lesson: first, fighting was properly gendered as male so that female fighters, though alluringly heroic, were barbarous; and, secondly, the barbarous past was over. The same rumors flew through medieval Europe about women of the Celtic past, such as the battle goddesses whom we have already encountered hovering over Gaulish fields, or the amazon-like fighters so skilled in the martial arts that they trained the greatest male heroes of saga, or the pseudo-historical queens who led armies to defeat entire provinces.[61] These heroines and their deeds, too, were set safely in an ancient pagan past where they could send lessons to early medieval audiences but cause no real trouble for real men and women.

It was easier for early medieval peoples, reflecting upon their pagan, bloody past, to insert women into the stories of the barbarian period and its wars than to imagine such women loose in their own, present day. It was also more appropriate, in their minds, to put such women in saga and poetry than in histories. Later composers of fictions must have been much more comfortable recording traditions of shield-maidens and fighting queens than were men who actually witnessed the acquisition of power by Germanic tribes and the organization of their kingdoms. By the twelfth century or so, when Brynhildr and her Celtic sisters became popular again, they were no longer threatening but titillating phantoms from a reimagined and very distant past. Tribal ethnogeneses had advanced far beyond the needs of the fifth and sixth centuries by the time such heroines hit the page. Yet some small reality might lie at the core of Byrnhildr and other warrior-women. Although no substantial evidence exists for the regular participation of women in invasions or any kind of warfare − as we have seen, the contemporary historical sources were almost completely silent about their presence − it may be that Germanic and Celtic women participated as witnesses and inciters

[61] See, for instance, tales of Queen Medb: Cecile O'Rahilly, *Táin Bó Cúailnge: Recension I* (Dublin Institute for Advanced Studies, 1976); trans. Thomas Kinsella as *The Táin* (Oxford University Press, 1970); see also Charles Bowen, "Great-Bladdered Medb: Mythology and Invention in the *Táin Bó Cuailnge*," *Éire-Ireland* 10 (1975), 14–34; Tomás Ó Máille, ed. and trans., "Medb Cruachna," *Zeitschrift für Celtische Philologie* 17 (1927), 129–46.

in invasion and fighting.[62] The mere fact that later medieval writers
could look to their ancient past and find the names and personae of
these women warriors still strong in the tradition reveals the muscle
of these women who won kingdoms and repelled enemies. They
endured in barbarian stories and poetry beyond the written word for
centuries, revised and recreated until their stories began to appear in
written bits of *Edda*, spare bardic poems, and finally in the formal
prose, on precious vellum, of the twelfth and later centuries.

HISTORIES OF BARBARIAN QUEENS

The more prim, church-trained historians of Francia may or may
not have savored the tales of shield-maidens and invading queens.
Nonetheless, all the tribal historians of the very early Middle Ages
told some marvelous stories about real women. Just as women of
the epics served to remind early medieval men and women of their
glorious past and their more civilized present, so the tribal historians
used women and gender to explain the historical progress of the new
kingdoms. Gregory of Tours composed his share of dynamic heroines, but he never breathed a word about women bearing arms or
flying as soldiers over the battlefield. By the time he authored his
history, during the twenty long years of his sixth-century episcopate,
the Merovingian Franks had set up an expanding kingdom, issued
laws, turned Christian, and engaged in numerous civil and external
wars. Gregory began his history with the Creation of the world, as
most early medieval historians did, but his focus was actually on recent
events. He aimed to tell the story of Francia. The characters of his last
chapters were those whom he had spied on for decades and whom he
knew by sight, including several influential queens. All these characters ended up in his history, along with Gregory's observations
of miracles and natural wonders, and some behavioral parables. The
Bible served him as model, as much as classical histories. We have
seen what biblical narrative made of women; sometimes women in
scripture were heroines, sometimes symbols, and often villainesses.
In other words, all the ambivalence of saga-writers about forceful
women also entered the early medieval histories. If the women of
histories were different, if they had different aims and methods, they

---

[62] See Ammianus Marcellinus, Dio Cassius, and Tacitus in Tierney, "The Celtic
Ethnography of Posidonius"; for method, see Helen Solterer, "Figures of Female
Militancy in French Literature," *Signs* 16:3 (1991), 522–49.

still simultaneously frightened and attracted their audiences simply because they wielded force. They were not just unusual for being fighters and leaders. They were also attractive, scary, and salutary. Many of Gregory's women and the women of other early histories were very real. Their existence is supported by other documents outside the literary tradition. Despite their literary trappings, tales of barbarian politics, like sagas of barbarian women, can also inform us about women's abilities, men's estimation of these abilities, and the restrictions placed upon women trying to exercise their skills. Stories of early medieval queens and noblewomen can also help us learn more about larger political structures and personal relations in past periods.

Like any other wife, a Merovingian Frankish queen of the fifth or sixth century was entirely dependent upon her husband for status and wealth, although she normally brought a substantial dowry with her. While peasant girls may have contributed a cow to the marriage, princesses might have brought chests of jewelry and extensive estates. Unlike peasant women, who married locally, a queen often came of a people distant from her new home and possibly hostile to her new husband. Her role was theoretically that of what the Anglo-Saxons called "peaceweaver," someone who bound unfriendly peoples together in a political alliance. A native-born, Romanized noblewoman might, for instance, be wed to a new lord of her territory, however barbarous and Germanic. A girl from Burgundy might marry a man from Thuringia. Her job, then, was to join her people and his. Her best chance at success was that of any wife: the production of sons, within a properly sanctioned, legal marriage, who could succeed to their father's position and property, and who could draw on the support of both of their kin-groups, which would unite behind them. The royal wife was also a facilitator and negotiator, who had to charm her husband and maintain happy relations with her kin and his. If she managed to outlive her husband and remain queen, and had borne acceptable sons, then she might achieve new kinds of influence as a widow and regent. Of course, she needed a legal guardian to guide her through the public, legal aspects of her job. Queens also often needed kinsmen with loyal soldiers to support them and protect their children until the latter could rule for themselves. When Clothild, widow of Clovis, wished to pursue politics or feuds, she called upon the very sons she had nurtured to manhood; like anyone else in the kin-based society, she picked and chose those allies who served her purposes, even though her grown-up sons by now had gained the right to represent her, legally and politically.[63]

Brunhild and Balthild were two more Frankish queens who managed to survive and prosper under this system.[64] Brunhild was one of Gregory of Tours's most prominent characters, and was still alive when he wrote. She was a Visigothic princess born around 550 who married King Sigibert of the Frankish kingdom of Austrasia (half of Clovis's old kingdom) in 566. Sigibert chose her specifically for her background. He was annoyed with his relatives, who were consorting irresponsibly with slave-girls. His uncle Theudebert, in particular, had engaged himself to a princess years earlier, but never married her because of his infatuation with his mistress, Deuteria. According to Gregory, Deuteria was well aware of the perils involved in being the concubine, not the legal wife, of a Merovingian monarch; she had a daughter by Theudebert whom Deuteria put in a cart and hurled into the Meuse river when the girl grew old enough to attract the desirous looks of her father.[65] Brunhild, by comparison, seemed thoroughly respectable. Her sister, Galswinth, also married well but tragically, as it turned out; she wed Sigibert's cousin, Chilperic, but found that he was more interested in his concubine, Fredegund. When she asked to return home with her dowry, he had her throttled so that he might marry Fredegund and keep Galswinth's loot.[66]

Brunhild's career began more happily. She governed together with Sigibert until his assassination, when her son was taken into safekeeping and her daughters sent to a monastery. She acted as regent for her son, Childebert, while marrying Sigibert's nephew, Merovech, in an obvious attempt to maintain control over what was, in her eyes, her kingdom. (This displeased her old enemy Fredegund, who had become the third wife of Merovech's father.) She allowed or rejected matches for her offspring and arranged for their accession to royal power, later acting again as regent for her grandsons. She also kept up her own connections with Byzantium to the east, and the Visigothic kingdom to the west. She corresponded with the bishop of

[63] Stephen D. White, "Clotild's Revenge: Politics, Kinship and Ideology in the Merovingian Blood Feud," in Cohn and Epstein, *Portraits of Medieval and Renaissance Living*, 107–30.

[64] Janet Nelson, "Queens as Jezebels: The Careers of Brunhild and Balthild in Merovingian History," in *Medieval Women*, ed. Derek Baker and Rosalind Hill (Oxford: Blackwell, 1978), 31–77.

[65] Gregory of Tours, *Historia*, III.22–26.   [66] Ibid., IV.28.

Rome, told other bishops what to do, and carried out a longstanding vendetta against Fredegund, who had become a mighty queen in her own right.[67] Gregory's history ended before Brunhild's death, but the *Liber Historia Francorum* of a century-plus later took a dimmer view of Brunhild's involvement in politics and her fitting finish:

When [Chlothar II] saw [Brunhild] he said: "O enemy of the Lord, why have you done so many evil things and dared to kill so many of the royal line?" Then the army of the Franks and Burgundians, joined into one, all shouted together that death would be the most fitting for the very wicked Brunhild. Then King Chlothar ordered that she be lifted onto a camel and led through the entire army. Then she was tied to the feet of wild horses and torn apart limb from limb. Finally, she died. Her final grave was the fire. Her bones were burnt. The king, in fact, having made peace all around, returned home.[68]

For Gregory, Brunhild's politics were just tolerable in a good cause. For supporters of the other Merovingian house such as Fredegund's son Chlothar, however, Brunhild was one more scheming woman contributing to the civil strife that ripped Francia apart. She violated all sorts of norms by causing violence and seizing power, and deserved both the vicious death and desecration she got. She was admirable for her strength and loyalty to her children, but in other ways she was an anachronism from the world of saga, a would-be woman warrior who belonged to a less civilized past. The life of St. Columbanus, written by the monk Jonas around 640 and a probably source for the *Liber Historia*, cast Brunhild as an aged, charmless Jezebel who battled against righteous kings and prophetic saints and fully deserved her appalling end.[69]

Fredegund came off better in the *Liber Historia Francorum*, composed among her Neustrian sympathizers. The historian of this eighth-century text granted her a serene burial in the basilica of Saint Vincent the martyr at Paris.[70] But she rated particularly poorly in Gregory's earlier account. Besides instigating the murder of Brunhild's sister, she also ordered assassination attempts on Brunhild's children. Once, when Fredegund had been packed off to a country manor for her part in misruling her husband's kingdom, she was, Gregory wrote,

[67] Ibid., v.1–3, 18, *et passim.* [68] *Liber Historia Francorum*, 96 (sec. 40)
[69] Jonas, *Vita Sancti Columbani*, in *Passiones Vitaeque Sanctorum Aevi Merovingici*, ed. Krusch and Levison, 62–108; trans. Dana Carleton Munro as *Life of St. Columban by the Monk Jonas*, Translations and Reprints from the Original Sources of European History 2 (Philadelphia: University of Philadelphia, 1895).
[70] *Liber Historia Francorum*, 96 (sec. 37).

"very depressed because much of her power had been brought to an end, and yet she considered herself a better woman than Brunhild."[71] She cheered herself up by sending a clerical assassin to the court of Brunhild, who discovered him and packed him off home again. Fredegund was then even more depressed, so she had the man's hands and feet cut off. She also never got along very well with her daughter, Rigunth. After Fredegund tried to marry the girl to a Visigoth – Rigunth made it halfway to Spain, but was plundered of her dowry and returned in disgrace – the mother continuously squabbled with her child. Rigunth, not so pleasant herself, had the habit of insulting her mother and reminding her of her slavish origins. Fredegund responded casually by leading her daughter into the treasure room and declaring, "You can take all your father's things which are still in my possession and do what you like with them." When Rigunth plunged into a chest full of ornaments and jewels in order to grab what she could, Fredegund slammed the lid on her neck and leaned on it with all her might, pressing the edge hard against the girl's neck so that "her eyes were soon standing out of her head." The servants intervened and soldiers dragged the princess outside, but the ladies continued to quarrel and beat each other. The main cause, according to Gregory, of Fredegund's displeasure was "Rigunth's habit of sleeping with all and sundry."[72]

Gregory's women were not all so unholy. Clothild, wife of Clovis, appeared as a patient missionary to the volatile pagan king, suffering the deaths of infant sons and never wavering in her Christian faith. When Clothild sought revenge, in Gregory's eyes she was justified.[73] Radegund was also a model of womanly, if not queenly, virtues; although she made a lousy queen (she neglected her duties as wife and co-ruler and instead spent her time hiding in the privy, performing penance) she became a famous and well-respected abbess and saint. Indeed, her vita served as the model for several later biographies of good queens as well as for hagiographies of queenly saints.[74]

But many of the females who attained power in Gregory's *Historia* did so by means of sex and other feminine machinations, provoking Gregory's mixed response. Even those who never gained much influence taught lessons about the dangers of female influence. Amalsuntha,

---

[71] Gregory of Tours, *Historia*, VII.19.   [72] Ibid., IX.34.

[73] White, "Clotild's Revenge," 127–28.

[74] Pauline Stafford, *Queens, Concubines, and Dowagers: The King's Wife in the Early Middle Ages* (Athens: University of Georgia Press, 1983), 9–12.

3 Radegund and Chlotar. In the upper register, Radegund offers hospitality; in the lower register, she prays privately

a noblewoman who ran off with a slave, ended by murdering her mother. Ingoberg, wife of king Charibert, tried to shame the two shepherdess concubines of her husband, and found herself dismissed from both royal court and marriage. Marcatrude, consort of Guntram, Charibert's brother, poisoned the son of his other woman. Susanna,

wife of Bishop Priscus, ran mad and loose-haired through the city of
Lyons, confessing her sins and calling upon St. Nicetius to help her.
The nuns of Poitiers engaged in what Gregory called a satanic revolt
against their abbess, hiring cut-throats to abduct the abbess and loot
the nunnery. Other women were simply victims, even though they
also sometimes misbehaved, such as Deuteria's daughter or the girl
assaulted by Duke Amalo until her wounds stained the bed of rape.
Likewise, Charibert's third wife (and widow) had to offer herself first
to the Frankish king Guntram, then to a Goth, to avoid death or
the nunnery. These were desperate women struggling to survive in
the political milieu of the new kingdoms. There a woman's worth
depended upon her virtue, her dowry, her marriage, and her children, all of which every woman was constantly in danger of losing.
Even the villainesses were victimized; even the victims were sinners.
Both intra-Frankish politics and literary topoi influenced Gregory's
presentation of women, but Gregory's very selection of female characters was merely a tool in his crafting of the Frankish establishment.

One episode in Gregory's history seems to sum up all the victimized, victimizing women in the entire text: the story of Tetradia,
wife of Count Eulalius. She was a woman of mixed blood, noble
on her mother's side; he was a typical barbarian (although with a
Romanized name), in the habit of taking slave-girls to bed. He ignored his wife, except to "knock her about" when he came back
from his "midnight exercises." He ran into debt, sold off his wife's
dowry, and lost his neglected wife to his nephew Virus, with whom
she fell in love. Virus sent Tetradia off to Duke Desiderius, for
safety's sake, along with all her husband's property she could carry
and her oldest son. Eulalius managed to ambush Virus and kill him.
But Desiderius, who had lost his own wife, then married Tetradia.
Eulalius, in a fit of pique, abducted a nun from a Lyons convent and
married her, but his slave-mistresses were so jealous that they cast a
spell on him. Eulalius killed the nun's cousin, along with the kinsman
of his half-sister (whom his father had sired on a mistress of his own).
In fact, Eulalius committed so many crimes that Gregory had no room
to recount them all. Eventually Eulalius offered his son John to the
priesthood, in exchange for the help of the man he made bishop of
Rodez, in recovering his property via legal suit from Tetradia. (John,
clearly traumatized by his horrible home life, became an extreme
ascetic, subsisting on barley bread, wearing rags, and riding a don-
key about the diocese.) The courts met, ruled in Eulalius's favor, and

imposed a fine of four times the property's worth on Tetradia. However, the dismissed and beaten ex-wife got her own considerable paternal inheritance back.[75] In all these scandalous events, Tetradia evinced no will of her own as did the villainesses of Gregory's stories. But she seems to have played a savvy game and was able, with men's protection, to use the legal process to get what she needed, if not all she wanted. She ended up married to a better man and in charge of what was left of her own property, with no punishment from the authorities or censure from the Christian guardian of the Frankish past for the elopement that set her career in motion.

In other regions and decades, the game was the same as in this emblematic episode from Gregory's *Historia*, even if the rules and players were a bit different. Behind the spite of chroniclers and the devotion of hagiographers, all of whom played local politics in their estimations of strong women, we can observe a theme in the literature of queens and noblewomen: Women survived and even attained influence or wealth by practicing modest subversion with the help of sympathetic and powerful men. For instance, Balthild, queen of a slightly later Frankish generation, governed like Brunhild through her offspring and with the help of sympathetic ministers and bishops, but was a far meeker figure in Frankish literature. We know of her not through rousing histories, such as Gregory's, but through her vita, as a saint. Her hagiographer tells us that God conferred upon Balthild "the grace of prudence" and "vigilant care," which she used to mother her princes, confer with priests and monks, and keep "intimate counsels secret" when entrusted to her; she "humbly and assiduously suggested things to the king."[76] In addition, she made some theological decisions, prohibiting heretical beliefs and the sale of church offices, and outlawing infanticide. She rewarded her followers, both ecclesiastical and secular, with estates and gold.[77] Some documents outside the Frankish canon suggest a dark side to Balthild's character, though, which may be the typical aspersion cast upon an active female politicker by an opponent. The vita of St. Wilfrid, written by an Englishman before 720, made Balthild responsible for the martyrdom of Wilfrid's mentor, Archbishop Dalfinus of Lyons. In this version she was an "evil-hearted queen" who "persecuted the church

---

[75] *Liber Historia Francorum.*, X.8.
[76] McNamara and Halborg, *Sainted Women of the Dark Ages*, 270.
[77] Ibid., 271, 273–74.

of God" and had nine bishops executed.[78] Yet in Frankish sources Balthild remained a meddling but goodhearted queen whose interfering presence at court became intolerable to the magnates of her kingdom, so she retired (possibly forcibly) to a convent and became, eventually, a saint – not a bad way for a queen to finish her career, and much more pleasant than Brunhild's end. Brunhild, Balthild, and other queens of early Europe relied on churchmen as allies, and vice versa. High-ranking clerics were often kinsmen of the noblewomen who helped place bishops and abbots in power and endowed their churches with estates and goods. Bishops, in turn, advised noblemen to support their queens' agendas, working as messengers and councillors, and pulling strings to support their benefactresses.

In other areas, churchmen were less helpful than secular male allies. In early Anglo-Saxon England and Ireland, where inheritance customs allowed distant adult male relations to inherit the royal office, under-age sons of kings could not accede to the kingship. Queens were thus unable to become regents. Bishops also carried less weight in the secular and ecclesiastical politics of these regions. Likewise, where bishops lacked authority to participate in local government, queens' contributions to governance tended to diminish.[79] In these areas, queens attained status and influence in other ways, with the support of other men. Unfortunately, we have nothing like the Frankish histories to help us plot their careers. Bede, the best source for Anglo-Saxon politics, lacked interest in women who were neither saintly nor royal. If a laywoman did not help to convert her territory to Christianity, or become a famous nun or abbess, Bede had little to say of her. Villainesses served no function in his history.

Fortunately, Bede is not our only source for Anglo-Saxon queens. The *Anglo-Saxon Chronicle* made a few provocative references to royal ladies of power. King Peada assumed kingship of the Mercians in 655, it tells us, but did not rule for long; he was betrayed by his queen. Whether she slipped him poison, as Merovingian women were wont to do, or sold him out to another, more desirable man, or simply cast her political lot with an anti-Peada party, we cannot know. In 672, the chroniclers wrote, "died King Cenwal; and Sexburga his queen

[78] Eddius Stephanus, *Vita Sancti Wilfrithi*, ed. and trans. Bertram Colgrave (Cambridge University Press, 1927), 5 (cap. 7); trans. David Farmer in *The Age of Bede* (Harmondsworth: Penguin, 1988.

[79] Nelson, "Queens as Jezebels."

held the government one year after him." Yet nothing explains her circumstances. In 697, the Southumbrians slew Ostritha, the queen of Æthelred, the sister of Everth. In 722, "Queen Æthelburga destroyed Taunton."

These events appear coded in the politics of the *Chronicle*, unexplained until we practice the detective work of unraveling prior and succeeding events that surrounded the acts of women. The entries reveal that queens managed to take temporary control of kingdoms and armies when men lost their grasp. The most famous regent among Anglo-Saxon princesses was Æthelflæd, daughter of Alfred the Great, who governed Mercia jointly with her husband until his ill health and then his death in 911 left the kingdom in her hands. She assumed all the public powers that went with governance until her own death in 918. She maintained the laws, oversaw the army, and played politics with other rulers of England, including her brother Edward, king of Wessex and effectively England.[80] Still, her subjects called her "Lady of the Mercians," not queen of Mercia. When it came time to pass on her power, she made sure that her kingdom devolved to her brother, king of Wessex, rather than her own daughter. Hers was a singular power created by herself and few maternal predecessors, but not something she had inherited as a property to be bestowed on her female offspring in her own name.

The charters issued by kings, sometimes jointly with their queens, sometimes witnessed by their queens, also testify to the involvement of Anglo-Saxon royal ladies in owning, overseeing, and granting properties to ecclesiastical communities. They further demonstrate royal women's participation in the actual legal process, as well as affirming these few women's lordship over both land and law.[81] Given the involvement of Anglo-Saxon noblewomen in their native churches and monasteries, it is not surprising that queens should exercise such powers. Except for the few queens who seized or were handed authority by counselors when their husbands disappeared, most Englishwomen participated in public politics by involving themselves in the churches. Like the Frankish women who played politics with bishops, Anglo-Saxon women also found the outlet for their ambitions in ecclesiastical arenas; or, to put it another

[80] Mary Dockray-Miller, *Mothers and Mothering in Anglo-Saxon England* (New York: St. Martin's Press, 2000), 55–70.
[81] *WEHD* 1, 452, 464, 478, *et passim*.

way, they chose a religious vocabulary for their ambitions, as we shall see in the next chapter.[82]

Anglo-Saxon England and earlier Merovingian Gaul/Francia set the tone for the parameters of women's political involvement elsewhere in Europe. Once they had secured a position as queen or high-ranking lady, they might wield influence derived from their own family's wealth and status and that of their husbands – but only so long as their kin and mate remained in power and they themselves remained in favor with their man. Queens who gracefully and gratefully accepted the benefits of male favor and wielded them within the guidelines set by both local politics and gendered expectations fared well in written histories; those who misbehaved earned reputations, still with us, as jezebels and mistresses of evil. And those whom royal men barely noticed left scant trace in the histories.

In Lombard Italy, barbarian women appeared in written memory as far less colorful figures than the women of Francia. Paul the Deacon told many stories of Lombards courting, and of wives taken and discarded, but said little of women actually using their positions to wield influence. One charming anecdote described the courtship of the Bavarian princess Theudelinda and the Lombard Authari. Rather than sending an emissary to assess his betrothed, Authari went to her father's court disguised as his own messenger; when he grasped her hand in greeting, he took it to his face and traced his features with her fingers. She blushed, but realized that he must be her future husband. When trouble came to Bavaria before their wedding could take place, Theudelinda fled with her brother to the Lombard court, and was met with all joy and ceremony by Authari.[83] Yet Paul neglected to tell his readers that Theudelinda had been previously engaged to Childebert, king of the Franks, who was at constant war with the Lombards. Still, he admitted that when Authari had died, the Lombards "allowed her to remain in her royal dignity, advising her to choose for herself whomsoever she might wish from all the Langobards; such a one, namely, as could profitably manage the kingdom."[84] She wooed him with wine and blushing kisses and elevated him, as any sovereignty goddess might have, to kingship. Theudelinda did not rule the Lombards but she earned enough of their respect to select and validate their next king.

[82] Dockray-Miller, *Mothers and Mothering*, esp. 9–41.
[83] Paul the Deacon, *Historia Langobardorum*, III.30.   [84] Ibid., III.35.

When he died, she acted as regent for her son Adaloald for ten years until he went insane. After that, Theudelinda dropped out of Paul's history. As a bride, a wife, and a mother, she could hold her own in the tribal memory, but once she lost her men, she, too, disappeared.[85]

Like her sisters elsewhere, Theudelinda derived much of her influence (and her place of honor in Paul the Deacon's history) from her interest in Christian institutions. She was a great patron of churches in Lombardy, handing over property and making sure of their orthodox orientation. She was a correspondent of Pope Gregory the Great and reader of his theological works. In a letter quoted by Paul, the pope praised Theudelinda's efforts at peacemaking among the Lombards, urging her to continue with her good works; he wrote a parallel letter to her second husband, Agilulf. Like Theudelinda, a few other women entered Paul the Deacon's text as obedient and generous Christian mothers, daughters, and holy women.[86]

Like Gregory the Great, though, Paul also taught by negative example. A good woman in history was merely symbolic, rather than an individual with a genealogy, a homeland, substantive contributions to the wellbeing of her people, and a life of experiences. To balance Theudelinda, lending both literary and gender symmetry to his narrative, Paul also told of Romilda, wife of the duke of Friuli, who defended her city after her husband's death. Her heroics were short-lived, however, as was she. Although queens were allowed, as the historian Pauline Stafford has put it, "the direction of immobile warfare centered on fortifications," they were not allowed to sleep with the enemy.[87] Romilda promised the town to the king of the invading Avars if he would marry her. After sacking the city, he kept her for one night before giving her to his men for their pleasure. Then he had her impaled on a stake, which he referred to, most sexually, as a fitting husband for her. Her daughters, however, "did not follow the sensual inclination of their mother," by which Paul disapprovingly meant her lust for both Avars and control of her husband's dukedom. When the Avars came for the daughters, the girls hid the raw flesh of rotting chickens under their clothes, which repelled the barbarians, who figured that all Lombard women smelled terrible. As Paul handily suggested, "By this stratagem then the noble girls,

---

[85] Ibid., IV.41.   [86] Ibid., IV.2, 21.
[87] Stafford, *Queens, Concubines, and Dowagers*, 118.

escaping from the lust of the Avars, not only kept themselves chaste, but handed down a useful example for preserving chastity if any such thing should happen to women."[88] The mother sought any means to continue her rule of men's territory and thus ended disastrously; the daughters disappeared into chaste historical oblivion.

LESSONS IN BARBARIAN HISTORY

In men's histories of the fifth, sixth, seventh, and eighth centuries, both bad and good women of earlier times attained their influence through their men, who had, in turn, inherited it from the barbarian fathers, who had, in their turn, taken it from Romans and other natives. The histories of Paul, Gregory, Bede, and other chroniclers, named and anonymous, recounted invasions and the creation of barbarian kingdoms in similar two-step terms for every new territory: invasion, then organization. Even when men well familiar with Roman ways slipped into control, their historians described a violent invasion. Everywhere, according to the histories, men came as warriors to overwhelm the waning *romanitas* of a civilized region. But not so many men came as historians would have us believe. Tribal ethnogenesists and some later scholars assumed that vicious masses poured over the old imperial borders. More likely, several thousand warriors led the way, perhaps followed more slowly by their kin; or the new rulers of the disintegrating empire had long lived within its borders, and simply assumed power.

The silence of tribal histories about women's participation is simply another indication of the barbarians' need for martial histories. The solid evidence of archeology suggests that while a few women may have migrated and invaded, most women and men tried to get on with their lives while their rulers supplanted one another. Periodic violence disrupted this plan. No doubt women were killed and taken as slaves again and again as the newcomers established themselves, raid by raid, as the lords of Europe, or while the new kings of European kingdoms fought over their borders. But not every village was burned, and not every field was trampled. Not every woman ended as a casualty of the barbarian take-overs, the defense against the Huns, or Frankish expansion. As material evidence and legal codes show, some women married the newcomers, and many more simply adopted

---

[88] Paul the Deacon, *Historia Langobardorum*, IV.37.

their names, dress, and laws. As wives, mothers, and daughters they lived by men's rules which decreed their status, regulated their legal business, and passed them from man to man.

Once barbarians had become legitimate rulers of the continent and its islands, royal and noble women gained entry into their tribal histories. Like lower-class women, princesses and queens had to work within their formally immobile roles as lovers, wives, and daughters of barbarian rulers. That a few managed to wield influence, sometimes in the absence of men, sometimes in milieux complementary to men's political arenas, is testament to their ambition and skill. For these efforts, historians and saga-writers were often quick to condemn such notable women even while making them a prominent part of the texts. That queens and other forceful women managed to push their way into the later chapters of the written histories of early medieval peoples is even greater proof of their authority.

Yet the narratives of early medieval Europe leave us with scanty evidence for the personal lives of these women, and their personalities remain mostly symbolic in the histories. As the ambivalence of Gregory of Tours, Bede, Paul the Deacon, and other chroniclers toward women suggests, the barbarian historians were no admirers of women. Historians used their female characters didactically to drive home political and religious morals, just as writers and audiences of saga employed the shield-bearing, sword-wielding heroines of more obviously fictional texts to send many messages about gender, politics, tribal identity, and history. Women characters in the histories of the early medieval literary world told about power and politics in the new West, but they also instructed readers and listeners in both the benefits and dangers of allowing women to play at warrior and king. Put a good woman in a man's place and she might, like the Germanic Valkyrie heroine Brynhildr, fight fiercely for her lord. Yet she might, also like Brynhildr, disobey, go where she wanted, and end up encircled by flames and shields, unavailable to all but the most doomed men. Give her men's prerogatives and she could, like Queen Brunhild of the Franks, keep her husband's kingdom together to pass on, so responsibly, to the sons and grandsons she nurtured into leadership. But she might also, like Brunhild, pursue personal vendettas and cause civil strife beyond bloody imagining. A certain kind of fickle, sly politics was always gendered female in the barbarian histories.

Given the fact that women were undependable, as Christian doctrine declared, the historians used their female characters to teach necessary lessons in gender history to the new rulers of Europe. Rulers and lawmakers needed to protect their women and themselves by limiting women's mobility to palace or farmyard under the watchful eyes of legal male guardians, to court and cloister women under male guidance. But the historians also knew a deeper truth. In societies where people did not always obey the laws, did not always follow the principles embodied in laws, it was not always possible to keep women where they belonged nor to control what, exactly, women and men took away from the sagas and tribal histories of their barbarian fathers and mothers. In such a setting the memory-keepers and lawmakers could only condemn and vilify, but not control the women who traveled the barbarous landscape.

3

THE THEORY AND PRACTICE OF RELIGION

•

It is an arbitrary practice of historians to divide the study of religious experience from the rest of daily life. Women of the early Middle Ages did not necessarily distinguish between spiritual moments and other hours of the day. Some sought blessings before hauling water from the well, hung sacred tokens on their walls or around their necks to prevent violence and illness, took advice from the Bible and the great theologians of the ancient past, or appealed to saintly intercessors in matters great and small – please make my baby live, please help me govern wisely, let me improve my stitches, make him love me, give us justice, stop this war. To segregate the elite women who practiced religion as professionals from the rest of women, and to imply that professionals felt or thought religion differently from other women, is also a mere scholarly device. It is a post-Enlightenment anachronism, too, to believe that those who did the job of religion by vowing themselves to God were more religious than others. Medieval women learned in Christianity left us very few documents and almost no evidence that allows us to probe the souls of other unwary believers.

Yet the religious stances of women were certainly distinct from those of men. To say so is neither hermeneutic, nor arbitrary, nor polemical, but merely true for early medieval Europe.[1] Even the best

---

[1] For polemics: Janet Nelson, review of Jane Tibbets Schulenburg, *Forgetful of Their Sex: Female Sanctity and Society, ca. 500–1100, American Historical Review* 105:4 (October, 2000), 1366–67; M. S. Leach, review of Jo Ann McNamara, *Sisters in Arms: Catholic Nuns Through Two Millennia, First Things* 74 (1997), 59–60. For historiography: Felice Lifshitz, "Gender and Exemplarity East of the Middle Rhine:

of Christian men, along with Jewish and Muslim men, purposely engaged in religion in ways that included but limited women. Especially when Christian clerical leaders practiced religious reform, as they did in the Francia of Charlemagne and Louis the Pious or the England of Wulfstan, they tended to doubt and check women. Unlike women's legal and political enfranchisement, however, women's religious experience was impossible to curtail simply because women did not always acknowledge doctrinal constraints. Women did not rebel against or reject formal religion, but strategized within its limits and continued to nudge those limits of belief and practice. They were helped by men of the church who lauded, valued, assisted, and collaborated with them. Although male clerical leaders openly praised a particular kind of holy female, a few women further resisted by exemplifying and accepting other modes of holiness. When institutional reforms within the church or attacks by "godless" men from without threatened the profession of religious women and the very faith of secular women, they nonetheless persevered in believing and practicing.

During the early Middle Ages, Christian leaders were still defining and organizing their doctrines, stabilizing their institutions, constructing their laws, and proselytizing. So far, there was no effective pope, no centralized church, no national churches, no Vatican commanding a continent of the faithful. There was, however, a great deal of disagreement about authority within the churches and much regional variety in orthodoxy and orthopraxis. Consequently, Christian women found more freedom of religion – not choice of religions, but endless opportunities to experience the variety of (dis)organized Christianity – in Europe between 500 and 900 than in any other period in pre-modern history.

RELIGIOUS THEORIES OF WOMAN

Most women in Europe after the sixth century were born to Christianity. Although plenty of Europeans maintained beliefs and religious

Jesus, Mary, and the Saints in Manuscript Context," *Early Medieval Europe* 9 (2000), 325–43; Hans-Werner Goetz, *Frauen im frühen Mittelalter. Frauenbild und Frauenleben im Frankenreich* (Weimar: Böhlau, 1995), esp. 19–20. For church leaders' opinions on women: Joyce Salisbury, *Church Fathers, Independent Virgins* (London and New York: Verso, 1991); Lynda Coon, *Sacred Fictions: Holy Women and Hagiography in Late Antiquity* (Philadelphia: University of Pennsylvania Press, 1997).

habits from beyond Christianity, the empire officially converted after Constantine allowed Christianity in 312. Gaul was largely Christian by 400, Ireland by 500, Italy and Spain orthodox Christian rather than Arian by 600. The Anglo-Saxons converted in the seventh century, Germany during the eighth, Scandinavia not until after 1000. Few Jews lived even in southern Europe yet, and no Muslims appeared there until the eighth century. Women's choices lay largely in how, and how intensely, to believe and practice Christianity. Should they integrate the old ways of their ancestors into their Christian lives? Convert to more public practice, perhaps take a vow of celibacy, poverty, obedience? They might move to a community of other vowed practitioners, but could choose to join men as well as women. Perhaps they could live in a local house of kinswomen or sail to a determined settlement of strangers far from home, even across the sea. They might become leaders of Christian communities, with duties and rights that lay far beyond the walls of their cells, among their secular neighbors. Women could not select from the same variety of official Christian roles as men could, but the range was wide. They could become Christian wives or mothers, ascetics, pilgrims, abbesses, mediators and negotiators, scholars and teachers, or saints.

Yet religious women, like their sisters in secular life, could not escape their community's expectations or their culture's understanding of them as women. Women vowed to the religious life avoided some of the limitations on legal franchise and property-holding, but not many, not often, and not always formally. Their vocations did not always protect them. They eluded only some of the suspicions about women implicit in the laws and explicit in narrative and gnomic literature. More difficult to avoid were the Christian theologians in every generation who were always ready to criticize all women, even clean-living celibates. The Christian literati's recurring denunciations of the inherent sinfulness and frailty of women influenced rules for professional religious life and the actual practice of that life. In the writings of some ecclesiastics, women themselves were made to mouth the limited capabilities of, and necessary limitations upon, themselves. Thus Ælfflæd, royal abbess of Whitby, told a self-denigrating story of how St. Cuthbert sent her a linen cincture to cure her of a debilitating illness. According to Bede, who retold her tale, Ælfflæd also used it on a nun who lay deathly ill, then hid it in her cupboard. But when she looked for it later the cincture had disappeared by an act of God, lest Ælfflæd and her nuns misuse it and misunderstand its powers.[2] The miraculous, even in the hands of an acknowledged holy woman, became perilous to Christian souls, at least in Bede's text.

Some Christian women may have believed themselves to be more susceptible to evil than were men. Some, like Ælfflæd, may merely have believed that all Christians were susceptible to sins of ignorance. But some women and men continued to reject the gender inequality inherent in theology. They cherished feminine spiritualities. They promoted what they perceived as a womanly quality of nurturing, and created maternally organized religious communities for women and men, or for women only. Similarly, European women who were not Christian professionals, as well as the few who were not even Christian, resisted limitations put on their religious experience by Christian leaders and political powers. Not only professional religious women, but all women faced the scrutiny and constraints of writing and ruling men in an increasingly Christian Europe and the ever-more-organized churches of the early Middle Ages.

Modern scholars of Christianity have tended to blame Jews for the misogynous streaks apparent in early Christian doctrine. They point to the Torah and Talmud for proof, touting Christianity in its earliest forms as liberating to women oppressed by the letter, as well as the spirit, of the old law.[3] Yet not all Jewish canonical texts condemned women. Although the Talmud reminded readers that woman is "a pitcher of filth with its mouth full of blood – yet all men run after her," at the same time, the rabbis praised mothers and wives who maintained the ritual purity of Jewish households.[4] For every passage in the Torah about evil, seductive, impure women, another existed to praise women's purity, goodness, and faith. For every evil example of a sinful woman, a heroine graced the pages of Hebrew scripture. For almost every denigrator among the sages there was an enthusiast. And plenty of passages in the Talmud and Torah simply referred neutrally to women going about their Jewish lives.

[2] Bede, *Life of St. Cuthbert*, xxiii; trans. Bertram Colgrave in *Two Lives of Saint Cuthbert: A Life by an Anonymous Monk of Lindisfarne and Bede's Prose Life* (Cambridge University Press, 1940; reprint Oxford: Clarendon, 1991), 230–35.

[3] Judith Plaskow, "Feminist Anti-Judaism and the Christian God," *Journal of Feminist Studies in Religion* 7:2 (1991), 99–108; Katharina von Kellenbach, *Anti-Judaism in Feminist Religious Writings* (Atlanta: Scholars Press, 1994), esp. 28–37.

[4] B. *Shabat* 152 a, cited by Judith Romney Wegner, "The Image and Status of Women in Classical Rabbinic Judaism," in *Jewish Women in Historical Perspective*, ed. Judith R. Baskin (Detroit : Wayne State University Press, 1998), 68.

The practical effect of ambivalence was women's exclusion from the foundation of the religion and from its basic rituals. Such exclusion still shocks some modern readers, although given the consistent stance on women of all pre-modern legal codes throughout the ancient and medieval worlds, one more example of early medieval disenfranchisement should come as no surprise. It is quite true that the Babylonian Talmud, the document that became the basis for Jewish practice throughout Europe and the rest of the known world during the Middle Ages, observed some distressing differences between the nature of the sexes, and between men's and women's observance of religious law:

All obligations of the son upon the father, men are bound, but women are exempt. But all obligations of the father upon the son, both men and women are bound. All affirmative precepts limited to time, men are liable and women are exempt. But all affirmative precepts not limited to time are binding upon both men and women. And all negative precepts, whether limited to time or not limited to time, are binding upon both men and women.[5]

This declaration actually comes from *Mishnah*, the jurists' handbook produced about 200 CE and then commented upon by the scholars of the Babylonian Talmud between 200 and 600. By precepts, the translator meant the injunctions and prohibitions that formed the basis of Jewish observance. For example, the obligation to recite various prayers was an affirmative commandment limited to time; certain prayers had to be performed at specific times during the day. "From what time may they recite the evening Shema?" asked the *Mishnah* regarding the recital of *berakhot* or blessings:

From the hour that the priests come in to eat of their Heave-offering, until the end of the first watch; these are Rabbi Eleizer's words, but the Sages say, Until midnight...

2. From what time may they recite the morning Shema? From the time one can distinguish between blue and white...
3. The House of Shammai say, In the evening every man must recline and recite, and in the morning, they must stand...
4. In the morning one recites two blessings before Shema and one after it, and in the evening two before it and two after it, one long and one short...[6]

---

[5] Ross S. Kraemer, *Maenads, Martyrs, Matrons, Monastics: A Sourcebook of Women's Religions in the Greco-Roman World* (Philadelphia: Fortress Press, 1988), 67.

[6] Barry W. Holtz, ed., *Back to the Sources: Reading the Classic Jewish Texts* (New York, 1984), 132–33. See also Judith Baskin, "Women and Judaism," in *The Encyclopedia of Judaism*, ed. Jacob Neusner et al. (Brill and Continuum, 2000), vol. 3, 1478–1502.

The *Shema* is the most important, monotheism-affirming prayer of Judaism: "Shema Yisroyal, Adonai elohenu, Adonai echod!" (Hear O Israel, the Lord is our God, the Lord is One!). The *Mishnah* assumed by its language that men, not women, repeated the *Shema* at dawn and nightfall. They also decreed that women were exempted from performing this time-bound precept as part of their ritual observance.

Exemption became disqualification. Like other regularly scheduled events in daily Jewish life, the greeting of God and the world at the break of day and at day's closing was the privilege of men. Elsewhere in the text, *Mishnah* prohibited women from performing as synagogue leaders, teachers, or judges, and even from creating their own *chavurot* or study groups. Since the sages also believed women to be incapable of grasping law and theology, there was no need to teach them the single most important duty of every Jew: to read the Torah.[7] Jewish women benefitted, as the Talmud put it, by "sending their [male] children to learn Torah in the synagogue, and their husbands to study in the schools of the rabbis, and by waiting for their husbands until they return from the schools of the rabbis."[8] Although plenty in Jewish religious culture was oral – including the interpretation of *halakhah* (law) and *haggadah* (religious traditions of the rabbis), the written Torah became the basis of post-Destruction Judaism. Yet women could not approach Torah except through men's repetitions of its passages and oral elaborations upon it.[9]

It is difficult to find evidence as to how Jewish women reacted, especially in such sensitive areas as belief. Most of the Jews of the early Middle Ages lived outside Christian Europe. Those who dispersed to Europe (mostly in Italy and then Spain) beginning in late Antiquity probably lived according to the same Talmudic precepts as those in Egypt, the Middle East, and elsewhere. References from literate Jewish communities of the East depicted women mostly in domestic roles. Marriage contracts, divorce decrees, wills, learned authorities' responses to legal inquiries (*responsa*), all focused on women in relation to their children, their property, and their men. One *responsum* from the late eleventh century proved that women still practiced basic rituals of Judaism in simpler, less informed ways than

---

[7] Wegner, "Image and Status of Women," esp. 74–75.

[8] Babylonian Talmud, *Berakot* 17a; Wegner, "Image and Status," n. 45.

[9] Stefan C. Reif, "Aspects of Medieval Jewish Literacy," in *The Uses of Literacy in Early Medieval Europe*, ed. Rosamond McKitterick (Cambridge, 1990), 134–55, esp. 136–37.

their men. Rabbi Isaac ben Menachem, writing in the 1060s, described women of northern French communities who observed a shorter fast on Yom Kippur than men did. "It is better that they transgress the law innocently, rather than knowingly," he ruled, "we do not reprove them for doing so."[10] Only an occasional text spotlit a learned woman, such as the deserted wife in eleventh-century Egypt mentioned in *genizah* documents who kept herself and family by running a school.[11] The documents do show that women in ancient and medieval times donated money and other items, such as books, mosaics, and even buildings, to their synagogues, even if they were not allowed to study there.[12]

Yet we cannot know whether women turned literate skills to prayer. Once Jews moved north to France and Germany, nary a woman literate in the Torah appeared in the written record before the eleventh century. The scholar Rashi's daughter supposedly took down his dictation in eleventh-century France. The twelfth-century Rabbi Eleazar ben Judah of Worms remembered it as exceptional for his six-year-old daughter Hannah to recite the *Shema*.[13] Besides these exceptions, if Jewish women composed prayers or considered theology in the early Middle Ages, no one recorded it.[14] Whether the domestic practice of Judaism – the religion of the household and family, which is so much a part of modern Judaism, complementary to the religion of the synagogue – originated in this period, in Europe, with women, we cannot be sure. The Talmud ordered the

---

[10] Irving A. Agus, ed., *Urban Civilization in Pre-Crusade Europe: A Study of Organized Town-Life in Northwestern Europe During the Tenth and Eleventh Centuries Based on the Responsa Literature* (New York: Yeshiva University Press, 1965), vol. 1, 307–08; for dating, 159. Compare, however, 766–67 on the fast at Purim.

[11] Moses Maimonides, *Responsa of Moses ben Maimon*, vol. 1, ed. Yehoshua Blau (Jerusalem, 1958), no. 34, no. 45; cited in Judith Baskin, "Medieval Jewish Women," in Baskin, ed., *Jewish Women in Historical Perspective*, n. 25.

[12] Baskin, "Medieval Jewish Women," 6–8, 107 (n. 48, reference to donation of books from the thirteenth-century *Sefer Hasidim*); Kraemer, *Maenads, Martyrs, Matrons, Monastics*, 112, 116.

[13] Cited in Moritz Güdemann, *Geschichte des Ehrziehungswesens und der Cultur der abendländischen Juden während des Mittelalters u. der neueren Zeit*, vol. 1 (1880–88, repr. Amsterdam: Philo Press, 1966), 189; Baskin, "Medieval Jewish Women," 104, n. 42.

[14] Later in the Middle Ages, some Jewish women attained – and were urged to attain – basic Hebrew literacy: Judith Baskin, "Some Parallels in the Education of Medieval Jewish and Christian Women," *Jewish History* 5 (1991), 141–51.

keeping of the Sabbath by women, with bread and lamps or candles as we have now. And the *mikvot* (the ritual bath-houses of Jewish women, where they cleansed themselves each month after menstruation and after childbirth) found in medieval Speyer and other German communities retained the same basic shape and structure as the bathhouses of ancient Palestine, and as *mikvot* around the world today.[15] By and large, though, we cannot find women's practice of Judaism before about 1050, and even then Jewish women's own voices remain rare and faint. If the Jews were distinct among Christians in the early Middle Ages, then Jewish women were even more – as the Talmud accuses them – "a separate people."[16]

Yet it took no Jews to instruct Christian writers in ambivalence about women. The Torah's ambivalence was not the only source of Christian theologians' distrust of women. From the start, Christians were more than willing to discard most of the basic precepts of Judaism in their reinterpretation of the Torah and construction of a new religion. They also rejected social customs of the Jews, such as polygamy (which lingered into the eleventh century, when Rabbi Gershom of Mainz ruled against it). Christians decried divorce by decree at either husband's or wife's insistence, as well as the levirate, the custom whereby a widow might marry her dead husband's brother and bear a child attributed to her first spouse.[17] Ambivalence about women's very nature was by no means limited to Jews. It was so ubiquitous that it influenced every major religion of the classical Mediterranean world. With the whole weight of Greek and Roman philosophy, Torah, and custom in the ancient empire behind them, the earliest Christian writers were quite ready to interpret their own sacred canon as both a condemnation and a cautious celebration of women. Even St. Paul, famous for his reliance on the spirit rather than the letter of the law, suggested, "Let your women be silent in the churches." Paul had written in the first century of Christianity, when

[15] Guenter Stein, *Judenhof und Judenbad in Speyer am Rhein* (Munich: Deutscher Kunstverlag, 1978); Hannelore Kuenzl, "Die Architektur der mittelalterlichen Synagogen und rituellen Baeder," in *Judentum im Mittelalter, Ausstellungskatalog zur Ausstellung vom 04.05–26.10.1978 im Schloss Halbturn*, ed. Jakob Allerhand (Eisenstadt: Kulturabt. Des Amtes d. Bgld. Landesregierung, 1978), 40–59. See also R. R. Emanuel and M. W. Ponsford, "Jacob's Well, Bristol, Britain's Only Known Medieval Jewish Ritual Bath," *Transactions of the Bristol and Gloucestershire Archaeological Society* 112 for 1994 (1995), 73–86.

[16] *B. Shabbat*, 62a.

[17] Agus, *Urban Civilization*, 620–21, 638–39, 644–45, 698–99, 705.

the Corinthians were struggling to control female heretics crying out in tongues and prophecies. Yet he had more than a little distrust of all women in the back of his mind.[18] Paul declared that there was "neither male nor female in Jesus Christ," but he also announced that women should veil themselves in church and should not presume to instruct their husbands.[19] There was nothing unusual nor particularly Jewish in the thoughts of Paul and his companions about women.

The history of Christian men's ideas about Christian women remains full of disturbing tensions and confusions. To be sure, interpretations changed according to period, region, culture, and commentator, but always supplied an easily available canon of censure. Late antique and medieval authorities absorbed Paul's thoughts about the gendered equality of souls but took his negative injunction in a more practical sense. They prohibited women from becoming teachers and preachers or holding any authoritative role in their churches. As early as the second and third centuries, Christian apologists were urging women to maintain traditional postures as housewives in normative families rather than attempting radical new lifestyles, such as residence in celibate communes or leadership positions among Christian congregations.[20]

The greatest and most popular Christian thinkers of the Middle Ages set down opinions of women that helped to organize the practices of all expanding Christendom. Their estimation of women as members of the church ran the gamut from misogyny to breathless admiration. By and large, the extreme opinions rather than the more qualified or neutral observations of women caught the eyes of later theologians. "You are the Devil's gateway," announced Tertullian, bishop of Carthage in the second century, to female Christians:

You are the unsealer of that forbidden tree. You are the first deserter of the divine law. You are she who persuaded him whom the Devil was not valiant enough to attack. You destroyed so easily God's image, man. On account of your desert, that is death, even the Son of God had to die.[21]

---

[18] Constance Parvey, "The Theology and Leadership of Women in the New Testament," in *Religion and Sexism: Images of Women in the Jewish and Christian Traditions*, ed. Rosemary Ruether (New York: Simon & Schuster, 1974), 123–37.

[19] I Timothy 2:8; I Cor. 11: 3–15; see also I Timothy 2:15.

[20] Margaret Y. MacDonald, *Early Christian Women and Pagan Opinion: The Power of the Hysterical Woman* (Cambridge University Press, 1996), 133–43.

[21] Tertullian, *De Cultu Feminarum*, I.1; trans. in Rudolph Arbesmann, Sister Emily Joseph Daly, and Edwin A. Quain, *Tertullian: Disciplinary, Moral, and Ascetical*

Tertullian came to believe that the only path for a virtuous woman was voluntary virginity. St. Paul had tolerated marriage for women and men who could not remain virgins, reminding early Christians that it was "better to marry than to burn" with lust. But he believed that the best Christians, the role models for the rest, remained celibate.[22] For a woman, the benefit of virginity was androgyny, according to the Fathers. A woman who could control her natural tendency to sin, particularly by sexual act, was no longer a woman, but a better Christian. Tertullian's statements were hardly ambiguous, but it is not clear how well early medieval theologians knew them. Only one ninth-century manuscript represents the gateway text before humanists rediscovered it in the fifteenth century.[23]

Not all early theologians thought women were more prone to sexual sin than men. Some, if they seemed to write in such terms, were actually using women as a symbol of all fallen humanity. St. Augustine (354–430), bishop of Hippo and the greatest favorite of medieval theologians, believed everyone hovered on the verge of sexual sin. Augustine often considered such things in theoretical terms, although he also agonized over his own sexual past in his famous *Confessions*. In *De Genesi ad Litteram*, he theorized that if Adam and Eve had sex in Paradise, they would have done the deed lustlessly without realizing or sensing it. No libido prevailed in the Garden. Adam had been innocent of his uncontrollable erections. If the first man and woman had sex, it would have been purely for reproductive reasons.[24] In Augustine's real world, however, men got erections because women inspired them. Women were not evilly sexual beings themselves but weak extensions of the male body. Men could either control them, helping women to salvation by denying them sinfully sexual pleasure, or fall victim to their carnal urges. Unfortunately, according to Augustine, women were prone to pleasure. The only solution was complete denial and total celibacy, which Augustine was pretty certain good men could achieve (despite his own rather

Works, Fathers of the Church: A New Translation 40 (Washington, DC: Catholic University Press, 1977), 118.

[22] I Cor. 7:9; Peter Brown, *The Body and Society: Men, Women, and Sexual Renunciation in Early Christianity* (New York: Columbia University Press, 1988), 54–57.

[23] Lifshitz, "Gender and Exemplarity," 327–28.

[24] Augustine, *De Genesi ad Litteram*, 9.5.9; 11.42.59; *De Civitate Dei* 14:10; *The Literal Meaning of Genesis*, trans. John Hammond Taylor (New York: Newman Press, 1982), vol. 2, 79–80, 175–77; Brown, *Body and Society*, 399–403.

sordid early life), but which he believed to be even more difficult for women.[25] Of course, Augustine was a prolific writer and had much more to say about sexual sin and sin in general, as well as about the religious lives of Christian women. Elsewhere, he described how his own mother, Monica, served as his role model and even brought about his conversion to Christianity.[26]

The other great inspiration from medieval thinkers on the subject of women was Jerome (340–420), a contemporary of Augustine who lived in Rome until he took his difficult temper and harshly voiced opinions to Jerusalem. Truculent, vehement, and a beautiful writer, he moved in the highest social circles of Rome on the verge of its fall. He treated women as intellectual and spiritual equals; most of the letters he left to the medieval world were originally directed to upper-class Christian women, such as his friends Paula, Eustochius, and Marcella. He also became the greatest champion of religious virginity for women. He wrote frequently about the horrors of marriage, his disgust for child-bearing, and the glories of chaste, independent widowhood. He described courses of education for Christian girls. He tutored women. He even offered advice to women he had never met, yet his message was always the same: remain a virgin, or if that is impossible, choose celibacy. Avoid fancy dress, jewelry, rich food, and socializing with any but other virgins or chaste widows. Jerome criticized so-called Christian widows who did not practice what he preached. "Look at them as they ride in their roomy litters with a row of eunuchs walking in front," he warned,

see their red lips and their plump sleek skins: you would not think they had lost a husband, you would fancy they were looking for one. Their houses are full of flatterers, full of guests. The very clergy, whose teaching and authority ought to inspire respect, kiss these ladies on the forehead and then stretch out their hand – you would think, if you did not know, that they were giving a benediction – to receive the fee for their visit. The women ... prefer their liberty as widows. They call themselves chaste nuns and after a diversified dinner they dream of apostles.[27]

[25] Augustine, *Confessions*, VI.12.21–22; *De Sancta Virginitate*, esp. 43; Brown, *Body and Society*, 392–95. See also Averil Cameron, *Christianity and the Rhetoric of Empire* (Berkeley: University of California Press, 1991), 71–73, 171–80.

[26] Augustine, *Confessions*, IX.8; trans. R. S. Pine-Coffin (New York: Dorset Press, 1988), 192.

[27] Jerome, *Epistolae*, XXII; trans. F. A. Wright, *Select Letters of St. Jerome* (New York: Putnam, 1933), 85.

Jerome saw Christian virginity as a new option, never realized before Mary bore Jesus who brought salvation, and as a chance to do something with otherwise useless lives:

> In the old days, as I have said, the virtue of continence was confined to men, and Eve continually bore children in travail. But now that a virgin has conceived in the womb a child, upon whose shoulders is government, a mighty God, Father of the age to come, the fetters of the old curse are broken. Death came through Eve: life has come through Mary. For this reason the gift of virginity has been poured most abundantly upon women, seeing that it was from a woman it began.[28]

Through Mary came redemption, just as through Eve, destruction. Jerome was also one of the first Christian writers to use the image of Jesus as bridegroom for the ordinary virgin, which became so popular with medieval authors. But the connection he made between Mary and the practice of virginity became the most influential idea in the gender ideology of Christianity: the duality of Mary and Eve, the inherent tension of virgin versus temptress. The concept of the dual nature of all women drew on old traditions of ambivalence apparent in both Jewish theology and classical philosophies, but combined it with a new Christian praise of virginity. Christian theologians after Jerome applied his ideas to European societies that had long practiced gender asymmetry. The Christianized doctrine of women's dual nature became useful anywhere that political ideology already disenfranchised or systematically subordinated women. Theologians developed a series of images related to Eve, the Magdalen, the whore of Babylon, and other wicked figures from their religious canon which expressed the corrupt aspect of femininity and thus the worst of humanity. Yet, at the same time, they used Mary to express the feminine side of Christianity and, hence, to symbolize the good side of women. The old Tanakh idea of Israel as a woman became the church married to Jesus. The soul became feminine in relation to the male Logos, or word made flesh. Sophia became the female personification of the wisdom of God. Mariology, the worship of Mary herself, emerged as a strong theme in Christian writings and practice after the fourth century, and traveled wherever the faith went.

Paul, Augustine, and Jerome were only the most famous and popular of the church fathers with something to say about the nature of woman and her position within Christian communities. Their

[28] Ibid.

opinions and others informed the decisions of religious leaders about women's participation in everyday religious practice. Tertullian had complained about groups that allowed women extensive participation in Christian ritual – by which he meant participation as free as that of men. "They have no modesty," he warned, "they are bold enough to teach, to engage in argument, to enact exorcisms, to undertake cures and, it may be, even to baptise!"[29] By Tertullian's time, few Christian communities let women officiate at the sacraments, although various heretical communities continued to do so; their dissident customs and beliefs about women continued to surface in later medieval heresies. But most Christian leaders wondered, as had Greek and Roman philosophers before them: Could women ever be as capable with religious ideas, as spiritually sensitive, as good as men? Could they properly learn theology? Participate in all rituals? Practice their own versions of Christianity? Some theologians were encouraging. Others had their doubts about women's abilities and good nature.

Their ideas had direct effects on the lives of women. Throughout the medieval period, ambivalent theology informed politics and society, and structures even more elusive to modern historians, such as mentalities, in a way that we can scarcely appreciate. When missionaries carried their theology into the reality of legal disenfranchisement and systematic sexism in early European societies, the workable result was a limit on women's Christian practice. Some of the earliest church councils, such as the Synod of Elvira (305), focused more on controlling women's sexual behavior than on encouraging their participation in rituals and leadership. By 441, according to the Council of Orange, women could no longer take part in leading rituals in Christian churches.[30] Whereas deaconesses of the early church had administered sacraments to women, instructed women catechumens, and baptized women, by the early medieval period deaconesses had few if any specific functions. Queen Radegund, wife of Chlotar, became a deaconess but only achieved recognition and security among her religious colleagues as an abbess under vows.[31] Women never had

---

[29] Tertullian, *On Baptism*, 17 in Alexander Roberts and James Donaldson, eds., *The Anti-Nicene Fathers* (Grand Rapids: Eerdman, 1975–76), vol. 3.

[30] Orange, canon 25 (26) in C. Munier, ed., *Concilia Gallica*, Corpus Christianorum Series Latina 148 (Turnholt: Brepols, 1963), 84.

[31] McNamara and Halborg, *Sainted Women of the Dark Ages*, 75, 88–89; McNamara, *Sisters in Arms*, 98.

become priests. In the fifth century, too, the assault on the position of *episcopa* or *episcopessa* (bishop's wife) began.[32] In 494, Gelasius, bishop of Rome, wrote disapprovingly to officials in southern Italy of women who dared to conduct services and take their places at the altar.[33] Women lost their status as bishops' wives by 567, when the Council of Tours ruled that women must be removed from clerical households, except to do the housework. Wives of bishops, theologians ruled, were to take a veil and a vow when their husbands were consecrated.[34] Writers such as Gregory of Tours cast suspicion on bishops' wives in the sixth century, as we have seen with Gregory's story of the crazy Susanna, wife of Bishop Priscus.[35] The council that met in Gregory's city of Tours in 567 was only one gathering of clerics to prohibit the cohabitation of bishops with their wives, and to order such women to live in celibate communities like nuns. Women continued to marry priests in some parts of Europe, and may have performed informal functions as priests' wives until the eighth or ninth century. But clerics gathered into councils and synods constantly prohibited the presence of women in priests' houses.[36] Carolingian rulers and their clerical reformers reiterated these restrictions, adding that women should not assist in churches by decorating altars or cleaning vessels and linens because they polluted all they touched with the stain of their sinful sex.[37]

By the early Middle Ages, the only professional religious roles left to Christian women were those of virgin, penitent, and widow under vows of chastity. Women seized upon and used these roles in ways many and marvelous. They occasionally usurped men's clerical jobs and tried to revive the ancient offices they had once performed. But even as nuns and abbesses, even as famous saints, Christian women faced pragmatic limits on their practice of religion. Men's opinions of them as a group defined by gender brought them disgrace even

---

[32] Ross S. Kraemer, *Her Share of the Blessings: Women's Religions Among Pagans, Jews, and Christians in the Greco-Roman World* (Oxford University Press, 1992), 174–90.

[33] Gelasius, *Epistola* 1.14, in *PL* 59; cited in McNamara, *Sisters in Arms*, 59.

[34] Council of Tours, 567, canon 14 (13), in C. De Clercq, ed., *Concilia Gallica*, Corpus Christianorum Series Latina 148A (Turnholt: Brepols, 1963), 181.

[35] Gregory of Tours, *Historia*, IV.36.

[36] Jo Ann McNamara, "Chaste Marriage and Clerical Celibacy," in *Sexual Practices and the Medieval Church*, ed. Vern Bullough and James Brundage (Buffalo: Prometheus Books, 1982), 22–33.

[37] *MGH Conc.* 2, Council of Soissons, 5; *MGH Capit., Capitularia Regum Francorum* 1, 347–48.

though great theologians and rulers of the church disagreed on the details of women's practice. "A woman may not take a vow without the consent of her husband," wrote the penitentialist and bishop Theodore in the 690s, echoing general opinion. "Women shall not in the time of impurity [menstruation] enter into a church, or communicate – neither nuns nor laywomen; if they presume to do this, they shall fast for three weeks . . . in the same way shall they do penance who enter a church before purification after childbirth, that is, forty days."[38] Yet Gregory the Great, asked the same question by missionaries to Britain in the sixth century, had reaffirmed the rights of pregnant and newly delivered women to enter the church and accept baptism.[39] Such matters continued under discussion throughout the early medieval centuries, for the very biological and spiritual natures of women raised questions about their practice of Christianity that would never arise for men.

NON-CHRISTIAN WOMEN'S PRACTICES

Jewish women, Muslims, pagans, and heretical Christians fared no better in the religious theories of men. No legalist or theologian from these religious groups left any clues about women's actual experience of religion. As we have seen, the practice of the indigenous religions of ancient Europe is still mysterious to historians. Women worshiped at shrines and performed rituals at home, but whether they were kept from public observance or religious leadership we cannot know for certain. If we cast back to classical sources for evidence that (what we call) paganism was more open to women and strong female symbolism, it may seem that women took a greater role in the non-Christian religions of northern Europe than they did in organized, patriarchal religions of the ancient Near East. Tacitus, for instance, claimed at the end of the first century that a Germanic prophetess-priestess lurked in the woods of the north. A shaman named Veleda, like a precursor to the stylite saints of the fourth century, inhabited a tower whence she dropped her judgments upon her devotees below. Likewise, Strabo feared the women of the sacred Breton isle who processed annually to a temple, bearing roofing materials in their arms;

---

[38] Penitential of Theordore, xiv.7, xiv.17, in McNeill and Gamer.
[39] Bede, *Historia Ecclesiastica*, XXVII.8. See also Janet Nelson, "Les femmes et l'évangelisation au ixe siècle," *Revue du Nord* 269 (1986), 471–85.

if one of their number fell and dropped her sacred load, the others tore her to pieces. If a man dared enter their isle, he was killed.[40] Writers throughout the Middle Ages continued to suspect that women practiced rituals that were distinctly un-Christian. As late as the twelfth century, Gerald of Wales, the indomitable Norman reporter in Ireland, claimed that St. Brigit's nuns performed some dubious rites, which later scholars have taken as pagan-inspired devotion to the goddess Brig.[41] Early medieval commentators, especially canonists such as Abbot Regino of Prüm (*c.* 845–916) and the eleventh-century bishop Burchard of Worms, continued to complain of women gathering to perform pagan ceremonies. But it is impossible to know whether Regino and others reported genuinely pagan practices, and whether customs were linked to previous pagan observances. We cannot be sure that the gatherings were woman-specific. Most important, the evidence does not demonstrate that any of these practices empowered women in the public performance of a more gender-symmetrical religion than either Christianity or Judaism. In their systematic descriptions of pagan religion in pre-Christian Europe, classical writers tended to write of women's participation only tangentially; Caesar's famous account of druidic practice in Gaul, for instance, mentioned only men performing priestly functions.[42] And medieval commentators were quick to cast irregular practices as pagan, and to blame women for them.

Muslim women, like Jewish women, hardly entered into the history of early medieval Europe outside of Iberia. Women had been Muslims since Islam had existed, of course. Women were among the original sixty-four who pledged to follow the Prophet. The Qur'an considered the spiritual worth of women equal to that of men. "Enter into Paradise," it declared, although addressing men, "you and your wives, with delight . . . Who so does that which is right and believes, whether male or female, him or her will We quicken to happy life."[43] The holy book especially revered chaste wives and loving mothers,

[40] Strabo, *Geographia*, 4.4.6.
[41] John T. Koch and John Carey, *The Celtic Heroic Age: Literary Sources for Ancient Celtic Europe and Early Ireland and Wales* (Malden: Celtic Studies Publications, 1994), 18–19, 38, 267.
[42] Caesar, *De Bello Gallico*, VI.13–14; ed. Wolfgang Hering, Bibliotheca Scriptorum Graecorum et Romanorum Teubneriana (Leipzig: Teubner, 1987); trans. Carolyn Hammond as *Seven Commentaries on the Gallic War* (Oxford University Press, 1996), 126–27.
[43] Qur'an, 43:70; 16:97.

and ordered men to treat both of these kinds of women with love and respect.[44]

Muslim women came to Iberia in the eighth century with or as invaders. They were not, like the Jews, perceived as outsiders or interlopers into an already established community. They and their men created a society that tolerated, if sometimes with suspicion, those of other faiths. As a result, Iberia became a place where some women demonstrated their religious initiative by choosing Islam. Notaries in the city of Córdoba drew up model documents in the tenth century to guide women through the legal and social ramifications of becoming Muslims.[45] Such certificates dealt more with the obligation of new Muslims to divorce non-Muslim spouses who refused to follow in conversion than with the spiritual experience of religion. Legal professionals were well aware that women might convert in order to discard an unwelcome husband, or to marry a better one, or to acquire property rights under Islamic law. But notaries did not need to examine a convert on her knowledge of the Islamic creed any more than a Christian bishop of the sixth century would grill a female convert on her catechism. Still, the matter continued to bother the organizers and interpreters of Islam, for as late as the fifteenth century a commentator on the process of conversion pointed out that belief was no business of the courts, nor even of husbands:

We trust the sincerity of the converted women when they manifest their creed and their Islam. Only God knows their secrets. Unless a man is convinced that there is a weakness in his wife's belief, he should not interrogate her about this. He is encouraged to teach her what she ignores in that respect. Some of the jurists, whose model of behavior is followed, say that during the writing of the marriage contract, the witnesses should examine the creed of the woman because weak creed is common among them. They should do that and so guide a large number of people to the true creed. I myself, God willing, intend to write a concise book, using a simple language for simple people, employing logic and traditional evidence which their brain could grasp.[46]

Like Christian writers, though, this commentator assumed that husbands and male witnesses to marriage contracts did actually understand religion more thoroughly and on a higher intellectual level than the most zealous female convert.

[44] Ibid., 30:21; 4:19; 4:1; 2:187.
[45] Maya Shatzmiller, "Marriage, Family, and the Faith: Women's Conversion to Islam," *Journal of Family History* 21 (1996), 235–65.
[46] Cited in Shatzmiller, "Marriage, Family, and the Faith," 254.

The need for a legal model suggests plentiful conversions. Male authorities wanted help in drawing up an official document to verify conversions, which were common enough that one model sufficed for all cases. Yet, despite the model, women were individuals who chose to convert one by one, voluntarily and legally. Earlier legal and theological texts from Arab lands had dealt with women's conversion, especially when women's husbands remained pagan. The Prophet himself invited wives of pagans to convert.[47] But in the Muslim kingdom of al-Andalus (southern Spain) in the tenth century, conversion had serious enough consequences that it could never have been merely a spiritual and social act; to leave a Christian or Jewish family and choose Islam meant losing the very family that was the basis of community and political organization, the source of all support for a woman, and moving into a new milieu that might not always be entirely welcoming. Stories of kings and caliphs who married formerly Christian women, and which reviled the queens for their political intrigues and overt sexuality show how wary the Muslim community could be of new members.[48] The social consequences of conversion, along with the fact that the legal model provided for spouses who did not convert – that is, for wives as well as husbands who chose not to follow the Prophet and thus rendered themselves liable to divorce from a new Muslim spouse – shows that women must have thought long and hard about their decisions.

Further, Muslim theology of the Middle Ages must have made the decision even more difficult. Islam did not assure women - converts or those born to the faith – any more equality of practice and leadership than the other religions of Europe. Muslim thinkers and leaders deemed women's nature inferior to that of men, just as in Judaism and Christianity. Ibn Rushd (d. 1198), writing from Córdoba later in the Middle Ages, noted disapprovingly that

> The competence of women is unknown, however, in these cities since they are only taken for procreation and hence are placed at the service of their husbands and confined to procreation, upbringing, and suckling. This nullifies their [other] activities. Since women in these cities are not prepared with respect to any of the human virtues, they frequently resemble plants in these cities. Their being a burden upon men [in these cities] is one of the causes of poverty of these cities. This is because they are to be found there in double the number of

---

[47] Ibid., 240.
[48] Maria J. Viguera, "On the Social Status of Andalusi Women," in *The Legacy of Muslim Spain*, ed. Salma Khadra Jayyusi (Leiden: Brill, 1994), vol. 2, 716–19.

men, while not understanding through [their] upbringing any of the necessary actions except for the few actions – like the art of spinning and weaving – that they undertake mostly at a time when they have need of them to make up for their lack of spending [power].[49]

Ibn Ru<u>sh</u>d believed that women's spiritual potential was limited by men who neglected to educate them. What spiritual epiphanies women enjoyed, or what tortures of the soul they suffered, as Muslims no one recorded. The scribes told only what happened to women born into Islam or to women who had defined their new lives as Muslims, not how they reacted.

As for heretics, there were not many in pre-1000 Europe. In late Antiquity, orthodox Christians often accused them of allowing women greater freedom, both religious and social. Yet the complaints of these early Christian writers echoed the dismay of Romans about all Christians in the first centuries CE, suggesting that Christians borrowed formulaic accusations from the texts of their own accusers. Several Roman commentators, for example, had blamed Christian men and women for orgies, and Christian women for promiscuity. They also believed that Christians allowed their women to teach and proselytize. Celsus, the second-century opponent of Origen, supposedly wrote of Christians (although we have only Origen's report of his words):

Whenever [Christians] get hold of children in private and some stupid women with them, they let out some astounding statements as, for example, that they must not pay any attention to their fathers and schoolteachers, but must obey them; they say that these talk nonsense and have no understanding, and that in reality they neither know nor are able to do anything good, but are taken up with mere empty chatter. But they alone they say, know the right way to live, and if the children would believe them, they would become happy and make their home happy as well.[50]

Classical pagans blamed Christians for the same offenses that Christians found in medieval heretics. They accused women of usurping the roles of father, master, and teacher in order to spread their outrageous doctrine among the unlearned. It is true that women in the barbarian north helped spread the Christian faith to their husbands and families. Heretical wives and mothers of later centuries seem

---

[49] Cited ibid., 712.
[50] Origen, *Contra Celsum*, III.55, trans. Henry Chadwick (Cambridge University Press, 1965), 165.

also to have participated in dissident Christian groups by performing the age-old tasks of hostessing church leaders and teaching their
children.[51] In the Middle Ages, though, church officials were more
worried about women who violated social norms. They chastised
women who transgressed their allotted roles to claim the functions of
clergymen. Yet such accusations were no more true, by and large, of
heretics than of others. Neither orthodox nor heterodox Christians
were especially radical in their treatment of women. Neither allowed
women to officiate. At any rate, it was hard to spot a heretic amidst
the variety of Christian practice existing in the early medieval period.
Women roamed the margins of Christianity, just as men did, in that
disorderly world. Only the occasional woman got herself noticed and
accused of outrageously anti-religious behavior, such as witchcraft,
before the millennium.[52] Whether this came of her choice or bad
luck, no commentator mentioned.

WOMEN'S HERITAGE IN CHRISTIANIZING EUROPE

Women had their own practices, interpretations, and choices to
make about religion, whether Christian or not, no matter what
men thought. In Iberia they could even choose safely not to be
Christian. Elsewhere, they could decline orthodoxy by continuing
pre-Christian customs or simply by not being observant. By the
seventh or eighth century, when most of Europe had become in
some sense Christian, women who chose that faith could look upon
their Christian history with some satisfaction about their spiritual
achievements. Stories circulated in the tribal histories about how
their ancestresses had been the first to accept the faith, dogging the
earliest male missionaries and demanding of their kin that they be
allowed to take religious vows.

To a certain extent, what the classical literati had worried about –
women sweet-talking their families and slaves into conversion – actually did occur in the barbarian West, according to the official
histories. Newly Christian ladies persuaded kings to receive the faith.
Queens worked their virtuous wiles upon their royal husbands, virgin saints upon their kinsmen, and mothers on their sons. Women

---

[51] Emmanuel LeRoy Ladurie, *Montaillou: The Promised Land of Error* (New York:
Braziller, 1978), 194–99.
[52] *WEHD* 1, 563.

who became nuns and abbesses also acted as missionaries and as emissaries of Christian communities to a larger, wilder, heathen world. Genovefa stood up to Huns, Frankish kings, and even other Christian officials. She also resisted the natural elements, in defense of, and as example to, her converts. She was not the only female missionary to move as the new religion's ambassador across the pagan landscapes of Europe. Abbess saints established convents as fortresses to protect their vowed sisters against demons, lusty bandits, and nuns' own disapproving kinsmen. All of these women acted as harbingers of Christianity, and also as what the historian JoAnn McNamara has called "living sermons": their stories proved didactic for women and men across the Christian territories, persuading others to conversion and to ever-more-meaningful Christian lives.[53] What is more, when these women died, their histories lived on in manuscripts, repeated at religious gatherings to inspire even more conversions.

Women did not finish with the effort of conversion once northern Europe had formally turned to Christianity. Although Christianization began as soon as clerics existed to record it, the process continued throughout the Middle Ages. It took more than the six or seven centuries of the early Middle Ages to bring full conversion – whatever that may mean in the practical sense of belief and practice. From the point of view of clerical reformers, the faith never fully infiltrated the minds and lives of ordinary people; we might better understand these believers as making choices and defining their own religious lives. Histories and saints' lives continued to offer up examples of pagans or lapsed adherents seeking a better life, and of ordinary souls turned to a higher calling. In all periods, women took part in expanding and deepening religious conviction among their neighbors and kin, and Christian documents featured females as exemplars.

The pious queen or noblewoman was a favorite example of medieval religious writers throughout the ages. As early as the fifth century, St. Pátraic (Patrick of Ireland) wrote of noble virgins who cast themselves at him, begging for help in evading their families and taking a vow of chastity to the Christian god.[54] In the seventh century, the saint's biographer, Tírechán, turned the motif of women's

---

[53] Jo Ann McNamara, "Living Sermons: Consecrated Women and the Conversion of Gaul," in *Medieval Religious Women*, vol. 2: *Peace Weavers*, ed. John A. Nichols and Lillian Thomas Shank (Kalamazoo: Cistercian Publications, 1987), 19–38.

[54] Ludwig Bieler, ed. and trans., *Patrician Texts in the Book of Armagh*, Scriptores Latini Hiberniae 10 (Dublin Institute for Advanced Studies, 1979), 99–101.

conversion into a gently heroic saga. Pátraic and his bishops surprised the two daughters of king Lóegaire washing at the well, "as women are wont to do." When the ladies inquired about his background, Pátraic reproved them and suggested they ask instead about his god. So the women obliged:

Who is God and where is God and whose God is he and where is his dwelling-place? Has your God sons and daughters, gold and silver? Is he ever-living, is he beautiful, have many fostered his son, are his daughters dear and beautiful in the eyes of the men of the earth? Is he in the sky or in the earth or in the water, in rivers, in mountains, in valleys? Give us an account of him; how shall he be seen, how is he loved, how is he found, is he found in youth, in old age?

And Pátraic answered with a creed:

Our God is the God of all men, the God of heaven and earth, of the sea and the rivers, God of the sun and the moon and all the stars, the God of high mountains and low valleys; God above heaven and in heaven and under heaven, he has his dwelling in heaven and earth and sea and in everything that is in them; he breathes in all things, makes all things live, surpasses all things, supports all things . . .[55]

As the girls wondered at Pátraic's theology, he suggested that they join "the heavenly king." They agreed, but only if they could see their bridegroom face to face. Pátraic baptized them, gave them the eucharist, and then they died. Their druid foster-fathers were incensed when they found out what the Christian missionary had wrought, but these pagans also soon followed the example of the girls. They converted and, rather than dying, accepted the monastic tonsure. The princesses were buried in a *ferta* or *relic*, the Irish words for a mound which later had a shrine atop it where other Christians could come to honor the saintly converts. The story was didactic, of course. The women, whom Pátraic first converted, then converted their near male relations with their selfless example, and continued after death to bring others of their community to Christianity. They remained present among their neighbors and family – physically, in the mound; spiritually, in the holy immanence of saints; and literarily, in the text, throughout the Middle Ages.

Conversion by royal female example occurred throughout pagan and Arian territories. Clothild of Francia and Bertha of Kent both brought their pagan husbands to the faith. Clothild tried preaching to her husband, Clovis, and when that did not work, she begged him at least to let her baptize the babies she bore him. Her first child died after his christening and she almost lost the second, as well. Clovis blamed the church. Clothild only won out after Clovis came near to disaster in a battle and pledged to accept Christianity if he won. Clovis turned to bishop Remigius, not to Clothild, for instruction; he took Constantine for his model, rather than his queen. But Gregory of Tours as well as the ninth- or tenth-century hagiographer of the queen remembered her as instrumental to the conversion.[56] And Gregory's history taught several lessons to later readers: those who accepted the faith, by whatever means, could look forward to political success as well as precious offspring. What is more, although it took a bishop to make Clovis official, the simple but superior wisdom of Christianity came to Clovis through his woman.

Likewise, it was Bertha, the Frankish princess who married Æðelbehrt in the seventh century and brought her bishop to England with her, who first persuaded the king to interview Christian missionaries landing on his shores. Likely, Bertha and her bishop knew in advance of the newcomers' arrival. Æðelbehrt gave the missionaries a fair hearing and very reasonably allowed them to set up a community near his court but without committing himself and his kingdom to conversion. Only after the monks began to preach to the locals and to conduct regular services attended by Queen Bertha did Æðelbehrt finally agree to be baptized himself.[57] Bede was more subtle in telling the queen's story than Gregory of Tours, but his text taught the same lesson to women: they could be instrumental in the Christianization of husbands, kings, and whole peoples by gentle argument and modest example. Conversion was, in these stories, a gendered act; for kings, it meant admitting that the ways of tradition and ancestors were inferior to the personal insights of a peaceable, literate Other, represented by women, sometimes even foreign (but more civilized) women brought into a territory as wives. Historians such as Bede and Gregory were casting their kings as catechumens at the feet of their own humble but inspired wifely teachers, who were themselves simple witnesses like the women at Jesus' tomb. In the context of a learned Christian tradition that already taught the paradox of Eve and Mary, this was a breathtaking bit of literary casting-against-the-grain.

---

[56] Gregory of Tours, *Historia*, II.20–22; *MGH SRM* 2, 341–48.
[57] Bede, *Historia Ecclesiastica*, I.25.

Queens were not the only conduit of Christianity, but some did actually did promote the faith. Other kinds of documents besides histories show that, through the rumor of their deeds as well as written accounts, queens took the examples of other queens. Long after Clothild brought her husband to Christ, Bishop Nicetius of Trier wrote a letter to Clotsinda, her granddaughter, queen of the Lombards in the 560s. He wanted Clotsinda to use her influence to lead her husband Alboin and all the Lombards from heretical Arianism into the orthodox fold. He prepped her with doctrinal arguments to use in favor of orthodoxy. He pointed out that the Arians were afraid to use Roman basilicas since they knew in their hearts that they, not the Romans, were the heretics. He reminded Clotsinda of the efficacy of orthodox shrines, where genuinely blind and lame believers were healed and demoniacs were whirled in the air before being cleansed of their evil spirits. Most persuasively, Nicetius provided Clotsinda with a precedent:

You have heard how your grandmother, Lady Clothild of good memory, came into France, how she led the Lord Clovis to the Catholic Law, and how, since he was a most astute man, he was unwilling to agree to it until he knew it was true. When he saw that the things I have spoken of were proved he humbly prostrated himself at the threshold of the Lord Martin and promised to be baptized without delay ... You are not ignorant of the what riches he and his sons possessed in the world. Such an admirable man as King Alboin is said to be, when the world offers him such glory, why is he not converted, or why does he come late to ask for the way of salvation? ... I beg that you not be idle; clamor without ceasing, do not cease to sing ... I pray that you so act that you both make the Lombard people strong over their enemies and allow us to rejoice at your salvation and at that of your husband.[58]

Nicetius not only knew his history of conversion and Clothild's role in it, but he knew that Clotsinda had heard the tale too, and he deemed it her duty to reenact her grandmother's historic role. Clotsinda's salvation, that of Alboin, and that of all the Lombard people depended not upon manly warfare but upon the queen's ceaseless clamoring. The alternative, continued heresy, meant not only hell but the destruction of the kingdom. Only the queen could save her people.

---

[58] Ed. W. Gundlach in Corpus Christianorum Series Latina 117 (Turnholt: Brepols, 1962), pp. 419, 422–23; trans. J. N. Hillgarth in *Christianity and Paganism, 350–750: The Conversion of Western Europe* (rev. edn., Philadelphia: University of Pennsylvania Press, 1986), 79–80.

Once Europe's rulers became nominal Christians, the clergy also expected women to make their men into better Christians. Pope Boniface exhorted Æðelburh of Northumbria (daughter of Bertha of Kent) in a letter much like that of Nicetius to Clotsinda, sending along a comb and a mirror as extra encouragement. It was her duty to uphold the Christian law of wedlock, he reminded her, in which the two made one in flesh, by converting her husband Edwin – for how could it be said that they shared oneness if her husband's "detestable error" alienated her from Christianity?[59] Sometimes, however, it took more than sweet talk from a well-groomed, queenly wife to turn her kingly husband from error. Edwin required deliberation with his followers before he would convert, according to Bede, who told the story. But Bede, famously, rarely gave women credit for proselytizing or for much else, so it is difficult to tell whether the Anglo-Saxons resisted the Christian blandishments of their women and followed a different model of conversion, or whether Bede simply wanted to remember that men brought men to Christianity in England. For her part, Æðelburh supposedly retired to found the monastery of Lymminge.[60]

St. Radegund's husband needed even more coddling to turn over a new leaf, according to Gregory of Tours and other documents from the time. Radegund became a famous example of the queen turned saint and influential ecclesiastic against all sorts of manly objections. As a child in the Thuringian court, she was won in a lottery among Merovingian princes who had killed her family and captured her in a raid in 531. Chlotar, who acquired her, had her brought up on one of his farms. She tried to escape but eventually was forced to marry her captor and live as his wife for about ten years. "She played the part of a wife," as one hagiographer put it, "only to serve Christ more devoutly acting as a model laywoman."[61] But after the king murdered her only surviving relative, her brother, she withdrew to one of her own estates. Hearing that Chlotar wanted her back, she first persuaded bishop Medard of Noyon to veil her as a deaconess and then took refuge in a convent that she had founded for other women at Poitiers. From there she persuaded Bishop Germanus to prevent Chlotar from coming after her. Chlotar released Radegund

---

[59] Bede, *Historia Ecclesiastica*, ii.11.
[60] Sarah Foot, *Veiled Women II: Female Religious Communities in England, 871–1066* (Aldershot, UK and Burlington, VT: Ashgate, 2000), 111–15.
[61] McNamara and Halborg, *Sainted Women of the Dark Ages*, 87.

from her marriage vows although he could well have snatched her back forcibly. As repeated secular and religious laws against the abduction of formally veiled nuns demonstrates, plenty of men did not hesitate to find (or recapture) a wife in the cloister, and both secular leaders and churchmen often supported their rights to do so.[62] Perhaps Chlotar was dissuaded by Radegund's ascetic habits even when she remained with him; she used to rise in the small of the night, ostensibly to visit the privy, where she crouched beneath a hair shirt and prayed on the cold stone floor. She stayed away from the dinner table, attending to the candles in the sanctuary, and always rushed to wash the feet of holy men when they arrived at the palace. She also gave away whatever treasure came to hand. Indeed, courtiers made fun of Chlotar, saying that he was married to a *monacha* (nun) rather than a normal queen.[63] Whether shame or piety motivated the king, he eventually even endowed Radegund's monastery at Poitiers.

Once safe in her women's community, Radegund continued to govern the women and estates of Ste. Croix at Poitiers even though she appointed another woman as abbess. She saw that her nuns were educated and was herself a writer of letters and poetry. She was also an avid collector of holy relics, including a bit of the Cross after which she named the monastery.[64] She involved herself in secular politics, always urging her kinsmen on the outside to a better life. She intervened in the feud among her husband's Merovingian heirs; when she could not put a stop to warfare, at least she could offer refuge to victims of strife. The daughters of her stepsons fled to her, but the violence of the times followed them right to the walls of Poitiers, which was burnt during the civil wars of the late sixth century. Indeed, after Radegund's death, the convent itself was torn apart by the feuds of royal nuns.

Yet Radegund's written legend may have served later generations as an example of better-behaved female religious among their own

---

[62] See Gregory of Tours's story and his position on the issue: *Historia*, IX.33.

[63] Ibid., 72–74.

[64] Baudonivia, *Vita* in McNamara and Halborg, *Sainted Women of the Dark Ages*, 16; ed. Paola Santorelli, *La Vita Radegundis di Baudonivia* (Naples: Dauria, 1999); K. Cherewatuk, "Radegund and the Epistolary Tradition," in *Dear Sister: Medieval Women and the Epistolary Genre*, ed. K. Cherewatuk and Ulrike Wiethaus (Philadelphia: University of Pennsylvania Press, 1993), 20–45; Fortunatus, XII.28, trans. Judith George in *Venantius Fortunatus: Personal and Political Poems* (Liverpool University Press, 1995), 120–21.

people. There was a time, the queen's hagiographers, correspondents, and Gregory of Tours pointed out, when queens brought Christianity and its institutions to the people, rather than abusing the church in pursuit of personal or family gain. They did it as respectable royal mothers and daughters. As the nun Baudonivia put it when writing of Radegund, she "no longer remembered that she had a family and a royal husband," but preached to her nuns "Daughters, I chose you. You are my light and my life." Baudonivia herself was "the smallest of the small ones she nourished familiarly from the cradle as her own child at her feet!"[65]

After Radegund, women of the Frankish nobility and the female elite of other cultures continued to convert their families, but to higher forms of Christianity rather than to the religion itself. They even hauled their families into the cloister. Sadalberga was an heiress pushed into marriage by her parents. After her first husband died, she took another, but ended up bringing her husband, her children, her brother and his wife, and one of her daughter's suitors, into monastic communities. St. Aldegund faced her parents' opposition to a religious vocation, too, but ultimately had her way; her sister, with a husband and two daughters, and Aldegund's mother also joined up.[66] Austraberta's (d. 703) hagiographer recorded how people in her neighborhood were so enthused by the saint's example that they "came to offer sons and daughters to God" and "many hurried to the monastery themselves, relinquishing their own marriages, casting off husbands and wives" only to be followed by the very spouses they had rejected.[67] In England, royal women commonly joined the communities of their relatives. The earliest English minsters in Kent and Northumbria were all founded on family property in the 630s and 640s by wives, sisters, and daughters of kings. Some English princesses entered religion as living memorials of the devotion of male relatives; Ælfflæd, daughter of Oswiu of Northumbria, joined a religious settlement because her father had pledged her in return for success in the battle of Winwæd. Her widowed mother joined her when Oswiu finally died in the 670s.[68] Perhaps Ælfflæd had no choice about moving into a religious community but her decision

---

[65] McNamara and Halborg, *Sainted Women of the Dark Ages,* 91; see also 86.

[66] McNamara, *Sisters in Arms,* 131–32.

[67] McNamara and Halborg, *Sainted Women of the Dark Ages*, 314.

[68] Bede, *Historia Ecclesiastica*, II.9, III.24, IV.26.

to remain there may well have been her own. The dedication of her mother's widowhood was surely influenced by Ælfflæd's example as well as that of other Anglo-Saxon dowager queens.[69]

Whereas royal and noble women were supposedly left to convert by quiet word and modest deed, kings could force their people to convert, or make it dangerous for ordinary farmers and workers to resist the preachings of clergymen. Once the Franks took up Christianity, they made laws forbidding the paganism they had cast off. King Childebert ruled in the middle of the sixth century that "any men who, once admonished, shall not at once cast out images and idols, dedicated to the devil, made by men, from their fields or shall prevent bishops from destroying them, shall not be free, once they have given sureties until they appear in our Presence."[70] The Lombard lawmakers merely decreed that a soothsayer pay his or her *wergeld* for practicing the old ways.[71] Visigoth rulers were harshest on pagans in a Christianizing Spain, ordering magicians and weathermakers to be given two hundred lashes, scalped, dragged through ten villages as a warning to others, and then deposited in confinement.[72] In England, where the king's fighting men still seemed to carry weight in decisions affecting the whole people, King Edwin supposedly consulted his nobles (but only the men) after he heard the missionary Paulinus preach. But after his entire council went over to Christianity, Edwin did not stop one of them − a former pagan "priest" − from leaping up, jumping on a horse, and racing to the nearest pagan site of worship, where he and his companions burnt it to the ground.[73] Throughout the Continent and the northern islands, the decisions of kings and nobles were supported by churchmen whose own extensive social rules forbade relapse into paganism. Clerics promoted Christian marriage by allowing a man to take a Christian wife if his pagan mate deserted him. They also condemned fornication with nuns, assigned severe penances for magical practices, and tried to prevent practicing Christians from doing business with heathens in

---

[69] Sarah Foot, *Veiled Women I: The Disappearance of Nuns from Anglo-Saxon England* (Aldershot, UK, and Burlington, VT: Ashgate, 2000), 41–45.

[70] Alfred Erwin Boretius, ed., *Capitularia Regum Francorum* (Hanover, 1883), 2–3; trans. Hillgarth, *Christianity and* Paganism, 108.

[71] Franz Beyerle, ed., *Die Gesetze der Langobarden* (Weimar: Böhlau, 1947), 139–40; trans. Hillgarth, *Christianity and Paganism*, 109.

[72] S. P. Scott, trans., *The Visigothic Code (Forum Judicum)* (Boston, 1910), 204.

[73] Bede, *Historia Ecclesiastica*, II.13.

their own communities.[74] Women, then, appeared in histories and hagiographies as the inspiration of Christian conversion, while men made the rules for its practice and preservation.

But rich and influential women had other means for conversion, too, which early medieval historians left untold or unemphasized. Donation and endowment were major ways for women to establish Christian practice as well as confirming their devotion. Any kind of gift, from a necklace to major estates, established a woman's faith and provided an example for others.[75] Ladies throughout Europe helped to make Christianity visibly important when they built and garnished Christian edifices and supported religious communities. Queens and princesses who retired to monasteries needed appropriately deluxe surroundings for their good deeds. The major feuds between Berthegund and her mother at Ingitrude's community at Tours, for instance, revolved around the monastery's extensive property.[76] The contents of Ste. Croix at Poitiers were so attractive to the soldiers of one rebellious noble nun that they looted the place while she quarrelled with the abbess; convents everywhere were well known as targets of the greedy and impious.[77] Families were concerned about the amount of property that accompanied their women into religion, and rightly so. English and continental charters from the seventh century onward similarly show how noblewomen contributed to Christianity materially and spiritually.[78]

Only the massively wealthy could give away family land without negative repercussions. According to her hagiographer, queen and saint Balthild "showered great estates and whole forests upon [religious communities] for the construction of their cells and monasteries," including the "special community of God" at Chelles (664–65)

---

[74] McNeill and Gamer, 246, 275, 306, 77.

[75] See also Bitel, *Land of Women*, 172–73; Cogitosus, *Vita Sanctae Brigidae*, PL 72: 789–90; Charles Plummer, ed., *Vitae Sanctorum Hiberniae* (Oxford: Clarendon, 1910), 2: 254–55, 256, 260, for building projects at Cluain Brónaig.

[76] Gregory of Tours, *Historia*, IX.33. See also the reference to the well-housed and well-fed Berthefled, ibid.

[77] Ibid., X.15.

[78] *WEHD* 1 79 *et passim*; Janemarie Luecke, "The Unique Experience of Anglo-Saxon Nuns," in Nichols and Shank, ed., *Peace Weavers*, 58, n. 5; David Herlihy, "Land, Family and Women in Continental Europe 700–1200," *Traditio* 18 (1962), repr. in *Women in Medieval Society*, ed. S. Stuard (Philadelphia: University of Pennsylvania Press, 1976), 28–32.

where she would retire.[79] Some women, including Balthild, chose to patronize women's houses. The royal nuns of Kent accumulated enough resources from their own property and by seeking donations from their ruling kinsmen that they could sponsor St. Boniface's missions in Germany. Abbess Eadburh of Thanet ruled a double monastery with extensive lands, a fleet in the isle's harbor, and a large, expensive scriptorium and library. Eadburh thought nothing of Boniface's request that she have Peter's epistles copied in gold for him, "that the Holy Scriptures may be honoured and reverenced when the preacher holds them before the eyes of the heathen," in addition to books and vestments that she had already sent.[80] Archeological remains confirm the story of generosity found in texts; the foundations of numerous women's settlements bely the silence of Bede and other Anglo-Saxon writers regarding the number and size of nunneries.[81] Royal women, supported by their kinsmen, had many good reasons to subsidize religious communities, including the promotion of saints' cults important to their families, the maintenance of coherent family properties, and the safe placement of extra daughters.[82]

Still, religious motives informed every vocation and every donation. Ordinary women gave what they could, including their labor. One poverty-stricken virgin swept the pavement of Austraberta's shrine every Saturday and strewed flowers and herbs to sweeten the air of the sanctuary because she had nothing else to give.[83] Others spread the faith. Any mother could have passed on the good word to her babies. We know that queens did so. Judith, embattled wife of Louis the Pious, prepared both her son, Charles the Bald, and her daughter Gisèle for their careers as, respectively, emperor and abbess.[84] Even in the ninth century, King Alfred's mother brought him to piety and literacy by giving him, along with her smiles, a book of songs even

---

[79] McNamara and Halborg, *Sainted Women of the Dark Ages*, 271. See also the donations of Queen Ingoberg in Gregory of Tours, *Historia*, IX.26.

[80] Boniface, *Epistolae* XIV, trans. Edward Kylie in *The English Correspondence of Saint Boniface* (New York: Cooper Square, 1966), 90–91; Dockray-Miller, *Motherhood and Mothering*, 24–27.

[81] Roberta Gilchrist, *Gender and Material Culture: The Archaeology of Religious Women* (London: Routledge, 1994).

[82] Karl Leyser, *Rule and Conflict in an Early Medieval Society: Ottonian Saxony* (London: Arnold, 1979), 64; Foot, *Veiled Women I*, 43–49.

[83] McNamara and Halborg, *Sainted Women of the Dark Ages*, 325.

[84] Nelson, "Les femmes et l'evangelisation," 475–76.

before he could read it.[85] Numerous saints, male and female, were first tutored in the faith by their birth or surrogate mothers, just as Baudonivia learned at Radegund's kindly knee. Irish saints, both male and female, learned their faith from surrogate mothers, too, by whom they were fostered and instructed in religious communities.[86] Women remained responsible for the early nurture and education of their children throughout the early Middle Ages, before and after the Carolingian reforms. Women also turned up in saints's lives as concerned mothers who brought their ailing children to thaumaturges for healing; after being restored to health, patients and their families either made generous donations to the saints' foundations or even joined the saints' communities as nuns or monks.

Although mothers could teach their children, no woman was allowed to preach formally, even if she took the vow of a nun. Women could not perform sacraments or take an official role in new churches. They could, as abbesses, go into the world to feed and minister to the ailing, or accept pilgrims and travellers in the public spaces of their religious settlements. But ordinary nuns were not supposed to have much truck with the world once they had left it, according to the rules composed for their communities by bishops and monks. Largely by their examples in life and, after life, in the texts that recorded their deeds and the churches and minsters that displayed their generosity and piety, religious women helped to convert Europe to Christianity. Once Europe was nominally Christian, women worked constantly to reinspire it to greater faith and better practice. Wives and mothers were called upon to nag their kinsmen with the method that their clerical advisors called "ceaseless prayer."

RULES FOR CHRISTIAN LIVING

A devout woman of the eighth or ninth century, reflecting upon the Christian past of her mothers, had multiple exemplars and guidelines for behavior available to her. She had the theology of those many-voiced scholars, canonists, and liturgists who handed down the sometimes conflicting directives. She may not have read them herself or even obeyed them to the letter, but she surely received

---

[85] Asser, *Life of Alfred,* chaps. 23–25, trans. and ed. in Simon Keynes and Michael Lapidge, *Alfred the Great* (Harmondsworth: Penguin, 1983), 75–76.

[86] Bitel, *Land of Women,* 99–100.

messages regarding Christian behavior from those who did. These templates, along with local traditions, allowed women to shape their participation in Christianity. A Christian woman of the early Middle Ages was reminded of her intellectual insufficiency and her tendency toward certain kinds of sin, as explained by the church fathers, when choosing her religious program. Monastic rules referred to all human failings but also to particularly feminine weaknesses. Penitentials laid down prayers and fasts as penalties for sins. Conciliar decrees and canons based precepts upon the principle of female inferiority. Lives of both male and female saints further illustrated the frailty of women. A good Christian also needed to consider the demands of social ties, economic obligations, and political affiliation. Custom, expectations of those about her, and the demands of daily life also helped determine what of the liturgy and sacraments meant most to an ordinary laywoman. Her age, her class, questions of property, and the bonds of the landscape that kept her close to home influenced her, too. Attitudes within and without the church pointed her toward the services she sought from Christian clerics and saints, and led her to interpret the rules for her behavior.

In turn, her gender identity shaped the kinds of religious opportunities a woman created for herself and what she demanded of Christianity and its official leaders. For example, just as a wife was supposed to keep her unruly husband on the path of righteousness, so a woman's traditional role as peaceweaver among disparate kin-groups made a female religious figure like Radegund an obvious choice for a mediating role among feuding factions.[87] Just as princesses adorned themselves with jewels and fine robes to mark their status as royal wives and daughters, so when they went to the convent their gifts of jewels marked them at once as converts to a new life, high-ranking ecclesiastics, and powerful links to politicians in the neighborhood.[88] Social expectations also led women, more than men, to seek the aid of saints in certain crises. Thus a couple's inability to have children or a woman's desire for miraculous cure of her illness brought believers to shrines of saints for holy intercession.

We know the rules for Christian living in the seventh, eighth, and ninth centuries. Besides the canons and decrees left by councils and synods of clerics from across Europe, and decisions rendered

[87] Wemple, *Women in Frankish Society*, 45.
[88] Bonnie Effros, "Symbolic Expressions of Sanctity: Gertrude of Nivelles in the Context of Merovingian Mortuary Custom," *Viator* 27 (1996), 1–10.

on all sorts of matters by bishops (including the pope) and kings, priests and monks also developed handbooks of penance. Irish and British churchmen first wrote them in the sixth century and later brought them to the Continent, where the texts became extremely popular among pastors and monks alike (not always different men in the very fluid ecclesiastical organization of the early Middle Ages). These handy books listed sins to which Christians were prone and the prayers and other penances that believers were to perform to expiate their offenses. Unlike legal codes, then, which often tried to legislate for all possible crimes, and therefore are not always accurate guides to behavior of people in the past, penitentials supposedly responded to the actual behavior of individuals within Christian communities. Whereas the laws demanded public negotiation of infractions by numerous people representing both perpetrator and victim, the penitentials were private sentences for privately confessed sins. Of course, churchmen were as imaginative as lawmen; nothing was to stop an inventive author, gathering momentum while describing sins of the flesh, from adding a few exotic infractions of his own devising. Also, the rules were for those who professed Christianity and actually confessed their sins to clergymen. We have few clues as to whether most layfolk obeyed or even knew of the rules. Certainly other kinds of texts, such as the tribal histories, depicted people sinning with abandon – most early medieval monarchs, for instance, committed more than a venal sin or two in their time. Some of their infractions came of plain evil or heedlessness, others of the difference between formal Christian ideal and local practice. Nonetheless, enough of the material in the penitentials is alike to suggest some patterns of concern on the part of ordinary Christian clergy and behavior on the part of their congregants. And the handbooks themselves were widespread and well copied. Editions of penitential tracts circulated around early medieval Europe and remain today in many major archives.[89]

The penitentials had much to say about everyday life for kings, nobles, peasants, and slaves, for clerics, nuns, and laypeople, including women. The texts covered some of the same categories of transgression as secular lawcodes, but their approach to crimes, the process by which misdeeds were judged, and punishments assigned differed substantially from that of secular codes. One of the most popular tracts was the *Penitential* of Theodore, composed in England in the

[89] McNeill and Gamer, 56–57.

later seventh century, which treated theft, manslaughter, false oaths, ownership of slaves, and matters relating to marriage, among other ordinary concerns. Unlike secular rules, however, according to which criminals paid fees for their offenses, penitentials decreed prayers, fasts, and even exile as penalties. According to Theodore's *Penitential*, a murderer was to perform either ten or seven years' penance, which involved severe fasting and even excommunication from sacraments; other penitentials set the penalty at permanent exile. But if the culprit slew a monk or cleric, the exact nature of his punishment was not decreed by a king but set down by his bishop, in addition to any penalties negotiated under secular laws. Even if he slew a victim while engaged in warfare decreed by his lord, he was to do forty days' penance, something unimaginable by secular standards, which took military service as an obligation of all free men.[90] If the malefactor kidnapped a monk (a sin listed by Theodore under the category "Of Thieving Avarice"), he was to enter a monastery or become a slave in recompense. A man who abandoned his first wife to marry a second was to do either seven years' hard penance or fifteen years' light penance, which involved more limited fasting, even though the custom was common enough in early medieval societies bent on reproduction, and legal under most circumstances by secular rulings.[91]

The penitentials also treated a variety of topics never covered by secular laws, mostly having to do with the practice of religion and sexual matters. The rules covered drunken excess and heresy, idol worship, and the appointing of churches. Several of the penitentials laid down penalties for the consumption of horseflesh, for instance; others ruled on the desecration of Christian spaces and ritual objects. But rules for sexual behavior and reproduction, more than any other kind, caught the attention of penitentialists and those who used their works. Perhaps a quarter or more of any text treated sexual matters. Besides hinting at the practice of sex in Christianizing societies, the writers of penitentials indicated the importance of sexual behavior in determining the identity of good Christians. Just as ascetic lifestyles had marked out Christians from other Jews or Romans in the first and second centuries, and as celibacy had come to denote the ecclesiastical elite of bishops and monastic personnel, so a more moderate sexual schedule within the context of legal monogamy signified the ordinary Christian in a slowly converting European society. What is more,

[90] Ibid., 187.   [91] Ibid., 186, 196.

the penitentials displayed an obvious double sexual standard. Not everyone deserved the same punishment for the same sin, for some evils were considered worse when the malefactor or victim was a woman. Penitentialists such as Theodore promoted the stable, monogamous, Christian couple as the basis of organized society. Adultery, fornication (sex between two people not married to each other), masturbation, lust, nocturnal emissions, incest, rape, bestiality, and homosexual and lesbian sexual activity were all taboo, according to these rules. But some sins were more taboo than others, and thus demanded more severe penances. Simple fornication with a virgin brought a man one year's penance. Fornication with a married woman called for two years' penance followed by two years during which the sinner practiced penance during the three forty-day fasts (before Easter and Christmas and after Pentecost) and three days a week during the rest of the year. But sexual activity of man with man or beast brought ten years' prayer and fasting, or fifteen, according to other authorities. Recidivists called down heavier penalties; men involved in homosexual acts received different punishments depending upon whether they were penetrating or penetrated. Masturbation or mere lust, as solo acts, commanded a forty-day penance. Incest was among the worst sins for man or woman, but "the worst of evils" was "he who ejaculates into the mouth of another," which, according to some rulemakers, brought a life of penance.[92] What is more, all these sins, from trivial to appalling, brought heavier penalties to men in orders. Bishops, presbyters (priests), or deacons who admitted fornication were to be degraded from their ranks in the church and perform their penances; fornication with a virgin brought a priest not one year's, but seven years' penance.[93]

Although confessors were willing to believe in women's sinfulness, the writers of penitentials aimed their texts, as did authors of secular laws, at the legal standard: the adult male. Women's vices appeared in the texts as variations of the basic design. Cases of simple fornication always involved a male sinner and female partner. Incest was primarily a sin of men with their mothers and sisters, and only secondarily of women with their sons or brothers. Theodore, for instance, distinguished the case of a mother and her male child, but not a father and his small daughter.[94] Women's vices also called forth an entirely

---

[92] Ibid., 186.   [93] Ibid., 192–93.   [94] Ibid., 186.

different schedule of punishment. Women practicing homoerotic acts with women earned three years' penance, while women's masturbation brought the same three years, rather than the forty days earned by a man. Other penitential tracts ignored the possibility of lesbian acts or women's masturbation entirely, either disregarding it as harmless or refusing to imagine it.[95] On the other hand, all the tracts had plenty to say about adulteresses (including women who wished to end one marriage and begin another), fallen nuns, and women practicing abortion or infanticide. The writers of penitentials condemned all these acts and ascribed serious penances to each.

Theodore and his colleagues were intent upon teaching Christians that sex outside of Christian marriage was sinful. The same theologians who had pronounced opinions upon the nature of woman also had much to say about sexuality in general and its effects upon a Christian population, which laid the groundwork for the working rules of daily behavior encoded in penitentials. But some religious notions about virtue and social order were more acceptable to ordinary believers in northern Europe than others. Incest taboos, for instance, along with laws against adultery and laws limiting the sexual freedom of women, were fairly standard in secular legal codes. But none of the secular laws had much to say about masturbation or nocturnal emissions, nor did they set higher penalties for clerics than for laymen caught in sexual offenses. What is more, Christian writers' abhorrence of divorce and multiple marriages (either serial, as in a married woman remarrying, or simultaneous, as in polygyny) had no echo in the laws. Penitentialists routinely ordered adulterous women to return to their husbands and take up their wifely duties again while performing their assigned penances. Lawmakers, on the other hand, allowed men to discard adulterous wives and remarry. And all those penitentials about fornication were aimed squarely at men who lived and slept with more than one woman, as many noblemen of early Europe were prone to do whenever they had the chance.

Did these rules reach ordinary parishioners, living on their farms in the isolated reaches of the countryside? It may not even be fair to call most Christians of early Europe parishioners. By the seventh or eighth century, the religion had officially spread to every corner of western Europe except Scandinavia and parts of Germany; bishops and monks, such as the famous Boniface and his lesser-known kinswoman

---

[95] Ibid., 185.

Leoba, had gone out from the older heart of Christendom to evangelize the eastern frontier, while the new, more efficient kings of Christian empires were forcibly converting conquered armies of remaining pagans. Yet the proportion of clergy to believers remained low, and the quantity and quality of parish services must have varied considerably. The letters of literate churchmen in this period are filled with complaints about the lack of resources, man-power, and support from the ruling powers. Bede suggested that priests in northern England be allowed to preach and say mass even if they could not read Latin, so desperate were congregants for leaders.[96] Boniface, from the wilds of Germany, wrote to friendly nuns back home, begging for gospels and other supplies. If the saints' lives are to be believed, people did not attend mass or other rituals with any regularity. They came to church when they needed something – a cure, a blessing on the crops, a baptism or funeral. And the pentientials suggest that Christians were unconcernedly performing every sort of sexual sin imaginable despite the efforts of churchmen to influence custom.

And yet most women in the countrysides of western Europe were Christian in some way. Eddius Stephanus, a seventh-century scholar from England, told a story about a woman who sought out Bishop Wilfrid of York while he was "out riding on a certain day, going to fulfill the various duties of his bishopric, baptizing and also confirming the people with the laying on of hands."[97] Wilfrid was a rural pastor who had to take his office to his flock, riding wherever they might be. A woman was waiting for him in one of the small villages through which he had to pass – not in church, but along the roadside. She sat moaning with grief, clutching the rag-wrapped corpse of her first baby. When the bishop rode by, she pulled away the cover to reveal the tiny body. According to Eddius Stephanus, she hoped that the bishop would not notice the dead child and by his accidental blessing would bring it back to life. What could really have passed through her mind, waiting there for the man who was just a man, doing his job, slipping off his horse and stopping in the mud to pray over this one, bless that one? Perhaps Eddius imbued his character with more faith than she possessed, if she even existed outside his story. Wilfrid confirmed the baby with the rest of the gathered faithful. Yet, in the narrative, the bishop hesitated, guessing

---

[96] *WEHD* I, 734.
[97] Eddius Stephanus, *Life of Wilfrid*, xviii; trans. J. F. Webb in David Farmer, ed., *The Age of Bede* (Harmondsworth: Penguin, 1965), 124–25.

her purpose. He wondered humanely whether it was his business to try to imitate the redeemer and resuscitate a life, or whether he must add to the mother's desolation. Eddius wrote,

> But the mother fell to earth before the face of the bishop on his perceiving what she had done and, weeping bitterly, she boldly adjured him, in the name of the Lord his God, by virtue of his holiness to raise her son, to baptize him and free him from the mouth of the lion. With such words she never ceased to adjure him again and again, by all the holiness of bishops, kneeling and kissing his feet, embracing and bedewing them with bitter tears, saying, "Most holy man, do not destroy the faith of a bereaved mother but help thou my (un)belief, raise him up and baptize him and he will live to God and to you. By the power of Christ, do not hesitate!"

Like a queen nagging her pagan spouse into Christianity, the mother ceaselessly and boldly adjured Wilfrid to attempt a healing blessing. The bishop lost his doubt and baptized the revived child, bidding the mother bring him to his monastery at age seven or so to become a monk. The mother never did, perhaps because she could not bear to. She fled the region to avoid losing her son. Eventually the bishop's officer came to fetch away the boy, who lived as Eodwald Bishop's Son in the monastery of Ripon until he died in the great plague.

In other episodes and other saints' lives, mothers were not so ungrateful. They dedicated healed children as nuns and monks in humble thanks for blessings received. They also took the advice of saints and other churchmen about all sorts of problems, thus negotiating among custom, gender expectations, and the possibilities of Christianity. Thus Adomnán, writing in the late seventh century of St. Columcille of Iona, told how the saint indulged in a little marriage counseling. Columcille was visiting some Christians on a remote island off the Scottish coast, travelling like Wilfrid to find Christians wherever they might be. He stayed with a married couple and found that the wife refused to sleep with her husband because he was so ugly. He preached at her a little from the gospel, but she replied, "I am ready to perform all things whatsoever that you may enjoin on me, however burdensome: save one thing, that you do not constrain me to sleep in one bed with Lugne. I do not refuse to carry on the whole management of the house; or, if you command it, even to cross the seas, and remain in some monastery of nuns." The woman took Columcille's holiness for authority, even though he was not her bishop but abbot of a local monastery. She accepted that her only release from marriage was the life of a religious celibate, as canons and penitentials regulated, rather than divorce. She expected the saint to be able to make an informed and canonically correct decision about her situation. Columcille indeed knew his canon law and hence refused to allow ugliness as grounds for a separation, no matter how heavy a penance the woman was willing to undertake. "It is forbidden that that should be separated, which God has lawfully joined," he pointed out. Then he suggested that the three of them pray and fast together, while the wife conceded that Columcille could, indeed, bring about the impossible. The next day, Columcille asked her: "Woman, are you today as you said yesterday, ready to depart to a monastery of nuns?" And she replied, "I know now that your prayer concerning me has been heard by God. For him who I loathed yesterday I love today." And, Adomnán concluded, "the dues of the marriage-bed, which she had formerly refused to grant, she never again denied."[98]

Both Christian rules and hagiography, then, seem to suggest a rural landscape where most women called themselves Christians, or were called so by the professional religious who passed through and wrote about their settlements. Bishops, priests, monks, and also holy women brought word of Christian mores and taught the practice of formal rituals, according to which ordinary Christians were to construct their daily lives. The more devout or needy may have made the extra effort of travelling to find clergy, rather than waiting for clergy to come to them. They journeyed to a shrine to consult the monks or nuns guarding a saint's relics for advice and help with a problem. They sought out a confessor with a penitential handbook and ashamedly recounted a sin, taking the prayers and fasts of penance as just desert. Some, of course, lived near enough a church to take advantage of its custodians more regularly; perhaps an ancestor had founded a nunnery on an extra estate, or a missionary had come through and built a little church which was blessed with a priest sent from somewhere more civilized. Wherever a Christian building existed with Christian personnel inside, it had to be supported materially with the dues, tithes, rents, and gifts of grateful congregants and clients. Wilfrid expected the mother of the restored baby to dedicate his life to God's service. No doubt Columcille expected happy couples – both the subjects of Adomnán's story and later readers of the tale – to give donations in thanks for God's blessings and clerical marriage counseling.

---

[98] Adomnán, *Life of Columba*, ed. and trans. A. O. Anderson and M. O. Anderson (London: Nelson, 1961), 436–41.

Sometimes even devout women were caught by custom and ex-
pectation, and thus unable to leave their houses to find succor from
a cleric. Even so, the clerics in charge expected women to find ways
to participate in Christianity as best they could, and to recompense
churchmen for what they gave. Bede told the story of Cuthbert,
roaming the countryside and encountering a familiar sheriff. The
sheriff was ashamed to present his wife's case to the saint, even though
she languished at death's door, because she was possessed of a devil.
He knew that a couple in such a situation could be shunned or cast
out by their community. Certainly the prestige conferred by the sheriff's office would suffer. The sheriff asked only that Cuthbert send a
priest to give his wife the last rites, so that the thaumaturge himself
would not have to see her howling, gnashing, and thrashing about.[99]
Of course, Cuthbert ended up healing the woman. The sheriff's wife
in Bede's story of Cuthbert could do nothing in thanks except give
him hospitality, and that was sufficient. We can be sure that later audiences of the story knew enough to donate to Cuthbert's church
when they wanted a miracle.

Christianity reached into the lives of ordinary women in many
ways but to varying depths. Some women who must have been at
least nominally Christian resisted the rules of the faith when such interfered with their practical lives. For instance, when clerics forbade
them from washing clothes or their hair on the sabbath, some were
willing to ignore regulations. Ordinary women chose the extent of
their belief and practice as well as whether or not to be Christian.
But Christian rulemakers expected both more and less of women
than of men. By nature, women behaved worse, especially in some
categories of sin, yet men remained the primary target of penitentials. Ecclesiastical leaders wanted female converts to define Christian
lives for themselves, despite the gendered limits imposed by their
surroundings and by the religion itself.

THE BEST OF CHRISTIAN WOMEN

Some women dealt with the restraints of Christian living just as
queens overcame political checks, by ignoring and exceeding them.
It was no coincidence that forceful religious women were often of the
highest nobility or even royalty. For a small percentage of European

---

[99] Bede, *Life of Cuthbert*, xv, ed. Colgrave, 203–07.

women in the early Middle Ages, the most meaningful Christian life came with a formal vow of asceticism. As soon as Europeans had become Christians, they began to wonder how to become even better Christians. They learned that the solution, perfected in the deserts of Egypt, was the purely abstinent life of withdrawal from society, practiced either privately under vows at home or in the communal endeavor of monasticism. Any man or woman with enough faith and willpower could do it. At least, that was what saints' lives and theology showed ordinary believers. As usual, Christians at the radical edge observed a less rigid gender segregation than those at the center. And, just as predictably, a woman needed a certain amount of wealth and status in order to be able to give them up.

Both Jesus and St. Paul had taught that, while marriage and a pious social life were acceptable, the sexless life lived in voluntary poverty and isolation from non-believers was better. Practitioners of asceticism wrote rules for others who would imitate them, beginning as early as the third century with Pachomius' rules. Many others revised the path to holiness: Basil, Cassian, the anonymous Master, Columban, and, most famous of all, Benedict of Nursia and his namesake, Benedict of Aniane. All taught the abandonment of worldly goods and concerns. Some writers wrote especially for women, including Augustine, Caesarius of Arles, Donatus of Besançon, Walderbert and, later, the author of the *Regularis Concordia*. Whenever a reformer wished to renovate the monastic life, he wrote a new rule. Men also wrote letters of advice to women religious, as Jerome had done for his matronly friends, and later bishops and abbots showered nuns with words both stern and good. But women also had the collective memory of those who had already successfully practiced the most difficult of Christianities: St. Pátraic's stories of young girls begging to take vows of celibacy, and the history of saints such as Radegund, who overcame severe opposition just to be allowed to live according to their consciences. Tales of other women provided models for those who wished to give themselves over to the professional pursuit of Christianity. And, of course, practitioners of the devout life existed throughout Europe as contemporary examples for others who would join them.

Yet, just as the concerns and constructs of the world shaped a laywoman's experience of Christianity, social custom and Christian ideology affected the conduct and aims of female religious professionals. Laws determined whether or not women could choose the religious life, or whether their male guardians might prevent them. Women who wanted grandchildren were reluctant to let their daughters choose celibate lives.[100] The suspicions about women's nature that permeated one strain of Christian thinking affected women's opportunities for organizing and governing their communities. Abbesses, for instance, were increasingly prohibited in the early Middle Ages from ruling communities that included men, whereas men continued throughout the Middle Ages to oversee women's groups. Even royal and noble women often depended upon their kinsmen to endow settlements where they might become religious professionals. They counted on men to work the lands attached to their monastic estates and to defend them by politics and by arms. They even needed men to perform many of the official Christian rituals that defined their seasons and their lives, since ecclesiastical leaders had long ago ruled that women themselves could not say mass, could not conduct funerals, could not even veil a sister when she came to take her vow.

Still, professional religious women retained choices about their vocations, including the choice not to obey men's rules. First, they could choose to take up the Christian life. Church leaders consistently supported women's rights to select virginity over the married life and valorized the role of religious celibate. Further, women could choose where and how to pursue their careers. St Genovefa lived at home, in her godmother's house, and with other vowed women at different points in her life. Some women joined communities, some opted for a lonelier life, while some like Genovefa moved from one state to another over the course of their careers. Kentish and Northumbrian royalty chose to found, join, and govern joint minsters or monasteries of women and men. Women in Francia generally created exclusively female communities. Still, these communities needed to decide upon their functions as a group: would they become pilgrimage centers or schools or dedicate themselves to the memorializing of royal dynasties, or all or none of these?

Male ecclesiastics never hesitated to provide guidelines for women religious and to try to help govern women's communities. Men's rules for the ascetic life were deceptively simple. St. Benedict's sixth-century Rule, which was used widely by both men and women throughout the Middle Ages, was a primer for abbots and abbesses. Like a father's words to a loving son, like a teacher's advice to his

---

[100] *Vita Aldegundis* in McNamara and Halborg, *Sainted Women of the Dark Ages,* 238.

small pupil, wrote Benedict, his precepts contained "nothing harsh or burdensome." Monks and nuns were to leave their kin and belongings behind when they entered a religious community. Titles and names were to lose meaning for them in their new family. They were to divide their days between prayer and manual labor, but to save time also for reading and learning – and apparently, as the writings of Baudonivia, the scholarship produced at the English houses of Whitby and Barking, and the manuscript illumination of the tenth-century Ende of Tabarà show – for manuscript illumination. They were to remain celibate, to choose poverty, and to be charitable (in the sense of cooperative and generous) to those within their community and on the outside. Above all, they were to obey their superior. Newcomers were to be tested for their sincerity of vocation. Guests were to be accommodated. The sick and young were to be nurtured. Those who went astray were to be encouraged, reprimanded, and, if necessary, punished.

Rules for women were based on those for men. Some abbesses took what they wished from Benedict's Rule and the guidelines of others. In Gaul, where the influence of Irish missionaries was strong, St. Columban's stricter ideals crept into the practice of some communities.[101] But other women demanded more gender-specific direction. St. Radegund used a rule written by Caesarius of Arles, a sixth-century bishop whose sister Caesaria gathered like-minded women into a community. Caesarius perceived a need for rules designed specifically for women's communities "because many customs in monasteries of young women seem to differ from those of monks."[102] But the primary difference between Caesarius' rule and that of Benedict was its first chapter: "The first point of observance is that no one shall leave the monastery until her death." For the sake of her soul and virtue, once a woman entered the walls of her new community, she was not even to advance as far as the basilica, where she could glimpse the door to the outside, so dangerous to her was the lure of the world left behind.[103]

Both men's opinions of women and the practicalities of constructing a women's community influenced the creation of later rules for

---

[101] Jo Ann McNamara and John E. Halborg, *The Ordeal of Community: The Rule of Donatus of Besançon and the Rule of a Certain Father to the Virgins* (Toronto: Peregrina, 1993), 8–9.

[102] Caesarius of Arles, *Rule for Nuns*, trans. Mary Caritas McCarthy (Washington, DC: Catholic University of America Press, 1960), sec. 2.

[103] Ibid., sec. 1.

4 Ende, Beatus of Gerona, *c. 975*, "Woman and dragon." One of several brilliant illuminations created by the tenth-century nun Ende of the Iberian monastery of Tábara.

nuns. A century after Caesaria, in a rougher and even less Romanized age, the abbess Gauthsruda needed a slightly different rule for her house, founded by her widowed mother in the same part of Gaul. She called upon her brother, Bishop Donatus, to produce a guide drawing on the precepts of earlier rulemakers. "You have enjoined me to heap up and promulgate all that is proper for the care of the female sex," wrote her brother, "saying that the rules for preaching fathers are less fitted for you since they were written for men and not for women." The rule of Caesarius for his own sister did not serve, since it was composed for patrician women of late Antiquity who enjoyed more "stability of place" than Gauthsruda, who was trying to survive the Thuringian and Merovingian feuds of the seventh century. Her nuns might need to disperse suddenly for protection or for economic reasons. So Donatus humbly but willingly created a practical rule organized into chapters with "enlightening titles," each chapter accompanied by "an apology for my vileness." He enjoined obedience, not only of nuns to the rule, but of his sister to her brother's instruction: "take care to keep without resistance each of these statutes you peitioned for all time." Gauthsruda was to read it often to all her sisters, correct her juniors, and entreat her elders to follow the rule.[104]

Despite the claims of Caesarius and Donatus that their rules were tailored for women, their suggestions for the religious life read much like those of Benedict. Donatus characterized the abbess as parent to her pious brood, acting prudently to correct their sins but always remembering mercifully that "the bruised reed is not to be crushed." None in the monastery should follow the will of her own heart, wrote the bishop. None should contend, none should refuse. All should subjugate the individual to the communal whole. Yet none should presume to pursue individual affections, either. She who took the hand of another woman in pleasure, walked together with her, or called her affectionately "little girl" was to receive blows for corrupting her selfless devotion to the larger group. Widows, along with "husband-leavers or clothes-changers," were to be accepted as well as virgins but only if they gave up all of their goods. None should create anything, none had a private bedroom or even a cupboard with a key. The women were to spend their days in silent labor, prayer, and reading. Above all, no man was to be let into the monastery except, of

---

[104] *PL* 87, 273–98; trans. McNamara and Halborg, *Ordeal of Community*, 36.

course, the bishop, the suppliers, the priest, deacons, aged lectors of praiseworthy life, artisans or their assistants, and the occasional visitor. If, God forbid, a nun broke the rules repeatedly, her worst punishment was excommuncation. Not ejection from the settlement, as in men's rules, but isolation from the solidarity of sisters during prayers, work, and meals was her penalty.

Together, the women were to practice what the historian Jo Ann McNamara has called the "ordeal of community." They struggled to create something that normally existed in early medieval society only by default: a house dominated by women. By adhering to the rules set down for them by men, by obeying the mother commissioned to gently and lovingly enforce the rule, by subjugating their own identities and wills to the greater good, by lowering the self and raising the eyes to heaven, and by never contending, individual women collectively enabled the community to survive. As McNamara has also pointed out, it must have taken a great deal of self-control for women who had made the decision to join such a community – a decision possibly opposed by their families, and which conflicted with centuries of social practice – to then so completely submit themselves to the liminalized whole.[105] Men were used to making decisions for themselves. For women, to decide upon a vowed Christian life took a stubborn determination which they were expected immediately to sublimate.

And yet, stubbornness and determination were essential qualities for a professional religious woman. In fact, the history of religious women in the Middle Ages was one long ordeal, not only of community, but of strategizing around the often restrictive ideology and rules of the ecclesiastical hierarchy, as well as the suspicions of secular neighbors and clerical colleagues. Women managed to pursue the religious life all across Europe during the Middle Ages, primarily by playing the same old roles as other women. As their rules announced, abbesses were mothers to their nuns, but they also acted as mothers and kinswomen to the neighbors and family they left behind in the carnal world. They nurtured children and laypeople, kept house for clerics, managed their farmyards and estates. They were spinners, weavers, cooks, and peacemakers. They labored at vestments and embroideries for their brother clergy.[106] They were also, unusually

---

[105] Ibid., 5, 30.
[106] Besides the Kentish nuns' supply for St. Boniface, see Mildred Budny and Dominic Tweddle, "The Maaseik Embroideries," *Anglo-Saxon England* 13 (1984),

for women, readers – or, at least, some of them were able to read, even write, and use texts to help in their holy lives. One vita of Radegund came from the pen of her spiritual daughter, Baudonivia; other saints' lives recounted episodes in which nuns copied books, exchanged books, and used books for ritual purposes, including the guidance and instruction of men and women, as well as maintaining correspondence with brother and sister professionals across Christendom. Nuns kept scriptoria where highly educated and skilled professionals manufactured books for themselves and others. They produced fine gospels, the theology of church fathers, ecclesiastical history, sacramentaries, vitae, and personal letters.[107] Nuns and other holy women helped in the conversion of Europe, just as did their married sisters, through the persuasion and teaching of men and other women. While only a few women, already endowed with status from their secular context, were able to enjoy genuine political power as ecclesiastical leaders, many more used traditional feminine postures as students, dependants, and muses to wield considerable influence in other, subtler ways.

The life of St. Leoba (died *c.* 782), the eighth-century Englishwoman gone to Germany, written a half-century later (838) by the monk Rudolf of Fulda, gives an excellent thumbnail sketch of nuns in the early Middle Ages.[108] By Rudolf's time, his Germany had been rather thoroughly evangelized so that Rudolf had to look to the recent missionizing past for charismatic subject matter. Like many hagiographers, Rudolf got his material from women and men who knew the saint or the traditions of her house, but posterity preserved his text rather than their notes. What is more, his own theories of sanctity and religious behavior influenced his depiction of his heroine, so that she ended up looking as much like St. Martin as an Englishwoman of

---

65–96; Mildred Budny, "The Ango-Saxon Embroideries at Maaseik: Their Historical and Art-historical Context," *Mededelingen van de Koninklijke Academie voor Wetenschappen, Letteren en schone Kunsten van Belgie* 45 (1984), 57–113.

[107] Rosamond McKitterick, "Nuns' Scriptoria in England and Francia in the Eighth Century," *Francia* 19 (1992), 1–35; McKitterick, "Frauen und Schriftlichkeit im Frühmittelalter," in *Weibliche Lebengestaltung im frühen Mittelalter*, ed. H.-W. Goetz *et al.* (Cologne and Vienna: Böhlau, 1991), 65–118; Bernhard Bischoff, "Die Kölner Nonnenhandschriften und das Skriptorium von Chelles," in *Mittelalterliche Studien: Ausgewählte Aufsätze zur Schriftkunde und Literaturgeschichte*, 3 vols. (Stuttgart: Hiersemann, 1966–81), vol. 1, 17–35.

[108] Rudolf of Fulda, *Life of Leoba*, in *The Anglo-Saxon Missionaries in Germany*, ed. C. H. Talbot (New York: Sheed & Ward, 1954), 204–26.

the eighth century.[109] Still, some useful details about how religious women operated lurk in the text.

Leoba, by Rudolf's account, was the only child of desperate parents. Her noble mother Æbba eventually had a dream of ringing a church bell, which her old nurse interpreted as a forthcoming pregnancy that would bring a daughter who must be dedicated to the religious life. Like Hannah, who dedicated Samuel to the temple, she was to give up her baby without any hesitation or any intervention on the part of the child's father. Although the child was precious enough to be called Leoba or "beloved," her mother handed her over to Mother Tetta of the double monastery at Wimbourne "to be taught the sacred sciences." The girl "grew up and was taught with such care by the abbess and all the nuns that she had no interest other than the monastery and the pursuit of sacred knowledge." Jests and romance were not for her; she preferred memorizing the gospel (whether from a written exemplar or by repetition, the text does not specify). She fasted and prayed and worked. She imitated the goodness of her sisters. Her reward was a vision: a purple thread, originating in her bowels, snaked out of her mouth. She wound the thread round and round into a great ball until she was exhausted from the labor. An aged and prophetic nun at Wimbourne explained that the thread was Leoba's wise counsel which she would enact throughout her life, just as she wound the ball of thread in the dream. The ball itself was the divine mystery, turned now toward earth by good works and now toward heaven through contemplation – down to neighborly love, up to love of God. The implication, according to the old prophetess, was that Leoba's words and deeds would be appreciated in lands far away. Nothing in the dream or Rudolf's description of it indicated gendered restrictions on Leoba's powers or mission; on the contrary, it signified authority granted by God. However, the dream, its interpretation, and Leoba's eventual enacting of her mission all took place in the company of women only.

Leoba was called by her kinsman, Boniface, to join him in his mission abroad. Despite her own abbess's objections, he set her up as abbess at Bischofsheim, where she promptly forgot both her home country and her former colleagues there, and set out to teach nuns to become missionaries for the monastic life. At the same time, Leoba

---

[109] Julia Smith, "The Problem of Female Sanctity in Carolingian Europe c.780–920," *Past and Present* 146 (1995), 3–37.

continued to learn: not only Old and New Testaments, but the writings of the church fathers, conciliar decrees, and all of church law. She even had young nuns read to her as she napped. When they tried to catch her dozing by misreading passages, she opened her eyes and corrected them (a trick learned from Martin and other saints). She set such a positive example that "many nobles and influential men gave their daughters to God to live in the monastery in perpetual chastity; many widows also forsook their homes, made vows of chastity and took the veil in the cloister."

Yet even Leoba was not exempt from envy and suspicion. The devil tried to tempt her nuns from their ascetic lives and, when unable, brought disrepute upon Bischofsheim through a beggar girl. The "poor little crippled girl" ordinarily sat at the monastery gate taking charity from the nuns, even scraps from Leoba's table. She succumbed to fornication and became pregnant. When she bore her child, she wrapped it in rags and cast it into a pool near the nunnery, thereby killing the baby as well as poisoning the local water source. A neighbor woman found the corpse and "burning with womanly rage" began immediately to denounce the nuns: "How admirable is the life of nuns, who beneath their veils give birth to children and exercise at one and the same time the function of mothers and priests, baptising those to whom they have given birth." The accuser suggested that the community locate any missing nun and punish her for the crime. The entire village was ready to blame the nuns; they caught up with Sister Agatha, who had been away visiting kin, and reviled her for the infanticide. Leoba calmly reacted with prayer. She ordered all the sisters to enter the church and pray with their arms extended as crosses, singing through the psalter. Then they were to process three times daily around the monastery, bearing their crucifix, calling on God to prove them innocent. Preparing for the third procession, Leoba approached the altar and demanded that God protect them. Immediately, the fornicating beggar was consumed by flames – or so it seemed to her – and called out her guilt. "So it came about," decided Rudolf, "that the reputation of the nuns . . . was greatly enhanced and praise was showered on them in every place." This was Leoba's first public miracle in Germany, and it "came to the ears of everyone." Her next, equally impressive, miracle was to put an end to a storm at the request of a mob of pleading, hysterical lay neighbors cowering in her church.

Boniface pleaded with her, too. When he prepared for his mission to Frisia, where he was eventually ambushed and killed, he exhorted

Leoba not to abandon her new territory by returning to England. She must not mind her own weakness, loneliness, or the long years of monastic life ahead of her, but must persevere with the help of their colleagues at the monastery of Lull. He even promised to have her buried next to him when her time came. Despite Boniface's faith in her and despite her extraordinary life, his friends at Lull still had certain rules about women that even Leoba could not escape. Although she came there to pray, she was the only female allowed within the private spaces of the men's monastery. She came only in daylight and in the company of a nun more ancient than she. Eventually, though, Boniface's promise was honored. Exile, miracle-maker, and exemplar of virtue, friend to saints and intimate of Charlemagne's queen, Leoba rested in a tomb near that of her kinsman at the monastery of Fulda. Her vita, spread at first as memories among her acquaintances then produced in written formula by Rudolf, ensured her reputation as a female version of St. Martin: a thaumaturge and weathermaker, an impresario of rituals, and a nurturer whose authority extended largely to her community of sisters and the peasants in its vicinity. She commanded but never preached, sang psalms but never the mass, negotiated with local laypeople but followed Boniface and the brothers at Lull unquestioningly. Anything less predictable would never have flowed from Rudolf's pen onto the pages of her life.

STRATEGIES FOR COMMUNITY ORGANIZATION

Leoba's house, brimming with learning, shining with its patroness's sanctity, infused with evangelizing zeal, was nonetheless subject to the same harassment as communities of religious women throughout Europe. Other communities of women were not so lucky as Leoba's group. They had more trouble maintaining their reputations, their resources, and their support from Christians beyond their walls. Monastic communities for women increased steadily from the time of conversion until the eighth century; the greatest period of monastic foundation for women in England, France, and Belgium before the year 1000 was between about 600 and 700, after which there was a sharp decline in new houses until after the new millennium.[110] Yet

---

[110] Jane Schulenberg, "Women's Monastic Communities, 500–1100: Patterns of Expansion and Decline," in *Sisters and Workers in the Middle Ages*, ed. Judith Bennett *et al.* (repr. Chicago: University of Chicago Press, 1989), 208–39, esp. 213; Bruce Venarde, *Women's Monasticism and Medieval Society: Nunneries in France and England, 890–1215* (Ithaca: Cornell University Press, 1997), 8.

even the best year for new foundations saw fewer than twenty new establishments in these areas. The disparity in numbers between female and male monasteries grew between 700 and 900, when Vikings targeted religious houses, particularly women's communities. According to some calculations, after 850 only ten per cent of 167 women's communities in Francia survived.[111]

Many explanations have been advanced to account for the rise and decline of women's religious communities. Women never were able to gain as much land as men, goes one story; hence the smaller number of their houses, and hence the poverty of those that existed. Noblemen supported nunneries only so long as their kinswomen inhabited them or the religious women there maintained the memory of the family with liturgy and prayers.[112] Yet hagiography along with charters and wills constantly recorded the endowment of women's houses and the many ways in which women and men avoided legal parameters of inheritance to give women land and incomes. We have seen that royal and noble English and Frankish women gave generously to women's communities. The assumption that women's religious vocation dwindled in the ninth and tenth centuries because of lack of noble interest, or the economic and social need for women to perform other jobs in society, or the devastation of Viking attacks, may be just a misinterpretation of the source material's focuses. Documents such as the Kentish charters or the Merovingian vitae are simply different in character and subject matter from the kinds of texts available from later periods.

Good evidence suggests, in fact, that religious women continued to join communities and secular women to endow them throughout the early Middle Ages. In England, the will of Wynflæd, a noblewoman of the mid-tenth century, bequeathed one pound (an impressive amount) from her considerable holdings to the nunnery at Wilton, and an entire estate at Chinnock to the nunnery at Shaftesbury.[113] The latter house was supposedly endowed by King Alfred for his daughter Æthelgifu, who also received two estates and a hundred pounds at her father's death.[114] Wynflæd's daughter Ælfgifu, wife of King Edmund, was buried there. The kind of multi-generational involvement with particular houses so characteristic of earlier Anglo-Saxon

---

[111] McNamara, *Sisters in Arms*, 149.

[112] Bitel, *Land of Women*, 170–75; Kathleen Hughes and Ann Hamlin, *Celtic Monasticism: The Modern Traveler to the Early Irish Church* (New York: Seabury Press, 1981), 7–9.

[113] *WASW*, 10–15.   [114] *WEHD* 1, 534–37.

royal women seems to have continued, then, into the tenth century though at different sites. Whereas the seventh-century prominence of Kentish minsters reflects the importance of the southern kingdom in England, the dominance of Wessex is obvious in the success of Wimbourne and Shaftesbury.[115] Certainly royal women in Francia, the German territories, England, and Ireland had no trouble finding the funds and property with which to begin major religious settlements, even if later sisters had difficulty maintaining their endowments against contesting heirs, encroaching lords, and ecclesiastical overseers, not to mention stray marauders. Radegund's problem was never resources, but her successors faced that dilemma; in the ninth century, Louis the Pious limited her convent's right to accept new nuns, possibly because it could not feed them, but more likely because Louis focused his religious charity elsewhere, upon other women. Yet the nunnery was still thriving in the fourteenth century, when it was devastated by invading Englishmen, and in the fifteenth century, when it fortified the villages on its properties.[116] In other words, women remained religious, but their foundations, their style of religious endowment, their means of community organisation, and even their religious functions shifted with politics. This was at once a compliment to the dynastic importance of women's communities and a blow to those communities whose inhabitants were out of power or favor.

In addition, not every religious woman lived in a major monastery founded by royalty and supported by royal properties, and such women are harder to find than properly organized women in communities noted down in writing or commemorated in stone. In England and Ireland, women normally shared their settlements with men in what have been called "double" houses; they also inhabited minsters, which were royal churches with priests attached. Both kinds of foundations had pastoral functions. Archeological and textual evidence together suggests possibly sixty or seventy mixed-sex communities in England in the eighth and ninth centuries. This does not even include the kind of family monasteries complained about by Bede in his letter to Ecgbert, or disapproved of by Theodore in his penitential: "It is not permissible for men to have monastic women under them, nor women, men; nevertheless, we shall not overthrow that which is the

[115] Barbara Yorke, "'Sisters Under the Skin?' Anglo-Saxon Nuns and Nunneries in Southern England", *Reading Medieval Studies* 15 (1989), 95–117, esp. 100–01.
[116] McNamara, *Sisters in Arms,* 164; 389.

custom in this region."[117] What is more, it appears that double houses
and minsters were far more common outside the well-documented
parts of the island, places to which Bede and others did not stretch
their pens, and where only stray references or archeological digs can
reveal their past presence. They existed elsewhere in Europe, too,
as at Chelles, which was a training ground for the Kentish abbesses.
Perhaps, like Chelles, most of them eventually became dominated
by male ecclesiastics. Vowesses may well have lived near them, still
attached to them by ritual and daily interaction, but unnoticed by
the recorders of deeds, charters, and histories.[118]

Women's communities were never numerous compared to those
of men, but they seem to have dwindled in number with the coming of Viking, Saracen, and Magyar raiders. In England, forty-one
women's communities disappeared from the documents during the
ninth and tenth centuries. By the time the Normans came in 1066
to take their turn at conquering England, only nine women's houses
existed, so far as the written records show.[119] On the Continent,
Hincmar of Reims mourned the abduction of nuns, but not necessarily at the hands of northmen.[120] In Irish saints' lives of the Viking
period and later, episodes often told of consecrated women gratefully
bestowing their foundations upon male saints; whether this was hagiographer's code for the shift of a nunnery to a male monastery, or
merely a statement of affiliation between the communities, remains
unclear.[121] Elsewhere, Muslims killed nuns in Spain, and Magyars
murdered women of Switzerland and Germany. Although raiders
and invaders attacked men's houses, too, women's communities may
have been more vulnerable to both physical attack and the economic
aftermath of devastation, since they often lacked the resources or
support to rebuild.

Even before the reform and the destruction that preceded it, however, clerics had begun to doubt the wisdom of allowing religious
women and men to inhabit the same settlement. Bede had complained about the nuns of double houses. Coldingham had burned,

---

[117] McNeill and Gamer, 204.

[118] Sally Thompson, *Women Religious: The Founding of English Nunneries after the
Norman Conquest* (Oxford: Clarendon, 1991), esp. 44–79; Foot, *Veiled Women*
I, 74–84.

[119] Schulenberg, "Women's Monastic Communities," 222.

[120] Hincmar of Reims, *Collectio de Raptoribus*, PL 126, 1017–36.

[121] W. W. Heist, *Vitae Sanctorum Hiberniae*, Subsidia Hagiographica 26 (Brussels:
Bollandists, 1965), 102, 126, 192, 402.

he decided, "by reason of the wickedness of them that dwelt therein, and especially of them which seemed to be the elders thereof."[122] Boniface had insisted that women not be allowed to live in priests' houses, meaning not only relatives of priests but also women vowed to religion, which was an effective damper on informal mixed communities.[123] In 796 the Council of Friuli affirmed private vows of celibacy, which allowed women to practice as nuns at home. But the emperor Louis the Pious prohibited such vows, preferring to install religious women in properly organized convents run with solid rules.[124] Hrabanus Maurus, archbishop of Mainz in the ninth century, also endorsed the elimination of small, informal houses of religious women which relied on a resident man or two to help keep them going.[125] Besides expressing disapproval in histories and rules, churchmen told hagiographical tales to illustrate the problems inherent in mixed-sex communities. St. Daig of the Irish, for instance, was resident in a mixed community, according to his eighth- or ninth-century vita. Rumors sent a neighboring abbot to observe the goings-on in Daig's settlement, where he espied sinless virgins carrying burning coals in their garments, proof positive that men and women lived and prayed blamelessly together. Nonetheless, the story's end found Daig setting up a separate community for nuns under his remote guidance.[126] Even for saints, who would never succumb anyway, it was better to obey the conciliar decrees about gender integration and maintain segregated communities.

With the reorganisation of the English church in the tenth century, exclusively female cloisters began to appear in England, as at Shaftesbury.[127] Before that, small family foundations supporting women simply disappeared when consolidated with men's larger houses. Religious women disappeared from written memory when reformers converted double foundations to regular men's monasteries. The new English rule for the tenth and later centuries, the *Regularis Concordia* compiled at Winchester, prohibited men from

---

[122] Bede, *Historia Ecclesiastica*, IV.25.

[123] Mansi, *Concilium Germanicum VII*, vol. 12, 367; McNamara, *Sisters in Arms*, 159–60.

[124] *MGH Leg. Sect. III: Concilia* 2: cap. 4, p. 191.

[125] *Epist. Fuld. Frag.*, 6, in *MGH Epist. 5, Karol. Aevi* 3, 518.

[126] Heist, *Vitae*, 392–3.

[127] Roberta Gilchrist, *Gender and Material Culture: The Archaeology of Religious Women* (London: Routledge, 1994), 22–36.

living in women's communities.[128] Similarly, Carolingian reformers ordered small women's communities to be either dissolved or consolidated.[129]

At the same time that they were being sent to fewer, consolidated, women-only communities, religious women were ordered to begin living more cloistered, less active lives, although whether they submitted is another question.[130] Beginning in the middle of the eighth century and repeatedly during the early ninth century, Carolingian councils directed all religious professionals to follow the Benedictine Rule. Henceforth women could be nuns, canonesses, or pious laywomen, but their choices were considerably narrower than they once had been.[131] If they chose the regular, ruled life of Benedictine nuns, then they were to stay within the cloister's walls rather than indulging in pastoral activities. Throughout Europe (except Ireland), the Benedictine Rule became the official guide to the monastic life for women and men until the invention of new orders after the year 1000. When the later reforms began in the great and gorgeous monastery of Cluny, a further restriction was placed on women religious: their prayers became less efficacious and less preferable to patrons than those of monks, who could not only chant their prayers but could sing the mass for the souls of the departed.[132] Women could entreat God to aid their friends and relatives, but laypeople preferred to subsidize the more exclusive and important rituals of male ecclesiastics.

Nonetheless, this great cloistering ordered by church leaders and mourned by some historians did not necessarily prevent women from enjoying a fulfilling religious life. Women escaped both the rules and the suspicions of others. Repeated Carolingian regulations against the preaching and even the offering of mass by women suggests that women were still taking Christianity into their own hands during the

---

[128] Thomas Symons, ed., *Regularis Concordia Anglicae Nationis Monachorum Sanctimonialiumque* (London: Nelson, 1953), 3–4.

[129] Schulenberg, "Women's Communities," 225; *MGH Capit. Duplex legat. Edictum* no. 19, I 69; Carl J. Hefele and Henri LeClercq, *Histoire des Conciles d'après les documents originaux* (Paris: Letouzey et Ané, 1938), vol. 4 : 2, 685.

[130] Jane Schulenberg, "Strict Active Enclosure and Its Effects on the Female Monastic Experience (ca. 500–1100)," in *Medieval Religious Women*, vol. 1, *Distant Echoes*, ed. John Nichols and Lillian Thomas Shank (Kalamazoo: Cistercian Publications, 1984), 51–86.

[131] *MGH Leg. Sect. II, Concilia II:* 4.7, 60, 230, 255 *et passim*.

[132] McNamara, *Sisters in Arms*, 207–09.

worst Viking depredations and the furious council-making of religious reformers.[133] The Carolingian vita of St. Odilia of Hohenburg
described how she built a hospital and an accessible monastery for
pilgrims and invalids. She then gave her nuns a choice of lifestyles:

> I know dearest sisters and mothers that you are most swift to endure every
> hardship and difficulty for Christ's name. But I fear that if we choose the
> regular life it will put a curse on our successors because, as you know, the great
> difficulty of procuring water makes this place inconvenient and improper for
> the regular life. Whence it seems to me, if it is pleasing to your gentleness,
> that it would be better for you to live the canonical life.[134]

Despite regulations, Odilia's followers simply chose to remain attached to the world and minister to visitors. Other nuns found ways
of continuing their chosen work despite the many rules of men.
St. Moninne, in northern Ireland, only went out veiled to visit local
Christians by night so that she should never see men. Thus, according to her eleventh-century biographer, she satisfied the increasingly
complex protocols of gender interaction for holy women, and yet
maintained an active, pastoral life.[135]

Some women vowed to religion continued to live invisibly to contemporary ecclesiastics and to modern historians alike when they set
up little cells near the dwelling of a hermit, or remained in family
homes practicing privately. The penitential of Ecgbert (Bede's correspondent) referred to religious women "in orders or not, married or
single, virgin or woman, canoness or nun."[136] Bishop Wulfstan, an
English reformer writing in the early eleventh century, maintained
the same categorical division among professional religious women.[137]
In Gaul, from the time of Genovefa, women could vow themselves
to chastity and poverty and yet inhabit a room or house belonging
to their parents, or move to a nunnery or monastery without taking
official orders. Queens regularly took up residence in women's communities when they lost their husbands. Some took refuge there
between spouses, or when politics drove them to sanctuary, and they

[133] Nelson, "Les femmes et l'evangelisation," 482–483.
[134] *MGH SS* 6, 24–50; McNamara, *Sisters in Arms*, 176–7.
[135] Ulster Society for Medieval Latin Studes, "The Life of St. Monenna by
Conchubranus," *Seanchas Ard Mhacha* 10 (1980–81), 136–39.
[136] Arthur Haddan and William Stubbs, ed., *Councils and Ecclesiastical Documents
Relating to Great Britain and Ireland*, 3 vols. (Oxford University Press, 1869), vol. 1,
417; Gilchrist, *Gender and Material Culture*, 27.
[137] Michael Swanton, trans., *Anglo-Saxon Prose* (London: Dent, 1975), 198–99.

must have brought their allies and servants with them. And the rules against women departing the cloister addressed a problem, in the eyes of rulemakers, that might have been merely a lifecycle choice in the eyes of religious women. Enough fallen nuns littered the hagiography to make clear that women moved in and out of official religious settlements with some frequency, no matter what ecclesiastical officials said. Like individual religious women, their communities, too, may have undergone cyclical changes. Sometimes nunneries became men's communities, or had their holdings dispersed among heirs to the estate; sometimes the cycle swung the other way, and women's communities grew or accumulated property.

Like laws, men's rules were just ideals and theories, implying but not necessitating restriction upon individuals. How many people in the medieval world were affected, ultimately, by the Council of Friuli's decrees or by Hrabanus Maurus' huffing and puffing? Perhaps not many. Only a tiny percentage of Christians ever chose the celibate life. Only an indeterminable fraction of those were women. Not all women vowed to celibacy fully observed the ninth- and tenth-century reforming rules that sought to limit their religious practice even more thoroughly than the earlier disapproval of theologians. And yet the rules were not so harsh for religiously vowed men. The reformers of the Carolingian period and late Saxon England sought to organize men's practice too, but did not shut men in the cloister, or discredit the efficacy of their prayers, or try to prevent their active work among laypeople. Men who wished an active Christian vocation could always (if they had the resources) choose the priesthood. Women could not; nor could they become priests' or bishops' wives, nor even deaconesses as easily as they once had. The places where they might become celibate nuns with like-minded sisters dwindled in number until at least the year 1000.

STRATEGIES FOR SPIRITUAL SATISFACTION

Women who vowed themselves to Christianity were like other women in their inability to function as men. On account of both social surroundings and a misogynist strain in formal Christian thought, they were disenfranchised in the realm of the spirit as well as the realm of the law. But they managed, nonetheless, to participate as professionals in rituals designed to promote the wellbeing of all Christian society. They aided men, and men aided them, in the maintenance of

5 Processional cross of the Abbess Mathilda and her brother, Duke Otto of Saxony, who are portrayed in Enamel at the bottom of the Cross

Christian institutions. The famous abbesses of the Continent and the islands provided hospitality for travelling bishops and missionaries. They educated the offspring of the nobility. They offered refuge to women fleeing the carnal life, protection from men they despised, respite from poverty, politics, or anything else that was chasing them. They ran hospitals, curing local peasants and converting them in the process. When they could, they practiced the scholarly life, reading and copying books, and producing fine works of art.

And in all these endeavors, women worked closely with men, sometimes in loving and comradely cooperation, sometimes simply strategizing around their brothers' restrictions and disapproval. Bede, who complained about the disruptive nuns of joint-sex communities, also wrote stories of wise abbesses sitting down to learned conversation at dinner with visiting bishops and abbots. The saints' lives showed abbesses and their nuns joining in prayers and the sacrament together with the priests and monks of their communities, or of neighboring monasteries. The great missionary Boniface is famous for relying on the services and loving letters of his holy sisters back home to sustain him during his trials in Germany. By and large, men wrote these stories of women who were able to work with men in religion.

European women of the early Middle Ages experienced a Christianity no more monolithic or single-minded than the modern versions. The variety of beliefs and practices which constituted Christianity, and the multitude of cultures which hosted the religion, meant that the religious life of a woman at one end of Europe varied vastly from that of her sister at the other end. One condition shared by Christian women everywhere in Europe, whether vowed celibate or penitent sinner, noble or slave, was the suspicion of theologians and rulemakers. But the flexible limits and often contradictory theologies of Christianity allowed women the room to maneuver and to define meaningful religious experiences within an orthodox framework, and even to exercise some influence as religious professionals, despite the boundaries set by male leaders and thinkers. Although their choices and cultures were different, Muslim, Jewish, and pagan women may have found some similar spiritual space by negotiating between the patriarchal communities they inhabited, the misogyny that pervaded their religions, and their personal needs. For we know, from the frustrating hints of the evidence, that women participated in, donated to, and infiltrated churches, synagogues, mosques, shrines, theologies, and other holy places.

4

SURVIVAL BY KINSHIP, MARRIAGE, AND MOTHERHOOD

—————— • ——————

Daily survival was never a sure thing for any woman in medieval Europe, whatever her age or station. Appalling mortality rates, low life expectancies, and high sex ratios from the early Middle Ages make grimly clear how dangerous it was to be born in Europe before the modern millennium. Accidents that annoy us now ended the lives of both child and adult back then. Harsh winters or dry springs brought famine among animals and humans. "Very great mortality among cattle throughout virtually all Europe, and death for very many people, too, including Rotrud, the emperor's daughter, and Pippin, his son," noted a Carolingian annalist in 810.[1] And warfare, constant and ubiquitous, brought death for princess and slave.

It was hard to survive and a challenge to help others to do so. Most taxing of all was bringing new souls into the world. Women died in childbirth or from its complications in numbers barely comprehensible to historians, although explicable to earlier observers. The Mishnah reminded Jews that women perished in travail on account of three transgressions, "because they are not meticulous in the laws of menstrual separation, in the dough offering, and in the kindling of a lamp [for the Sabbath]."[2] What else besides moral trespass could explain the constant disasters that beset women? Babies – sinless in

[1] *Annales Laurissenses Minores*, ed. Georg Pertz in *MGH SS* 1, 114–23; trans. P. D. King in *Charlemagne: Translated Sources* (Kendal, UK: P. D. King, 1987), 166.
[2] *B. Shabbat*, 2:7 in Jacob Neusner, trans., *The Mishnah: A New Translation* (New Haven: Yale University Press, 1988), 182.

Jewish eyes but tainted from birth according to Christian doctrine – succumbed to diseases that today cause barely an anxious thought.

Anglo-Saxon poets composed lovely but grim lyrics that reflected the dark perils of life and lifegiving in the medieval world. Painful social constraints, blind aspirations, the inevitability of violence and death, even bad weather, were all motifs in early English poems. A few of the verses, such as "Wulf and Eadwacer" and the "Wife's Lament," treated the special woes of women. One of the greatest, composed in the eighth century, described a mother's reaction when her wretched son Grendel staggered home to die. She prowled the drinking hall of King Hrothgar, called Heorot, where Beowulf had ripped an arm from her son, aiming to reclaim the gory limb:

His mother, still ravenous and gloomy at heart, purposed to go on a sorry journey to avenge the death of her son. She came then to Heorot where the Ring-Danes slept all around the hall. Immediately then there came a reverse for the warriors, once Grendel's mother made her way in. The terror was the less dreadful by just so much as the power of women, the war-terror of a female, is less than that of an armed man when the patterned blade of a hammer-forged sword, stained with blood, mighty of edge, shears through the boar-crest above opposing helmets.[3]

In her panic, the mother took both the arm and an armed warrior. To the poet and his audience, this was no normal nurturer but an alien spirit in the likeness of a woman, a "walker in the wasteland" like her hideous son, Grendel. She was no wife, but a dark mirror-image of a mateless mother wrought by the literate – an anti-woman made up to horrify beer-swilling Englishmen and women hiding from winter in their halls. But she shared with other, ordinary mothers – both in the poem and beyond the text – a simple determination to protect her offspring. When that was impossible, as the poet put it, "she would avenge her child, her only son."[4] Her poetic identity made it possible for her to fight back as common mothers could not. She dueled the hero Beowulf when he invaded her underwater lair, plunking herself

---

[3] *Beowulf*, xviii, ed. and trans. Michael Alexander (New York: Penguin, 1995), 95–97.

[4] Ibid., xxii; Janice Grossman, "Tropes of Femininity and Monstrosity in Old English Poems, *Old English Newsletter* 28, 3 (Spring 1995), A20–A21; Dockray-Miller, *Motherhood and Mothering*, 88–96.

down atop him and almost stabbing him to death before he slashed off her head and sent her to join her son.[5]

Grendel's mother was no more representative of women in the years approaching 1000 than queens and saints. Nonetheless, this famous childbearer serves as an instructive introduction to the common conditions of medieval women. In the early Middle Ages most women were sexual partners to men and parents of children. Their social roles were their primary vocations; their most respected jobs were marrying, reproducing, and mothering. Be they wealthy wives or cast-out monsters, their communities handed them the same imperatives. Yet marriage and motherhood were difficult tasks, given the violence of environment, ill health, and men. Conceiving, bearing, and protecting children was what they had to do, often without sufficient support from spouse, kin, or anyone else. Grendel's mother, like many a medieval woman, was left to defend her offspring without benefit of caring mate, protective family, or allies of any other kind.

Women, like men, sought to build order in the midst of the medieval precariousness of life. They could not easily use men's tools of public law or physical force although at times they resorted to both. Women aimed mostly to make their families and households secure and then to help preserve their communities. A woman who bore legitimate babies and ushered them through the hazards of childhood to adulthood with all the vocational training and material resources she could muster was a successful woman. Grendel's dreadful mother could not manage, but many more ordinary women did.

KINSHIP AND FAMILY

Family, in the modern western sense, did not exist in the Middle Ages. In one sense, people living together made a deceptively modern-seeming nuclear unit. Men and women clustered inside the walls of a single house or settled behind the enclosing ditches of a settlement were usually related by blood, marriage, or relations imitative of these, but servants and slaves were also part of the *familia*. Indeed, the word's original meaning in Roman society was the slaves of a single household; in medieval Europe, all the residents of a monastery or nunnery

---

[5] 'Ofsæt þa þone selegyst': ibid., 94–95; Fred Robinson, "Did Grendel's Mother Sit on Beowulf?" in *From Anglo-Saxon to Early Middle English: Studies Presented to E. G. Stanley*, ed. Malcolm Godden *et al.* (Oxford : Clarendon, 1994), 1–7.

might also make a *familia*. Rare estate censuses from before 1000 suggest that average households held not the eighty or ninety members of a large monastery, but between 3.5 and 6 members.[6] Households were also linked to other households by ties of blood, loyalty, and affection. Individuals felt strong connections to those who shared their ancestry but lived elsewhere. Any household or conjugal family was a smaller piece of a larger, more complex group. Family was, at once, the people with whom one lived and the scores of people to whom one was related. Each unit within these overlapping "families" had a different function and meaning for the individual who participated in it.

In the early Middle Ages, a woman was born into a social group composed of kin on her mother's and father's sides. She remained one of this family, to a varying extent, even when she married and set up another household and acquired another kin-group. She knew who her relations were, although modern historians cannot always figure out who, exactly, was in any woman's family.[7] The French historian Marc Bloch long ago tried to describe family by scrutinizing the network that focused on any given individual (ego) living in the early Middle Ages. Each person had an immense but variable group of known relatives attached to him or her in concentric rings of closeness. Often enough, they were also neighbors, tenants, lords, or allies of another sort as well. In this anthropologically based view, the family was cognatic because people did not differentiate especially between relations on mother's and father's sides. Both kinds of kin were important, since children could inherit property from either parent (although normally daughters' inheritance from either side was more limited than that of sons.) A child could not marry his or her cousin from either side of the family to the seventh degree of kinship (later, after the Fourth Lateran Council in 1215, the fourth degree), although people often chose spouses from the first permissible degree of kinship in order to ensure the cohesion of the larger kin-group and to keep property within the group. And members from both kins were responsible for protecting ego, just as he or she was obliged to

---

[6] Richard R. Ring, "Early Medieval Peasant Households in Central Italy," *Journal of Family History* 4 (1979), 2–25, esp. 9; Russell, *Control of Late Ancient and Medieval Population*, 151–52.

[7] Hans-Werner Goetz, *Life in the Middle Ages: From the Seventh to the Thirteenth Century*, trans. Albert Wimmer (Notre Dame: University of Notre Dame Press, 1993), 24–29.

protect or support them. In such a system, a woman had so many relatives linked to her in such intricate ways that she could not possibly know and use all of them, support them all, or be friends with them.[8] Every individual had to choose, from among her entire network of relations, those that were beneficial and attractive. No individual's family was identical to another.

Gender influenced choices. For a woman, a powerful uncle might be a useful advocate in a legal dispute, but for friendship and advice a girl would probably turn to her aunt. Merovingian and Anglo-Saxon women followed mothers, daughters, sisters, aunts, and cousins into religious communities, thus selecting the most intimate relations of their lives as well as careers in a single decision. An uncle might be less willing to invest affection in her than a woman would because she could not fight for him, swear an oath for him, or work his fields. Still, if she came from a high-class background or had married extremely well, he might be interested in her. The status of kinfolk helped with both her choice and his; a mighty lord or a wealthy abbess was always handy as a relation. Affection played its part, too. Someone who lived near and was familiar and loveable, not to mention a work partner, was also a potentially important relation no matter how close or distant the blood tie; a third cousin next door might be more intimate a crony than an aunt in the next village. What is more, given early medieval mortality rates, households and relationships were in constant flux. The composition of an individual's group changed frequently as members died, left, or were born. The cousin who survived might be more dear than the sister who did not, or a sister who went off to spend her adolescence in the lord's weaving house. Hence, at any given time, a woman had a theoretical or potential family stretching beyond her social horizon, and a recognizable, more immediately useful family group including perhaps just her conjugal household, neighbors, and a few very special, more distant relatives. Throughout her life, and even after, she continued selecting and discarding allies. Some English wills from the ninth and tenth centuries show the results of women's lifelong decisions; a cup here, a carved box there, rewarded female allies for a lifetime of loyalty and love.[9]

But the choice of meaningful kin did not always belong to ego, especially if she were a woman. Families were obliged to rally around

[8] Marc Bloch, *Feudal Society*, trans. L. A. Manyon (Chicago: University of Chicago Press, 1961), 134–42.

[9] *WASW*, 10–15. Compare the situation in Germany: Leyser, *Rule and Conflict*, 58–61.

a kinsman in legal trouble, swearing oaths on his behalf, and were liable for the crimes and fines of a defaulting member. If a branch of the family became embroiled in a feud, as the traitor Ganelon's kin did in the eleventh-century adventure about Carolingian events, the *Chanson de Roland*, ego might find him or herself caught up in the cycle of revenge and counter-attack that absorbed as many relatives as an endangered individual could muster. In this romance of eighth-century events, Ganelon was the traitor who betrayed the hero Roland to the Saracens. Charlemagne executed the evildoer's entire family after Ganelon lost a judicial duel in his own defense.[10] The Irish annals and Welsh chronicles, as well as the Icelandic sagas, are full of early medieval feuds resolved ultimately by death after death.

The greatest possible extent of any large kin-group, in fact, was determined not by any individual's choices, but by legal theorists and practitioners who decided which of its members were obligated to take part in a feud. Legal retribution was one of the group's most important functions because of the decentralization of early medieval governments. Even though barbarian kings throughout Europe established codes in their names, trying to reserve the powers of punishment to their governments, families continued to prosecute feuds. Frankish laws allotting payment of *wergeld* and fines for murder, for instance, adjudged portions of the compensation to sons or near heirs, widow or mother, and *proximiores* (near relatives) who were further divided into maternal and paternal kin. Most lawcodes worked out a complicated schedule for the percentage of compensation due parents, uncles, brothers, and more distant kinfolk involved in the action. Such codes reflected scholarly theorizing about the hierarchical nature of kin connections.[11] Those closest to an individual had the heaviest duty as well as the greatest potential compensation on his or her behalf. The premise behind laws regarding feuds was that threat of compensation would compel peace; relatives of a potential offender would prevent a crime or, at the very least, bring the offender to justice so as not to incur (more) fines and revenge killings.

Legal codes varied slightly on the question of kinship obligations, which suggests some diversity in theoretical families across Europe. In

---

[10] Patricia Terry, trans., *The Song of Roland* (2nd edn., New York: MacMillan, 1992), 146.

[11] Alexander Murray, *Germanic Kinship Structure: Studies in Law and Society in Antiquity and in the Early Middle Ages* (Toronto: Pontifical Institute of Mediaeval Studies, 1983), 135–49.

areas where lordship or kingship was strong, kin-groups were smaller. Where lords could not protect their followers, extended relations had to do the job. Yet even where lordship remained primitive, kin-groups were constantly changing shape and refining their functions during the early Middle Ages. Irish law, for instance, originally distinguished the largest kin-group, *fine*, as a group so extensive and vague that it had later to be subdivided into the *derbfine* (descendants through male line from a single great-grandfather), *gelfine* (from a great-great-grandfather), *iarfine* (from a great-great-great-grandfather) and other annoyingly petty juridical refinements. In other words, the *fine*, while once useful and still legally crucial, was not a viable or easily identified group.[12] The same was true for what historians and anthropologists have come to call the *Sippe*, or largest Germanic kin unit. Yet all early medieval laws envisioned the greatest extent of kin as the basis of society, containing functional smaller families and their responsibilities and rights based on blood ties.[13] As usual, then, lawmakers imagined the possible and ideal while individuals were left to enact realities.

Medieval legal codes, however impractical, reflected lawgivers' attempt to cope with the dangers they perceived in the day-to-day world. Women and men of late Antiquity, by contrast, had been surrounded by so many legal protections of the Roman state that they could function as smaller conjugal units. But people in early medieval societies could not afford to lose their cousins and aunts and uncles, their in-laws, or their grandparents. In legal terms, at least, families had to be large to survive and to move property from generation to generation. Families even supplemented blood ties with relationships modeled on the natal family: godparentage, fosterage, adoption, clientage and, later, vassalage. Legally, a man or woman could not escape family easily. Frankish law had an elaborate ritual for the bizarre exception who wanted to sever certain kinship ties: He had to come before a judge, break four alder branches over his head, throw the pieces into the four corners of the room, and swear that he forwent oathhelping, inheritance, and all the affairs of his kinsmen. If they died or were harmed, he got no inheritance or fines; if he himself died, the property, *wergeld*, or fines went not to his kin, but to the state treasury of the king. The alder was the tree of misfortune.

[12] T. M. Charles-Edwards, *Early Irish and Welsh Kinship* (Oxford: Clarendon, 1993), esp. 33–88.

[13] *Pactus Legis Salicae*, lxviii; trans. Drew, *Laws of the Salian Franks*, 130; Murray, *Germanic Kinship*, 140–41.

To break the branches and throw them away symbolized an attempt to protect an unfortunate individual from the almost certain violent and unavenged death awaiting the kinless and outlaws.[14] Women, of course, could not legally dissociate themselves from any kinsmen except by being cast out. They were stuck with what they were born to, including the male guardian, be it father, brother, uncle, or distant kinsman, who controlled their *mundium*. They needed men to represent them in legal affairs, to vouch for them in public, and to support them economically. It was as difficult to shed a father or brother as it was to get rid of a husband. Besides, why would most women want to do such a thing? They would be unimaginably friendless without their male protectors, at the mercy of anyone who wished to harm them.

Although they were enmeshed in family, women's participation in the obligations of kinship were different from men's. A woman might be caught up in a feud and find herself abducted, or she might receive compensation for a slain son or husband, or be compensated for if murdered. She might even instigate a feud as the female characters in sagas did. When Brynhild lost her bid for Sigurdr, she started a whole cycle of murder and vengeance with her evil words, and she was not the only Scandinavian female to do so; the inciter was a familiar motif in Old Norse literature.[15] Neither she nor more normal women could formally participate in the prosecution or finishing of the feud, however, even though Brynhild was herself a Valkyrie.

Nor could women claim family inheritance as men could. Although both sides of the cognatic kin-group were important to sons and daughters, most early medieval laws nonetheless limited the amount of land that a female might inherit from her male relations, as we have seen – with the notable exception of the Visigoths, who allowed daughters to participate in partible inheritance.[16] Yet it is a profound irony, unremarked by modern medievalists, that a society so obsessed with reproduction and the passing on of property, and so concerned with the limits of family and its obligations, should theoretically curtail so severely the number of potential heirs. Women received property from relations as gifts, as pre-mortem inheritances from their guardians, as dowries, and through financial transactions.

---

[14] *Lex Sal.*, lx; Jacques LeGoff, "The Symbolic Rite of Vassalage," in LeGoff, *Time, Work, and Culture in the Middle Ages* (Chicago: University of Chicago Press, 1980), 237–87; see also Murray, *Germanic Kinship*, 149–55.

[15] Jochens, *Old Norse Images of Women*, 174.   [16] *Leges Visigothorum*, IV.2.1.

But the bulk of the land was destined, by law, to go to sons. Still, as with other conditions of life, women's inheritance rights varied by both region and period. Eighth-century documents recording land transactions show that women comprised about fifteen per cent of the buyers, sellers, and givers of land in northern Europe; in the ninth century, their number declined to less than ten per cent.[17] Carolingian legal action against divorce may have had something to do with the numbers in Charlemagne's empire. Under earlier Frankish custom, women had few legitimate reasons beyond impotence or adultery for leaving their husbands. When women were no longer able to divorce their husbands by law, they could not acquire new settlements of property that came with remarriage, nor could they gain control over their own dowries and do what they pleased with the land. In other words, women's control of land, never widespread, dwindled with religious reforms of married life during the Carolingian period. Increasing restrictions on the rupture of marriage contracts may have influenced other rules about women's property. Even the number of women acting as co-donors with their rich husbands declined in the ninth century.[18]

Elsewhere in both northern and southern Europe, the chronology of women's inheritance depended upon many other variables. In southern Italy, for instance, women of the ducal family of Gaeta inherited houses and land along with their brothers during the tenth century. But when the ducal family no longer acquired new land in the next century, merely handing down what it had already got, women more often inherited moveable goods which they took to their husbands' families as dowries. Those who received such property were noble women of great wealth whose kinsmen had estates to spare. When a family depended upon its farm to survive, both in the present generation and in generations to come, daughters were even less likely to get a piece of it. Families had to be judicious about who might manage the estate best and most closely associate it with their ancestral name; a woman leaving the house to marry another man was not usually the best choice in times when the family fortune and identity depended upon land. Where kinship bonds remained most extensive and strongest, neither men nor women could alienate land as freely. In such circumstances, when other institutions such as lordship or the state competed with family ties, individuals could give

---

[17] Herlihy, "Land, Family, and Women in Continental Europe," 116–18.
[18] Wemple, *Women in Frankish Society*, 109–110.

land to the church, sell property, or leave portions to their daughters
and other kinswomen who, in turn, could choose what to do with
their land. In ninth-century Brittany, for example, daughters inherited some sort of goods or small bits of land from their fathers and
even succeeded to the patrimony when sons failed. When uncles or
cousin tried to challenge the inheritance, Breton women took them
to court and won.[19]

The very size and shape of the family as well as inheritance customs
also depended upon the amount of land available for parceling out to
heirs. In northern Europe, where smaller families set up new farms
on the edges of perceived wilderness, the amount of land necessary to
support their members helped to determine the membership of the
group. Younger sons went out to work on the lord's farms until property became cleared for their farms; young women departed for other
men's households. The situation was complicated further by the institutions of slavery, Christianity, and, in northern Francia, the manse
system. The records of the great ninth-century abbatial estates there
show that many young women worked as semi-enslaved domestic servants on the master's demesne only until they became nubile; then, if
they were lucky, they moved into huts on the lord's estates with male
partners and set up their own dependent households of nuclear-style
families. They became partners with their husbands in the farming of
their lords' lands and the creation of another generation of serfs, passing hut and field to their children.[20] In southern, more Romanized
rural areas, families continued to live in multi-generational or complex households, farming the same cluster of fields for centuries,
passing the estates down within the group. Daughters were more
likely to share some control over the family lands while remaining
with their husbands at home. More often, though, it was daughters
who left and sons who continued living with their parents. Under
either system, however, the northern manorial estates or the southern
farms, the normal flow of property bypassed women.[21] Only when
women were rare and precious did land routinely accompany them

[19] Patricia Skinner compared the situations in Gaeta during the tenth and eleventh
centuries: *Family Power in Southern Italy: The Duchy of Gaeta and Its Neighbors,
850–1139* (Cambridge University Press, 1995), 57–84; Wendy Davies explicated
Breton charters in the ninth century: *Small Worlds: The Village Community in Early
Medieval Brittany* (London: Duckworth, 1988), esp. 70–73.

[20] Devroey, "Men and Women in Early Medieval Serfdom."

[21] Michael Mitterauer and Reinhard Sieder, *The European Family: Patriarchy to
Partnership, from the Middle Ages to the Present* (Oxford: Blackwell, 1982), 24–47.

to marriage. Even then, a woman often held the property in trust for her children, and automatic inheritance (rather than inheritance by will or decree) went to the descendants of her father or to her husband rather than to her offspring.

Thus, when ego was a woman, both her participation in family and her choice of beneficial relations were based on principles different from those of her male relations. She was not normally a potential heir who could maintain the family's name upon a particular bit of territory. Nor was she a legal player who might swear oaths in support of her kinsmen. Her own effective blood-family was a smaller unit, focused legally on the man at its head who held her guardianship. When he died, he delegated his protective power to his son or son-in-law or some other man, who passed it to yet another. If she were a slave or some sort of servant, she also answered legally to another man, her lord or master.

Her best hope was marriage, whereby she might start a household with the combined capital of her dowry and her mate's inheritance. She could also complete what was, from her family's perspective, an important job of linking them to another family, acting as ambassador to the new group into which she married – and most women did, indeed, get married. Theirs, too, was the crucial task of reproduction. If women did not cooperate in the process of marriage and mothering, no family could endure. If they refused matches, fought with their in-laws, or bore no children, the family died out. No one could survive without a family of some sort, but the question for women was: which sort?

MARRIAGE AND OTHER SEXUAL UNIONS

The instability of political and economic environments and the flux of kinship shaped every woman's life. Women built order from the bottom up, beginning within their households. The usual way to create a new household was for a man and woman to marry – or attach themselves in some other kind of sexual union – and settle down in a house with their combined goods, earned or acquired from their kin, and then to produce children. Some women worked together to make religious communities; other women never managed their own households but remained part of another woman's. But most men and women organized themselves to form families, households, and generations. Theologians, lawmakers, and leaders of society all participated in creating, maintaining, and perpetuating families through the institution of marriage. Everyone shared guidelines and good motives. But for women, marriage and motherhood were also the way to ensure personal survival and seek opportunities for happiness and profit – or, at least, satisfaction from a job well done.

A woman had to be ready to accept a contract of marriage when the head of her family decided to send her to another man. Except in the cases of great female scarcity or among the highest aristocracy, a woman and her guardian began to consider her marriage after she reached puberty. Everyone heard stories of princesses wedded at ages ten or twelve, forced into bearing the next king even before they had themselves finished with childhood. The unfortunate Rotrud, Charlemagne's daughter, was betrothed at nine although the marriage never happened.[22] Jews in early medieval Cairo also practiced child marriage, finding precedents in the Talmud; whether the Jewish communities that began to appear further north did so, we cannot know.[23] More often, it was not scripture but a lack of women that lowered ages at marriage. While the Visigoths were still constructing their kingdom in Iberia, their laws defined the *aetas perfecta* (perfect age) at marriage as twenty for men, fifteen for girls.[24] The same theoreticians disapproved of a larger age gap. The child-wife of a mature man could not begin to produce babies; and if a groom were too young and the bride mature, jurists explained, she might be sexually exploited by the father or older brother of the groom. Families also had to worry about an older mother producing deformed children and, as eleventh- and twelfth-century Spanish laws pointed out, the reversal of natural order that occurred when a more experienced woman married a younger man.[25]

Nonetheless, chartularies and the few population surveys of the early medieval period suggest that both girls and boys were marriageable from ages fourteen or fifteen, when they were officially no longer children.[26] Tenants on monastic estates at Farfa in early ninth-century

---

[22] Stafford, *Queens, Concubines, and Dowagers*, 55.

[23] S. D. Goitein, *A Mediterranean Society: The Jewish Communities of the Arab World as Portrayed in the Documents of the Cairo Geniza*, vol. 3: *The Family* (Berkeley: University of California Press, 1978), 436.

[24] *Leg. Vis.* I, IV.I.4.

[25] Heath Dillard, *Daughters of the Reconquest: Women in Castilian Town Society, 1100–1300* (Cambridge University Press, 1984), 56.

[26] Herlihy, *Medieval Households*, 74–78.

Italy, where the monks kept meticulous records, tended to marry fairly early, around twenty years old. Likewise, on the major estates of Francia, girls (*puellae*) left domestic service at marriageable age, moving to small farms where they became *ancillae coniugati* (married servants or dependants).[27] Although toward the end of the Middle Ages Europeans adopted a marriage pattern more familiar to moderns, marrying in their mid-twenties, early medieval men and women tended to marry and die earlier.[28]

Families also remembered church rules when negotiating a marriage, although they did not always abide by ecclesiastical dicta. Theologians prescribed the permanent physical and spiritual union of two Christians for the sole purpose of reproduction. Bishop Jonas of Orléans, writing in the ninth century, scolded married people who had sex for the fun of it, when their real task was procreation. In the ninth and tenth century, Frankish kings backed church decrees concerning the indissolubility of marriage, such as the Council of Trosly's declaration in 909: "Impurity, adultery, sacrilege and murder have overwhelmed the world!"[29] Kings also supported the right of the church to regulate and prevent divorce (Council of Tours, 1060), and the degrees of kinship within which parties were forbidden to marry (Council of Rome, 1059). By the eleventh century, when several reform movements had begun to gather momentum among church leaders, ecclesiastics also ruled that their own kind could not marry women or take them as concubines (Council of Paris, 1023). They aimed to maintain clerical purity but also to prevent children of clerics from inheriting church property.[30]

Theologians and penitentialists, such as Burchard of Worms, wrote chapters on the creation of proper marriage relationships – who should do it, how they should do it, and what ramifications the

---

[27] Ring, "Early Medieval Peasant Households," 14; Devroey, "Men and Women in Early Medieval Serfdom," esp. 22–25.

[28] J. Hajnal, "European Marriage Patterns in Perspective," in *Population in History: Essays in Historical Demography*, ed. D. V. Glass and D. E. C. Eversley (London: Arnold, 1965), 101–43; Russell, *Control of Late Ancient and Medieval Population*, 151.

[29] Mansi, 17A–18A, 263–307 (Concilium Troslejanum); *New Catholic Encyclopedia* online (1996), www.allmax.com/advent/cathen/03481a.htm.

[30] Mansi, 19, 343, 422 (Concilium Parisiense); Jean Verdon, "Les sources de l'histoire de la femme en Occident aux xe–xiiie siècles," in *La Femme dans les civilisations des Xe–XIIIe siècles: Actes du colloque tenu à Poitiers les 23–25 sept. 1976* (Poitiers : Université de Poitiers, 1977), 130–31.

process had on everyone in both families and their communities.[31] Mostly, Burchard concentrated on how marriages might go wrong at any stage in the process. If a woman did not protect her virginity before marriage, and did not intend to marry the man who had polluted her, she was subject to fifteen years' penance before she could take Holy Communion again. A man should not have a wife and a concubine simultaneously because it was like having two wives and therefore constituted bigamy. A madman and a madwoman could not marry, but if somehow they did, divorce was not permitted.[32] The aim of Burchard's restrictions was to limit sexual unions to monogamous, community-sanctioned, legal partnerships between sane men and women which produced legitimate children.

Mothers and fathers took more account of secular law and custom when they arranged marriages for their girls. By the ninth century, many of the original barbarian lawcodes were no longer practical guidelines but documents expressing antiquarian principles of law formed in a golden past.[33] Yet, as recommended in the early codes, marriage remained a multi-purpose contract aimed at creating a social union, a reproductive unit, and a production and property-holding unit or household economy. Like all property matters, marriage involved the members of a larger family group. Officially, women and their potential grooms hardly participated in the process of selecting their mates, although they gradually won these privileges over the centuries.

Politics at the village level must also have influenced the choice of candidates for a girl's marriage partner. Perhaps she and her family watched the available men for some time before her parents finally chose the best of the lot. Perhaps she herself weighed in with an opinion based on affection, or an assessment of her groom's resources, or some other estimation. If her father chose against her will, a woman could take measures to secure her own choice of spouses. Some historians have argued that early medieval laws against the abduction and marriage of women reflect elopement rather than actual kidnaping and rape.[34] Laws that regularized elopements and abductions

---

[31] Burchard of Worms, *Decreta*, Book 9, in *PL* 140: 815–30; Book 19.5, 957–60.
[32] Ibid., Book 9, 817–19.
[33] Murray, *Germanic Kinship*, 128–29; Kelly, *Guide to Early Irish Law*, 225–238.
[34] Rebecca Colman, "The Abduction of Women in Barbarian Law," *Florilegium* 5 (1983), 62–75; Dillard, *Daughters of the Reconquest*, 135–147, esp. 141; William G. Lockwood, "Bride-Theft and Social Maneuverability in West Bosnia," *Anthropological Quarterly* 47:3 (1974), 267.

appeared in several codes; the Burgundians, for instance, ordered an abductor to pay three times the normal marriage fee to keep his willingly kidnaped girl.[35] The ninth-century laws of King Alfred of England legislated against the man who eloped with a nun without the permission of the king or bishop; although the malefactor was to pay a fine of 120 shillings, the laws went on to regulate the inheritance rights of the ex-nun and the children she bore her alleged kidnapper.[36] But other rules made sure that abduction, elopement, and rape — which lawmakers treated as largely the same offence — did not happen regularly. The Burgundians also allowed parents of a stolen woman to do whatever they wished with the abductor and to disinherit a girl who ran off. The Franks ordered extremely high fines for kidnapers and rapists and for their accomplices; if the villain was a semi-freeman or a servant of the king, he lost his freedom and became the slave of her family.[37] Later laws of the twelfth century and after maintained the same principles, adding only the stipulation that a woman had to make a public outcry when she was taken, else she might be thought to have run off with her captor.[38] The acknowledgment that some women took part in their own abductions was built into all medieval legal codes, as was the belief that men took wives by force.[39]

Yet it was in no one's best interest to make a dubious match. A woman whose husband could not support her, could not be friendly with her own family, or whose family might disinherit her and her offspring was in trouble, for the future of both families lay with her children, who had to be legitimate and accepted by all parties. It did her no good to bear children to a man she loved, then to be unable to provide material goods and kinship alliances for them. In a legal sense, the essence of marriage was a betrothal sanctioned by both families, and the heart of betrothal was neither love nor sex, but a contract.

Hence, the entire decision-making procedure was complex and perilous. It was further encumbered by the exchange of property that accompanied the marriage. Objects and promises accompanied a bride from one house to another. The making of the contract for

---

[35] Katherine Fischer Drew, trans., *The Burgundian Code* (Philadelphia: University of Pennsylvania Press, 1972), XII.4.

[36] *WEHD* 1, 410–11.   [37] Drew, *Laws of the Salian Franks*, XIII, 78.

[38] Emilie Amt, *Women's Lives in Medieval Europe: A Sourcebook* (New York: Routledge, 1993), 56; Dillard, *Daughters of the Reconquest*, 135–47.

[39] Binchy, *Corpus Iuris Hibernici*, 505, 518.

a sexual union – the betrothal – was a long process of negotiation over exchanges of property, and was a far more important legal event than the marriage ceremony itself. In situations where women were generally less valued (culturally or because the sex ratios were low), a fiancee brought a dowry or bridewealth to her new husband, which might include land, animals, household goods, or money. This was the norm in late antique provincial societies. But in societies where women were scarce and valuable, a bride received gifts conveyed by deed or certified before witnesses: domestic animals, clothing, jewelry, coins, a strongbox, a bed with fine covers, household utensils and other moveables. This was the norm in late Roman society, and became ordinary in early medieval societies, too. Some Merovingian princesses got estates as dowries, or piles of gold. Rigunth, daughter of Fredegund, for instance, had coffers of gold and jewels as well as an extensive retinue before her wedding procession to Spain was robbed by her own followers and, later, her uncle Guntram.[40]

Small or large, at least part of the dowry usually remained the bride's property. If the union dissolved – which happened less frequently after ninth-century Carolingians and their bishops began tightening the bonds of monogamy – she had rights to some, if not all, of it. Older Frankish laws had required a woman to compensate her first husband's family with typical feminine possessions such as furniture and linen; presumably, these were part of her dowry.[41] In England, under Æðelbehrt of Kent's seventh-century laws, a woman could leave her husband and take her children and half of her goods with her. Where divorce lingered longer as a possibility, as in Wales, a woman got a fixed amount of the capital she had brought to the marriage, which increased with the number of years she had been married to the lout she was leaving. Irish women, who also were able to opt for divorce throughout the early Middle Ages, did best of all in property settlements. They took their own property and a percentage of the family profits based on the labor they had contributed to the household economy. Jurists assumed, for instance, that women who kept sheep and made cloth from the wool, and kept cows to make milk products, deserved a percentage of the couple's lambs and calves. But even while it remained possible divorce required good reasons, such as one partner's entry into the monastic life or other disasters. Again Ireland remained the exception. There a man's

[40] Gregory of Tours, *Historiae*, VI.45, VII.9.   [41] *Leg. Sal.*, tit. 100f.

impotence, tendency toward indiscretion (telling secrets about his wife's sexual performance), or even mere incompatibility was reason enough.[42] "One easily divorces what was never united," declared the wife in the English poem "Wulf and Eadwacer," who preferred her lover Wulf.[43] But she meant emotionally. Near the year 900, it was increasingly harder for women in England or on the Continent to gain a legal divorce, let along take back their property, given the efforts of ecclesiastics to promote indissoluble marriage bonds.[44]

Hence, there was a multitude of details to work out in order to create a stable union and to prevent unhappy squabbling over property. An English legal text of the later tenth century laid down an elaborate model for the entire negotiating process:

> How a man shall betroth a maiden and what agreement there ought to be:

1. If a man wishes to betroth a maiden or a widow, and it so pleases her and her kinsmen, then it is right that the bridegroom first according to God's laws and proper secular custom should promise and pledge to those who are her advocates that he desires her in such a way that he will maintain her according to God's law as a man should maintain his wife; and his friends are to stand surety for it.
2. Next it must be known to whom belongs the remuneration for rearing her. The bridegroom is then to pledge this, and his friends are to stand surety for it.
3. Then afterwards the bridegroom is to announce what he grants her in return for her acceptance of his suit, and what he grants her if she should live longer than he.
4. If it is thus contracted, then it is right that she should be entitled to half the goods [given as brideprice] – and to all, if they have a child together – unless she marries again.
5. He is to strengthen what he promises with a pledge, and his friends are to stand surety for it.
6. If they then reach agreement about everything, then the kinsmen are to set about betrothing their kinswoman as wife and in lawful matrimony to him who has asked for her, and he who is leader of the betrothal is to receive the security.[45]

All the relevant issues of betrothal were carefully considered by the writer of this legal guide, who was probably under the influence of the reformer Bishop Wulfstan. The exchange of payments to the groom, the bride (including the down-payment on a baby) and her

---

[42] Binchy, *Corpus Iuris Hibernici*, 507–508, 510; Bitel, *Land of Women*, 126.

[43] Robert K. Gordon, *Anglo-Saxon Poetry* (New York: Dutton, 1954), 83.

[44] Goetz, *Life in the Middle Ages*, 36–40.   [45] *WEHD* I, 431.

kinsfolk, and the necessity of witnesses and securities to ensure the contract were all carefully set down. The writer further specified that if the bride moved to another district, away from the protection of her parents, her family and friends were to be given assurance that she would not be harmed. (Perhaps this is a reference to the marriages across English and Scandinavian borders taking place during the eleventh century, under Knut's Anglo-Danish rule.)[46] If the bride committed an offence, her guarantors could help her compensate the victim, rather than having her suffer the punishment of those who could not afford to pay. If all went as planned and the contract pleased everyone then, as the writer put it, the kinsmen "set about betrothing their kinswoman." The bride herself was able to give consent to the union, according to this passage; by the tenth century, churchmen in England and elsewhere had won some advances in their campaign for the rights of the betrothed to approve or reject their own unions. King Knut, under this same ecclesiastical influence, explicitly declared elsewhere in his laws that "neither widow nor maiden is to be forced to marry a man whom she herself dislikes, nor to be given for money."[47] But a woman's kinsmen and those of her groom remained the ultimate creators of the marriage. No woman married without their consent and impetus.

Public betrothal – what later canonists called "promises in the future tense" – was binding. Early in the Middle Ages, years could pass before a couple celebrated a formal sacramental marriage, if they ever even bothered. If the parties involved changed their minds, there were penalties to pay and even more dire consequences to suffer, especially if they had indulged in sexual consummation. If a Frankish man left his fiancee to marry someone else, he had to recompense the slighted family (not the woman herself) with a big fine of sixty-two solidi.[48] In some lawcodes, a woman who refused an arranged marriage to take a different husband merely cost her family a heavy fine, but in other codes she committed a crime as heinous as adultery and was liable to similar punishment.[49] Officially, Frankish laws prohibited forcing a woman to marry against her will, but such rules suggest that some young people submitted unhappily to their parents' wishes

[46] Pauline Stafford, "The Laws of Cnut and the History of Anglo-Saxon Royal Promises," *Anglo-Saxon England* 10 (1981), 173–90.

[47] *WEHD* 1, 429; Wemple, *Women in Frankish Society,* 31–37.

[48] Drew, *Laws of the Salian Franks,* LXVa, p. 126, also 191.

[49] Binchy, *Corpus Iuris Hibernici,* 25, 47; Drew, *Burgundian Code,* LII, pp. 59–60.

and, once the deal was made, tried to escape it. A betrothed woman who ran off with another man could, in some regions, according to the earliest barbarian codes, be enslaved.[50]

Still, most couples must have been satisfied with their parents' choices for them. No chronicler or poet recorded any chaos of adultery and fornication. Laws prohibited both offenses but histories and epics refer to sexual indiscretions, if at all, as unusual enough to be worth writing about. On the contrary, the normal social unit was the married couple and its consequent kin. Weddings were a marker of a kin-group's growth. The betrothal or wedding, or both, were normally celebrated by the entire community and marked with ceremony – maybe a great banquet with copious drinking, singing, dancing, and plenty of obscene jokes to enhance the fertility of the union.[51] The couple may have signified their union with symbolic gifts, possibly a ring. They may also have exchanged a kiss on the mouth, which was a medieval symbol for all sorts of unions – the same kiss united a lord and his vassal. Thus were man and woman formally joined, even without benefit of religious ceremony, despite the insistence of some priests that they be included in the proceedings, perhaps just by blessing the couple. Often enough, two young people joined by their families began living together immediately (if they had not been already), without a formal wedding.

Sex completed the business. Expressing the churchman's view, Archbishop Hincmar of Reims put it in 860, "A true coupling in legitimate marriage between free persons of equal status occurs when a free woman, properly dowered, is joined to a free man with paternal consent in a public wedding [followed by] sexual intercourse."[52] Hincmar may have been influenced by the fraught politics of his moment, for he wrote when the Emperor Lothar II was trying desperately to divorce his legally wedded and bedded wife, Thietberga, in order to marry another woman, Waldrada. Nonetheless, the bishop's theologically based opposition turned up elsewhere in clerical writings before 1000.[53] Secular lawgivers agreed that sexual intercourse completed the marriage process, ordering a public payment to the

---

[50] Drew, *Laws of the Salian Franks*, XIII.8, p. 78.

[51] Burchard mentions feasts, songs, obscene gestures, and jokes at wedding celebrations: *Decreta*, Book 2., 132, in *PL* 140: 648.

[52] Hincmar of Reims, *Epistolae*, 22 136, in E. Perels, ed., *Hincmari Archiepiscopi Remensis Epistolae*, *MGH* (1975).

[53] James A. Brundage, *Law, Sex, and Christian Society in Medieval Europe* (Chicago: University of Chicago Press, 1987), 188–95.

bride after her first night with her groom. In Germanic cultures, he was supposed to give his wife a *Morgengabe* (*morgengifu* in Anglo-Saxon), literally a morning gift, as a token of thanks for coming as a virgin to the nuptial bed and leaving it otherwise. The groom thus signified his grateful certainty that the first child of the union would undoubtedly be his. In fact, if a betrothed woman was found not to be a virgin, she was liable to severe penalties including slavery or even death, according to the earlier Germanic laws. She had exposed her family to fines and shame. At the very least, she was likely to be dumped by her potential spouse and sent back home. If a bride was not a virgin at wedding, the parentage of children was uncertain, the whole family and its inheritance schedule thus endangered, and the validity of marriages in general were threatened – in short, society and its orderly reproduction were at risk.

In practice, of course, plenty of experienced women and men must have entered into marriages. That same Lothar II, for instance, had his marriage to Thietberga annulled at a synod in Aachen in 862, then claimed Waldrada, who had already borne him a son, as his legal wife. Churchmen forced Lothar to take Thietberga back; then the pope annulled the marriage on the condition that neither Lothar nor Thietberga swear never to marry again, while Waldrada herself was excommunicated. Still, Lothar died on the way home from persuading a new pope to grant him divorce and remarriage.[54] For Lothar, Waldrada, and their supporters, the couple's marriage was quite legal.[55]

When arranging a marriage, one thing fathers, mothers, kinsmen, women, the church, and lawmakers rarely took official notice of was love. (Regino of Prüm implied that Lothar II acted out of passion for Waldrada, but just as Hincmar sought theological justification for preserving Lothar's first marriage, Regino sought legitimate spiritual reasons for Lothar's second.) In medieval eyes, marriage was not the monogamous meeting of two hearts beating as one, or the fusion of two individual minds promising eternal love. Yet, just because their families participated does not mean that men and women eliminated affection from the process, or were themselves passive players shunted from one house to another, or that their desires were unimportant

---

[54] Regino of Prüm, *Chronik Anno 864–869*, ed. Reinhold S. Rau, Quellen zur karolingischen Reichsgeschichte (Berlin: Rutten & Loening, 1956–), 192ff./218ff., cited in Goetz, *Life in the Middle Ages*, 38–39.

[55] Stuart Airlie, "Private Bodies and the Body Politic: The Divorce Case of Lothar II," *Past and Present* 161 (1998), 3–38.

to all concerned. We cannot appreciate the entire complex process by which most people came to select spouses. We do know that men and women fell in love, sometimes with their spouses, and that others helped them find their soul-mates. Even before the explosion of love lyrics and romances in the eleventh century, medieval literature expressed a man's love for his woman, and more rarely a woman's for her man, both within marriage and without. Poems and stories were not reticent about sexual desire, either. In epics and stories, mere rumor of men's bravery or women's beauty caused the opposite sex to seek them as sexual partners.[56] The nobility and royalty of Europe married for both politics and love. Charlemagne, for example, lived with his first common-law wife apparently because she pleased him, but discarded her at his mother's urging to marry a Lombard princess, then dumped his second woman after a year to take yet another wife.

Is it a coincidence that men, their minds trained on farming or war or both, courted their women in the language of combat or farming while women often phrased their affection in contrast to the bonds of kin? "Praise the features of the fair girl," counseled the Norse *Eddas*, "Who courts well will conquer." The same text told the story of Odin seeking to seduce Billing's daughter, who made her own choice about loving the one-eyed god:

> I thought my wooing had won the maid,
> That I would have my way.
>
> After nightfall I hurried back,
> But the warriors were all awake,
> Lights were burning, torches blazing:
> So false proved the path.
>
> The guards were sound asleep:
> I found then that the fair woman
> Had tied a bitch to her bed.
>
> Many a girl when one gets to know her
> Proves to be fickle and false
> That treacherous maiden taught me a lesson,
> The crafty woman covered me with shame,
> That was all I got from her.[57]

---

[56] As in the ninth- or tenth-century *Tochmarc Becfhola*: Máire Bhreathnach, "A New Edition of *Tochmarc Becfhola*," *Ériu* 35 (1984): 59–81; see also Bitel, *Land of Women*, 44–56.

[57] Paul B. Taylor and W. H. Auden, trans., *The Elder Edda: A Selection* (New York: Random House, 1967), 51.

In pastoral Ireland they used the language of cows to make the same points. "That is a fine young heifer going by," remarked the hero Noísiu of his lover-to-be, Deirdriu, in the eighth-century Irish tale of their elopement.[58]

By contrast, heroines loved men despite the objections of their guardians, with no care for the consequences.[59] Deirdriu, Noísiu's lover, was raised in seclusion to marry King Conchobar of Ulster. But one day outside her cottage she spotted a crow hovering over the blood of a calf newly slaughtered on the snow and remarked that she "could love a man with coloring like that." Her loving fostermother told her where to find a dark-haired, white-faced, red-cheeked man and the rest was cruel destiny, including death for the eloping sweethearts. Similarly, Iseult and many other lovers carelessly took their men by deception or seduction, causing permanent damage to family and community.[60] Women, even in the earliest versions of these stories, disregarded all the careful maneuvering of families to pursue the men that struck their fancy. The poets who told their tales were not always unsympathetic. When the narrator bewailed the woman's exiled, faithless husband in the Old English "Wife's Lament," her distress was on display for the audience to pity, although there was plainly nothing anyone could do to help her.[61]

Love was difficult to include in marriage because it was uncontrollable and could interfere with women's other loyalties. Love also entered only incidentally and informally into the matter of legal mating. Even if couples commonly grew to care for each other, matrimonial affection had no place in laws and other guidelines. Love and lust, as we shall see, occasionally guided other kinds of unions which did appear in laws and ecclesiastical canons. But men and women had to work hard to make an affective marriage amidst the obligations of family and kinship and the overwhelming necessity of producing children. Along with her attachment to her husband, every wife had to remember her other duties to her natal kinsmen, her chosen allies and, above all, her babies.

---

[58] R. I. Best and O. Bergin, ed., *The Book of Leinster*, 6 vols. (Dublin Institute for Advanced Studies, 1954–83), vol. 5, 1162–70.

[59] Penny Schine Gold, *The Lady and the Virgin: Image, Attitude, and Experience in Twelfth-Century France* (Chicago: University of Chicago Press, 1985), 37–42.

[60] Best and Bergin, *Book of Leinster*, vol. 5, 1162–70.

[61] Gordon, *Anglo-Saxon Poetry*, 79–80.

The process of betrothal and marriage changed throughout the Middle Ages. Churchmen of the eleventh century tried to recreate marriage as a spiritual and religious – although not necessarily a more affective – event marked by religious ceremony. The great Christian institutional reforms of the period, inspired by clerical leaders' desire to eliminate secular legal influence upon ecclesiastical organization and property, nonetheless brought the infusion of Roman legal concepts into ecclesiastical law. The resulting canons governed every aspect of Christian moral and sexual behavior, including marriage. Clerics decided that both morals and sexuality were the province of church courts rather than secular judges. Reformers urged chastity upon the clergy, who needed to be pure to transmit holy sacraments to ordinary people and to set an example for the behavior of their flocks. While priests were to give up wives and mistresses, secular rulers tainted by carnal lust were to keep their hands off church offices, and the entire secular population was to abstain from anything but the sanctified procreative sex of marriage. The reforms of such great leaders as the monks of Cluny and Pope Gregory VII were, of course, more complex in aim and effect than a simple prescription of morally safe sex. Their impact upon actual marriage practice, let alone sexual behavior, is difficult to measure since Christians rarely related their sins to the men who wrote the rules.

Reformers intended primarily to set standards for Christendom which, if believers adhered to them, would persuade everyone of both the sacramental nature of marriage and the clergy's right to regulate sexual acts. Gratian (fl. 1140), the great harmonizer of previous Christian decrees, was most concerned about the necessity of age requirements at betrothal, public ceremonies conducted or sanctioned by clerics, the necessity of monogamy and exogamy, the issue of consent among the parties, and especially the importance of consummation in making a marriage.[62] But other canonists and theorists of the central Middle Ages, such as Peter Lombard, promoted the significance of consent in a Christian union over consummation, and emphasized the enduring bond formed when spouses promised themselves to each other.[63] Only in the twelfth century did the highest clergy express an understanding of marriage as a sacrament. In the thirteenth century, banns and ecclesiastical ceremonies became

[62] Brundage, *Law, Sex, and Christian Society*, 183–87, 229–42.
[63] Ibid., 187–88.

required; before that, marriage remained a public family affair made permanent through private sexual union.[64]

To some extent, ordinary folk changed behavior in accordance with reformers' rules. The French medievalist Georges Duby suggested that by the twelfth century two models for unions were popular: the ecclesiastical model, based on proliferating church rules, and the older lay model, which remained more fluid and dissoluble as well as under control of family groups.[65] Like most textbook formulations, Duby's model is too rigid to accommodate the wide variety of marriage styles that occurred in early and later medieval Europe. But he is right that in the twelfth century a canonically formal ecclesiastical model had been added to the possibilities. Further, while Duby rightly argues that legal and theoretical interpretations of the marriage bond and its forms changed, he is wrong to limit such change to the period after 1100. Marriage styles shifted constantly, especially during the Carolingian moral reform and again during the Gregorian reforms when economic development, urbanization, and the intellectual revolution that included the codification of canon law utterly transformed Europe.

Throughout the medieval period, marriage retained one most important purpose: the creation of a sanctioned conjugal unit that would produce and support the next generation, either within or despite Christian standards. When ages at marriage rose for both men and women, economics had as much to do with it as canon laws that set a minimum; ages escalated when times were hard but dropped again when a bride and groom could expect prosperity in their youth. Secular laws of marriage changed under church influence, too. The Carolingians were neither the first nor last rulers to collaborate with ecclesiastical authorities and try to regulate sexual relations and prevent fornication (defined as sex with a partner not married to the perpetrator), adultery, incest, polygyny, and divorce.[66] Social factors, in turn, affected such laws and religious rules, though. On the frontiers of Christian Spain in the twelfth and thirteenth centuries, where

[64] Gratian, *Decretum* C. 27 q. 2 c. 33–34, d.p.c. 39, in *Corpus Juris Canonici*, ed. E. Friedberg and A. Richter, 2 vols. (Graz: Akademische Druck- und Verlagsanstalt, 1959); Dillard, *Women of the Reconquest*, 38; J. T. Noonan, "Marital Affection in the Canonists," *Studia Gratiana* 12 (1967), 479–509; idem, "Power to Choose," *Viator* 4 (1973), 419–34.

[65] Georges Duby, *Medieval Marriage: Two Models from Twelfth-Century France* (Baltimore: Johns Hopkins University Press, 1978), esp. 3–22.

[66] Wemple, *Women in Frankish Society*, 76–80.

women were as scarce as in barbarian Gaul, the adultery and abduction of precious young women brought serious legal penalties; but fornication by a young, unattached man and a low-class or mixed-race girl remained a mere peccadillo for him and a disgrace for her.[67]

For women, marriage had some obvious continuities through the Christian centuries. The sexual double standard, the high valuation of women's reproductive role, and the largely theoretical nature of women's consent to marriage all endured in pre-modern Europe. For their legal unions with men to be happy, women depended upon sympathetic parents and benign spouses, but also their own resourcefulness in influencing the choice of marriage partners and the conduct of their marriages. Otherwise, they suffered the whims of dictatorial kinsmen and husbands with little recourse to law or other authority. They exercised agency in marriage only by choosing either to obey or to subvert the restrictions placed upon the whole process. Later medieval lives of female saints are full of brave women who resisted wrong marriages; these women succeeded in imposing their contrary wills rather than submitting to undesirable unions. But others went willingly, wanting to marry, knowing that formal legal union with a man and the consequent production of children was their best hope for survival, prestige, social contribution, and some measure of independence.

SURVIVAL BY MARRIAGE

Because their opportunities for public life were different and more limited than those of men, and because their inheritance rights and ability to govern were legally curtailed, women's most useful weapons in the fight for peace and order became family, kinship, and marriage. Only when she prepared to wed did a woman receive the substantial goods or property (dowry or pre-mortem inheritance) that made her a person of substance. Only sheltered by a formal union could a woman produce legitimate children, her most valuable treasures and the object of many of her struggles. Yet just as women's familial functions differed from those of men, wives and mothers had to balance their aims with their obligations to other family members attached by both blood and marriage.

Once a woman finally found a mate, she did what her brothers never accomplished: she left her natal kin, without any ceremony of

[67] Dillard, *Daughters of the Reconquest*, 135–47, 178–79.

rejection, no breaking of the alders, no public humiliation. On the contrary, marriage was her surest way of remaining a fully respected member of her natal kin. All she did was join a second family and, normally, enter a new home. In most areas of Europe she went to live with her husband's family but remained more or less legally attached to her blood-kin, as the bride in the tenth-century English contract did. Her first family retained rights to compensation if she were a victim of harm and could interfere if her new family mistreated her. Whether her family's affections went with her to her new home is harder to say. And did she come to love her new family? Most people in pre-modern Europe were so profoundly attached to their birth-places that the reverberations of departure must have been intense both for the one leaving and for those left behind, even if the traveler was only a bride going across the village or down to the next farm.

The English contract-writer cited earlier was rightly concerned that when an individual left the familiar she was bereft of the pro-tections she had enjoyed from babyhood. She could not entirely rely on her new kin for what she had lost. Yet the contract also served to remind her blood-kin that they still had responsibilities for their de-parted daughter, something they might be prone to forget. Laws reg-ulated exactly how much responsibility kinfolk continued to have for their married (or otherwise sexually attached) kinswomen. Variations derived not only from regional differences, but also from the legal nature of women's ties to their new households. A free woman prop-erly married to a free man in permanent monogamy integrated more thoroughly into her affinal group (her in-laws) – at least officially – than, say, a secondary wife or concubine with a less comprehensive contract.

Although church rules forbade other arrangements, the early Franks, English, Irish, and Welsh had all practiced what historians have called *Friedelehe*, a contractual relation based on mutual consent. In such an arrangement, women could choose their partners more freely. The arrangement still formally shifted a woman to a new household where she benefitted by some sort of morning-gift but got no dowry; her family retained legal responsibility (*mundium*, Ger. *Munt*) for her. When she got into trouble – as victim or malefactor – it was her father or his surrogate who had to protect her, not her lover.[68] Although the liaison was legal it could also be terminated

---

[68] Aline G. Hornaday, "Early Medieval Kinship Structures as Social and Political Controls," in *Medieval Family Roles: A Book of Essays*, ed. Cathy Jorgensen Itnyre (New York: Garland, 1996), 21–37, esp. 25.

more easily by the partners since it included no elaborate exchange of property, although any children of the match could inherit their father's property, or at least contend for it. Earliest Germanic laws formally recognized *Friedelehe* as only one of three kinds of legal sexual unions, along with *Raubehe* (marriage by capture) and *Kaufehe* (marriage by purchase.) If a man kidnapped his bride or the two arranged to elope, this was *Raubehe*. The couple probably negotiated their union made without the involvement of kin, and possibly without even the future bride's collaboration. But the laws still formalized such unions with the payment of fees to her guardian by the groom or his kin. The third type of union, *Kaufehe* (or *Muntehe*) was actually the normative exchange of bride and her legal guardianship for properties, dowry, *Morgengabe*, or whatever else accompanied and signified the new family unit.[69]

Nonetheless these three Germanic "marriages" were similar to a variety of other kinds of more or less permanent ties between a man and a woman, ranging from brief encounters to lifelong companionship. Early medieval legal distinctions among types of sexual unions merely show how lawmakers sought to control the whole process of union and reproduction, including the participation and consent of the parties involved and the distribution of exchanged properties. Irish laws, for instance, distinguished at least nine kinds of legal sexual unions, including what jurists called a "visiting" relationship, in which a woman lived at home with her own natal family and had only periodic sexual contact with her mate so that she might bear his children. Such a range of acceptable legal relationships meant that relative promiscuity was acceptable to the Irish of both sexes. Under Irish laws, men could simultaneously have many wives and concubines, while women could divorce their husbands fairly easily in order to break and reform unions. The job of negotiating among different kin-groups became a high-stakes game for the most influential Irish noblewomen, who helped or destroyed their families by making and breaking political marriages. The famous

[69] Janet Nelson, "Early Medieval Rites of Queen-Making and the Shaping of Medieval Queenship," in *Queens and Queenship in Medieval Europe: Proceedings of a Conference Held at King's College London, April 1995*, ed. Anne J. Duggan (Woodbridge: Boydell, 1997), 301–16; Brundage, *Law, Sex and Christian Society*, 128–31; Wemple, *Women in Frankish Society*, 12, 35, 111; Rudolf Köstler, "Raub-, Kauf- und Friedelehe bei den Germanen," *Zeitschrift der Savigny-Stiftung für Rechtsgeschichte, Germanistische Abteilung* 63 (1943), 95–98.

tenth-century princess Gormflaith became the wife of four Irish
provincial kings in succession, depending upon which man could
offer her and her kinsfolk the best political terms and military alliance.[70] Politics and the fundamental need for reproduction enabled
these women to ignore the very rules set up to promote the legitimate production of heirs. Rather than coming to the marriage bed
as virgins, such political players brought their experience, their royal
names, and the influence of their kinsfolk as dowries. They then set
about their jobs of producing children who would help cement the
marriage alliance. But only queens and princesses took such demanding positions. A similar set of conditions existed in late Anglo-Saxon
England, where queens enjoyed controlled primary access to their
husbands but wellborn concubines of the king also might enjoy high
status and enormous wealth. Concubines advised English monarchs
and attested charters, thus remaining influential among their natal
kin.[71]

Elsewhere in Europe a man might have more than one such
woman, bound to him by *Friedelehe*, concubinage, or pure lust, as
well as a wife, whereas under any and all laws, a woman could only
engage in one recognized longterm sexual relationship at a time with
a man. Such an imbalance of sexual ties existed wherever a double
standard flourished – which is to say, everywhere. Anthropologists
call it "resource polygyny" when wealthy, powerful men keep more
than one woman. In such situations, many poor and powerless men
thus have no women.[72] But even rich men had only so much property to spare their partners and offspring. When a woman was but
one partner of several to her man, each with children, the fight for
family property could become a desperate battle among half-siblings,
as many a king's son found to his sorrow. Women who mated with
men of high status faced the possibility that they would have to share
him with other women, fight viciously for the support of their children, or find themselves cast back upon their blood-kin when a new
favorite expelled them from the master's house. The sexual partners

[70] Binchy, *Corpus Iuris Hibernici*, 7–8, 21–22, 505.

[71] Christine Fell with Cecily Clark and Elizabeth Williams, *Women in Anglo-Saxon England and the Impact of 1066* (Bloomington: Indiana University Press, 1984), 65; Henrietta Leyser, *Medieval Women: A Social History of Women in England 450–1500* (New York: St. Martin's Press, 1995), 44; Stafford, *Queens, Concubines, and Dowagers*, 60–71.

[72] Herlihy, *Medieval Households*, 55.

of wandering soldiers or shepherds, by contrast, did not suffer the competition or enjoy the support expected by noblewomen who shared a man. Women faced further restrictions on their sexual practice. Most of the barbarian codes frowned upon the "fornication" of an unmarried woman with a man, be he married or single.[73] In some areas, laws declared the exact extent of a fallen woman's membership in her original household and its kin network. Elsewhere, she was disgraced and dependent upon the goodwill of her family.[74] Even in Ireland, with its liberal attitudes toward a variety of sexual liaisons, the word for secondary wife, *adaltrach*, derived from the Latin for "adulteress." But churchmen everywhere condemned polygyny when it interfered with marriage and orderly reproduction. Early medieval penitentials ordered stiff penalties for fornication, although not so stiff as for incest or adultery. While ordinary folk and even lawmakers might have ignored ecclesiastical disapproval for the sake of reproduction, secular laws came more and more to echo Christian insistence on monogamy after about 800. But who was to police women who wanted sex with men legally denied them? Lascivious noble ladies, wayward nuns, and willing servant-girls were all popular characters in later medieval romances and fabliaux.

Although we cannot know how the legality of unions affected most women's choices or any particular woman's heart, we can explore the effect of social constraints on a woman's place in her community. The early medieval literati relentlessly probed the difficulties of married women who tried to balance their loyalties to husband or lover, children, affines, and natal family. Though the English called such women peaceweavers, their stories and poems more often depicted unsuccessful women whose families unraveled, rather than serene mothers knitting families together in amity. Both blood-kin and in-laws made demands upon the woman at the tense center of two social groups, and both suspected her of favoring the other. Neither supplied as much help as she needed, especially if she had made a legally dubious connection with her man. One classic case of the woman caught between kin and in-laws in conflict comes from *Beowulf*, providing yet another example of the depressing Anglo-Saxon world view.

[73] McNeill and Gamer, 18, 94, 184–85, 335.
[74] Binchy, *Corpus Iuris Hibernici*, 232, 856, 915; Bitel, *Land of Women*, 90–91; see also Margaret Clunies Ross, "Concubinage in Anglo-Saxon England," *Past and Present* 108 (1985), 3–34.

The poet told the story-within-a-story as a warning to audiences both inside and beyond the verse. A princess named Hildeburh, sister of Danish kings, married Finn, king of the Jutes. When her brother Hnaef visited her, a fight broke out between his men and the troops of his host and brother-in-law. Hildeburh lost both Hnaef and her son to the bloodshed. "Not without cause did Hoc's daughter lament the decree of destiny when morning came," the poet put it, "and she might see, under the sky, the slaughter of kinsmen – where before she had the greatest of world's joy." Hildeburh watched son and brother burn on the same funeral pyre. Eventually, Jutes killed Finn, too.[75] Hildeburh mourned for her men, one after another. She could not persuade either side to make peace, could not argue away the hostility, and could not even use her son – who united both houses – to end the fight. Yet, as the poet's mournful tone indicated, she and other women were expected to bring about order when male-headed families sought to disrupt it. Neither the poet nor Hildeburh expected her to be passive. She had accepted her marriage in the first place; after the disaster, she purposefully put her son and brother on the same pyre, thus possibly inspiring the revenge upon her husband, and finally chose to accompany her blood-kin home.[76] Hers was just one episode in a long tale of women and men making bad choices that led to instability and violence. In the second "branch" of the *Mabinogion*, a Welsh story-cycle with equally ancient roots, an evil brother willfully cast his nephew into the hearthfire in order to incite violence between his brother, a Welsh king, and his brother-in-law, an Irish king, sparing no thought for his sister who was bound to them all. She too became a victim of the circumstances, although her royal brother eventually rescued her.[77]

Real women could and did successfully seek equilibrium among their kin and in-laws, though. Royal widows and dowager mothers could wield considerable negotiating power among their children and other kinsfolk. Ottonian queens and princesses seem to have outlived their husbands by decades and managed to pass on inheritances from both sides of their families to their children, thus demonstrating how determined mothers could use their multitudinous kinship

[75] *Beowulf*, xv–xvii. [76] Dockray-Miller, *Motherhood and Mothering*, 96–100.
[77] Derick Thomson, ed., *Branwen Uerch Lyr* (Dublin Institute for Advanced Studies, 1976), 14; Jeffrey Gantz, trans., *The Mabinogion* (Harmondsworth: Penguin, 1976), 66–82.

ties to support the next generation. Oda was the granddaughter of Otto, *dux* of the Liudolfing family, who married King Zwentibold of Lotharingia. When he died in 900 Oda married Zwentibold's enemy, Count Gerhard, who fell in battle in 910. Her cousin, Gerberga, married Duke Giselbert of Lotharingia, but he drowned in the Rhine during battle. She then wed Louis d'Outremer, who played politics in Lotharingia until he died in 954 while hunting a wolf.[78] While the historian Karl Leyser describes these women as "taken" and "carried off" by their second husbands, any lady who outlasted her husband and kept her dowry had a good chance of doing some of her own taking and making some of her own decisions. Presumably, for the widows to marry, stay married, and inherit from their second husbands they must have gone at least somewhat willingly. They could hardly have escaped the savvy politics of the Ottonian house from which they sprang. Ottonian noblewomen not only outlived their husbands and other kin, but wielded great influence and inherited property, which they spent setting up, staffing, and endowing major convents.[79]

If peaceweaving was difficult for legal, high-status wives, it was nearly impossible for women in less formal relationships. In fact, the consequences of polygyny ranged from humiliating to fatal. Coexistence with other wives or concubines of a single husband must have been difficult for women, even when they were kept in separate households. Early in the barbarian period, Gregory of Tours had told tragic tales of women struggling to retain the favor of Merovingian dukes and princes, even killing each other to keep their places. Irish laws of the eighth and later centuries, so indulgent of liaisons and polygyny, permitted a man's chief wife (*cétmuinter*) to injure second wives who insulted her, suggesting the hostility common among rivals to a man's affections and property. Women frequently quarreled over their men. One saint's life of the eleventh century or later told of a devout nobleman who retired to a distant island to escape his two wives, who caused such a ruckus that they made his life hell.[80]

However amusing the hagiographer found such a situation, contests could get serious since the stakes were often very high. Women were fighting for nothing less than their lives and the lives of their

[78] Leyser, *Rule and Conflict,* 53.   [79] Ibid., 73.
[80] Binchy, *Corpus Iuris Hibernici,* 7–8; Plummer, *Vitae Sanctorum Hiberniae,* vol. 1, 147–48.

children, not to mention the fortunes of their blood-kin and all their allies. Laws everywhere defined and regulated the rights of legitimate heirs. Where the rules allowed leeway in determining which of a man's offspring inherited his property, women worked hard to ensure the prosperity of their children. What, the jurists must have wondered, if a man left only bastards by two different women? What if he had a boy by his mistress and only daughters by his primary wife? What if his illegitimate son was an adult, while his wife's son was a baby? Could his brother or daughter succeed him if he had no legitimate sons? Such issues were not always clear legally or politically. Matters became more complicated when men formally divorced and remarried, when widowers took new wives, and when clerics and kings together finally brought canon law into secular law and ended legal divorce.

Determined women could help influence the outcome of complicated cases with paternity and property suits, or could stay married despite husbands who wished to divorce or annul, if only they had the backing of kinsmen or churchmen. When Thietberga, the unfortunate wife of Lothar II of Lotharingia, could not become pregnant and Lothar tried to discard her for Waldrada, he needed a legitimate reason. His Carolingian forebears had legislated against frivolous divorce. He tried accusing Thietberga of incest with her brother, but she proved her innocence through trial by ordeal. Although Lothar forced her to admit not only incest but an astonishing pregnancy by means of femoral intercourse (without issue), she eventually won out because she had the support of bishops and popes. As we know, even with help from a different pope, Lothar died before he could recoup his position.[81] At stake for Thietberga was her position as queen, the reputation of her family, and the status of any children she might eventually bear. For this, she risked ordeal, imprisonment, and torture, not to mention public humiliation. A century later, Ælfreda, mother of Æðelred Unræd, went even further. She secured the English crown for her son by having his half-brother, Edward the Martyr, murdered. Ælfreda was a properly married second wife, but jealous and fearful of her step-children nonetheless, and willing to commit the most heinous sin to protect her own. More virtuous noblewomen played a similar game, diverting property to chosen heirs. English wills from the Anglo-Saxon period record the cases of Leofgifu, Wynflæd, and

---

[81] Wemple, *Women in Frankish Society*, 85–87.

Ælfgifu, all of whom made sure to leave property to kinswomen or female friends.[82]

Women were willing to battle their own men and other women for what they wanted in marriage and motherhood, but were not always so successful as Thietberga and Ælfreda. One woman, no less tragic than Grendel's mother, could do little more than survive her husband and render her imperiled son some stoic advice, although she too was exceptional among women. She was Dhuoda, a noblewoman of the highest birth who had married Bernhard of Septimania, the Frankish emperor's right-hand man until around the year 830. Unfortunately, Bernhard was not only a bad politicker but earned the hatred of all the contenders in the quarrel over imperial succession, and was further rumored to be sleeping with the Empress Judith. He was eventually captured and killed by his enemies at court. Before that, though, he offered his and Dhuoda's sixteen-year-old son to one of the emperor's sons as a hostage. Bernhard undertook all of this without consulting his wife.

In the winter of 841, Dhuoda began writing to her child William from their house at Uzès, where Bernhard had left her, and from which he had taken their second infant before Dhuoda could even name him. The *Manualis*, as she called her work, was a marvel of allusion and erudition. Dhuoda knew her Bible, her theologians, her grammarians. She counseled William on the Trinity, on prayer, on the respect due even a father such as Bernhard. She advised him about how to endure temptations and trials, avoid bad habits, receive gifts from God, and the benefits of prayer. She asked for his prayers for herself and listed the dead members of her husband's family so that William might include them in his petitions to the Almighty. "I am thinking now," she wrote to her son with some irony,

of those stories I have heard read and also of some of my relatives, and yours, also, whom I have known; they were powerful in this world and are no more. Perhaps they are with God because of their merits, but they are not present in body on earth. For them and for others I pray on bended knee: Requiem aeternam.[83]

She ended her work, as Jesus ended his, with the words *Consumatum est*, "It is finished."

[82] *WASW*, 10–15, 20–23, 77–79.
[83] Dhuoda, *Liber Manualis*, ed. and trans. Marcelle Thiebaux (Cambridge University Press, 1998); trans. in Katharina Wilson, ed., *Medieval Women Writers* (Athens: University of Georgia Press, 1984), 1–29, esp. 15.

Dhuoda was a classic peaceweaver, or would have been, had she been at liberty to pursue her vocation. She knew the histories of her family and her in-laws. She was well aware of the politics of status, although she also disdained the game of men who were "no more." She, with her motherly knowledge, prayed for her sinning in-laws and advised her son to avoid their mistakes. Take my words, she counseled her son, not those of your father. But William seems not to have absorbed the advice of his educated mother, who was herself as much a captive as he. Dhuoda finished the manual in 843; William's father and Dhuoda's husband, Bernhard, was executed in 844. William himself was beheaded for political reasons six years later. Even the grown second son, also called Bernhard "Hairypaws," may have ended the same way.[84] Since Dhuoda was no walker in the wilderness, like Grendel's mother, but only a lady in a nobleman's hall, it seems that all the mother and wife could do was wish them well and offer them her exquisitely phrased advice. Despite her status as chief and only wife, despite all her good efforts, and despite her rare erudition, she was defeated in her search for social stability and the safety of her children by him to whom it should have mattered most.

Dhuoda and other embattled wives had allies in the churchmen who tirelessly combated polygyny in all its forms. Ecclesiastics finally achieved some success with pervasive Christian improvements around the millennium. Church leaders, such as Pope Gregory VII, pushed for celibacy among clerics, tried to release churches and ecclesiastical personnel from the hands of lay noblemen, and struggled to regulate the moral, sexual, and marital life of laypeople. All sorts of new mentalities, ideas, attitudes, and practices spread throughout Europe, which were bound to affect the practice and concept of marriage, and women's part in it. The battle over spousal consent and the nature of betrothal was one effect of reform; the increasing popularity of monogamy was another. But even in monogamy, women had to work hard to create stable households and peaceable communities.

Theologians attempting reform after the millennium were struggling with a temporary resurgence of paternal authority among elite families. Around the eleventh and twelfth centuries, a new family

---

[84] *Annales Sancti Bertini* (Annals of St. Bertin), in *Annales et Chronica Aevi Carolini*, ed. Georg Pertz, *MGH SS* 1, 864; Janet Nelson, *Charles the Bald* (London: Longman, 1992), 211–12; Constance Bouchard, "Family Structure and Family Consciousness Among the Aristocracy in the Ninth to Eleventh Centuries," *Francia* 14 (1986), 639–58.

form appeared in the West: the agnatic lineage, or the patrilineage. It differed from old-style cognatic kin-groups in several important ways. Patrilineal families were organized around a line of descent from the father's family and became essentially a fellowship of males whose community stretched backward and forwards in time. Women were no longer the nodules through which passed the surest kinship ties; daughters became marginal members of their fathers' lineage, not lynchpins in horizontal alliances. After a woman's marriage to another man, her children left her kin-group entirely for her husband's family, whereas in barbarian cultures both maternal and paternal kin held importance and bestowed inheritance. Patrilineage was ancestor-focused, tracing its descent through the male line back to a known founder, whereas the *cognatio* was ego-focused: the line of relationship ran from ego in both directions, through males and females, to the accepted limits of kinship, making each kinship group unique to an individual, redefined with each generation. Agnatic lineage acquired new members over time, but remained a stable group. With such new families came the invention of genealogies, designed to support the existence of dynasties and their claims to political and noble status. Along with genealogies came coats of arms, mottos, and family names.[85]

When dynasties gained arms, women lost claim to whatever shares in their patrimony they had once enjoyed. Neither sons nor daughters inherited from maternal kin so frequently. Fathers provided dowries, but if they also had sons, little else. However, when rich nobleman had no sons, they might produce highly eligible heiresses whose control over their own property made them very desirable wives. One famous example was Eleanor of Aquitaine. In 1137, as an adolescent, she married King Louis VII of France, and her dowry doubled the size of his kingdom. When her marriage was annulled, she married the king of England. When she quarreled with Henry of England, she returned to Aquitaine and ruled on her own until he shut her in a tower.[86] Thus, in this feudal age as in earlier times, the best brides

---

[85] Georges Duby, *The Chivalrous Society* (Berkeley: University of California Press, 1977), esp. "Lineage, Nobility, and Knighthood: The Mâconnais in the Twelfth Century – A Revision," 59–93, and "The Nobility in Medieval France," 94–111; Georges Duby, ed., *A History of Private Life*, vol. 2, *Revelations of the Medieval World* (Cambridge, MA: Belknap Press, 1988), 90–91.

[86] Amy Ruth Kelly, *Eleanor of Aquitaine and the Four Kings* (Cambridge, MA: Harvard University Press, 1950), 157, 189–91.

were prizes to be won by noble warriors. But after the millennium, men of good birth wanted women for the prestige they brought to a noble lineage and their valuable possessions, including offspring. A wife need no longer be a skillful peaceweaver or a partner in armor. At the highest levels of medieval society, women added nothing special in themselves and took nothing from the patrilineage.

Other family forms continued to exist, especially among the lower classes. Since family structure influenced marriage and the status of women, a variety of marriage types and statuses of women also continued to coexist with new patriarchal models. Regional difference determined some of the contours of marriage, family, and status. On the frontiers of Christendom, as the next chapter argues, women were more important to mother's kin, father's kin, in-laws, and their own children. And everywhere, to be sure, people still relied on their mother's family for informal kinds of support. The coexistence of two or more kinds of family for each individual raised all sorts of new questions: how large a dowry could a father spare for his daughter? How many resources should he expend on the career of his younger son? How could a wife protect her sons against his participation in the demands of lordship, such as military service? How assiduously should she cultivate her own relatives and her affines (in-laws)? Such difficult questions caused tensions for families, but only within such fluid, tense situations could women still find important social roles to fill, choosing which relatives with which to ally themselves, which children to support, whom to love, to honor. As always, the more confusion within the social system, the less rigidly people applied their rules about gendered behavior. The cracks in the system benefitted women of the later Middle Ages at both ends of the hierarchy. From queens to slaves, women all along the spectrum found ways to profit by their prescribed social roles.

THE DANGERS OF MARRYING AND MOTHERING

In the early Middle Ages, cosmic stability depended upon family harmony and chaste women, so that a man could rely on his kinsmen and never doubted who his sons were. "Mothers are creators" in the godly sense, announced the ninth-century Irish writer of the prologue to *Cáin Adomnáin* (The Law of Adomnán).[87] Reverence

---

[87] Kuno Meyer, ed. and trans., *Cáin Adamnáin: An Old-Irish Treatise on the Law of Adamnán* (Oxford: Clarendon, 1905), 5.

for motherhood generated ideals that sustained medieval spirituality. The Virgin Mary became an object of widespread veneration, not to say worship, as early as the seventh century in Britain and Ireland, and her cult flourished everywhere with the courtly society of the second feudal age. One hymnist sang:

> Bride of the most excellent lord of Heaven . . . Lady of the heavenly host . . . you alone among all people having the courage of your persuasions, gloriously determined that you would offer your maidenhood to the ordaining Lord and grant it him without sin. None comparable has come, no other above all mortals, a ring-adorned bride who with pure heart then sent the sublime offering to the heavenly home.[88]

Via this icon of motherhood, medieval people supposedly revered their mothers.

If theorists and idealists noticed any tension between theoretical motherhood and its practice by ordinary women, none admitted it. Nonetheless, churchmen and other composers of documents realized that in their violent world the near-impossible tasks delegated to wives and mothers were made more difficult by certain kinds of harm afflicting only women. Medieval people did not lack an ability to distinguish right from wrong, and may have regretted or even hated physical mayhem. But they were not shocked to see it applied to women in a daily context. Since they evaluated violent crime according to the social origins of both the perpetrator and the victim, evil inflicted upon women, especially lower-class women, could never surprise them. In fact, the sources took it for granted. The motif of wives and mothers dragged off to be manhandled or enslaved was as common as that of babies spitted on soldiers' spears. Simeon of Durham, writing a century after the event, described the Danes' assault on Canterbury in 1011, recalling that "matrons dragged by the hair through the streets of the city, at last were thrown into the flames and perished. Infants torn from the mother's breast were carried on pikes, or crushed to pieces by a wagon driven over them." Likewise, in 1070, Simeon recorded that Malcolm of Scotland pierced babies on pikes, beheaded aged men and women, and drove maidens into slavery, except those women who, "worn out by running in front of their drivers further than

---

[88] Jackson J. Campbell, ed., *The Advent Lyrics of the Exeter Book* (Princeton University Press, 1959), IV.53, vol. 2, 278ff.

their strength would bear, falling to the earth, perished even where they fell."[89]

While men faced death in battle and women may have counted among the casualties, women rarely died with weapons in their hands in the midst of fighting. Men might ride from the field of battle and burn women in their houses or carry them off into slavery but only extraordinary, threatening monsters such as Grendel's mother took up arms to defend themselves, much less attack. Throughout the Middle Ages, women warriors such as Fredegund, who led her troops against Austrasia and Burgundy, or Joan of Arc, who was burned for wearing men's armor, remained uncomfortable wonders. The Latin literate must have known the story of the indomitable Brunhild who, according to Gregory of Tours, rose with "a vigor that would have become a man" and tried to interfere in a man's war. "Stand back, woman!" cried her diplomatic opponent. "It should be enough that you held regal power when your husband was alive. Now your son is on the throne, and his kingdom is under our control, not yours. Stand back, I say, or you will be trodden into the ground by our horses' hooves!" The queen prevailed temporarily, but her attempt to participate in warfare only to the extent of stopping it caused outrage among her soldiers and allies, according to Gregory, and among his readers, too, we must assume.[90] By the approach of the millennium, women, like peasants, were not to pick up sword or ax, but to survive by other means.

But it was difficult for women to survive when they might so easily fall victims to sexual violence or physical abuse even within their own communities or households. Lawmakers and canonists decried rape, although as we have seen, they confused it with sexless abduction and theft. They also considered the problem of wifebeating. Hincmar of Reims, the ninth-century bishop and advisor to Carolingian monarchs, warned of the destruction brought by husbands upon their wives. Men accused their wives of adultery and then led them "to the slaughterhouse to be butchered, and they bid the cooks to kill them with swords as it is the practice with sheep

[89] Amt, *Women's Lives in Medieval Europe*, 95–96.

[90] Gregory of Tours, *Historia*, VI.4; Ross Balzaretti discusses the distress of lawmakers over female or unmanly violence in "These Are Things That Men Do, Not Women: The Social Regulation of Female Violence in Langobard Italy," in *Violence and Society in the Early Medieval West*, ed. Guy Halsall (Woodbridge: Boydell, 1998), 175–92.

and pigs, or they personally murder them with the edge of their own swords, cutting them to pieces."[91] Hincmar wrote his dreadful words in the midst of considering the issue of Lothar II's divorce, while his colleagues in Christianity were beginning to debate vigorously the whole issue of marriage's end. Abuse was not a just cause for divorce, Hincmar and the others decided. But churchmen sought other means to protect women come to harm through bad marriages. In 895, the Council of Tribur opened churches as sanctuaries to women fleeing abuse.[92] Irish laws continued to allow a woman to divorce a wifebeater, despite the pleading of canonists to preserve Christian marriage.[93] Jewish leaders were divided about wifebeating, even though the Talmud did not specifically prohibit it. Sages from the Middle East and Spain regarded severe or chronic abuse as grounds for divorce on the woman's part, but many considered it a husband's prerogative to beat a wife who neglected her chores, thus endangering the entire household economy and the social order upon which the community was based. Rabbi Shmuel Hanaggid advised husbands in eleventh-century Spain, "Hit your wife if she dominates you as a man and raises her head." Although later northern European rabbis despised spousal abuse as "the way of the gentiles," many scholars, gentile and Jewish, acknowledged that men commonly hurt the women most intimately connected to them.[94]

Slavery also brought abuse and death to women, who were more likely to become and remain slaves than men. The early medieval narratives, such as Gregory of Tours's history and hagiography, suggest that aristocratic women who survived warfare often ended up as unwilling sexual partners in the beds of their conquerors. Radegund, who became queen of the Franks, was one famous example. When Chlotar wiped out her family, the ruling house of Thuringia, he hauled the child captive off to his estates to raise her to be his wife. Only after years of miserable marriage did she escape to a nunnery. At the lower end of the social spectrum, peasant women were

---

[91] *PL* 125: 657; Wemple, *Women in Frankish Society*, 104. See also Gregory of Tours, *Liber de Martyribus*, trans. Raymond van Dam as *Glory of the Martyrs* (Liverpool University Press, 1988), 92–93.

[92] Wemple, *Women in Frankish Society*, 104.

[93] Binchy, *Corpus Iuris Hibernici*, 47: 'ben fora fuirmither ainim coisc'; H. Wasserschleben, ed., *Die irische Kanonensammlung* (Leipzig: Tauschnitz, 1885), 186–87.

[94] Avraham Grossman, "Medieval Rabbinic Views on Wife-Beating, 800–1300," *Jewish History* 5:1 (1991), 53–62.

captured as slaves well into the Middle Ages, as Simeon of Durham's account suggests. *Cáin Adomnáin*, although issued around 700 to protect all women, described in its later preface the condition of slave-mothers: "*Cumalach* was the name for women until Adomnán came to emancipate them, and this was the *cumalach*: the woman for whom a pit was dug at the head of the sluice-gate so that it hid her nakedness. One end of the crossbar was supported by her until the grinding of the load was done."[95] According to the *Cáin*, women had to hold burning candles aloft in their bare hands while warriors feasted, were forced to live in mud huts outside the protection of fortified houses, and even had to fight men's wars, bearing babies on their backs. Slavery was a gendered issue in the minds of ninth-century Irish writers: to be powerless and exposed was to be female.[96]

Such pornographic fantasies tell us much about churchmen's aversion to female slavery, and about the kinds of violence they thought women vulnerable to in the barbarous past and their own turbulent present. No one in the ninth century could seriously imagine his own women fighting, performing such monstrous manual labor, or being exiled to a hut beyond the community. Wives and mothers did not live outside, but at the heart of the household. But the nakedness of the women in the story attributed to Adomnán suggests that the Irish writer, who so valued mothers, was also well aware of the persistent exposure of mothers and other women to specially gendered kinds of violence throughout the medieval centuries. Everywhere in Europe, women were still slaves in the ninth century and later. Even though Christian legal theorists prohibited taking baptized slaves, the trade in female slaves remained brisk.[97]

---

[95] Meyer, *Cáin Adamnáin*, 2.

[96] Máirín Ní Dhonnchadha, "The *Lex Innocentium*: Adomnán's Law for Women, Clerics, and Youths, 697 A.D.," in *Chattel, Servant, or Citizen: Women's Status in Church, State and Society. Papers Read Before the XXIst Irish Conference of Historians, Held at The Queen's University of Belfast, 27–30 May, 1993*, ed. Mary O'Dowd and Sabine Wichert (Belfast: The Queen's University of Belfast, 1995), 53–76.

[97] Susan Mosher Stuard, "To Town to Serve: Urban Domestic Slavery in Medieval Ragusa," in *Women and Work in Preindustrial Europe*, ed. Barbara Hanawalt (Bloomington: Indiana University Press, 1986), 39–51; see also Ruth Mazo Karras, "Desire, Descendants, and Dominance: Slavery, the Exchange of Women, and Masculine Power," in *The World of Work: Servitude, Slavery, and Labor in Medieval England*, ed. Allen J. Frantzen and Douglas Moffat (Glasgow: Cruithne Press, 1994), 16–29; Devroey, "Men and Women in Early Medieval Serfdom."

All acts of medieval violence, whether willful or accidental, domestic or public, were gendered. The infrastructure of Christendom, based on the theoretical superiority of men and the political invisibility of women, necessitated such a state. Women were more subject to violence and more helpless to prevent it; more plagued by disorder and less able to correct it. But the kinds of violence that occurred were also gendered. Men succumbed more often to mishaps in the field, while women were more likely to fall down wells or meet injury in the farmyard.[98] When food was low, women were more likely to drop from hunger, or to starve first. Parents practiced gendered infanticide in some parts of medieval Europe, eliminating female mouths that needed to be fed before they killed boy babies.[99]

Yet wives and mothers made all life possible, as early medieval Christians acknowledged in their devotion to the Virgin Mary. How was it possible then to permit and accept the violence done to ordinary women? The Virgin Mother's status as virgin childbearer (*parthenos* Matthew the evangelist called her, quoting Isaiah) was one signal that human motherhood was not all it was cracked up to be.[100] Mary was the ideal, escaping normal conditions of wifedom and motherhood, which fell without exception upon ordinary women. Eve's biblical punishment by travail, so popular in manuscript illustrations, was another hint at the distance perceived by medieval people between the ideal motherhood of the Virgin and the mothers one met every day in the neighborhood. In some illuminations, the serpent enticing Eve to her life of labor had the same feminine features as the first woman: woman led herself to sin and thus to the possible redemption of reproduction. That old binary ideology which cast women as virgin and whore, lifegiver and destroyer, crawled from the ancient world where it was born into the thoughts of medieval men and women. Women might make marriages, households, and babies, but that never made them saints in early medieval eyes. Only after they had given up wifehood and its implicit sexuality could they achieve sanctity, as saints Radegund and Balthild did; only later

[98] Barbara Hanawalt, *The Ties That Bound: Peasant Families in Medieval England* (Oxford University Press, 1986), 145.

[99] Clover, "Politics of Scarcity."

[100] Matt. 1:23; Isaiah 7:14; Jaroslav Pelikan, *Mary Through the Centuries: Her Place in the History of Culture* (New Haven: Yale University Press, 1996), 16–18 *et passim*; Marina Warner, *Alone of All Her Sex: The Myth and Cult of the Virgin Mary* (London: Weidenfeld & Nicolson, 1976), 45 *et passim*.

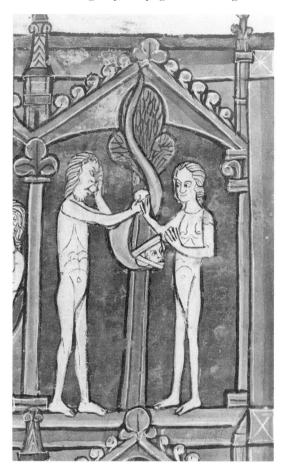

6 Serpent with the face of Eve in the Garden of Eden.
From a thirteenth-century English psalter.

in the Middle Ages did secular wives become religious models.[101] In
the meantime, ordinary wives and mothers were just as capable of
committing evil as any subject of Christendom.

Gnomic literature and riddles took a wry view of the old double
ideology, suggesting that some medieval people must have sensed
the irony of it. The *Eddas*, which praised a good wife to the skies,
also taught that the end of the world would bring brothers fighting
brothers and whoredom for women of the family.[102] Irish wisdom
literature advised men on how to find a reliable wife: "Do not marry

---

[101] Smith, "Problem of Female Sanctity," esp. 25–26.   [102] *Elder Edda*, 150.

the short fat one," the texts advised, or the gossipy, thieving, wanton one, for she would ruin your life.[103] The Old English Maxims advised women on how to obtain lovers without losing their reputations, while at the same time warning men that women were prone to such duplicity, as well as greed: "A lady must, with secret craft, have a woman seek out her lover, if she does not wish it to come about among the people that she is obtained with rings."[104]

THE SUBVERSION OF MOTHERHOOD

Yet, as many writers lamented without humor or irony, the failure of good mothers and wives to keep the peace and maintain their chastity meant catastrophe for all. In 1014, Bishop Wulfstan, the English reformer, despaired at the devastations of the Scandinavians. However, rather than physical destruction, rather than the destruction of mothers and wives, Wulfstan was worried about depredations on the native English character:

> Here there are, as we said before, manslayers and murderers of their kinsmen, and murderers of priests and persecutors of monasteries, and traitors and notorious apostates, and here there are perjurers and murderers, and here there are injurers of men in holy orders and adulterers, and people greatly corrupted through incest and through various fornications, and here there are harlots and infanticides and many foul adulterous fornicators, and here there are witches and sorceresses, and here there are robbers and plunderers and pilferers and thieves, and injurers of the people and pledge-breakers and treaty-breakers, and, in short, a countless number of all crimes and misdeeds.[105]

Violence from without caused violence within, theorized Wulfstan. The ravages of invaders caused good men to kill and drove good women to sexual crimes and magic.

Just as women were susceptible to gendered violence, they also perpetrated their own specifically female acts of violence. Although women were formally included in the laws against theft and murder – and were punished for such crimes when caught – laws and penitentials

---

[103] Roland M. Smith, ed. and trans., "The *Senbriathra Fithail* and Related Texts," *Revue Celtique* 45 (1928), 52–53.

[104] Exeter Maxims, 42b, cited in Carolyne Larrington, *A Store of Common Sense: Gnomic Theme and Style in Old Icelandic and Old English Wisdom Poetry* (Oxford: Clarendon, 1993), 133.

[105] Wulfstan, *Sermo Lupi ad Lupos*, ed. and trans. Melissa J. Bernstein, http://www.cif.rochester.edu/~mjbernst/wulfstan/noframes.html, (1996), ll. 121–30.

more often condemned women as adulteresses, infanticides, abortionists, and magicians of love and sex. Their worst crimes were destructively aimed at their most fundamental social roles of wife and mother. Just as gnomic literature assumed women were faithless, and as Wulfstan railed against the whores and witches of eleventh-century England, so other theologians connected women with crime, magic, and sex. Burchard of Worms worried that women were prone to divination and incantation, employing benign magic to protect themselves, their men, their property, and their livelihoods. They directed evil magic at men and what men held dear, notably babies and other lovers.[106] "Save me," pleaded a prayer ascribed to St. Pátraic, "from the spells of women and smiths and druids!"[107]

Perhaps women did resort to spells to protect themselves from disorder and violence. Certainly, they committed all of men's crimes except armed battle. Gregory of Tours knew plenty of Merovingian harpies ready to assassinate their husbands, lovers, sons, and grandsons. Early medieval courts kept no records of inquest, but later medieval English coroners' rolls proved that women were perfectly capable of all kinds of violence.[108] Of course, most early medieval writers could not believe that women committed major brutalities, and the very real restrictions upon women's mobility and public life probably led females more readily into other subversive acts such as magic and other secret offenses. More often, laws aimed merely to keep miscreant women from breaking their marriages through violence or greed, or from murdering their babies. Laws forbade abortion and infanticide. Penitentialists, too, prohibited abortion. A ninth-century Iberian tract attributed to Vigila of Alveda condemned women who consumed abortifacient potions to penalties for homicide, one penalty for each abortion.[109] Burchard also associated practices destructive of orderly marriage with magic. He railed, for instance, against women who used sorcery to prevent their lovers from taking legitimate wives, casting spells to make the men impotent. Others, Burchard insisted, killed their husbands with magical tricks such as rolling naked in honey and wheat and then using the grain to make an enfeebling bread. They might even snuggle down

---

[106] Burchard, *Decreta*, Book 10.24 in *PL* 140: 836.

[107] Whitley Stokes, ed. and trans., *The Tripartite Life of St. Patrick and Other Documents Relating to the Saint* (London: Eyre & Spottiswoode, 1887), vol. 1, 50–51.

[108] R. F. Hunnisett, *Bedfordshire Court Rolls* (Bedfordshire Historical Record Society, 1961), cited in Amt, *Women's Lives*, 190–91.

[109] McNeill and Gamer, 304.

for the night in their husbands' arms, then rise and fly like wraiths from the bed through closed doors to kill people, feast on their flesh, and revive them with hearts of straw or wood.[110] Women's crimes may have been the result of their inherent evil, as misogynist theologians theorized. Their misdeeds may have been born of the world in which they lived, where no single act of violence could cause shock. The stresses of marriage and mothering may have driven them to crime. But surely some of their transgressions were sheer subversion. Not all medieval women wished to marry and to mother, or thought of themselves first as the partners of men and mothers of children. Women had other jobs. They had aims besides reproduction. Some women managed to run from marriage and motherhood to religious communities. Others chose to live as outcasts, harlots, and witches, inhabiting the borderlands of communities. There probably were women who prepared meals for the Fates, who used the turf from beneath a man's footprint in a spell to kill him, and who drove stakes through the hearts of unbaptized stillborns.[111] Someone had to learn these practices and pass them on, while ordinary women kept house and children.

We also find hints in the evidence that women used marriage and mothering for other specifically feminine ends. Groups of mothers, like co-workers, may have come together and shared consciousness in social or political solidarity, much as pre-revolutionary French mothers later gathered and rioted for bread. It is not enough, then, to understand that most women were mothers or that people believed women ought to mother, and respected them for it. The evidence of legal records that punished women for crimes against marriage and motherhood will never reveal why women committed such offenses. Too few women left us notes about their personal responses to the pressures of married life. No one recorded their objections to the notions of lawmakers and theologians regarding motherhood and its sacral qualities. Dhuoda was but one exception, and even she wrote in a code of theology and allusion that disguised her emotions.

Nonetheless, the sources show clearly that women had problems reconciling the necessities of marriage and mothering with their responsibilities as daughters and kinswomen, participants in the household economy, and creators of social order in the larger community.

---

[110] Ibid., 339–41.
[111] Burchard, *Decreta*, Book 19.5, in *PL* 140: 960–62; McNeill and Gamer, 339–40.

They were both helped and hampered by laws and customs, which protected and restricted them. Sometimes men allowed women into their families and communities; sometimes they excluded women on the very basis of their womanhood or motherhood. At other times, only certain groups of women, defined by blood relationship or marital status, were allowed to participate in larger social structures, such as inheritance and legal suits. When women ignored their limits and their assigned roles by refusing marriage and motherhood, or denying their kin, the risks were high. They were cast as criminals and monsters, deprived of children and property, bereft of all love, condemned to wander the wastes of an unwelcoming world.

5

THE TAKE-OFF: MOBILITY AND ECONOMIC OPPORTUNITY

Beginning at the end of the eighth century, native Europeans began to brave the edges of their continent, pressing across seas and deserts. By the ninth century they had reached Iceland. By the eleventh century, they were climbing into boats and sailing out to the Holy Land, down to Africa, and beyond. They raided and emigrated southward through Spain, and they infiltrated pagan territory in the Balkans. But the Scandinavians had already learned to sail the seas in their long, shallow boats with the flexible keels. Their landlocked neighbors had also been crossing the frontiers of local wildernesses for hundreds of years. Although the continent's population declined at the start of the Middle Ages, people never stopped moving, traveling, resettling. Armies, pilgrims, and poets all wandered the tracks and seaways as far as Rome or Jerusalem. Within Europe, whenever local conditions were favorable, people moved about: farmers cleared new fields, extended their pastures up the mountainsides, and took their surplus goods to trading centers at villages, manor houses, or monasteries. But genuine sustained economic growth and the mobility that accompanied it began only after the last external invasions of Vikings, Saracens, and Hungarians, bringing the familiar combination of population increase and movement, agricultural expansion, long-distance trade, and urbanization.

The geographic, demographic, and economic boom that began around the eleventh century must have proved shocking to the inward-looking cultures of the medieval West, even if it did not begin as suddenly as historical retrospect suggests. Such expansion in all

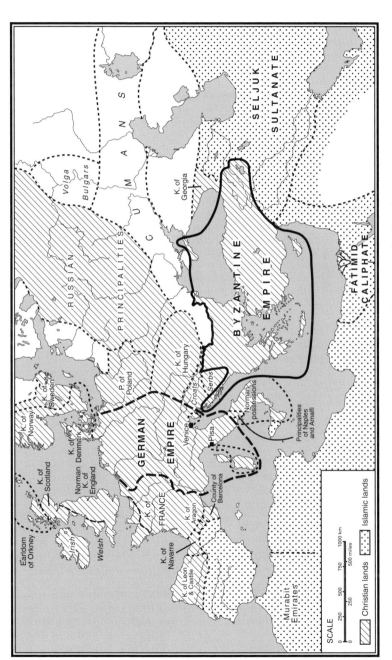

Map 2 Europe c. 1200, showing Iberian and other kingdoms

directions was what twentieth-century French historians, borrowing from economists, have called the "take-off."[1] But for historians of women, take-off should mean literal mobility, for mobility was the basic condition for economic opportunity. Women experienced economic change and achieved increased autonomy, rewards, or satisfaction only when they took off, bidding farewell to traditionally gendered labors and going to new sites of labor. As long as they remained within the households and farmyards of their ancestors (or their husbands), as long as their agricultural chores and craft work remained undervalued within economic systems, as long as they remained excluded from the mysteries of men's labor, women did not directly participate in any episodic or sustained economic growth. Most women spent most of their time at the customary tasks of childbearing and rearing, clothworking, and household and farmyard chores, all dictated by what remained, for them, a largely subsistence economy and rigid ideologies of gendered labor.

Three kinds of economic frontiers lured women to increased profits and new employment. One was the actual edge of Europe, especially the territories that were empty of people or inhabited by non-Christians. For medieval Christians, any territory not under the rule of the Trinity invited invasion and settlement. A second kind of frontier opened when Muslim invasions and Viking raids ended and the resident population began to grow, thanks to a steadily increasing agricultural surplus. Europe's underutilized wildernesses of wood and meadow, marshes, hillsides, and coastlines invited (re)settlement. The third frontier was urban. It lay in the deteriorated Roman cities, the episcopal settlements and monasteries, the trading *vici* and defensive *burghs*, and the palaces of old Europe. Jewish women found these frontiers as well as Christians, coming from the ancient world to the urban borders of the new Europe in increasing numbers after 1000.

All three of these frontiers formed a kind of meta-frontier for women, not a geographical line found on any map but a consequence of the same take-off: the frontier of women's economic opportunities. The real surprise for historians is that women were actually among the voyagers and colonizers and entrepreneurs, and that for a few generations some women gained new jobs, more vocational options, more profits, and relative prestige. Although women's jobs

---

[1] Duby, *The Early Growth of the European Economy*, 257–70.

and roles largely remained subject to age-old social restraints, and although ideologues and rulemakers thought about women in largely the same theoretical ways, the structural transformations taking place after the last invasions allowed some women to slip past the guardians of custom and ideology and to escape the traditional limits people placed on women's work. New settlements, militarized areas, colonies, and urban centers were volatile social and political sites where women seized their chances. Sometimes women went to new places only because, in the expanding medieval economy, old places and conventional tasks could not support them or win the husbands they desired. The villages that had contained them no longer provided for them. But on the most extreme frontiers – not the volcanic landscapes of Iceland, but the streets and close-set houses of evolving cities – women's possibilities remained diverse for longer than elsewhere in the heart of old rural Europe. Cities had only begun to be necessary when the early Middle Ages came to an end, but women were already taking advantage.

Although tracking their mobility allows us to understand changes in women's work during the early Middle Ages, however, it reveals no permanent advance. In fact, terms of advance, expansion, or progress are not very appropriate for the *longue durée* of women's pre-modern history. Some admirable accounts of women's past tout a teleology of female rights and status, including increasing or decreasing economic participation, but such histories too often ignore the experience of women in favor of diagnosing their agency or victimhood.[2] Frontiers, however defined, never remain frontiers for long. No matter how far Europeans journeyed from their native lands, and no matter how exotic the territories they mapped, seized, and settled, they always brought along the baggage of gendered culture. They successfully recreated their homelands and domesticated frontiers wherever they went. Even when women found freedom on the

[2] Judith Bennett, "Theoretical Issues: Confronting Continuity," *Journal of Women's History* 9 (1997), 73–94. For transformative history: Gerda Lerner, *The Creation of Patriarchy* (New York: Oxford University Press, 1986); eadem, *The Creation of Feminist Consciousness: From the Middle Ages to Eighteen-Seventy* (New York: Oxford University Press, 1993); Edith Ennen, *Frauen im Mittelalter* (Munich: Beck, 1984); David Herlihy, *Opera Muliebria: Women and Work in Medieval Europe* (New York: Temple University Press, 1990); Wemple, *Women in Frankish Society*. See also Barbara Hanawalt, "Women and the Household Economy in the Preindustrial Period: An Assessment of *Women, Work, and Family*," *Journal of Women's History* 11 (1999), 10–16.

boundaries of Christendom or escaped into the shadows of city lanes, they were ultimately halted by embedded laws and customs. Ancient social roles came to influence their occupation of new physical and social geographies as well as their jobs. Increased mobility and general economic expansion on either side of the millennium allowed a minority of women on the move to take up new jobs for a generation or two, but ultimately nothing could permanently alter the gendered division of labor, which remained a boundary more solid than any wall.

THE HOMELAND OF WOMEN'S WORK

To analyze women's work in the early medieval period means resorting to generalizations without much chronological or regional specificity or proof. Women stayed mostly at home to work. Their most important jobs were biological reproduction, cloth production, and house- and farmyard work. A lack of documentary evidence has led economic historians either to ignore women in the period or to depict women's labor as supportive to men in their onerous and premier task of producing enough food for everyone. All of the major interpreters of the medieval economy either exclude or reduce women's participation in the economy.[3] More woman-oriented studies of the period tend to focus on more dynamic topics than the economy, such as power, literacy, sanctity, or culture, where women's participation is both more exciting and more thoroughly documentable. The few good studies of medieval women's work concern the late medieval period in regions where the serial records are extensive, especially England.[4] We can certainly blame this historiographical hole on scanty evidence. But another cause is historians' need to detect change.[5] Women's work did not change in any meaningful way during the seven centuries of the early Middle Ages. Medieval

[3] Roberto Lopez, *The Commercial Revolution of the Middle Ages, 950–1350* (Englewood Cliffs, NJ: Prentice-Hall, 1971); Duby, *Early Growth of the European Economy*; Herlihy, *Opera Muliebria*; M. M. Postan and H. J. Habakkuk, gen. eds., *Cambridge Economic History of Europe* (Cambridge University Press, 1966–89), vols. 1–3.

[4] Judith Bennett, ed., *Sisters and Workers in the Middle Ages* (Chicago: University of Chicago Press, 1989); Hanawalt, *Women and Work in Preindustrial Europe*; Martha Howell, *Women, Production, and Patriarchy in Late Medieval Cities* (Chicago: University of Chicago Press, 1986).

[5] Bennett, "Theoretical Issues: Confronting Continuity," 73–74.

writers tended to ignore the unchanging and so do historians of the Middle Ages.

There were no frontiers of opportunity for women to cross, at least until they were released from the farmlands of early medieval Europe. Nowhere were women-as-a-group bound explicitly by law from leaving their farms. Nowhere were they utterly deprived of property or barred from economic transactions. Yet the distribution of land among families, a tendency toward patrilineality in most of Europe and, above all, a traditional division of labor presented formidable boundaries to mobility and economic opportunity. The image of Eve, half-naked and dolefully nursing her babe while Adam poked at the ground with his mattock or digging stick, adorned most of the illuminated Bibles in medieval Europe. Women did not necessarily spend the greatest amount of time on nurturing and training children, provisioning of the household and farmyard, or clothwork. Nor were these necessarily the most satisfying occupations for women. But medieval theorists saw women first as reproducers (rather than producers), and secondly as provisioners and clothworkers. Women learned this vocational lesson from childhood, both in practice and as received wisdom, and passed it on to the girls of their families and region who came after them.

Gender worked forcefully to regularize women's tasks before and after the millennium. This was true of women in Charlemagne's kingdom, with its densely populated royal estates and well-organized villages, as well as in the first Germanic settlements with their scatterings of farms and nucleated clusters of houses. It was the way of life in Anglo-Saxon and Irish lands, where settlements tended to be small and isolated, and in northern Italy and Iberia, where population centers might grow relatively large, and just about everywhere else in medieval Europe. Jewish women did as Christian and Muslim women; townswomen, peasants, nomads, and slaves all lived and labored in ways that were essentially the same.[6] Old worked much as young did. Noblewomen simply managed larger households than did poor women, though performing many similar labors. Although Æthelbehrt's laws of seventh-century Kent referred to "grinding-slaves" (the women who pounded grain in querns), women

---

[6] Gavin Hambly, "Becoming Visible: Medieval Islamic Women in History and Historiography," in *Women in the Medieval Islamic World: Power, Patronage, and Piety*, ed. Gavin Hambly (New York: St. Martin's Press, 1998), 22–23.

7 Adam and Eve at labor from the Moutiers-Grandval Bible, created in the mid-ninth century at Tours. Eve nurses her baby in a vine-draped bower while Adam works in the field

of all stations made bread for their families.[7] Wives and maids, children and nuns, all labored at the same jobs day after day, year after year, generation after generation, to keep house, keep family, keep prosperous, keep the community together.[8] Even when women's property rights within and outside of marriage changed in the years after 1000, especially with the new influence of canon law, their basic occupations remained the same.[9]

Most women needed no specialized training for labors within or outside of marriage, but only what other women knew and passed on to them as they grew. Peasant girls learned from their mothers and other kinswomen not only clothworking, but the care of chickens and other farmyard animals, milking, cooking, brewing, and other necessary labors. In the country, they went with mothers and older female relatives to the fields, learning to weed, harvest, and bind sheaves. Older women of their communities – mothers-in-law, aunties, neighbors – also taught the added tasks, which came with maturity, of producing a family and training daughters to join the workforce. A young woman from a poorer family might have to specialize in, and spend more time at, the lowest of these many occupations in the employ of another in order to earn money for a dowry. She might work for years before accumulating enough to be an attractive bride, perhaps laboring as a dairymaid or a shepherdess for a well-to-do neighbor. But her accumulated skills were capital for the marriage, too. Most women would eventually work as wives; fewer than ten per cent of women in medieval Europe never married.[10] A wife's jobs complemented those of her husband, who had trained with the men surrounding him to till and plant, harvest and herd, or to craft, trade, or kill for a living.

Gender divided the marital partners' workspaces. In the country, marriage partners only worked in the same space at similar or related tasks at specific periods of the year such as during harvest. One ninth-century German estate survey from Friemersheim described how a peasant family adjusted its gendered labors: "the woman must

[7] *WEHD* 1, 392.

[8] Judith M. Bennett, *Women in the Medieval English Countryside: Gender and Household in Brigstock Before the Plague* (Oxford University Press, 1987), 3–17; Herlihy, *Opera Muliebria,* 185–91.

[9] Verdon, "Les sources de l'histoire de la femme," 153–56.

[10] Barbara Hanawalt, "Introduction," in Hanawalt, *Women and Work,* vii–xviii; also the argument of Judith Bennett, *Women in the Medieval English Countryside.*

bind the sheaves, gather them, and pile them in fives . . . her husband returns two piles to the grange of the manor. The remainder she keeps herself."[11] Women might also help with the sowing in spring, carrying seed in baskets or gathered in a fold of their skirts and scattering it by hand in the furrows. They took on such tasks seasonally, when men needed extra hands, just as they took their produce – beer, bread, cloth, eggs – to market only when they had generated a surplus or when their household needs demanded, rather than as a vocation. Likewise, women could plough, reap, thatch, and build when the labor market demanded. But agricultural tasks were as gendered as other labors and even when women went to men's workspace, they did not, and were not supposed to, perform men's agricultural tasks. Gerald of Aurillac, according to Odo of Cluny, was so appalled when he observed a woman driving a plough that he ordered his servant to give her the money to hire a male laborer.[12] It is significant, too, that illustrations of labor in the fields from late Antiquity until the nineteenth century commonly depicted men reaping with scythes, but not women, who more commonly gathered sheaves.[13] The authorities were happier when women managed this perceived casual labor and extra jobs around their main work at home. Their co-workers were usually also women. Women met at wells to wash their clothes, ovens to bake their bread, and gathered with their spindles and children to chat and spin.

Women mostly worked at different tasks in different places from men. Some divorce laws placed husband and wife in utterly separate spheres of work, dividing a couple's equipment according to the appropriate labor of each partner. The tenth-century Welsh laws ascribed to King Hywel Dda assigned pigs to the husband and sheep to the wife because the man kept swine in the woods while she took the sheep (and the children) to the highlands in summer. Milking and cheesemaking equipment were hers since she controlled the dairy; drinking cups were his since he was master of public display. He got

---

[11] Günther Franz, *Geschichte des deutschen Bauernstandes vom frühen Mittelalter bis zum 19. Jh.*, Deutsche Agrargeschichte 4 (Stuttgart: Ulmer, 1970), no. 43, 110–11; see also Goetz, *Life in the Middle Ages*, 140–52.

[12] Odo of Cluny, *Vita Geraldi Auriliacensis*, PL 133: 655–56.

[13] Michael Roberts, "Sickles and Scythes: Women's Work and Men's Work at Harvest Time," *History Workshop* 7 (1979), 3–29, esp. 5. Roberts gathered 125 representative illustrations of harvesting, among which women appeared with scythes in only ten; of these, one was clearly allegorical, one in the Luttrell Psalter more decorative than accurate, and the rest from the period after 1400.

8 Men with scythes and a woman (Virgo?) gathering. From "August" in the Liège
Book of Hours. These tidy reapers and their symbolic female companion were the
closest most medieval artists came to creating images of women's work in the fields

the chickens while she took the flax, linseed, wool, butter, cheese,
and some flour. Only the bedclothes were more difficult to sort,
since other factors intruded upon the division of goods according to
the division of labor. Although she had probably woven and sewn the
linens, laundered them, given birth in them, and tended the sick who
lay upon them, post-divorce ownership depended upon who (else)
had slept upon and under them.[14] In Irish laws of roughly the eighth

[14] D. Jenkins, trans., *The Laws of Hywel Dda* (Liverpool University Press, 1954),
44–45.

century the produce of the couple's flocks was split between them, too, with the ex-wife always gaining some percentage of cows, sheep, and their products even when she had not contributed animals to the flock originally.[15] Much later in the Middle Ages, records of legal disputes refined but retained the gendered division of equipment and labor. For instance, women worked as brewers in England at least, where court records adjudicated cases of aletasters and alemakers, the latter being women and the former men.[16]

Men and women's labor differed by time as well as space. Men pursued a steady course, whether they were peasants or urban workers. They began jobs, acquired skills for those jobs, and continued to work at them until old age or death. Marriage and family could add to or detract from their profits, but did not change what they did. Just like the sword, the plough belonged to men and not because women were too weak to guide it. The stick or knife that clove the earth had been part of a male sexual metaphor since ancient Greece, bound up with theories of reproduction and notions of male prowess in sex, war, and the creation of civilization. In Anglo-Saxon England, sticks and swords were the subject of common lewd riddles recorded in expensive manuscripts, which identified them as male, while women in the jokes were housewives and bakers who grabbed, massaged, or received such protrusions. The riddles were an amusing reminder – or critique? – of the hierarchical division of labor.[17]

Similarly, in Jewish communities, learned tradition reminded teachers and students that clothwork demeaned and demasculinized males. According to the Book of Samuel, a cursed household contained "a male who handles the spindle, or a male slain by the sword, or a male lacking bread."[18] Clothwork, weakness in conflict, and lack of a woman to feed him were all inappropriately effeminate, even disastrous, for a male. Put another way, a man spinning was as bad as a dead or starving man. Everywhere in Europe and the Mediterranean world, skilled crafts other than clothwork were limited

---

[15] Binchy, *Corpus Iuris Hibernici*, 507–08.
[16] Judith Bennett, "The Village Ale-wife: Women and Brewing in Fourteenth-century England," in Hanawalt, *Women and Work in Preindustrial Europe*, 20–21.
[17] Kevin Corssley-Holland, ed. and trans., *The Exeter Riddle Book* (London: Folio Society, 1978), 45, 49, 67, 68, 77, 84.
[18] Sam. 3:29; Miriam Peskowitz, *Spinning Fantasies: Rabbis, Gender, and History* (Berkeley: University of California Press, 1997), 72.

to men from late Antiquity on. Metalworking, carpentry, boat-building, manuscript production were normally the gnosis of men. The technological innovations that allowed for agricultural expansion in the second half of the early Middle Ages belonged to men, too. Water mills increased the profits on large estates before 1000. A portion of such profits may have trickled down to the women of the lord's family. Mills saved female slaves from grinding labor. But the mill itself was built and managed by men. Mills were rare until the eleventh century when landowners began to invest more heavily in their construction. England, for instance, had some six thousand mills by 1086. Peasant women brought grain to be ground by the miller, but did not operate the machinery. Likewise, the application of iron to the plough – the introduction of coulter, share, and mouldboard – allowed men to penetrate more easily and deeply into the land, but did not change the schedule of thrice-yearly tillings or the amount of time women spent in the fields.[19] A wife or daughter might learn part, but not all, of the mysteries of ploughing, milling, or craftworking, but she could never be a full member of the masculine guild that passed on and regulated its secrets.

Unlike men, women changed jobs with periods of life. Unmarried women, who were never recognized agents in the economy, always worked at lower-status jobs whether at home or in others' workshops, farms, or houses. After marriage they found opportunities in new contexts of their own household economies, which they created together with their spouses. Queens had the important jobs of displaying their husbands' wealth and giving it away to warriors, other nobles, visitors, religious professionals, and the destitute. This duty derived, though, from their very common wifely duty of keeping track of the household supplies.[20] Most wives, besides keeping family and house, might also perform labors complementary to those of their husbands in order to add to family income: for instance, brewing, weaving, serving at another household, or taking in piecework. Only married women could enter into the larger markets beyond their farmyards or town doorsteps. Finally, in widowhood, some women had genuinely expanded opportunities to become economically independent; but even then their economic activities might be restricted by local custom, the pressures of remarriage, or law. In

[19] Duby, *Early Growth of the European Economy*, 186–92.
[20] Stafford, *Queens, Concubines, and Dowagers*, 99–114.

later medieval England, local laws allowed widows to keep almost everything of their husband's. Hence widows were in high demand as marriage partners. Of course, widows might choose whether or not to remarry. Their need to carry on the business of their lost husbands might, for example, push them to find a suitable partner in the same business. If they decided against a second husband, they had to hire men to do their husband's chores, such as ploughing or traveling to markets.[21]

What little statistical evidence remains for agrarian labor supports the traditional picture of women working in their homes at their weaving and childrearing, even after the end of the early Middle Ages. The best way to sense any variations in women's work in pre-industrial economies is to consult the serial records such as wills, contracts, notarial records, tax documents, legal records. However, few such documents exist for the period before 1000. Later medieval records, in combination with stories and poetry, yield a blurry picture of peasant women at work in their villages – not the most wretched wanderers nor necessarily the greatest ladies, but women attached to prosperous farmers and well enough off to eat, but not so well off as to afford much leisure. The historian Barbara Hanawalt has used these records to recreate the lives of rural working women in England in the fourteenth century, which may reflect backwards on women of earlier centuries. Records of accidental deaths in coroners' inquests of the manorial courts in Northamptonshire show where women worked and thus what women did during their work-days. Women's work was much less dangerous and prone to accidents than men's; only 22% of accidental deaths investigated by the courts were suffered by women. But the same records show where unfortunate women met their ends. Accidents in the house accounted for 21% of women's deaths in the records, while only 8% of men's accidents happened in their houses. When women went out, it was to familiar and nearby destinations, for the purpose of completing domestic chores like fetching water. Deaths by drowning in the public well took 5.9% of women, but just 1.6% of men; in the public pond where they did their washing, 10% of the women in the records drowned, but only 5% of the men. Men were more likely than women to die in fields, forests, mills, and construction sites. In other words, in death as well as in life women stayed near home. The fact that the number

---

[21] Hanawalt, "Introduction," x–xii.

of men's deaths rose during harvest seasons (July and August), while women's deaths did not, also places women more safely at home or, more likely, performing the less dangerous tasks of gathering sheaves or gleaning.[22]

The same records hint at an ordinary workday, for instance, indicating the periods when labor was most taxing. Women had few accidents at dawn compared with their men, who went off to the fields at cock's crow. Women got a slower start. But women had more accidents during their mornings, and noon brought many disasters for both sexes because workers were already tired, hungry, and careless. Afternoon was safer for both, possibly because they rested. Accidents increased in evening, though, and night was a real killer: 40% of all accidents occurred to women at night, compared with 34% of men's mishaps. Were they exhausted from their day's labors, or was it too dark for them to see their way? At any rate, women worked hardest in the morning, at noon, and at evening, when they fetched water, prepared meals, fed or milked animals, and brewed beer. Night deaths were not from work but from fires, collapsing houses, or because clumsy women fell into the hearth, into furniture, or out of windows. The lifecycle had no influence upon work-related accidents; by age two or three, the accidental death pattern of children matched that of adults of the same gender. In childhood, girls were learning to do what women had always done, were doing it close to home, and were doing it apart from men, but in domestic spaces shared with other women.

Is such evidence meaningful for women of five hundred years earlier? Probably. Despite the grand shifts in European population, agriculture, and technology of the tenth and later centuries, despite the new spaces and activities open to women, people continued to divide their tasks according to gender. The pervasive ideologies of medieval Europe, born of classical, Germanic, and Christian ideas about the inferiority of women, still dictated the pattern of everyday life. The high value placed by early medieval communities upon birthgivers in times of demographic contraction also helps explain why women were tied to the house and labors nearby. But men were also afraid of feminine competition.[23] When the European population finally

---

[22] Barbara Hanawalt, *The Ties That Bound: Peasant Families in Medieval England* (Oxford University Press, 1986), 141–55.
[23] Power, *Medieval Women*, 60.

began to expand in a multi-century cycle, and men and women moved to towns, men still became the burghers who organized and ran the town and regulated the economy. After the millennium, when people in towns took up new kinds of production for new markets, men actively discouraged women from entering their guilds or organizing their own guilds. They also debarred women from public positions where they might influence regulations upon their labor, or gain knowledge of men's labor.[24] Women maneuvered around economic restrictions, just as they navigated around limitations upon religious practice, but they could not avoid either the rules or their connotations of ideology.

THEORIES OF FEMALE LABOR

Theories of women's work are almost as informative as serial records of their production might be. Not surprisingly, the traditional culture of early medieval labor derived from existing gender ideologies, followed by the limitations of the agricultural-intensive economy of pre-modern Europe. That the same ideologies of women's labor prevailed in ancient Greece and throughout the massive empire of the Romans should give interpreters pause. Livy and Jerome also heaped encomia upon modest women who remained quietly at home spinning. Epitaphs and grave steles from across the Roman empire depicted clothworkers as feminine paradigms. Mythologists showed the goddesses, saints, and noble heroines spinning, weaving, and sewing.[25] Even in such widely divergent economic conditions as archaic Greece and the international, urbanized, Europe-encompassing empire, women bore children, kept house, and made cloth, or should have done, according to theorists.[26]

---

[24] Jo Ann McNamara, "City Air Makes Men Free and Women Bound," in *Text and Territory: Geographical Imagination in the European Middle Ages*, ed. S. Tomasch and S. Gilles (Philadelphia: University of Pennsylvania Press, 1998), 143–58.

[25] Livy, *History* (*Ab Urbe Condita*), 1.57; Jerome, *Instructions for Rearing a Virgin Christian Daughter*, 107; Plato, *Republic* 616 c, d; Ovid, *Metamorphoses*, 6; *Proto-Evangelium Jacobi* 10.1; all cited in Peskowitz, *Spinning Fantasies*, 199, nn.18–22.

[26] See, for example, the various texts collected in Mary R. Lefkowitz and Maureen B. Fant, ed., *Women's Life in Greece and Rome* (repr. Baltimore: Johns Hopkins University Press, 1992), 16–19 (epitaphs, 2nd century BCE to 4th century CE), 33 (Juvenal), 84 (Xenophon), 165 (Suetonius), 168 (Diogenes Laertius), 170 (5th century BCE epigram), 198–201 (Xenophon).

9 Marble *stele* showing a lady of Palmyra with her spinning, third century

Above all, according to the prescriptive sources of all these cultures, women were not to wander. A mobile woman was a woman who did not work, hence got into (sexual) trouble and ruined the household based on cooperative labor of husband and wife. Christian penitentialists decried women who wandered and those who worked on Sundays.[27] Churchmen meeting in Nantes in 660 reprimanded

---

[27] McNeill and Gamer, 272, 287.

"miserable women" who attended public political gatherings but "ought to be sitting among their girls of the cloth shop and ought to be talking about their wool processing and their textile labors and about women."[28] Even the poets agreed that women prone to destructive mobility should be occupied with the duty of clothmaking and working. One Anglo-Saxon aphorism announced that "Fæmne æt hyre bordan geriseð", "It befits a wife to sit at her embroidery."[29]

Meanwhile, the rabbis who wrote and read the Mishnah recalled Proverbs 31 to configure both gender and gendered labor. "Who can find a virtuous woman?" asked the biblical writer. Her virtue lay not so much in character as in domestic skills: seeking wool and flax and working them well and willingly; rising before dawn to cook for the family; farming when necessary; working late at night with her spindle and distaff to produce clothing, tapestries, linens, and girdles, and selling the surplus to neighbors to add to the family income. "These are the labors that the wife does for her husband," the rabbis of the Mishnah elaborated. "She grinds, and she bakes and she launders; she cooks, and she nurses her child; she tends the bedding and she works in wool."[30] Similarly, the women of Muslim communities in Iberia must have known what the Prophet had said about clothwork. "Sitting for an hour employed with the distaff is better for women than a year's worship; and for every piece of cloth woven of the thread spun by them, they shall receive the reward of a martyr."[31]

Charlemagne, master of the Christian West, agreed. When he considered in the early ninth century what women should do to earn their keep on his estates, he decided that they should be clothmakers. They should not be "blacksmiths, goldsmiths, silversmiths, shoemakers, turners, carpenters, sword makers, fishermen, boilers, soap makers." Men were the ones who "know how to make beer, cider, perry, or other kind of liquor good to drink, bakers to make pastry for our table, net makers who know how to make nets for hunting, fishing, and fowling, and other sorts of work – men too numerous to be designated."

---

[28] *PL* 132: 317; Herlihy, *Opera Muliebria*, 42–43.
[29] Louis J. Rodrigues, ed. and trans., *Anglo-Saxon Verse Charms, Maxims, and Heroic Legends* (Pinner: Anglo-Saxon, 1993), 112–13.
[30] Peskowitz, *Spinning Fantasies*, 95–96.
[31] *Ma qāma* 40 in BN 3929, f. 134r, cited in Shirley Guthrie, *Arab Social Life in the Middle Ages: An Illustrated Study* (London: Saqui Books, 1995), 155.

Such were men doing men's jobs of crafting, baking, brewing, and fishing. Men made "whatever is prepared or made with the hands – that is, bacon, smoked meat, sausage, partially salted meat, wine, vinegar, mulberry wine, cooked wine, garum, mustard, cheese, butter, malt, beer, mead, honey, wax, flour," all with "the greatest cleanliness."

Women on the king's estates needed all the materials for clothing their cohabitants, as Charlemagne ordered his steward, "For our women's work they are to give at the proper time, as has been ordered, the materials – that is, the linen, wool, woad, vermilion, madder, wool combs, teasers, soap, grease, vessels, and the other objects which are necessary." The emperor's admonitions against the work of women on Sundays revealed just what women did during the week: "card wool, break flax, launder in public or shear sheep."[32] Just as Charlemagne's men fed and protected the community, women covered its adults, children, and furniture with textiles they spun, wove, sewed, knitted, and embroidered.[33]

An Irish theorist of the ninth century actually linked cloth production and reproduction, the two most important (in churchmen's eyes) jobs of women, and sanctified the entire symbolic system of gendered labor by equating weaving mothers with the Virgin Mary. The author of *Cáin Adomnáin* (The Law of Adomnán), although promoting an older seventh-century law against harming women and other non-combatants, interpreted the earlier law in terms of preserving women and the fruits of their labors. In the introduction to the law itself, an angel ordered St. Adomnán:

> You shall establish a law in Ireland and Britain for the sake of the mother of each one, because a mother has borne each one, and for the sake of Mary mother of Jesus Christ, through whom all are. Mary besought her Son on behalf of Adomnán about this law ... for the sin is great when anyone slays the mother and the sister of Christ's mother and the mother of Christ, and her who carries the spindle and who clothes everyone.[34]

For this writer, every mother was as holy as the mother of Jesus just because she bore and clothed her offspring. Indeed, a woman could

---

[32] *Admonitio Generalis* of 789, lxxxii, trans. P. D. King in *Charlemagne: Translated Sources* (Kendal: P. D. King, 1987), 219.

[33] *De Villis*, in H. R. Loyn and John Percival, *The Reign of Charlemagne: Documents on Carolingian Government and Administration* (London: Arnold, 1975), 69–70.

[34] Meyer, *Cáin Adamnáin*, 22–25; Bitel, *Land of Women*, 103–110.

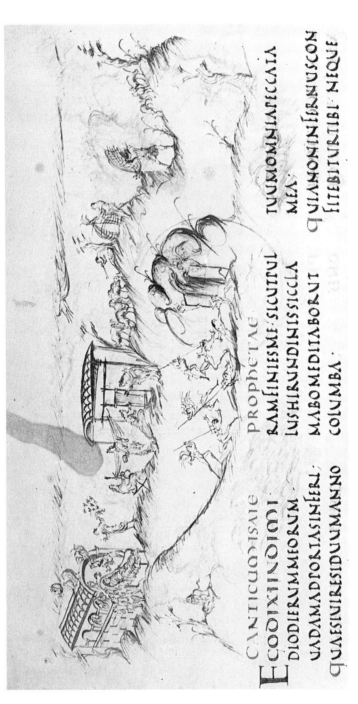

CANTICUOISAIE PROPHETAE
E GODIXINDIMI DIODIERUMMEORUM UADAMADPORTASINFERI QUAESIUIRESIDUUMANNO

RAMSINIESME SICUTUL IUSHIRUNDINISSICCLA MABOMEDITABORUT COLUMBA

TUUMOMNIAFECCAIA MEA QUIANONINFERNUSCON FITEBITURTIBI NEQUE

10 An illustration of Isaiah 38 from the ninth-century Utrecht Psalter. The Latin text, which begins *Ego dixi in dimidio dierum meorum ad portas inferi*, is brought to life with illustrations of specific images from the biblical text. The spinners and weaver, which illustrate verse 12 ("Like a weaver I have rolled up my life, and he has cut me off from the loom") are accompanied by shepherds, birdcatchers, and devils going about their own work

earn sainthood in Ireland for acting as another (male) saint's seamstress and cook.[35]

Women continued to win praise for their work with cloth after the great economic changes of the central Middle Ages. Men's great "take-off" had little effect on this area of women's economic experience. The romances of Marie de France and Chrétien de Troyes depicted ladies in terms of their ability to weave and embroider.[36] Bishops, such as Marbode of Rennes in 1100, lauded housewives who clothed their families as well as men of religion: "Who draws out the wool and the linen?" he asked. "Who turns the spindle? Who prepares the skein of yarn? Who does the weaving? These things accomplished for our benefit are so advantageous that, if they were lacking, the quality of our life would decline."[37] Even long after women had yielded their places as prime cloth producers for Europe, and after men had either "put out" or organized women's labor into new kinds of workshops or factories, or taken over their jobs as cloth producers, women's identity was still bound up with cloth production and the finishing and decorating of textiles. One of the fourteenth-century Wife of Bath's virtues was that she "had swich an haunt" for clothmaking that she surpassed the great producers of Ypres and Ghent, according to Chaucer.[38] In other words, long after the early medieval period a good housewife, with her innate talent and skills learned at her mother's knee, could still outperform an urban workshop run by men. And centuries after Europeans had acquired the new technology that helped shift the subsistence basis of their economy to one based on industry, trade, and the circulation of money, the symbolism of Adam and Eve at work remained the same: Adam was relegated to the poor man's stick, symbol of all Christians' spiritual poverty, while Eve, when not nursing, appeared with the simple equipment for women's other main job after reproduction.

---

[35] Whitley Stokes, ed. and trans., *Félire Óengusso Céli Dé* (London: Harrison & Sons, 1905), 42–43. The saint is supposedly fifth century while the text is probably no earlier than 900.

[36] Marie de France, *Le Fresne*, in *The Lais of Marie de France*, ed. and trans. Glyn S. Burgess and Keith Busby (Harmondsworth: Penguin, 1986), 61–67; Chrétien de Troyes, *The Knight with the Lion or Yvain (Le Chevalier au Lion)*, trans. William W. Kibler (New York: Garland, 1985), 360–61; see also Amelia E. Van Vleck, "Textiles as Testimony in Marie De France's *Philomena*," *Medievalia et Humanistica* n.s. 22 (1995), 31–60.

[37] *PL* 171: 1701; trans. Herlihy, *Opera Muliebria*, 76.

[38] Chaucer, *Canterbury Tales*, General Prologue, l. 447.

She carried the spindle, for the spinning of yarn which women wove or knitted into cloth. No matter what the variety of women's work by region, period, or point in the lifecycle, the spindle characterized women's labor as it had since Creation. In the minds of early medieval artists and writers, clothwork and childbearing flattened class, regional, religious, and chronological diversity to form from all women one, ideal, woolworking and flaxworking woman.

At the end of the early Middle Ages, ordinary wives and daughters still expected to make or embroider cloth. Even in the seventh century, women may have been producing cloth for markets and monasteries, but a major loss to women of later medieval centuries was the management of their own clothwork as men developed the textile industry. After they helped to form the weavers' guilds of medieval cities they were joined and eventually dominated by men in all aspects of cloth production. Female clothmakers reacted in diverse ways to recapture economic opportunity. Women formed their own guilds in some major towns but were later banned by guilds from all but ancillary participation in most of them.[39] Although women were active as weavers in Toulouse in the later thirteenth century, by 1335 a census in the same city could not detect a single woman engaged in the cloth industry. By the thirteenth century, the most common occupations for urban women in Paris were servant and peddler, although many also labored as dressmakers, silkworkers, and spinners.[40] In smaller towns, where cloth production was insignificant, women in the textile industries did not even count: in late fourteenth-century Exeter, for instance, women worked as servants, brewers, merchants, and prostitutes, but not as weavers, according to court records.[41]

---

[39] *Cambridge Economic History of Europe,* vol. 2, *Trade and Industry in the Middle Ages,* 622–24. For the governance of women's guilds in thirteenth-century Paris see Etienne Boileau, *Les Métiers et corporations de la ville de Paris, XIIIe siècle,* ed. R. de Lespinasse and F. Bonnardot (Paris: Imprimerie nationale, 1879).

[40] Herlihy, *Opera Muliebria,* 94–97, 146, 159. By 1427, when the Florentines conducted their great *catasto* or census of households in the city and its regions, most women with declared occupations were servants (103), with women in any kind of cloth business – from hosemaker to weaver – numbering about two-thirds as many (69). Women heads of households with occupations counted for only one-half of one per cent of the entire number of women running their own households.

[41] Maryanne Kowaleski, "Women's Work in a Market Town: Exeter in the Late Fourteenth Century," in Hanawalt, *Women and Work in Preindustrial Europe,* 143–64; also Bennett, "Village Ale-Wife," 20–36; Helena Graham, "A Woman's Work . . . :

Although cloth production left many women behind when it entered the urban economy, or involved women as workers on single, low-skilled and ill-paid aspects of the process rather than as crafters of the entire process, individual women and groups of women continued to work in the industry throughout the pre-modern period.[42] Although it made economic sense to men to occupy the gross production of cloth throughout Europe, women's skills at textiles and clothing were still recognized, utilized, and understood as essentially feminine. Every early medieval queen could produce fine needlework and some were justly famous for it. Edith, wife of Edward the Confessor, dressed him in her own handiwork and was an expert spinner.[43] Even when women were paid too little for their work, they won respect for what everyone perceived as their inherent talents, whether applied to the family's shirts or the fine embroidery of ladies' bonnets. Thus was essential femaleness associated with the artistry of cloth. Even in the twentieth century, in Danish weaving school every girl's first task was to weave her household linens and her own trousseau.[44]

Throughout the early Middle Ages, women's economic experience must have varied with that of men in their families and villages. When men were bound as semi-servile dependents, tilling and hoeing for their lords, this affected both women's jobs and their rewards; when men could opt for another, better lord, or to fight in an army instead, or to haul extra produce to sell at a regional monastery, their kinswomen shared in production and profits or, at least, shifted their own work to accommodate men's labors. When a man seized the opportunity to move to a Newtown or Villeneuve, or a German peasant decided to try his luck on the Slavic frontier, and brought

Labour and Gender in the Late Medieval Countryside," in *Women in Medieval English Society*, ed. P. J. P. Goldberg, (Stroud: Alan Sutton, 1997), 126–48.

[42] Jeffrey Hamburger, *The Visual and the Visionary: Art and Female Spirituality in Late Medieval Germany* (New York: Zone Books, 1998), 87 *et passim*; also Hamburger, *Nuns as Artists: The Visual Culture of a Medieval Convent* (Berkeley: University of California Press, 1997); Olwen Hufton, *The Prospect Before Her: A History of Women in Western Europe, 1500–1800* (New York: Norton, 1996), 96; W. H. Crawford, "Women in the Domestic Linen Industry," in *Women in Early Modern Ireland*, ed. Margaret MacCurtain and Mary O'Dowd (Edinburgh University Press, 1991), 236–54.

[43] Stafford, *Queens, Concubines, and Dowagers*, 107.

[44] Elizabeth W. Barber, *Women's Work: The First 20,000 Years: Women, Cloth, and Society in Early Times* (New York: Norton, 1994), 30–31.

his family along, the women clearly adjusted their workspaces and schedules. Different kinds of women had different jobs. There were rich and poor women in early medieval Europe, women who controlled property and those who were penniless, women living in rural isolation and women occupying palaces, women particularly adept at brewing or thatching or illuminating manuscripts, and women whose expertise lay in ruling vast territories. There were women who performed the same tasks, day after day, all their lives, just siting their labors in different households in at particular points in their lives, or shifting emphasis with the seasons. Yet, with the possible exception of women vowed to Christianity, all these women shared considerable similarities and continuities in their work. They expected and were expected to reproduce, if physically possible within acceptable sexual unions. All were expected to spin, weave, knit, sew, or embroider. To paraphrase one of the most influential Christian gender theorists, St. Paul: in the gendered ideology of early medieval labor there was not nearly as much division among Jew and Gentile, slave and free, as there was between male and female.

MOBILITY

Mobility was the key to the differentiation among labors for both women and men. Yet women always had less of it than men during the early Middle Ages. When men were highly mobile, as when Germanic raiders or Scandinavian Vikings boarded ship and attacked foreign lands, women rarely went with them, though they followed after. When men were barely mobile, as with the farming and herding peasants who comprised most of the early medieval population, women's travel, migration, voyaging, rambling, or itinerancy was practically nil. Partly, the mass movement of external invaders and immigrants between the fourth and tenth centuries had kept early medieval people of both sexes in isolated rural communities and prevented them from moving around or passing beyond Europe's established edges. Migrations at the end of the Roman empire abated just in time for Germanic settlers to build farms before Muslims erupted in *jihad* into Spain and along the Italian coasts. Saracens colonized the Mediterranean, building empires in northern Africa and Iberia. All that was golden in early medieval Iberia came with the Arab conquest and the willingness of the invaders to allow Christians and

Jews to cohabit the peninsula with themselves. This flourishing of art and architecture in a distinctive Hispano-Arabic style, of literature and sciences and politics, turned the Arab territories into the most sophisticated civilization of Europe before 1000. The Muslims and Jews of Iberia were no more enlightened than their Christian counterparts, however, about the roles and status of women. As in the rest of Europe, women took no official part in government, religious leadership, or the control and management of economic resources. As we have seen, powerful queens and mistresses of kings were characterized by Muslim chroniclers as sexually rapacious and disdainful of a political order created by God.[45]

Even as al-Andalus flourished, the Scandinavians began to get restless. Beginning in the late eighth century, Scandinavian pirates appeared off the coast of England. Vikings raided the monastery of Lindisfarne, off the northeast coast, in 793 and Iona, off the west of Scotland, in 795. "It is nearly 350 years that we and our fathers have inhabited this most lovely land," lamented Alcuin, an Englishman in Francia, "and never before has such a terror appeared in Britain as we have now suffered from a pagan race, nor was it thought possible that such an inroad from the sea could be made."[46] Alcuin may have misremembered his Anglo-Saxon history, but he had a realistic understanding of the threat of Scandinavian sea-raiders. By 800, Charlemagne was maneuvering to prevent attacks on the Frisian shores of his empire. The first emperor of the Franks managed to repel most of the early assaults but when his sons let his kingdom fall apart, the Vikings took advantage. They descended repeatedly and fiercely, storming up the rivers of France, as well as penetrating Britain and Ireland via estuaries. They began to winter abroad, building encampments that eventually became port towns and trading centers, and using them as bases for breaching the interior of Europe. Unlike earlier migrations of Germanic fighters and their families, which moved in almost geologic time across Europe, these Scandinavians came in small, rapid groups of men whose sole purpose was, at first, to raid. Women were not among these Vikings although contemporary chroniclers cast them as frequent targets of Viking murder, rape, and abduction. The

---

[45] Viguera, "On the Social Status of Andalus Women"; Mernissi, *Forgotten Queens*, 45–49.
[46] *WEHD* I, 193; P. H. Sawyer, *Kings and Vikings: Scandinavia and Europe, A.D. 700–1100* (London: Routledge, 1982), 78–79.

inmates of one English convent were reputed by Roger of Wendover
to have sliced their own noses off to prevent sexual assault by disgusted
raiders who then killed all the nuns.[47] But monasteries of men were
destroyed or sent into exile, too, and entire villages of women, men,
and children devastated by marauders.

But even the Vikings settled, sometimes in exchange for annual
tribute, sometimes for land, sometimes because they had simply carried off everything they could find in a region. As with the earlier Germanic migrations, the Vikings first came in male-dominated
warrior groups followed by the mixed-sex settlement of traders and
farmers. In Ireland, the northmen eventually became entangled in
the already bloody tribal politics of the island. Irishwomen married
Scandinavians and Vikings took Irish names. In England, the newcomers annually charged outrageous amounts of money for their
good behavior, demanding £10,000 by 991; but in the resulting peace
they also built the Danelaw, a colony with its own language, customs,
and rulers. In that same year, English warriors fought the famous battle of Maldon against Scandinavians, and poets celebrated it as native
men's Christian heroism and loyalty to their lord. But at the same time
as chroniclers were lamenting invasion and touting English nation-
hood, Danes were happily farming and trading from their strongholds
in the north of the island; they, too, began to live as natives of an
Anglo-Danish world, ranging back and forth between England and
other points around the Scandinavian seas and battling to drive off
new invaders. Eventually, under the prosperous rule of Knut (k. 1016)
and his Norman wife Emma (Æthelgifu), a Dane would govern all
England as a model Christian monarch. Like many other rulers of
England before him, Knut issued a lawcode based on the provisions
of earlier kings, meant to maintain traditional Christian order. He
chose his queen for her useful familial connections, the children she
would give him, and the unthreatening prestige she lent to his royal
image as ruler of an empire that stretched from the German border
to Wales. She chose him for the political status he lent her, which
she continued to wield via his son.

---

[47] Roger of Wendover, *Chronica sive Flores Historiarum*, ed. H. O. Coxe, 4 vols.
(London: English Historical Society, 1841–42), vol. 1, 300–02; Jane Schulenberg,
"Heroics of Virginity: Brides of Christ and Sacrificial Mutilation," in *Women in the
Middle Ages and Renaissance: Literary and Historical Perspectives*, ed. Mary Beth Rose
(Syracuse University Press 1986), 29–72; but see Foot, *Veiled Women I*, 71–84,
esp. 73.

11 Knut and Emma, from the *Liber Vitae*

Other invading men came from different directions to plague Europeans with violence before the year 1000. Saxons attacked Charlemagne's kingdoms from the north. Magyars came through Hungary in the middle of the tenth century, raiding and burning, and fully believing that they could not be defeated unless the heavens collapsed or the earth swallowed them.[48] Slavs pounded the eastern frontiers. And, despite Frankish victories in the south, the Muslim leaders of Iberia continued throughout the Middle Ages to consider their northern borders quite fluid. Even after the creation of a Pyreneean marchland manned by Christians, warfare between Muslims and the kingdoms of Navarre, León, and Aragon continued without any certainty of the eventual *reconquista*. Out at sea, pirates harried the coasts of Italy as long as Arabs and Turks ruled the Mediterranean, routinely raiding and razing the cities of Provence.

Of course, despite the threat of external invasions, small bands of European travelers had moved constantly within their neighborhoods, and even across and beyond the continent during the early Middle Ages. The literate among them brought home their knowledge of the hinterland to early medieval geographers, who used this information along with classical texts to define the peripheries of Europe by contrast with the core of Christian civilization. The maps that began to appear more regularly after the year 1000 always depicted a world focused on Jerusalem, surrounded by Europe, Africa, and Asia, and constrained by the mysterious waters of Ocean on all sides. It was theoretically possible to escape such a map by taking ship and sailing to the edge of the page.

However, throughout the very early Middle Ages, few men and no women had boarded their vessels in order simply to go. St. Brendan (or Brénainn, d. *c.* 580) and other fervent navigators with a tenuous grasp on the carnal life had risked the trip, but even saintly adventurers eventually hoped to land, at least in their popular legends.[49] What is more, as a holy old nun explained to St. Columbanus, such permanent exile was only for men.[50] Wanderers without a purpose, like women without work, were dangerous according to sponsors of legal codes. The laws of King Wihtræd of Kent (*c.* 695) declared that "if a traveler from afar or a foreigner leave the road, and he then neither shouts nor blows a horn, he is to be regarded as a thief to

---

[48] Adalbert, *Continuatio Regionis*, year 955, l.168, in *Quellen zur Geschichte der sächsischen Kaiserzeit*, ed. Albert Bauer and Reinhold Rau (Darmstadt: Wissenschaftliche Buchgesellschaft, 1971), 212–13.

[49] Carl Selmer, ed., *Navigatio Sancti Brendani Abbatis* (Notre Dame: University of Notre Dame Press, 1959).

[50] Jonas, *Vita Sancti Columbani* (Life of St. Columbanus), in *MGH SRG*, 156.

12 Psalter map, *c.* 1250. Jerusalem sits at the center of the world

be either killed or ransomed."[51] Legitimate itinerants sailed, rode, or walked from one place to another for specific reasons: to emigrate, to trade, to proselytize, to visit as pilgrims. They never stopped doing

[51] *Leges Anglo-Saxonum, 601–925*, ed. Karl August Eckhardt, Bibliotheca Rerum Historicarum, Corpus Iuris Europensis, no. 13 (Göttingen: Musterschmidt, 1974), 65.

these things during the long centuries of the early Middle Ages, but fewer people regularly traveled, and less often, between the ebbing of the Roman empire and the end of the first Christian millennium. It was simply too difficult, too dangerous. Even men rarely journeyed alone but preferred instead to move in bands or armies. Seventh-century Anglo-Saxon laws recognized the necessary aggression that inspired travel, good and evil. The laws identified all groups of armed vagrants as either bandits or armies depending upon how many men they contained.[52]

A small but coherent body of travel literature, mostly concerning trips to Rome and Jerusalem, circulated through pre-millennial Europe as a vademecum for the most dauntless souls.[53] Until the eve of the first crusade, noblemen and a few adventurous women sailed and trekked to the sites of Christ's birth and death. Indeed, the crusade was itself a pilgrimage of sorts. St. Boniface advised the abbesses of England to seek peace in Rome if they could not find it at home; but he also sternly wrote to the archbishop of Canterbury about the peril that matrons and veiled women met en route to the Holy City. He advised the archbishop to forbid English women's "frequent journeys back and forth to Rome. A great part of them perish and few keep their virtue."[54] Like St. Columban's abbess friend, Boniface apparently believed that female travel was a chancy business. The chroniclers' obits of kings and queens who died on treks to holy places are proof that Europe's pious elite journeyed when they absolutely needed to. Other devout Christians sought out saints' shrines, although perhaps not such distant ones as the tombs of Peter and Paul. Besides the road to Rome, the great transnational pilgrimage routes to European shrines such as Compostella or the slightly less famous Canterbury or St. Patrick's Purgatory were phenomena of the romanesque period.[55] More often, before 1000, people crossed only a kingdom or a region to reach a famous sanctuary.

Daughters of monarchs who married into another kingdom's nobility also covered great distances to reach their weddings. Some of

[52] *WEHD* 1, 400.

[53] John Wilkinson, trans., *Jerusalem Pilgrims Before the Crusades* (Warminster: Aris & Phillips, 1977); see also the numerous volumes of the Palestine Pilgrims' Text Society (London, 1896–97; repr. New York, 1971).

[54] M. Tangl, ed., *Die Briefe des heiligen Bonifatius und Lullus*, *MGH Epistolae I* (Berlin 1955), 27, 78; see also Hollis, *Anglo-Saxon Women and the Church*, 146–50.

[55] Seymour Phillips, "Medieval Background," in *Europeans on the Move: Studies on European Migration 1500–1800*, ed. Nicholas Canny (Oxford: Clarendon, 1994), 9–25, esp. 22.

their countrymen must have accompanied them. Beowulf, himself a great voyager, told the story of Hildeburh of the Scyldings who left to live in the house of a foreign king, as we have seen. When trouble and tragedy descended upon their uneasy households, women took ship and went home again or else fell victim to evil in-laws.[56] Some marital migrations worked, though. Bertha, a Merovingian princess of the seventh century, married the only English king taken seriously by the Frankish ruling houses, Æðelbehrt of Kent; Judith of western Francia also married an English king in the ninth century. Within England, Northumbrians wed Mercians, West Saxons wed East Saxons, East Anglians wed Northumbrians. When family and politics demanded, women mobilized. When families resisted women's marital or sexual choices, a few women eloped, judging by barbarian laws against this impermissible movement.

Despite suspicious lawmakers, drifters of all sorts – traders, crafts-people, musicians and poets, magicians, wandering preachers, eloping lovers, and any number of outlaws, criminals, and raiders – roamed the local wilderness between settled communities. These were mostly men, though. The Irish celebrated one or two footloose female poets and seers. There was Liadain, who supposedly trysted annually with a male colleague before rejecting her lover for a nun's robes and then dying for love of him.[57] But the tenth-century story implies more criticism of Liadain's early career than historical documentation of her life and death. On the other hand, a whole literary genre grew up in Ireland to celebrate men on the move, such as Fionn mac Cumhaill (Finn McCool) and his landless young followers. These were the *fian*-bands of mercenary warriors biding time until they could quit wandering and settle with women behind the fences of farmsteads. Women represented stability for such mobile men. Nonetheless, with the *fiana* moved other women, according to the tales: official wives, eloping lovers, camp-followers.[58] When armies moved constantly throughout Ireland and other territories in the seasons of war, women followed them, although usually not very far. Men went only to raid a neighboring kingdom's cattle pastures,

---

[56] *Beowulf*, ed. Alexander, xvi.

[57] Kuno Meyer, ed. and trans., *Liadain and Cuirithir: An Irish Love Story of the Ninth Century* (London: Nutt, 1902).

[58] Kuno Meyer, ed., *Fianaigecht: Being a Collection of Hitherto Inedited Irish Poems and Tales Relating to Finn and His Fiana* (Dublin: Hodges, 1910; repr. Dublin: School of Celtic Studies, 1993); Joseph F. Nagy, *Wisdom of the Outlaw: The Boyhood Deeds of Finn in Gaelic Narrative Tradition* (Berkeley: University of California Press, 1985).

knock down a fort, or support their leader in a bid for extra-regional rule. Early medieval European armies seldom crossed seas or mountain ranges to exert their aggression (the troops of extraordinary rulers like Charlemagne and Knut presenting rare examples).

In a sense, the raids of outsiders unsettled Europeans, jolting them into mobility. The historian Georges Duby has argued that Viking and Saracen raids did not affect agriculture much, since peasants were used to running off to hide when one lord attacked another on their property. But when the invaders came repeatedly by sea to harass dependent farmers, women and men fled their ancestors' farms for generations. Brittany and Yorkshire were hard hit this way. Elsewhere, families left lords who could not protect them for new masters elsewhere who imposed less onerous conditions of service.[59] But Europeans only had the resources and leisure to venture beyond their regional boundaries after the Scandinavians had turned to settlement, trade, and kingdom-making more often than raiding. The sustained economic expansion of the eleventh century inspired international trade. The Christians of northern Iberia began to invade and colonize the territories that had once sent raiders northward into their own kingdoms. The princes of Germany went on the offensive against Hungarians and other tribes from the east. All these population movements were part of a new phase of consistent, broad-based European mobility. This time, instead of outsiders sweeping through the old Roman heart of Europe from its borders to its center, those in the center began to test the known peripheries and even to pass over the edges of the map. Women journeyed in three directions: to the unsettled interiors of the continent and to its emerging urban centers; to its wild edges; and over the borders to non-Christian parts of the world. At this time of steadily increasing mobility for men, women gained not only a larger range of movement but better economic opportunities and the possibility of improved status, if briefly.

THE URBAN FRONTIERS OF WOMEN'S LABORS

With the economic take-off around the eleventh century, a small but growing number of both women and men began to leave farms and move into larger communities where they found new kinds of work. These towns were not the rudimentary villages built in

---

[59] Duby, *Early Growth of the European Economy,* 116–18.

lords' forests, but they were not the lost Roman cities of the very early Middle Ages, either. Some 3000 "towns" grew in medieval Germany, although 2800 had populations of less than a thousand. In England, only London contained more than 10,000 souls in the later Middle Ages. Paris was the only real city of France. Milan and Florence were the only Italian cities to top 100,000 in the fourteenth century.[60] No records reveal how many people lived in towns during the eleventh century, and how many newcomers were men and how many were women. Only late in the Middle Ages, after the plague, do the documents give good evidence about the rate of migration, but most records ignore both short-term migrants and women, who were more likely to be the short-termers anyway. Sparse documents, such as scattered depositions from ecclesiastical courts, suggest the percentage of women going to towns, their age, their origins, and their occupations. In the late medieval (1357–1507) region of York, for instance, most of the women mentioned in the documents had come to town as late adolescents, and most came from within a day's walk of town.[61] But whether this post-plague region, with its shifts in agriculture and pasturing and its high demand for skilled laborers, represented patterns common throughout Europe at an earlier period is doubtful.

Yet as soon as population centers began to grow, women everywhere found genuinely unprecedented opportunities for work in town. On the urban frontiers of old Europe, the astonishing, new concentration of people and markets created a demand for goods and services, thus freeing some women from traditional household and farmyard work to fill such demand. Women modified their traditional labors to fit different markets, strategizing around expectations that they should marry, bear children, and nourish and clothe them. Indeed, in some late medieval towns, such as Nuremberg, Basel, and Rostock, women were forced to do something other than marry and bear, since the sex ratios were somewhere in the 120s and marriageable men were scarce. This was the great phenomenon known to early twentieth-century historians as the *Frauenfrage*, the "woman-question." The question was, apparently, how women managed to survive so well in such great numbers, and what they did

[60] Fritz Rörig, *The Medieval Town* (Berkeley: University of California Press, 1967), 111–12.

[61] P. J. P. Goldberg, *Women, Work, and Life Cycle in a Medieval Economy: Women in York and Yorkshire, c. 1300–1520* (Oxford: Clarendon, 1992), 280–94.

without men.[62] The answer is that women tried to seize the chance, as men did, to profit by change at the start of a new Middle Ages and throughout subsequent urbanized centuries. They did so by adapting traditional skills, or by working in town for one period early in their lifecycles, or in rare cases by inventing innovative occupations in town. But their inability, ultimately, to break down the gendered division of labor eventually sent women back into the house, into familiar occupations, and under the management of men.

Wherever women moved to the urban frontiers of Europe, they escaped the restriction of the old, agrarian ties that had bound them in place. But then, so did men. The incentives granted by lords of towns to their inhabitants – such as the legal freedom from serfdom that came with living a year and a day in the city – applied to men and women both. The earliest German charters granting rights to citizens appeared in Bremen in 1186 and Stade in 1209. Such charters confirmed what had been happening for decades, allowing townspeople to avoid the customary dues of labor owed to their rulers. Women also benefitted by laws allowing them to inherit property in growing towns, as in Pamplona in Christian Iberia. The eastern German nobles began the same practice in the later eleventh century, when Bishop Burchard in Halberstadt granted the right of succession to merchants' daughters, and Duke Conrad of Zähringen announced that widows and their children must be able to inherit dead men's goods.[63] It was more important to the lords and leaders of towns that the community should prosper and that women should remain satisfied, permanent citizens than that women's property rights be restricted (another way, perhaps, of limiting women's movement). Women also shared with men the struggle for such freedoms waged against their feudal lords. The monk Guibert of Nogent described how eighty women were among the crowds that stormed their lord's palace in the town of Amiens in 1115. In such situations, gender did *not* transcend class: earlier in the rising at Laon in 1111, according to Guibert, a noblewoman had fallen into the hands of a female mob and "was seized, beaten with their fists, and stripped of the costly

[62] Ibid., 115; Karl Bücher, *Die Frauenfrage im Mittelalter* (revised edn., Tübingen: Laupp, 1910).
[63] Erika Uitz, *Women in the Medieval Town* (London: Barrie & Jenkins, 1990), 14–22.

clothes she was wearing; she was scarcely able to reach the abbey of Saint-Vincent clad in a nun's habit."[64]

Yet the documents of urbanizing Europe suggest more continuities than novel possibilities for women's work after the agrarian expansion of the tenth and eleventh centuries. Towns were not so severely separated from arable or wilderness as urban spaces are today. Even such a flourishing city as Paris was surrounded by thick woods. Vegetable gardens and henyards dotted the lots between houses. The boundary between town and country was fluid enough to permit peasants and their animals inside city walls, and to encourage easy movement from farm to town and back. As a result, city women could keep at their country chores within the gardens and adjacent fields of towns. Women could also come to town for short periods in their careers and return home to become farmwives again. No statistics exist to demonstrate whether women were, in fact, more mobile than men and whether women penetrated the urban frontier more easily and regularly than men. But it would not be surprising, given that women already expected to change work according to place and lifecycle, training in one place for maturity elsewhere. Above all, women were not traveling far enough to shed completely the customs that governed their work. Towns created concentrated populations with demands to be met, but were not wildernesses where all the laws and traditions of gender had to be recreated in order for the community to survive.

Kinship continued to guide a townswoman's labors. Although some women found new jobs, their tasks were mostly supportive to their guardians and masters rather than independent professions. A woman might be allowed to assist or even substitute for a man in a butcher's shop or a goldsmith's shop but would not likely to manage or master either business. Women also helped men pursue new trades and specialized crafts by preforming traditional services of cleaning, laundering, feeding, and childcare. Women still learned their vocations within the household from other women connected to them by kinship, real or surrogate. A girl might learn the tasks of the family shop from her sister married to a craftsman. Mistresses, as surrogate mothers, taught their female servants how to clean and

---

[64] Guibert of Nogent, *Memoirs*, in John F. Benton, ed. and trans., *Self and Society in Medieval France: The Memoirs of Abbot Guibert of Nogent* (repr. Toronto: University of Toronto Press, 1984), 179, 206.

launder, while orphan girls learned from matrons in hospitals how to be domestics. Midwives, who practiced a rare female-specific craft, took girl apprentices. A master goldsmith did not teach his skills to the women in his house, but his wife might tutor them in assisting and cleaning up after the master. Merchants rarely bestowed their literacy and numeracy upon their daughters, but merchants' wives taught girls how to bring goods to market or watch the trading to see which products were popular.

Living arrangements promoted the familial and familiar routine. Young women who went or were sent to town lived either with family members or their employer's family, but never alone. Until industrialization, the dominant model of economic organization in Europe was the household, just as it had been the model for early medieval farms and estates.[65] In town, as well as in the country, women were expected to work until they married and set up their own homes either in a town or, more likely, back home in their villages. When the rural economy had no place for young, unmarried women – when, for instance, families needed more resources than they could give a girl for her marriage – they went to the lord's house or else to town to find employment that matched their abilities, until they might gather resources for dowries to make them more attractive wives.

Some women were successful at using provincial skills in fresh settings, others less so. In return for the opportunity to go elsewhere and pursue better economic futures, rural women sometimes settled for bad terms of urban employment as servants, prostitutes, or even slaves.[66] Among the emerging merchant classes of northern Italy, traditional culture placed heavy restrictions on women's participation in the new economies, limiting them to refinements of traditional roles. Although records only made this clear after 1000, the later evidence may still suggest what working life was like for women

---

[65] Indeed, the domestic model proved the key to industrialization in Spain. See Marta Vicente, "Artisans and Work in a Barcelona Cotton Factory (1770–1816)," *International Review of Social History* 45 (2000), 1–23; eadem, "Images and Realities of Work: Women and Guilds in Early Modern Barcelona," in *Spanish Women in the Golden Age: Images and Realities*, ed. Alain Saint-Saëns and Magdalena Sánchez (Westport: Greenwood 1996), 127–39.

[66] Susan Mosher Stuard, "Ancillary Evidence for the Decline of Medieval Slavery," *Past and Present* 149 (1995), 3–28.

in an earlier period.[67] In the governing communes of the eleventh- and twelfth-century northern Italian towns women lacked even the indirect influence accorded them by noble privilege, but they could still take part in the new economy if they were property-owners, heirs, and donors.[68] Notarial documents recorded women pursuing litigation, making marriage agreements, and investing.[69] Similarly, in German towns, some women found new things to do within their roles as wives and daughters. They kept their family's businesses going when their merchant husbands left on buying trips, just as crusaders' wives managed their noblemen's estates. They checked local markets to see who was buying and selling what, relaying information back to the masters of their households. Documents from the early thirteenth century show that widows and daughters of bankers and traders took to the business themselves, once their husbands or fathers were out of the way.[70]

Women were conscious enough of economic opportunity to take advantage when changes in population, settlement patterns, and men's labor practices allowed them to. Over the long haul of the Middle Ages, women benefitted early in the process of expansion and urbanization, lost out when towns began to draw an abundance of male laborers, yet profited again when wars or major pandemics eliminated male competitors. Again, late medieval English evidence reveals patterns useful for looking back upon earlier centuries.[71] In the view of one historian, P. J. P. Goldberg, Englishwomen were able to make choices at certain points in the economic cycle of expansion and contraction inspired by population change. A housewife might brew and deliver beer, sell her extra wool, and keep house for a neighbor, all to make a living and all while raising her children. When male labor shortages occurred, women joined the public workforce in increasing numbers. Those in the small towns and cities of England made good,

---

[67] Most of the Italian serial documents were written after 1200 or even later; the Florentine *catasto* counted 60,000 households, but not until 1427–30. By then a good quarter of the population of the area lived in those cities which had never really disappeared through the long centuries of Goth and Lombard control.

[68] Herlihy, "Land, Family, and Women," 28–32.

[69] David Herlihy, "The Towns of Northern Italy," in *Medieval Women and the Sources of Medieval History*, ed. Joel T. Rosenthal (Athens: University of Georgia Press, 1990), 133–54.

[70] Uitz, *Women in the Medieval Town*, 14–22.

[71] Goldberg, *Women, Work, and Life Cycle in a Medieval Economy*, thesis outlined, 8–9.

since they helped create items such as beer or cloth, and services, such as laundering and housecleaning, were purchased with higher wages. But countrywomen lost opportunities when labor-intensive agriculture gave way to other pastoral pursuits, so that workers had to seek employment elsewhere – the towns, of course. When farmers no longer needed dairymaids or threshers as they once had, when the population was larger and spread across the fields, women adapted by going to town to make a living. After major outbreaks of bubonic plague in the mid- and late fourteenth century, women outnumbered men in several northern English towns such as Hull, York, and Carlisle. Now working women produced goods and services, but married later and had fewer babies, and the demographic decline continued until the economy could no longer sustain it. Yet the pattern reversed again in the 1400s, so that men used laws to preserve themselves from female competition. By the end of the fifteenth century, women were adding to the population again, whether they liked it or not. Only during that tumultuous hundred years were women in York and other English towns able to turn economic necessity into economic choice.

Women everywhere in the early Middle Ages profited by temporary shortages of men, however much they mourned men's absence. For women these changes translated into the relative freedom to choose work over marriage or remarriage, or skilled work over domestic service, only in the short periods when demographics made it possible. Critics of this paradigm of short-term economic autonomy for women point out the continuity in low wages for women compared to men, or the restriction of women to the lowest-skilled jobs within particular industries.[72] Nonetheless, given the enduring effects of the gendered division of labor in medieval Europe, any cyclical increase in mobility and expansion of opportunities for women, even if their options and wages never matched those of men, was historically significant.

Women did create some new occupations in the burgeoning economy of millennial Europe. Prostitution was not actually new, of course, but did not flourish where the population was too sparse to support the practice. Early medieval penitentials and laws reprimanded "harlots" and "adulteresses" but it was not until after

---

[72] Sandy Bardsley, "Women's Work Reconsidered: Gender and Wage Differentiation in Late Medieval England," *Past and Present* 165 (1999), 3–29; Bennett, "Confronting Continuity," 73–94.

1000 that towns began to regulate prostitution and either prose-cute, evict, or profit by women who sold sex for money.[73] At the other end of the medieval moral scale, religious women also found new jobs in or near the city. Hospitals and foundling homes appeared more frequently after the eleventh century, staffed by nuns and other vowed women. Alkmonton, Amour Dieu, Baldignano, Bar-sur-Aube, Carrow, Castle Donnington – foundations from across Europe – and many other foundations for women or for both sexes appeared after 1100 to house and care for lepers and other chronically ill.[74] Beginning in the eleventh century, beguines (urban women vowed to religion but living at home or in small groups in private houses) depended upon the property and skills of women to support themselves while following an independent Christian program of prayer and asceticism. They lived mostly in Belgium, Flanders, and northern Italy, and hence worked at what those regions were best known for, such as the cloth industry, or else as caregivers to the sick. Their history, however, belongs properly to the later Middle Ages and the resurgence of choices for professional religious women.

Around 1000, when women everywhere in Europe took a temporary leave from the traditionally rural site of their labors to participate in the new economies of the cities, Jewish women lived the exception. Jews were not normally country-dwellers, so Jewish women did not travel back and forth between town and farm according to economic cycle and lifecycle. Their frontiers kept them away from Christian parts of town, out of churches where Christians gathered and, ordinarily, out of the spaces where Christian leaders determined their fates. But the shift in population that inspired urbanization affected them too. Increasing ease of travel allowed for contact among Jewish groups in towns across Europe and beyond. As their communities within communities grew they adapted to economic changes taking place everywhere, and as a result the traditional boundaries of Jewish women's labor loosened.

The rabbis dealt with many ethical questions involving the participation of Jewish women in business. One case discussed by a student of Rashi (1040–1105) described a well-to-do woman who was part of the retinue of the local ruler. The Christian lady demanded her

---

[73] Leah Otis, *Prostitution in Medieval Society: The History of an Urban Institution in Languedoc* (Chicago: University of Chicago Press, 1985), esp. 1–24.

[74] *http://matrix.bc.edu* (Monasticon: keyword, "hospital.")

company on a journey that happened to take place on the fast before Purim, so the woman went to ask her rabbi whether she could
substitute another day for fasting instead. The rabbi answered simply
that she could not "separate [herself] from the group". Despite the
responsibilities of her position, she must observe custom with the rest
of the Jewish community.[75] Rabbi Gershom advised participants in
another case concerning a woman who deposited her valuables with
a neighbor woman from whom they were stolen. The loan and the
theft took place without the involvement – or even knowledge, apparently – of their husbands. A third case discussed by Rashi himself
involved two brothers in a business partnership who were joined by
boy and his mother, all four of whom split the profits three ways (the
mother and boy sharing a third).[76]

Ordinarily Jewish wives were responsible for domestic duties, as
the Torah and Talmud demanded, as well as contributing to family
businesses. However, some daughters of prosperous merchants were
mobile in a different way, traveling to distant towns for arranged
marriages. Brides from Italy married men from Germany, and even
came from beyond Europe to new homes in the West, their only
link to their new communities being their faith and the antipathy of
Christian neighbors.[77] Women also moved from house to house or
among towns when they divorced; unlike Christian custom, Jewish
law demanded that women who had good reason be allowed to
leave their husbands with their property intact. A few Jewish women
in England were mobile and wealthy (before Edward I expelled all
Jews in 1290.) They owned land and houses, conducted business in
partnership with male relatives, and even brought court proceedings
against both Jews and non-Jews. In the typically small communities of
medieval England, which had thirty or forty families at most, women
often had to fill in for, and assist, their men in business.[78] Yet only the
greatest exceptions among Jewish women were visible to Christian
record-keepers, typically as villainesses who crossed a frontier just
as hostile as the great divide between men's and women's labor: the

---

[75] Agus, *Urban Civilization in Pre-Crusade Europe*, vol. 2, 766.
[76] Ibid., vol. 2, 610–11; vol. 1, 298–306.
[77] Judith Baskin, "Strategic Alliances and the Human Factor: Migration and
Marriage in Two Jewish Societies," forthcoming.
[78] Barrie Dobson, "The Role of Jewish Women in Medieval England," in *Christianity
and Judaism*, ed. Diana Wood (Oxford: Blackwell, 1992), 145–68.

border between Christians and non-Christians.[79] For a Jewish woman to leave the relative security of her own community – even though Jewish communities in Christian towns were increasingly vulnerable to personal and mob violence during the crusades – was disastrous for most Jewish women, unless they crossed the religious and cultural boundaries permanently and converted to Christianity. But to do so meant they never returned to home, family, and the religion that made them, since Christian laws severely punished apostates.

All women in the Middle Ages made choices about religion, marriage, and work, thankfully most not so dramatic as conversion and the betrayal of family and community. Often enough men tried to influence or restrict those choices with laws, because of their convictions about women's nature or because of their own economic aims. Every wife and daughter had the choice of whether to work, how hard to work, and what to work at, even if the alternatives were dreary or deadening. After 1000, many chose to go to new places to work: Europe's edges, Europe's towns. Whether sitting and spinning in their huts at the field's edge, or helping to harvest newly cleared fields, or laboring in the markets of an economically revitalized Europe, women participated in the take-off. Adult women, women trained by women, were not only agents in the sense of making personal choices but were agents of the momentous economic changes taking place on the Continent during the middle centuries of the Middle Ages, as were men. But they were agents in distinctly gendered ways, with distinctly gender-specific results, whether they dwelt at the center of Europe or on its periphery.

THE EDGES OF EUROPE: ICELAND

In the minds of medieval writers, disorderly frontiers existed wherever Europeans sailed or trekked into (what they perceived as) undomesticated wilderness. Where no Christian churches or sturdy houses stood to tame the landscape, where no priests lived to preach Christian morals, where no Christian kings or soldiers kept the peace, nature alone governed the beasts and pagan peoples succumbed to the land and spirits. No civilized men had imposed biblical order upon the ancient forests of the European heartland, on the ocean

---

[79] For twelfth- and thirteenth-century examples, see Baskin, "Jewish Women in the Middle Ages," 108–09.

just off a long-settled coast, or beyond the traditional boundaries of the Continent and its Mediterranean motherland. But once men and women settled, transforming landscape into properly distributed property, and built their shelters, which became domestic spaces, they could replicate their homeland and begin civilization anew. Just as women moving to newly dense population centers within Europe might seize upon unusual chances for jobs and rewards, so women in colonial settlements could, during the period of organizing and building, take economic advantage of social relationships and political structures that were fluid and changeable as the weather. Women profited by relaxed rules and unkept customs to improve their status, influence, and wealth.

The Scandinavians were the first Europeans systematically to colonize uninhabited lands. They had infiltrated already settled territory during their earlier invasions. In England, Danes imported farmers for the Danelaw, while in northern France Duke Rollo of Normandy brought workers to the land burnt and cleared by his raiders.[80] Around the same time, in the tenth century, Scandinavians continued on to Iceland by way of sparsely populated northern Scotland and its islands, which they had also peopled, passing thence to Greenland and the shores of what would one day be a new world. Although women and men who arrived in Greenland and Newfoundland found indigenes whom they called *skraelings* ("wretches"), Iceland had supported only the odd Celtic hermit or two, long gone.[81] Hence, when their historians wrote the story of their arrival, several centuries after its fact, they created an ethnogenesis of the Icelanders that was unlike the origin story of any other group of medieval immigrants. Icelanders knew that they had not come to their island as barbarian invaders. They displaced no natives. They formed no kingdom, but became a colony of farmers, herders, and fishers. Their island's history was composed not to justify an invasion but as propaganda in reaction to the greater Scandinavian powers that were to dominate them politically and economically later in the Middle Ages. Most unusually, women participated more fully and freely in both the settling of Iceland and in its written history than in any other migration of peoples within medieval Europe.

[80] *Cambridge Economic History of Europe*, vol. 1: *The Agrarian Life of the Middle Ages* (Cambridge, 1966), 65.
[81] William W. Fitzhugh ed., *Vikings: The North Atlantic Saga* (Washington, DC: National Museum of Natural History, 2000), esp. 164–65, 213.

According to *Laxdaelasaga*, the great epic of Iceland's earliest years written about 1250, a woman was among the first farmers arriving in the tenth century. Called Unnr (or Auðr) the Deep-minded, daughter of Ketil Flatnose, she sailed from Scotland with all her surviving kinsfolk, followers, and wealth. She wandered the island's coasts for a while, leaving place names behind her wherever she touched the virgin land. Where she lunched became Daymealness, and where she lost her comb, Combness. Finally, she tossed the pillars of her high-seat (the chair that signified her status as head of household) into the water and watched them float ashore to a suitable settlement site, where she chose to build her home. According to the many historical sagas of Iceland, she was doing nothing extraordinary.[82] Other women and men came to the new world of Vikings when, like Unnr, they lost spouses or parents to violence and their homelands held no further prospects. Indeed, Unnr herself had fled the Orkneys, where she had previously settled, after her husband and son died and she felt unable to protect their property or to guard a young grandson and unmarried granddaughters. Unnr decided that her future lay over the seas in a new land without traditional enemies and legal restrictions to hamper her highly traditional obligation of protecting her dead husband's things. According to her story, Unnr considered, reasoned, and chose, never questioning whether the Icelandic frontier was available to her. The evidence may be relatively late and offered in the form of historical romance, but the generations of Icelanders on either side of its writing, who kept Unnr's tradition orally and then read of it in saga, believed that her participation was essential to the (re)creation of civilization. She was able to use the alliance of families, signified by her marriage and her grandchildren, to people and govern the island.

Some Scandinavianists have argued that in Iceland Europeans had a chance to experiment with social and political organizations unencumbered by the customs of the homeland; other scholars believe, however, that the Icelanders brought with them to the new land the customs of the old, including gender relations.[83] For instance, when

---

[82] A. Margaret Arent, trans., *Laxdaela Saga* (Seattle: University of Washington Press, 1964), iv–v, pp. 7–9; Jochens, *Women in Old Norse Society*, 62–63.

[83] Jesse Byock, *Medieval Iceland: Society, Sagas, and Power* (Berkeley: University of California Press, 1988), esp. 51–76; Margaret Clunies Ross, *Prolonged Echoes: Old Norse Myths in Medieval Northern Society* (Odense University Press, 1994); Fitzhugh, *Vikings*, 164–74.

they took ship, the newcomers adorned their prows with familiar carved beast-heads, jaws gaping, to frighten the sea-monsters that would capsize a boat and devour its sailors. When they approached Iceland, the voyagers removed the jawed beasts in order to accommodate the *landvaettir*, the spirits of the landscape that could choose to ease or prevent successful settlement. If they brought their aesthetics, beasts, and religious beliefs to Iceland, surely the settlers carried, too, their notions of women, women's jobs, and women's relations with men. Unnr may have settled in the normal (which is to say, men's) way, but her story was unusual among accounts of settlers because she lacked divine inspiration from a patron such as the god Thor in choosing and naming her territory. No *landvaettir* contacted her to help or hinder her settlement. Unnr was without any spiritual justification in her settling, unlike most of the men mentioned in the sagas of Iceland.[84]

All of the new Icelanders' notions regarding the nature of the landscape, the ways in which a settler could claim and define his or her territory, and the greater meaning of the landtaking (*landnám*) were gendered. These notions informed both settlement and later Icelanders' histories of it. The landtaking was a migration of between 10,000 and 20,000 men, women, and children from Norwegian territories to Iceland over the course of about sixty years (870–930).[85] It was unique among early medieval population movements because it occurred fairly rapidly but included both sexes and resulted in permanent settlement. But the *landnám* was also the process of coming to know the land, claiming it for one's family, and assuming ownership by defining and labeling parts of it. Although women's participation in the *landnám* was unusual among colonizations, nonetheless in Norse and Icelandic texts the whole business was typically a public male duty. Unnr acted in place of her lost husband and son when she settled her new farms, just as other women took on male characteristics in the sagas when performing men's projects. She acquired land, had her followers build farms and fence pastures, and provided an inheritance for her affines' descendants, her husband's offspring,

---

[84] Margaret Clunies Ross, "Land-Taking and Text-Making in Medieval Iceland," in Tomasch and Gilles, *Text and Territory*, 159–84; Gillian R. Overing and Marijane Osborn, *Landscape of Desire: Partial Stories of the Medieval Scandinavian World* (Minneapolis: University of Minnesota Press, 1994), 82–86.

[85] Byock, *Medieval Iceland*, 2–3.

rather than for her own blood-kin.[86] Icelandic laws of the twelfth century acknowledged the legal ability of ordinary women to do what Unnr had done, but also placed limits upon them: while a man could take as much territory as he and his men could carry lit torches across in a day, a woman could claim only as much as she might lead a two-year-old heifer around on a day in spring.[87] His was the flame that lit the landscape for all to see and take; hers was the cow that bound her to homestead and fields nearby.

What is more, once women settlers had taken up residence in their new houses, their jobs were much the same as those of women left behind in Norway. Indeed, they recreated Norway in Iceland. The basic social unit of Icelandic society was the *hjón*, the household with its marital couple, children, spare relatives, servants, and slaves. In its earliest form, the household economy split its labor in two: men went out and created or gathered resources from what the landscape offered while women processed the landscape's products. Although settlers initially farmed the land, they quickly found that they had to practice intensive manuring to make the soil yield grain. They turned instead to herding for survival, along with fishing and gathering. Icelanders ate meat and dairy products and fish, which women turned into food, accompanied by berries, seaweed, and the eggs of seabirds. Women's primary chores, besides producing and nurturing children, were milking and making cheeses, running the dairy at home or herding in the uplands in the summer, laundry and bathing services, generally managing the house, farmyard, and stores, and most important, cloth production. Clothes, the hangings to line their walls, packs, sails for the ships they navigated away from the island, and even one of Iceland's most important exports came from the small portable looms of women, at least until the eighteenth century. Women kept the new communities of Iceland from running out of food, clothing, and new generations of Icelanders.[88]

The women of Iceland, then, gained economic opportunities by sailing away to a new home. Early settlers claimed land with, or in

---

[86] Carol Clover, "Regardless of Sex: Men, Women, and Power in Early Northern Europe," *Speculum* 68 (1993), 363–87.

[87] Byock, *Medieval Iceland*, 55–56.

[88] Jochens, *Women in Old Norse Society*, 116–40; Nana Damsholt, "The Role of Icelandic Women in the Sagas in the Production of Homespun Cloth," *Scandinavian Journal of History* 9:2 (1984), 75–90.

place of, their men. Later they produced one of the island's most important trade goods. But their fundamental tasks within the Icelandic economy did not necessarily lend women authority or liberty from the social restrictions that followed them from Scandinavia. Women made the cloth, but did not always own it; their men shipped and distributed it in foreign lands. Although in the Icelandic sagas women were notoriously visible, even dominant, and scholars have made much of their freedom to move about the stories, the literature is still more suggestive of life than undeniable proof of its details. Female characters seem to be sexually unrestricted but their actions conveyed messages about morality to medieval readers. The inciters, warrior women, prophetesses, and adulteresses of the many sagas come of story, with as much historical reality as the monstrous queens of Gregory of Tours's history or the miracle-makers of saintly vitae.[89]

THE CHRISTIAN EDGES OF EUROPE

Scandinavians went to Iceland to stay, which demanded domestication of the land and its new settlements, which required women. When Europeans went to the other edges of Christendom, they did so with more ephemeral aims, more violence, and fewer women. The first generations of Icelanders were the exception, while colonists of eastern Europe, Iberia, and the Holy Land followed the traditional pattern of including women only after conquest ended and domestication began. Beginning in the early Middle Ages and continuing for centuries, adventurer aristocracies charged out of the old Frankish empire eastward, beyond the Elbe and the marks (counties) on its Slavic borders; northeast to Europe's Celtic fringes in Scotland, Wales, and the most remote island of Ireland; southwest over the borders of Iberia; and southeast into other Muslim territories, or what Christians called the Holy Land. On the Saracen and pagan frontiers, where Europeans encountered inhabitants in the lands they coveted, the process of (re)taking the land and its consequences were different for women than in the fresh territory of Iceland, although conquerors and crusaders brought as much gendered baggage with them as the Icelanders. Fewer European women accompanied men to the Holy Land than were left behind to cope with their demasculinized homes

---

[89] Jochens, *Women in Old Norse Society*, esp. 161–70; Clover, "Maiden Warriors and Other Sons."

and communities. On the shifting frontiers of Christian–Muslim
conflict in Iberia, women actively colonized with their men, thus
gaining some considerable legal and economic advances, although
making little headway in changing men's minds about their nature
and capabilities. Where men aimed at conquest, women took little
part and gained little; where they colonized, women participated and
gained economic choices.

Only the first crusade took place during the early Middle Ages.
Even this statement is debatable depending on the parameters of the
early medieval period and the question of whether such a thing as a
crusade could be part of it. In some sense, the very definition of the
early Middle Ages incorporated the inward-looking tendency that
gave way to such enterprises as crusading. Certainly, the first crusade
was an innovative, large-scale, international, aggressively colonialist
organization of people and resources unlike any other since Rome's
empire or, at least, since its reinvention during Charlemagne's reign.
On the other hand, ideas motivating the first crusade – religious
reform, penitence, conquest, and conversion – were nothing new to
medieval Europeans. Like all wars, the first and subsequent crusades
were for men. When Pope Urban II preached the first crusade east in
1095, both men and women responded, but the pope had been talking
to knights. Robert of Rheims reported that Urban tried to dissuade
women from going along unless they had the specific permission of
their guardians.[90] One vowed to take up the cross in a written charter
of the late eleventh century, but the bishop of Toulouse told her that
"it would be better for her to build a house in honor of God so
that the poor of Christ might be received," so she endowed a local
monastery instead.[91] Nonetheless, couples such as Robert Guiscard
and his wife, and Baudouin of Boulogne and his, together took the
pledge to make a pilgrimage to the heart of Christendom.[92]

Women of other kinds and lower classes felt the urge to contribute
to the recovery of Jerusalem, or to take part in the adventure of

[90] Robertus Monachus, "Historia Iherosolimitana," *Recueil des Historiens des Croisades, Historiens Occidentaux*, iv, 281, 288, 317; cited in James A. Brundage, "Prostitution, Miscegenation and Sexual Purity in the First Crusade," in *Crusade and Settlement: Papers Read at the First Conference of the Society for the Study of the Crusades and the Latin East*, ed. Peter Edbury (Cardiff: University College of Cardiff Press, 1985), 57–66, n. 10.

[91] Giles Constable, "Medieval Charters as a Source for the History of the Crusades," in Edbury, *Crusade and Settlement*, 77 and n. 41.

[92] Régine Pernoud, *La Femme au temps des Croisades* (Paris, 1990), 17–19.

the journey. Several chroniclers noted wives, daughters, nuns, and prostitutes among the ranks. In fact, Anna Comnena, daughter of the Byzantine emperor, observed around the year 1140 camps full of both male and female barbarians – by which she meant Europeans – crowding the riverbank of her city. Likewise a Westerner, Fulcher of Chartres, sounded a common theme of temptation when he described how the first crusading army of 1096 brought along women (but whether European or local he does not specify) and then ejected them from their ranks "lest perhaps, defiled by the sordidness of riotous living, [crusaders] should displease the Lord". According to Fulcher, invaders of both sexes expired in the desert on their way.[93] Fulcher and others attributed crusader defeats to the simple fact of fornication. In order to triumph, the fighters had to be free of pollution spread by women.[94]

While men fought, women followed with supplies, nursing skills, and sexual services. Female adventurers to the Holy Land and other sites of European expansion did not ordinarily engage in actual conquest, which was none of their business. A few reports of women with weapons survived from the later crusades. But for women to engage in crusading battles was unthinkable except in emergency, disaster, or fantasy. Still, tales of Amazon princesses, which had tickled the imaginations of western writers from Antiquity throughout the early Middle Ages, moved to the Holy Land with Christian invaders. The alluring Other of oriental women was born in the crusades; the first stereotype was not the willing odalisque so prominent in later centuries, but a fighter.[95] Saracen chroniclers of the third crusade noticed

---

[93] Fulcher of Chartres, *Historia Iherosolymitana: Gesta Francorum Iherusalem Peregrinantium ab anno Domini MXCV usque ad annum MCXXVII, Recueil des Historiens des Croisades* (Paris, 1886), i.xv–xvi; trans. Frances Rita Ryan in *A History of the Expedition to Jerusalem, 1095–1127*, ed. Harold A. Fink (Knoxville: University of Tennessee Press, 1969).

[94] Brundage, "Prostitution, Miscegenation," 58.

[95] Jacqueline de Weever, *Sheba's Daughters: Whitening and Demonizing the Saracen Woman in Medieval French Epic* (New York: Garland, 1998). In 1180, Jacques de Vitry wrote of women-warriors among the Alans who were "much dreaded by the Saracens, and have often by their inroads done great damage to the Persians, Medes, and Assyrians, on whose borders they dwell, being entirely surrounded by infidel nations . . . Their noblewomen, like the Amazons, bear arms in battle like knights." Jacques de Vitry, *Historia Iherosolymitana*, trans. Aubrey Stewart as *The History of Jerusalem A.D. 1180 by Jacques de Vitry* (London, 1896, repr. New York:

European women participating in the bloodshed. However, the Arabs were propagandizing about the barbarity of the westerners and the immorality of the Christian cause. What better way to describe western degeneracy than to point out women amongst the warriors?[96] Arab writers had their own traditions of female fighters who armed themselves and went to battle with or against men, which may or may not have filtered down to European writers.[97]

Yet when western women tried to accompany men in the ranks and to fight, the result was "upheaval," according to Anna Comnena, looking back on previous invasions by western Europeans. Led by Peter the Hermit, a mass of men, women, and children descended upon Christian Nicaea and massacred its inhabitants, impaling and dissecting babies and torturing the aged. Later, the disorderly crusaders were ambushed by Turks and the "mass of [their] bones" was "a mountain of considerable height and depth and width."[98] Anna Comnena was a Christian Easterner educated in the same classical gender differences that influenced Westerners. In her eyes, the presence of women in the troops could only doom a military mission. A similar sentiment prevailed in Fulcher's account of the initial storming of Jerusalem in 1099, although instead of Christian fatalities, he described the Muslim victims of crusading wrath. At the end of a day of bloodshed, after the Europeans had captured the town and its Sepulchre, the holiest spot in Christendom, nearly 10,000 Saracens were beheaded at the Dome of the Rock. "If you had been there your feet would have been stained to the ankles in the blood of the slain. What shall I say?" demanded Fulcher. "None of them were left alive. Neither women nor children were spared."[99] Women

---

AMS Press, 1971), 3:83–84 (ch. 49). Cited in Vincent DiMarco, "The Amazons and the End of the World," in *Discovering New Worlds: Essays on Medieval Exploration and Imagination*, ed. Scott D. Westrem, ed. (New York: Garland, 1991), 77.

[96] Helen Nicholson, "Women on the Third Crusade," *Journal of Medieval History* 23 (1997), 335–49; see also Sharon Bryant Neal, "Las Donas e las feminas, las tozas avinens: Women in *La Cansi de la Crozada*," *Tenso: Bulletin of the Société Guilhelm IX* 10 (1995), 110–38.

[97] Remke Kruk, "The Bold and the Beautiful: Women and 'Fitna' in the 'Sīrat Dhāt al-Himma': The Story of Nūrā," in Hambly, *Women in the Medieval Islamic World*, 99–116.

[98] Anna Comnena, *The Alexiad of Anna Comnena*, trans. and ed. F. R. A. Sewter (Harmondsworth: Penguin, 1969), 11–312.

[99] Fulcher of Chartres, *Gesta*, I.xxvii.

belonged neither on the victorious nor losing sides in this battle. If they dared be present, they could not escape the horrors that befell them.

Hence, while small numbers of women went on crusade, or accompanied the crusaders, or followed the crusaders who came to Jerusalem and other eastern cities, and even joined soldiers in new homes in captured territory, most crusaders were men. Some Franks took up farming in rural areas and married converted Muslim women, to the dismay of Fulcher and other writers. A total of about a quarter-million Westerners settled in the occupied territories of the Middle East, mostly in urban areas.[100] The Christian lords of conquered territory attempted in the twelfth century to create plantations on estates outside Jerusalem and the other major cities. Archeological evidence indicates where these eighty or more towns existed, what kinds of houses and churches were built, and even when the towns were destroyed.[101] But the rubbish of the past cannot tell whether the immigrant farmers lived with women from Europe, local Christians, or women of other religions. Certainly, no European women who went east on the first crusade intended to settle, and few men aimed to bring their wives, mothers, sisters, or daughters to live forever in the East. They planned instead to return to Europe. They did not need women to help domesticate the territory they conquered because they desired only to reach and take Jerusalem and cast themselves before the Sepulchre in utter penitence.[102] Once they had arrived in the East, they did not find a landscape of Christian ruins manned by infidel warriors, as they had imagined, but plenty of native Muslim, Jewish, and even Christian women and men to be conquered and ruled. Although Palestine became a place to build kingdoms and gain estates and income – and where a few women inherited kingdoms – it was not initially a place where most civilized knights would wish to live permanently.

Both Christian and Arab chroniclers accused the other side of lusting after its own women, and enemy women of being promiscuous. However, instances of actual sexual boundary-crossing were reported less often than prohibitions against it. Christian visionaries accused crusaders of losing battles because of their contact with

<hr>

[100] Phillips, "The Medieval Background," 18–19.
[101] Denys Pringle, "Magna Mahumeria (al-Bīra): The Archeology of a Frankish New Town in Palestine," in Edbury, *Crusade and Settlement*, 147–168.
[102] Constable, "Medieval Charters," 74–75.

Muslim women (as well as with Christian women). Arabs storytellers depicted Frankish slaves as cunning and fickle when it came to serving their Muslim masters or even granting their sexual favors.[103] Crusaders were even more disapproving of extramarital sexual contact unless it was rape, which was routine treatment of captured women on both sides. According to the Council of Nablus in 1120, some decades after the first crusade, a Christian woman who willingly had intercourse with a Muslim man suffered severe penalties, but if she were raped she escaped punishment. Nablus also legislated, however, against Christian settlers who raped Muslim women in their own households or the houses of others.[104]

The crusaders' own women stayed at home by choice or by order of their men during the wars of invasion. Stephen of Blois charged off on the first crusade, leaving his wife Adèle behind to receive a letter from him describing his ill-fated adventures on behalf of God. Adèle apparently approved of his crusading since she had funded his trip. According to the medieval historian Orderic Vitalis, when Stephen fled the hopeless situation in Antioch and returned to Adèle, she helped persuade her fifty-plus-year-old husband with caresses and stern words to return to the Holy Land, where he met his end.[105] Orderic also pointed out that Adèle "honorably governed" the count's holdings while he was absent.[106] Other women were less sanguine about men going while they stayed behind. French poetry from the period never sang of women urging crusade, but represented only the longing and grief of women bereft of courageous men. "She wept beside the spring and gave a heartfelt sigh," wrote Macabru (1147), whose lovelorn character sang:

Jesus, king of the world, my great sorrow grows because of you, for the shame perpetrated against you causes me great grief: the best men in all this world are going off to serve you, but this is what pleases you. It is with you that my lover is going away, the handsome, the noble, the worthy, and the powerful; all that

---

[103] Yvonne Friedman, "Women in Captivity and Their Ransom During the Crusader Period," in *Cross Cultural Convergences in the Crusader Period*, ed. Michael Goodich *et al.* (New York:Lang, 1995), 85–87.

[104] Council of Nablus (c. 13–15), in Mansi xxi, 264.

[105] Ordericus Vitalis, *Historia ecclesiastica*, ed. and trans. Marjorie Chibnall, 2 vols. (Oxford: Clarendon, 1968–80), 10.19.

[106] Ibid., 11.5; Kimberly A. LoPrete, "Adela of Blois: Familial Alliances and Female Lordship," in *Aristocratic Women in Medieval France*, ed. Theodore Evergates (Philadelphia: University of Pennsylvania Press, 1999), 7–43, esp. 20.

is left to me here is my sorry plight, my frequent longings, and my tears. Oh! Cruel was King Louis who issued the summonses and edicts through which sorrow entered my heart![107]

The trials of wives such as Adèle of Blois were made worse by being left in charge of property and children. Without the public authority that came from being a man in a warrior society, some women were apparently helpless to protect even themselves, let alone estates or babies. One premier historian of the crusades, Jonathan Riley-Smith, listed with horror the consequences for several women – or at least, for women's men:

> The experiences of kin, particularly women, left behind for several years to manage estates and bring up families, surrounded by rapacious neighbours and litigious relations, could be horrific, and judicial records reveal a depressing inventory of the injuries of every sort to which they were exposed. William Trussel's wife was murdered six weeks after he had left on crusade in 1190 and her body was thrown into a marl pit. Peter Duffield's wife was strangled while he was on the Fifth Crusade, and Ralph Hoddeng came home to find his daughter and heiress married to one of his peasants.[108]

Wives murdered and daughters married to peasants were terrible crimes, indeed, perpetrated against a lord of the land (although the daughter in question may not have thought so.) Urban II promised to protect the crusaders' women and property while they were away, but noblemen responded by making legal provisions for guardians of their estates and their women while they were at war, whether killing Saracens and storming Acre or fighting fellow Europeans.

Yet whenever men left home, their castles and houses became the domain of women, a kind of temporary frontier where gender rules flexed. Some women seemed to have managed quite well and even taken advantage of such situations.[109] Adèle was, after all, the daughter of the king of England (William the Conqueror), immensely wealthy in her own right, and had been sharing comital duties with her much older husband since their marriage began. The ability of noble

[107] Macabru, "A la fontana del vergier," ll. 8–28; http://www.cam.org/~malcova/troubadours/marcabru/mcbr1.html; also cited by Michael Routledge, "Songs," in *The Oxford Illustrated History of the Crusades*, ed. Jonathan Riley-Smith (Oxford University Press, 1995), 103.

[108] Jonathan Riley-Smith, "The State of Mind of Crusaders in the East, 1095–1300," ibid., 72.

[109] Paulette L'Hermite-Leclercq, "The Feudal Order," in *Silences of the Middle Ages: A History of Women*, ed. Christiane Klapisch-Züber (Cambridge, MA: Balknap Press, 1992), 346–47.

women to run households and estates, and the willingness of men to rely upon them, should come as no surprise since everyone in medieval Europe expected women to be mistresses and managers of their homes and goods. Women of the highest nobility trained as rulers to succeed their husbands as regents while their children were still small. Lawmakers had routinely granted women the power to manage estates and engage in business for the sake of their men, so long as men gave assent. Peasant women in prosperous households stored the harvest, oversaw the flocks, grew vegetables, and governed the house while helping out with work in the farmyard. Just as Unnr took land in Iceland because she had no husband to do so for her, so Adèle and other crusaders' women were ready to rule bits of Europe in the absence of men who normally assumed or at least shared control.

The politics of women filling in for kings and noblemen occurred in an oddly gendered milieu where class and training allowed women to transcend some traditional restrictions. The documentary sources often assumed women's responsibilities without recording much about how women felt when they took on the roles of regents and managers. The nature of medieval marriages, arranged as contractual partnerships for women of consequence, may have helped practical women to carry on without being devastated by the absence of mates. Yet aristocratic marriages could inspire affection, and women must have missed their men even if they did not indulge in the excesses of troubador grief. Although one romantic sculptural example comes slightly after the early Middle Ages, it exemplifies the supporting role of women left behind in any war: a wooden statue from northern France still shows an aged Hugo I of Vaudémont clasped in the bolstering embrace of his wife, Anna. Hugo had left in 1147 to crusade in the East and returned between 1161 and 1163 to die, poor but comforted by his marital partner, in the shabby robes of a pilgrim knight. The statue, as art historians explain, reveals the reciprocity of marriage emerging in church literature of the twelfth century. But it also suggests that women with resources knew how to maintain their places in patriarchal society and muster their feminine strength for gain while their mates were far away.[110] Someone, after all, commissioned and paid for that ennobling portrait of the lady of Vaudémont, which stood as a lesson to all wives left at home by men.

---

[110] Ibid.

13 Hugo and Anna of Vaudémont (?) or "The return from the crusades," from the cloister of Belval, *c.* 1150

METHODS OF COLONIZATION

On eastern and other frontiers, temporary gender imbalances cast women into three categories: those who came along, those already there awaiting the disruption and intrusion of men, and those left behind to assume the duties and temporarily acquire the rights of men. Women in any of these situations were not necessarily choiceless or victimized, although they could be; but women did not initiate or invite invasions. Nearer than Jerusalem, for instance in Sicily, Normandy, Iberia, eastern Germany, Poland, and Ireland, the situation for women varied by culture, religion, and politics. On the eastern edge of Europe, lords of newly taken lands appealed to others of their own sex to join them on lands unpopulated by Christian souls, but with no thought of bringing women along:

These pagans are the worst of men but their land is the best, with meat, honey, and flour. If it is cultivated the produce of the land will be such that none other can compare with it. That is what they say who know about it. So, O Saxons, Franconians, Lotharingians, and Flemings, here you will be able both to save your souls and, if you will, to acquire very good land to settle.[111]

Not only could good noblemen gain land, but they could kill pagans and earn space in the afterlife, as well. But such crusaders within Europe had as little intention of bringing their women to share in the abundance of Wendish territory as they did of hauling them to the Holy Land. Who, then, was to perform the work of women on farms? Native slaves and tenants, presumably. Among the Sorbs and Poles, a social hierarchy inspired by the German colonists quickly took hold: a prince ruled a territory supported by various lords who dominated native soil-bound or enslaved producers. As in the oldest Germanic class systems, women were simply attached to each of these classes, laboring beside their men.[112]

Intermarriage sometimes secured the incomers' hold on newly acquired territory. The degree of sexual mixing varied widely by specific situations and such factors as the organization of local

---

[111] H. Helbig and L. Weinrich eds., *Urkunden und erzählende Quellen zur deutschen Ostsiedlung im Mittelalter*, 2 vols. (Darmstadt, Wissenschaftliche Buchgesellschaft, 1968–70), vol. 1, no. 19, pp. 96–102; trans. Robert Bartlett, *The Making of Europe: Conquest, Colonization, and Cultural Change, 950–1350* (Princeton University Press, 1993), 136–37.

[112] *Cambridge Economic History of Europe*, vol. 1, 449–51.

families and their religious preferences. As the historian Robert Bartlett has pointed out, immigrant groups almost always included more men than women, so newcomers' marriage into local aristocracies was a means of gaining the cooperation of local elites. No crusader in his right mind would marry an infidel in Jerusalem and its territories, but invaders married local women in Ireland and Sicily, thus gaining the alliances, rights to lands, and shared prestige of recognized leaders. The Norman knight Robert Guiscard wed a daughter of the prince of Salerno, while in Ireland the Cambro-Norman Richard Fitzgilbert de Clare (nicknamed Strongbow) married Aífe, daughter of Diarmait mac Murchadha of Leinster. Likewise, Matilda, daughter of the king of Scotland and a descendant of the great West Saxon ruling house, left a convent to marry Henry I, son of the Norman William the Conqueror of England. On the eastern frontier of Germany, margraves of Brandenburg routinely married Christian Slavic women, thus gaining the patronage and alliance of local men and women of power.[113]

On a less elevated level, another pattern of landtaking occurred whereby women ran the home farm while men left under the patronage of these colonizing lords to develop new lands. Men moved locally to farm the "wilderness" of woods and marshes, as well as beyond the bounds of Christian occupation. As early as the eighth century, the high sex ratios of Carolingian estates (the same evidence used by some historians to claim high rates of female infanticide) could be explained by the fact that most women stayed home or upon the lord's demesne and remained uncounted, while men went back and forth between home and frontier farms where estate managers counted them.[114] Christian settlers in eastern Europe and Iberia often maintained estates in their homelands while setting up new farms in unmapped territory, presumably leaving managers – their women – behind to keep the revenues, which they might need to invest in new estates, flowing.[115] Like the aristocratic ladies of crusading knights, farmers' wives filled in for their men until new landscapes had fulfilled their promise of agriculture or pasturage. Only then did women from elsewhere arrive and permanent colonization occur.

---

[113] Bartlett, *Making of Europe*, 55–56.
[114] Jean-Pierre Devroey, "Men and Women in Early Medieval Serfdom: The Ninth-Century North Frankish Evidence," *Past and Present* 166 (2000), 3–30.
[115] Bartlett, *Making of Europe*, 137–38.

No improvements in technology assisted farmers in their work of reclamation, so neither the gendered division of labor nor methods of cultivation changed substantially; all that lords of the wasteland could offer were better terms of employment. After the example of earlier raiders who came to stay and imported peasants to cultivate land, the lords of eleventh-century Europe encouraged farmers to clear the wilderness by releasing them from traditional dues of service. Bavarian bishops recovered lands after Hungarian invasions in this manner. In France, monasteries encouraged the development of new villages under their jurisdiction. Even where lords did not give good terms, they could still attract peasants to the wilderness. Where farmers set up economically independent households, as on French lands where they enjoyed the chartered status of relatively free men, they were more likely to take their families with them. And once *villes neuves* were set up, they attracted whole new households. In eastern Germany, Flemings and Dutchmen became the "locators", initial settlers, who secured parcels of land and later recruited both men and women to build homesteads in their villages, which were governed at a distance by the lords of these colonial territories. This kind of major reclamation only began in the eleventh century, gathering momentum later in the Middle Ages. After 1200 or so, freed from feudal dues and church tithes, more and more families were able to start new lives on the frontier.[116] Both gender and generation influenced the timing of peasants' move into uncleared territory, along with the balance of population growth and the exercise of feudal powers, whereas gender alone prevented the majority of women from marching off on wars of conquest.

The same sequence of conquest and colonization, bringing first to men and then to women the opportunity for migration and economic improvement, occurred in Iberia, where settlers took over or created towns as often as farms. Louis the Pious had followed his father, Charlemagne, in trying to expand Carolingian borders into the peninsula, but the marchland between the empire and the Muslim caliphate at Córdoba consisted mostly of tiny, irrepressible kingdoms until the eleventh century. After al-Andalus collapsed into several *taifas* (kingdoms) in 1009, the men of northern Iberia began the *reconquista* against what they called Saracens, led by the kingdoms of Navarre and León. The reconquest took centuries (Granada did not fall to the Christian kingdom until 1492) and was never a straight-forward matter of Christian armies marching inexorably southward. In the twelfth century, politics in Iberia were complicated by the arrival of two different groups of north African Muslims, conflict among the *taifas*, and constant feuding among the Christian king-doms, as well as a papal decree of crusade in Spain.

Nonetheless, Christian reorganization of the landscape occurred soon after each Christian advance, and men and women from the north (re)settled the peninsula just as Westerners moved over the German frontiers and into other perceived wild edges of old Europe. The repeopling of the peninsula also required defending the land and making it productive, for which purpose the new lords of Iberia had initially to entice farmers and laborers locally and from the Midi with promises of freeheld fields, although later labor conditions changed for the worse, as everywhere in Europe during the high Middle Ages.[117] Women helped with the earliest *repoblación* (colonization) on the edges of León and Navarre by moving with fathers and hus-bands to the towns of the borderlands, where they earned legal lib-erties and property for their efforts. But only once towns had been captured could women move into men's houses there. Lawmakers of the northern Spanish settlements encouraged women to follow their men in order to keep soldiers from roving, and to produce the pop-ulation necessary for civic development. In their opinion, a woman in the house meant a man would stay.[118]

Accordingly, laws of newly Christian towns in the centuries fol-lowing 1000 induced women's migration by recognizing their in-vestment in territory and neighborhood. Visigothic law had left a strong tradition in Christian communities allowing daughters to in-herit property alongside their brothers. The *fueros* (settlement char-ters and/or customary codes) of frontier communities encouraged women to work with men to attain and expand holdings taken from either wilderness or Muslims. In Soria, women who helped clear and plant the wilderness gained a percentage of the profits. Further south in Cuenca, where children could inherit mother's or father's prop-erty, wives got an even better deal: both spouses in a marriage shared equally in the profits of improvement, even if the wife contributed none of the heavy labor or original capital.[119] Lawmakers and town

---

[117] Archibald Lewis, *The Development of Southern French and Catalan Society, 718–1050* (Austin: University of Texas Press, 1965), 382–97.

[118] Dillard, *Daughters of the Reconquest*, 12–35.

[119] Ibid., 73–74.

fathers must have recognized both the necessity of including women in stable colonization and the contribution women made simply by entering a household and helping produce a family. Like a lord and tenant who created a partnership for improving property, sharing the planting and its harvest, husband and wife also devised a legal and economic unit for the Christian colonization of Iberia.

Nonetheless, even in this arena of renewed economic opportunity for women, wives and daughters continued under the guardianship of their men and were represented by them in legal dealings. In general women were both valuable and vulnerable to their men. As elsewhere in Europe, husbands could legally beat their wives. The scarcity and value of women made them liable to abduction. Non-Christian women who stayed in conquered lands, or entered Christian territories from the south, suffered worse crimes. How ironic that a few centuries earlier, a woman might have improved her social and economic status by converting to Islam, whereas now a *mudéjar* or Muslim woman was subject to bigotry and harm on account of her faith.[120] In fact, on both sides of the religious border, Christians and Muslims maintained flourishing slave markets peopled by unbelievers. On the other hand, a free Christian woman's value remained high as a wife and precious as a daughter once she had married. Her family tended to keep a protective eye on its daughter and her property even when she left the natal home for a new household or a new town.[121] Although every Christian on the margins of Christendom had a chance at increased wealth and improved status, and although the consequences of *reconquista* were not unique to women, the nature of women's opportunities and the advantage they might take of the situation were determined by their sex. They could, as always, become heiresses, wives, and widows, but it was simpler and more profitable to do so on a recognized frontier.[122]

---

[120] Shatzmiller, "Marriage, the Family, and the Faith," 252–53.

[121] Dillard, *Daughters of the Reconquest*, 94ff.

[122] An example from slightly later in the second millennium makes this most clear: In Bonifacio, a town founded in 1195 by Genoese merchants overlooking the strait between Corsica and Sardinia, the widow and daughter of a skinner named Armano could write, in 1239, "We Orenga and Riccafina, mother and daughter, wishing to undertake with the benefit of inventory, the administration of the goods which belonged to the late Armano, skinner . . . desired to make and inventory or repertory of said inheritance" – then list at length the skins, cloths, finished garments, tools, cheese and wine, and debts belonging once to Armano, now to them. R. Lopez and I. Raymond, ed. and trans., *Medieval Trade in the Mediterranean World* (New York: Columbia University Press, 1955), 95–97.

GENDERED THEORY OF PEOPLING: IRELAND

The last military frontier of early medieval Europe was on its chronological and geographical edge, what an Irish saint had once called "the edge of the known world," but securely within Christendom, in Ireland. Although the Norman invasion of Ireland began in 1167, the involvement of women in the process resembles earlier population movements in Europe. What is more, texts from the same time teach a complex lesson about the gender of invasion and conquest, and of labor and mobility. Tradition tells that Irishwomen accommodated the invading foreigners of the twelfth century by marrying them or by joining their newfangled religious orders as continental-style nuns, both responses helping the invaders to become, in the traditional phrase, more Irish than the Irish. By contrast, the Norman invaders of Britain remained a relatively separate, French-speaking, outsider class for generations. But in Ireland, the daughters of newcomers quickly began marrying the natives, too. Women on both sides of the ethnic divide facilitated assimilation of invaders and invaded, as had women in Gaul in the fifth century, British women in the sixth century, and Irish women a century or two earlier among the Danes of Dublin and other Viking ports.[123]

In fact, the first accommodation of Norman interlopers involved a woman and her marriage. The Cambro-Normans came across the water to Leinster, in the southeast, in 1167 at the request of an Irish provincial king, Diarmait mac Murchadha. Mac Murchadha offered his daughter Aífe along with the inheritance of his own kingdom to a Norman knight from the Welsh marcher lands, Richard Fitzgilbert de Clare, in exchange for support in war against other Irish rulers. This might have been a great advance for Aífe and her status as heir in preference to her brothers, had her father meant it. But de Clare (called Strongbow by contemporaries) got only the girl, not the kingdom. Since he and his fellow Normans had come to colonize, they began to wage war for land, imposing a new feudal structure and territorialism foreign to the backwaters of Ireland, and a conforming Christianity that the locals met with ambivalence. Norman knights swore allegiance to the Plantagenet king of England, as did conceding Irish leaders. After a century of struggle, the Normans had established lordships and castles throughout most of the island.

[123] Seán Duffy, *Ireland in the Middle Ages* (Dublin: Gill & MacMillan, 1997), esp. 147–48.

They spoke a new language and practiced a different law. But after two centuries, Norman towns and government had begun to recede back towards Dublin and a shrinking frontier-land known as the Pale. Those left outside the boundary had long before begun to act more like Irish tribal lords than European knights; they spoke Irish inside their stone towers, named their daughters and sons with Irish names, and made the same sorts of shifting political commitments that their Irish neighbors made.

In a sense, the quick assimilation promoted by women may have limited their chances to gain on this borderland of Europe. Women were on the outside and the inside of the Pale, but acquired no special privileges anywhere, just as Aífe failed to profit in property by her marriage to Strongbow. Heiresses could be found in both legal systems of this frontier-within-a-frontier, but the laws of both the Normans and Irish were patriarchal and tended normally to disperse land to males. Both sides practiced a Christianity that did not indulge women. In the few towns of Ireland, founded by Vikings and later commanded by Normans, women had no greater economic opportunities than women elsewhere in the heart of old Europe. It seems, at first, that Ireland was the exception among borderlands and their opportunities for women.

However, the self-reflective revision of contemporary Irish literature during the colonization of Ireland makes clear just how gendered the process of invasions, settlement, and reorganization actually was. Europeans conceived of their entry into "wildernesses" and "frontiers" within the framework of an ancient mythology of relations between men and women, custom, legal ideologies, and traditional divisions of labor. This mythology helps explain why the mobility and economic opportunities for women varied so greatly in the take-off, and why results for women were so diverse by place and cultural circumstances.

Around the time of the initial Norman incursions, the Irish synthesized their centuries-old mythologies into a proper tribal ethnogenesis in which, as in the Icelandic histories, women figured prominently as settlers and leaders. In this reimagined history of the ancient peopling of Ireland, drawn from ancestral tales as well as the Bible and Christian histories, invasions occurred in explicit gender terms. The very act of invasion was cast as either male or female, along with the relations of peoples to landscapes and the success of any given invasion. In reality, the ancient Irish had come to their island over the centuries of the Bronze and Iron Ages in groups of immigrants and colonists. Medieval writers had never needed to justify any conquests, nor were they able to produce any single tribal memory of how, exactly, people had come to their land or taken it from the original inhabitants. But in order to fit the Irish into the grander schemes of Christian expansion which they knew were taking place beyond Europe, learned men of the early Middle Ages made up a series of maritime *gabála* or "takings" based on a wild amalgam of Celtic myth and biblical cosmology, which one (or more) enterprising twelfth-century scholar later rewrote into a *Book of the Taking of Ireland* (*Lebor Gabála Érenn*).

He began at the beginning: "In principio fecit Deus caelum et terram," in the beginning God created heaven and earth. After that the rest of creation occurred over the seven days, followed by the Fall and the rest of world history up to Noah, whose descendants peopled Ireland along with the rest of the newly washed world. Noah's grandchildren launched the first of a series of five cyclic landings, settlements, namings, conquests, and depopulations of Ireland, culminating with a sixth successful, permanent taking by the sons of Míl Espaine of the Gaedil. The clan of Gaedil were suspiciously Hebrew-like in their history, including a sojourn in Egypt where they languished in servitude, an alliance with a friendly daughter of Pharaoh (named Scota, after whom the Scotti, the Irish themselves, were named), a leader who died before bringing his tribe to the promised land which he sighted from atop a mountain, and the eventual occupation by the chosen of this rainy land of milk and honey.

According to the *Lebor Gabála*, Cesair, granddaughter of Noah, was the leader of the first peopling after the flood. As in other European schemes, a woman was able to lead a settlement venture so long as it never involved warfare; as with Unnr in her own story, the fertile significance of a female figure civilizing the land was not lost on its writers and readers. Cesair headed out for Ireland with three boat-loads of colonists (like the Anglo-Saxons of Bede's history), but two ships were wrecked en route. The third held Cesair, forty-nine other women, and only three men: her father Bith, her brother Ladra, and Fintan. The men divided up the women "for peace and for reason." But Bith and Ladra soon expired. Ladra succumbed to "female excess" or, alternately, from "the oar-shaft that penetrated his buttock." Either way, sex was the end of him, which is but one of many hints that Cesair's peopling failed on account of immorality, the creation of improper social ties, and gender imbalance. Cesair herself fell dead of heartbreak. Flood took the rest of the women, and only Fintan endured, possibly underwater, until the next *gabál*.[124] The successful invasions, according to *Lebor Gabála*, were led by men. Cesair's troops were followed by the Partholonians, who all succumbed to plague. Next came the Nemetians who fell to the Fir Bolg, who were conquered by the Tuatha Dé Danann (Tribe of the Goddess Danu), who were driven underground by the last triumphant boats bearing the sons of Míl Espaine. These last were also descendants of the friendly Scota, princess of Egypt. They became the fathers and mothers of the men and women of Ireland, moving in a great biblical mass from the Continent to Ireland.[125] They had success because they were chosen by God, which they signified by practicing normal social and gender relations. Their wives did not inflict "female excess" upon them, nor did their women practice the witching spells of the women of the Tuatha Dé. The women of the Irish were neither adulteresses nor virile men-women. But the Milesians knew also that the peaceful domesticity of women was necessary for the phase of settlement that followed men's invasions. They thus organized and named the Irish landscape, and then worked it as family farms. Nothing was lacking from this gender-balanced and successful peopling but the perfection of Christianity which came, some years later, at the blessing hand of St. Patrick (Pátraic), as had been ordained.

The Irish of the twelfth century were not invading any new frontiers, although their own island was suffering reorganization by Norman invaders. They were not offering their women any special opportunities in this millennial age of frontiers. But in the imagined history of invasions of Ireland, women taught a vital lesson to the audiences of *Lebor Gabála*. The more aggressive and visible the women in an invasion, the less successful the whole venture. Women had no rightful place in the first phase of invasion and conquest. Only when they followed their men to help with the peaceful reorganization of

---

[124] R. A. S. MacAlister, ed. and trans., *Lebor Gabála Érenn: The Book of the Taking of Ireland*, 5 vols., Irish Texts Society (Dublin: Irish Texts Society, 1932–56; repr. London: Irish Texts Society, 1993), vol. 2, 188–89.

[125] Ibid., vol. 5, 1–135. See also Lisa M. Bitel, "Landscape, Gender, and Ethnogenesis in Pre(norman) Invasion Ireland," in *Inventing Medieval Landscapes*, ed. Michael Wolfe and John M. Howe (University Press of Florida, forthcoming.)

the invaded landscape were women acceptable and the colonization itself viable. In this belief, the Irish were no different from continental crusaders or the Christians of the *reconquista*, or even from those Frankish immigrants into Gaul many centuries before. In the age of expansion, the Irish literati generated a gendered history of invasion and conquest while their own women, with the collusion of their guardians, seized the opportunity to marry Norman conquerors and make what they could – within law, custom, and the traditional division of labor – of a frontier situation.

All the narratives of conquest, invasion, and colonization around the edges of Christian Europe included women, but most usually and most successfully in the second phase of settlement after initial invasion. Spanish laws recognized the participation of women in the *repoblación* that followed *reconquista*. Icelandic sagas granted women fresh lands in imitation of men, but soon settled them down as wives and mothers. Crusaders took their brides to the omphalos of the civilized world, but not to fight. And Irish intellectuals envisioned their origins in terms of the proper and improper participation of females. Europeans seemed to recognize that the extraordinary movements of the time necessarily jolted people from the safety of their homes and homelands. The seismic shifts even moved women, who had always been more inclined or more conditioned to stay behind. Women were on the move. But they were not going as crusaders and conquerors. Stories of women on crusade and failed Irish invasions proved the disasters that crossing such gender frontiers could cause. Women went as unequal partners in colonization, to perform the same roles and tasks that they had always performed: to recreate, as wives and mothers, domestic and community stability, once men's wars were done. They may have more readily reaped more profits, but their jobs were the same as ever. The only place where some women actually experienced a more significant disruption in occupation and status was nearer to home, in the new towns of old Europe. There, the flexibility of tasks, the general mobility and increase in the population, and occasional losses of men in a constantly changing urban milieu allowed women some temporary gains.

CONCLUSION: THE GOLDEN AGE OF WOMEN'S LABOR

Was there ever a golden age for women searching out new economic opportunities for their own profit and enjoyment? The historian David Herlihy argued for the early Middle Ages. Others have found it in the post-millennial Europe of the frontiers.[126] Economic historians always seem to be looking for a period when women had some equality in the workforce or, at least, gained respect for their labors. For women's historians, the search for a golden age of women's labor is another way of seeking that lost utopia of (near-)gender symmetry that we hope, some day, to stumble upon in the past.[127]

Some scholars have taken the search all the way back to hunter-gatherers, arguing that women's contributions in the stone age were more important than those of male hunters, since women provided the bulk of food for any community. No one survived on meat back then, but everyone ate the nuts and berries plucked by women toting their babies. More recently, archeologists have found evidence for women and men hunting together with nets for game. Others, such as the nineteenth-century theorist Friedrich Engels, argued that when people settled down to practice agriculture, men and women both worked the land until men got the bright idea of producing surplus, which compelled them to reduce women to reproducers of heirs to the profits. Further, men brought in the metal tools that allowed them to dominate women and each other. Women were banished from the fields, men took over production using that most male of tools, the plough, and they cultivated large fields far from their huts, a practice which could not be easily accommodated to women's reproductive and nurturing role. How was a mommy with a thirty-pound child on her back able to labor equally with a bigger, stronger man? Because their productive capacity was lower, women became less valued in plough societies except when they could bring wealth to a marriage and produce babies, which formed part of the conjugal unit's capital.[128] Recent historians have produced variations upon this nineteenth-century theme, rearranging the causes and effects of gendered labor or locating its origins in a different period.[129]

But the search for a chronology of gendered labor is as culture-encrusted as Adomnán's *cáin* or Charlemagne's dictum about spinners or medieval theories of housewifely duties. Medieval people before and after the agricultural expansion of the tenth century and the commercial revolution that followed valued women's contributions

[126] Herlihy, *Opera Muliebria*; Goldberg, *Women, Work, and Lifecycle in a Medieval Economy*.
[127] Eller, *Myth of Matriarchal Prehistory*, 41–55.
[128] Engels, *Origin of the Family, Private Property, and the State*.
[129] Gerda Lerner, *Creation of Patriarchy*; Alice Clark, *Working Life of Women in the Seventeenth Century* (repr. New York: Kelly, 1968).

to their economy. They knew that women provided domestic skills that balanced men's agricultural or craft skills. Everyone realized that women's contributions to the home economy were indispensable, and that well-defined roles for men and women were mutually productive. Yet none of these skills empowered women politically, or brought women control over resources or expenditures, or allowed women to shed their identification with domestic duties. Women could and did participate in dissident movements, such as heretical affiliations and peasant risings, but even rioting for bread or preaching to the neighbors did not cause significant change to people's domestic interpretation of women's labor in the Middle Ages. Even when women gained the mobility that allowed them to participate in new ventures on the frontiers of the European economy, they could not pass on their gains to the women of future generations. As the demographic cycles of late medieval England demonstrate, long after the take-off older, stronger patterns returned women to what they were thought to do best, bear and raise babies at home. Women gained no chance to rebel against this economic culture until the early years of industrialization, when young women flocked again to cities – with not always happy results, and at risk to their health, morals, and even lives.

If women at the turn of the first Christian millennium never progressed evenly toward either an increase or decrease in economic autonomy, the evidence suggests at least oscillations in women's economic opportunities. Improvement might as well be measured by increased mobility, more variety of options, leading to more satisfaction and rewards, as by control over their own situations. At certain conjunctures of social and political history, economic opportunities seemed to open, briefly, for individuals and communities of women with enough sense to seize them. Women in Iceland experienced such a phenomenon when they set up their own homesteads. Women moving with partners to the borders of Christian Iberia occasionally took such an opportunity. Most obviously entrepreneurial were the first women to leave the domestic context that had contained them for centuries and would continue to cloister most of their sisters for centuries to come, and to venture into new towns, even if only for long enough to earn a dowry. It did not matter to women what kind of town reinvigorated a region and its economy, only that such growth seemed to offer new work in new places, in new professions, and with new freedom to learn and profit. *Stadtluft macht frei,* "Town air makes one free," declared nineteenth-century writers about the Middle Ages. This was true for certain lucky women, too, at least for a time, in specific ways. Ultimately, the gendered culture of women's work caught up with them on the city streets, too, but not at the same pace in every city.

More women were on the move after 1000 than at any time previously in Europe's medieval history. Men had migrated before, in armies and hordes, but not women. Yet, whether on the edge of Europe itself, or in new fields and cities within the Continent, or on the social and religious marchlands of Jewish and Muslim communities, wherever they went, women continued to make themselves into settled mothers and wives, living and working much as their own mothers had. Women could do little else, given that they were not a coherent, self-conscious social class. As long as an expanding Europe was still mapped by tiny, discrete micro-economies bursting into life, where "progress" was a word without meaning, women's best longterm opportunities for profit and prestige came from adapting the work they had always done to fit local circumstances. Whatever individual pioneers accomplished at the end of the early Middle Ages, generations of women still inhabited a distinctly patriarchal *longue durée*.

6

CONCLUSION: CONCERNING FAMOUS
WOMEN BEFORE AND AFTER 1100

·

In this age of historical re-enactments, Renaissance Faires, virtual reality games in ancient settings, and cinematic reproductions of the past, the early medieval period has not attracted much notice. Women of the Middle Ages attract much more. Joan of Arc has starred in several bad films over the last few decades. The queens of later medieval England, especially Eleanor of Aquitaine, regularly merit historical novels. Hildegard of Bingen is a media sensation, inspiring concerts, recordings, websites, and many books both scholarly and silly. Heloise, eleventh-century abbess of the Paraclete and lover of Peter Abelard, has likewise infiltrated modern memory and media; almost as many pilgrims still flock to her ornate neo-Gothic tomb at Père Lachaise in Paris as attend the grave of the rock-star Jim Morrison. Yet no one recalls the fallen nuns or raging queens of Francia with such romantic affection as they bestow upon Heloise or Eleanor. No warrior women of early Ireland or Gaul storm modern imaginations like Joan of Arc, whose short life has generated so many biographies, fictions, and films. Even witches come to us from the later Middle Ages while earlier magic-makers remain lost and anonymous, not proper witches at all. The few early medieval saints who remain objects of veneration, such as St. Brigit or Genovefa, owe their fame more to early modern revisions of their cults than to their origins.

Women of Europe before 1100 have failed to capture modern imaginations, even though some forceful women left their marks on the collective history of Europeans before the end of the first

Christian millennium. Popular memory has forgotten, but the written past still includes, Queen Radegund, the saintly, and the Queens Brunhild and Fredegund, who played a racier game of politics, along with Clothild who converted her husband to Christianity. Notable holy women marched from the documents purposefully into this book: not only Brigit and Genovefa, but Leoba, the miracle-worker who wanted so desperately to be buried with her dear cousin Boniface. The noble mother Dhuoda who tried to save her son and the monstrous mother who bore and avenged Grendel dwell in these pages. The frontierswoman Unnr sailed into these chapters and Cesair, the antidiluvian settler of Ireland, drowned in the words of Chapter Five. These were the movers and shakers – literally – of the early Middle Ages. Some were real women who broke or exceeded rules and norms, rattling the men who organized and ruled them, and some were just figments of what women might be. But all of them impressed the literati who wrote their stories.

Women in early medieval Europe gained fame with the power of political influence, and acquired power only when birth, wealth, education, or marital circumstance allowed. They were queens, holy women, but also rulebreakers and troublemakers. These were the roles in which contemporary men and women could imagine women of influence. Queens and noblewomen manipulated traditional family ties to wield authority and influence. Abbesses and saints escaped customary restrictions on secular wives and daughters, although they accepted other constraints. Religious and secular women used relations with male leaders of churches and political territories to establish their authority. Female miscreants broke into history because they acquired influence in neither of the acceptable ways. The literati were shocked into taking notice of them. Finally, a very few females themselves were able to transcribe their own legacies, usually in the same terms established by male colleagues. They too were holy women and noblewomen whose texts were similar enough to those of men that men kept and recopied their manuscripts.

But why even such notable women remain harder to revive in our collective recollection while the later Middle Ages produced so many more memorable characters is hard to figure. Perhaps it is because the kingdom-building and new patrilineal structure of the later Middle Ages created a new, smaller cadre of rich and powerful women. Or maybe the great mental expansions of the eleventh and later centuries produced what historians have called the discovery of the individual, including the famous woman. Or maybe increasing literacy created a demand for new genres and more stories about women. All these suggestions are, and have been, subjects for histories of the later medieval period.

But surely, too, the very nature of memory and fame in the early Middle Ages contributed to the obscurity of women. Even the select few who won celebrity among their contemporaries before 1100 fall back, like Eurydice, from our historical vision, fading away while the singers of their tales, their Orpheuses, are bright and loud in our historical consciousness. Abbess Hild is almost gone, the Venerable Bede remains; we know of Dhuoda but not the noble mothers of other victims of Carolingian politics. Even the fearsome beast who dueled Beowulf has no identity beyond that of Grendel's mother. Who can repeat all the names of Charlemagne's consorts? As we have seen repeatedly in this book, the documents and material artifacts from the period are scarce, difficult to use and, in the case of texts, largely authored by men who found most women hardly discernible. The politics, social organization, and culture of the early Middle Ages helped to cast women to the outskirts of political and intellectual life – the seat of history – then and now.[1]

Almost more important, our own modern construction of history has clouded our memory of women's early medieval past. We continue to study what the tribal historians wrote, although we know that they forgot to bring along their women. We rely on hagiographers, the decrees of episcopal councils, monastic theologians, rabbinical *responsa*, and letter-writers to tell us how people chose and lived religion. Archeological remains allow us to include women, but hardly to view the spread of Christianity in feminine terms. What shall we say of queens and noblewomen, their ways of marriage and work, their households? We analyze what laws and rules can reveal. While these documents supply useful evidence to historians sensitive to a gender-inclusive past, scholars still find it hard to conceptualize distant centuries from a woman-centered perspective, following a woman-inspired chronology, if such a chronology can even exist. The alternative seems to be the cyclical time or near-stasis favored in feminist approaches, organized in topically divided chapters.[2] The

---

[1] Geary, *Phantoms of Remembrance*, esp. Conclusion, 177–81.
[2] As one example, the popular survey by Bonnie Anderson and Judith Zinsser, *A History of Their Own: Women in Europe from Prehistory to the Present* (revised edn., New York: Oxford University Press, 2000).

literati who permitted only select women to enter the documents – and even fewer to join their ranks – also contributed to our very notions of history: the way time moved from war to war and reign to reign, decline to renaissance; the start-to-finish, birth-and-death biographies of society's leaders and heroes; the changes in markets and technologies masterminded by men; and the paradigm shifts of major thinkers. This kind of history demands observable change. Although we pride ourselves on ceaselessly updating our historical information and methods, both our popular and our scholarly past remain a teleology of men, sometimes adorned with famous women.

We cannot entirely escape our inherited historiography, no matter how many qualifying footnotes we add or how much critical common sense we apply. For too many generations, teachers and students of history, female and male consumers of history, have collaborated in the creation of this past. For generations, lecturers have told the story of the Middle Ages to students, who in turn have repeated its beginning in the Fall of Rome and its end in the Renaissance. Orpheus has tugged us into the twenty-first century at such a rate that we can hardly peer out of the shadows. All we can do is our best, applying our latest theories and most sensitive political consciousness to the past – using the lens of gender, as the historian Joan Scott has suggested; concentrating on the changes in women's experience rather than searching out transformations in their status, as Judith Bennett has argued; maneuvering between orality and literacy, informal and formal pasts, and navigating the gendered nature of memory in the Middle Ages, as Elisabeth Van Houts has done.[3] The simple conceit of this book has been a differently organized history of women, revealed by gently deconstructing men's chronologies of men's deeds and their occasional comments about women. I have assumed that women contributed to the making of these sources even when the documents ignored women. I have often relied on queens, holy women, and rulebreaking monsters to represent the general experience of women.

But this leaves us with one more puzzle to serve as a conclusion to the history of European women over seven centuries: why famous women appeared after 1100, and how women from before 1100 might

---

[3] Joan Scott, "Gender: A Useful Category of Historical Analysis," in *Gender and the Politics of History*, ed. Joan Scott (New York: Columbia University Press, 1988), 28–50; Bennett, "Theoretical Issues"; Elisabeth Van Houts, *Memory and Gender in Medieval Europe 900–1200* (Toronto: University of Toronto Press, 1999).

become more famous. When European men finally noticed the frontiers of Christendom, when they began breaching the geographical,
spiritual, and mental limits that had contained and protected them
for many generations, they also breached the gendered frontiers of
fame. Later in the Middle Ages new genres of formal written memory
began to include more women and to present women in revised categories of good and evil. After the eleventh century, when Europeans
went on the prowl, the restless minds of a few literate women awoke
to the possibility of their own posterity and that of their sex. They
began to write, in their own voices, of women's experiences, desires,
and aims.

The early medieval literati's concept of notorious women, later
medieval women's writings, and modern gender ideologies have all
influenced our current affection for certain kinds of famous women.
Medieval shifts in the nature of elite women's power and in women's
power to make memory has shaped our own desire to remember
famous women. Together these medieval and modern memories
explain why readers are still lured by Joan and Eleanor, but not by
Brunhild and Radegund. The increase in visibly powerful, famous,
and sometimes self-explanatory women beginning around 1100 re-
minds us of what we are missing from our story of early medieval
women, from the European past generally, and from our own practice
of history.

MAYHEM AND MEMORY

The *Elder Edda* (a twelfth-century compilation of earlier poems)
reminded Icelanders that

> Cattle die, kindred die,
> Every man is mortal:
> But the good name never dies
> Of one who has done well.
>
> Cattle die, kindred die,
> Every man is mortal:
> But I know one thing that never dies,
> The glory of the great dead.[4]

The lives of cattle and men are fragile, only collective memory
remains. For the Icelanders, stuck on their volcanic rock, only the

---

[4] Taylor and Auden, *Elder Edda*, 47.

sustainers and the sustained mattered in the end: the cows that produced the milk and the men who drank it. If we fool with the pronouns, we could add the women who milked the cows to this poem, and the babies they reared to become the next cohort of men. We could also supply the ponies they rode and the dogs that accompanied them. Undoubtedly the poet imagined women and horses and dogs among his men and cattle. But his audience approved the more succinct statement of mortality, else the verse would never have lasted long enough to be recorded as an *edda*, a nugget of traditional wisdom. Survival was so uncertain at any moment of an early medieval day that, as the historian Elisabeth Van Houts has pointed out, men and women needed each other to generate the collective memory of themselves.[5]

Women could help maintain public memory but only in limited ways. Historians and hagiographers relied on female witnesses to events for their written reports, but rarely acknowledged the contribution, since women lacked the authority of higher-ranking sources.[6] Although historical detectives are finding more and more manuscripts, even historical documents, actually authored by women during the early medieval period, female chroniclers rarely signed their names.[7] Women may have collaborated in poetic versions of the collective past, but in heroic versions of their community's history, women appeared only to mourn fallen warriors and kings. The lone female in the tenth-century *Battle of Maldon* groaned, "He was my kinsman and lord."[8] Women, unlamented themselves, lamented their men. One ninth-century Welsh poet caused the princess Heledd to cry out for her lost brother Cynddylan: "The hall of Cynddylan is dark tonight, without fire, without bed; I shall weep a while, I shall be silent after... the hall of Cynddylan it pierces me to see it, without roof, without fire; my lord dead, myself alive..."[9] But the fate of

---

[5] Van Houts, *Memory and Gender*, 2.   [6] Ibid., 38–39 *et passim*.

[7] J. L. Nelson, "Perceptions du pouvoir chez les historiennes du Haut Moyen Âge," in Rouche and Heuclin, *Les femmes au Moyen Âge*, 77–85; McKitterick, "Frauen und Schriftlichkeit im Frühmittelalter"; Bischoff, "Die kölner Nonnenhandschriften." See also Van Houts's bibliography, *Memory and Gender*, 185–86.

[8] *WEHD* 1, 93–97; Pauline Stafford, "Kinship and Women in the World of *Maldon*: Byrhtnoth and his Family," in *The Battle of Maldon: Fiction and Fact*, ed. Janet Cooper (London: Hambledon Press, 1993), 225–235.

[9] K. H. Jackson, ed. and trans., *A Celtic Miscellany* (Harmondsworth: Penguin, 1986), 251–52; Ifor Williams, ed., *Canu Llywarch Hen* (Cardiff: University of Wales Press, 1935).

Heledd – captive? casualty? – is unknown. Such women participated in political narratives as sympathetic figures only when they were manless victims.

It may be that women used material objects rather than texts to keep the memory of others and to spur the memory of themselves. Historians differ, for instance, about whether or not women were primarily responsible for the preparation of dead bodies, which would also make them memory-keepers.[10] Women cleaned, buried, and mourned dead men. After King Harold caught an arrow in the battle of Hastings, immortalized in the Bayeux tapestry, his mother Gytha came to beg the Normans for his body according to *The Song of the Battle of Hastings*.[11] One extraordinary set of pictures from the *Sacramentary* of Bishop Warmundus of Ivrea, finished around 1000, depicted a woman involved in all the stages of death and burial of men, watching, mourning, and lamenting.[12] That women may have recovered and prepared each other's bodies remains only scholarly speculation, not the subject of medieval poetry. Certainly, women sponsored the building of shrines and tombs. St. Genovefa was neither the first nor the only woman to erect a basilica over her favorite saint. Women in Scandinavia commissioned carved stones to commemorate men in the family, or their own accomplishments.[13] Women also paid the monks of Ottonian houses to commemorate the royal dead in *Libri memoriales*. As the comparative patronage of men's and women's monasteries demonstrates, male ecclesiastics were considered more effective at commemorative prayer than females, although we might consider the patronage of monks by noblewomen to be a kind of partnership in memory-keeping.[14] Monks wrote in their books the names of the deceased and their kin, including mothers and sisters, for whom the brothers continued praying regularly through the years.[15]

---

[10] Van Houts, *Memory and Gender*, esp. 13–14, 94–98; Geary, *Phantoms of Remembrance*, 48–80.

[11] C. Morton and H. Muntz, ed. and trans., *The Carmen de Hastingae Proelio of Guy Bishop of Amiens* (Oxford: Clarendon, 1972), 36–39.

[12] *Il sacramentario del vescovo Warmondo di Ivrea* (Ivrea, 1990); see also Schmitt, *Raison des gestes*, 223; Geary, *Phantoms of Remembrance*, 54–59.

[13] Birgit Sawyer, *The Viking-Age Rune-Stones: Custom and Commemoration in Early Medieval Scandinavia* (Oxford University Press, 2001); Van Houts, *Memory and Gender*, 97–100.

[14] McNamara, *Sisters in Arms*, 207–09.

[15] Leyser, *Rule and Conflict*, 50–51; Geary, *Phantoms of Remembrance*, 51–73, esp. 62.

14 Sacramentary of Ivrea, woman mourning

Without frequent access to memorial books or histories, and without the funds to build memorial architecture, women were left with
the feminine medium of needlework to commemorate the deeds
of their men. The Anglo-Saxon wills mentioned hangings created,
owned, and bequeathed by women to women. Ælfflæd, widow of
the hero at Maldon, Byrhtnoth commissioned a hanging embroidered with the "memory of his bravery", which she later donated to
the monastery at Ely. A similar tapestry – although not necessarily
accomplished by women – helped the Anglo-Saxons who made it
and the Normans who kept it recall the battle of Hastings.[16] A few
women moved among the male figures on this particular piece of
cloth, including a mother and her son caught in the conflict. The
tapestry shows one scene of a frantic woman grasping her son's hand
and trying to escape while two men set fire to her house. But where

[16] Van Houts, *Memory and Gender*, 102–03.

15 Woman and son in a burning house, from the Bayeux tapestry, eleventh century

could she hide? Who would protect her? Men and war surrounded her, flames descended upon her head. She was not a unique victim, but her sympathetic memorial is rare. Although plenty of women died as horribly as men, in public memory they figured most often as unnamed casualties rather than fallen makers of history.

Even when women were officially remembered in formal media, their passing was not elaborated upon as in the epitaphs of Roman women centuries before, or inscribed in the burial sculpture of the romanesque, but merely noted in the prayerbooks of churchmen and women. Long ago, in imperial Rome or even as late as sixth-century Cappadocia, a tombstone might read lovingly and appreciatively, "Here lies Maria the deacon, who in accordance with the statement of the apostle reared children, practiced hospitality, washed the feet of the saints, distributed her bread to the afflicted. Remember her, Lord, when you come in your kingdom."[17] But in the memorial registers of the medieval West, the few inscribed women waned to mere names. Famously pious women were the exception. Very early in the Middle Ages some saints, such as Radegund, happened to begin

---

[17] Kraemer, *Maenads, Martyrs, Matrons, Monastics*, 223.

their careers as queens; by the end of the period, queens achieved sainthood not for miracles but for exemplary lives of piety and charity, as was the case with Margaret of Scotland.[18] Some of the wives of Ottonian emperors became saints: the two wives of Otto I, Edith and Adelheid, and Cunegunda, wife of Henry II.[19] Churchmen and a few churchwomen wrote the stories of these saints, as Baudonivia commemorated her Mother Radegund, and queens sometimes commissioned the vitae, but even the number of women saints and their written vitae declined after the tenth century.[20] And, frustratingly, early medieval female authors rarely left their own names on the manuscripts, purposely losing themselves to the humility of historical anonymity. Baudonivia was a proud exception.

Genre contributed to the gendering of public memory. Writers of historical narratives and epic poetry focused on heroic public leaders, who tended to be major participants in warfare. Convention required a certain amount of brutality and chaos, well as the drama of combat. Monks who composed chronicles and annals were interested in feuds and murders as well as natural disasters, because such events were not only lurid and exciting, but also the traditional stuff of history. Poets preferred not to sing of dull daily events like women's unchanging work. Their readers and listeners colluded: sagas about the happy domestic life nurtured by homebound wives and mothers would not have attracted much of an audience. People could remember mundane continuities because they lived them. Likewise, lawyers wrote laws for audiences interested in preventing violence and disorder, not to commemorate the peace and stability that it was women's duty to promote. Even hagiographers depicted the melodrama of miracles rather than the unstinting everyday goodness of their subjects. Cattle die, kinsmen die, and both made better subjects of poetry than women.

Authors' purposes, audiences' interests, and the gendering of memory all came of the same patriarchal culture set on a landscape of violence. Not all dangers derived from the hysterical imagination of

---

[18] Lois Huneycutt, "The Idea of the Perfect Princess: The *Life of St. Margaret* in the Reign of Matilda II (1100–1118)," *Anglo-Norman Studies* 12 (1989), 81–97.

[19] K. Ciggaar, "Theophano: An Empress Reconsidered," in *The Empress Theophano: Byzantium and the West at the Turn of the Millennium*, ed. Adelbert Davids (Cambridge University Press, 1995), 62.

[20] Jane Schulenburg, *Forgetful of Their Sex: Female Sanctity and Society, ca. 500–1100* (Chicago: University of Chicago Press, 1998), 63.

the literati, and the gendering of protagonists in the documents was probably quite realistic. Men made politics, war, and history. Europe before the millennium consisted of societies organized hierarchically, as we know, by both class and gender. Nobility brought the right to bear arms, but only to men. The governments of kingdoms and lordships, and even of the deconstructed empire of Charlemagne, were all based on what Georges Duby has called an economy of gift and pillage – gifts from those with great power to those with less, and pillage of the powerless by the stronger (indeed, Duby thought the system lasted until 1200). If an individual did not have the resources and birth-right to remain a fully functioning member of a family group and a community, if he or she could not buy protection through labor, rents, tributes, or ransom, then he or she lost kin affiliation, refuge, life, memory. Lawmakers acknowledged this fact of life-and-death with penalties based on the *wergeld* system, whereby a malefactor paid money or goods for his or her crimes. If the criminal could not pay, kinsfolk paid; if the criminal had no obliging kin, she or he was enslaved or killed. Churchmen admitted the same principle with their penitentials: it prescribed fasting and exile as punishment for the sin of murder, because of the impurity with which it stained a good Christian and his entire community.

When violence occurred, those responsible paid for it, one way or another, unless powerful enough to escape retribution. The weaker the individual, the lower her status, the more legal restrictions placed upon her public participation in society, the more vulnerable she was to violence and less visible she was to memory. Cattle died, kinsmen died, but when most women died they succumbed anonymously without the option of raising an army or a sword in the hope of a memorable end. In the period of conversion to Christianity, they might have gone into the ground with a bauble or a tool to mark individual identity, depending upon their status and their family's affection for them, but once they became Christian even that marker of memory was denied them.[21]

Plenty of women appeared in histories, poetry, sagas, chronicles, charters, legal codes, and all the other documents produced in early medieval Europe, but not as the principal makers of politics and history. Both the women and men who predominated in the sources were upper class, even royal. Women themselves may have controlled

---

[21] Effros, "Symbolic Expressions of Sanctity."

unwritten histories made more durable in stone or textile. They may well have collaborated in shaping and approving formal, public histories. But in the official historical memory of Europeans, only three broad types of early medieval women appeared as protagonists of the past: she who subverted the order that medieval people worked so hard to bring about; the queen who maintained order on behalf of her man; and the holy woman who radiated peace, and occasionally written documents, from within her cloister gates. This was the legacy of early medieval memory-makers to the historians of the later Middle Ages and all who came after.

WOMEN OF POWER

The great structural changes that followed agricultural and demographic expansion and the reorganization of European landscapes did not erase the sexism of written memory. But the mobility that brought some women more property and profits, prestige, or access to education also forced a revision of public memory. First, a small class of regents and heiresses acquired new forms of political influence and consequently intruded upon traditional accounts of the heroic past. Secondly, educated women helped to create new genres of learning that made more room for diverse individual histories, including those of women. Together, these two shifts in public memory contributed to the lasting celebrity of the heroines of the later Middle Ages. As for monsters, the same kinds of women became notorious, but suddenly there were more of them – the sluts and scolds and viragos of the early Middle Ages but also heretics, witches, and transgendered troublemakers such as Joan of Arc.

In Chapter Four I reminded readers how changes in inheritance patterns, particularly the nobility's new interest in patrilineages in many parts of the Continent, deprived many women of a share in family property but also endowed a very few women with great wealth and influence as heiresses, even as genuine wielders of royal power. The process began, as so many medieval changes did, in the borderlands – Iberia and the kingdom of Jerusalem, where politics, religious ideas, racial categories, and social relations were already in flux.[22] In León, for instance, Elvira Ramírez (*c.* 935–after 982) was the first of

---

[22] Lois Huneycutt, "Female Succession and the Language of Power in the Writings of Twelfth-Century Churchmen," in *Medieval Queenship*, ed. John C. Parsons (New York: St. Martin's Press, 1993), 198–201.

several female regents of the Iberian kingdoms. Elvira was the sister of Sancho the Fat and aunt of the succeeding king, Ramiro III. She was also an abbess and an accomplished politician who negotiated treaties with the caliph at Córdoba to the south. She was the co-signatory on charters and other documents during her brother's reign and the subsequent early reign of young Ramiro. Three charters referred to her as *regina* (queen), and she gave judgment in the royal court, a power always reserved for kings before Elvira appeared.[23] No contemporary histories revealed the sources of Elvira's power or accounted for her rise. The lack of any male heirs except Ramiro from among the newly consolidated families related to Sancho the Fat meant that the child had to reign after his father died and needed someone reliable – not another competitive man – to help him. The old Visigothic custom of forcing kings' widows into nunneries meant that Ramiro's mother could not act as regent, at least initially. Perhaps it was Elvira's personality that allowed her to take advantage of venerable laws and new politics in the frontier kingdom of León for about ten years. But something happened in 975 that either killed Elvira or more likely put her back in her cloister. An army of Christian warriors from Navarre, Castile, and León beseiged the Muslim fortress at Gormaz and though they expected easy surrender, suffered a rout. Elvira disappeared from the records and Ramiro's mother took over as regent until she, too, returned to seclusion in 980.[24]

Elvira was merely the first of a string of queens and other great ladies who played a new kind of public politics. Queenship changed in the centuries around 1000. As kingship became more centralized, bureaucratic, and ceremonial, and kings themselves more remote, queens went with them. From influential peaceweavers, wielders of their own property, and mistresses of the family household – a household that focused on palaces and could comprise whole countries and their treasuries – queens became loving consorts of rulers whose primary power was intercession on behalf of petitioners.[25] As lady of the king's bed, the queen controlled intimate access to his ear. Matilda

[23] Roger Collins, "Queens-Dowager and Queens-Regent in Tenth-Century León and Navarre," ibid., 84–85.

[24] Ibid., 86–87.

[25] Jo Ann McNamara and Suzanne Wemple, "The Power of Women through the Family in Medieval Europe, 500–1100," in *Women and Power in the Middle Ages*, ed. Mary Erler and Maryanne Kowaleski (Athens: University of Georgia Press, 1988), 81–101.

(d. 1118), wife of Henry I of England and sister-in-law of Countess Adèle of Blois, was a woman well aware of the changes in queenly roles that transformed her own job and that of her mother, Queen Margaret of Scotland. Once married and consecrated, Matilda travelled with Henry, acted as his vice-regent when he was away, and kept her own household with her own officials. She also commissioned literature that promoted the queenly image she fancied in her saintly mother and in her own dutiful self.[26]

Likewise, the enemies, Adelaide, wife of Otto I and her daughter-in-law, Theophano, may have wrangled over control of parts of the empire and over the emperor himself during the reign of Otto II, but together they effectively maintained rule in the direct line of three emperors, contrary to previous traditions which permitted other royal males to inherit power in the absence of an adult heir. Although they battled over Italy, which was Adelheid's widow-property, Theophano triumphed via influence over her husband as *consors regni* (co-ruler) and after his death as regent for her son, Otto III. Theophano died first, though (991), and Adelheid succeeded her as regent until 994, when Otto III had her ejected for preventing memorial masses on behalf of his mother.[27] Their effect on the shape of imperial rule and the role of the empress was considerable and calculated, savvily employing bishops and foreign rulers to support their respective positions.

Countess Matilda of Tuscany (1046–1115), another well-documented powerhouse, was also a considerable heiress. She commanded troops and oversaw the reconciliation of Pope Gregory VII and Emperor Henry IV at Canossa after their battle over temporal power and church reform. A lovely picture from Matilda's own gospel book shows the emperor kneeling to an enthroned Matilda while the churchman points to her; she, meanwhile, extends a reassuring, benedictional hand to Henry from above. The influence of women such as Elvira and the two Matildas (as well as a third Matilda, the daughter of Matilda and Henry I, claimant to the English throne, wife

---

[26] Lois Huneycutt, "Intercession and the High-Medieval Queen: The Esther Topos," in *Power of the Weak: Studies on Medieval Women*, ed. Jennifer Carpenter and Sally-Beth MacLean (Urbana: University of Illinois Press, 1995), 126–46. See also Huneycutt, "Images of Queenship in the High Middle Ages," *Haskins Society Journal* 1 (1989), 61–71.

[27] Odilo Engels, "Theophano, the Western Empress from the East," in Davids, *Empress Theophano*, 28–48.

Rex ROGAT ABBATEM MATHILDIM SUppLICAT ATQ;

16 Matilda of Tuscany

of Emperor Henry V, and mother of King Henry II) was based on their connections. Just like early medieval queens, they were born of noble families and, except for Elvira, also married reigning leaders in order to produce more kings or dukes. They also gave birth to daughters whom they used as they had been used, in political marriages or abbatial positions to support family interests. But the way that queens exercised their influence after about 1000 began to change. They gained control of those precious portals to their husbands' attention, allowing access only to supplicants they themselves favored. Just as importantly, they acted as regents when their husbands were away or dead, and their children were too small to rule for themselves. In this way, the queens infiltrated such formal histories as those of Orderic Vitalis and William of Malmesbury.

The rituals by which clerics ordained queens from the end of the ninth century also marked a sacralization of queen's roles and the institutionalization of their duties as representatives of kings. Such rites expressed traditional pious wishes for the fertility of the royal couple, sustained by both the marital fecundity and the general chastity of the king's wife. Ermentrude, first wife of Emperor Charles the Bald, was one of the earliest to receive a crown by ordination although not until they had been married for twenty-four years. Her sons had all died, were dying, had rebelled against their father or, in Carloman's case, were tonsured, so the entire kingdom's wish for another child from the queen was poignantly apparent in the liturgy composed in 866 by Hincmar of Reims:

> May the Lord almighty, who blessed Adam and Eve, saying: "Go forth and multiply" . . . bless you and him your spouse in the future, so that according to the command of the Lord it may be brought about that "two are one flesh," "what God joined may no man separate," and may He bless you "with the dew of heaven and the fatness of the earth."[28]

Hincmar used the ordination of an abbess, with all the implications of governance and virtue that the religious office carried, as a model for his queenly ordination. However, the ceremony performed before nobles and ecclesiastics still focused publicly on the queen's ability to bear children.[29] Abbesses, too, held power derived from their noble births and family wealth, and their relations to powerful men within and outside of their kin; they responded to the authority of bishops and abbots as wives did to husbands. But they had purposely given up sons, the greatest treasure of laywomen and the source of political influence once other kinsmen had died. Instead, religious women wielded power over brothers and sisters and their offspring, as had the royal abbesses of Kent so many years before.[30]

---

[28] Richard A. Jackson, ed., *Ordines Coronationis Franciae: Texts and Ordines for the Coronation of Frankish and French Kings and Queens in the Middle Ages*, vol. 1 (Philadelphia: University of Pennsylvania Press, 1995), 86. See also Nelson, *Charles the Bald*, 210.

[29] Nelson, "Early Medieval Rites of Queen-Making."

[30] Johanna Maria Van Winter, "The Education of Daughters of the Nobility in the Ottonian Empire," in Davids, *Empress Theophano*, 86–98.

Queens in the years after 1000 came to share in an institution of queenship that lent them the potential for genuine power. Scholars have debated whether medieval queens were meek mead-bearers, pawns in family political games, honorary men who transcended gender, or active participants in and makers of events.[31] Some have even argued that queens lost power when kings and bishops together centralized and sacralized the position of kings and reduced the mediating function of queens.[32] Queens' political fortunes and access to power varied widely across the years and regions of Europe, depending upon the organization of queens' families, the nature of their connections to kings, the popularity of their relatives and themselves, their resources, their personalities, and sheer circumstance. But when they ruled, they did so based on their participation in the kingly cult of dynastic power, via titles that marked them as co-governors with their men, sanctified by coronation or ordination.[33] They used their authority as king's women to rule in several different situations, especially when their men allowed them to share power, when their men were too weak to stop them, or when their men died.

New trends in the public memory of ruling women took visual form, too. Beginning in the eleventh century, the artists of Europe recognized a different kind of queenship with pictures. Emma (d. 1052), wife first of Æthelred Unræd of England and then of Knut, conqueror of Æthelred and his kingdom, and ruler of an Anglo-Danish empire, took her place beside her second spouse in a page of the *Liber Vitae* of New Minster Abbey (see Fig. 11). Emma, called by her English name and her title Ælfgifu *regina*, stands to the viewer's left but to Jesus' right, across an altar from her husband. A crowd of clerics watch from below. An angel deposits a veil upon her head while another sets a crown on Knut. Above the couple and the altar, Christ floats in a mandorla with his mother Mary to his right, above Emma, and St. Peter to his left above Knut. Mary and Emma wear almost identical clothing. The artist was suggesting four vertical or horizontal pairs in the picture: Emma and Knut, Mary and Peter;

---

[31] M. J. Enright, "Lady with a Mead Cup: Ritual, Group Cohesion and Hierarchy in the Germanic Warband," *Frühmittelalterliche Studien* 22 (1988), 170–203; J. M. Wallace-Hadrill, *Early Germanic Kingship in England and on the Continent* (Oxford: Clarendon, 1971), 92–93; Pauline Stafford, "Emma: The Powers of the Queen in the Eleventh Century," in Duggan, *Queens and Queenship*, 3–26, esp. 6–12.

[32] McNamara and Wemple, "Power of Women," 83–101; McNamara, *Sisters in Arms*, 217.

[33] Duggan, "Introduction," in *Queens and Queenship*, xxi.

Peter and Knut, Mary and Emma. By this identification Emma shared the motherhood and virtues of the Blessed Virgin and through her gained a special relationship with Jesus. Her connection to the Son of God was similar to the tie she would make with the sons, invisible in this picture, that she bore Knut. The king, meanwhile, shared characteristics not with Jesus but with Peter, his rock and successor. In a sense, Emma outranked Knut just as Mary outranked Peter in intimacy with Jesus. Emma had a closer tie with Jesus through Mary. The artist was reminding viewers, too, that the kingship came to Knut, a usurper, through Ælfgifu, the anglicized wife of his predecessor Æthelred.[34] Emma fulfilled that promise not only with the births of sons but by favoring her son by Knut over her son by Æthelred when she engaged in politics.

Emma also took a hand in writing her own story, which is why we know so much more about her than about Elvira Ramírez or earlier queens. She commissioned the *Encomium Emmae* (Praise of Emma) in 1041 to justify her political choices as a mother and queen, although her author had trouble explaining events that eventually led to one of her sons being murdered so that another could take the English throne.[35] But Emma's patronage of a biographer puts the queen's perspective at the core of her history. Other manuscripts commissioned by women did the same by commemorating their patronesses' views and deeds in written histories, but also by acting as tangible, visible memorials to the women. Matilda's vita of her mother, Margaret of Scotland, is one example. The Books of Hours so popular in the later Middle Ages also signified the lives of women powerful and wealthy enough to command the creation of beautiful manuscripts, many of which featured portraits as visual memorials to their patronesses.[36] The frontispiece of the *Encomium Emmae* did the same in a drawing of the enthroned queen receiving a book from the kneeling author, watched by two royal sons peeking out of the picture's frame. The very existence of Emma's book, as well as its contents, constituted her fame.

[34] Stafford, "Emma," 3–4.
[35] Stafford, "The Portrayal of Royal Women in England, Mid-Tenth to Mid-Twelfth Centuries," in Parsons, *Medieval Queenship*, 143–67. See also Stafford's book developed from both articles cited here, *Queen Emma and Queen Edith: Queenship and Women's Power in Eleventh-Century England* (Oxford: Blackwell, 1997).
[36] See the articles in *Selected Proceedings of the St. Hilda's Conference 1993*, ed. Lesley Smith and Jane H. M. Taylor, vol. 2, *Women, the Book, and the Worldly* (Cambridge: D. S. Brewer, 1995.)

17 *Encomium Emmae*, frontispiece

Women's full realization of the potential of royal wifedom and motherhood became possible only when early medieval tribal kingdoms developed into the expanding, centralized, proto-national units of later Europe. Women became official queens and regents: not just wives of kings, as early medieval chronicles often styled them, but *reginae* (queens) and even *reges feminei* (feminine kings). Such changes in title and status occurred only after shifts in family structure allowed women to participate in focused dynastic politics rather than weave peace between sprawling cognatic kingroups. In the same period,

clerics were working to reform marriage laws so that women formally had some voice in the selection of their spouses, and could also
expect monogamous unions from law-abiding husbands. But only
when women recorded their own voices, whether indirectly through
their commissioning of particular works or through their own pens,
did they attain fame for their own political acts and thus promote the
recalling and commemorating of other royal and powerful women.

WOMEN OF WORDS

At around the same time that they became able to rule kingdoms and,
in the absence of brothers, inherit vast estates, women burst into written conversation. The increasing literacy of an emerging mercantile
culture helps explain the change. More people were literate; more
people were writing and producing more kinds of writing.[37] But new
kinds of individual consciousness in the literature also contributed,
especially an interiority unglimpsed in documents since the classical
period. No one would argue that individuals did not exist during the
early Middle Ages, of course, but literacy was rarer and writers then
had expressed self-awareness differently.[38] A woman like Hugeburc,
who wrote in 778 an account of the pilgrimage of St. Willibald to
Jerusalem, disguised her voice in her text and even hid her name in
a cryptogram undiscovered until 1931.[39]

Still, a very few exceptional women put their name and their feminine perspective to their works before 1000. Hrotsvit of Gandersheim
(932–1000) was the earliest known poet and playwright in Germany.
She produced her works for her sisters in the nunnery, who acted
out some of the pieces, thus sharing in Hrotsvit's production of texts.
Hrotsvit's poem about the martyr Pelagius took the traditional con-
ventions of the vitae and gave them a gendered twist. Her virgin
martyr was no long-suffering woman but a young man pursued by a
homosexual Saracen. When the Moorish ruler tried to kiss Pelagius,

---

[37] See, for instance, Michael Clanchy, *From Memory to Written Record: England 1066–1307* (Oxford University Press, 1993).

[38] Colin Morris, *The Discovery of the Individual, 1050–1200* (Toronto: University of Toronto Press, 1972).

[39] Bernhard Bischoff, "Wer ist die Nonne von Heidenheim," *Studien und Mitteilungen zur Geschichte des Benediktinerordens* 49 (1931), 387–97; Peter Dronke, *Women Writers of the Middle Ages* (Cambridge University Press, 1984), 33–34; see also Van Houts, *Memory and Gender*, 42–43.

he punched the persecutor in the mouth. Hrotsvit's drama was a critique of the semi-pornography of some early medieval vitae, which so luridly depicted women being sexually threatened. While a female saint might not have been able to defend herself within the parameters of traditional hagiography, the feminized victim in Hrotsvit's text could swing away.[40]

Once women began to write, they also began to put women in their words, to write about women's interests and even to write for women. Rather than serving as images in men's literature or modeling their works after those of men, women began to create a written consciousness of their own and even to create their own genres. Others in the Christian communities of Germany followed Hrotsvith's examples and wrote specifically so that their sisters might read. Hildegard of Bingen (1098–1179) was among the first to record her mystical experiences and her own interpretation of these in written words. "Behold in the forty-third year of my age," she recalled,

while with a trembling effort and in great fear I fixed my gaze upon a celestial vision, I saw a very great splendour, from which a voice from Heaven came to me saying: "O fragile man, ashes of ashes and dust of dust, say and write that thou seest and hearest. But because thou art timid in speaking, and simple in expounding, and unlearned in writing these things, say and write them not according to the speech of man, nor according to the human intellect and will, but according to that which thou seest and hearest in celestial matters from above, in the wonderful things of God."[41]

God himself told her not to write as a man, in the "speech" or written forms of men, but simply to record what came to her through divine inspiration – or inflammation, as what may be her own illustration of the process revealed. In the frontispiece to *Scivias*, from which this excerpt comes, Hildegard drew herself with head literally afire from above. Her caption read, "In the year 1141 of the incarnation of Jesus Christ the Son of God, when I was forty-two years and seven months of age, a fiery light, flashing intensely, came from the open vault of heaven and poured through my whole brain . . . And suddenly I could understand what such books as the psalter, the gospel, and the other catholic volumes of the Old and New Testament actually set forth."

[40] Elizabeth Petroff, ed. and trans., *Medieval Women's Visionary Literature* (Oxford University Press, 1986), 120.

[41] Hildegard of Bingen, *Scivias*, ed. Aldegundis Fuhrkotter (Turnholt: Brepols, 1978); trans. Columba Hart and Jane Bishop, The Classics of Western Spirituality (New York: Paulist Press, 1990).

18 Hildegard's vision, from *Liber Scivias*, manuscript (now lost) composed *c.* 1165

In the picture, Hildegard set down the story of her visions and other texts while, imprisonned by the frame of the image, her confessor and secretary Volmar watched. Hildegard seemed to be keeping a cautious eye on her scribe, lest he interfere with her own account of her past.[42]

Hildegard was right to fear interruption and restriction. Her irregular career made monks, bishops, the pope, and Bernard of Clairvaux wonder what she was up to, and they all read her *Scivias* and other

[42] Marilyn Stokstad, *Art History* (Abrams, 1999), fig. 15–36.

mystical writings, her scientific texts, and her hymns with a close eye for deviance. After all, she had been raised as a cloistered noblewoman, literally shut away with a single female tutor, until together they had formed a community at Disibodenberg. But later, when Hildegard commanded this community as abbess, she began to take orders from a higher authority than the abbot of the attached monastery. Apparently God recommended that she move her community to a hill at Rupertsberg. The monks and abbot "conspired together to prevent and thwart us," she wrote later. "They also said that I was deceived by some illusion."[43] Rather than resisting, Hildegard was opportunely struck by total paralysis. Only after the abbot came to nudge her, which produced no reaction except his belief in her vision, and after local noblewomen helped secure the bishop's permission for the nuns' move to Rupertsberg, did Hildegard get her way.[44] Thereafter, she continued to write and to administer her community until her death, after which her vita – as well as the people who had met her, who read her story, and who wondered at her works – gained her a cult following.

The core of her life's story probably came from Hildegard herself around 1170 when she was seventy-two, although it was subsequently revised by three monastic editors.[45] The process had been slightly different in the earlier Middle Ages, when St. Leoba's story was related by three of her sisters to a monk who made notes, after which Rudolf of Fulda constructed a narrative out of the notes. Hildegard, by contrast, dictated the essentials herself in a voice still recognizable beneath the monastic rewriting. Hildegard's was a distinctly eleventh-century feminine inspiration which had few models in the written canon. Before her, few religious female or male professionals since St. Augustine had described their personal experiences. Sustained self-examinations had only just begun again, after a long early medieval lapse, in the eleventh century.[46]

Hildegard, however, did not offer her own life events as a message to other Christians, although she referred to her past in order to

---

[43] *Vita Sanctae Hildegardis*, ed. Monika Klaes (Turnholt: Brepols, 1993), cap. 2.

[44] Sabine Flanagan, *Hildegard of Bingen, 1098–1179: A Visionary Life* (London: Routledge, 1989), 1–11.

[45] Barbara Newman, "Hildegard and Her Biographers: The Remaking of Female Sainthood," in *Gendered Voices: Medieval Saints and Their Interpreters*, ed. Catherine Mooney (Philadelphia: University of Pennsylvania Press, 1999), 16–34.

[46] Benton, *Self and Society*, 7, 35, 37.

justify her impudence in meditating upon other subjects. She demonstrated her worthiness to think and write with diverse autobiographical proofs: the message sent in flames, her long childhood history of visions denied, her lack of formal training, her fear of the very endeavor and its consequences, even the form taken by her writing, which was not in the language of men. When the writing itself did not suffice as justification, divine will caused an illness that proved the authenticity of her voice and gave her permission to record her thoughts. But Hildegard did not set out to write her life-story. Instead she, like the other female religious writers who followed her example, described an internal journey. When women did recount their days, it was to support these other passages, as Hildegard did when she mentioned the visions of her childhood. Only when confessors and editors intervened did women remember their personal pasts as Christian history, as Elisabeth of Schönau did for her brother Ekbert. More often, men recorded women's lives. They did so not in Hildegard's mystical tongue but in what Hildegard called the language of men, in order to validate and publish women's spiritual experiences for the benefit of other women and men.[47]

No one in the years around 1100 actually addressed women's past consciously as gendered history, but a few newly prominent female voices began to tell of women's experience or, at least, a woman's experience. A woman called Heloise (b. 1100) met Abelard (b. 1079) when she was a teenager, learned philosophy from him, had sex with him, had a child by him, and after they both entered religious communities continued to work and correspond with him. She became an abbess and unofficial theologian at a time when women could not train to be the latter. Most modern readers know Heloise simply as the discarded lover of Abelard, but in 1143 Peter the Venerable, abbot of the great monastery of Cluny, recalled Heloise's career as one of improving scholarship, not one of scandal that forced her into the religious life. "I had yet not quite passed the bounds of youth and reached early manhood," he wrote to her,

when I knew of your name and your reputation, not yet for religion but for your virtuous and praiseworthy studies. I used to hear at that time of the woman who although still caught up in the obligations of the world, devoted all her application to knowledge of letters, something which is very rare, and to the

[47] Mooney, *Gendered Voices*, passim, esp. Introduction, "Voice, Gender, and the Portrayal of Sanctity," 1–15.

pursuit of secular learning, and that not even the pleasures of the world, with its frivolities and delights, could distract her from this worthy determination to study the arts . . . You have surpassed all women in carrying out your purpose, and have gone further than almost every man.[48]

Peter remembered the precocious young scholar who excelled at letters, not the young woman who fell to her tutor's seductive charms. She chose the conventional way to remain a scholar by entering the cloister, but her reasons made her, as Peter points out, unusual.[49]

Once knowledge of her affair with Abelard had become public, Heloise argued that they should not marry; to further his career, prevent her own humiliation, and maintain their passionate love, they should remain unwed lovers. According to Abelard, she cited Christian fathers and classical philosophers to prove her point. "Who can concentrate on thoughts of Scripture or philosophy," she apparently demanded, "and be able to endure babies crying, nurses soothing them with lullabies, and all the noisy coming and going of men and women about the house?"[50] Abelard, who reported this conversation, read her concern as for him, but who is to say she did not fear such a life for herself? Later in life, she read Abelard's epistolary account of their shared history and criticized his version of their past: "I hoped for renewal of strength, at least from the writer's words which would picture for me the reality I have lost. But nearly every line of this letter was filled, I remember, with gall and wormwood, as it told the pitiful story of our entry into religion and the cross of unending suffering which you, my only love, continue to bear." She disagreed with his penitential acceptance and regretted having to give up Abelard and the sexual life in order to pursue knowledge, and she wrote him a letter to say so. But when he replied severely, she decided to separate her past and carnal self from her later and intellectual self: "I will therefore hold my hand from writing words which I cannot restrain my tongue from speaking," she told Abelard. "Would that a grieving heart would be as ready to obey as a writer's hand!" She added, "The more fully any thought occupies the mind and distracts it from other things, the more worthy should be the subject of such a thought and the more important it is where we direct our minds."[51] She had her own history distinct from that of

---

[48] Betty Radice, trans., *Letters of Abelard and Heloise* (Harmondsworth: Penguin, 1974), 277–78.

[49] Ibid., 70–74.   [50] Ibid.   [51] Ibid., 109ff.

Abelard, her own interpretation of the past to write, and her own future to shape after Abelard turned from her. She also was ready to express a feminine perspective on marrying and childbearing that other, less learned women of the earlier period may have shared. All these she incorporated into letters, allowing us an unique entry into a medieval woman's heart and mind.

Although Heloise was an innovator, she did not create a new literary genre specifically for women. She used an ancient epistolary form and she wrote to men. If she corresponded with other women or wrote literature for them, we do not know it (although she did beg Abelard to compose a monastic rule for her sisters, as she considered them too weak to follow monks' rules). Other female writers of the period, such as the anonymous daughter of the great Jewish talmudist Rashi (d. 1105), learned men's disciplines of theology and law to assist men, not in order to write for women. Likewise, Herrad of Hohenburg (1130–96) prepared an encyclopedia, gathering and arranging bits of knowledge and images originally produced by men over the centuries. Yet to write in the voice or style of men, or even in support of men's own writing, was not to write *as* men. Each of these women made feminine statements simply by composing with a pen. Herrad's selection of available scholarship was her own expression; Rashi's nameless daughter made her intellectual mark when she noted down his decisions; Heloise poured her heart into her letters.

One woman at the end of the early Middle Ages came close to analyzing women's experiences in a womanly voice, with her stories of men and women in love and marriage. Her name was Marie, called "de France" because historians know nothing more of her than that she came from that region. No one knows when, exactly, she was born or died, although her work probably appeared in the late twelfth century; the earliest manuscript containing her *lais* (tales in the form of poetry) comes from the early thirteenth. She used the first person writer's voice in her tales, and once mentioned herself by name: "Hear, lords, the words of Marie who, when she has the opportunity, does not squander her talents."[52]

Marie produced twelve *lais* about the adventures of ladies and knights, selected from the songs performed in Breton noble houses but transformed by her pen into tales for the highest literate elite.

---

[52] *Guigemar*, ll. 3–4, in Glyn S. Burgess and Keith Busby, trans., *The Lais of Marie de France* (Harmondsworth: Penguin, 1986), 44.

Unlike the romances of Chrétien de Troyes, who wrote lengthy stories of Arthurian heroes from a distinctly male point of view around the same time, Marie's stories offer a feminized perspective. In the prologue to the *lais*, Marie pointed out that "Anyone who has received from God the gift of knowledge and true eloquence has a duty not to remain silent: rather should one be happy to reveal such talents." Hildegard claimed authority for her writings based on God's command to reveal them in a new language. Marie's authority to write came from a greater assurance in her own talents, her knowledge and eloquence. Following the great authors of Antiquity, she argued, it was a worthy undertaking to study ancient texts and explicate them with translations and glosses. But, she believed, too many others were doing this kind of thing so she decided to write *lais* instead, "to perpetuate the memory of adventures." She even ordered the king, to whom she dedicated her work, not to consider her presumptuous. She deemed herself worthy and able to do the kind of work reserved for male scholars trained in monasteries and, by the time she was writing, the urban schools for theologians and philosophers. She rejected that labor, though, for another kind of writing that privileged the non-academic, non-canonical adventures of women and men together, and which could express the romantic past of women in a way that philosophy or traditional religious narratives never could. She was consciously recording this past: "In days gone by these valiant, courtly and noble men composed lays for posterity and thus preserved them from oblivion," she wrote, but it was Marie who lent the *lais* the permanence of written history.[53]

Women burst into song around Marie's time. Trobairitz, women poets, composed love songs to be performed at court. We know the names of about twenty of them. But the noble love songs of women were not always public; women composed under pseudonyms and recorded no verifiable personal events. They recounted loves won and lost, mostly illicitly, and even in the chivalrous atmosphere of the court could not reveal any genuine private histories.[54] Troubadors elsewhere wrote in the personae of women, but were actually men acting out women's laments at unfaithful lovers or imitating women's pleasure at men's attentions. Even women's prayers most often found

[53] *Equitan*, ll.1–2, ibid., 56.
[54] Peter Dronke, "The Provençal Trobairitz: Castelloza," in Wilson, *Medieval Women Writers*, 131–33.

manuscript form at men's hands, for instance the *tkhines*, special supplications for Jewish women's problems recorded at the end of the Middle Ages. Were they really the pleas of women, or what men imagined women would pray for?[55] The *chansons de toile* supposedly sung by women at needlework may have just been men's auditory hallucinations of women's songs.

There was no evolution of women's writing consciousness, no definite beginning point or goal of full literary voice achieved centuries later. And yet the very idea that women might sing, compose, and write of events and histories specific to women was new (with the possible exception, long ago, of Baudonivia's work) to the later Middle Ages. Heloise disapproved of Abelard's version of their combined history; Hildegard invoked an authority higher than bishops and abbots for her work; Marie revised men's oral and written forms of romance to write women's stories. Each act of defiance, however humble, gave evidence of women's new visibility and audibility after 1000. In the courts of great queens such as Eleanor of Aquitaine, a writer like Marie might flourish and experiment. In the interstices of reformed Christian institutions and new sorts of Christian spirituality, Hildegard had room to express knowledge imparted by God to the benefit of women and men throughout Christendom. When education moved out of the cloister, Heloise got some and used it to remember, in written form, her past. Modern scholars argue about how innovative these and other women writers of the Middle Ages were, whether they wrote for men or women, whether they even wrote their own texts (for a long time, historians suspected that Abelard might have composed Heloise's letters.) The point is not how we see and read these women, though. The point is that, after 1100, they left us their individual lives so that we might actually argue about them.

The end of the early Middle Ages allowed select women to emerge into the light of historical individuality. The new queens and heiresses, the literate women who wielded pens, and, particularly, the women who told women's own stories forced themselves into their generations' collective histories. The few who did this in the eleventh or twelfth century were followed by more women with increasing

---

[55] Leo Jung, "Literature for Jewish Women in Medieval and Later Times," in *The Jewish Library*, vol. 3: *Woman*, ed. Leo Jung (New York, 1943), 213–43; Baskin, "Jewish Women in the Middle Ages."

appeal for modern descendants. Heloise's brave stand against male authority, Hildegard's pursuit of a specifically feminine spirituality, Eleanor of Aquitaine's determination to rule in a man's world, and Joan of Arc – who has evolved from the nationalist martyr of Jules Michelet's nineteenth-century history to the feminist shaman of more recent interpretations – represent only the latest versions of popular affection and historical rediscovery. The strange nexus of patrilineal royal politics, new individualist mentalities, and increased access to literacy produced these heroines of the later Middle Ages. Yet their emergence into history had its costs, too, since their newfound prominence reduced the women who came before to a horde of mysterious saints, royal wives, and working mothers imprisoned in an utterly different kind of historiography.

THE GENEALOGY OF WOMEN

Alas for the less-than-famous women, the scholars and saints, the queens and peasants, the good girls and troublemakers, of the early Middle Ages! The women of later centuries added their own shadows to the cloud of men obscuring their ancestresses. Still, perhaps women of the early Middle Ages will not always live in the shade of historical speculation. They probably had their own histories and stories spread among themselves, and perhaps some day scholars will happen across the manuscripts or artifacts that reveal these tales. Women may have colluded in the histories produced by men, persuading them to include accounts of women's experiences via the formal constructs of men's texts. Our methods may become so refined that we can rescue the hidden histories. Women may have written the histories that we call men's, so perhaps we will discover the secret name of another woman in the margin of a manuscript and break the monopoly on early medieval history held by Gregory of Tours, Bede, and the undeserving others. We may also find new kinds of evidence to give us women's past: objects, art, bodies, or news from the landscape itself. Or we may simply revise what we know of the early Middle Ages, telling the story in another way, and thus spreading the fame of its women to larger audiences, giving Medb the due of Eleanor, Hild the renown of Hildegard.

For many reasons, women of the early medieval west are not important to most of us now. Eileen Power (d. 1940) wrote in her radio lectures on medieval European women that "the position of women is often considered a test by which the civilisation of a country or age may be judged."[56] We no longer think so, although we still seem to believe that the fame of individual women is a good substitute for measuring their status. And our instinctive reaction, probably molded by the philosophy and theology of the early Middle Ages, may still lead us to disapprove of cultures that "mistreat" their women. But scholars now would never presume to judge a society simply because it asked women to carry large burdens, labor together with men in fields, or work in factories. We would not immediately condone a community or nation that prevented its women from ruling or working in order to protect them from harm. We would not necessarily distinguish, as Power did, between the theoretical and legal positions of an elite regarding women, and the everyday lives of women, assuming that under liberal laws regarding gender all women must flourish. The issues of women's rights, women's equality, and women's voices still concern us since they are still more or less curtailed in almost every society on earth, but we do not all believe that our history can teach us how to dismantle the patriarchy. We do not even all agree that women's rights are curtailed, that patriarchy exists, or that women should have what men have, think what they think, or act as they do.

Yet the origins of our gender system lie in the earliest Middle Ages, not the later Middle Ages or any period before or after. As Suzanne Wemple pointed out several decades ago, this was when the crucial combination of a dominant Christian religion, Germanic custom, and Roman ideologies joined to form a formidable gender system. Christian leaders perfected their policies on women then. Governments and ethnic groups took shape in Europe that ultimately produced the nations and ethnic identities of today. The art and literature and, most importantly, the written history that came into being among the educated elite of the West still wield unavoidable influence. All of these developments took place in a cultural context that denigrated women as intellectually and morally inferior, legally disenfranchised women, and defined power as something women could never officially have. We took no direct path from early medieval Europe to the western world today, but we are haunted by the men and women who lived in Europe between about 400 and 1100 CE. Even our memory of them – and consequently, our memory of more

[56] Power, *Medieval Women*, 9.

recent generations – has been shaped by their own preferences for the deeds and thoughts of men.

Like all books, this book has merely signaled the beginning of a process of remembering. Each time a historian writes, she starts again to reconstruct the lines of descent from women and men of the past to herself. I have gone back beyond the famous women of the later Middle Ages to record the names of women who went before them, a few of whom commanded kingdoms, resisted men's institutional authority, or carried pens and wrote of women. But I have also sought the hidden memories of women who never ruled, never wrote, never told their names. I do once more what historians have been doing since long before the early Middle Ages: examine the books and fragments to discover what women and men left behind. This published act of recollection preserves what little is left of early medieval women, so that other memory-keepers can make new testaments to women gone before when they read this book, put it in a footnote, or revile it in a review. Merely retelling the stories keeps women alive in our collective memory, and our collective past keeps us all alive. From my fingers to God's ear, and to the eyes of the women and men who will read this book.

BIBLIOGRAPHY

——————— • ———————

In both footnotes and Bibliography, primary source citations are to dual-language editions when possible; editions in the original language when useful; and otherwise to English translations.

PRIMARY SOURCES

Adalbert. *Continuatio Regionis*, in *Ausgewählte Quellen zur deutschen Geschichte des Mittelalters*, vol. 8, *Quellen zur Geschichte der sächsischen Kaiserzeit: Widukinds Sachsengeschichte, Adalberts Fortsetzung der Chronik Reginos, Liudprands Werke*, ed. Albert Bauer and Reinhold Rau. Darmstadt: Wissenschaftliche Buchgesellschaft, 1971, 190–231.

Adomnán. *Life of Columba*, ed. and trans. A. O. Anderson and M. O. Anderson. London: Nelson, 1961.

Aethelwold. *Regularis Concordia Anglicae Nationis Monachorum Sanctimonialiumque*, ed. Thomas Symons. London: Nelson, 1953.

Ammianus Marcellinus. *Ammiani Marcellini Rerum Gestarum Libri Qui Supersunt*, ed. Franz Eyssenhardt. Berlin: Vahleln, 1871.

Amt, Emilie, ed. *Women's Lives in Medieval Europe: A Sourcebook*. New York: Routledge, 1993.

Annales Laurissenses [Annals of Lorsch] *Minores*, ed. Georg Pertz, *MGH SS* 1 (1826), 114–23.

Annales Sancti Amandi [Annals of St. Amand], in *Annales et Chronica Aevi Carolini*, ed. Georg Pertz, *MGH SS* 1 (1826), 6–14.

Annales Sancti Bertini [Annals of St. Bertin], in Annales et Chronica Aevi Carolini, ed. Georg Pertz, *MGH SS* 1 (1826), 439–54.

Arent, Margaret, trans. *Laxdaela Saga*. Seattle: University of Washington Press, 1964.

Asser. *Aelfredi Regis Res Gestae*, in *Alfred the Great: Asser's Life of Alfred and Other Contemporary Sources*, trans. and ed. Simon Keynes and Michael Lapidge. Harmondsworth: Penguin, 1983.

Augustine. *Confessions*, trans. R. S. Pine-Coffin. New York: Dorset Press, 1986.

Augustine. [*De Genesi ad Litteram*] *The Literal Meaning of Genesis*, trans. John Hammond Taylor. New York: Newman Press, 1982.

Augustine. [*De Civitate Dei*] *City of God*, trans. David S. Wiesen, Loeb Classical Library. Cambridge, MA: Harvard University Press, 1965.

Augustine. *De Sancta Virginitate*, Corpus Scriptorum Ecclesiasticorum Latinorum, vol. 41. Vienna: Tempsky, 1900.

Baudonivia. *La Vita Radegundis di Baudonivia*, ed. Paola Santorelli. Naples: Dauria, 1999.

Bede. *Vita Cuthberti*, in *Two Lives of Saint Cuthbert: A Life by an Anonymous Monk of Lindisfarne and Bede's Prose Life*, ed. and trans. Bertram Colgrave. Cambridge University Press, 1940; reprint Oxford: Clarendon, 1991.

Bede. *Historia Ecclesiastica Gentis Anglorum, Historia Abbatum, Epistola ad Ecgberctum, Historia Abbatum Auctore Anonymo*, ed. Charles Plummer, 2 vols. Oxford: Clarendon, 1896.

Bede. *Baedae Opera Historica*, 2 vols., ed. and trans. J. E. King. New York: Putnam, 1930.

Benton, John F., ed. and trans. *Self and Society in Medieval France: The Memoirs of Abbot Guibert of Nogent*. Toronto: University of Toronto Press, 1984.

Beowulf, trans. Michael Alexander. New York: Penguin, 1995.

Best, R. I. and O. Bergin, eds. *The Book of Leinster*, 6 vols. Dublin Institute for Advanced Studies, 1954–83.

Beyerle, Franz, ed. *Die Gesetze der Langobarden*. Weimar: Böhlau, 1947.

Bhreathnach, Máire. "A New Edition of *Tochmarc Becfhola*." *Ériu* 35 (1984), 59–81.

Bieler, Ludwig, ed. and trans. *Patrician Texts in the Book of Armagh*, Scriptores Latini Hiberniae 10. Dublin Institute for Advanced Studies, 1979.

Binchy, D. A., ed. *Corpus Iuris Hibernici*, 6 vols. Dublin Institute for Advanced Studies, 1978.

Binchy, D. A., ed. and trans. "Bretha Crólige," *Ériu* 12 (1938), 26–27.

Boileau, Etienne. *Les Métiers et corporations de la ville de Paris, XIIIe siècle*, ed. René de Lespinasse and François Bonnardot. Paris: Imprimerie nationale, 1879.

Boniface. *Epistolae*, ed. M. Tangl in *Die Briefe des heiligen Bonifatius und Lullus. MGH Epistolae* 1 (1955).

Boniface. *Epistolae* xiv, trans. Edward Kylie in *The English Correspondence of Saint Boniface*. New York: Cooper Square, 1966.

Boretius, Alfred Erwin, ed. *Capitularia Regum Francorum*. Hanover, 1883.

Burchard of Worms. *Decretum*, in *Opera Omnia*, PL 140 (1880).

Caesar, Julius. *De Bello Gallico*, ed. Wolfgang Hering, Bibliotheca Scriptorum Graecorum et Romanorum Teubneriana. Leipzig: Teubner, 1987. Trans. Carolyn Hammond in *Seven Commentaries on the Gallic War* (Oxford University Press, 1996).

Caesarius of Arles. *The Rule for Nuns of Saint Caesarius of Arles*, trans. Maria Caritas McCarthy. Washington, DC: Catholic University of America Press, 1960.

Campbell, Jackson J., ed. *The Advent Lyrics of the Exeter Book*. Princeton University Press, 1959.

Cassius Dio Cocceianus. *Historia Romana*, ed. and trans. E. Cary and H. Foster as *Dio's Roman History*. New York: MacMillan, 1914–27.

Chaucer, Geoffrey. *Canterbury Tales*, trans. and ed. David Wright. Oxford University Press, 1985.

Chrétien de Troyes. [*Le Chevalier au lion*] *The Knight with the Lion or Yvain*, trans. and ed. William W. Kibler. New York: Garland, 1985.

Chronica Minora Saec. IV. V. VI. VII., ed. Theodor Mommsen, *MGH AA* 9, 3 vols. (1892–98).

Cogitosus. *Vita Sanctae Brigidae*, *PL* 72 (1878).

Comnena, Anna. *The Alexiad of Anna Comnena*, trans. and ed. F. R. A. Sewer. Hamondsworth: Penguin, 1969.

Concilia Gallia, ed. Charles Munier and Charles de Clercq, Corpus Christianorum Series Latina 148A. Turnholt: Brepols, 1963.

Corpus Medicorum Latinorum, multiple vols. Berlin: In Aedibus Academiae Scientiarum, 1915– .

Crossley-Holland, Kevin, ed. and trans. *The Exeter Riddle Book*. London: Folio Society, 1978.

Dhuoda, *Liber Manualis: Handbook for Her Warrior Son*, trans. and ed. Marcelle Thiebaux. Cambridge University Press, 1998.

Donatus. *Regula ad Virgines*, *PL* 87 (1863), 273–98.

Drew, Katherine Fischer, trans. *Laws of the Salian Franks*. Philadelphia: University of Pennsylvania Press, 1991.

Drew, Katherine Fischer. [*Leges Langobardorum*] *The Lombard Laws*. Philadelphia: University of Pennsylvania Press, 1973.

Drew, Katherine Fischer. *The Burgundian Code*. Philadelphia: University of Pennsylvania Press, 1972.

Epstein, Isidore and Josephy H. Hertz, trans. and ed. *The Babylonian Talmud*. London: The Soncino Press, 1935.

Ford, Patrick, trans. *The Mabinogi, and Other Medieval Welsh Tales*. Berkeley: University of California Press, 1977.

Fortunatus, Venantius. *Venantius Fortunatus: Personal and Political Poems*, trans. Judith George. Liverpool University Press, 1995.

Fredegarius Scholasticus. *Fredegarii et Aliorum Chronica. Vitae Sanctorum*, ed. Bruno Krusch, *MGH SSRM* 2 (1888).

Fulcher of Chartres. *Historia Iherosolymitana: Gesta Francorum Iherusalem Peregrinantium ab anno Domini MXCV usque ad annum MCXXVII*, Recueil des Historiens des Croisades. Paris, 1866.

Fulcher of Chartres. [*Historia Iherosolymitana*] trans. Frances Rita Ryan in *A History of the Expedition to Jerusalem, 1095–1127*, ed. Harold A. Fink. Knoxville: University of Tennessee Press, 1969.

Gantz, Jeffrey, trans. *The Mabinogion*. New York: Penguin, 1976.

Gelasius. *Epistolae et Decreta, PL* 59 (1862), 13–140.

Gerald of Wales. *Topographia Hibernica*, ed. J. F. Dimock. Rolls Series vol. 5. London: Longman, 1867.

Gerald of Wales. [*Topographia Hibernica*] *History and Topography of Ireland*, trans. John J. O'Meara. New York: Penguin, 1982.

Gildas. [*De Excidio Britanniae*] *The Ruin of Britain and Other Works*, trans. Michael Winterbottom. London: Rowman and Littlefield, 1978.

Gratian. *Decretum*, in *Corpus Juris Canonici*, ed. E. Friedberg. and A. Richter, 2 vols. Graz: Akademische Druck- und Verlagsanstalt, 1959.

Gregory of Tours. [*Liber de Martyribus*] *Glory of the Martyrs*, trans. Raymond van Dam. Liverpool University Press, 1988.

Gregory of Tours. *Historia Francorum*, ed. Wilhelm Arndt and Bruno Krusch, *MGH SSRM* 1 (1884).

Gregory of Tours. [*Historia Francorum*] *History of the Franks*, trans. Lewis Thorpe. Harmondsworth: Penguin, 1974.

Gundlach, W., ed. *Epistulae Austrasiacae*, in *MGH Epistolae* 3, *Epistolae Merowingici et Karolini Aevi* (1892).

Gwynn, E. J. and W. J. Purton, ed. and trans. "The Monastery of Tallaght," *Proceedings of the Royal Irish Academy* 29 C (1911), 115–79.

Gwynn, L., ed. and trans. "De Síl Chonairi Móir," *Ériu* 6 (1912).

Haddan, Arthur and William Stubbs, ed. *Councils and Ecclesiastical Documents Relating to Great Britain and Ireland*, 3 vols. Oxford University Press, 1869.

Hefele, Carl J. and Henri LeClercq. *Histoire des Conciles d'après les documents originaux*, vol. 4. Paris: Letouzey et Ané, 1938.

Helbig, Herbert and Lorenz Weinrich, ed. *Urkunden und erzählende Quellen zur deutschen Ostsiedlung im Mittelalter*. Darmstadt: Wissenschaftliche Buchgesellschaft, 1968–70.

Heist, W. W. *Vitae Sanctorum Hiberniae*, Subsidia Hagiographica 26. Brussels: Bollandists, 1965.

Hildegard of Bingen. *Scivias*, ed. Aldegundis Fuhrkotter. Turnholt: Brepols, 1978; trans. Columba Hart and Jane Bishop, *Scivias,* The Classics of Western Spirituality. New York: Paulist Press, 1990.

Hillgarth, J. N., trans. and ed. *Christianity and Paganism, 350–750: The Conversion of Western Europe*. Rev. edn. Philadelphia: University of Pennsylvania Press, 1986.

Hincmar of Reims. *Collectio de Raptoribus*, in *PL* 126, 1017–36 (1900).

Hincmar of Reims. *Hincmari Archiepiscopi Remensis Epistolae*, ed. H. Perels, *MGH Epistolae* (1975).

Hunnisett, R. F. *Bedfordshire Court Rolls*. Bedfordshire Historical Record Society, 1961.

Jackson, K. H., ed. and trans. *A Celtic Miscellany*. Harmondsworth: Penguin, 1986.

Jackson, Richard A., ed. *Ordines Coronationis Franciae: Texts and Ordines for the Coronation of Frankish and French Kings and Queens in the Middle Ages*, vol. 1. Philadelphia: University of Pennsylvania Press, 1995.

Jenkins, D., trans. *The Laws of Hywel Dda*. Liverpool University Press, 1954.

Jerome. *Select Letters of St. Jerome*, trans. F. A. Wright. New York: Putnam, 1933.

Jonas. *Vita Sancti Columbani*, ed. B. Krusch, *Ionae Vitae Sanctorum Columbani, Vedastis, Iohannis, MGH SRG* (Hanover, 1902).

Jonas. [*Vita Sancti Columbani*] *Life of St. Columban*, ed. and trans. Dana Carleton Munro. Philadelphia: University of Philadelphia Press, 1895.

Jordanes. *Iordanis Romana et Getica*, ed. Theodor Mommsen, *MGH AA* 5:1 (1882).

Jordanes. [*Getica*] *The Gothic History of Jordanes in English Version*, trans. C. C. Mierow. New York: Barnes & Noble, 1960.

Justinus, Marcus Julianus. *Epitome of the Philippic History of Pompeius Trogus*, Books 11–12, *Alexander the Great*, trans. John Yardley and Waldemar Heckel. Oxford: Clarendon, 1997.

King, P. D., ed. and trans. *Charlemagne: Translated Sources*. Kendal: P. D. King, 1987.

Kinsella, Thomas. *The Tain*. Oxford University Press, 1970.

Koch, John T. and John Carey, ed. *The Celtic Heroic Age : Literary Sources for Ancient Celtic Europe and Early Ireland and Wales*. Malden: Celtic Studies Publications, 1994.

Kraemer, Ross S., ed. *Maenads, Martyrs, Matrons, Monastics: A Sourcebook of Women's Religions in the Greco-Roman World*. Philadelphia: Fortress Press, 1988.

Leges Anglo-Saxonum, 601–925, ed. Karl August Eckhardt, Biblotheca Rerum Historicarum, Corpus Iuris Europensis, no. 13. Göttingen: Muster-schmidt, 1974.

Lefkowitz, Mary R. and Maureen B. Fant, eds. *Women's Life in Greece and Rome*. Repr. Baltimore, MD: Johns Hopkins University Press, 1992.

Leges Visigothorum, ed. Karl Zeumer, *MGH Leges* 1 (1902); trans. S. P. Scott as *The Visigothic Code (Forum Judicum)*. Boston, 1910.

Lex Ribuaria, ed. F. Beyerle and R. Buchner, *MGH Leges* 3, 2 (1954).

Liber Historiae Francorum, ed. and trans. Bernard S. Bacharach. Lawrence: Cornado Press, 1973.

Lopez, R. and I. Raymond, ed. and trans. *Medieval Trade in the Mediterranean World*. New York: Columbia University Press, 1955.

Louis J. Rodrigues, ed. and trans. *Anglo-Saxon Verse Charms, Maxims, and Heroic Legends*. Pinner: Anglo-Saxon, 1993.

Loyn, H. R. and John Percival, ed. *The Reign of Charlemagne: Documents on Carolingian Government and Administration*. London: Arnold, 1975.

Lucan. [*Pharsalia*] *The Civil War*, trans. S. H. Braund. Oxford University Press, 1992.

Macalister, R. A. S. and John Carey, ed. and trans. *Lebor Gabála Érenn: The Book of the Taking of Ireland*, 5 vols., Irish Texts Society. Dublin: Irish Texts Society, 1932–56; reprint, London: Irish Texts Society, 1993.

Maimonides, Moses. *Responsa of Moses ben Maimon*, vol. 1, ed. Yehoshua Blau. Jerusalem, 1958.

McNamara, Jo Ann and John E. Halborg, trans. *The Ordeal of Community: The Rule of Donatus of Besançon and the Rule of a Certain Father to the Virgins*. Toronto: Peregrina, 1990.

McNamara, Jo Ann and John E. Halborg with E. Gordon Whatley, trans. *Sainted Women of the Dark Ages*. Durham: Duke University Press, 1992.

Marie de France. *Guigemar, Equitan, Le Fresne*, in *The Lais of Marie de France*, ed. and trans. Glyn S. Burgess and Keith Busby. Harmondsworth: Penguin, 1986.

Meyer, Kuno, ed. and trans. *Liadain and Cuirithir: An Irish Love Story of the Ninth Century*. London: Nutt, 1902.

Meyer, Kuno. *Cáin Adamnáin: An Old-Irish Treatise on the Law of Adamnán*. Oxford: Clarendon, 1905.

Meyer, Kuno. *Fianaigecht: Being a Collection of Hitherto Inedited Irish Poems and Tales Relating to Finn and His Fiana*. Dublin: Hodges, 1910; repr. Dublin: School of Celtic Studies, 1993.

Morton, C. and H. Muntz, ed. and trans. *The Carmen de Hastingae Proelio of Guy Bishop of Amiens*. Oxford: Clarendon, 1972.

Murphy, Gerard, ed. and trans. *Early Irish Lyrics, Eighth to Twelfth Century*. Oxford: Clarendon, 1956.

Neusner, Jacob, trans. *The Mishnah: A New Translation*. New Haven: Yale University Press, 1988.

Ó hAodha, Donnchadh, ed. *Bethu Brigte*. Dublin Institute for Advanced Studies, 1978.

Ó Máille, Tomás, ed. and trans. "Medb Cruachna," *Zeitschrift für celtische Philologie* 17 (1927), 129–46.

O'Rahilly, Cecile, ed. and trans. *Táin Bó Cúailnge: Recension I*. Dublin Institute for Advanced Studies, 1976.

Odo of Cluny. *Opera Omnia*, PL 133 (1881).

Ordericus Vitalis. [*Historia Eecclesiastica*]. *The Ecclesiastical History of Orderic Vitalis*, trans. and ed. Marjorie Chibnall. Oxford, Clarendon, 1968–80.

Ordericus Vitalis. [*Historia Ecclesiastica*] *The Ecclesiastical History of England and Normandy*, trans. Thomas Forester. Repr. New York: AMS Press, 1968.

Origen. *Contra Celsum*, trans. Henry Chadwick. Cambridge University Press, 1965.

Pactus Legis Salicae, ed. Karl A. Eckhardt, *MGH Leges* 4,1 (1962).

Paul the Deacon. *Historia Langobardorum*, ed. Georg Waitz, *MGH SSRG* 48 (1878).

Paul the Deacon. [*Historia Langobardorum*] *History of the Langobards*, trans. W. D. Foulke, ed. Edward Peters. Philadelphia: University of Pennsylvania Press, 1974.

Petroff, Elizabeth, ed. and trans. *Medieval Women's Visionary Literature*. Oxford University Press, 1986.

Plummer, Charles, ed. *Vitae Sanctorum Hiberniae partim hactenus ineditae ad fidem codicum manuscriptorum . . . prolegomenis notis indicibus*, 2 vols. Oxford: Clarendon, 1910.

Radice, Betty, trans. *The Letters of Abelard and Heloise*. Harmondsworth: Penguin, 1974.

Regino of Prüm. *Chronik Anno 864–869*, ed. Reinhold S. Rau, Quellen zur karolingischen Reichsgeschichte. Berlin : Rutten & Loening, 1956–.

Regino of Prüm. *De Synodalibus Causis et Disciplinis Ecclesiasticis*, ed. Hermann Wasserschleben. Leipzig: Engelmann, 1840; repr. Graz: Akademische Druck- und Verlagsanstalt, 1964.

Roberts, Alexander and James Donaldson, eds. *The Ante-Nicene Fathers: Translations of the Writings of the Fathers down to A.D. 325*, multiple vols. Grand Rapids: Eerdmans, 1974–77.

Rodrigues, Louis J., ed. and trans. *Anglo-Saxon Verse Charms, Maxims, and Heroic Legends* (Pinner, 1993).

Roger of Wendover. *Chronica, sive Flores Historiarum*, ed. H. O. Coxe, 4 vols. London: English Historical Society, 1841–42.

Rudolf of Fulda. *Life of Leoba*, in *The Anglo-Saxon Missionaries in Germany*, ed. C. H. Talbot. New York: Sheed & Ward, 1954.

Sacramentario del vescovo Warmondo di Ivrea: fine seculo X, Ivrea Biblioteca capitolare, MS 31 LXXXVI. Ivrea: Diocese of Ivrea, 1990.

Saxo Grammaticus. *Saxonis Gesta Danorum*, ed. Jorgen Olrik and Hans Raeder. Copenhagen: Levin & Munksgaard, 1931.

Saxo Grammaticus. [*Gesta Danorum*] *The History of the Danes*, trans. and ed. Peter Fisher and Hilda Davidson. Cambridge: D. S. Brewer, 1979.

Selmer, Carl, ed. *Navigatio Sancti Brendani Abbatis, From Early Latin Manuscripts*. Notre Dame: University of Notre Dame Press, 1959.

Sidonius Apollinaris. *Letters and Poems*, ed. and trans. W. B. Anderson. Cambridge, MA: Harvard University Press, 1936–65.

Smith, Roland M., ed. and trans. "The *Senbriathra Fithail* and Related Texts," *Revue Celtique* 45 (1928), 52–53.

Stephanus, Eddius. *Vita Sancti Wilfrithi*, ed. Bertram Colgrave. Cambridge University Press, 1927; trans. David Farmer in *The Age of Bede*. Harmondsworth: Penguin, 1988.

Stokes, Whitley, ed. and trans. *Félire Óengusso Céli Dé*. [*The Martyrology of Oengus, the Culdee*] London: Harrison & Sons, 1905.

Stokes, Whitley. *The Tripartite Life of St. Patrick and Other Documents Relating to the Saint*. London: Eyre & Spottiswoode, 1887.

Stokes, Whitley. "The Death of Crimthann Son of Fidach and the Adventures of the Sons of Eochaid Muigmedón," *Revue Celtique* 24 (1903), 172–207.

Strabo. [*Geographica*]. *The Geography of Strabo*, trans. Horace Leonard Jones. Cambridge, MA: Harvard University Press, 1960–70. 7 vols.

Swanton, Michael, trans. *Anglo-Saxon Prose*. London: Dent, 1975.

Tacitus. *Annales, Germania*, in *The Complete Works of Tacitus*, trans. A. J. Church and W. J. Brodribb. New York: The Modern Library, 1942.

Taylor, Paul B. and W. H. Auden, trans. *The Elder Edda: A Selection*. New York: Random House, 1969.

Terry, Patricia, trans. *The Song of Roland*. 2nd edn., New York: MacMillan, 1992.

Tertullian. *De Cultu Feminarum*, trans. Rudolph Arbesmann, Sister Emily Joseph Daly, and Edwin A. Quain in *Tertullian: Disciplinary, Moral, and Ascetical Works*, Fathers of the Church: A New Translation, vol. 40. Washington, DC: Catholic University Press, 1977.

Theodoricus Wirzburgensis. *Theodoric's Description of Holy Places: circa 1172 A.D.*, trans. Aubrey Stewart, Palestine Pilgrims' Text Society. London, 1896; repr. New York: AMS Press, 1971.

Thomson, Derick, ed. *Branwen Uerch Lyr: The Second of the Four Branches of the Mabinogi*. Dublin Institute for Advanced Studies, 1976.

Ulster Society for Medieval Latin Studies. "The Life of St. Monenna by Conchubranus," Seanchas Ard Mhacha 10 (1980–81), 136–39.

Vita Genovefae Virginis Parisiensis, in *Passiones Vitaeque Sanctorum Aevi Merovingici*, ed. Bruno Krusch and Wilhelm Levison, *MGH SSRM* 3 (1902), 204–38.

Vita Galli Confessoris Triplex, in *Passiones Vitaeque Sanctorum Aevi Merovingici*, ed. Bruno Krusch and Wilhelm Levison, *MGH SSRM* 4 (1913).

Vita Radegundae, in *Fredegarii et Aliorum Chronica. Vitae Sanctorum*, ed. Bruno Krusch, *MGH SSRM* 2 (1888).

Vita Sanctae Hildegardis, ed. Monika Klaes. Turnholt: Brepols, 1993.

Vitry, Jacques de. [*Historia Iherosolymitana*] *The History of Jerusalem A.D. 1180 by Jacques de Vitry*, trans. Aubrey Stewart. Repr., New York: AMS Press, 1971.

Wasserschleben, F. W. H., ed. *Die irische Kanonensammlung*. Leipzig: Tauchnitz, 1885.

Williams, Ifor, ed. *Canu Llywarch Hen*. Cardiff: University of Wales Press, 1935.

Wilson, Katherina, ed. *Medieval Women Writers*. Athens: University of Georgia Press, 1984.

Wilkinson, John, trans. *Jerusalem Pilgrims Before the Crusades*. Warminster: Aris & Phillips, 1977.

Wulfstan. *Sermo Lupi ad Anglos*, trans. and ed. Melissa J. Bernstein at http://www.cif.rochester.edu/~mjbernst/wulfstan/noframes.html. 1996.

SECONDARY SOURCES

Agus, Irving A., ed. *Urban Civilization in Pre-Crusade Europe: A Study of Organized Town-Life in Northwestern Europe During the Tenth and Eleventh Centuries Based on the Responsa Literature*. New York: Yeshiva University Press, 1965.

Airlie, Stuart. "Private Bodies and the Body Politic: The Divorce Case of Lothar II," 161 (1998), 3–38.

Amory, Patrick. "The Meaning and Purpose of Ethnic Terminology in the Burgundian Laws," *Early Medieval Europe* 2 (1993), 1–28.

Anderson, Bonnie and Judith Zinsser. *A History of Their Own: Women in Europe from Prehistory to the Present*. Revised edn., New York: Oxford University Press, 2000.

Bachofen, J. J. *Das Mutterrecht*. 2nd edn., Basel: Schwabe, 1897.

Barber, Elizabeth W. *Women's Work: The First 20,000 Years: Women, Cloth, and Society in Early Times*. New York: Norton, 1994.

Bardsley, Sandy. "Women's Work Reconsidered: Gender and Wage Differentiation in Late Medieval England," *Past and Present* 165 (1999), 3–29.

Barnwell, P. S. "Emperors, Jurists and Kings: Law and Custom in the Late Roman and Early Medieval West," *Speculum* 168 (2000), 6–29.

Bartlett, Robert. *The Making of Europe: Conquest, Colonization, and Cultural Change, 950–1350*. Princeton University Press, 1993.

Baskin, Judith. "Jewish Women in the Middle Ages," in *Jewish Women in Historical Perspective*, ed. Judith Baskin, 94–114. 2nd edn., Detroit: Wayne State University Press, 1998.

Baskin, Judith. "Some Parallels in the Education of Medieval Jewish and Christian Women," *Jewish History* 5 (1991), 141–51.

Baskin, Judith. "Women and Judaism," in *The Millennial Encyclopedia of Judaism*, ed. Jacob Neusner *et al.*, vol. 3, *1478–1502*. Brill and Continuum, 2000.

Bennett, Judith M. "The Village Ale-Wife: Women and Brewing in Fourteenth-Century England," in Hanawalt, *Women and Work in Preindustrial Europe*, 20–36.

Bennett, Judith M. *Women in the Medieval English Countryside: Gender and Household in Brigstock Before the Plague.* Oxford University Press, 1987.

Bennett, Judith M. "History that Stands Still: Women's Work in the European Past," *Feminist Studies* 14 (1988), 269–83.

Bennett, Judith M. "Medievalism and Feminism," in Partner, *Studying Medieval Women*, 7–29.

Bennett, Judith M. "Theoretical Issues: Confronting Continuity," *Journal of Women's History* 9 (1997), 73–94.

Bennett, Judith, ed. *Sisters and Workers in the Middle Ages.* Chicago, 1989.

Berger, Pamela C. *The Goddess Obscured: Transformation of the Grain Protectress from Goddess to Saint.* Boston: Beacon Press, 1985.

Berkey, Jonathan. "Women in Medieval Islamic Society," in *Women in Medieval Western European Culture*, ed. Linda E. Mitchell, 95–111. New York: Garland, 1999.

Biddick, Kathleen. "Genders, Bodies, Borders: Technologies of the Visible," in Partner, *Studying Medieval Women*, 87–116.

Bischoff, Bernhard. "Die kölner Nonnenhandschriften und das Skriptorium von Chelles," in Bischoff, *Mittelalterliche Studien: Ausgewählte Aufsätze zur Schriftkunde und Literaturgeschichte*, 3 vols. Stuttgart: Hiersemann, 1966–81.

Bischoff, Bernhard. "Wer ist die Nonne von Heidenheim?" *Studien und Mitteilungen zur Geschichte des Benediktinerordens* 49 (1931), 387–97.

Bitel, Lisa M. *Isle of the Saints: Monastic Settlement and Christian Community in Early Ireland.* Ithaca: Cornell University Press, 1990.

Bitel, Lisa M. "*In Visu Noctis*: Dreams in Early Medieval Hagiography and Histories, 500–900," *History of Religions* 31 (1991), 39–59.

Bitel, Lisa M. *The Land of Women: Tales of Sex and Gender from Early Ireland.* Ithaca: Cornell University Press, 1996.

Bitel, Lisa M. "Women in Early Medieval Northern Europe," in *Becoming Visible: Women in European History*, ed. Renate Bridenthal et al., 105–128. 3rd edn., Boston: Houghton Mifflin, 1998.

Bitel, Lisa M. "Landscape, Gender, and Ethnogenesis in Pre(norman) Invasion Ireland," forthcoming in *Inventing Medieval Landscapes*, ed. Michael Wolfe and John M. Howe. University Press of Florida.

Bloch, Marc. *Feudal Society*, trans. L. A. Manyon. Chicago: University of Chicago Press, 1961.

Blondiaux, Joel. "La femme et son corps au haut moyen-âge vus par l'anthropologue et le paléopathologiste," in *La Femme au moyen-âge*, ed. Michele Rouche and Jean Heuclin, 115–38 Publication de la Ville de Maubeuge, Diffusion Jean Touzot, 1990.

Bouchard, Constance. "Family Structure and Family Consciousness Among the Aristocracy in the Ninth to Eleventh Centuries," *Francia* 14 (1986), 639–58.

Bowen, Charles. "Great-Bladdered Medb: Mythology and Invention in the *Táin Bó Cuailnge*," *Éire-Ireland* 10 (1975), 14–34.

Braudel, Fernand. *The Mediterranean and the Mediterranean World in the Age of Philip the Second*, trans. Sian Reynolds, 2 vols. London: Collins, 1972.

Brenneman, Walter L. and Mary G. Brenneman. *Crossing the Circle at the Holy Wells of Ireland*. Charlottesville: University Press of Virginia, 1995.

Bridenthal, Renate and Susan Mosher Stuard, eds. *Becoming Visible: Women in European History*. 3rd edn., Boston: Houghton Mifflin, 1998.

Brown, Peter. *The Cult of the Saints: Its Rise and Function in Latin Christianity*. Chicago: University of Chicago Press, 1981.

Brown, Peter. *The Body and Society: Men, Women, and Sexual Renunciation in Early Christianity*. New York: Columbia University Press, 1988.

Brundage, James. *Law, Sex, and Christian Society in Medieval Europe*. Chicago: University of Chicago Press, 1987.

Brundage, James. "Prostitution, Miscegenation and Sexual Purity in the First Crusade," in Edbury, *Crusade and Settlement, 57–66.*

Bücher, Karl. *Die Frauenfrage im Mittelalter.* 2nd edn., Tübingen: Laupp, 1910.

Budny, Mildred. "The Ango-Saxon Embroideries at Maaseik: Their Historical and Art-Historical Context," *Mededelingen van de Koninklijke Academie voor Wetenschappen, Letteren en schone Kunsten van Belgie* 45 (1984), 57–113.

Budny, Mildred, and Dominic Tweddle, "The Maaseik Embroideries," *Anglo-Saxon England* 13 (1984), 65–96.

Burns, Robert I. "The Significance of the Frontier in the Middle Ages," in *Medieval Frontier Societies*, ed. Robert Bartlett and Angus MacKay, 307–30. Oxford: Clarendon, 1989.

Byock, Jesse. *Medieval Iceland: Society, Sagas, and Power.* Berkeley: University of California Press, 1988.

Cameron, Averil. *Christianity and the Rhetoric of Empire: The Development of Christian Discourse.* Berkeley: University of California Press, 1991.

Camille, Michael. *Image on the Edge: The Margins of Medieval Art.* Cambridge, MA: Harvard University Press, 1992.

Chance, Jane. *Woman as Hero in Old English Literature.* Syracuse University Press, 1986.

Charles-Edwards, T. M. *Early Irish and Welsh Kinship.* Oxford: Clarendon, 1993.

Cherewatuk, K. "Radegund and the Epistolary Tradition," in *Dear Sister: Medieval Women and the Epistolary Genre*, ed. K. Cherewatuk and Ulrike Wiethaus, 20–45. Philadelphia: University of Pennsylvania Press, 1993.

Ciggaar, Krijna. "Theophano: An Empress Reconsidered," in Davids, *Empress Theophano*, 49–63.

Clanchy, Michael. *From Memory to Written Record: England 1066–1307*. Oxford University Press, 1993.

Clark, Alice. *Working Life of Women in the Seventeenth Century*. New York: Routledge; repr., New York: Kelly, 1968.

Clover, Carol. "Maiden Warriors and Other Sons," *Journal of English and Germanic Philology* 85 (1986), 35–49.

Clover, Carol. "The Politics of Scarcity: Notes on the Sex Ratio in Early Scandinavia," in Damico and Alexander, *New Readings on Women in Old English Literature*, 100–34.

Clover, Carol. "Regardless of Sex: Men, Women, and Power in Early Northern Europe," *Speculum* 68 (1993), 363–87.

Coleman, Emily R. "Medieval Marriage Characteristics: A Neglected Factor in the History of Medieval Serfdom," *Journal of Interdisciplinary History* 2 (1971), 205–21.

Collins, Roger. "Queens-Dowager and Queens-Regent in Tenth-Century León and Navarre," in Parsons, *Medieval Queenship*, 79–92.

Colman, Rebecca. "The Abduction of Women in Barbarian Law," *Florilegium* 5 (1983), 62–75.

Condren, Mary. *The Serpent and the Goddess: Women, Religion and Power in Celtic Ireland*. San Francisco: Harper and Row, 1989.

Constable, Giles. "Medieval Charters as a Source for the History of the Crusades," in Edbury, *Crusade and Settlement*, 73–89.

Coon, Lynda. *Sacred Fictions: Holy Women and Hagiography in Late Antiquity*. Philadelphia: University of Pennsylvania Press, 1997.

Crawford, W. H. "Women in the Domestic Linen Industry," in *Women in Early Modern Ireland*, ed. Margaret MacCurtain and Mary O'Dowd, 236–54. Edinburgh University Press, 1990.

Damico, Helen and Alexandra Hennessey Olsen, ed. *New Readings on Women in Old English Literature*. Bloomington: Indiana University Press, 1990.

Davids, Adelbert, ed. *The Empress Theophano: Byzantium and the West at the Turn of the Millennium*. Cambridge University Press, 1995.

Damsholt, Nana. "The Role of Icelandic Women in the Sagas in the Production of Homespun Cloth," *Scandinavian Journal of History* 9:2 (1984), 75–90.

Davies, Wendy. *Small Worlds: The Village Community in Early Medieval Brittany*. London: Duckworth, 1988.

Devroey, Pierre. "Men and Women in Early Medieval Serfdom: The Ninth-Century North Frankish Evidence," *Past and Present* 166 (2000), 3–30.

de Weever, Jacqueline. *Sheba's Daughters: Whitening and Demonizing the Saracen Woman in Medieval French Epic*. New York: Garland, 1998.

Dhonnchadha, Máirín Ní. "The *Lex Innocentium*: Adomnán's Law for Women, Clerics, and Youths, 697 A.D.," in *Chattel, Servant, or Citizen:*

Women's Status in Church, State and Society: Papers read before the XXIst Irish Conference of Historians held at The Queen's University of Belfast, 27–30 May, 1993, ed. Mary O'Dowd and Sabine Wichert, 53–76. Belfast: The Queen's University of Belfast, 1995.

Dillard, Heath. *Daughters of the Reconquest: Women in Castilian Town Society 1100–1300*. Cambridge University Press, 1984.

DiMarco, Vincent. "The Amazons and the End of the World," in *Discovering New Worlds: Essays on Medieval Exploration and Imagination*, ed. Scott D. Westrem. New York: Garland, 1991.

Dobson, Barrie. "The Role of Jewish Women in Medieval England," in *Christianity and Judaism: Papers Read at the 1991 Summer Meeting and 1992 Winter Meeting of the Ecclesiastical History Society*, ed. Diana Wood, 145–68. Cambridge, MA: Blackwell, 1992.

Dockray-Miller, Mary. *Motherhood and Mothering in Anglo-Saxon England*. New York: St. Martin's Press, 2000.

Dronke, Peter. "The Provençal Trobairitz: Castelloza," in *Medieval Women Writers*, ed. Katharina Wilson, 131–33. Athens: University of Georgia Press, 1984.

Dronke, Peter. *Women Writers of the Middle Ages*. Cambridge University Press, 1984.

Duby, Georges. *The Early Growth of the European Economy: Warriors and Peasants from the Seventh to the Twelfth Century*. Ithaca: Cornell University Press, 1974.

Duby, Georges. *The Chivalrous Society*. Berkeley: University of California Press, 1977.

Duby, Georges. *Medieval Marriage: Two Models from Twelfth-Century France*. Baltimore: Johns Hopkins University Press, 1978.

Duby, Georges, ed. *A History of Private Life*, vol. 2, *Revelations of the Medieval World*. Cambridge, MA: Belknap Press, 1988.

Duby, Georges, and Michelle A. Perrot, ed. *A History of Women*, vol. 2, *Silences of the Middle Ages*, ed. Christiane Klapish-Züber. Cambridge, MA: Belknap Press, 1992.

Duffy, Seán. *Ireland in the Middle Ages*. Dublin: Gill & Macmillan, 1997.

Duggan, Ann, ed. *Queens and Queenship in Medieval Epic: Proceedings of a Conference Held at King's College London, April 1995*. Woodbridge: Boydell, 1997.

Economou, George D. *The Goddess Natura in Medieval Literature*. Cambridge, MA: Harvard University Press, 1972.

Edbury, Peter, ed., *Crusade and Settlement: Papers Read at the First Conference of the Society for the Study of the Crusades and the Latin East*. Cardiff: University College of Cardiff Press, 1985.

Effros, Bonnie. "Symbolic Expressions of Sanctity: Gertrude of Nivelles in the Context of Merovingian Mortuary Custom," *Viator* 27 (1996), 1–10.

Eisler, R. *The Chalice and the Blade: Our History, Our Future.* Cambridge, MA: Harper & Row, 1987.

Eller, Cynthia. *The Myth of Matriarchal Prehistory: Why an Invented Past Won't Give Women a Future.* Boston: Beacon Press, 2000.

Emanuel, R. R. and M. W. Ponsford. "Jacob's Well, Bristol, Britain's Only Known Medieval Jewish Ritual Bath," *Transactions of the Bristol and Gloucestershire Archaeological Society* 112 for 1994 (1995), 73–86.

Engels, Friedrich. *Origin of the Family, Private Property, and the State.* Chicago: Kerr, 1902; repr. New York: Pathfinder, 1972.

Engels, Odilo. "Theophano, the Western Empress from the East," in Davids, *Empress Theophano,* 28–48.

Ennen, Edith. *Frauen im Mittelalter.* Munich: Beck, 1984.

Enright, M. J. "Lady with a Mead Cup: Ritual, Group Cohesion and Hierarcy in the Germanic Warband," *Frühmittelalterliche Studien* 22 (1988), 170–203.

Evison, Martin. "Lo the Conquering Hero Comes (or Not)," *British Archaeology* 23 (Apr. 1997), http://www.britarch.ac.uk/ba/ba23/ba23feat.html.

Fell, Christine, with Cecily Clark and Elizabeth Williams. *Women in Anglo-Saxon England and the Impact of 1066.* Bloomington: Indiana University Press, 1984.

Finley, M. I. *The Ancient Economy.* Revised edn., Berkeley: University of California Press, 1999.

Fitzhugh, William W., ed. *Vikings: The North Atlantic Saga.* Washington, DC: National Museum of National History, 2000.

Flanagan, Sabina. *Hildegard of Bingen, 1098–1179: A Visionary Life.* London: Routledge, 1989.

Foot, Sarah. *Veiled Women I: The Disappearance of Nuns from Anglo-Saxon England.* Aldershot, UK and Burlington, VT: Ashgate, 2000.

Foot, Sarah. *Veiled Women II: Female Religious Communities in England, 871–1066.* Aldershot, UK and Burlington, VT: Ashgate, 2000.

Franz, Günther. *Geschichte des deutschen Bauernstandes vom frühen Mittelalter bis zum 19. Jh.,* Deutsche Agrargeschichte 4. Stuttgart: Ulmer, 1970.

Friedman, Yvonne. "Women in Captivity and Their Ransom During the Crusader Period," in *Cross Cultural Convergences in the Crusader Period,* ed. Michael Goodich et al., 85–87. New York: Lang, 1995.

Gauthier, Nancy. "Le paysage urbain en Gaule au Ve siècle," in *Grégoire de Tours et l'espace gaulois: actes du congrès international, Tours, 3–5 novembre 1994,* ed. Nancy Gauthier and H. Galinié, 49–64. Tours: Revue Archéologique du Centre de la France, 1997.

Geary, Patrick. *Furta Sacra: Thefts of Relics in the Central Middle Ages.* Princeton University Press, 1978.

Geary, Patrick. *Before France and Germany: The Creation and Transformation of the Merovingian World.* New York: Oxford University Press, 1988.

Geary, Patrick. *Phantoms of Remembrance: Memory and Oblivion at the End of the First Millennium*. Princeton University Press, 1994.

Gilchrist, Roberta. *Gender and Material Culture: The Archaeology of Religious Women*. London: Routledge, 1994.

Gimbutas, Marija. *The Goddesses and Gods of Old Europe 6500–3500 B.C., Myths and Cult Images*. Revised edn., Berkeley: University of California Press, 1982.

Godden, Malcolm *et al.*, ed. *From Anglo-Saxon to Early Middle English: Studies Presented to E. G. Stanley*. Oxford: Clarendon, 1994.

Goetz, Hans-Werner. *Frauen im frühen Mittelalter. Frauenbild und Frauenleben im Frankenreich*. Weimar: Böhlau, 1995.

Goetz, Hans-Werner. *Life in the Middle Ages: From the Seventh to the Thirteenth Century*, trans. Albert Wimmer. Notre Dame: University of Notre Dame Press, 1993.

Goetz, Hans-Werner *et al.*, ed. *Weibliche Lebengestaltung im frühen Mittelalter*. Cologne and Vienna: Böhlau, 1991.

Goffart, Walter. *The Narrators of Barbarian History (A.D. 550–800), Jordanes, Gregory of Tours, Bede, and Paul the Deacon*. Princeton University Press, 1988.

Goitein, S. D. *A Mediterranean Society: The Jewish Communities of the Arab World as Portrayed in the Documents of the Cairo Geniza*, vol. 3, *The Family*. Berkeley: University of California Press, 1978.

Gold, Penny Schine. *The Lady and the Virgin: Image, Attitude, and Experience in Twelfth-Century France*. Chicago: University of Chicago Press, 1985.

Goldberg, P. J. P. *Women, Work, and Life Cycle in a Medieval Economy: Women in York and Yorkshire, c. 1300–1520*. Oxford: Clarendon, 1992.

Gordon, Robert K. *Anglo-Saxon Poetry*. New York: Dutton, 1954.

Graham, Helena. "A Woman's Work . . . : Labour and Gender in the Late Medieval Countryside," in *Women in Medieval English Society*, ed. P. J. P. Goldberg, 126–48. Stroud: Alan Sutton, 1997.

Graves, Robert. *The White Goddess: A Historical Grammar of Poetic Myth*. London: Faber and Faber, 1948.

Green, Miranda. *Symbol and Image in Celtic Religious Art*. London: Routledge, 1989.

Green, Miranda. *Celtic Goddesses: Warriors, Virgins, and Mothers*. New York: Braziller, 1996.

Groenman-Van Waateringe. "Wasteland: Buffer in the Medieval Economy," in *L'Homme et la nature au Moyen Age: paléoenvironnement des sociétés occiden- tales: actes du Ve Congrès international d'archéologie medievale tenu à Grenoble (France), 6–9 octobre 1992 (Société d'archéologie médiévale)*, ed. M. Colardelle, 113–17. Paris: Editions Errance, 1996.

Grossman, Avraham. "Medieval Rabbinic Views on Wife-Beating, 800– 1300," *Jewish History* 5:1 (1991), 53–62.

Grossman, Janice. "Tropes of Femininity and Monstrosity in Old English Poems," *Old English Newsletter* 28 (Spring 1995), A-20–A-21.

Güdemann, Moritz. *Geschichte des Ehrziehungswesens und der Cultur der abendländischen Juden während des Mittelalters und der neueren Zeit*, vol. 1, *Geschichte des Ehrziehungswesens und der Cultur der Juden in Frankreich und Deutschland von der Begründung der jüdischen Wissenschaft in diesen Ländern bis zur Vertreibung der Juden aus Frankreich (X–XIV Jahrhundert)*. Vienna: Hölder, 1880–88; repr. Amsterdam: Philo Press, 1966.

Guterman, Simeon L. *The Principle of the Personality of Law in the Germanic Kingdoms of Western Europe from the Fifth to the Eleventh Century*. New York: Lang, 1990.

Guthrie, Shirley. *Arab Social Life in the Middle Ages: An Illustrated Study*. London: Saqui Books, 1995.

Hajnal, J. "European Marriage Patterns in Perspective," in *Population in History: Essays in Historical Demography*, ed. D. V. Glass and D. E. C. Eversley, 101–43. London: Arnold, 1965.

Halsall, Guy. "Female Status and Power in Early Merovingian Central Austrasia: The Burial Evidence," *Early Medieval Europe* 5 (1996), 1–24.

Halsall, Guy, ed. *Violence and Society in the Early Medieval West*. Woodbridge: Boydell, 1998.

Hambly, Gavin R. G., ed. *Women in the Medieval Islamic World: Power, Patronage, and Piety*. New York: St. Martin's Press, 1998.

Hamburger, Jeffrey. *Nuns as Artists: The Visual Culture of a Medieval Convent*. Berkeley: University of California Press, 1997.

Hamburger, Jeffrey. *The Visual and the Visionary: Art and Female Spirituality in Late Medieval Germany*. New York: Zone Books, 1998.

Hanawalt, Barbara. *The Ties That Bound: Peasant Families in Medieval England*. Oxford University Press, 1986.

Hanawalt, Barbara. "Women and the Household Economy in the Preindustrial Period: An Assessment of Women, Work, and Family," *Journal of Women's History* 11 (1999), 10–16.

Hanawalt, Barbara, ed. *Women and Work in Preindustrial Europe*. Bloomington: Indiana University Press, 1986.

Heather, Peter. "Disappearing and Reappearing Tribes," in Pohl and Reimitz, *Strategies of Distinction*, 95–116.

Hennessy, William. "The Ancient Irish Goddess of War," *Revue Celtique* 1 (1870–72), 32–55.

Herlihy, David. "Ecological Conditions and Demographic Change," in *One Thousand Years: Western Europe in the Middle Ages*, ed. Richard DeMolen, 3–43. Boston: Houghton Mifflin, 1974.

Herlihy, David. "Land, Family and Women in Continental Europe 700–1200," *Traditio* 18 (1962); reprinted in *Women in Medieval Society*, ed. Susan Mosher Stuard, 28–32. Philadelphia: University of Pennsylvania Press, 1976.

Herlihy, David. "Life Expectancies for Women in Medieval Society," in *The Role of Women in the Middle Ages: Papers of the Sixth Annual Conference of the Center for Medieval and Early Renaissance Studies, State University of New York at Binghampton, 6–7 May 1972*, ed. R. T. Morewedge, 1–22. Albany: State University of New York Press, 1975.

Herlihy, David. *Medieval Households.* Cambridge, MA: Harvard University Press, 1985.

Herlihy, David. *Opera Muliebria: Women and Work in Medieval Europe.* Philadelphia: Temple University Press, 1990.

Herlihy, David. "The Towns of Northern Italy," in *Medieval Women and the Sources of Medieval History*, ed. Joel T. Rosenthal, 133–54. Athens: University of Georgia Press, 1990.

Higham, Nicholas J. *Rome, Britain, and the Anglo-Saxons.* London: Seaby, 1992.

Hill, Bridget. "Women's History: A Study in Change, Continuity, or Standing Still?" *Women's History Review* 2 (1993), 5–22.

Hollis, Stephanie. *Anglo-Saxon Women and the Church: Sharing a Common Fate.* Woodbridge: Boydell, 1992.

Holtz, Barry W., ed. *Back to the Sources: Reading the Classic Jewish Texts.* New York: Simon & Schuster, 1984.

Hornaday, Alice G. "Early Medieval Kinship Structures as Social and Political Controls," in *Medieval Family Roles*, ed. Cathy Itnyre, 21–38.

Howell, Martha C. *Women, Production, and Patriarchy in Late Medieval Cities.* Chicago: University of Chicago Press, 1986.

Hufton, Olwen. *The Prospect Before Her: A History of Women in Western Europe, 1500–1800.* New York: Knopf, 1996.

Hughes, Kathleen, and Ann Hamlin. *Celtic Monasticism: The Modern Traveler to the Early Irish Church.* New York: Seabury Press, 1981.

Huneycutt, Lois. "The Idea of the Perfect Princess: The *Life of St. Margaret* in the Reign of Matilda II (1100–1118)," *Anglo-Norman Studies* 12 (1989), 81–97.

Huneycutt, Lois. "Images of Queenship in the High Middle Ages," *Haskins Society Journal* 1 (1989), 61–71.

Huneycutt, Lois. "Female Succession and the Language of Power in the Writings of Twelfth-Century Churchmen," in Parsons, *Medieval Queenship*, 198–201.

Huneycutt, Lois. "Intercession and the High-Medieval Queen: The Esther Topos," in *Power of the Weak: Studies on Medieval Women*, ed. Jennifer Carpenter and Sally-Beth MacLean, 126–46. Urbana: University of Illinois Press, 1995.

Itnyre, Cathy Jorgensen, ed. *Medieval Family Roles: A Book of Essays.* New York: Garland, 1996.

James, Simon. *The Atlantic Celts: Ancient People or Modern Invention?* Madison: University of Wisconsin Press, 1999.

Jewell, Helen M. *Women in Medieval England*. Manchester University Press, 1996.

Jochens, Jenny. *Women in Old Norse Society*. Ithaca: Cornell University Press, 1995.

Jochens, Jenny. *Old Norse Images of Women*. Philadelphia: University of Pennsylvania Press, 1996.

Jones, A. H. M., ed. *A History of Rome Through the Fifth Century*. New York: Harper & Row, 1970.

Jung, Leo. "Literature for Jewish Women in Medieval and Later Times," in *The Jewish Library*, vol. 3, *Woman*, ed. Leo Jung, 213–43. New York: Bloch, 1943.

Karras, Ruth Mazo. "Desire, Descendants, and Dominance: Slavery, the Exchange of Women, and Masculine Power," in *The World of Work: Servitude, Slavery, and Labor in Medieval England*, ed. Allen J. Frantzen and Douglas Moffat, 16–29. Glasgow: Cruithne Press, 1994.

Kellenbach, Katharina von. *Anti-Judaism in Feminist Religious Writings*. Atlanta: Scholars Press, 1994.

Kelly, Amy Ruth. *Eleanor of Aquitaine and the Four Kings*. Cambridge, MA: Harvard University Press, 1950.

Kelly, Fergus. *A Guide to Early Irish Law*. Dublin Institute for Advanced Studies, 1988.

Kelly-Gadol, Joan. "The Social Relation of the Sexes," *Signs: Journal of Women in Culture and Society* 1 (1976), 809–23.

Köstler, Rudolf. "Raub-, Kauf- und Friedelehe bei den Germanen," *Zeitschrift der Savigny-Stiftung für Rechtgeschichte, Germanistische Abteilung* 63 (1943), 95–98.

Kowaleski, Maryanne. "Women's Work in a Market Town: Exeter in the Late Fourteenth Century," in Hanawalt, *Women and Work in Preindustrial Europe*, 143–64.

Kraemer, Ross S. *Her Share of the Blessings: Women's Religions Among Pagans, Jews, and Christians in the Greco-Roman World*. Oxford University Press, 1992.

Kreutz, Barbara. "The Twilight of *Morgengabe*," in *Portraits of Medieval and Renaissance Living: Essays in Memory of David Herlihy*, ed. Samuel Cohn and Steven Epstein, 131–47. Ann Arbor: University of Michigan Press, 1996.

Kruk, Remke. "The Bold and the Beautiful: Women and 'Fitna' in the 'Sīrat D̲h̲āt al-Himma': The Story of Nūrā," in Hambly, *Women in the Medieval Islamic World*, 99–116.

Kuenzl, Hannelore. "Die Architektur der mittelalterlichen Synagogen und rituellen Baeder," in *Judentum im Mittelalter: Ausstellungskatalog zur Ausstellung vom 04.05–26.10.1978 im Schloss Halbturn*, ed. Jakob Allerhand, 40–59. Eisenstadt: Kulturabt. des Amtes d. Bgld. Landesregierung, 1978.

Lamb, H. "Climate from 1000 B.C. to 1000 A.D," in *The Environment of Man: The Iron Age to the Anglo-Saxon Period*, ed. J. Jones and G. Dimbleby, 53–65. Oxford: British Archaeological Reports, 1981.

La Rocca, Cristina. "Using the Roman Past: Abandoned Towns and Local Power in Eleventh-Century Piemonte," *Early Medieval Europe* 5 (1996), 45–69.

Larrington, Carolyne. *A Store of Common Sense: Gnomic Theme and Style in Old Icelandic and Old English Wisdom Poetry*. Oxford: Clarendon, 1993.

Leach, M. S. Review of McNamara, *Sisters in Arms*. *First Things* 74 (1997), 59–60.

LeGoff, Jacques. *Time, Work, and Culture in the Middle Ages*. Chicago: University of Chicago Press, 1980.

Lerner, Gerda. *The Creation of Feminist Consciousness: From the Middle Ages to Eighteen-Seventy* New York: Oxford University Press, 1993.

Lerner, Gerda. *The Creation of Patriarchy*. New York: Oxford University Press, 1986.

LeRoy Ladurie, Emmanuel. *Montaillou: The Promised Land of Error*. New York: Braziller, 1978.

Lewis, Archibald. *The Development of Southern French and Catalan Society, 718–1050*. Austin: University of Texas, 1965.

Leyser, Henrietta. *Medieval Women: A Social History of Women in England 450–1500*. New York: St. Martin's Press, 1995.

Leyser, Karl J. *Rule and Conflict in an Early Medieval Society: Ottonian Saxony*. London: Arnold, 1979.

L'Hermite-Leclercq, Paulette. "The Feudal Order," in *Silences of the Middle Ages: A History of Women*, 346–47. Cambridge, MA: Belknap Press of Harvard University Press, 1992.

Lifshitz, Felice. "Gender and Exemplarity East of the Middle Rhine: Jesus, Mary, and the Saints in Manuscript Context," *Early Medieval Europe* 9 (2000), 325–343.

Lockwood, William G. "Bride-Theft and Social Maneuverability in West Bosnia," *Anthropological Quarterly* 47:3 (1974), 253–69.

Lopez, Roberto. *The Commercial Revolution of the Middle Ages, 950–1350*. Englewood Cliffs, NJ: Prentice-Hall, 1971.

LoPrete, Kimberly A. "Adela of Blois: Familial Alliances and Female Lordship," in *Aristocratic Women in Medieval France*, ed. Theodore Evergates, 7–43. Philadelphia: University of Pennsylvania Press, 1999.

Lucas, A. T. "The Sacred Trees of Ireland," *Journal of the Cork Historical and Archaeological Society* 68 (1963), 16–54.

Lucy, Sam. "Houswives, Warriors and Slaves? Sex and Gender in Anglo-Saxon Burials," in *Invisible People and Processes: Writing Gender and Childhood into European Archaeology*, ed. Jenny Moore and Eleanor Scott, 150–68. London: Leicester University Press, 1997.

Luecke, Janemarie. "The Unique Experience of Anglo-Saxon Nuns," in Nichols and Shank, *Medieval Religious Women*, vol. 2, *Peace Weavers*, 55–66.

Lysaght, Patricia. *The Banshee: The Irish Death-Messenger*. Dublin: O'Brien Press, 1986.

MacDonald, Margaret Y. *Early Christian Women and Pagan Opinion: The Power of the Hysterical Woman*. Cambridge University Press, 1996.

McCone, Kim. *Pagan Past and Christian Present in Early Irish Literature*. Maynooth: An Sagart, 1990.

McKitterick, Rosamond. "Frauen und Schriftlichkeit im Frühmittelalter," in Goetz *et al.*, *Weibliche Lebengestaltung im frühen Mittelalter*, 65–118.

McKitterick, Rosamond. "Nuns' Scriptoria in England and Francia in the Eighth Century," *Francia* 19 (1992), 1–35.

McNamara, Jo Ann. "Chaste Marriage and Clerical Celibacy," in *Sexual Practices and the Medieval Church*, ed. Vern Bullough and James Brundage, 22–33. Buffalo: Prometheus Books, 1982.

McNamara, Jo Ann. "Living Sermons: Consecrated Women and the Conversion of Gaul," in Nichols and Shank, *Medieval Religious Women*, vol. 2, *Peace Weavers*, 19–38.

McNamara, Jo Ann. *Sisters in Arms: Catholic Nuns Through Two Millennia*. Cambridge, MA: Harvard University Press, 1996.

McNamara, Jo Ann. "City Air Makes Men Free and Women Bound," in *Text and Territory: Geographical imagination in the European Middle Ages*, ed. S. Tomasch and S. Gilles, 143–58. Philadelphia: University of Pennsylvania Press, 1998.

McNamara, Jo Ann, and Suzanne Wemple. "The Power of Women Through the Family in Medieval Europe, 500–1100," in *Women and Power in the Middle Ages*, ed. Mary Erler and Maryanne Kowaleski, 83–101. Athens: University of Georgia Press, 1988.

Mallory, J. P. ed., *Aspects of the Táin*. Belfast: December Publications, 1992.

Mathisen, Ralph and Hagith Sivan, ed. *Shifting Frontiers in Late Antiquity*. Aldershot: Variorum, 1996.

Matrix: Sources for the Study of Women's Religious Life, 500–1500. http://matrix.bc.edu.

Merchant, Carolyn. *Death of Nature: Women, Ecology, and the Scientific Revolution*. San Francisco: Harper and Row, 1980.

Mernissi, Fatima. *The Forgotten Queens of Islam*, trans. Mary Jo Lakeland. Minneapolis: University of Minnesota Press, 1993.

Mitterauer, Michael, and Reinhard Sieder. *The European Family: Patriarchy to Partnership from the Middle Ages to the Present*. Oxford: Blackwell, 1982.

Mooney, Catherine. "Voice, Gender, and the Portrayal of Sanctity," in Mooney, *Gendered Voices*, 1–15.

Mooney, Catherine. *Gendered Voices: Medieval Saints and Their Interpreters*. Philadelphia: University of Pennsylvania Press, 1999.

Morris, Colin. *The Discovery of the Individual, 1050–1200.* Toronto: University of Toronto Press, 1972.

Murray, Alexander. *Germanic Kinship Structure: Studies in Law and Society in Antiquity and in the Early Middle Ages.* Toronto: Pontifical Institute of Mediaeval Studies, 1983.

Nagy, Joseph Falaky. *Wisdom of the Outlaw: The Boyhood Deeds of Finn in Gaelic Narrative Tradition.* Berkeley: University of California Press, 1985.

Nagy, Joseph Falaky. *Conversing with Angels and Ancients: Literary Myths of Medieval Ireland.* Ithaca: Cornell University Press, 1997.

Neal, Sharon Bryant. "Las Donas e las feminas, las tozas avinens: Women in 'La Cansi de la Crozada,' " *Tenso: Bulletin of the Société Guilhelm IX* 10 (1995), 110–38.

Nees, Lawrence. "Introduction," *Speculum* 72 (1997), 959–69.

Nelson, Janet. *Charles the Bald.* London: Longman, 1992.

Nelson, Janet. "Early Medieval Rites of Queen-making and the Shaping of Medieval Queenship," in Duggan, *Queens and Queenship,* 301–16.

Nelson, Janet. "Les femmes et l'évangelisation au ixe siècle," *Revue du Nord* 269 (1986), 471–85.

Nelson, Janet. "Perceptions du pouvoir chez les historiennes du Haut Moyen Âge," in *La Femme au moyen-âge,* ed. Michel Rouche and Jean Heuclin, 77–85. Publication de la Ville de Maubeuge, Diffusion Jean Touzot, 1990.

Nelson, Janet. "Queens as Jezebels: The Careers of Brunhild and Balthild in Merovingian History," in *Medieval Women,* ed. Derek Baker and Rosalind Hill, 31–77. Oxford: Basil Blackwell, 1978.

Nelson, Janet. Review of Schulenburg, *Forgetful of Their Sex. American Historical Review* 105:4 (October, 2000).

Newman, Barbara. "Hildegard and Her Biographers: The Remaking of Female Sainthood," in Mooney, *Gendered Voices,* 16–34.

Nichols, John A., and Lillian Thomas Shank, ed. *Medieval Religious Women,* vol. 1, *Distant Echoes*; vol. 2, *Peace Weavers.* Kalamazoo: Cistercian Publications, 1984–87.

Nicholson, Helen. "Women on the Third Crusade," *Journal of Medieval History* 23 (1997), 335–49.

Ní Dhonnchadha, Máirín. "The *Lex Innocentium*: Adomnán's Law for Women, Clerics, and Youths, 697 A.D.," in *Chattel, Servant, or Citizen,* ed. Mary O'Dowd and Sabine Wichert, 53–76. Belfast: Institute of Irish Studies, The Queen's University, 1995.

Noonan, J. T. "Marital Affection in the Canonists," *Studia Gratiana* 12 (1967), 479–509.

Noonan, J. T. "Power to Choose," *Viator* 4 (1973), 419–34.

Ó Coileáin, Seán, "Oral or Literary: Some Strands of the Argument," *Studia Hibernica* 17–18 (1977–78), 7–35.

O'Flaherty, Wendy Doniger. *Women, Androgynes, and Other Mythical Beasts.* Chicago: University of Chicago Press, 1980.

Ortner, Sherry. "Is Female to Male as Nature Is to Culture?" *Feminist Studies* 1 (1972), 5–31.

Otis, Leah. *Prostitution in Medieval Society: The History of an Urban Institution in Languedoc.* Chicago: University of Chicago Press, 1985.

Overing, Gillian R., and Marijane Osborn. *Landscape of Desire: Partial Stories of the Medieval Scandinavian World.* Minneapolis: University of Minnesota Press, 1994.

Parsons, John Carmi, ed. *Medieval Queenship.* New York: St. Martin's Press, 1993.

Partner, Nancy F., ed. *Studying Medieval Women: Sex, Gender, Feminism.* Cambridge, MA: Medieval Academy of America, 1993.

Parvey, Constance. "The Theology and Leadership of Women in the New Testament," in *Religion and Sexism: Images of Women in the Jewish and Christian Traditions,* ed. Rosemary Ruether, 123–37. New York: Simon & Schuster, 1974.

Pelikan, Jaroslav. *Mary Through the Centuries: Her Place in the History of Culture.* New Haven: Yale University Press, 1996.

Pelletier, André. *La Femme dans la société gallo-romaine.* Paris: Picard, 1984.

Périn, Patrick. "A propos de publications récentes concernant le peuplement en Gaule à l'époque mérovingienne: la 'question franque'," *Archéologie Médiévale* 11 (1981), 125–45.

Pernoud, Régine. *La Femme au temps des Croisades.* Paris: Stock/L. Pernoud, 1990.

Peskowitz, Miriam. *Spinning Fantasies: Rabbis, Gender, and History.* Berkeley: University of California Press, 1997.

Peyroux, Catherine. Review article: "Lands of Women? Writing the History of Early Medieval Women in Ireland and Europe," *Early Medieval Europe* 7 (1998), 217–27.

Phillips, Seymour. "The Medieval Background," in *Europeans on the Move: Studies on European Migration, 1500–1800,* ed. Nicholas Canny, 9–25. Oxford: Clarendon, 1994.

Plaskow, Judith. *Standing Again at Sinai: Judaism from a Feminist Perspective.* San Francisco: Harper & Row, 1990.

Plaskow, Judith. "Feminist Anti-Judaism and the Christian God," *Journal of Feminist Studies in Religion* 7:2 (1991), 99–108.

Pohl, Walter. "Telling the Difference: Signs of Ethnic Identity," in Pohl and Reimitz, *Strategies of Distinction,* 17–69.

Pohl, Walter, and Helmut Reimitz, ed. *Strategies of Distinction. The Construction of Ethnic Communities, 300–800.* Leiden and Boston: Brill, 1998.

Postan, M. M. and H. J. Habakkuk, ed. *The Cambridge Economic History of Europe,* vol. I, *The Agrarian Life of the Middle Ages.* Cambridge University Press, 1966–87.

Pounds, N. J. G. *An Historical Geography of Europe*. Cambridge University Press, 1990.

Power, Eileen. *Medieval Women*. Cambridge University Press, 1975; repr., Cambridge University Press, 1997.

Pringle, Denys. "Magna Mahumeria (al-Bīra), The Archaeology of a Frankish New Town in Palestine," in Edbury, *Crusade and Settlement*, 147–68.

Provost, Michel, ed. *Carte archéologique de la Gaule*. Paris : Académie des Inscriptions et Belles-Lettres, 1988–.

Raftery, Barry. Review of James, *The Ancient Celts*, *The Times Literary Supplement* 4967 (June 12, 1998), 9.

Reif, Stefan C. "Aspects of Medieval Jewish Literacy," in *The Uses of Literacy in Early Medieval Europe*, ed. Rosamond McKitterick, 134–55. Cambridge University Press, 1992.

Renfrew, Colin, and Katherine V. Boyle. *Archaeogenetics: DNA and the Population Prehistory of Europe*. Cambridge: McDonald Institute for Archaeological Research, 2000.

Riley-Smith, Jonathan, ed. *The Oxford Illustrated History of the Crusades*. Oxford University Press, 1995.

Ring, Richard. "Early Medieval Peasant Households in Central Italy," *Journal of Family History* 4 (1979), 2–25.

Ripoll López, Gisela. "The Arrival of the Visigoths in Hispania: Population Problems and the Process of Acculturation," in Pohl and Reimitz, *Strategies of Distinction*, 151–87.

Roberts, Charlotte A. and Keith Manchester. *The Archaeology of Disease*. 2nd edn., Ithaca: Cornell University Press, 1995.

Roberts, Lawrence D., ed. *Approaches to Nature in the Middle Ages: Papers of the Tenth Annual Conference of the Center for Medieval & Early Renaissance Studies*. Binghamton: Center for Medieval & Early Renaissance Studies, 1982.

Roberts, Michael. "Sickles and Scythes: Women's Work and Men's Work at Harvest Time," *History Workshop* 7 (1979), 3–29.

Robinson, Fred. "Did Grendel's Mother Sit on Beowulf?" in *From Anglo-Saxon to Early Middle English*, ed. Malcolm Godden *et al.* (Oxford University Press, 1994), 1–7.

Rörig, Fritz. *The Medieval Town*. Berkeley: University of California Press, 1967.

Ross, Margaret Clunies. "Concubinage in Anglo-Saxon England," *Past and Present* 108 (1985), 3–34.

Ross, Margaret Clunies. *Prolonged Echoes: Old Norse Myths in Medieval Northern Society*. Odense University Press, 1998.

Ross, Margaret Clunies. "Land-Taking and Text-Making in Medieval Iceland," in Tomasch and Gilles, *Text and Territory*, 159–84.

Rousselle, Aline. "Du sanctuaire au thaumaturge: La guérison en Gaule au IVe siècle," *Annales ESC* 31 (1976), 1085–107. Trans. as "From Sanctuary to Miracle-Worker: Healing in Fourth-Century Gaul," in Robert Forster and Orest A. Ranum, ed., *Ritual, Religion, and the Sacred.* Baltimore: Johns Hopkins University Press, 1982.

Roymans, Nico. *From the Sword to the Plough: Three Studies on the Earliest Romanisation of Northern Gaul.* Amsterdam University Press, 1996.

Russell, Josiah Cox. "Population in Europe," in *The Fontana Economic History of Europe: the Emergence of Industrial Societies,* ed. Carlo Cipolla, 25–41. London: Collins, 1973.

Russell, Josiah Cox. *The Control of Late Ancient and Medieval Population.* Philadelphia: American Philosophical Society, 1985.

Russell, Josiah Cox. *Medieval Demography: Essays.* New York: AMS Press, 1987.

Salisbury, Joyce. *Church Fathers, Independent Virgins.* London and New York: Verso, 1991.

Sawyer, Birgit. *The Viking-Age Rune-Stones: Custom and Commemoration in Early Medieval Scandinavia.* Oxford and New York: Oxford University Press, 2001.

Sawyer, P. H. *Kings and Vikings: Scandinavia and Europe, A.D. 700–1100.* London: Routledge, 1982.

Schmitt, Jean-Claude. *La Raison des gestes dans l'Occident médiéval.* Paris: Gallimard, 1990.

Schmitt, Jean-Claude. *Le Saint Lévrier: Guinefort, guérisseur d'enfants depuis le XIIIe siècle.* Paris: Flammarion, 1979. Trans. Martin Thom as *The Holy Greyhound: Guinefort, Healer of Children Since the Thirteenth Century.* Cambridge University Press, 1983.

Schulenberg, Jane. "Strict Active Enclosure and Its Effects on the Female Monastic Experience (ca. 500–1100)," in Nichols and Shank, *Medieval Religious Women,* vol. 1, *Distant Echoes,* 51–86.

Schulenberg, Jane. "Heroics of Virginity: Brides of Christ and Sacrificial Mutilation," in *Women in the Middle Ages and Renaissance: Literary and Historical Perspectives,* ed. Mary Beth Rose, 29–72. Syracuse University Press, 1986.

Schulenberg, Jane. "Women's Monastic Communities, 500–1100: Patterns of Expansion and Decline," in *Sisters and Workers in the Middle Ages,* ed. Judith Bennett *et al.,* 208–39. Chicago: University of Chicago Press, 1989.

Schulenberg, Jane. *Forgetful of Their Sex: Female Sanctity and Society, ca. 500–1100.* Chicago: University of Chicago Press, 1998.

Scott, Joan. "Gender: A Useful Category of Historical Analysis," Chap. in *Gender and the Politics of History.* New York: Columbia University Press, 1988.

Shatzmiller, Maya. "Marriage, Family, and the Faith: Women's Conversion to Islam," *Journal of Family History* 21 (1996), 235–65.

Sivan, Hagith. "'Roman–Barbarian' Marriage in Visigothic Gaul and Spain," in Pohl and Reimitz, *Strategies of Distinction*, 289–304.

Skinner, Patricia. *Family Power in Southern Italy: The Duchy of Gaeta and Its Neighbors, 850–1139* (Cambridge University Press, 1995), 57–84.

Slotkin, Edgar. "Medieval Irish Scribes and Fixed Texts," *Éigse* 17 (1978–79), 437–50.

Smith, Julia. "Did Women Have a Transformation of the Roman World?," *Gender and History* 12 (2000), 552–71.

Smith, Julia. "The Problem of Female Sanctity in Carolingian Europe c.780–920," *Past and Present* 146 (1995), 3–37.

Smith, Lesley and Jane H. M. Taylor, ed. *Selected Proceedings of the St. Hilda's Conference 1993*, vol. 2, *Women, the Book, and the Worldly*. Cambridge: D. S. Brewer, 1995.

Solterer, Helen. "Figures of Female Militancy in French Literature," *Signs* 16:3 (1991), 522–49.

Stafford, Pauline. *Queens, Concubines, and Dowagers: The King's Wife in the Early Middle Ages*. Athens: University of Georgia Press, 1983.

Stafford, Pauline. "The Laws of Cnut and the History of Anglo-Saxon Royal Promises," *Anglo-Saxon England* 10 (1981), 173–190.

Stafford, Pauline. "The Portrayal of Royal Women in England, Mid-Tenth to Mid-Twelfth Centuries," in Parsons, *Medieval Queenship*, 143–67.

Stafford, Pauline. "Kinship and Women in the World of Maldon: Byrhtnoth and his Family," in *The Battle of Maldon: Fiction and Fact*, ed. Janet Cooper, 225–35. London: Hambledon Press, 1993.

Stafford, Pauline. "Emma: The Powers of the Queen in the Eleventh Century," in Duggan, *Queens and Queenship*, 3–26.

Stafford, Pauline. *Queen Emma and Queen Edith: Queenship and Women's Power in Eleventh-century England*. Oxford: Blackwell, 1997.

Stein, Günter. *Judenhof und Judenbad in Speyer am Rhein*. Munich: Deutscher Kunstverlag, 1969.

Stuard, Susan Mosher. "Ancillary Evidence for the Decline of Medieval Slavery," *Past and Present* 149 (1995), 3–28.

Stuard, Susan Mosher. "To Town to Serve: Urban Domestic Slavery in Medieval Ragusa," in Hanawalt, *Women and Work in Preindustrial Europe*, 39–55.

Stuard, Susan Mosher, and Margaret Schaus. "Citizens of No Mean City: Medieval Women's History," *Journal of Women's History* 6:3 (1994), 170–98.

Thompson, Sally. *Women Religious: The Founding of English Nunneries after the Norman Conquest*. Oxford: Clarendon, 1991.

Thurneysen, Rudolf. *Irisches Recht*. Aus den Abhandlungen der Preussischen Akademie der Wissenschaften, Jahrgang 1931. Phil.-Hist. Klasse, nr. 2. Berlin: Verlag der Akademie der Wissenschaften, 1931.

Tierney, J. J. "The Celtic Ethnography of Posidonius," *Proceedings of the Royal Irish Academy* 60 C (1959–60), 189–275.

Tomasch, Sylvia, and Sealy Gilles, eds. *Text and Territory: Geographical Imagination in the European Middle Ages*. Philadelphia: University of Pennsylvania Press, 1998.

Turner, Alice K. *The History of Hell*. New York: Harcourt Brace, 1993.

Uitz, Erika. *Women in the Medieval Town*. London: Barrie & Jenkins, 1990.

Van Dam, Raymond. *Leadership and Community in Late Antique Gaul*. Berkeley: University of California Press, 1985.

Van Houts, Elisabeth. *Memory and Gender in Medieval Europe 900–1200*. Toronto: University of Toronto Press, 1999.

Van Winter, Johanna Maria. "The Education of Daughters of the Nobility in the Ottonian Empire," in Davids, *Empress Theophano*, 86–98.

Van Vleck, Amelia E. "Textiles as Testimony in Marie de France's *Philomena*," *Medievalia et Humanistica* n.s. 22 (1995), 31–60.

Venarde, Bruce. *Women's Monasticism and Medieval Society: Nunneries in France and England, 890–1215*. Ithaca: Cornell University Press, 1997.

Verdon, Jean. "Les sources de l'histoire de la femme en Occident aux xe–xiiie siècles," in *La Femme dans les civilisations des Xe-XIIIe siècles, Actes du colloque tenu à Poitiers les 23–25 septembre 1976*, 129–61. Poitiers: Université de Poitiers, 1977.

Verdon, Jean. *Les Femmes en l'an mille*. Paris: Perrin, 1999.

Vicente, Marta. "Artisans and Work in a Barcelona Cotton Factory (1770–1816)," *International Review of Social History* 45 (2000), 1–23.

Vicente, Marta. "Images and Realities of Work: Women and Guilds in Early Modern Barcelona," in *Spanish Women in the Golden Age: Images and Realities*, ed. Alain Saint-Saëns and Magdalena Sánchez, 127–39. Westport: Greenwood, 1996.

Viguera, Maria J. "Asluhu Li'l-Ma'Ālī: On the Social Status of Andalusian Women," in *The Legacy of Muslim Spain*, vol. 12, *The Near and Middle East*, ed. Salma Khadra Jayyusi and Marin Manuela, 709–24. Leiden: Brill, 1994.

Wallace-Hadrill, J. M. *Early Germanic Kingship in England and on the Continent*. Oxford: Clarendon, 1971.

Wallace-Hadrill, J. M. *The Frankish Church*. Oxford: Clarendon, 1983.

Ward-Perkins, J. "Etruscan Towns, Roman Roads and Medieval Villages: The Historical Geography of Southern Etruria," *Geographical Journal* 128 (1952), 389–405.

Warner, Marina. *Alone of All Her Sex: The Myth and Cult of the Virgin Mary*. London: Weidenfeld & Nicolson, 1976.

Wattenbach, Wilhelm, and William Levison. *Deutschlands Geschichtsquellen in Mittelalter*, multiple vols. Berlin: Hertz, 1894–.

Wegner, Judith Romney. "The Image and Status of Women in Classical Rabbinic Judaism," in Baskin, *Jewish Women in Historical Perspective*, 73–100.

Wemple, Suzanne. *Women in Frankish Society: Marriage and the Cloister, 500 to 900*. Philadelphia: University of Pennsylvania Press, 1981.

White, Hayden. *The Content of the Form: Narrative Discourse and Historical Representation*. Baltimore: Johns Hopkins University Press, 1987.

White, Stephen D. "Clotild's Revenge: Politics, Kinship and Ideology in the Merovingian Blood Feud," in Cohn and Epstein, *Portraits of Medieval and Renaissance Living*, 107–30.

Whitehouse, David. "Rome and Naples: Survival and Revival in Central and Southern Italy," in *The Rebirth of Towns in the West A.D. 700–1050: A Review of Current Research into How, When, and Why There Was a Rebirth of Towns Between 700–1050*, ed. Richard Hodges and Brian Hobley, 28–31. London: Council for British Archaeology, 1988.

Wickham, Chris. *Early Medieval Italy: Central Power and Local Society, 400–1000*. London: MacMillan, 1989.

Wolfram, Herwig. *The Roman Empire and its Germanic peoples*. Berkeley: University of California Press, 1997.

Wood, Ian. *The Merovingian Kingdoms, 450–751*. London: Longman, 1994.

Wormald, Patrick. "Lex Scripta and Verbum Regis: Legislation and Germanic Kingship from Euric to Cnut," in Wormald, *Legal Culture in the Early Medieval West: Law as Text, Image, and Experience*, 1–44. London: Hambledon Press, 1999.

Yorke, Barbara. " 'Sisters Under the Skin?' AngloSaxon Nuns and Nunneries in Southern England," *Reading Medieval Studies* 15 (1989), 95–117.

Young, Bailey K. "The Myth of the Pagan Cemetery," in *Spaces of the Living and the Dead: An Archaeological Dialogue*, ed. Catherine E. Karkov *et al.*, 61–86. American Early Medieval Studies 3. Oxford: Oxbow Books, 1999.

INDEX

Cambridge Medieval Textbooks

Already published

Germany in the High Middle Ages *c.* 1050–1200
HORST FUHRMANN

The Hundred Years War
England and France at War *c.* 1300–*c.* 1450
CHRISTOPHER ALLMAND

Standards of Living in the Later Middle Ages:
Social Change in England, *c.* 1200–1520
CHRISTOPHER DYER

Magic in the Middle Ages
RICHARD KIECKHEFER

The Papacy 1073–1198: Continuity and Innovation
I. S. ROBINSON

Medieval Wales
DAVID WALKER

England in the Reign of Edward III
SCOTT L. WAUGH

The Norman Kingdom of Sicily
DONALD MATTHEW

Political Thought in Europe 1250–1450
ANTONY BLACK

The Church in Western Europe from the Tenth
to the Early Twelfth Century
GERD TELLENBACH
Translated by Timothy Reuter

The Medieval Spains
BERNARD F. REILLY

England in the Thirteenth Century
ALAN HARDING

Monastic and Religious Orders in Britain 1000–1300
JANET BURTON

Religion and Devotion in Europe *c.* 1215–*c.* 1515
R. N. SWANSON

Medieval Russia, 980–1584
JANET MARTIN

The Wars of the Roses: Politics and the Constitution in England,
c. 1437–*c.* 1509
CHRISTINE CARPENTER

The Waldensian Dissent: Persecution and Survival,
c. 1170–*c.* 1570
GABRIEL AUDISIO
Translated by Claire Davison

The Crusades, *c.* 1071–*c.* 1291
JEAN RICHARD
Translated by Jean Birrell

Medieval Scotland
A. D. M. BARRELL

Roger II of Sicily
A Ruler between East and West
HUBERT HOUBEN
Translated by Graham A. Loud and Diane Milburn

The Carolingian Economy
ADRIAAN VERHULST

Medieval Economic Thought
DIANA WOOD

Women in Early Medieval Europe, 400–1100
LISA M. BITEL

Other titles are in preparation

CU00691283

A Patch of
Blue
And Other Stories

Dewi Williams

EsteemWorld Publications
United Kingdom

A PATCH OF BLUE and Other Stories
Copyright © 2010 By Dewi Williams

ISBN: 978-1-907011-12-2

First Published 2010 in the United Kingdom, by
EsteemWorld Publications

British Library Cataloguing In Publication Data
A Record of this Publication is available from the British
Library.

All rights reserved. Written permission must be secured from the publisher to use or reproduce any part of
the book except for brief quotations in critical reviews,
magazines or articles.

For further information or permission, address:
EsteemWorld Publications
United Kingdom.
E-mail: info@esteemworldpublications.com
www.esteemworldpublications.com

Printed in Great Britain for EsteemWorld Publications

CONTENTS

—0—

Dedication

For Hilary

My thanks to Luke, Hilary and especially Alan Marshfield for their help and support in the creation of this book.

A Patch of Blue

When it rains in Mid Wales, in the summer, in the cricket season, it invariably pours. If one is bothered to glance at the weather forecast shown on the Television, there nearly always appears the symbol of a dark cloud circling around the heart of the old country: a poised, hovering, chamber pot, the sword of Damocles, about to be emptied. The residents of the small town and the surrounding neighbourhood, members indeed of the cricket club, were used to this kind of weather and the captain of the team was the stalwart, the ever optimistic and ever challenging owner and proprietor of a small back street car repair shop, who would utter the familiar phrase.

"There's a patch of blue up there boys."

Like an ancient Biblical prophet, minus the cloak and beard, he was the only one who could spot this oasis in a grey desert of sky. When this statement was proffered his face would remain impassive but the blue eyes would twinkle like marbles. For home games it was not unusual to see the same man, a Mister Rowley Hall, clad in overalls, covered with oil, lean out of his car window to exclaim.

"Start without me boys! Got to finish servicing a car. Just changing the oil. Be along in a minute."

After a few overs had been bowled on an always drying wicket, unless of course it was raining at the time, he would reappear, his black hair a vivid contrast to the now daz whited cricket gear that graced his long, lean and slightly stooping figure.

The small town, although commonly and affectionately known as the village, at that particular time was a collection of houses, solid late Victorian villas, red bricked and double fronted, on three streets bisected by a

7

small river, a church, three chapels, a village school, a Post Office, two banks, a telephone kiosk, three butcher shops, a bakery, a cobbler, a chemist shop, four pubs two urinals: one official and the other a series of stone walls, and a motley collection of other small shops selling an assortment of items ranging from daily newspapers to seed potatoes.

There was also a Petrol Station which sold four star Esso and serviced cars, ran by a couple and their two sons. On the edge of the small town stood a tiny factory ran by the British Legion producing woollen garments like sweaters, scarves and caps. They also sold good valued rugs and blankets, rather coarse but hard wearing tweed that was made to last. There was a great sense of community guided by a vicar, a parson, policeman and the hand of providence.

The neighbouring county was dry on a Sunday so it was no secret that car loads of visitors crept into the village late on a Sunday afternoon to imbibe in an evening's drinking in the New Inn where often the singing in the front bar was sweeter than that of the bedraggled congregation across the road in the half empty cold stone Wesleyan chapel.

The cricket season was arranged with a few fixtures against other neighbouring villages, some sides in South Wales where the competition was fierce and the welcome sometimes chilly, a long trip into Lampeter where the sporting standard was much higher but the welcome was warm and a stop in the Half Way Inn on the way back would provide an added bonus. Rowley knew they had a piano in the bar and after a half of bitter shandy would spend an hour caressing the keys of the old upright and sing a selection of the old Welsh hymns. As is the custom in many parts of Wales: one drink leads to

8

another drink, one man starts to sing and in a few minutes a choir is assembled. The Lampeter pitch was of a very high standard, as smooth as a bowling green, the facilities modern although in one particular match the sun was setting right behind the bowler's arm which made it impossible for the facing batsman to see the ball. One of the boys played for forty five minutes in one match, scoring over twenty runs and never saw the ball at all!

Other village teams were lucky enough to share a common patch of land where thistles grew near the boundary, sheep shit littered the crease and rabbit holes made the bowler's run up rather a hazard and gave the attributes of a swing bowler a completely different dimension. Oh the joys of cricket in wet Wales: Tommy Jones, all five feet with stumper's pads up to his chest and Wellington boots on his feet, Dai Goliath rolling a cigarette in the slips catching a ball and continuing the process of cigarette making without blinking an eye, Dai Jones running off the field half way through an innings when the Fire Siren went off. Picture the scene, a helmet, a buttoned up jacket and batting gloves!

On this particular Saturday, a cloudless blue sky day, a fixture had been arranged to play the team from the neighbouring army camp near Sennybridge. In all probability this was to be a tough challenge pitting their skill, guile and wit against very fit and healthy young men and the village hoped to put up a good show and produce their strongest team. On the Wednesday before the long awaited day, the "selectors" congregated in Rowley's work yard as he lay on his back under an old Ford car. The selection committee comprised Hall, Bindy Davies, vice captain and postman and "GlynThe Factory", very knowledgeable although he did not play himself and who had connections with Glamorgan! What the connections were, one wasn't quite sure.

Bindy was as keen as mustard, analytical in his approach and Rowley was his hero. In fact Henry Rowley Hall was known in some circles as the King because of his initials and in Bindy's case, "O worship the King all glorious above" was as appropriate as water to a bucket! Bindy was hoping to eventually take over the captaincy of the cricket team and Rowley was grooming him in this direction. When Rowley's young teenaged son, Ian called them in for a mug of tea, the real process of selection took place. Who was available? Could we get a team? Were the boys home for the weekend and so on, let alone the prospect of losing some of the boys to the haymaking? But as it had rained most of the week the last question was omitted from the equation.

It was decided that Rowley would open the batting along with Nobby Smith from the factory who was fearless and as tough as teak. Mr Thorpe, a gentleman sheep farmer from up the valley would be at number three and Bindy would follow him at number four. Bindy gave this serious consideration blowing on his steaming mug of tea and he wanted to discuss tactics there and then. That would come later. Now it was selection time.

Over a packet of digestive biscuits and further mugs of tea, the team selection was completed. Norman Jones, a civil servant and farmer's son, was home. He would bat at number five and also open the bowling along with The Mad Banker, Alun Walters who would bat lower down in the order. Dilwyn Richards was home too. In a manner of speaking! He was in fact at university but was courting a local girl. He was a good fielder and, when on form, a good batsman. The rest of the team would be selected on who would turn up on the square at 12.30!

"Don't forget. Saccy Davies is keen to turn up. Dead keen so I think we ought to give him a game," said Glyn reaching for another biscuit. Saccy was in fact more than dead keen. With his presence he was formidable like a hawk with his thin frame and hooked nose. He contested every ball and he also paid homage to the King.

"Alun is an useful bowler!" said Bindy.

"Aye mun. As long as he is off the beer. He was seen singing standing on the window sill last Friday night in the back bar of The New Inn and was pretty hung over the next day," suggested Glyn.

"Took four wickets though."

Walters closed the door of the little bank behind him and pocketed the large bunch of keys. Glancing at his watch he realised he had a half hour to change from his crumpled suit, have a quick smoke and a swift lunch before meeting the others on the square where he now in fact stood. His eyes were sore and his head ached, the consequences of last night's exertions. Had not he and Charles Poole had a skinful in the Prince before arriving back in the village in the early hours? Charles, in his cups had been determined to make a speech despite the noise and merriment surrounding him. The opening gambit had been something along the following lines.

"Ladies and gentlemen. I have come here to address you, not undress you and to part in peace and not in pieces."

There followed hysterical giggling and silly derisive cheers from anyone daft enough to listen to his tirade. Charles was to drive the minibus to the game and he was sure to smuggle on to the bus several bottles of lemonade. Walters strolled up to the garage and met Charles serving petrol to a local farmer. Charles stood there head lowered, eyes watching the pump and he grinned sheepishly.

"Put it on the bill," stated the farmer stepping in to his Landrover as Charles muttered his acknowledgement and duly entered a figure into a dog-eared exercise book inside the little garage office. He replaced the stub of a pencil behind his ear.

"How's your head this morning?"

"Not so bad mun.We are the heroes of the night, hee hee. We would rather fool around than fight. A steaming piss up!"

"Okay to drive?" demanded Walters.

"No problem. We are the people!"

On the square, like explorers about to set out on a trip across a continent, the village cricket team assembled. Rowley, white shirted and smoking a small cigar sat at the wheel of his Ford Consul. He was accompanied by Bindy in the front seat and the back seat was made up of young Ian and Saccy sitting upright and his eyes darting here and there. Next to him was Nobby Smith sitting erect and motionless like a redundant totem pole. Others gathered around and tumbled on to the minibus clutching their carrier bags and assorted items of kit. Walters sat at the front with Charles, riding shotgun to his stage coach. He noticed that they were ten in number including the occupants of Rowley's car but realised they were about to collect Norman from the farm.

A few mid day drinkers emerged from the shadows of the Hotel that dominated the square, and wished the party well. Charles's hands were trembling when he took the wheel and there was a significant smell of stale alcohol in the air. He took a long swig from his lemonade bottle and lit a cigarette. Two young girls, nubile teenagers, passed on horseback, the hooves of the horses echoing across the square. Several heads turned in their direction and voices from the shadows were heard.

"I'd rather sleep with her than the policeman!"

"Cradle snatcher!"

"I wouldn't mind the best of three falls with her!"

The trek began with Rowley leading the way, right elbow perched on the open window of the car, followed by the minibus as they trundled slowly out of the village. The sun was shining and the air was filled with the scent of newly mown grass and the cooking aroma that filtered from the open doors of the houses. On the crest of the hill just south of the little town they stopped in order to pick up Norman. Rowley felt a slight panic within as there was no sign of Jones. He tooted the horn and the faces at the windows of the vehicles showed trepidation and uncertainty.

The conclusion drawn was that Norman would not be playing that day and as a result Rowley would now have to open the bowling as well as the batting and to make up the numbers, Charles, who was as competent with a cricket bat as a teddy bear with a paint brush, would have to field and bat at number eleven. Walters realised this too but did not wish to remind Charles of this until a little later. Meanwhile at the farm gate nothing could persuade Norman to change his mind and Arwel Yupp had the highly original idea that he had spotted a strange woman behind the farmhouse curtains. Arwel, a sixth form boy was a lad who knew a thing or two and had scored ninety eight not out last season only for Rowley to call a declaration in order to make a game of it! Arwel would not get an opportunity like that again to achieve his century.

The procession continued up along the Sugar Loaf

and crossed the county line. Here the view below was an unfinished oil painting and the dark clouds disappeared along with the birds of prey that had watched their departure. They moved on, top speed of forty five and swigs from a bottle of lemonade supplemented with long drags on Gold Leaf cigarettes. In front was Rowley driving slowly gliding around corners and a passenger from Charles's minibus would see the hands of the Rowley's occupants in great gestures as they argued the toss.

On the other side of Llandovery they re-entered their own county and slowly wound their way over a stream, through thick woods where bluebells grew in abundance until at last they arrived at the small Army training camp. They were met with a man, an obvious officer, sporting a white umpire's coat over his uniform. He barked when he spoke and for the first time in his life Walters felt he was glad he was working in a bank. Mr Thorpe, the English sheep farmer, who spoke with a pronounced accent was immediately at home and in a matter of seconds was in animated conversation with the officer. Dilwyn Richards, home from university and wearing a striped scarf to prove it, laughed at this scenario and stated in a loud stage whisper that the ruling classes always looked after their own. He was smiling when he said this, although he was not far from the truth, as one could never dislike Thorpe, or disrespect his batting prowess.

Into the changing room they filed rather self consciously passing through an area where several young soldiers sat around a table smoking cigarettes and playing cards. The visitors were studiously ignored and it was clear to all and sundry that they cared not a tinker's curse about cricket laying out the cards that were in fact pictures: of naked busty women. This blatant display of uncovered flesh was almost enough to put some of the younger members off their cricket. But not quite!

When Charles was asked if he would bat at number eleven, his face changed colour and his stammer increased. But since he was an accommodating young man, wanting to please, he reluctantly agreed and grinned rather weakly at the daunting prospect.

"You might not need to bat at all if they go in first and we pass their total," suggested Saccy whose eyes had lit up when he had spotted the card school. He looked around seeking the approval of others and a back up to this original statement. Keith Mardsen who was a nineteen year old semi invalided young man and earned a crust at the wool factory, offered his advice to try to placate Charles.

"I batted number eleven last week. The bowlers were totally knackered by then. I scored one not out."

"Does that improve your batting average then Mars? What is it now?"

"Three."

The only sound that followed was the snort of stifled laughter. Everyone in the team knew how seriously Marsden took his cricket even though he could not hit a hole in a wet Western Mail. Nobody dared to hurt his feelings. Because he lived in the village, he was looked after by others around him and was made to feel as important as if he were the acting Mayor.

The toss was lost and the village was invited to bat. Rowley, the King, would open along with Nobby Smith who had the determined air of a Brian Close about him. Poker faced and lantern jawed he slowly began to put on his pads. Then in the clamour and excitement of the changing room where the smell of socks mixed in with stale tobacco and body odour, the voices could be heard.

"Did you come down by car this morning Saccy or did you walk?"

"Came down on the tractor. Left it in Rowley's"

"Got yourself a box yet Mars? They come in four sizes. Large, medium, small and Marsdens!"

There was immediate raucous laughter and someone slung a dap across the room and it slapped against the whitewashed wall.

"Have you seen their captain? A black lad. A Cassius Clay look alike."

"He looks bloody dangerous!"

One or two went and had a look at the black athlete. Some of the boys had never seen a non white person in real life, had never been further afield than Aberystwyth and in a sense this was a novelty. The openers took to the field to small applause from a handful of people who sat around looking on. Saccy approached Walters and spoke to him in Welsh. He had not understood the joke about the box and Walters patiently explained it to him although he had some difficulty in finding the right Welsh word for genitals. It was lost in translation. Saccy's face was like the opening dawn of day and he blushed slightly and walked away muttering to himself in a true bachelor fashion.

The rest of the team emerged into the sunshine blinking at the light and sat around in small groups or practised some shots around the boundary. Walters tossed a few balls at Marsden and pretended to give a John Arlott commentary which amused the younger man. Someone spotted Charles on the far side of the field crossing over a hedge and disappearing from view.

"What's he up to now?"

"Don't ask! Charles! He's a bloody star!"

Cassius Clay opened the bowling. He was fast, swung the ball either way and struck terror and apprehension into the opposition. In his first over, Rowley managed a single and Nobby was hit by several short deliveries the ball thudding into his chest and ribs. Nobby showed no sign of pain and could have been mowing the lawn or playing poker. Clay glared at him with all the practised hostility of an experienced fast bowler and then tore up to his wicket. At the end of the opening over Charles reappeared on the far boundary seemingly wiping his hands with long bunches of green grass.

To the relief of the visitors, the other opening bowler was not as aggressive as the Clay character and as the game progressed it became easier to score runs off the other bowler. Richards sharpened his pencil and continued to do the scoring, in the score book that is. Rowley appeared to be finding his form whilst Nobby continued to offer stubborn resistance and scored a few singles here and there. When the score reached nineteen, Nobby was caught behind off a rising ball from Cassius Clay and then Bindy was cleaned bowled first ball, his stumps askew and his face crest fallen.

"Look boys! Is that a red Kite up there?"

"No no, kite is bigger, different colour and has a forked tail. A buzzard hawk! " Ian blinked behind his glasses. He was used to reading a lot of books.

"It's probably a vulture waiting to pick our bones after we get hammered by this team," said Richards with his tongue firmly in his cheek. Bindy wandered disconsolately around the boundary trying desperately to tie a knot in his disappointment and knowing he would have to wait another week before he could try again. First ball! A duck!

17

The afternoon passed with a slow laziness and the only sounds that were heard were leather on willow, a few hand clapped applause and the songs of birds that congregated in the hazels and oaks that surrounded the little cricket pitch. There seemed little evidence of army life with only the occasional barking of the umpire officer to signal a no ball or a not out decision.

Thorpe got ten and Rowley fourteen. Richards got a dozen and Walters acquired two boundaries before being trapped leg before. Arwel Yupp continued his form and scored an unbeaten eighteen whilst the remainder accumulated the princely sum of four between them. Charles, grinning like a new moon, faced one ball which flew over his head into the safe hands of the waiting wicket keeper. A grand total of seventy seven and their opening bowler, a class act, had taken seven wickets. Saccy had managed two runs and Mars just a meagre single before he was run out. Both now looked forward to tea.

During the interval where platefuls of cold ham sandwiches with white bread and mugs of strong sweet tea were served, tactics were discussed.

"They'll get seventy eight in no time," said Bindy studying the string of white fat that emerged from his sandwich.

"Now that's where you are wrong!" insisted the King, after all he was captain and had a responsibility towards his troops.

"That black lad is some cricketer, he played bloody Hamlet with our batting. Couldn't do a thing with him."

"I was puffing like an adder after twenty minutes."

Saccy devoured his sandwiches and searched everyone's plate for a second or third helping.

18

"Who is going to bowl instead of Norman?" he said innocently. There was a pregnant pause, a silence as everyone stopped chewing for a second.

"I will open with Alun. I'll try my off spin."

Rowley spoke with a quiet authority. It was anyone's guess who would be first change bowler. And so the village cricket team, replenished and refreshed, took to the field to try to bowl out the opposition.

To nobody's surprise the opening bat was none other than their opening bowler: The ubiquitous Cassius Clay. He glared at the visitors as he strutted to the crease and took his mark. He then made an elaborate pantomime of surveying the field, adjusting his cap, doing a bit of gardening before taking guard. Nobby was stumper and his open necked shirt revealed a few ugly red marks where he had been hit during his innings.

Rowley ambled up and bowled a short one on the leg side. It was pulled with nonchalant ease to the boundary for four. The close fielders began muttering to themselves that this would be all over in a half hour. The second ball was wide of the off stump and was square cut but straight at Walters fielding in the gully. In a flash of inspiration and good fortune, Alun hung on the ball as he fell heavily to his right and the score was four for one wicket. The batsman could not believe it and angrily hit the ground with his bat and stormed off cursing and swearing back to the pavilion. The boys gathered around Alun and congratulated him. The game was won there and then.

After Cassius Clay, the support acts showed no hint of talent. They may have been soldiers but as cricketers they had no backbone and no fight. The wickets tumbled to the cries of triumph and surprise, the match was a skirmish on the sands before the tide came in. Rowley and Walters took five wickets apiece and the opposition were all out for forty six. The Village Team returned to the pavilion to a steady applause and the welcoming handshake of the black lad who now smiled broadly and offered his congratulations.

A swallow swooped into the pavilion rafters like a visiting dive bomber and was spotted by Ian sitting there, arms folded ready to return home.

"What bird was that then?" said Walters.

"A swallow, of course," stated the bespectacled one.

"One swallow doesn't make a summer. One away victory doesn't make us invincible," said Richards collecting his kit. The boys were uncertain whether he was serious or not. They were never quite sure!

"One swallow doesn't make a pint either. Does it Charles?" said Walters.

"But I'll buy you one tonight. and a boom boom to go with it!"

"What's a boom boom?" enquired Mr Thorpe rather timidly.

"Double rum and black," replied Charles with a look of relish on his face.

"We are the heroes of the night. Never surrender," continued Charles, the fear gone now and the prospect of a drink in close proximity.

"We are heroes of the day as well," said Richards. Everyone realised that a famous, if unlikely, victory had been achieved and they would be talking about this day in years to come.

"Looks like we just made it Rowley. The clouds are gathering fast."

The shadows had indeed lengthened as the party returned to their transportation, each one basking in the glow of the success of the day, each one with individual thoughts of home and the long awaited Saturday night that lay before them. Some of the older men would return to their wives and family, the familiarity of television. Others gave a thought of the pub and Saccy thought of the unfinished book of Welsh poetry to read and cold meat left over from yesterday. There was the whiff of rain on the wind coming from the Beacons but Rowley turned his head to the sky and pointed out an area that only he could have spotted. In the grey sand hills of the sky was indeed a small watering hole, a little cushion of turquoise rimmed with silver.

"Now that's where you are wrong boys. There it is! A patch of blue."

And as usual, he was right. The King had spoken. Eleven faces turned to the sky and for a second the world seemed to stand still.

The Bike Ride

On his fourteenth birthday Enoch got a wonderful surprise. With some assistance from his Bopa Lawrence, his
mother and father presented him with a beautiful, brand
new, spanking, sparkling, shining, Raleigh bicycle. It
was cream and red in colour, had a three speed, a dynamo, mudguards, a hand bell, a pump, saddle bags at
the rear, a cushioned seat, straight handlebars and a plastic drinks container complete with a straw. Enoch was
delighted. How he had longed for any bike but to have a
brand new one was a dream come true. He never questioned the fact that the gift had cost money, teenage boys
seldom do, and he knew his father earned very little at
the "Cables" factory and his mother had to scrimp and
save to keep their little two up and two down terraced
house in order. There was no room in the house for the
bike so it was kept outside next to the "lav" and at night
when it looked like rain, Enoch would cover the bike
with his overcoat. Such was his passion.

Three streets away lived one of his pals in a semi detached house called Woodbine Villa, where there were
two toilets and three bedrooms as well as a shed. Here
lived the minister's son called Daniel but known to all as
Danny Boy. He was fourteen and a half and lived with
his parents and older brother and younger sister. Danny
Boy was the middle child and had all the symptoms per-
taining to that. He had just acquired a second hand bike
from a boy in the Grammar School who lived in Plas
Draw. His father had bought it for him for the princely
sum of three pounds and as in the case of Enoch, Danny
Boy had no indication of how the cash had been generated. Although the house in which he lived was spacious,
it belonged to the chapel and his father earned a pittance

as a priest. Danny had longed for a bike and had waited a long time for this one. It was in reasonable condition, a Raleigh, with a three speed and a gadget that measured the mileage you'd made. The machine had a drop handle in true racing style and metal shoes on each pedal to help the rider produce more speed when pumping away. Danny was chuffed as hell and could now visit so many butties in the neighbourhood, to play football in the winter, cricket in the summer and follow his country pursuits.

Danny Boy was just a little different from other boys in the vicinity. Firstly he spoke with a different accent and had been laughed at when he joined the Grammar school for wearing hob nailed boots. Having just moved from a rural idyll, Danny Boy was used to wearing this kind of footwear as all the farm boys did the same and he could not understand why the townie lads had poked fun at him. But the banter did not last long and the typical schoolboy teasing and torment ceased especially as Danny Boy had threatened to bloody someone's nose at one break time in the school playground. He was soon accepted by his contemporaries and as is customary, the attention to teasing and taunting went elsewhere. But deep in his heart the longing for the old home festered within him and occasionally a kind of melancholy surrounded him.

Enoch did not attend the grammar school, had cheerfully failed the eleven plus, was not interested in sport except for fishing but got on well with the gang of lads that frequented the streets. He liked nothing more on a Sunday night than to walk into town for a pie and coffee in the Bridge café. Here he would sit and smoke a Players Weights and watch the girls go by stalked by the "hard Boys" of the town. There were some hard lads

24

around at that time, dressed in draped jackets and brothel creepers. Boys you stayed away from. Enoch had yet to go out with a girl, although he longed to, but he was now testing the waters of adolescence after being acutely attacked by acne that had sneaked up on him when he wasn't looking. Along with a change of appearance and a semi crew cut in Basset's the barbers, his voice was having difficulty in establishing its own persona and occasionally when he spoke he sounded like Paul Robeson one second and Jimmy Clitheroe the next. He was fond of telling the others that he would be able to earn fifteen pounds a week just for brushing the factory floor in "Cables". Enoch had little ambition other than to have a girl friend, a job that brought in money and the pictures on a Saturday night. His favourite actor was Victor Mature although until corrected, politely, by Danny Boy, called him Victor Matcher.

On the other hand, Danny wanted to get away from his older brother, wanted a room of his own with pale blue walls and although he attended the Grammar school, was never completely at home there. Some of the inspired and motivated lads in his class were very bright and already talk of university and further education were the topics of the day. Danny, in the meantime had discovered rock and roll and had started to grease his hair and spend many a minute in front of the cracked mirror with a tortoise shelled comb. He had never been quite the same after having seen James Dean in "Rebel Without a Cause" in the Aberaman Hall and for days after, with his eyes narrowed, he walked around the house in a mumble and a slouch much to the annoyance of his family. And from then on he searched diligently for a teenage girl with black hair who might easily be mistaken for Natalie Wood. But then there was Algebra! This brought him back to earth with a bang and a snide remark from his teacher. When he tried to share his anxiety with Enoch he failed miserably. Enoch was ready to learn to read and write his own name and address but as for Algebra, as far as he was concerned it could have been an Egyptian brothel owner's undergarment.

One Sunday night, after having been to church or chapel, Enoch and Danny Boy rode into town, tethered their bicycles by the turn to the Cow Field Livery Stable and walked into the Bridge Café, or was it the Saloon? They ordered a pie and coffee each and sat at the back of the little café and watched the girls. When it was clearly apparent that no female threw a glance in their direction they abandoned the idea of hitting it off with a girl and decided to plan for the following Saturday.

"Do you fancy a bike ride up to the Beacons?" said Enoch in a black and white voice as if Othello were chatting up Gracie Fields. At the sound of the word "Beacons", Danny Boy's heart skipped a beat. The Beacons were in Breconshire, his home county.

"Great idea! We'll take some sandwiches and a bottle of pop and we will make a day of it. I'll show you where I come from."

"We won't be going that far. Take us about two hours going up and an hour coming back. It'll be downhill then all the way. What do you reckon?"

"Fair raring! We'll pop in and see Tony Moreno and have a drink in his dad's caff."

"Who's he?"

"A boy in my class. He's got an Italian accent.".

"Why is that?"

"Because he's Italian. Twpsin!"

"I only asked," Enoch answered assuming a Bernard Bresslaw accent looking dopey and hanging his head in affected shame.

Over one cigarette between them and a smoke ring blowing competition, they finalised the arrangements. The sandwiches would be placed in the saddlebag of the new bike and Enoch would fill his plastic liquid container with a drink of Dandelion and Burdock. Enoch would call for him at 9.30.

"Don't be late!"

"I'll be waiting. Ready to rock. Do you like Ben Hewitt?"

"Don't know him. Does he live in Top End?"

"He's a singer."

Danny suddenly reached for an empty coke bottle and pretended to sing, gyrating his hips. "'Not giving up nothing if I can't get something from you' Have you heard it?"

A few girls turned their head at Danny Boy's poor Presley like rendition, rolled their eyes to the ceiling and retreated to the comfort zone of their own private world of secret, female conversation.

"Never yeard of him!"

"He's never heard of you either."

As the Summer night darkened and dusk threw a grey blanket over the land, they checked their lights. Enoch caressed his bicycle making a show of assessing the tyre pressure with a little chrome gadget that passed for a fountain pen. Danny Boy tapped his tyres with the sole of his shoe, adjusted his dynamo and cocked his leg over the cross bar. Off they rode in a cloud of dust for home and bed.

Permission was granted for the teenage boys to venture forth on an expedition and the respective mothers

27

prepared a few sandwiches to sustain them on their perilous trip. They were sliced bread with black currant jam that smudged the white like blood stains and there was a green apple with skin like Enoch's grandfather and a piece of hard yellow cheese. Danny had bought a bottle of Corona pop and hoped he would be able to store it in Enoch's saddle bag. Enoch in the meantime had washed the frame of his bike, polished the chrome and repeatedly checked the tyre pressure. There was no sign of rain and a gentle breeze cooled the summer morning. At nine twenty nine he arrived outside Danny's house, saw the curtains move, and as he rang his bell, Danny appeared in white shorts and T shirt pushing his own bike from the alleyway at the side of his house. Enoch's saddlebag was crammed with the wrapped sandwiches, a rolled up plastic mac and Danny Boy's bottle of pop. From behind one of the windows Danny Boy's older brother grinned like a demented man and gave them both a v sign with the two fingers of his right hand. Danny Boy's mother came to the door and inspected Enoch. Her face was a statue and she sniffed at her son and spoke with some disdain.

"You be good now. Both of you. Mind you come back safe!"

Off they went in procession with Enoch leading the way straight backed and erect like some visiting general in an open car. They crossed the main road and took a turning along the disused canal bank where the water was oily black treacle like liquid, under the remnant of the railway bridge that had once been used by a single track to carry coal from a long since abandoned colliery. Following the track that ran parallel to the main railway line they rejoined the main road Here they rode side by side at a steady pace, past the red bricked Girls' Grammar. School, along Plas Draw and over the railway line past the Bridge Café. Manoeuvring through the Saturday morning shoppers and the few cars that veered along the streets, they continued past the Co-op, past the Fish shop where the smell was always prevalent, the Market, past Victor Freed's record shop where Danny Boy stopped for a second to view the adverts of the new releases. In the window there were musical scores, electrical goods and sheet music where pictures of carefully groomed crooners smiled at the onlookers and there were the latest record players in shining bright red. He wished he had the dosh to buy such a player but it was mere wishful thinking on his part. Enoch was waiting for him at the corner where every weekday morning, never mind the weather, a man with a ruddy complexion and open necked shirt would stand smiling, selling copies of the Daily Worker. It was understood that this man was a commie but Danny Boy paid little heed to that assumption. What was a commie anyway?

They cycled up past the Palladium cinema and then the Rex, past the swimming baths where the smell of chlorine filled the air, past the steepled church and ascended the Gadlys hill. Opposite the park where every summer they had motorcycle races, stood the Boys' Grammar School, a fine Victorian building with a clock tower. Danny Boy spat across the road in youthful rebellion and then looked around hoping nobody had seen him. It was a steady incline now and the boys had to change gear a few times, Danny Boy furiously pedalling backwards as this procedure took place whilst Enoch merely paused for a second and effortlessly changed his gear. They continued past rows of terraced houses, corner shops, the open cast site where heavy lorries and bulldozers stood parked in a higgledy fashion like Dinky toys on a sea of small coal, past the cemetery where grave stones and monuments perched like snails, the new estate where all the houses looked the same and then to the little village at the end of the valley where Tony Moreno's father had a café.

It was a small establishment; a rich aroma of ground coffee welcomed them. It had a few Formica topped tables, a faded menu, a fridge in one corner where there were rows of coke bottles their deep red contents glowing in the light, and a juke box. The two boys trooped in rather self consciously knowing full well they had not a penny to scratch their back sides with. A voice from the corner shouted.

"Danny Boy!. The pipes the pipes are calling. How ya doing?"

It was no other than Tony himself geared in a white T shirt, blue jeans and white socks with black slip on shoes. He looked like a teenaged Paul Newman.

"Hi Tony, this is my pal Enoch, we're off to the Beacons on a bike ride. Enoch this is Tony Moreno, he's in my form in school"

"Hiya Enoch," said Tony offering his hand with a side long grin.

Tony opened a bottle of coke and quickly poured the contents into two small glasses. He would have been at home in a bar in Sorrento serving customers with an easy charm. He knew quite well that the two boys were penniless and when Danny Boy made a gesture of reaching for a coin he swiftly lifted a shilling piece from the till, quickly checking that Papa Moreno was not in sight, and slotted it into the juke box. Tony waved his hand.

"On the house. But don't tell my old man!"

The two drifting cowpokes raised their glasses and sat solemnly in a corner. Tony pressed a few buttons

30

and the contraption groaned, then hissed as the disc came into view. All of a sudden there was an explosion of noise which made Danny Boy jump to his feet and wiggle his hips but Enoch sat impassive like a grey monument. When the music changed into a slower number Tony picked up a brown bentwood chair and began to dance slowly and suggestively smooching it around the little café floor.

"I wish I was embracing Mrs Michael, our lovely Maths teacher."

"She might be talent, but she can't teach me bloody Algebra."

"I dropped my pencil on the floor so I could admire the view. Belissimo."

When the record finished playing Enoch growled into his empty glass.

"Time to go. Thanks for the drink Tony."

"Prego. I see you Monday morning in class .Danny Boy. So long Enoch! Or is it Eunuch?"

They remounted their machines to the sound of another record booming from the dark interior of the café. Danny wondered where Tony's father was and would have liked to have stayed a little longer to hear the music and to absorb the company of the randy little Italian boy. But today his loyalty lay with Enoch.

As the morning grew, the sun came out, the air seemed fresher and the trees greener. They could even hear the songs of birds as a contrast to the raucous rhythms of the juke box. They cycled past a small primary school where Danny's old teacher from yesteryear had moved to. Was Mr Bowen still alive? Would he have remembered him?

They passed a sign post which indicated they had crossed into Breconshire and they saw the little pub where some six form boys had bragged about getting sloshed when on a geology trip. Now the road was steeper, the green fields now turned to gorse land where a few bedraggled sheep munched busily on the verges. The animals looked lost and bewildered their fleeces half torn and stained. There were craggy rocks and large stones and in the distance you could spot a solitary white washed farm or small holding. The wind had risen and the boys felt as if they were in another country. They stopped at a sign post where a narrow road veered to the left which would take them to an underground river and cave. They would visit that perhaps on another day. It was a dangerous place. Danny Boy's brother had been there with some pals and thought it very claustrophobic.

"I need a slash," said Enoch "What did he mean when he called me Eunuch?" he muttered relieving himself at the roadside soaking the green rushes and the sheep droppings that lay there like the contents of a half opened mince pie.

"Can't be anything bad can it? It's in the Bible isn't it? Eunuchs. Are you tamping about it?" said Danny Boy joining him in his irrigation project.

"Like airoil I am!"

"Okay then?"

Enoch buttoned his trousers and after checking, yet again, the pressure of his tyres got back into the saddle.

"Thought it was the name for a young sheep!" he muttered to himself.

It was time to eat. Danny felt the hunger in his stomach which mixed with the yearning for his old home and the stiffness in his limbs. He wanted to stop but they both agreed they would do so when they were able to view the reservoir that nestled above the plains of Merthyr. If only he had the verve, the stamina and courage to carry on until they were in Brecon itself and surround himself with the old familiar rustic accents. He promised himself that one day he would do this. There was little traffic on the winding road and they were now watched by birds that hovered and then soared above them. In the distance below they spotted the other road that was a straight grey ribbon and there it was sparkling in the sun; the reservoir. It was time to stop. Danny flung his bike on to the verge and raced into the heather and spread-eagled himself on to the ground. Enoch carefully placed his prized possession against a stone and wiped the bike down with a rag. He then retrieved the contents of the saddle bag and unhinged the plastic bottle containing the drink.

They found a suitable place about a hundred yards from the road that was sheltered from the wind and caught the sun. The smell of the gorse was strong, pungent and increased their hunger pangs. The dandelion and burdock drink tasted like wet plastic but Danny did not wish to hurt his friend's feelings so said nothing. The sandwiches were devoured in a trifling and soon they were hungry again. They lay on their backs hearing only the song of the birds whose melody rode along the gentle wind.

"Have a dekko at that!" said Enoch breaking the silence and tossing a small magazine at Danny. It was a little booklet, rather stained and well thumbed containing black and white pictures of half naked women who stood in a semi embarrassed pose gazing into the camera. Close scrutiny was made and various comments made. Enoch's eyes were ablaze as he pointed to one picture that was evidently a favourite of his. A heavily built woman in a bulging bikini stood holding two balloons in front of her. The next photo showed the balloons having

33

burst leaving her revealing her pendulous breasts. For a brief second Danny Boy had a vision of Mrs Michael standing holding her exercise books in front of her, totally naked except for her university gown and high heeled shoes and then he flung the book away in a mixture of arousal and acute embarrassment. Enoch retrieved the discarded item and carefully picked it up as if it was made of red hot iron and bent over the pages deep in a trance.

The silence hung heavily in the mid day sun. Danny Boy closed his eyes but the vision of the busty woman would not disappear. He tried to think of the saints, the picture on the wall of the vestry of Jesus holding a lantern but Mrs Michael stood in his way. Algebra would never be the same again. Then he heard voices in the distance. Like a young Comanche Indian buck he crept out of the hiding place and peered over the rim of the little copse. The voices were unmistakeable and a faint trace of cigarette smoke billowed from the crest of another dip.

Enoch was lying on his back muttering quiet obscenities to himself and gently caressing the middle pages of the Spick and Span.

"There's someone over there Enoch and I don't know what they are up to."

"Is my bike ok?" he jumped up to ascertain that his gleaming machine had not been stolen or tampered with, bobbing back down after ensuring himself it was all in order.

"I'm going to have a look. Might be a couple snogging. Much better than the book."

"For God's sake be careful. If they are doing something naughty, something very private and he catches you, you'll be peeing razor blades for a week."

"Tough call it! Watch this. Are you coming as well?"

"No."

Danny Boy suddenly remembered he had a kid sister and sat staring at the ground. Enoch crept towards the hidden spot, the rainbow's end, the unopened casket which could very well turn out to be an unopened tin of worms. Danny Boy could not sustain his sense of honour for very long and he stood to observe his friend creeping like a commando towards the enemy line. Enoch was now crawling on all fours and he suddenly stopped and lay perfectly still. Danny Boy thought about joining him and sharing in his view but the scythe of good sense fell before him. Enoch was urging him now to follow signalling with his arm and giving a thumbs up sign.

Suddenly there was a shout and Enoch scurried to his feet and made a run for it. Danny Boy espied the figure of a man rising awkwardly, his trousers around his ankles and a pair of braces dangling in the wind. A female rose to her feet her hair in a mess and bare flesh showing from a half turned down shoulder strap.

"Bollocks!" shouted Danny and he too bolted in the direction of the bikes. He slipped and stumbled. laughing and shouting at the same time seeing his pal's shirt flapping in front of him. He had never see Enoch, a non combative sportsman, run so fast before as if his life was in danger. It was! When they reached the road, they could see the man standing on the horizon, silhouetted against the sky his fist waving in their direction and the woman by his side straightening her clothes and one arm brushing back her hair.

It was like the start of the Tour De France as the two boys vaulted on to the machines and pedalled furiously away. After about a hundred yards they looked to see if they were being followed but there was no sign of any pursuing posse.

"Keep going and don't stop until I do!" said Danny at the top of his voice as he passed Enoch who looked perplexed. It was all down hill now, a film playing backwards and the wind, such as it was, was behind them. Their lives flashed before them as they hurtled down the mountain road no need now to pedal as they free wheeled in unison, laughing now and reckless as two rodeo riders. When at last they reached the relative safety of the streets and traffic they stopped.

"I can't tell you what I saw. Oh boy. What a star!" Enoch's voice was a soprano in waiting.

"Never seen anything like it. She was…"

"Don't tell me. It will only make matters worse," Danny interrupted him.

"Let's go home. I'm totally knackered now anyway."

"Did you like the book? Have to give it back on Monday. Where is it?"

"Don't know, must have left it behind. Well I'm not going back for it."

"Oh bloody hell. What am I going to tell him?" Enoch was now a baritone.

Enoch got on his bike in a sulk and slowly pedalled away. He realised also he would have to explain to his mother how he had lost the plastic bottle of his brand new bike, but as the machine picked up speed again he remembered what he had seen and how the fruitful, arousing images would stay with him for a long time to come. He could replace the plastic bottle easily or he could tell her that it had fallen off in the wind. He began to smile to himself and his good humour returned. What a day it had been? He loved his bike and thought Danny Boy was a good butty to have on your side. He wasn't quite sure about Tony Moreno. A bit too clever. A bit too chesty! He sat up in the saddle and whooped like a brave on a warpath.

"Race you to the Park Bug Cinema. First one there. Hey you! Wait for me!"

The Making of Mendel Matthias

Now that the summer season had returned, Mendel would be in work again and a trickle of money would soon be coming in. He needed the money after a long hermit like existence over the long dark winter nights in a sea side town on the west coast of Wales. Mendel lived alone in a small terraced house with a tiny secluded garden at the back where he could sit and read his crime detective stories and wrestle with the cryptic crossword puzzle. He only did this when it wasn't raining and where Mendel lived, it rained frequently, heavy drizzle that steered its course across the Irish sea. Mendel liked the rain. He liked the feel of it on his face when he went for his morning paper; he liked the taste of it between a lungful of cigarette smoke and the rain kept people away. Mendel wasn't too keen on people and was not comfortable in the company of strangers. He liked to keep his distance; not interfere; never offer an opinion. Too often they had let him down in one form or another as he had the tendency to take people at their word and inevitably this led to disappointment at first followed by a deep mistrust.

Outwardly Mendel gave the impression of a private man, genial and polite but seldom wanting to socialise or drink a pint or two in the tap room of the local bar. He once or twice had ventured to the pictures, the town had three cinemas, but had been constantly irritated by others around him who had chattered too loudly, eaten obnoxious pop corn which stunk the place out and he had been embarrassed by the behaviour of the various courting couples that had accommodated the back row. He had not seen another film since he had witnessed a screening of Trent's Last Case and had already spotted the murderer after ten minutes. He had little money to waste on such indulgencies and his neat green Pass Book from the local bank bore witness to this. He had less than thirty eight pounds to eke out over the next winter.

"Mendel! Mendel! Where are you?" a woman's voice echoed in his brain. Mendel sat up abruptly in his bed and blinked. He had heard his mother's voice calling to him in a curious mixture of self pity and aggression. But his mother was dead and had been for at least eighteen months. Mendel winced and then smiled to himself, glanced at the clock at his bedside table and went back to the safe haven of his sheets and blankets. The uneasiness of his dream stayed with him for a minute or two and then his mind relaxed and he felt the tension of his body ease and warmth entered his whole being. The guilt of having survived his mother eased into a strange sense of relief and a further incongruous sense of excitement at being able to do things for himself at last. The burden had been lifted. Getting up, he walked to the window and peering through the curtains observed a dry but windy day.

The routine of breakfast was the same every day whatever the season and whatever the mood. He would boil an old kettle on his gas stove and make a pot of tea. Whilst this was brewing the ritual of washing and shaving took place in the cluttered bathroom. Mendel would stare at his reflection in the mirror and scrutinise his lined face and thinning hair which he brushed straight back over his large forehead and realised in a few years he would receive his pension and then there would be no need for work at all. Each day he would wear a grey shirt and a striped tie a pair of fading flannels and a sports jacket which now accommodated a leather patch on both elbows. He looked like a redundant Maths teacher without the spectacles. At 7.50 exactly he would despatch a boiled egg from the saucepan and listen to "Lift up your hearts" on the Home service. In a strange way he took comfort from this programme where a kindly voice reassured him that all was well in the world. After the boiled egg and two pieces of bread and butter, thinly spread with marmite he would fill his thermos flask with strong tea and make his usual round of corn beef sandwiches for his dinner. After checking all the windows and doors Mendel Matthias would leave his little house locking the front door behind him at exactly 8.40.

It was a pleasant little walk to his place of work which took him eleven minutes or so, depending if he stopped to chat at the corner newsagent where he bought his daily newspaper and every Monday a large Players and a small box of England's Glory. At the end of the street he would turn the corner and head for the castle ground above the little harbour. He would be greeted each morning with the woeful cries of the seagulls as they swooped and dived in the sky above. By the ruins of the old castle was the putting green where Mendel was in charge until the last week of September. Here was his little wooden hut with a fence and small wooden gate in front. It opened at nine and in the height of the season was a popular venue for the visitors. There were 9 holes and the greens were kept in immaculate condition, cut and mowed at regular intervals. Many young children thought that Mendel, genial and smiling, lived in the little hut as he always appeared to be there, behind the wooden counter, come hell or high water. The interior of the hut smelled of cut grass, wood, fresh paint and stale tobacco, and in rows above Mendel's head were a number of putters and the tariff for the season. Behind the counter was a cardboard box of white golf balls and a packet of scoring tickets in a pale blue colour encircled with a rubber band. Beneath the counter were placed his thermos flask and sandwiches wrapped in greaseproof paper.

When the door was opened it was left ajar so he could see the visitors strolling around the castle grounds and glimpse the sea front and the edge of the pier. He was happy in this scenario of putting - green pleasure and as he observed the world about him he had a satisfaction of knowing he was getting paid for his time. When things were quiet, when perhaps the rain had prevented people from playing. he would read the paper from cover to cover, attempt the crossword or pursue his reading of detective novels.

He was quite the observer, enjoyed seeing children running wild amongst the ruined walls of the castle, attempting to stamp their names in tin on an ancient printing machine that stood by a moss covered wall. Some people he recognised from previous years when perhaps a Sunday school trip would arrive from the country and the boys would shout and laugh, their voices echoing around the area. One elderly retired farmer and his two sisters from Breconshire came every year for a week staying in the usual boarding house. Every morning they would sit on a particular wrought iron bench and watch the passers by, making a few comments on occasions and nodding to one another in agreement.

One fine June morning, well into the summer season, a young couple sat on the same bench in front of the putting green waiting for Mendel to arrive and open the door. He was about seventeen years of age and wore a black shiny leather jacket, a white T shirt, a pair of tight blue jeans and he wore on his feet red baseball type canvas shoes. When he stood up at Mendel's arrival, he appeared tall and lean but his face bore a wide smile and his eyes were twinkling. His companion was a young girl of around fifteen who wore a summer frock which did not fit her properly and emphasised the shape of her ample bust. Her shoes were white and pointed with stiletto heels and she was over made up, her black mascara contrasting with the pale blue colour of her dress. She remained seated and smoked on a long cigarette making a show of the whole thing drawing attention to herself blowing clouds of smoke into the air.

"Morning mister. Your first customer of the day. Two for the little lady and me."

He spoke with a Midlands accent and his smile was infectious.

"Morning to you too. Here we are then. Two putters and two balls and a scorecard each. There's a deposit on the clubs which you will get back when you've finished your game. Three shillings please. Thank you."

Mendel placed the putters on the counter and awaited the money.

"Nice place here. Such freedom! The air is great, wonderful. Long way from nowhere. Can't get over all these towns starting with a double el. But I'm from a town with two ells in it. Walsall!, Do you get it?"

The boy turned and swished the club through the air like a sabre laughing at his waiting girl friend.

It was still early and only a few people had finished their breakfasts and had not yet ventured out. Mendel watched the boy and his girl friend. He was full of fun and restless energy whilst the girl appeared bored, listless and found difficulty walking in her high heeled shoes. When she bent over to place her golf ball on the ground, Mendel noticed how her dress lifted to reveal a pair of stockings and an expanse of flesh beneath a few

43

coloured petticoats. Mendel tried not to look but was fascinated at the antics of the young couple. The boy looked so confident, full of assurance and his shoulders swaying as the music of his laugh hung on the sea breeze. Occasionally there was a loud groan as the little white ball rolled down a slope and into the long grass. Then there was a whoop of delight as the ball rolled into the hole making a plopping noise. When their game was over, the tall youth sauntered back to the hut with a pound note in one hand and the clubs in the other.

"I enjoyed that but my bird isn't really interested. Here's the balls and clubs and the pound should cover it."

"Thank you. I'll get you your change."

"No no. Keep it. Have a drink on me."

For a second their eyes met. The youth's eyes were a steely blue and to avoid any embarrassment Mendel offered him a cigarette.

"Thanks. I'm sorry I took so long with the game. Cynthia hasn't a clue about golf and I'm no Max Faulkner. More like Max Bygraves if you ask me."

Mendel struck a match and they lit the cigarettes. The boy had a small tattoo on his left hand just above the wrist. Mendel could read the inscription: "mother".

"Thanks for the fag. My name is Ricky. Ricky Weston. I could live here. The sea air. Better than the hole I come from. See you around sometime again eh mister? Off to the pier now and some music. See if that will keep her happy."

He made a face then sauntered down the pathway where the girl was waiting with a bored look on her face. She now sported a cotton head scarf on her head and her black hair looked an unnatural colour. Mendel did not approve and wanted to say something to her. To tell her

44

of how cheap she looked, how fast. She pointed to her wrist watch and made a rueful gesture. Arm in arm they disappeared down the incline and behind the castle wall.

When the day's work was over and the moon rose behind the castle and cast its reflection on the sea, Mendel decided to treat himself to a fish and chip supper and the few spare shillings burned a hole in his trouser pocket.

"Nice boy, too kind by half. Didn't think much of her!"

He pondered over the image of the young couple and the boy's generosity. There was an Italian fish shop in the street adjacent to the pier where it was reputed the helpings were generous, the haddock freshly cooked and the mushy peas were out of this world. That evening Mendel dined like a king and even left a six penny piece as a tip for the young dark haired waitress. After the meal he sat with his cup of tea and leisurely smoked a cigarette to end a nice day.

The train station was busy as the train hissed and snarled to a stop. It was the end of the line: World's end. A number of people got off as the hustle and bustle increased, whistles blew, porters shouted, children screamed and laughed as bags, trunks, trolleys were pushed and pulled in a sudden frenzy of excitement. After about five minutes of mayhem a woman stepped out of her carriage. She wore a white mac over her street clothes and she carried a pale blue hand bag, a shopping bag and she pushed a suitcase on wheels. On her head was a spotted head scarf and her shoes were also pale blue in colour with high heels. At a guess she was around fifty five years of age. She was the last to leave the train allowing the happy holiday makers to go about their business and to give her the time she needed. She was tired after her journey, needed a stiff drink to steady her nerves. It had been a long journey where she had had sufficient time to think, to reflect, to ponder and to plan for what was left of her future. In her bulging handbag was a brown envelope containing £200 in used five pound notes that she had withdrawn from the National Provincial Bank the previous day, along with the address that she had written down in black pencil on a scrap of paper, the keys to her house, a bright red lipstick, a compact, a hair brush, a Ronson cigarette lighter that smelled of petrol and assorted bits of paper and boiled sweets. She was leaving the past behind her.

The air was cool but dark clouds were gathering, threatening a down pour. She walked steadily along the crowded streets of the little town pausing here and there to check her whereabouts and collect her thoughts. She wished she had called for a taxi but at the same time she welcomed the cool fresh air of the seaside and the echoing cries of the gulls that swooped and dived around her.Winding her way through the streets she found herself near the castle grounds and in sight of the eternal sea. Nothing had changed here she thought. The same old grounds, the seats, the ancient castle ruins and the same old putting green. She stopped to rest on the seat where the iron had rusted but had been painted over in a vivid green. She could taste the salt on her lips and sensed that rain was in the air. She closed her eyes. Yesterday seemed far away in another land, another country where an alien tongue was spoken. She had left that world behind her. She reached into her coat pocket to retrieve a packet of cigarettes and searched for her lighter in her bag. Her mind was in the mountains as she dug into the depths of her handbag. The brown envelope was blocking the way. She absent mindedly pulled out the envelope and stuffed it into her coat pocket along with the half empty cigarette packet, found the little lighter and lit up. She breathed in the smoke feeling the tension of her body relax and she surveyed the scene.

Mendel looked up from his crossword puzzle and noticed the dark clouds gathering in the grey sky. He noticed also that the last few golfers had gone and the place was practically deserted. He would pack up soon especially if the heavens opened. He also observed the woman sitting alone on the bench, hunched in her own thoughts silhouetted against the drab background, smoke curling up from her cigarette. He returned to his crossword but he felt a sense of unease, an augury. The silence hung in the still air and then the rain started as suddenly as a thought. Slanting stinging rain that drummed on the roof of the hut and in a matter of seconds the wind rose and the storm broke. He went to close the door and saw the figure of the woman rise up from the bench.

"Quick in here!" he shouted as the woman looked up and began to clamber to the refuge of the hut. Mendel quickly slipped out the door the newspaper over his head and opened the little gate. In a few scampered seconds she was safe inside the door as the rain hammered outside. There was a curious aroma in the air, the smell of rain on grass added to nicotine and cheap perfume. Mendel found it difficult to contain his excitement, a strange emotion, a paradox, as he placed the soggy newspaper beneath the counter.

"Here. Let me take your coat. Best to take it off for a while until the rain eases off."

She removed her scarf revealing a fine head of hair, dark and bobbed. She slipped out of her coat, shook it and draped it over the side of the counter and the empty umbrella stand. For a second or two she looked a lot younger and Mendel noticed her figure. She was short but well defined in a middle aged sort of way. He did not know quite what to do so he defended his goal by talking about the weather. He was aware of his own voice as he forced the pace, not knowing what to say but wanting her female company at the same time. When she spoke her voice was deep and the accent unfamiliar. Mendel noticed also that she had a habit of fluttering her eyes in an unconscious manner when she concentrated to find the words.

"Do you know Victoria Street? I was told it was near the harbour behind the castle." She suggested a fleeting glimpse of a smile as she tidied her hair and adjusted her clothing. Mendel, in his sleuth like way, noticed she wore no wedding ring on her finger and that her nails were chipped and discoloured, There was also traces of nicotine stains on the first and middle fingers of her right hand. Here was a woman who did not wear a hat or gloves. He began to indicate the way to Victoria Street, drawing the instructions in pencil on the back of a score-card. There was something vaguely familiar about her. He wanted to ask questions but his good manners prevailed. He wanted in an unfathomable way to see her again for reasons he did know himself. The two people stood in a little arena of loneliness as the rain suddenly stopped and faint traces of steam rose from the saturated ground outside. The clouds were tinted with gold and silver.

"Thank you for your shelter and thank you for the directions. Perhaps we'll meet again. Bye-bye now and thanks again."

Mendel was lost for words. His attempt at conversation fell at the wayside as she clambered into her wet coat and collected her belongings. She did not turn to say a further goodbye but went slowly along the pathway pushing her wheels until she turned the corner.

The following morning he followed the same routine as he had always followed but today there was a spring in his step and a feeling of optimism within his sheltered heart; a heart which beat with a slightly faster tempo. The sun was rising and a new day promised. A clear day when the green would be busy and time would slip by quickly. Today he carried an umbrella despite the promising weather forecast and he appeared like a London commuter minus the bowler hat as Mendel Matthias moved on to his work. He opened his door and placed his little bag containing his thermos flask and sandwich behind the counter along with his daily newspaper. He opened the door wide to welcome the arrival of the fresh air when he noticed something half hidden in the corner near the stand where now he placed his unopened black umbrella. He stooped to pick up a brown envelope which when opened contained a wad of five pound notes. Mendel instinctively closed the door of the hut and sat down. He could feel his heart pounding beneath his vest and he felt a bead of sweat roll down his back. He gulped and had an urge to drink as his mouth was so dry. He laid the contents of the envelope on the counter and counted the cash. It totalled £200. A small fortune! He thought of what he could do with such a sum of money. He could live well through the winter and not have to worry about the next bill. He could take a trip to London as he had always wanted to do. He could visit the museum, go to the Airport and watch the planes landing and taking off. He could buy a new coat. A knock on the door brought him back to reality. He quickly returned the notes to the envelope and slipped the whole lot inside his newspaper and then placed the shebang into his bag.

"Are you open Mister?" said a voice.

"Yes, yes of course, just tidying up I was. Yes indeed! Now then what can I do for you?"

It progressed and developed into a long and seemingly never ending day. Every person that came into view was supposed to be the strange woman from the night before. Mendel waited on coals of fire relishing the thought that he would be able to please her by returning to her what was rightfully hers. Why had she not returned to claim her possession? Had she not missed the sum of money? He would wait for her. He would keep it for her. He would guard it with his life and then return it to her. But this was a Saturday and tomorrow the putting green would be closed because of the Sabbath. By the end of the afternoon there was still no sign of the mystery lady and when he closed the hut at the end of the day the brown envelope containing the cache of money was still under the counter. He would take it home and keep it locked up for her. He had an old tin box with a key that his mother had used to keep her ration book in as well as her will and a few personal trinkets. He would lock the tin and place it under his bed and tomorrow he would go to chapel and think about things, get his mind straight and decide on which course of action to follow.

The minister would have noticed that Mendel was absent for the morning service and he wondered if everything was well with one of his most faithful members, He conceded that it would be little use to pay Mendel a visit as it was unlikely that the door would be opened to him even though he was his priest. Mendel had other ideas. In mid morning he gently opened the door of his late mother's bedroom and silently entered. It smelled of decay, dust, damp and moth balls. Very little in the room had been altered since his mother's death and he still had not got around disposing of her clothes which hung in the old oak wardrobe. He felt a sense of unease as if he were intruding into his mother's personal space. In the bottom of the wardrobe was her old tin box which he now removed and carried down the stairs into the kitchen. He closed the curtains even though the sun shone outside and once more counted out the fivers. He could buy a television set perhaps? That would add a little pleasure to his life. Opening the box he discarded some dusty papers and a photograph of his mother, her lips like a button and a look of total disapproval on her face. He grinned at it and suddenly laughing out loud tore the picture into little pieces. He was about to deliver the same sentence on another picture when he realised it was an old school photograph taken when he was about ten years old. He smiled to himself and sat at the table to scrutinise the image. Some of the pupils he recognised immediately. One or two children were now dead. He recalled the names of some of his school pals. There were Miriam Davies, Aubrey Jenkins and Oliver Pittard. He observed the image of Gretta Lewis now married and living in Toronto. Others still lived in the neighbourhood and there was Alun Protheroe now a bank manager in Barmouth. Other faces he remembered but their names were lost in the relentless passing of time. Then he espied a little girl sitting in the front row who looked familiar but he could not put a name to. She had a shock off black hair and her eyes were half closed as if she were listening to something that nobody else was tuned into. Turning the photograph over there were the initials of all the children in the class. Who was this girl with the initials O.P? He left the photograph on the table next to

51

the neatly stacked money and emptied the contents of the box. He dusted the interior with his handkerchief and placed the money inside wrapped in the brown envelope. The package fitted like a glove. He then locked the box and placed it under his bed and closed the bedroom door.

Back in the kitchen Mendel went to the drawer and fished out a large magnifying glass and returning to the table had another look at the old school photograph.

"Elementary my dear Watson!"

He giggled like a schoolboy at his new found sense of humour holding the glass to his eye. Other names came back to him as he rediscovered his childhood days. They had not been happy days although he had been a reasonable scholar and an avid reader. They had teased him in school and one girl had been merciless towards him: a little spiteful girl whose father had been the assistant Post Master in the town. She had been a spoilt little brat who had insisted on calling him names.

"Mental! Mental! Mental Matthias!" she would cry making a funny face half closing her eyes in mockery and lifting the hem of her dress.

Suddenly the penny dropped! He remembered the pain and humiliation that she had caused him in front of her friends and to add salt to the wound she had stolen a little brass Victorian magnifying glass that had belonged to his Grand mother and which had been replaced by the very same one he now held in his hand.

"Olwen Parslow from the Post Office. The little shrew. That's her and she was the one I bumped into the other day. Well bless my soul!"

Mendel drew back the curtains allowing the light to flood the room and making himself a cup of tea he sat down to review the situation. His anger and pain at being reminded of his childhood humiliation was still a knife in his heart and now he was determined that the money would stay in the safety of his bedroom until he, Mendel, would decide what to do with it. He would let her suffer. Let her worry about having lost something. But then she did not remember him, had not recognised him some forty odd years later. He drew the conclusion that she did not care a tinker's curse about him and was only concerned about one person in her life: Herself. He decided that after tea he would take a walk along the promenade and perhaps stroll around the vicinity known as Victoria Street. He walked along the long promenade that stretched from the harbour behind the castle grounds to the foot of the steep hill where an ancient wooden cable car took willing paying passengers to the summit. There were droves of people milling around. Young women walked cheerfully arms linked together their dresses swirling in the evening breeze. Young children ran ahead of their dutiful parents, bobbing and weaving in a constant clamour of chat. The tide was high and in several places the waves would crash against the sea wall sending a spray soaring into the air over screaming and laughing onlookers. Mendel's spirits were high. He felt intoxicated by the events of the recent past and decided that this must be a turning point in his fortunes.

It was a lovely evening, the sea breezes picking up and the gulls riding on the wind as if on invisible merry go rounds. In the near distance he could hear the gathering crowd singing the old Welsh hymns, the refrain rising and falling on the wind. Some of the visiting colliers from South Wales would lead the community choral singing with gusto and a sense of spiritual brotherhood. He stopped and stood at the fringes of the congregation never venturing forward to be a part of it all but standing with one toe so to speak in the reverent water. Another hymn began and the emotion of the piece gripped Mendel's heart like a vice. He could not join the voices in song but he stood quietly, head bowing slightly as the tears flowed from his eyes. These were tears of sorrow, guilt, remorse and tears of relief. He saw his mother's troubled face as she shook her head in disapproval, and as the mountain stream of his tears tumbled, a smile slowly began to play on his lips and his heart warmed as a new life entered his whole body. The wing of an angel seemed to caress his face. The smile turned to laughter and then he too began to sing lifting his head to the heavens and his heart was a fledgling that had learned to fly.

Then, from the corner of his eye, he saw her: Olwen Parslow no less, standing with a man whose face he could not see. He noticed she was wearing the same coat that she had worn on the day she had entered his hut. Her arm was linked with the other man and as he turned towards her, Mendel recognised him. It was Frank Botwood who owned many properties in the town, had many business interests, a man of influence, reputation and power. A big wheel in a small town. Botwood was a man you could not trust. She had certainly landed on her feet, thought Mendel. He slipped away from the crowd and stood by the edge of the promenade, hands on the iron railings and looked towards the couple. Botwood was wearing a suit and a brown trilby hat and carried an umbrella. He had a smile like the permanent crease in a pair of trousers. As the couple walked towards him Mendel was about to greet them when he realised she had not recognised him. She had certainly seen Mendel but had looked right through him as if he were invisible. Perhaps I am invisible thought Mendel as the couple strolled by, arm in arm, Botwood swinging his umbrella as if keeping time to an imaginary tune. The choir had dispersed, the music over for another Sunday, the seagulls asleep and only the rumble and hiss of the sea questioned his astonishment.

Before he went to bed that night, Mendel collected several sacks from his garden shed and carefully folded all his mother's clothes from the wardrobe into them, tying each sack neatly with orange string. Then in cardboard boxes, all his mother's trivial personal belongings were stacked and stashed ready to be thrown away. As he busied himself with all of this, he hummed a tune beneath his breath as he systematically placed the sacks and boxes by the kitchen door. It was well past the witching hour before he turned out the light.

Mendel followed the same routine of breakfast and washing and in no time at all he was whistling his way to work at the putting green. It was yet another fine summer morning and as he turned the corner he saw the tall imposing figure of a policeman waiting for him at the gate. He appeared like a Dracula figure with the early morning sun behind him his face in shadow and a cape around his broad shoulders. Mendel's mouth went dry but he did not falter in his step and though he felt a bead of sweat roll down between his shoulder blades, kept a poker face and a cool head. He was a young copper, in his early twenties Mendel surmised, well over six feet with pale laughing eyes, a pock marked face and a South Wales accent.

"Mr Matthias? Can I have a few words with you? Inside if you don't mind."

"Certainly. Early worm is it?" replied Mendel with a crooked smile.

They stepped into the hut. Mendel opened the door and went behind the counter. She had reported him to the police? Or perhaps Botwood had and now he was for the high jump. Several thoughts flashed through his mind as he awaited the policeman's interrogation. The policeman was in no hurry and he watched attentively as Mendel prepared for the day arranging the golf balls and wiping the putters with an old cloth. At last he produced a black note book and a short stub of a pencil.

"You see a lot of people here I bet. How many can you remember?"

"One or two I suppose. Some come here every year. Holiday like?"

There was a silence broken only by the sound of a bumble bee trapped in the corner of the hut but still humming away. Mendel took out his handkerchief and evacuated the insect in one practised movement.

"You can get a very nasty sting from one of those," said the policeman.

"Aye. But I don't kill them. They don't live for long anyway".

Mendel waited. He lit a cigarette after having offered one to the officer, and continued to wait. Was the policeman playing with him? Was he just biding his time? The money in his box under the bed was still untouched and Mendel would say that he had kept it for safe keeping. He would tell the truth and get away with perhaps a caution or at the very worst a small fine.

"A sum of money has gone missing. Around two hundred pounds I'm told. A nice little bonus for some hard up chap. Two hundred quid can buy you a few nice things. I was wondering if you might offer some assistance in our enquiry?"

The policeman was scrutinising the rows of clubs as he spoke but Mendel had read too many detective stories to think for one minute that the policeman was not aware of what was going on.

"How can I help then?" said Mendel blowing a cloud of smoke in the direction of the door and picking a speck of tobacco from his lower lip.

"Well," began the policeman turning to face Mendel, "the Liberal Club was broken into a couple of nights ago and their money box containing cash was taken. We found this close to the scene of the crime and I thought of you."

The policeman placed a crumpled putting score card on the counter and continued to speak.

"It's one of yours. Am I right?"

"Oh yes one of ours. Without doubt."

Mendel tried desperately to conceal his sense of relief but the policeman was now in full flow.

"I was wondering whether you would recognise the man in the photo. He's a fugitive from justice. Escaped from Borstal and is reported to have arrived in the vicinity. I've got it here somewhere."

The policeman reached inside his tunic and produced a little black and white photograph of the suspect which he handed to Mendel. Mendel stared at the picture and recognised him at once. It was unmistakeably the boy Ricky who had given him a generous tip a few days ago and had gone off with the dark, dyed haired, young woman. Mendel made a scene of studying the face as the cop looked on nonchalantly.

"Ricky Nelson!"

"What? Ricky Nelson is an American singer !"

"Ricky something. Hang on, something to do with cowboys."

" Cowboys?"

"Ricky Weston! That's him alright, from Walsall, nice boy, wore a black leather jacket and a pair of daps like you wear when boxing or playing indoor sport."

"Basket ball!"

"Aye that's it Aye. Ricky Weston. Hope you collar him. Was in here last week with a bit of fluff, pardon me, a bit of a floozy. I've been reading too many detective novels."

The policeman wrote down in his black book a few particulars, licking the stub of his pencil and then began discussing the fortunes of Glamorgan Cricket Club. It was pretty clear that was in no hurry to leave the cosy corner of the world of Mendel Matthias and Mendel was now enjoying the younger man's company. The conversation drifted from the game of cricket to the increasing traffic problem in the town and the proposed one way system. Mendel knew by now that the money encased in the brown envelope, locked in his mother's box and resting under his bed, was his and his only. As the policeman stepped outside, he demonstrated a square cut to Mendel showing the precise position of his feet and the correct posture for such a shot. The morning was filled with laughter.

When September came and the trees in the park began to change colour and the holiday makers began to dwindle in number, Mendel read in the local paper of the forthcoming marriage of Mr Francis Botwood, a local businessman, to a Mrs Olwen Cowland formerly of Solihull. He pursed his lips and then smiled. She had landed on her feet alright but how long would it be before she would discard Frank Botwood like an envelope that is thrown away after the letter is read? He put down his paper and turned on his new television set. A voice from the flickering shadows shouted.

"Carry on London!"

This was followed by a fanfare and a shriek of helpless laughter from the occupant of the chair.

The Black Car

It was a black car. A black car is a rich man's car. This he had been told years earlier by a little man who had served him petrol although at that time he had been the proud owner of a 1956 Morris Minor the colour of apple green. The black car purred like a contented fat cat as it glided through the wrought iron gates of the big detached house in South Hertfordshire, the tyres making a crunching noise like a youth stuffing himself with crisps, as it rolled over the gravel of the driveway.

It was a pleasant, mild, mid June morning as the driver effortlessly manoeuvred his way to the junction of the Orbital motorway that encircled the city of London. So his last remaining Welsh aunt, on his mother's side, had passed away, quietly and dignified. She had slipped into the past at the age of 92 and the funeral was to be tomorrow in his home village near Swansea. Walters had to pay his respects, revisit his past and spend some time in the old world.

He had the time now to do this. He had made his money, had invested shrewdly in various enterprises and lived a comfortable life, owned several good suits, was a member of the club although in all honesty he admitted that sometimes he never felt truly at home in such an environment, felt he was not truly accepted as an equal, learning with some irritation to ride the banter and good natured jibes about his Celtic roots that occasionally were thrown in his direction like some wayward drunken local darts enthusiast. He was independent, owed nothing to anyone and nobody could come knocking on his door to lead him away. He slept at night despite the emptiness of his double bed and the warm softness of his double duvet cover.

On the M25 it was the usual stop and start, motorway madness and to ease the tension he put on a CD recording of Bruch's violin concerto number one. He particularly liked the adagio. The driving became easier as the music played, easing the aching in his shoulders. He smiled at his reflection in the rear view mirror, deluding himself as always about his receding hair and the puffiness of his jaw line. The hands on his steering wheel were gnarled and knotted like the branches of an oak tree. He grinned again as the car came to a halt at yet another hold up, reflecting that when he died his hell would be, to be stuck for ever on the M25, going nowhere with only Radio1 to listen to. Shuddering at the thought he remembered having read about a man from Kent, an elderly man who had decided to drive to Newcastle to see his son only to go around and around on the motorway for eight hours until sympathetically stopped by the Police and led to safety like a stray bewildered animal.

Near the Airport he joined the M4 and was now travelling west and going home. But where was home now? He left the question unanswered and concentrated on his driving listening again to the strains of the violin concerto. This motorway was less congested and he was able to easily cruise at a high speed allowing the car to float along as if in some underwater route. He was a considerate and careful driver, looked after his car and never opened the bonnet relying on the trust and benevolence of his dealer. When the bill was presented to him he simply signed the card and drove away.

To his left he could spot the outline of Windsor Castle with the union jack fluttering in the wind and soon the landscape changed to green fields and meadows, the occasional man made lake where a gaggle of wild geese rose in perfect formation and headed for the skies chattering like children as they went their merry way. He checked the speedometer and realised he was cruising sweetly at ninety five miles per hour and was in reality breaking the law. He slowed down to a more comfortable speed and deftly manoeuvred the buttons of the radio to find Radio Wales. In a matter of seconds he was entertained by some happy sounding presenter with a strong accent cracking jokes two a minute and talking to various people who phoned in to "be on the wireless". The personality of the disc jockey was infectious and he seemed to enjoy what he was doing spreading a sense of goodwill to all his listeners. There followed a competition where the beginning of a well known record would be played and a listener was invited to identify the singer and the song, to phone in with the correct answer and win a small prize.

"Here we go then. Who is this? If you know the answer, ring this number."

Jimmy Walters recognised the song immediately and chuckled to himself.

"Dream Lover, Bobby Darin,1959," he yelled and then waited for the response of the phone in competitor.

"Hullo! It's Sandra from Rhiwbina Cardiff. Alright love?. Who do you think this is?"

"Oh I know this. It's Bobby something ? Not Bobby Vee? Bobby Windsor?"

"Bobby Windsor? Good God love he was hooker for Ponty, Wales and the Lions. But It is Bobby something. Play it again for you."

"Bobby Shaftoe, Vinton? Bobby Rydell? oh help!"

"Give you a clue, he was married to Sandra Dee."

"Oh Bobby Darin. Dream Lover is it?"

"Well done!"

63

The opening of the song and the chanting echoing voices of the female backing singers always took him back to the bright red telephone kiosk where he used to phone her. That hot summer when during his trials at O Levels he had spent a half hour phoning her for his four coppers. Across the road some youngster had played the number one song, Dream Lover over and over and over. They had met at a record hop at the Settlement where for two bob you were invited to an evening's dancing to the records of the day. It was all adolescent innocence. The lads in the grammar school always looked forward to the Friday night and they assumed another identity, pretended they were somebody else with their pouting, posturing, DA hairstyles and jiving prowess. Dave Maddox was Pat Boone, whiter than white, Tony Tedaldi was a "Johnny Cool" with a strong Italian accent.

"But I want to love you, you are a violin in my hand, let me pluck your strings"

Nobody was quite sure how much of a success rate Tony had achieved with the opposite sex but he was a popular lad. There was Cyril Knibb who could pass for John Saxon and David James who was a Welsh Don Everly. Jimmy Walters thought he was James Dean in his white T shirt, blue jeans and a cheap. plastic smelling jerkin bought through his mother's catalogue. Although he was Jimmy, most of his pals called him Moses or Mose for short.

"Up the settlement on Friday then Mose? Alright then?"

"You bet. See you then."

The sun glistened on the white structure of the new Severn Bridge like a gigantic galleon emerging through the mists of time as the black car approached the border.

Walters smiled at the thought of having to pay to enter his native country and that the money was taken on the English side. He was no nationalist, never totally convinced by any politician of any party, but he noticed that the fee for crossing was almost as much as he had earned in a week when he had first started work. It was also a rather unique occasion, the sun shining in Wales. Hearing the old song had set his heart racing and now in total silence apart from the hum of the car engine and the ticking of the flashing indicators, his mind started to reminisce.

"Nostalgia has no future!" he muttered to himself but as he ventured further and deeper into his home country, the land of his fathers, his heart became lighter and for reasons unknown to him, he felt younger and the burdens of adulthood seemed a lesser load to bear. To his right he could see the imposing castle with the Red Dragon flag proudly erect.

David Maddox, a natural organiser, had invited some female friends from his particular neighbourhood to the hop on that auspicious Friday night. Mose had gone there with Amos Jones, his pal from up the street. After having danced to the slow songs, each guy holding on to his girl like a newly won prize, afraid to falter and let the trophy slip from his grasp, they had persuaded two girls: Tish and Janine, to let them escort them to the bus stop. It was raining with heavy gusts blowing up from the distant sea. Glowing Woodbines in the male mouths, shoulders hunched in the heavy drizzle, the four scurried to the bus stop as lights from traffic criss-crossed across the wet road reflecting like shooting stars.

Mose tried to imitate his dead hero, substituting the Aberaman Road for Times Square, but neither of the two girls seemed to appreciate this gesture and Amos had seen it all before. Then the red single decker bus came and went in a matter of minutes. The girls waved from the back seat. As it drew away in a roar of diesel fumes, Mose still tasted the fleeting sweetness of her soft kiss on his lips. Amos grinned and flicked his dap into a waiting puddle. It spun and hissed like a discarded Catherine wheel and then fell silent.

They walked home together to save on the bus fares, two lads, two innocent teenagers, exchanging ideas and plans for the morrow searching for a piece of gum to banish the smell of nicotine from their breath. When the entranced Mose hung up his coat to dry in the back kitchen he could still smell the trace of her perfume on his shirt and his senses reeled and ricocheted as he lay in bed that night thinking of her.

Walters had all day to get to Swansea, had booked in to a smart modern city hotel, so there was further time to kill and why hurry? Why worry? It was about eleven in the morning, the motorway quiet, so he turned off at the Merthyr junction and began to enter the valleys. It had been so long since he had visited this area remembering that in his teenage years he had spent time here, sown a few oats, perhaps not wild ones. Turning off the main road he searched in vain for familiar landmarks. Long gone were the old slag heaps that had dominated each mining village with its row upon row of little streets. Not so many years ago each village had boasted a rugby team, a choir, a chapel, a school and a colliery. Now the landscapes of this area were a revelation. There were small overseas owned factories producing who knows what, boarded up chapels that had once echoed to sweet singing and now the land had been reclaimed and new roads built and a galaxy of new cheap houses, identical in shape and size and each one wearing on its lapel the shell of a Television station, replacing the old rows of cottages.

He turned past an old garage with remnants of fading disused pumps, past the Welfare Hall, the Co-operative Society and over the bridge where the small river ran adjacent to the little railway line. The old road area was still narrow and he wondered where he might park his car for he felt like stretching his legs and breathing in the Welsh air. He suddenly remembered some of the old way and after manoeuvring the car at what seemed an impossible angle found himself at the bottom of a steep hill where familiarity smiled at him. He parked the vehicle where no yellow lines flashed a warning and after securing it with a flick of his remote control began his stroll.

From a corner shop an elderly man emerged carrying a newspaper under his arm. He was short, squat and wore a waistcoat unbuttoned, a blue collarless shirt and a pair of dark trousers. He stopped and looked at Walters in a quizzical but non threatening way. He invited Walters's conversation.

"Safe do you think to leave my car here?"

"Oh aye, safe as anywhere else around here. Nobody's going to potch with it. Nice car too. What brand is it?"

"Porsche"

"Alright for some!" he muttered without a trace of malice or envy.

"Haven't even got a bloody front porch but I did have a bike once. No good to me now. Cannot get my leg over if you know what I mean?"

Walters warmed to the old man's accent and manner and his sense of self mockery.

"You a local man? I'm trying to find Lyle street. Near the park I think. I used to ride the range around here some years ago. Changed a bit since then."

"Change! So quiet now mun. Like a bloody morgue it is and with the new road. you can get to Heathrow in a couple of hours. I am local. Used to work in the pits when I was a younger man. Down the "Duff" All closed now see. But it was alright and the money was pretty good. Then the missis got up the duff. Poor dab! Put an end to all that. You can do anything when you are young. Lyle Street? End of the road turn left to the top and then next street next to the park."

"The park. That's right. Still there I hope. Is the Rec still there too?"

"Oh aye. Still there like. A permanent fixture, bit like my old missis. Am off now. All the best butt. Hope she's still there."

The old man winked and smiled broadly before walking quietly away. Walters smiled reflectively. He had actually played rugby on the rec, once only although he wasn't much good, had merely made up the numbers.

The next day Mose and Amos had gone down to visit the area hoping to accidently come across the two girls. They had ridden their bicycles along the main road past the stinking washery where the smoke belched and the ash was thick on the ground. Tish had told him where she lived so Mose was adamant on seeing her again and perhaps even to admit that he had fallen in love with her. He struggled to remember every cliché he had read, every song he had heard about undying love. Amos was more cynical and lacked his companion's sense of ro-

68

mance. Despite the hostility of the furnaces the sky was a pale blue and sunshine played promising rock and roll on the tarmac.

When Tish stepped out of the door dressed in a white blouse and a black pencil skirt, Mose blushed and stammered whilst Amos looked on with a studied pose of cool sophistication despite the bicycle clips and plastic sun glasses. She seemed pleased to see Mose and took command of the situation with nonchalant ease. She was a debutante at a garden party. She was Lesley Benedict in Giant. The three teenagers readily agreed to call on Janine so that Amos might connect and perhaps they could make up a foursome. Mose welcomed this and he felt he needed the support of his butty, such was his inexperience with young women. When Janine appeared, her hair shining like butter, Amos was astounded, embarrassed and disgusted. He muttered under his breath.

"Bloody ankle socks, jailbait! Sod this. I'm off."

Immediately the butter melted as he mounted his Raleigh and pedalled furiously away abandoning his pal and his two female companions. One was blonde and the other was brunette. The blonde girl was indeed wearing white ankle socks that made her look thirteen whilst the dark haired girl wore black high heels. She looked nineteen. Mose was perplexed about this.

In the mid day sun, Walters entered Lyle Street. It looked small, diluted as if he were looking through water. The street was steep and at the top he could make out the gap in the wall to the path leading to the park. He trundled upwards seeing nobody and the air hung solemn and still that particular day. When he passed the door of the house where she had lived with her parents, there was nothing there to remind him of those long ago days.

There was no hint of recognition, no cast away souvenir and yet he knew that he had stood inside this little house, had listened to records in the small, cool parlour. He was conscious of his heart thumping and his mouth was curiously dry.

The entrance to the park was hardly more than a hole in the wall and he was amazed to observe that the bench was still there. This was the same bench where they had sat together holding hands. The wood was old but had recently been given another coat of dark green paint which failed to obliterate some graffiti of long ago.

"Gareth is God" and "Wales is not dead yet" were faintly discernable along with various declarations of undying love. He sat and breathed in the mid day air. The sky was a blotting paper blue. Overhead a bird of prey glided and swooped, surveying the panorama, a visitor from the hills of Breconshire, and in the distance he heard the faint drone of traffic.

A young woman came by, busily wheeling a child in a push chair. The fugitive infant reached out for the hand of the sitting stranger but the woman looked directly ahead, face solemn and taut as a totem pole, immersed in her own hectic world. He watched her disappear into the distance. She could not have been more than nineteen and already her thighs were large and the jeans she wore, too tight. His quiet contemplation was invaded by the presence of a little robin which appeared and strutted manfully in the dust and dirt of the pathway. The tiny bird, aloof and solitary wrapped itself in an orange coat of loneliness. Two boys hurtled by on mountain bikes, their hoods barely concealing their white shirted, striped tied, school uniform. They tore past him and followed in the wake of the young mother and child. The scythe of silence cut through the early afternoon.

Their romance grew along the clichéd avenues of fan magazines, popular love songs and teenage stories. The Friday night hop was now a priority and Mose was proud to show off his girl friend much to the envy and grudging respect of some of his pals. Tony Tedaldi even offered to buy her off him but his request was emphatically denied. Mose took her to the pictures, held her hand in the dark, wrote love letters when, in the week, school work prevented him from seeing her. He would ring her from the telephone kiosk at a pre arranged time and she would answer from a suitable call box near her street. He still cycled the two miles down whenever he had a stolen hour and their walks along the canal bank, the park and up on the mountain side were blessed with fleeting sunshine, white clouds and the rowan berries ripened as the locked doors of summer were slowly eased open. One afternoon in the precious freedom of a Saturday, she asked him a question.

"Jimmy, can I ask you something? Why is it that some of your pals call you Mose?"

He drew out a Bristol before answering, creating a little scenario from lighting the tipped cigarette by striking a match on his heel. He squinted and smiled cupping his hand around the flame like an old collier. He had once tried to light a match by inserting his thumbnail into the pink tip but had burned himself in the painful process and was now more inclined to adopt a more cautious approach. He played a defensive straight bat.

"My initials are J.E.W. So the boys in my form started calling me Jewey but I sounded as if I was one of Donald Duck's nephews and I wasn't too happy about it. But one day in Mr Luther James's RI class, Eddie Jones asked him who did he consider to be the most important Jew in the Bible. 'Moses I suppose' was the answer so

71

since then I became Moses or Mose for short and I've been taking the tablets ever since."

He snorted at his own joke.

"And what does the E stand for? Elvis?"

"Don't laugh. Emlyn."

He blew a smoke ring at her to suppress her giggles and she brushed it away with a wild flower she held in her hand.

"I prefer Jimmy."

Her smile was pert and arousing, her eyes like sloes. It was a magic moment.

Walters stretched himself and walked along the pathway for a little while noticing how very little had changed here over the years. The nettles and thistles still grew in wild abandon along the edges of the pathway and there were tiny wild flowers that blushed and bowed in the hedgerows. He felt an urge to urinate and for a second he almost considered unzipping and relieving himself on the spot. He chuckled to himself and the thought vanished into the air. He was a grown man now, did not behave like that. A motorway stop was not too far away.

What had happened to her? He reflected. Somebody had said she had married at nineteen to a man called Prosser, or it might have been Rosser, and had gone to live in Cardiff. Walters stood still for a second and despite his concentration and his selective powers of recollection he could not visualise her face now and only had an abiding memory of a teenage romance that had hardly developed to more than a secret kiss and a series of sweaty hand holding in the double two and nines in the back row of the Rex cinema. She had given him a snapshot of her taken in Pontypridd market wearing an overcoat. He had given her a picture of himself with Eddie

Jones and one or two others after having competed in a cross country championship. The photographs had long since gone. They had kissed but he had never touched her, not having had the verve and the confidence to attempt such an imposition. Anyway, people did not behave like that then.

Plans had been finalised for a day out in Barry Island on the Bank Holiday with Marian Coles and Charlie Grady making up a foursome Mose wasn't keen on Grady, a pain in the arse to put it bluntly, a boy who would light a fuse and then sneak away out of danger. He was a mitcher and because he was also Catholic, was excused School Assemblies along with Bob Servini and Tony Tedaldi. However, in order to please his girlfriend he agreed with the plan. He wanted to have gone as a couple, did not appreciate Grady's perverse sense of humour and rather insensitive attitude to life in general. Grady was a skiver and Mose felt he could not trust the rogue although he had met and danced with Marian a few times up the settlement. She was tidy. He felt a sense of unease and insecurity as if a storm was brewing.

Tish was very sympathetic about money, the lack of funds, and was happy enough to pay her own way so to speak. Mose's paper round in the morning earned him less than a pound a week and from that he had to pay his bus fares and buy cigarettes. Arrangements were made to meet in town and take the train to the coast and have a day at the sea side and the Barry Island funfair. A man about to be hanged can still enjoy a last hearty breakfast. John Donne had said that no man is an island, unless his name was Barry!

When they all met at eleven at the station, Mose felt cool in his newly pressed T shirt and blue jeans but was not pleased to see Grady who belched and farted in succession and never once offered anyone a cigarette from his packet of Senior Service. Being a Bank Holiday the train was packed and they had to stand but Mose noticed that almost imperceptibly the two girls stood near each other and the boys assumed the role of two other passengers. There was a distinct sense of unfamiliarity despite the holiday feeling that was in the air. There was laughter, gaiety and a hullabaloo of colour but Mose felt detached as if he were invisible and was watching a film. They walked and laughed together through the funfair, they thrilled to the Wall of Death, screamed on the scenic railway, battled on the bumpers and giggled on the ghost train. They were four young people giving the impression of enjoying themselves.

After some refreshments of chips and corona pop, it was time for the beach. Mose had dreaded this moment, was not a swimmer, hated the sand, the wind spoiled his hair style and furthermore he had no bathing costume. When the girls changed, the boys stood by smoking and staring away from the possible strip show. Tish appeared in a black one piece costume which did not fit her properly and contrasted vividly with the white of her thighs and arms.

Mose wanted to comfort her, put his jacket over her bare shoulders, was aware in a curious way that she was self conscious about her figure. Gallantly, he decided to buy her an ice cream and dutifully queued at the kiosk. When he returned the three were paddling in the sea. The wind rose and she stumbled, with a sudden scream, into the sea and the sand, giving a brief and intimate glimpse of a white breast and a pink, bud like lonely nipple. The three laughed uproariously as the proffered cornet slipped from her clutching fingers and fell like a discarded sympathy bouquet into a tangle of seaweed and salt water. The cornet bled and floated away. The tide came in and the tide went out.

Walters checked his mobile phone. It glittered like a fish out of water. There were one or two text messages from business colleagues which he could reply to later but no messages that were personal, no well wish for a safe journey to Wales, no words of condolence about his dead relative, no indication of the security of a loved one. He returned like a beaten dog, proverbial tail between his legs, to the entrance by the wall to Lyle Street. He touched the old grey stone. Its surface was cold, damp, and coarse. Bits of litter had gathered in the crevices, an empty, rejected crisp packet, soiled brown remains of a take away that had been used and then cast aside. Clouds were gathering in the North and he knew it was time to go.

"I shall not come back here again. No point really, Dream Lover where are you? Please don't make me dream alone."

He sighed and then laughed out aloud scaring a black cat that darted across the road and scurried out of sight.

Mose held her hand, almost for the first time, on that Holiday Monday, as they trudged back from the station. He knew something was wrong, something gone amiss, but he also knew that there was very little he could do about it. He had no capacity to change things and felt he was walking alone in the world and all around him were strangers in a strange land. He wanted to tell her how he felt but in his anxious state of mind decided to let it pass hoping that things would get better. They slowly walked to the top of Lyle street and he had the urge to kiss her, to hold her fiercely and never let her go.

"Let's go to the park."

"Alright, but only for a while. I'm very tired."

After they had kissed, her lips cold and salty from the sea, Tish told him quietly what she might have been rehearsing in her mind all day, that she did not want to see him again except perhaps only as friends. Jimmy was devastated. Dusk drew a dark curtain between them. He was transformed into a small child and he turned his face to the wall to hide his acute sense of embarrassment, misery and shame. When he began to weep silently, she placed a cold and lifeless hand on his shoulder but said nothing. There was nothing to be said. He searched for his clean handkerchief and began a desperate attempt at pulling himself together. He could only think that he had done his best, had been so proud of her, the envy of his class mates and now she was leaving him.

The spotlighted moon came out for the curtain call and shone on the young couple, a boy and a young woman who stood close to one another but who may as well have been divided by an ocean. When he finally controlled his emotions and started to reallocate his own voice she gently took the sodden handkerchief from his hand and kissed his cheek. He smelled her perfume then.

"I'll wash it for you and send it back to you in the post."

Jimmy never saw her again. True to her word, the handkerchief was returned, neatly pressed, enclosed with a letter on violet coloured note paper in bold upright black inked handwriting. At the bottom of the paper she had written.

"I'll always associate a little sadness with you."

She had signed her name with a flourish.

"Affectionately yours, Letitia."

At the grave side people huddled in small groups, black umbrellas jousting with the rain filled breeze. Walters stood alone on the edge as always. An observer in his own life. The choir sang an old sweet hymn and he congratulated himself on how well he remembered the words. He took a certain comfort from them, filling his big heart with pride and a rejoicing. When prayers were offered to the deceased, they were words of comfort for the loss of a loved one.

He shook hands firmly with several people, distant relatives, old friends of the family and some who were total strangers to him. He slowly walked to his car. It was a black car. A black car is a rich man's car.

Mitching on the Mountain

Wally had nearly completed his morning paper round. Having been up since just after six, he was looking forward to a cup of tea, a fried egg with a piece of fried bread and a quick wash before school. He cycled amiably along the narrow footpath that would lead to the railway level crossing. He was well within his time as he stopped and lifted his bike grabbing the machine where the fork and cross bar met and hauling it over his head to manoeuvre his way through the gates and across the line.

When he had quickly washed and changed from his jeans into grey flannel trousers, rushed through his breakfast, slurped his tea, he stood at the open door of his house to await the bus. As he lived near the convergence of two main roads he had the choice of bus routes: Top End or Bottom. He stood at the doorway until he espied the red single decker appear at the bottom road. His heart raced and he suddenly shouted to his mother busy in the kitchen.

"I need the lav and the bus is coming!"

He bounded upstairs to the toilet, sat on the seat and listened intently. When he heard the double ting ting of the bell and the groaning sound of the bus move slowly away, he flushed the toilet and hared down the stairs rushing out the door. His mother appeared looking agitated and flustered.

"You've missed the bus. What will you do?"

"I'll run after it and catch it at the next stop. Ta ra!"

Cagey studied himself in the little mirror that hung rather precariously over the fireplace, brushing his hair with fastidious movements ensuring his parting was neat and the waves in perfect symmetry. He made sure that the Windsor knot in his school tie was to his satisfaction

and that his brogue like shoes were shining. Square
jawed and eagle eyed he had the look of an up and coming army Cadet Officer. He yelled to his mother who
was busy somewhere in the house.

"See you later. I'm off to school. Ta ra!"

He closed the door of the terraced house and walked
briskly down the road past the little corner shop and the
alley way where in the winter the street gang had played
"kick a tin" with careless teenage abandon and much to
the disdain of the neighbourhood. Passing the urinal,
where the stink invaded the crisp June morning, by the
street lamp post he stopped by the wall and, carefully ensuring he wasn't been watched, furtively removed a
brick to retrieve his packet of half used woodbines and a
box of matches. With a sly grin he pocketed his cache
and strode down the street and around the corner, over
the canal bridge and into the woods to await the others.

The third member of the mitching team had also finished his meagre breakfast and was ready for the off. He
was polite to his mother who still grieved from the sudden death of her husband a mere twelve months earlier.
Winnie was a seemingly studious, serious boy who went
to a different school from the other three and carried
with him an air of detached sadness. Winnie finished his
piece of toast, carefully returned the loaf of Mother's
Pride to the allocated space, nodded to his older brother
and winked at his younger sister before moving to the
door.

"Work hard today Winford and don't be late for your
tea," said his mother solemnly, her hands in the sink.

He left the stifling back kitchen and ventured out on
to the road. There was no sign of his pal and close
neighbour Cagey, so Winnie, running as always, made a
grand detour. He turned right and then left up what was

commonly known as the Incline, a small, coal - covered single track wide enough for a car, leading up to a small holding and the rough gorse fields which were abound with stones and thistles. He loped like a long distance runner in perfect symmetry until he too joined the others at the chosen designated spot.

Jeffery Hock finished his breakfast and wiped his face with the linen napkin which had carefully been placed at his right hand side by his ever attentive and ever loving mother. It was clear that Jeff, or Effer Ock as he was known by his school pals, was an only child. He was a good looking lad, a year younger than the other three mitchers, and an outstanding footballer. Had he not played for the schoolboys against Swansea Schoolboys on the Vetch Field no less? And, added to this, he owned a real pair of wicket keeping gloves. Effer Ock was another version of Brighton Rock or even Blackpool Rock and occasionally, when his mother was present, Jeff. Wally, an avid fan of popular music once called him 'Ock Around the Clock.' But that was another story.

Effer Ock was not only, a little spoilt, but also bone idle. He smiled sweetly at his mother who kissed his cheek as he exited through the back door and into the garden. He brushed away the dampness with the sleeve of his school blazer and vaulted the gate and into the woods behind the detached house to make his own way to the mitchers' rendezvous.

So the four rebels met at the allocated spot and sat down to establish the agenda of their day. The first assignment was to establish what money they had between them although what little use was money as they planned to spend the summer schoolday on the mountain. They had a few shillings and Cagey had once again managed to trick his mother about the price of eggs that he had bought on her behalf from the little farm above the Incline. She must have been a bit stupid thought Winnie as the price of eggs seemed to change on a weekly basis. Cagey was cold and callous when it came to money but nobody said a word. Wally, whose conscience often reared, decided to ignore this trickery and having already lied to his mother an hour earlier was consequently heavy laden with guilt.

It was a Wednesday morning full of the mid week blues and what were the four lads going to miss from school? Wally and Cagey, both in the same form, would miss Chemistry and then History followed by Mathematics and Religious Instruction. Effer Ock, a form below, could not remember his time table and was too indolent to look into his school diary. He was not certain he carried the diary with him. Such was his indifference. It was all the same to him anyway biding his time until he could play for Swansea Town or even Cardiff City. Winnie was a little unhappy to be missing Geography and Economics but was glad not to have to sit through the boring sonorous voice of the History teacher.

"Let's make most of the day boys. We are only young once. I vote we have a look at the Black Hole first."

Cagey barked the instruction like an officer, his eyes glazed and a crooked grin across his face. He was clearly indulging himself and enjoying the sound of his own voice.

"Okay as long as we have a game of football on the golf course as well," piped in Effer, producing a grubby, well worn tennis ball from his blazer pocket. Winnie nodded in agreement and Wally shrugged his shoulders.

They traipsed along a rough trodden track which once might have been a road or a railway line and came across a folly like building shaped like a cube and built in red brick. It must have stood about twelve feet high and the same in width. Tall alder trees hid it from the main road and it was a place that Wally and Effer Ock had discovered walking home from the Ynys Stadium one day. It was agreed that Effer and Winnie would climb up the bare wall to investigate and Wally would keep guard as they all expected him to, including Cagey who still gave out orders brandishing a hazel twig like a swagger stick. Wally felt a sense of unease knowing the danger of this apparent disused mine. Had he not climbed to the summit on that particular day and looked in to the blackness of the shaft? Heaven help us all should one of the lads lose his footing and slip scream- ing into the darkness. The thought turned his stomach but he stood resolute and determined although his hands were soaked in a cold sweat.

The two lads gingerly reached the ramparts and Effer crawled across the top of the wall and slowly dipped be- low the surface. Nothing broke the silence. Cagey stood with his hands behind his back, his eyes narrowed, Wally watched the road and the track in case of intruders and Winnie crouched on the summit bowed like a heron silhouetted against the blue of the sky.

"Throw a stone in Winnie. Try to gauge its depth!" Cagey tossed a pebble up to his pal and Winnie caught it first go.

"Cannot hear a thing, it's bottomless as far as I can see. C'mon Effer get back up."

His voice seemed deeper and resonant as if speaking through a funnel. Effer Ock had precariously and un- wisely begun to descend into the darkness but changed his mind when the air turned sour and the total blackness shook his teenage faith that made him ask himself a few questions. He reappeared from the tomb his face white, brow wet with sweat and his eyes red. A Lazarus with a Welsh accent.

"I need a kick up the arse after that!" he exclaimed clambering down, his white school shirt, so carefully ironed earlier by his mother, now streaked with black and grey. For a second he looked like a lost child.

"Someone's coming!" yelled Wally from a clump of trees by the road and immediately all four high footed it through the undergrowth and found themselves on the edge of the golf course.

"Time for a spell," stated Cagey and they sprawled on the moss and fern that grew in the wood. The pleasant, verdant green of the golf course was a sharp contrast to the disused remnants of the forgotten, dangerous and abandoned mine. They regained their composure, Wally did not think it wise to mention the fact that, as the acting sentry on duty so to speak, he had not spotted an intruder but had merely wanted the retreat anyway. He was happier now, the gnawing in his stomach had diminished. The danger had passed. Effer wiped the stains with his white handkerchief and Winnie's eyes widened as he told the others what the view had been like. Like looking into an inkwell he had remonstrated.

"They should fill it in. It's obvious to me that it was once used as a pit shaft but found no coal so they moved on to other places. Lletty Shenkin perhaps or Groes or Dyffrun."

Wally spoke like a school master and the other boys said no more. Cigarettes were lit by Cagey and Effer but the other two declined. Effer still looked a little shaken as if he had come face to face with a demon and had survived to tell the tale. He inhaled deeply on his dap end until finally producing a pin from his blazer lapel. He placed the pin through the end of his cigarette and holding the pin with both hands was able to extract the last remains of nicotine. The others looked on shaking their heads with a smiling curiosity at this dexterity.

When they reached the golf course and had ensured that no early start golfers were in the near vicinity, the four removed their coats and began a game of football using the tennis ball that Effer had produced. Wally went in goal and the bunker behind the tee served as a suitable backdrop so that no ball had to be retrieved when a goal was scored. The other three passed and kicked and Wally dived and the others scrambled and slid, tackling and cursing and laughing and elbowing in total abandonment. The green, still wet with the early morning dew, soon was scorched and scudded with marks resembling the baize cloth of the snooker table in the Workmen's Hall when youngsters learning the game has miss potted and scoured the surface. Once again Wally felt the recurring sense of guilt and a quiet sense of shame. Winnie kept running, a constant windmill of energy in motion, Cagey tackled like a wild animal and Effer was delicate in his passing and relaxed, balanced, ball control. He was the only naturally gifted footballer amongst them.

"I think someone is coming. I hear voices," said Cagey with quiet authority. They began to collect their clothing in a slow and deliberate manner.

"Walk slowly and quietly. They might not spot us. But if I give the word run like billy-o to the oak tree by the stream. You know the one."

Figures could now be seen, thick set men carrying golf bags. The men stopped and looked in the direction of the shamed fugitives. One man pointed with his iron and all stood and stared.

"Time to vamoose," uttered Winnie.

"Like hairoil. Keep your composure," said Colonel Cagey throwing back his shoulders but increasing his step as they moved in unison in the direction of the woods. One of the men shouted something in their direction but the words were carried away by the rhythm of the wind. It was sufficiently ominous so the boys waited no more for Cagey's command but made a sudden dash for it, throwing caution to the elements.

"Run for cover men!" barked Cagey now demoted to an acting sergeant major and they scattered in all directions as if their very life depended on it. The golfers could be seen staring at the skid marks and remonstrating but they made no attempt to pursue the four boys who now whooped and howled like a horde of Apaches.

They stretched out once more under the shade of the old oak tree, each one preoccupied with his own thoughts, turning over in his mind their actions. They were intelligent and aware enough to know that what they had done on the golf course was an act of near vandalism but the thought was discarded and flung away like an empty cigarette packet.

"We will all get caught one of these days. Mitching school for one thing and messing about on the golf course, that's more serious like."

Winnie spoke like an older man and measured his words carefully.

"Don't give a duck's arse for the golfers anyway. Stuck up bloody Toffs.!"

"How do you work out they are Toffs Winnie? Did you get a good decko at them?" chimed Cagey with a seriousness that betrayed his earlier sense of adolescent bravado.

"Bet they never worked underground. Twelve hour shifts and never seeing daylight in the Winter, except on Sundays."

Wally was well aware that Winnie had recently lost his own dad not from direct injuries sustained in the colliery but his lungs had packed up through constantly breathing in the dreaded coal dust. He empathised with Winnie's anger and inner frustration. He was also conscious that Cagey was needling his best pal, probing for an avenue that would lead to an argument.

"It's okay Win. No need to get your moss off over a couple of golfers. They are the same as us I expect, no real difference, and anyway my pal Vernon Pugh's dad plays golf."

Wally's voice was reassuring and calm.

"What do you think Effer?" Cagey looked for another opening.

"Lend us another fag, I'm gasping!"

They all laughed dissolving the allusion of tension that had inadvertedly crept into their conversation.

"The ground cut up a bit but a shower of rain and it will be back to normal in a day or so. So what was it like playing against Swansea schoolboys then Eff?" said Wally who personally had failed to get into the team the previous year despite having performed well in the trial and having even scored a goal. and with his left foot too!

"Not much different than the Blaen Gwawr or Cae Pugh Very sandy though Lots of sand."

"Should have taken your bucket and spade mun. Come on let's get on."

Cagey realised immediately that Effer was not swallowing the bait so he decided that they should move on proceeding with their adventure.

Through the woods they stalked, slashing at the undergrowth with rotting pieces of wood and hammering a tree scaring the crows and magpies, lost in their own individual world, glad to be free from the boredom of school and the cruelty of some of the teachers. With each slash of his wooden cutlass, having discarded the swagger stick, Cagey visualised the faces of some of his teachers in front of him. He roared like a pirate and uttered their names in an assumed frenzy. How their heads rolled! "Rocky" was damned along with "Butch" a man never known to have smiled. Then it was "Curley" the completely bald History teacher who loved to bend the boys over the desk to smack their bums. They all fell to an inglorious death. Despite the thickness of the foliage, the leaves were covered with a fine filter of dust and dirt that had been carried on the wind from the furnace plant further down along the valley and clouds of dust arose as the boys proceeded like jungle fighters. It was a miracle that wild life survived at all in such a place but as they emerged from the other side of the wood and followed the narrow mountain path the air became cleaner and the breeze was pleasant and welcoming.

Cagey had said that their next port of call would be the big Islwyn rock on the side of the mountain. This big rock such as it was called was a landmark that could be spotted from the main road and was probably a distance of two miles away. Wally could identify it clearly on a dry morning when he rode his bike on the paper round and he had often thought of venturing there. Bits of broken unwanted machinery and stumps of trees together with a few unhappy looking sheep were their only companions as they trudged along, blazers flung over their shoulders, kicking at anthills, swiping at thistles and searching in vain for a few early seasoned hazel nuts. It was too early for wild berries. Everything was in a state of growing. According to Cagey one could collect wimberries here and in some places, wild, sweet blackberries.

They arrived at the rock and immediately clambered on to the cold smooth surface, standing tall to survey the landscape that lay before them. Down the valley they could see clearly the main road, the river, the canal, the rows of terraced houses, the scarred and blemished land, the pit head, the washery where the flames, the smoke and fumes clearly emanating in a dark cloud that hung on the breeze. In the distance a freight train carrying coal to Cardiff perhaps, puffed and chuntered. Silent whiffs of white appeared like distant smoke signals in a cowboy comic story. The sky remained a clear blue and the sun smiled tentatively. The only sound to be heard if they all held their breath for a second was the wind ruffling the rough grass on the hill side. Someone had carved their initials on the rock with a crude drawing of a heart pierced with an arrow: 'DW loves HK'.

The truant boys stretched out on the rock and allowed the visiting sun to warm their young bodies. No word was spoken for a little while and the thought of school, homework and the cruelty of teachers simply evaporated. In the distance the faint sound of an aircraft could be heard and Winnie broke the silence. Lying flat on his back, the sun trying to heal the acne traces on his face, he pondered loudly.

"I wonder where that plane is heading for?"

"As far away as possible from this bloody hole," muttered Cagey.

" America!"

"Could be butt. The pilot has to remember to turn left at Cefnpennar and keep going."

Cagey shifted his body half sitting up so that his head rested on his elbow. He was hungry for conversation.

"I bet there's some smart girls there boy. Lovely little chicks with hour glass figures all waiting to meet me and greet me."

"I'd rather spend some time with Cynthia," said Winnie.

"Who's she then when she's at home?" said Effer looking up and showing real signs of interest at the thought of girls and the strange mystery that surrounded them. Wally smiled to himself and said nothing. He liked to listen sometimes.

"I see her coming home from work everyday. Ten past six on the dot. Always dressed in a white blouse and a black pencil skirt with a split down the side showing a bit of leg like, oh! and those high heels tottering up the street and her arse winking at me. Click, clack, click, clack."

Winnie suddenly jumped up, raised his arms to the heavens and feet planted wide apart, shouted to the gods.

"Oh Cynthia my darling. Come up to my boudoir and help me with my homework! Oh, deductions, reductions and erections."

When the raucous laughter had subsided each boy retreated to the safety of his own curiously corrupt mind with bedroom sheets and pillows and Cynthia standing provocatively at the end of the bed. Of course the boys also conceded that she had a boyfriend. He was a tough guy and had served out in Cyprus no less.

"Don't let Nipper Lewis catch you eyeing her up. He's a bloody squaddie and knows a thing or two. Tough you had boy! Tough you had!"

The solemnity of Cagey's words brought the prospect of sexual fantasy to an abrupt end. The sun continued to show its face and even the surface of the rock was unusually warm.

"I can see the Ynys Stadium from here," stated Effer.

"Great if they have a Boxing promotion there again. Remember Jeff. You and me paying five bob each and then moving down to the ringside when nobody was looking. Redvers Sangoe! What a physique! What a body puncher. But boys, you'd never guess who was sitting at the ringside?" Wally spoke with a trembling voice.

"Sarah-Jane Tomboy? Maggie Fish? Dicky Bonk,? Billy Dog? Harry Seccombe?, or Prick Evans from Porth?"

"Don't be stupid Win. No honest now. You'll never guess. None other than the great Jimmy Wilde, the ghost with a hammer in his hand, a little white haired old man sitting on his own, quiet like, docile. I touched his shoulder."

There was another prolonged silence as they scrutinised the scenario below them. People busy at their work, grafting in the mines, sweating in the factories and here, the four boys, soon to become young men, were able to dream for a little while longer before the manacles of maturity and responsibility would forever hold them in their grip. It was Cagey who finally invaded the solemnity.

"Can't wait to get away from this part of the world. Might join the Civil Service, move to London, see the world. Have a bit of life. One day, who knows, I might become Sir Keith Griffiths. Think about that! Then what would Bunny Warren and the rest of them think? That would show them a thing or two. What about you blokes? Win?"

"Don't know and I don't care very much. Cables or Hoovers, as long as I earn some money."

Winnie was thinking of his mother for once and he knew he had a tacit responsibility for her and also for his younger sister.

"I want to play professional football. Hoping to get a trial soon. One or two blokes came around the house the other day to talk to my dad about it. They wore suits. So I'm waiting to hear…"

Effer's voice trailed off as the others looked on eyes wide in wonder.

"Good Job. Call it," muttered Cagey. They waited now to hear what Wally had to say. He was very quiet and insular as if he were entombed in a large ice cube. He cleverly changed the subject.

"Do you boys know that Ynys is Welsh for Island? So here we are looking at an Island In the Sun."

It needed very little prompting for the four to jump up and immediately break in to song.

"Oh Island in the sun, willed to me by my father's hand."

It was a spontaneous gesture as they all assumed the role of Harry Belafonte. Winnie, in true pantomime, fell to his knees and began to sing the verse cleverly inserting his own words as follows:

"I see woman on bended knee, cutting coal for the NCB," and he rolled off the edge of the rock to groans of derision and wild shouts from the rest. At which time they gathered their thoughts and proceeded to ascend the mountain singing now the Banana Boat Song trooping like adolescent sugar cane cutters in single file carrying their load until they reached the summit.

The wind had risen and dark clouds grumbled in the distance. Below them they could see the sprawl of the industrial area of Merthyr with the Hoover factory clearly defined. The landscape was again scarred and torn with row upon row of crooked looking buildings and criss-crossed terraced cottages. The ground on which they stood was boggy and rough, the grass, such as it was, coarse and wild. The sun had vanished and the temperature cooler. A single track railway line could be seen about half a mile away, an old line possibly not used as much now which would lead them back through a tunnel, back to the top end of their own village. Tired limbs and empty stomachs prompted them on to search for the station, if there was such a place, to perhaps get a train back home. Between them they decided to take a chance and find the train. They scrambled down the other side of the mountain crashing through the boulders and torn trees, sliding, stumbling and staggering forever in freedom. The wind dropped suddenly and the air was again warmer. They reached the single line and walked along it stepping and skipping over the black sleepers and the rusty steel.

It looked like a scene from 'High Noon' minus the horses and the cowboy hats. The four lads pushed back their shoulders and sauntered towards the little bricked building that masqueraded as a station. There were faded posters on the outside walls and a battered old milk churn near the door that was rusted around the rim. They huddled together outside and suddenly realised that they had very little money between them and it dawned on them that they might have to walk back all the way they had come. A man appeared in a grubby railwayman's uniform, a stub of a cigarette in one corner of his mouth and a sweat stained cap high on his grizzled head. He stood for a moment and eyed the intruders with a mixture of curiosity and suspicion. Cagey stepped forward.

"Excuse me sir. Can we get a train back from here through the tunnel like? You know up to the Top End. Save us walking all the way back over the mountain.?"

Cagey had spoken like an inquisitive child and Wally was impressed by his charm. He had some difficulty suppressing his smile.

"Walked over 'ave you? Lovely day for it. Nice to be young isn't it? Very good, very nice, very sweet. You boys mitchin'?"

There was no reply so the man continued, measuring his words carefully, enjoying the little game he was playing. When he spoke the fag end dangled and danced on his bottom lip.

"Too early for the whimberries. Aye, too early. The train do stop here and one is due in about ten minutes. Suppose you want tickets as well, four singles. Let me see. Follow me boys."

He threw away his dap end and spat noisily into the nettles that grew by the station door. The four escapees followed dutifully but such tension that might have threatened had flown away now over the trees and beyond like a bird set free from captivity. Cagey and the man went into another room and their voices could be heard. Cagey was explaining that his dad worked on the railway down in Taff's Well, a complete lie, and that as they were actually playing truant they lacked the funds to buy the tickets. He buttered up the little man by pretending to be impressed with the way he had concluded they were truants. The two figures emerged and the old man spoke again.

"Aye well, beings you come like. There will be room enough for you. Ticket office is closed like. Well never

94

open to be honest. But beings you come like. Mitching? I never done nothing like that when I was in school. Aye beings you come. Aye aye, very good, very nice, very sweet."

He trundled away talking to himself and the boys congratulated Cagey on his work, shaking his hand and patting his back.

The little train pulled in to the station halt making a lot of noise. There was a puff, a hiss, a clank and a shudder of steam and stink. It had one passenger carriage which was totally empty and four trucks containing pit props, glistening coal, gravel, and wooden crates. The train trundled to a stop and as the lads climbed aboard they could see the kindly railwayman in animated conversation with the driver. The two men exchanged cigarettes, the porter pointing in the direction of the boys and laughing, his shoulders shaking in the process. The mitchers were glad to sit down after their trek over the mountain even though the carriage was dirty and dusty, the wooden doors stained and cracked and the seats tattered and torn. Winnie began to sing.

"Last train to San Fernando." but his efforts were silenced by the protests of the other three. Winnie sat in the corner sulkily and longed for a drink and something to eat. After a shudder and a loud belch the little train began to roll out of the station yard. They stood by the open window and waved at the man who had been so kind to them. He grinned back, the fag end once more drooping from his lips. They flung themselves on to the seats and stretched out having the compartment to themselves. They felt they were riding on a first class ticket across an unknown continent, a stage coach west bound, rocking gently to the slow rhythm of the wheels. Would life be so free and easy ever again?

"Tunnel's coming up soon," stated Effer in his indolent manner. He glanced at the empty socket in the ceiling and grinned sheepishly.

"Winnie's afraid of the dark."

"Like horlicks I am. Stop potching and leave me alone."

Winnie was still smarting from his unwanted serenade but he relished the idea of the dark tunnel. In many ways he was still a little boy. So were the others. Suddenly it was total blackout and the smell of soot filled the compartment. From the darkness the voices emerged, supplemented with groans and sighs.

"Oh Cynthia!"

"Virginia Mayo."

"Rhonda Fleming."

"Jayne Mansfield."

"Pat Barclay. She works in the record shop."

"Dorothy Malone."

"Oh Cynthia. Again. and again."

"Gina Lollobridge on the river Kwai."

"Aneurin Bevan."

Daylight returned. The dawn broke again. They had passed through the tunnel and their adventure was nearly over, their journey concluded, their passage completed. They tumbled from the train slamming the door behind them and shouted their thanks to the driver who in turn gave them a thumbs up sign. The Halt was deserted. No one else got on and no one else got off. The train clanked and hissed as it pulled away and slowly disappeared from sight. Cagey carefully adjusted his tie and cleaned his shoes in the grass verge. Effer rolled a hand through his tousled hair. Winnie began to whistle and Wally cleared his throat. By the bushes next to the little lane that would lead to the Incline they all relieved themselves making a show of the procedure but secretly hoping they would not be spotted by any self respecting adult. They strode on down the Incline which would lead them to their respective homes. At the crossroads they stood for a second or two and then said their goodbyes.

When each young man returned from his odyssey and entered the door of his home, the table was laid out with his tea and each awaiting chair was adorned with a soft cushion.

The Visitor

The thin, bespectacled man of around forty five stooped over his old oak desk in the fading light of a mid winter's day. He pondered over an arithmetical problem and with his pencil stub, which he called a "black lead", scrawled a few figures on to the back of a brown used envelope. He was trying to balance the books with one hand whilst composing a short poem of four lines and a strict metre, with the other. He seemingly needed a conjurer's stick. He sighed audibly. Scattered across the surface of his desk was an array of papers, some neatly folded, others at a compromising selection of angles, amongst his pipe and tobacco pouch, an ink bottle, a sprinkling of chewed end pencils and a lovely old tortoise shell Waterman fountain pen which he used for completed works when on a sheet of white paper he would write, with a steady hand, the completed poem. He had won a number of small poetry competitions, a few pounds here and there, his name in the local paper, and now and again, a miniature bardic chair so small that even an infant child would find little use for it.

The daylight was fading quickly now and soon he would have to light the paraffin lamp that hung from the ceiling of his study. Before venturing on this, he added another piece of dead wood to the fire sending a sudden rush of sparks up to the dark recess of the chimney. A little yellow flame danced for a second and then disappeared in a puff of blue smoke. The room was filled with a curious aroma: his own body odour tinged with pipe tobacco smoke, the pungent smell of burning wood and the damp and dusty smell of old books that lay tightly side by side like standing spectators at a rugby match, along the whole length of one wall. Many books were a mixture of old and new; some had been purchased second hand at a small book shop in a nearby market town, and others had been given him by well meaning folk from the farming community in which he served. The Bible and Shakespeare were accompanied by a Dickens novel, a Hardy or two and several old battered books on medieval poetry as well as a variety of Theological works in both languages. Scattered around the cramped room were various old newspapers and magazines, pamphlets totally irrelevant and disposable other than to be used for kindling the fire in the cold mornings and to light the oil lamp when darkness enclosed him like a glove. He hummed to himself as he rose and went to the fire where he lit a spill and then attended to the lamp. He failed to hear the first knock at the door but when the process was repeated, he picked up a large torch and trundled out to the echoing cold hallway. He could not afford the luxury of a carpet and the polished, smooth, stone floor was like a sheet of ice. Absentmindedly he tapped the old dark wooden framed barometer than hung on a hook on the wall but did not bother to consult the result. He knew it was cold enough. He ran a hand through his thinning hair, adjusted his tie and opened the front door. It scudded and shook as the uninvited bitter wind entered. In the damp gloom he espied the figure of an elderly woman standing there in her loneliness. For a second she was a stranger and then the smack of recognition brought him to his senses. He beckoned her to come in and noticed she did not wipe her feet as she crossed the threshold.

He pushed the front door shut leaning heavily on it with his shoulder and making a mental note to put some oil on the hinges. He indicated to the visitor to enter his study but did not offer his hand. The woman eased her considerable bulk on to the bentwood chair that creaked under her weight and loosened some of her clothing in order to allow the heat to ease her coldness. The man noticed she was wearing a shapeless brown overcoat over a dark green cardigan and some skirt or other, her black Wellington boots glistened as the flames of the fire threw a reflection on to them. Her shoulders were covered by two sacks to keep the incessant drizzle away. She removed them now but left on her soft felt hat that once had been embellished with feathers. She wore no stockings and her legs were red from the cold with a purplish ring where the tops of her Wellingtons had left a mark like a miner's old wound. She sat looking at the floor. He knew her well enough and he felt neither intimidated nor embarrassed. She was younger than she looked, her face lined and strained. The man waited.

Tea was offered but declined. The man knew her well enough and realised that she had walked a fair few miles to pay him a visit. She had no bicycle and where she lived, with her older brother, no car had access to such a remote and lonely, wind swept spot. Each time he spoke she avoided his eyes, her attention drawn to other parts of the room which seemed to fascinate her. On the partition wall was a fading black and white photograph set in a heavy oaken frame of a Victorian couple dressed in funeral black staring into a solemn space. The man considered, to make conversation so to speak, pointing out the identity of the sitters but changed his mind when the woman's eyes turned to the Grandfather clock that stood like a sentinel in the far corner of the study, her gaze swooping over it like a bird on a wing.

"You have read all them books Mister Ellis? A job and a half. Need a long time to finish a job like that. Yes indeed!"

"I have read some of them but not all. Most are for reference purposes…"

His voice trailed off when he realised that her mind had moved on to other pastures. The only sound now was the gentle ticking of the clock, a gentle reminder of the passing of time, a slow and steady rhythm like a heart beat. He stooped to place another log on the fire adjusting its position allowing the air to do its job. Faint gossamer lines of steam rose from the woman's shoulders and the room smelled of the farm yard. He continued to wait.

He enquired tentatively about her brother and the grunt of a reply suggested there was little change in that department. It was difficult to put an age on her brother as it was with the sister. He could be forty. He could be sixty. They shared a small holding up in the remote part of the valley where it seemed to rain all the year round, where the river was a permanent flood and very little grew other than thistles and thorn bushes. He had visited them once, a pastoral duty, and had great difficulty in finding the place as there was no road and not even a path to the cottage that was joined to a cowshed. They kept a pig, a cow and a few Rhode Island Reds. Her brother did odd jobs, seasonal work mostly on the bigger farms although he was an adept hedger having won prizes in small agricultural shows and took a pride in his modest achievement although the craft was slowly and inevitably becoming a dying art in the neighbourhood. He had an inclination for strong beer and consequently any money that was earned was soon safely deposited behind the bar of the local tap room. He was well known in the area: often talking to himself whether sober or carrying a bellyful of beer. She said that she had little knowledge of his whereabouts but it was a safe bet that he was in some back bar. One Sunday he had attended chapel wearing a brown shoe on his left foot and a black one on the other. Mr Ellis had noticed this badge of eccentricity but in his wisdom had tactfully not mentioned it and the service had continued in the usual manner. She had not come to visit him to discuss her brother. This was patently clear so there was little else to do but wait.

How pertinent it might have been if he might have discussed with her the latest news, the state of the country, the regaining of the Ashes, the achievements of Stanley Matthews and the conquest of Everest. At least he had a newspaper and a radio as well as a library of books. He knew it was a pointless exercise to try to engage her in such a conversation. He understood too well the burden of illiteracy that both she and her innocent brother carried on their shoulders. When the warmth of the fire had eased the numbness of her body, she began to regale him with stories of local interest, her voice in a sing song rhythm and her toothless mouth making grotesque shapes as she struggled and wrestled with her vowels. It was mostly gossip, some of which might have been true and some which would stretch the imagination of the troubadour and the story teller. As she spoke her eyes appeared to change colour as she seemed to visualise what she was retelling and moved in unison with her words, her hands folded in front of her. Ellis felt his own eyes grow heavy and he hoped that his guest would soon make herself scarce. Then of course, as was natural to him, he experienced a twinge of guilt and a pang of remorse and nodded in agreement as she continued with her monologue. He had no choice but to wait. Then suddenly her monologue stopped as abruptly as it had begun as if she had learned it off by heart and had rehearsed it on her hazardous journey to the manse. She had nothing

103

more to say and Ellis heard the last of the smoking wood fall, clumping into the grate. He cleared his throat and spoke, his bass voice seemingly loud and resonant in comparison to the shrillness of his visitor's.

"I will fetch some more wood. Please excuse me for a moment."

He got up, tapped the decaying debris of the fire with his boot and picking up his torch, which he called a flashlight, stepped outside into the kitchen where the fire there had burned out. Gathering some more logs, his breath a grey trail in the beam of the light, he returned to the study where Jinny still sat, avoiding his gaze, motionless like a large bird of prey. He picked up a sheet of newspaper and placing it over the grate after having replenished it with dry tinder wood and a log or two, let the air relight the fire. He had done this many times and in a matter of seconds there was a blaze again in the hearth. Stars shot towards the darkness and shadows danced on the ceiling. He had a yearning to light his pipe and return to the complexities of his poem but knew that this was not the right way to go about his business. He was well aware of his calling, his responsibility and his duty as a shepherd to his flock. He would continue to wait. There was no other alternative.

Mr Ellis was quite comfortable with his sense of duty, had long come to terms with his calling and he felt he understood the people of his parish. He, along with the local Schoolmaster, were regarded as the educated men, scholars, respected and revered by the farming community. There was hardly a book to be found on the farms whenever Rev Ellis made his visits. There was invariably a family Bible and in one or two places perhaps a book about horses. Electricity had not yet chiselled a pathway to these remote places and only a few had the means of a car or a van. He knew that young men would seek him out to help fill in a form or two, compose a letter or indeed translate the contents of an important document to those who had no knowledge of the written word and could only write their name in a shaky and inexperienced hand. He co-habitated many of their secrets, was a guest to their lost dreams, their unfulfilled ambitions, their dull acceptances of things that could not or would not be changed. Everyone knew their place in a harsh and unyielding environment.

"And how is Rowena? Is she keeping well Miss Edwards?"

He was aware of the sound of his own voice and for a split second almost regretted having asked such a personal question. He was offering her a branch to cling to. A clouded look of suspicion filtered over her weather-beaten features and disappeared as fleetingly as it had appeared. The wild bird of silence hovered in the room. After a pregnant pause, Jinny replied.

"She be very good Mister Ellis, very sound health, have not seen her for a while .not since the November Fair, aye very sound..."

Her voice petered out. It became quickly apparent that she had not come to discuss her illegitimate child with the clergyman. She had accepted her fate, the cards that had been dealt her. She knew she had committed a sin and had paid the price for it, had been allowed to retain her membership of the chapel, but the infant was now off her hands and working. The burden had been rolled away. Mr Ellis had written a long letter of introduction "To whom it may concern," extolling the virtues of Rowena, her good conduct and her sense of honesty and trust. He had not written lies but had debated whether this was the right thing to do: her child with a

105

token gesture of education at fourteen to work in service at a prosperous farmhouse in a different county some twenty miles away where the climate was considerably kinder and the land more fertile. At least she would be well fed and would have a clean bed in which to sleep at night but the work would be never-ending. He considered it one step up from the work house. There was no other solution on offer, very little choice and Jinny had been determined to see her right. It had been a fruitless exercise to try to dissuade the mother. She was a fugitive from the truth.

Ellis had spotted her too at the November fair. She was a pale faced diminutive little girl, wouldn't say boo to a goose, shy and undemonstrative but she was with a boy of similar age, a tall stooping gangling youth who, when he walked, looked as if he were crossing a river on invisible stepping stones. Ellis sensed then that the girl had recognised him, but for reasons known only to her, had pretended not to. Jinny had never revealed the identity of Rowena's father and the Reverend Ellis had not had the audacity to pursue the matter. In the parish, tongues had wagged, various names had been whispered. The war had just begun and men were leaving to join the forces, but any conclusions that were drawn relating to the absent father's identity were secreted. She was not the first woman to have given birth to a child outside marriage and it was a foregone conclusion that she would not be the last.

When the clock struck the hour the woman stared at the time piece in wonder and amazement. It was a child opening a wrapped present at Christmas. He wondered if she could tell the time or did she live her life in tune with the season, the sun and the moon, the rain and the wind. She had not revealed to him what she was doing here in the house of the local minister. She had not asked for advice, no letter to translate, no simple problem to solve and she had not asked for him to remember anyone in his prayers nor to ask him to pray for her. The room was warmer now but she suddenly stood up and picking up the drying sacks readjusted her clothing ready for the long trek back in the now seemingly still black night. She was not afraid. She was renown in the area for having the ability to cross a mountain by night even when there was not enough light to see your own hand in front of you. The Rev Ellis offered some food or a glass of milk which were dismissed and he even offered the loan of a spare flashlight to help her find her way home. In the echoing cold hallway he heard her say.

"I walk with the fox Mr Ellis and fly with the owl." Then she was gone without a word of farewell, no wave of a hand, disappearing into the black night. There was no moon and not a single star winked in the sky. He could hear the steady song of the little river but there was no trace of the visitor as if she had not appeared at all but had been a figment of his poetic inspiration: a vision.

He shoved the door closed and stepped back into the cocoon of his study. He whistled quietly under his breath and began to question whether he had fulfilled his professional obligations, whether his visitor had gone away feeling better and filled with a renewed spirit. He concluded that he had done his best under the circumstances, had listened and had waited. He had given Jinny the opportunity to confide in him if she had so wished but his attempts had fallen on stony ground.

He concluded that he must complete the poem as he sat down again at his desk and picking up the scrap of paper casually reached for his tobacco pouch. His hand touched something solid and he found, half hidden behind a sheaf of papers and a book, a blue cardboard sugar box. Gingerly he prised it open and to his amazement, discovered four small chicken eggs individually wrapped in brown paper but delicately positioned so that they had remained perfectly formed and undamaged. They were like priceless pieces of jewellery.

Where Snowdrops Weep

He actually enjoyed getting out of bed in the morning. Unlike so many of his teenage contemporaries who held on to their adolescent dreams beneath the blankets, he loved the prospect of confronting a new day, a new dawn and he had a job of work to do. He was a paper boy and he loved it. It was always exciting. No matter what the weather held in store, come wind rain or shine he was up at an instant and ready to embrace the morrow. How he loved the silence of the early morning, the small house, as cold and grey as the ashes in the hearth, and having the place to himself. At this time of the day there was nobody to interfere with his business, no reminders for long overdue homework, and no taunts from older brothers, no demands for spare cash or unwanted sweets from younger sisters. The house was his domain.

Luckily he had a bedroom to himself; hardly more than a box room which contained the iron framed single bed with the solitary pillow, a chair on which lay his shirt and jeans, white socks and his crumbled pair of black slip on shoes. Under the little bed was a cardboard box which stored his few treasured possessions: a pen knife, a football magazine, some fading black and white snapshots of pals, a torch with no battery, a small tin of assorted marbles and a few copies of old magazines that had pictures of scantily dressed young women posing in the most unnatural and oblique positions staring with feigned allure at the camera. So when he arose, he stepped straight into his jeans, pulled on his socks, thrust an arm through his shirt sleeve and was downstairs in a jiffy. Lighting the gas stove in the scullery, he made himself a cup of tea using a little metal strainer, cut off a chunk of bread and finished dressing. The dawn had hardly begun but it was difficult to tell what the weather would unfold because of the predominant smoke and fumes from the tin plating factory and colliery that permeated the street where he lived. It was bitterly cold when he opened the unlocked back door and the frost was heavy on the ground. He gauged the pressure of the tyres on his bike by pressing them with his thumb and forefinger and, checking his watch, wheeled the bike out to the street. He was away.

There had been a heavy frost during the night and the early morning cold air took his breath away. The streets and houses were ghostly and the branches of the few trees in the neighbourhood were like birds' legs, a tangled assortment of heron and stork. He crouched over the drop handlebars of his bike and crossed the main road and took the pathway along the side of the railway line. It was a short cut that he knew well and he swore that he could complete this route with his eyes closed. He ensured this morning however that he watched where he rode as there was ice in several places and he did not want to come a cropper. Presently he arrived at the foot of a bridge which he called "echo bridge". He stopped here for a rest and to practise his singing skills. He let the bike drop to the ground and suddenly standing with his legs apart and arms reaching to the sky burst into song.

"You are my destiny. You are what you are to me."

His voice, sounding a little like Paul Anka, resonated in the eeriness of the still early morning. He threw back his head and sang as loudly and as emotionally as possible hearing in his tousled haired head the deafening applause as he once more remounted the bike and continued along his way. A man approached him mufflered against the cold and a flat cap pulled down over his face and the dap end of a cigarette stuck behind his left ear. The boy veered to the side to pass him and he heard the man shout out.

"Early morning start boy! Enough noise to wake the birds. Who the hell do you think you are? Johnnie bloody Ray?"

There was no malice in the remark and the boy blushed, grinned to himself but continued his journey to work. From under the bridge the path soon joined the main road that led to the small industrial town. There was a constant stream of traffic now and the light was beginning to brighten. Directly he completed his journey, parking his bike outside he stepped in to the local newsagents. As usual he was on time.

He enjoyed his little job as a paper boy and the manager of the shop, a Mister Morris, nodded to him as if to say well done and that he was on time as usual. He was proud of his punctuality and had learned the bitter lesson about promptness and doing the right thing. He might have been a bit of a rebel in school, a clown and a performer, but as far as his role of paper boy was concerned, he had made his mark and he wanted to keep his job. Money was always short. When he joined a football club in two villages away, on the other side of the small town, playing on a regular basis as a winger, he was chuffed despite the fact that he had to catch two buses to get to the club and there were no shower facilities. But to his dismay one Saturday he missed the connecting bus and was fifteen minutes late arriving at the ground. His frustration and bitter disappointment was compounded when a younger boy had been given the coveted role of outside left in his place and he was left to stand and look on as the team played without him. He remembered quite clearly the look of triumph on the rival boy's face as he bent tying the long laces of his football boots. He vowed he would never be late again for anything in his life.

Football was important to the paper boy. He had put himself forward to represent the town in the schoolboy championships but sadly had not been selected despite having performed quite well in the trials. Some of the lads from his school had been picked and he felt a sense of envy as well as rancour. Many of the trialists, potential stars of tomorrow, had had their father there in support and to urge them on and also to butter up to the selectors. Nobody from his own home had shown much interest in his sporting prowess but he shrugged off this indifference. He had played to the best of his ability but conspicuous in the fact that it was clear that nobody was watching him. He started out playing on the right wing and even scored a goal from a left footed volley from thirty yards out which surprised everyone including himself. They then moved him to play at left back much to his disappointment. He never heard another word from those men in raincoats who had huddled around the saw-dusted touch lines, not a word of commiseration or a thank you for having turned out. His life would go on regardless!

He loved the smell of the shop floor and the feel and warmth of the stacked newspapers. He enjoyed getting his hands dirty as he expertly sorted out the deliveries. He counted out the Mirrors, the Heralds, the Chronicles, the Sketches, the Western Mails and the odd quality paper like the Times and the Telegraph. He scoured the back pages to read the sports items to devour titbits about Ivor Allchurch and John Charles, Dick Richardson and Joe Erskine and whether Duncan Edwards was continuing to make progress after the terrible crash at Munich which had robbed the young man of so many of his comrades. All the paper boy's pals at school had been upset by this especially as the pictures of the young dead footballers were printed in all of the newspapers. Their innocent young faces were akin to the ghosts of the Somme from another generation. He sorted the papers whilst on his knees in the semi darkness of the shop floor, listening at the same time to the chat and banter emerging from the manager, Mr Morris who sold the daily papers to the early morning workers. He did not care for Mr Morris, found him creepy and sly.

Morris was a man in his early forties, pale faced and balding with always a bead of sweat on his high forehead. He was always very polite to the customers but the paper boy could see him give a v sign from under the counter whilst thanking the customer for his time and money. Morris was a classic example of a million men stuck in a job that paid a paltry salary and a job which was despised. The paper boy hoped that he himself would not find himself in a similar situation when he got a real job. He kept clear of the two faced Morris whose sharp tongue could cut like a carving knife.

As he continued marking up the papers, using the stub of a pencil, one of his school pals arrived to do his round. This was a boy with a man's body and the face of an angel who played second row rugby and certainly knew a thing or two. As usual he was a few minutes late and Morris scowled at him as he sauntered into the shop after having hurled his bike on to the outside wall. Morris said nothing but made a theatrical gesture of looking at his watch and rolling his eyes. The two boys exchanged greetings and the rugby player offered him a cigarette.

"No thanks Tango. Have given it up."

113

"Oh aye? How long?"

"Three days. Am bloody gasping."

The paper boy watched his pal as he too began marking up the papers for his round, observed how the smoke from the lit cigarette drifted lazily upwards into the upper darkness of the room and how his eyes narrowed in concentration.

"Any news on Edwards?"

"Battling. So it says here, but distressed."

They continued their sorting in silence each boy preoccupied with his own thoughts. The rugby boy was known as Tango in school. Nobody seemed to know the origin of the nick name and he was considered a real character, a hard man on the field but gentle in the school yard, his reputation speaking volumes so that nobody bothered him or had the temerity to try to provoke him. His famous line on the rugger field was.

"Never mind the bloody ball, let's get on with the game!"

The silence of their concentrated effort was broken by the sound of voices from the door way. It was Morris the manager having words with the old timer of the party: Cadwyn Phillips known as Caddy to all and sundry. Forty years earlier Caddy had been a Lance Corporal in the Great War and now in the late Autumn of his years was reduced to the rank of a paper boy.

"You gave them a Sketch instead of the Mirror Caddy."

"Sorry Mr Morris! Anyway it's same thing only different."

The last sentence was muttered almost under his breath but Morris had heard him and was not prepared to let it go. Here was an opportunity to unleash his frustration and old Caddy was the whipping boy. The two

114

schoolboys said nothing but they had heard it all before. It was little use to feel sorry for the old man, let alone feel a sense of injustice as to the way Morris spoke to him. The old man came into the gloomy room and began to fussily mark up his round. He grumbled to himself muttering remarks about being picked on and that life was not fair.

"He'd better watch out. One of these days. I boxed when I was in the army you know."

"Bloody Salvation Army!" yelled Morris, "just don't do it again alright?"

The old man turned to the boys seeking some form of solidarity but was confronted by shy grins and a shaking of heads.

"Up there you want it!" he proclaimed, pointing to his forehead, "down there you got it!" he continued pointing in the direction of his groin. The laughter broke the silence and eased the feeling of uninvited tension that had entered the shop.

The cold air was a stinging slap full in the face when he stepped out of the shop and he was soon on his way, the heavy bag slung over his shoulder. He knew the route well, had his routine, where to leave the bike, which house had easy letter boxes, which had none, which had dogs and which had milk bottles to avoid when the mornings were dark. The slumbering had now stirred. The Bridge Café was open and already had customers although he suspected that the juke box was not switched on. He glanced at his watch and was on time. He freewheeled past the Co-op, the red bricked Drill Hall and delivered to the row of railway cottages, two up and two down little terraced houses adjacent to the railway line. Smoke rose from the chimneys and lights were turned on in the bedrooms. He kept a wary eye for one of his customers who demanded his paper as he went to catch the train to work. This was a fussy little man, smartly dressed in a suit and tie with a small moustache and brief case. If he confronted him he would have to dig deep into the bag and retrieve the paper and put him out of his routine. But this morning he avoided the little man. He proceeded past the Girls Grammar school and turned into an area where the houses were bigger. Here some of his teachers lived, and the local Member of Parliament, in a row of semi detached villas with a little lawn in front and a large porch.

He was well on time now and as he pedalled past the Council offices where there was tennis courts and up the rising lane known as Snowdrop Hill to the doctor's house which stood on the edge of the golf course. This would be his final delivery of the morning. The frost was still heavy on the ground and the bunker on one of the greens looked like a sponge cake covered with a trace of castor sugar. Further down the valley where the colliery stood, the coal tips were lined with frost so much that it was like a miniature mountain range. He felt his heart racing and a shiver played tricks on his spine. She had been there every morning for the last few days appearing at the bedroom window like a ghostly vision to torment him and to arouse his sensuality.

His stomach churned as he parked his bicycle at the foot of the driveway. He carefully took out a copy of The Times and folding it neatly walked up the gravel path and soon slid the paper easily through the letter box. He heard the echoing thud as it hit the tiled floor and he turned and walked back to the gate. It clanged as he closed it and he retreated into the shadow of the horse chestnut tree. In the space of about five seconds the light switch was flicked on in the same upstairs window and the same apparition appeared. From his voyeuristic, secluded spot he could see quite clearly, although her face was always well hidden, the contours of her shapely figure which sent his senses reeling. She moved gracefully to the window, a negligee half open at her bosom revealing the deep secretive shadows of her large breasts. She inhaled deeply and suggestively hands on her large hips. Then the curtains were closed as abruptly as the light had been switched on. The private show was over and it had lasted no more than thirty blissful seconds. He knew it was pointless waiting for a reprise so he reluctantly stepped out from his lair and checking that he in turn was not being watched, sloped off on his bike.

He never mentioned his little secret to any of his school pals fearing they would either not believe him or it turn would ridicule him or call him a fantasist. He never dared to mention it to his girl friend either although their relationship, such as it was, was rather tenuous to say the least. She was a tidy girl, fair haired and sweet natured called Maggie Brown and he had been going out with her for several weeks. Their liaison was little more than a walk in the Cow Field or the park and an occasional evening at the pictures. He had plucked up enough courage to have kissed her once and although he had wanted to do so again, his shyness and lack of confidence determined that he play it safe. Maggie's mother sometimes worked in the market stalls selling vegetables every Wednesday and Saturday and she always gave him a warm smile whenever he ventured into her sight. What would Maggie have thought of him knowing he was spying at a half naked older woman? He blushed at the thought and immediately tried to dismiss it. But the image of the doctor's wife continued to invade his thoughts and concentration at school was even worse than normal.

117

If only he could see her face, if only she would strip off completely? Someone had said that the doctor played rugby for an important club and was regarded as a possible candidate for the national team. The red light was flashing! So the lady of mystery had appeared every morning at exactly the same time for the last ten days or so: except of course on Sundays.

At school, the day was as long as it always was with overcrowded classrooms, dusty and dry teachers, unsmiling, tie knotted, not long back from the war and quietly going mad with boredom and who lived up to their nick names: "Pike", "Slasher" and "Tojo". It was confrontational all the way, sarcasm, dry wit, brooding tension and physical violence. Then there was an elderly teacher who was probably dreaming of a pension and gardening, a Mr Davies who was known as Will Hay as he bore a striking resemblance to the comic film actor from another time. He was no comic either and although bumbling and somewhat eccentric in manner could suddenly become very aggressive. The paper boy remembered how Will Hay had asked a boy, who had let off a stink bomb in class, to step out to the front of the classroom and ordered to remove his spectacles. The boy had meekly obeyed and then was clouted around the head with a series of open handed slaps. So, one had to be careful with him but there was a way of diverting him. That particular morning he was trying to interest the lads about the Magna Carta until a timid little lad in the front desk asked a pertinent question.

"Sir? Do you think Wales will beat England in the rugger international?"

"But of course boy. Beat them? Very simple. I will explain to you boys how they are going to do it. Sit up and pay attention!"

118

The bait had been taken and for twenty minutes the class was entertained by the lecture from the so called history master. The English king was relegated and in his place was a modern day Owain Glyndwr in a rugby shirt fighting a different battle against the mighty oppressor.

School, despite the respite from Will Hay had been boring and predictable. The boy continued to refrain from smoking and was even able to maintain his deference despite the break visit to the "dubs." He told nobody about the doctor's wife although her image continued to infiltrate his thoughts especially when a grubby copy of a dirty book was passed around in one of the lessons. All he was asking himself was, how long was this masquerade going to continue and was she going take it further? What if he knocked on the door and said he was unwell? Would she take him in and nurse him, hold him in her arms until he felt better? The possibility of sexual seduction sent his mind into a spin. Each morning she had appeared in a different undergarment of a variety of colour but never showing her face and feeding him with only tantalising glimpses of her ample body. She was playing with his teenage affections but he was riddled with self doubt and guilt and did not know which way to go.

He paid for the two tickets, the silver coins wet from his hand and he and Maggie Brown entered the upstairs of the local cinema. He was nervous, tense, wanted to blow his nose but had forgotten to ask his mother for a clean handkerchief. The young girl looked pretty; her fair hair parted at the side, her figure slim and trim half hidden by a fawn coloured overcoat. Despite her attractiveness he was embarrassed and looked around hoping he would not see anyone he knew. He had combed his hair and wore a jacket and tie. He did not possess a smart overcoat and had almost frozen at the bus stop. The film was in vivid Technicolor, over made up faces, a terrible plot and every middle aged woman on the screen was the doctor's wife. Not only did he feel uncomfortable, but the anxiety was immediately attached to the little girl who sat solemnly by his side staring wide eyed at the silver screen.

When the interval came and the lights went up she excused herself and went to the toilet. He did not have enough money to suggest an ice cream and he slumped further into his seat wrapped in the blanket of self pity and embarrassment. When the film came to a close, they hurriedly departed just before the national anthem started up and there was a prolonged silence as he walked her home that night. He had failed to hold her hand let alone pluck up the courage to kiss her. He knew he would not be seeing her again and his heart was aching though there was also a feeling of relief. She was very sweet about it all and they both agreed that the "romance" was over but they would, in true teenage fashion, remain as friends.

Life continued without the pretty presence of Maggie Brown but the haunting and disturbing image of the doctor's wife continued. It was the same pattern every morning with no further development as to how much naked flesh was open to viewing. The Paper Boy had started smoking again, the money which he had set aside for Maggie now appropriated to tobacco. He selected Players Weights instead of Woodbine but there was little difference in the flavour as was there in their price. The weather was typical of February: windy and wet one day, hard frost the next and occasionally the signs of Spring when the yellow beak of the blackbird complemented the wild daffodils that grew around the fringes of the golf course. Then it all changed.

Tango was early for once which has astounded Mr Morris and surprised the Paper Boy. Tango sat with a cigarette, the open paper in front of him. He looked pale and there was a seriousness about him.

"What's up Tango? You look like you've seen a ghost."

"He's gone. Died last night."

"Who's died?"

"Duncan Edwards. My hero! He fought for nearly a fortnight. The doctors couldn't believe how strong he was. Aye! he's dead."

Tango passed him a cigarette and the paper boy took it without a word lighting it from Tango's own. They sat silently, immersed in their own melancholy. The smoke from the cigarettes drifted towards heaven, making shapes like blue angels The paper boy has seen Edwards play once, had remarked how muscular and strong he was and how even from a half back position could score goals with either foot. He had also noticed how Edwards had rolled up his shorts in a style copied by a thousand schoolboys and now the warrior was dead. He had played for England as a teenager and now at the age of twenty one was gone. Morris, for once, realised that the boys had been shaken by the news, were clearly upset, and although he looked at his watch decided not to re-mind them of their responsibilities. Caddy too, was quieter than usual and kept his distance although he continued to talk to himself like a running commentary at a race meeting.

"I will see you in school butt," said Tango with quiet resignation.

"Yes, thanks Tango!"

121

The paper Boy worked in silence and in sorrow, grateful for the cigarette and the quiet strength of his rugby playing pal. Then to his further surprise old Caddy came and placed a hand on his shoulder.

"I knows how you must be feeling lovely boy. But you have to, well, accept it like. His time is up. When I was at Mametz Wood, I saw boys who was younger than him, snuffed out, hardly older than you, just boys they was, hadn't lived, had done nothing. But you have to get up and get on with it! I had to."

The old Veteran's voice trembled a little and then faded away. The Paper Boy saw the old man's eyes, grey and overflowing with humanity. Perhaps he wasn't such an old fool after all.

"Thanks Caddy. You're a star!"

The rain, heavy drizzle, was sweeping up the valley when he finally got on his bike and began his round but he could not rush; his heart heavy, his legs weary and his mind in a quandary. As he finally reached the summit of the hill and approached the doctor's house it seemed that the road was awash and that in the hedgerows were the first signs of Spring, where little birds began to sing and where snowdrops wept. He sensed that she would not appear that sad and rain drenched morning and he was right. He waited under the horse chestnut tree where the buds were blooming but she did not come to the window. He knew he was a little later than usual but felt this was no legitimate excuse and that in some perverse way she too had let him down. He reached for another cigarette but changed his mind and crushed the packet in his fist, releasing his pain, his anger and his frustration. He struggled with his emotions; fought back the tears and then suddenly he cleared his throat and yelled an obscenity into the morning rain. The filthy word seemed to boom across the sodden golf course and bounce down the valley below.

She never appeared again, in stark reality or in a soft dream. Soon afterwards his round was changed for a little more money and his paper boy prowess was used in a different locality. Tango was given the sack for poor timekeeping and dissent. Caddy continued to grumble and fuss and Morris managed to keep his two faces clean wiping away the sweat with a white handkerchief. Will Hay had got his prediction wrong with the rugby the result had been a boring draw game much to his disappointment. He saw Maggie's mother in the market and received a knowing smile of sympathy when he greeted her although he would never saw Maggie again.

Spring came as promised; the clocks moved forward and the days grew longer. One afternoon on the way home from another tedious day at school he made a detour and took the road towards the doctor's house. The horse chestnut was in full bloom but the roadside were devoid of flowers. In the garden of the doctor's house he spotted a woman probing about by the rose bushes. She sported a green headscarf, a pair of Wellingtons on her feet and upon her shoulders she wore a shapeless gabardine overcoat. As he pushed his bike past the gate she looked up but did not give him a passing glance of recognition. He thought she looked as old as his mother and she ignored him completely when he shouted a hello. He watched her walk wearily to the front door, her body stooped in quiet resignation, open it and without turning step inside closing it behind her.

He asked Mr Bassett for a semi crew. He grinned sheepishly as his hair was sheared and in ten minutes stood outside the shop door looking like a surprised hedgehog. In a few weeks his hair would grow and he would train it so that he would look a bit like Don Everly. When he stepped into the Bridge Café a young red headed girl looked up and made a comment about his hair.

"What's up then Ginger?" he retorted with a grin.

"It's not ginger it's auburn!"

She smiled and indicated for him to sit next to her and her female companion. A familiar song was playing on the Juke Box, the room was full of colour that promised summer, he had a few bob in his pocket and a pretty girl had smiled at him.

"Do you like Paul Anka?" she asked.

"My favourite singer." he remarked looking unblinkingly straight into her pale blue eyes. He knew it was the truth.

One More Saturday Night

The battered and bruised saucepan was stuck in a pre-
carious position on the open fire. The fire was made up
of dead wood and a few lumps of coal so that every so
often a green and blue flame would rise up and lick the
side of the utensil like some prehistoric creature. The
saucepan contained three large potatoes that were now
well and truly boiled so that when the little stout man
pricked them with a fork they disintegrated. He poured
the contents through an old strainer and threw the water
outside the open back door of his farm house and
placed the remains of the potatoes on to a blue plate
that contained several thick slices of cold ham. He then
added a little milk from an enamel jug he kept in the
scullery and sat down in an old wooden chair without a
cushion, by the fire to eat his meal balancing the plate
on his lap.

The light was fading but he was in no hurry to light
the oil lamp as he contentedly shovelled the food into
his mouth. Some of the chickens had entered the room
but he did not mind their company as they clucked and
cooed and pecked at the thick dust on the stone floor.
They were gentle creatures and were his friends. He
would talk to them from time to time in a low soothing
voice that an adult would use to an infant. The living
room was large with a window and a door which led to
the parlour , which was never used, and the stairs that
led upstairs to the bedrooms. One wall was occupied by
an old Welsh Dresser that was adorned with a selection
of antique plates and an array of jugs. There was also a
fading sepia photograph of a young woman with pale
sad eyes that seemed to be looking at a scene from a far
away land. The little man glanced at the picture as he

chewed on his cold ham and tried to remember his mother. A piece of wood in the fire suddenly crackled and fell into the grate sending up a series of sparks as it died. The ash was a clear thick grey like the colour of a wood pigeon.

Having finished his meal, he slowly got up and hobbled into the scullery scraping the remnants of the food into a tin bucket he kept inside the door. The bucket was half filled with potato peelings, pieces of crusty bread, egg shells, bacon rind and tea leaves. The chickens followed him like children as he stepped outside and ventured to the pig sty. The pig heard him coming, recognised him immediately and knew there was food. The animal grunted and rolled over in his excitement as the contents of the bucket were dispersed amongst the debris and stinking mess. The little man spoke to the pig in the same voice as he had used to the chickens. He ensured the pig was safely locked in for the night and then proceeded to do the same for the Rhode Island Reds. There were foxes in the vicinity although they were seldom seen.

When he returned to the house he made sure the fire was out and putting on a cap filled the pockets of his jacket with a packet of Players and a box of matches, a few pound notes and a varied selection of silver coins. They would buy him a few drinks. After all it was a Saturday night. His sheepdog, already confined to the cowshed, barked furiously wanting to be freed and wanting to chase after sheep and rabbits when he heard the noise. He soon calmed down at the command of his master. He locked the door and decided to secrete the key inside the barn door. He thought to himself that perhaps later, well in his cups, he might not remember where he had left the key. He chuckled to himself as he brought out his old bicycle that would take him down the narrow untarred road through a series of four fields to the main road. He tied his blackthorn stick to the cross bar with a piece of thick cord and with some difficulty mounted his old bicycle. The late afternoon was quietly reaching for the overcoat of evening when he rode off.

The grass was long on either side of the roadway and as usual very wet. The evening was fresh and the smell of pine wood and lilac filled the air. After a short summit of about fifty yards it was downhill all the way, unless the gates were closed, along the edges of the fields. It was a non stop ride even if a little bumpy. He had come off a few times when the front wheel had hit a large stone or he had skidded where the rain had created slippery mud. His left hip was giving him some gyp and he wondered whether he had made the right decision when he had opted not to have a replacement hip back in the spring. Various trusted friends of his, and in particular the young woman called Deidre, had arranged a date where he would have the operation, a routine job he had been assured, but at the last minute he had changed his mind. Now, to his added discomfort, the pain had increased and he knew in his heart that sooner or later he would have to sell up and acquire another place in the small town where there were shops, other people and where he would never be alone. He laughed out loud as the slope increased and the speed took him down the hill, the wind in his ears and the sudden sting of early evening rain slashing his face. The bike wheels hissed like geese. He parked his machine under an oak tree, untied his stick and lit a cigarette. Then he stood at the roadside waiting for a familiar face that would take him the three miles or so to the small town.

Presently a little A35 van stopped and the swathes of rain could be seen very clearly in the headlights as the engine ticked over nicely. A voice from the gloom called out, a reassuring voice that was familiar to the little man. In a matter of moments he was huddled in the passenger seat, cap slewed over one eye, cigarette hanging on the precipice of his bottom lip and his stout stick at an angle. The driver was a local farm worker, lived with his wife and children in a cottage a few miles down the road and was a quiet, friendly, young man. They drove on in silence and the little man was glad of a lift into town. The pain in his left hip eased a little and he began to look forward to a drink of beer.

"I'll drop you off on the square. Off to see Dennis, might see you later!"

"Righto boy. See you directly. Thank you very much for the lift!"

When he entered the main door of the Hotel, his boots echoing on the cold stone floor, he was greeted by Deidre who worked there during the evenings as general bar maid. She was a down to earth, no nonsense young woman of about thirty, with a genuine ready smile. Tonight she was wearing a pair of jeans that were slightly too small and which emphasised the ampleness of her hips and waistline. She recognised him immediately and her smile filled the reception area.

"Hullo Mally. How are things?"

"Very sound Deidre. Oh yes very sound. I have a few more letters for you to see if you don't mind like?"

Deidre emerged from behind the little counter and taking him by the arm led him into a small room where there were empty armchairs, a selection of small tables

128

and a silent television set. She took a few letters from the little man and after having opened them studied them briefly. They were unimportant letters trying to sell things which the little man neither needed nor wanted. Mally noticed that the young woman's right hand was red stained and he asked with some concern in his voice.

"Cut yourself?"

"Oh no! Was collecting blackberries this afternoon and have not washed my hands properly. Naughty girl aren't I?"

She smiled openly at him and her affection for him was clear and genuine like the sparkling water that flowed from the hills in the neighbourhood. Mally remembered the blackberries and for a second a feeling of sorrow engulfed him. All those years ago he had been on the hill picking the wild fruit with his mother when they had stood and watched a funeral procession below them in the valley. How vividly he remembered the line of figures in black, the horses, a few cars and the solemn singing carried on the wind. A week later they buried his mother. Now a stone had been erected at her grave and Mally had relied on his young friend to sort out the business which Deidre had undertaken with sincerity and business like professionalism. It was as if she had read his mind when she spoke again.

"I have seen the gravestone. A very tidy job done I'd say. If you pop down one day next week with your cheque book we will go and see the Mason and settle the account. I'll take you in my car. Now go and enjoy a drink. The back bar is pretty busy tonight."

Mally was in no hurry, the beer would not get cold, and he enjoyed the comforting presence of the young woman. He replaced the letters inside his coat pocket and stood in silence inviting conversation.

"She was very young. Your mother? Thirty four. It's no age. And how old were you when she passed away?"

"Eight."

There was a loud chorus of greeting when the little man entered the warmth of the back bar and immediately, someone offered him a stool at the counter which he accepted raising his stick in a mock salute, the cigarette dancing on his bottom lip. The room was fairly crowded and the familiar smell of wood smoke filled the air. Several farm boys sat on the settle in front of the long table playing a lively game of cards. Many wore their flat tweed caps despite being indoors and one or two sported a tie with a horseshoe design. There were shouts of joy when a trump appeared coupled with groans of dismay as a trick was either won or lost. In the far corner by the window, where the blinds were drawn, a few men played a keen game of darts, silence when a throw was made and banter when the target was hit or occasionally a wayward dart would pierce the outer ring of the board.

"Shout your score please!"

"Puncture!"

A few old men stood with their backs to the open fire and now and again a fresh log was placed precariously on the blazing flames.

"How bistee sirry? What you having Mall?"

"Half an Alberts, thank you boy."

The proprietor grunted to himself as he poured the drink and took a few coins from the pile that stood on the counter in front of the swarthy man who had bought Mally a drink.

"Cheers Tommy. Good health!"

He sipped the beer, an Abbots ale which Mally had sweetly mispronounced. He liked the taste of beer. Tommy sat crookedly on the bar stool hooded eyes staring at all and sundry. Sometimes they challenged, sometimes they beckoned. He was a generous man, would do you a good turn at the drop of a hat but did not suffer fools or any man who dared to wear the imposter's cloak. His hair long and straight was as black as a crow. He sipped his pint of dark mild and lit another cigarette. Cigarette smoke mingled and mixed cordially with the wood smoke from the fire and the fragments of broken conversation could be heard, the mulled and half muffled voices within the tavern rising and falling as the evening progressed. It was a timeless scene. Someone coughed and cleared his throat noisily.

"Weather's turning. No more runner beans. It will be November Fair before you know it."

"They tell me it's snowing in Jordan! Heard it on the six o clock news."

"Hot place that. I was out that way during the Great War."

"Long train journey wasn't it?"

"No, went on a big ship, hundreds of us boys. Never been out of the country before. Adventure!"

"Some bloody adventure alright. Most of us never got back. I am one of the lucky ones."

"Aye Mesopotamia! That's where it was. That's in the Old Testament that is."

"Where's that then?"

"No idea. I don't want to go back there I can tell you for a fact."

"It's near Utopia."

"No that's in Scotland."

131

"I see there's a big fight on next Tuesday. Howard Winstone."

"Big fight on tonight."

"Who's that then?"

"Me and the missis."

Mally returned the compliment and bought his pal a pint and replenished his own glass. He felt a whole lot better as the alcohol began to have its effect. The pain in his hip was still causing him some discomfort so after a few more swift halves he ordered a small bottle of cherry brandy and poured the contents into a wine glass. What could be better on a Saturday night? A glass of good ale, a small glass of brandy and a packet of cigarettes along with convivial company. Several old comrades greeted him and one or two men who sat alone said nothing but watched everything that was going on in the tap room, their eyes darting here and there, not missing a trick.

It was another Saturday night in the little country town of no purport, a small town that was a sanctuary for some strangers who had come to the area and had forgotten to catch the lonesome and elusive train back to where they had started from. Not many people asked too many questions, the local bobby was glad to have peace and quiet and the days passed into months and then to years. Changes were slow and the passing of the seasons was an endless chain of events as the colours faded, the rain washed away the winter, and spring would come again. The bar was a personification of the area. Mr Lessanne was an exiled Frenchman, he also was a survivor of the Great War, who liked his little nip on a Saturday night but when the nips became bites he would shed a tear and produce from a brown wallet a fading photograph of a plain woman who he acknowledged as his late and lamented wife. One or two men in the town called him the Patron which delighted Mr Lessane and made the old man smile. Someone referred to him as Maigret which also warmed his heart. Nobody asked what he was doing so far away from home and hardly anyone in the small town could offer a sprinkling of the alien language. Sometimes he would engage in conversation with a man called Ezzard who fixed wrist watches and spoke slowly with a slight stutter and a Northern accent. He too was a victim of conflict having spent some time in Burma during the Second World War. He never talked about his experiences there and nobody dared to ask him. Both men, despite their age gap shared a common bond.

The little town embraced not only those who made a contribution to the life of the little community but also to the lost and the lonely who had nowhere else to go and whose guiding candle had long since been extinguished. There were others, silent as stone statues, who sat alone and made no attempt at conversation. One man, an infrequent visitor, would sit all night at a table chuckling to himself over a pint of beer never taking any notice of others around him who named him The Laughing Cavalier. There was a Polish refugee who had a small holding somewhere in the vicinity, who had a long thin face, lined and lean, an aquiline nose but who had the eyes of a poet. He was the only person in the bar who might sip large vodkas for the duration as if he were drinking tea. Nobody had the cheek to ask what visions he could see or from what he was running away.

Presently Mally rose to his feet and made his excuses. He needed to relieve himself and instead of simply stepping outside the back door to the smelly urinal,

proceeded into the front bar to be greeted enthusiasti-
cally and cordially by another gathering of a local
group of people. There was the town's Bank Manager
in a suit and tie along with others who felt perhaps they
were of a better class of people than those who frequented the iniquitous back bar. These were men with a
touch of pop and took their station in life with some solemnity. They were willing to pay the extra few coppers
for their drink in the front bar. It was noticeable that
their wives were always absent. Mally grinned and
nodded at them and picked his way down the stairs to
the toilets in the basement below.

"He's looking alright. Should have had his hip done
when he had the chance. Deidre had sorted it for him.
Or so they say."

"Mally is his own man. Independent. A free spirit."

"Talking of free spirits. It's your shout. Mine's a
whiskey with a dash of lemonade."

There was a spontaneous spattering of laughter
though it appeared that some of the joviality and small
talk was at times a little forced. Their heads were
turned as a young woman dressed in a black skirt, long
black boots and a dark polo necked sweater popped her
head through the doorway. She should have been wearing glasses as she screwed her eyes and made a face as
she looked around the room. She was very self conscious and she flushed deeply when she heard a voice
from the corner.

"He's up the in the Bell love and he's got his ca-
tarrh with him."

There was another outburst of laughter as the young
woman turned on her high heel and stamped out of the
door.

"There'll be some fireworks later, one way or another and I am not talking about Match of the Day."

There was a murmur of assent and then the men stood in silence, tumblers in hand, each preoccupied with their own thoughts, each taking a tentative step into the darkness of their own private room. Deidre surveyed it all from the relative safety of the bar but she knew she was in safe hands here despite the men's eyes who watched her every move.

"He wouldn't have the operation to his hip then? Why is that Deidre?"

"You'll have to ask Mally that. I'm pretty sure he'll tell you why."

At that moment Mally returned from visiting the toilet. He was out of breath from climbing the stairs and his face was like a blemished plum.

"We were just talking about you Mr Rhys," suggested the Bank Manager.

"It's when you are not talking about me is the time to fret," Mally retorted in a flash. The manager smiled at Mally's quick witted reply, ordered a round of drinks and with due respect to his customer included a cherry brandy for Mally. As they sipped their drinks, in through the door shuffled a young man with a face like the half moon, craters included. He brushed a hand across his forehead, grinned openly shrugging his shoulders muttering and complaining about the weather. He had a nervous habit of adjusting and readjusting his collar and stained tie and he had the exact money in his hand for his usual drink of half of bitter and a double rum and blackcurrant.

"Alright tonight then Wyndham? Usual is it?"

"Half of Albright and a double rum and black. I think you'll find the right money there."

He handed Deidre the collection of coins which she automatically placed in the till without checking.

"Did you get the result of your blood test Wyndham?"

"All clear!"

"It wasn't Captain Morgan positive then?"

Sooner rather than later, the subject of Mally's refusal to have his hip operation would come up. The group of people waited with some anticipation for Mally to begin his account. He was a figure of fun to them, a comical character, and an invisible border line between affection and contempt was easily crossed especially when the line was often indistinguishable. Deidre, who had a genuine affection for the little man, kept a wary eye on the proceedings and interjected now and again when she thought the conversation was taken too far. Mally was by now in full swing and enjoying himself to the delight of the onlookers. This was free entertainment and a far better alternative to anything the television sets might offer.

"The night before I was to have the operation I was sitting there in my pyjamas along with a few other clients sipping a cup of tea that the pretty little nurse had given me. Pretty girl she was, not as pretty as Deidre mind, when the doctor came round to see us. He was the top man. Very important chap. He was the what you call it? The magician!"

"The physician?"

"That's the man. Big sorted chap in a nice suit with a spotted dicky bow tie and a whiskery face. He took a good long look at us sitting there. Like children we was on a Sunday School bench. He stared me full in the face, his whiskers shifting back and forth, eyes like pellets and he pointed a finger at me and said. 'I'll be cut-

136

ting you up tomorrow,' and I said back to him 'Shut thy eye boy! Like hell you will!' and I got up like a shot and went off to bed."

There was a burst of laughter and a farmer's voice called out

"Good for you Mally! Well done you! Good ol' kid then!"

"I put the bugger in his place. Those bloody whiskers that done it for me! He looked like a fish! All the best boys!"

He lifted his glass in a toast, emptied the contents with one swallow, made his exit from the stage and swayed away into the relative comfort of the back bar where he knew several more drinks awaited him.

The place was almost full, the card and darts games still in progress and the fire crackled and hissed. The pleasant drone of conversation filled the room. Mally loosened his collar and he felt a bead of sweat run down his back. The pain in his hip had eased considerably by now, the alcohol was doing its duty, and although his cheeks were hot he felt quite light headed. It was one more Saturday night, the best day of the week, and he was as happy as Larry and amongst friends. He wondered whether the singing would start soon and he spotted a local exponent of the art trying to round up a choir. He was a sheriff in a western picture doing his best to cajole and organise a posse from the reluctant and obdurate townspeople. He would sidle up to a man and elbow him in the ribs talking two to the dozen. Some old wag remarked that he had an alarm clock on every tooth and could not sing in tune anyway. Another proclaimed that he was stone deaf. One of the drinkers stated that the clocks were moving back soon but it would make very little difference here in the bar where little notice was taken of country licensing hours. Stop Tap was when you stopped drinking or when the beer or, more often than not, the money ran out.

The back door was pushed open making a scraping noise in the process and in walked a very tall, very pale, scrawny young man, thin as a bean pole, dressed in a poor imitation of a Mississippi gambler. He sported a long dark jacket and an unmatching waistcoat, a white shirt, a string tie and a broad black hat. In his dream this was a roving cowboy entering the town saloon, not looking for trouble but ready for it if the opportunity presented himself. In reality; a friendly innocent forestry worker that had never got into a fight, had no girl friend, a hard and honest worker who listened to cowboy songs and loved the music of Hank Williams.

"The Man from Laramie has just ridden in."

"Howdy partner. Still riding on the range? On the cooker?"

The lad walked forward to the questioner narrowing his eyes in mock menace and replied.

"Howdy hombre! I am mighty fine, yes sirree. Just call me Luke the Drifter, that's my handle 'Unless you've made no mistakes in your life, be careful of stones that you throw,' am mighty fine boy mighty fine."

"What's the weather like up there Tex?"

"Saddled your horse boy?"

"Ok you cayhoots. Have your fun. 'I've been down that road before, be careful of stones that you throw,' Adios hombre. Hasta la vista commanchero! Or, if you prefer? Up yours!"

There was a small explosion of friendly laughter and the customers returned to their business of cards, conversation and beer. The tall stooping young man grinned his way through the throng and disappeared into the front bar where he would continue acting out his Western scenario to anyone who cared to listen.

"I've seen him on a horse. He be a good rider. He becomes part of the horse."

"Well don't tell me which part! Let me guess."

Mally looked on in wonder and amusement as Tex ambled past him ready to catch the next stage coach.

"I thought he was a visiting preacher in that long black coat. Bible puncher. Yes indeed! Amen! We had one here years ago. Tried to baptise me in the river. He couldn't get my head under the water for long enough. I think he gave up in the end."

Was this a cue to start the singing? A tall fair headed man with an open honest face, pale eyes and broad shoulders pitched the tune and was soon joined by one or two. The fair headed man tried to placate the others, encouraging them not to force the music but be gentle with the refrain. A bearded, roughly dressed young man, joined them and stood rigid as his deep bass voice resonated around the room. The harmony was immediate and spontaneous and in a matter of minutes a small choir was assembled. The tunes were old and familiar, like favourite items of clothing that even though were worn and tattered were comfortable and snug and never thrown away. Mally listened in wonder and some of the melodies reminded him of child hood days, woods and meadows and the fleeting image of his long lost mother drifted into his consciousness. Another joined the party, a weasel faced middle aged man, well in his cups, black hair heavily greased, face newly shaven, insisted on singing a solo and room was made for him. The fair headed man called for order and the rendition began. It was his party piece.

"Where is my wandering boy tonight?"

The sentiment was heavy and familiar, and there was rapturous applause at the end where the long faced man's colour turned to purple and his teeth shone like a dog. The singing continued, sometimes sweet and melodious, sometimes ragged and out of time but always with gusto and enthusiasm especially when fuelled by strong drink. There was a farmer, a postman, a bus driver, a forestry worker, a lorry driver, a green grocer, the milkman and a butcher. Some eyes were closed in rapture and concentration and others seemed to ascend a mountain for a view of the promised land. Then came the favourite to end all favourites:

"For ever and ever, my heart will be true."

Mally loved this old song with its simple lyric and sentiment. At the bar along side Tommy, he laughed out aloud. Many people had left by now and it was only the serious drinkers and ones who had nobody waiting for them at home were left. Mally thought about going home but his brain was befuddled and he laughed again.

"What's up Mal?"

"I tried singing that song to a girl once. Years ago it was. I could not remember the words and she laughed."

"Lovely song. You old dog you. I sing like a drain so my old teacher once told me. So what happened to her?"

"She came up now and again on a visit but she wouldn't stay. She was a nice woman. Tiny little thing she was. She worked in service up at the big house. A tidy girl who went to church instead of chapel. She'd pay a visit. But she wouldn't stay. I wonder what became of her."

"Waste of time. I should know. Still paying out every month, never get enough. Waste of time women! Have another. One for the road."

It was late by now. There was always one for the road even though it was not always clear where the road led. The fire had almost burned itself out. The singing had come to an end and the remaining half a dozen people clung to their drinks and thought about tomorrow. Deidre came in from the front bar wearing an overcoat. She approached Mally who by now was almost asleep on the stool, his cap at a rakish angle and his eyes half closed.

"You can stay here tonight. I have arranged it with Gordon. I am off now. I will look in tomorrow morning and I'll run you back. The first bedroom on the first floor. He's put a bucket there. Ok Mally?"

She reached out and touched the little man's face, looked imploringly at Tommy and the young fair haired man, then turned and went out the door.

"We will have one more then boys. I am in the chair."

The final drinks were assembled and the silence was heavy now in the back bar. The embers glowed, the room was cooling fast and there were three left. Mally, Tommy, and the fair haired young man who loved to sing. They had taken this journey many times before. It was one more Saturday night and all was well with the world. Mally began to sway on his stool and the two men either side of him formed the front row of a scrum. He was escorted up a short flight of stairs to the allocated bedroom. Tommy carried his stick.

The tin bucket was behind the door. They stretched Mally out on the single bed and between them removed the little man's boots. One of his socks had a hole and a pink toe protruded like a new potato. They covered his body with a blanket and ensured that there were no matches in his pockets. The little man was breathing steadily and he looked happy and contented. They left a light on, placed the bucket near the bed and closed the door behind them as they stole away.

Outside, the town square was deserted. The two men stood hunched in the doorway. One or two cars were parked haphazardly at the side of the road. A few windows in the street were lit. The wind had risen and the rain swept in great gusts across the scene whipping into their faces. Water poured like a small brook down the street and gurgled into the drain The two men exchanged a goodnight, shook hands briefly and went their separate ways each vanishing in opposite directions into the gloom. It was just one more Saturday night.

Goodness And Mercy

Mister Miller was most particular about everything he did. Whether it was making an early morning pot of tea, choosing an appropriate tie to match a shirt, ironing and pressing his clothes or, in this case, watering the plants and flowers of his garden, he was fastidious to the point of fussiness. It was a quiet, still, May morning and the sun was in a state of semi slumber, so it was the right time to do the watering. Miller lived alone as he had done since leaving the stifling existence of a smug, self righteous provincial town for the sprawl of North London. Making the break had been a clean and painless exercise, had not felt the searing cut of the scalpel and he had been more than willing to turn his back on the past. The past however did not always turn its back on him.

He stopped for a second to listen to the visiting birds that were welcome in his garden. He had erected a bird stand in one corner of the lawn, had hung from a nail in the birch tree a selection of seed and nut so that he attracted a mixed variety of his feathered friends. He recognised the species that dined there and those he was unsure of would be looked up with great patience in his little bird spotting book. Here he might record in neat black ink, the date of the discovery and any little bits of information that would be of interest to only him. There was no one else. Today there were finches, a solitary robin, several sparrows, a female blackbird, a wood pigeon, a collection of blue and yellow tits, a starling, two magpies and lo and behold a gold crest.

He loved his flowers and his greenery: delphiniums, geraniums, yellow roses, clematis, border petunias as well as a substantially sized lawn with trimmed borders. As he sprayed the water from his can he felt again the gnawing ache in his limbs and he stiffened as a sudden twinge of pain caught him in the small of his back. He snorted to himself as a thought entered his head. There was little chance of his attending the local doctor's surgery knowing that he would be told it was his age and he could be prescribed a selection of tablets. Besides there were fussy women at the reception desk who saw themselves as prissy, patronising, philanthropists and spoke with loud voices as if they were leading a team of hockey players! This kind of behaviour he would not tolerate.

He returned inside after having secured the back door, drawing the locks and turning the key to his satisfaction and made himself a cup of coffee. He then carried his cup to the table and placed it carefully on the table mat and began to browse through the assortment of local papers. It was a Friday morning and this was his weekly ritual. After glancing with half an eye on the local news and gossip, the adverts, the pictures and the innumerable and numbing sports results, he found the obituary pages.

Picking up a blue felt pen from the collection in his desk drawer he began to scrutinise the pages until he was able to ring one or two suitable names. He liked funerals. He chose carefully not wanting to give himself away, not wanting an invasion of his well kept and preserved privacy. He preferred funerals of men of a similar age, non military men as he had no affinity with the forces, had thanked the lord that he was young enough to have escaped conscription and avoided the retired colonels and puffing officers. There were rules that he played the game to. He knew the bus routes to all the churches and graveyards in the local neighbourhoods. He did not want to stay too close to home. On a local map which had been enlarged and photocopied for him by a helpful Librarian, he had drawn in another of his felt pens a boundary using a radius of about eight miles.

He never was quite sure what the attraction of other men's funerals was to him but he accepted it, brushed aside any questions and continued without too much self analysis. He enjoyed the peace and tranquillity of a church, the sense of shared compassion, the mutual feeling of loss and he loved the literature of the holy books and sometimes the words of a clergyman. Music too was like warm water and the traditional hymns were never too much to take: Abide With Me, The Day Thou Gavest and The Lord's My Shepherd all stood the test of time. Once he had inadvertently attended a funeral where at the end of the service a recording of a crass and tasteless pop song had been played with its sentimental lyric and nursery rhyme tune and people had turned to each other to shake hands or even kiss. This he had found embarrassing and nauseating.

He would always arrive early, avoid any conversation, wrap himself in a coat of assumed grief and would always sit at an end pew staring straight ahead. Sometimes he would assume a different identity to protect himself and occasionally he would wear a false moustache expertly glued on in the bathroom mirror. He liked to use, only if necessary, a false name and some of the handles he prescribed were Crafer, Morton and Benson. He always closed his eyes and bowed his head when the priest prayed and took solace from this, tried to look into his own troubled heart although when the prayers were uttered in rote, like children learning their tables, his fingers were unconsciously crossed. When

145

the priest said in the eulogy for the dear departed that all would be welcome for refreshments afterwards in the local Golf Club or Welfare Hall, Miller's heart would leap and he immediately looked forward to the free food and drink.

The catering was a lottery. In one place he had made an early exit having managed only a milky cold cup of tea along with dry tuna sandwiches in white sliced bread. On other occasions hot soup had been served with a delicious range of cold food ranging from smoke salmon to spicy chicken. He relished the food and often joined in the conversation as if he had known well the deceased and whenever he found himself in a tight spot and that the lid of his pretence was about to be lifted, he would assume solemnity and choke back the crocodile tears excusing himself as he sought refuge in the gentlemen's toilet. He always got away with it.

To cover his tracks he always ensured that he avoided direct contact with the priest in case his face became familiar and that his true identity revealed. Father McLaughlin had officiated in three funerals that Miller had attended in the last few months and as a young man with a future, this priest did not miss a trick. Here was another reason why Miller kept an account of all the funerals he had graced. In a little note book that he hoarded in his desk drawer. he recorded, very neatly in black ink, the name of the deceased, the time of the service, the Church and town and most of all the catering facility where a mark out of ten was awarded. This was marked in a HB pencil at the side of the entry.

Some people might suggest that this way of life was somewhat eccentric bordering on bizarre but in Miller's own mind it was a means of passing the time in his retirement, a chance to wear a suit and tie, a scenario in which he enjoyed assuming the role of another, to be seen as a pillar of society, to be respected by fellow mourners and to have, as a bonus, most of all a free meal. On the odd and ear marked occasion when he addressed these questions to the image that stared back at him in the bathroom mirror, his answer was that he was hurting nobody and in fact might even be giving support to those who grieved and at the end of the day it was nobody's business but his. Who was going to ask questions? He lived alone, had few friends and his family consisted of a long lost cousin living a hundred miles away.

A few Fridays later. whilst following his usual behaviour pattern of watering his plants and flowers, he spotted a strange and unfamiliar bird in the silver birch tree. He paused and slowly placed the watering can down feeling again the numbing pain in the small of the back. Tentatively he turned to step back into the kitchen to retrieve his bird book but as suddenly as he had appeared the strange bird took flight and soared heavenward.

There had been a vivid flash of green and yellow and Miller wondered if it was a rare bird from the African continent that had lost its way in transit. When he later scrutinised the book he failed to establish the beautiful creature's identity and was succumbed once more to exercising his fervent imagination.

That same morning, whilst examining the Obituary column of one of the local rags he came across a surname that he had not seen in years but a name that certainly lit a match inside his heart and a strange feeling overtook him. Why was his heart missing a beat and why was there a bead of perspiration on his brow? All those years ago, another life time it seemed, there had been a boy at school called Mihailovic. Marcus Mihailovic, known by most of his contemporaries as Sparky. Here was a young man whom everyone considered to be of Polish extraction who was a free spirit, a proven athlete, a natural communicator with strong broad shoulders, black hair greased back in the fashion of the time and had played Romeo in the Boys Grammar School's adaptation of the Shakespearian classic. But as it was a school for boys, the female roles were taken by the junior pupils whose voices were still unbroken.

Something had inspired young Miller to read for the part of Juliet and despite the lewd remarks, the jeering and the jostling of his contemporaries was pleased and surprised to discover that he had passed the audition. Maurice Miller had discovered his true vocation. To his delight he found that he learned his lines quickly and effortlessly. accepting the direction of the English Master without a qualm. The strenuous and very demanding rehearsals took place after school but the lad was in his element. All the other players were fine, loved the sword play of the rival gangs and one of the older boys performed the role of the Nurse with a half beard which was shaved off in time.

What the boy had not realised, however, was that whilst giving the part all of his concentration, he was falling in love with the young man who played opposite him and this strange, visiting, emotion that stirred within him, was both exhilarating and terrifying. During the love scene, where they in fact did not kiss, Miller recalled the intoxicating aroma of Sparky, a concoction of musk, nicotine, brylcreem, hot breath and sweat. Although he found the whole experience disturbing he wanted desperately to open the door to his new found happiness and allow the stranger in. It was unrequited love. To make matters worse some of the older boys re -christened him 'Mandy' much to the schoolboy relish of the cast and crew.

When the play finished its short run of four nights Miller's world seemed to disintegrate although he had received high praise for his portrayal of the doomed girl, he also had to fend off the well aimed insults that were hurled at him by those around him who lacked sensitivity and grace. Ironically, and in particular, the leading man had made it patently clear that he was not interested in developing any kind of friendship with little 'Missy Mandy' and had, at the end of the show, punched the fair haired lad in the face as if to emphasise the point. It was like cracking a walnut with a crowbar.

To compound the feeling of restless incomprehension, Miller had found himself, a few nights later entwined with a girl at a party at the Church Club. He had allowed himself the privilege of drinking a bottle of Bulmer's in the graveyard, without the consent of the vicar, and willingly fell to the mercy of an older girl. When she had unceremoniously uncupped her bra and placed his hand on her cold breast he had felt a sense of revulsion and disgust and when she had shrieked with laughter at his embarrassment, he had fled, stumbling through the looming lopsided gravestones until he slipped to the floor, burst into tears and promptly threw up.

He lay there recovering, his shirt stained with vomit and tears, trying desperately to keep a check on his anger. He despised the young woman, so brazenly confident of her raw sexual power; he hated the arrogant and strutting Romeo who had so blatantly rejected his affec-

tions, he despised the school, the uncaring and mis-
guided masters for allowing him to become a figure of
scorn, subjected to such a torment; but above all he
loathed himself. As he sat there in a tangle of twisted
emotion and as the moon waltzed above him, he made a
calculated decision. From now on he was not perhaps
certain of what he wanted in life but he was absolutely
certain of what he did not want.

The funeral service of this Mihailovic was to take
place on the following Wednesday morning at a Catholic church which was known to Miller. He would find
his way there without any difficulty, knew the bus
routes and their connections, some of the drivers were
familiar to him, some spoke to him with cheerful abandonment whist others were dour and serious and
checked his bus pass like a Gestapo officer. To his
added pleasure the local Golf Club was arranging the
post service refreshments.

Sitting at his desk he planned his day like a military
exercise, consulting the bus time tables and writing
down the times into a little black book. He then exam-
ined closely his bank statement, noting the various entries of his standing orders, his direct debits and the few
dividends received from a small but profitable share
portfolio. Wednesday would suit him well and he
hoped that the food on offer would be as agreeable as
the other times he had been there. When he attended to
his garden that evening as dusk drew shadows all
around him, he felt again the nagging twinges of pain in
his body and he wondered what the near future held for
him.

As he lay in bed that night he began to reminisce
about his unhappy schooldays. Why did he torment
himself with the recollections of spiteful remarks, silly

nicknames, innuendo, accusations about his private life and filthy jokes about lifting shirts and being up the pole? It had offended him, disgusted him and all those years later he felt he carried the cloak of shame and humiliation that had never been quite able to shake off. The self depreciation had never really left him. Some consolation had been found in a prestigious Theatre club he had joined. It was an association that accepted unquestionably the misfit, the misunderstood. A haven. Miller had made a few friends there and was secure in the theatrical world knowing he was respected; admired even.

He stepped out of his bed and reached for his dressing gown and slippers. He was wide awake although it was gone midnight and usually at this hour he would be safely asleep. In the shadows of his lounge he opened the curtains and saw his lawn and garden bathed in moonlight. It was a mild night and he opened the window a little to let in the air. He could smell the faint flower fragrances and he felt a sense of aloneness. He put on a piece of music and stood silently by the window drinking in the beauty of the night. The piece was by Donizetti: Una Furtiva Lagrima. As the moon rose higher a furtive tear traced its way down his left cheek. The fleeting shadow of a young animal slunk its way across the garden and vanished into the foliage by the silver birch. It might have been a cat or even a small, half grown fox. As he climbed the stairs he thought once more of the boy that had been called Sparky. Notwithstanding the bitter sweet memory of Romeo and Juliet and the pain of spurned affection, he still clung by his fingernails the image of the young Adonis winning the one hundred yards race final in the school sports, his head held at an angle as he breasted the tape, eyes half closed in concentration, a silver St Christopher medallion glinting in the sun and his black hair sticking to his forehead. What had become of him? Very soon after that, the young man's family suddenly moved from the area, the torch that Miller had carried for him was extinguished and placed aside as Sparky left the school and was never seen or heard of again.

On that particular Wednesday morning, Miller rose a little earlier than normal, ironed and pressed a clean lemon coloured shirt, polished his shoes and selected a light grey herring bone suit from his wardrobe. The irritating weather girl on the television, all glittering teeth and dyed hair, had reminded the viewers that they might need to take an umbrella today as if it was any of her business to tell him how to behave. He snorted and shouted at the television before silencing her tirade by the press of a button.

"If I wish to get soaked to the skin it's my business!" and he laughed out loud at his sense of outrage and noted the irony of the situation of laughing all the way to a funeral. Having washed and dressed, brushed his thinning fair hair and looking as immaculate as a visiting matinee idol, he stepped outside and proceeded to the bus stop. He carried on his arm a rolled up black umbrella even though it was clear day, just in case.

The church was two thirds full when Miller arrived. Several small groups of people stood outside, speaking in hushed tones either waiting for family and friends or simply delaying their entrance into the church. As was his custom, Miller kept his head low as he entered and took the white order of service card from an usher dressed in funeral black. He was desperate to look at the picture on the front to search for any connection with his memory but placed the pamphlet in his pocket and took a pew sitting at the end as always. The congregation rose to sing the entrance hymn and Miller again declined the opportunity to glance in the direction of the coffin or the enlarged photograph of the deceased. He was afraid of being disappointed.

When the priest began his greeting and introduction, it became very clear to Miller that this was not the funeral of a man he had once known in his adolescence and despite the initial smack of rejection he began to feel a sense of relief. He was a happier soul, grateful for the things he had, his home, his possessions and his health and when they sang The Lord's My Shepherd he felt in his heart that perhaps life had a meaning after all. The words "Goodness and mercy all my life shall surely follow me." rang out echoing around the church and Miller felt elation in his heart. He scrutinised the photograph of the deceased, searching for some semblance of memory, something to trigger off a response but found nothing. It was not Sparky.

During the communion hymn he excused himself and with the minimum of fuss steered a path to the exit. The fresh air caressed his face as he stepped outside. He spoke to no one and no one spoke to him. He decided that he would walk to the golf club which was about a mile and a half away. The physical exercise would do him good and he hated the undignified finality of a crematorium, the lack of ritual, the façade of a church where recorded organ music reminded him of some tacky television show from an earlier age. He knew the route to the Golf Club, had travelled this way before and he had plenty of time on his hands. The sun was high and birds sang, seemingly oblivious to the pain and suffering of the world. He smiled as he recognised the songs of the blackbird as it perched on a telegraph pole, its yellow beak prominent against the black background.

He remembered how different it had been forty or so years earlier when he had turned his back on the Grammar School life, opting to leave school with a small clutch of "O" levels and seek a new life in London. How simple it had been to get a job with an insurance firm, a position that required very little brain power for a young man with no ambition other than a quiet life and to be left alone. There had been ample opportunities for promotion over the succeeding years which Miller had either ignored or politely declined and although his salary increased steadily he was happy enough to walk through his career.

He seldom had stopped to think about what others in the firm thought of him. They perceived him as a bit of a character, an odd bod, an asexual eccentric but as his work was always of a high standard, his reliability unquestioned and his attendance and punctuality impeccable, his colleagues grudgingly learned to respect him; the snide remarks thrown in his direction became less frequent, attempts at trying to change his ways diminished and in general he became an integral part of the organisation.

Over the years one or two females had shown a vague romantic interest in him and had tried to encourage Miller to join the social club, to make small talk in the canteen, to join in on company outings, to have a drink after work. But all their attempts had fallen on stony ground. He made a distinction between his private life and the public one. His friends were few but he liked it that way.

He was hungry when he arrived at the entrance to the Golf Club. The fresh air had whetted his appetite. A few sportsmen, dressed to the nines, were practising their putting skills on a side course and the car park was full to overflowing. There were many mourners in the vicinity exiting from vehicles, milling around, jackets removed and some smoking furtively before entering the premises and Miller felt the familiar tightening of his stomach and the wave of anxiety that travelled through him.

There was a sign which read "Funeral" and an arrow pointing in the appropriate direction. There was a general hum of conversation as he entered the large function room. At the far end was a set of French Windows opening out to the greens where the sun sparkled. There was a well stocked bar where two men in white jackets served the customers; two long tables where an assortment of cold food was expertly laid out on crisp white cloths and there were a number of tables where people sat around eating and drinking. In the toilet he washed his hands thoroughly and inspected the image in the mirror. He was satisfied with his appearance.

He had perfected his role play. He would simply stand in line with his plate in hand and help himself to what was available. He liked Scotch Eggs, tomatoes and cold chicken. He collected a serviette, a cold soft drink and found a table as far away as possible from the main food area. It was impossible to sit alone on such occasions and he knew he would have to make polite conversation whenever necessary. From where he was seated in a darkened corner, he had a good surveillance position so that he was able to view what was happening around him.

A young couple sat opposite him but after a cursory nod in his direction showed only an interest in themselves, guzzling food as if they had not eaten in days.

She was berating her companion about something, speaking rapidly, her nose twitching with her mouth full of food. A strand of lettuce hung from the corner of her mouth and she wiped it away quickly with a cloth and continued to chide her husband or boyfriend. Miller could not ascertain whether she wore a wedding ring. Looking around the crowded rooms he assured himself that there was nobody there that he knew. In the corridor he glimpsed a young man who had removed his jacket, studiously playing the fruit machines. From the expression on the young man's face it did not look as if he were winning. The gambler took out a twenty pound note from a wallet and Miller watched him carefully place the money into the waiting jaws of the machine like a sacrificial ritual.

Miller had failed to notice that there were several children in the room, some clinging to their mother's hand whilst one or two ran around on the balcony outside where the steps led to the greens. He would allow himself one alcoholic drink on funeral occasions; usually a large gin and tonic and subsequently he rose from his seat to make his way to the bar. He had failed to spot a little girl carrying a plate of ice cream come dashing towards him the plate slipping from her tiny hand and the contents spilling over his shirt and trousers. His immediate instinct was of anger but he instantly controlled his emotion and began to gather up the plate and the remnants of the ice cream. He smiled meekly as the child stared at him with wide eyed bewilderment. Miller fished for his handkerchief and began to wipe himself down when he heard a man's voice.

"Very sorry! Are you alright? Here. Let me help you."

Miller, on his knees, looked up and felt light headed as he stared at the vision of a young man looking down at him. As he began to rise, the vision spun, blurred and then the lights went out.

When he came to, he found, to his acute embarrassment, that he was seated surrounded by a sea of perplexed and anxious faces. He hoped he had not appeared like an abandoned beached whale. The man who had been the reason for the loss of oxygen was now standing in front of him as clear and as defined as the memory of the lost love. A glass of brandy was placed in Miller's hand and he was ordered to drink it by the younger man. Miller dutifully did as he was told and sipped the drink feeling the recovering warmth shudder through his body.

"Where's the St. Bernard?" he asked meekly with a ridiculous grin.

"I must have lost my balance. Am so sorry, causing an upheaval like this."

"It's ok. My name is Steffan. Steffan Mihailovic and this is my daughter Tina. Say hullo to Mister?"

"Miller. Maurice Miller." He was astounded that he had given his real name. The little girl smiled at him and to his greater sense of absurdity Miller found himself conversing with a child.

"Hullo Tina. And how old are you?"

"Four and three quarters!" she replied breaking the ice with the radiant smile of an angel.

Miller felt twenty years younger. It was a combination of the contents of a large brandy and the intoxication of seeing the young man who so resembled the Romeo of his long lost youth. He had the same broad shoulders, the pale blue eyes that seemed to glow, the shock of black hair which was also greased and brushed

157

back at the sides. What Miller did not particularly like was the little gold earring that pierced his left lobe. There was no sign of the little girl's mother but Miller was desperate to involve Steffan in conversation, any kind of chat that would keep him here.

For the first time in many a month Miller was speaking the truth to people, opening up his heart and pleading for the stranger to enter his life. He insisted on buying Steffan a drink and at the bar he hoped he had enough money to pay. As it happened, the drinks were still on the tab of the deceased's family. Steffan was waiting for him when he returned with another brandy for himself and a pint of lager for his new found friend.

They stepped outside where to Miller's irritation, Steffan lit a cigarette. Although Miller detested the obnoxious smell of tobacco. he was peculiarly reminded of the sensual aroma that had surrounded Sparky all those years ago and he was determined not to lose the interest of Steffan who appeared to show a genuine concern for the older man. They found an empty table on the balcony and sat down facing the greens. In the distance could be seen rolling greens of the golf course, trees, golfers moving like giant insects across a green desert. Steffan was a good listener and Miller found himself opening his heart to this stranger that had shown him kindness. He watched the younger man sip his beer and studiously smoke his cigarette. He noticed that he wore an identity bracelet on his right hand and a silver watch on his left but there was no ring on a finger.

"Are you retired Mister Miller?"

"Oh yes, life of leisure you might say. Get up when I want and go to bed whenever. And you? You work?"

158

"I'm a self employed. A humble landscape gardener. Here! Have a card."

Miller took the little card and glancing at it noted the address and telephone number.

"Can give you my e mail address if you want?"

"No. That will be fine. I do not have a computer thank you. But I might need the assistance of a gardener."

About three weeks passed before Miller decided to pick up the telephone and contact the gardener. It was a fact that he needed someone to tend to the garden, rearrange it, mow the lawn, cut the grass and destroy the weeds and keep it in good shape. When it was agreed that the gardener would visit him on the Friday evening after his day's work, Miller was delighted and began to make plans in his usual meticulous way. Steffan asked if he could bring his daughter too and although Miller was a little disappointed at this, had wanted the young man's company to himself, he added his confirmation.

When he did his weekly Waitrose shopping he added a few more items to his list: some cans of lager, a carton of mixed flavoured ice cream and frozen raspberries. He had never subjected himself to such luxury but there was a new sense of purpose in his life, a reason for being alive and someone else to think about other than his precious self.

When Steffan arrived, carrying his daughter in his arms, Miller observed that he was twenty minutes late, was unshaven and had obviously stopped for a drink or two after work. Undeterred, Miller ushered his guests through the house and onto the patio outside the back door. It had been a nice day but now dark clouds obscured the early evening sunshine. A small garden table was laid for drinks and on it a pad and pen had been placed so that notes could be taken by the men if necessary. He looked quite different in his working clothes; sleeves rolled up, indistinct tattoos on forearms, heavy boots and tough denim jeans and the remnant of a roll up dangling from his lips. It was quite a contrast from the suited young man he had met at the funeral. Miller opened a can of lager and gave it to the gardener who nodded and poured the contents expertly into the waiting glass. Tina was given a smaller drink of orange juice and was allowed to play on the grass skipping away in her own world clutching a little rag doll and talking to herself as the two men discussed business.

Adolescent butterflies danced and cavorted amongst the flowers to the delight of the wide eyed child who chased after them gurgling with laughter. When the business was concluded and arrangements settled, Miller fetched the raspberries and the ice cream. It had been a very long time since he had played host to any visitor but tonight he was more than happy to do so. He sensed that Steffan, who had probably been working hard all day, was now more visibly relaxed and the two men sat either side of the table, Miller resplendent in a straw hat and the child happy to sit on the grass making a red and white mess with the dessert. It was like a scene from a Chekhov play, the silver birch trees, the setting sun and the air of melancholy that hung over them all. Miller got up and strolled to the child who sat with a bowl of ice-cream in her lap. Miller bent down gingerly, removing his hat, to speak to her.

"Is it nice Tina?"

"You don't like ice cream," she replied spooning ice cream into her mouth.

"Oh I do. I love ice cream. It's my favourite."

"No you don't. You don't like ice cream," staring at the figure that towered over her, she finished, with great relish the whole bowl and then wiped her mouth with the back of her hand. The sound of laughter was a genial intrusion to the evening bird song's serenade.

Slowly a business relationship began to develop between the two men. Steffan found the whole experience a fascination whilst Miller was hoping that the younger man would become a trusted friend. Sooner or later he would have to ask the question. And so, the arrangements were finalised. The gardener would arrive every two weeks, always in the mid morning, parking his little van on Miller's driveway. He always paid the young man in cash, the money secreted in a brown envelope and passed to him without a word.

Miller looked forward to their meeting, prepared strong Columbian coffee as he anticipated the sound of the van and enjoyed his company. On this one particular morning it started to rain heavily and Steffan had to abandon the mowing and take sanctuary in the kitchen where Miller poured him a mug of coffee. Steffan sat rather moodily staring at the rain which came down like needles. The question asked was like a body blow.

"Why did you come to my cousin's funeral? You did not know him and none of us know you. What's the game mate?"

Miller felt his stomach turn over and a shortage of breath almost overcame him.

"It's a long story. Shall I start from the beginning?"

Steffan sat without moving and without any sign of emotion as Miller began telling him about the boy called Sparky. It was as absurd a story as he'd ever heard but there was earnestness in Miller's monologue that made him acknowledge that it could only be the truth, strange and obtuse as it may have appeared. Miller spoke slowly and deliberately as if he were in a courtroom choosing his lines carefully without actually declaring undying love and desire, whilst Steffan listened with deep concentration until the ambiguity of silence prevailed. Miller stood up suddenly and left the kitchen for a minute or two returning directly with a large photo album which he placed on the table.

"Let me show you my theatrical pictures. I am a bit of a thespian you know."

The younger man did not respond to the remark other than to raise his eyebrows and wipe his stubble. The album contained impressive, professionally taken photographs of Miller in a number of acting roles where he looked handsomely distinguished in one and equally roguish in another.

"This is me as Iago in Othello, Astrov in Uncle Vanya and here's a good one. Pastor Manders in Ghosts. Do you know it?"

"I saw the film with Demi Moore and Patrick Wassisname in it. Don't remember a Pastor."

"Different play dear boy! Ibsen. Here, have a look at this one and see if you recognise anyone in it."

He indicated a small crumpled, fading black and white snapshot of a group of schoolboys where Miller and Sparky stood in the centre of a make shift stage surrounded by an assortment of supporting actors. Miller watched the young man's face as he scrutinised the image, hoping for a flash of recognition or some reaction. Instead he tasted the acid sting of disappointment.

"Where are you in this one? I don't see you. And who is the pretty little blonde bird?"

"The little blonde bird as you call her, is me, fourteen in a wig. And that is Romeo. Sparky. Your dad?"

"I need a leak. Excuse me a minute please."

"Of course. Use the downstairs one. You know where it is."

The clatter of his boots echoed around the kitchen and the rain continued to shed its tears on the outside window. Miller stepped to his desk and retrieved a little jewel box which he placed in the pocket of his trousers. He poured another coffee and waited for the man to return. Mihailovic emerged, after what had seemed a long time, from the outside toilet wiping his hands on his jeans and glancing at his watch. Time was money and he had not got all day to sit and listen to the rambling anecdotes of an ageing luvvie who was left hand drive to boot and as nutty as a fruit cake.

"Let me show you one more thing as I know you have to go soon."

He produced the jewel box which made Steffan laugh out loud and remark.

"Sorry Mister Miller. Already married mate and about to be divorced. Ha ha!"

Miller smiled broadly at the attempt at wit by the film fan. He indicated for him to sit down then opened the lid of the box and handed it to him. To his astonishment Steffan saw a small tooth lying there on a soft bed of red velvet.

"When your father punched me in the face all those years ago he dislodged a tooth. I have kept it since. Not quite sure why. Something to do with fairies perhaps? He needn't have done that to me. All I wanted Steff was to be his friend, but he had other ideas I guess. He was as confused as me. Wish I could tell him that now. You have to tell me whether he is still alive and if..."

163

"He's dead. Got himself killed in a car crash in Spain of all places, about ten years ago."

It was time for Miller to listen now as he was fairly certain that this would no doubt be the first and last time he would hear the story of Sparky. He waited whilst Steffan gathered his thoughts and cleared his throat.

"My grandfather was from Serbia, or Yugoslavia as it was known in those days, but soon after the war was over he came to England and married my grandmother. She was from Essex somewhere. They moved from place to place wherever my grandfather could get work so they say. My dad and I were never close. He had joined the Merchant Navy and had fallen in love with foreign travel I guess and he divorced my mother when I was about fourteen. She burned a lot of things after he went, clothes and pictures and that and little things. She didn't want to be reminded of him, always bringing her down as guys often do. So I lost touch with him and when the news came of his death I felt nothing, no sense of loss. As far as I was concerned, he had died a long time ago. Now my mother is dead too and my wife is about to divorce me. Great life eh? I have access to Christina. My little gel. Or Tina as we call her. So Marco, I mean Marky, or Sparky as you called him, was not an influential figure in my life."

"Did he ever mention me?"

There was a note of desperation in Miller's voice as he searched for an answer from the young man.

"Let me get my tools now the rain has stopped."

Whilst the tools were gathered and despatched to the little van, Miller returned the album and the jewel box that contained the tooth, to the desk closing the drawer gently but with a firm finality. His whole body ached and he needed to lie down and have a sleep to take away the weariness of it all. The young man returned and stepped back into the kitchen.

"He mentioned that when he was in school he was pretty wayward, a bit of a tear away, showed me a cross he always wore around his neck that some girl had given him on his fourteenth birthday. He liked the girls and they liked him. He said he had been a bit of a sod to a younger boy when he was in the fifth form. I think the boy could have, must have, been you Maurice. I think he was sorry for the way he had messed up. Repentant. That's the word. Thank you for the coffee. It will be half term in a couple of weeks. I'd like to bring my little princess with me. If it's okay with you?"

"Yes of course. I'd be delighted. Come earlier I'll make breakfast for the three of us. Bacon and eggs, sausages, and baked beans and mushrooms and ice cream. We'll have a picnic on the lawn even if it rains."

"Even if it rains! That's handsome mate. I look forward to it."

So the morning came and as in all fairy stories, the sun began to shine. Everything in the garden was growing. Spring had sprung alright and the birds were having a singing competition in between scoffing themselves. Miller was cooking in the kitchen, with the door wide open, to let out the fumes and he sang to himself. He wore an apron and his straw hat. On the dot, his visitors arrived and they came echoing down the alleyway to the backdoor. The little girl ran to the older man and hugged him. It was difficult for him to conceal his happiness. She had made him a present: a drawing of a horse, an unusual horse as it was purple in colour and had a neck as long as an inquisitive giraffe. He quickly found some drawing pins and mounted in on the wall for all to see. Steff had brought a bottle of wine and some quiche and he looked as if he had stepped out of the bath, all spruced and clean shaven.

Little Tina helped her dad to lay the table outside on the lawn and he pointed out to her the various birds that sang. When they had finished the breakfast and Tina had another piece of toast, complete with marmite, they decided a stroll on the lawn was next on the menu. Miller decided to show her the flowers in his garden whilst Steff collected the plates and began to stack them in the washing up bowl.

It was then the fox cub appeared over in the corner of the garden where the silver birch grew. The young fox stopped in its tracks and stared at the little girl and the man in the straw hat. The child froze and met the stare, eyes like saucers, slowly gripping Miller's hand in a mixture of fear and excitement. The little fox with the reddish brown brush sniffed and with a quick turn slunk back into the shadows of the hedgerow. The beautiful little girl looked up and smiled at Miller, her eyes blue and full of wonder. A small white cloud obscured the sun for a moment and Miller pointed it out tracing with his finger the silver lining that could be seen. She looked up too and continued to hold his hand in hers.

Two Green Leaves

It was hardly more than a mountain stream which became a river when it reached the foot of the valley and was joined by two smaller tributaries. The smaller brooks chattered and protested until they were embraced by the parent and immediately their noise was placated like a mother would when comforting her two crying infants. Surrounded on both sides by deciduous trees, ancient oaks and towering beeches, hand in hand with blackthorns and hazels, the convergence of water created a natural, dark, pool deep enough for young men to swim in during the summer months and appropriate enough for the small holders and hill farmers to wash their flocks before the annual shearing. It was also a place where sometimes a leisurely walk would take place on a Sunday afternoon and an ideal place for courting couples too.

The countryside was in full bloom, blossom abounding, birds in harmony with nature, their songs of joy, innocent to the troubled world, filling the air. Swallows swooped and dived, feeding on the wing, butterflies danced drunkenly on the early morning breeze and occasionally a kingfisher flashed upstream in a splash of blue and orange.

The dawn was breaking and as the first shoots of sunlight were mirrored on the placid surface of the pool, a young woman could be seen sitting as silent as a stone statue on a large boulder at the river's edge. Here the current was smooth and steady as she dangled her bare feet in the water. She was nearly seventeen. She was slowly pinning up her fair hair that had fallen down upon her shoulders and she was practised and precise in her movement and manner. She screwed up her eyes in concentration, her mouth full of pins as she completed the ritual. She had removed her boots that now stood in waiting under a blackberry bush along with a small brown suitcase and a pair of men's black hob nailed boots.

Almost in mid stream, on another boulder, chipped and moss-covered, sat a young man in a pair of brown corduroy trousers and a collarless shirt, his bare feet also cooling in the water. He was shaving. She watched now, with a deep attentive look as he gingerly held a small mirror in one hand and expertly shaved with a cutthroat in his right hand. She was fascinated by the way he expertly manoeuvred the blade around the contours of his young face. She returned to looking at the river's slow flow and she sighed deeply. To her eyes, the colour of the water was like the strong tea she had poured so many times from the silver pot in the dining room of the big house. She knew that soon she would have to go back to her place of work naively hoping that nobody had noticed her absence. She did not want to return but she had little choice. But for the present, she did not move and continued to stare into the dark water deep in thought.

He wiped the edge of his razor on the seat of his breeches and carefully secreted it into his pocket. He too sighed deeply, the memory of the night before still precious and immediate in his mind. He also was in no hurry to move but considered that he had made up his mind after having weighed up the pros and cons and after having spoken to both the Vicar, who had been very understanding and had simply listened, and to the Major, his employer, who had been not only understanding but supportive too. To his eyes the river looked the colour of the strong beer that was served in the tap room of the tavern he occasionally frequented. It was a rich dark colour with the specks of foam that swirled on the surface. He sat hearing only the lull of the river and in the distance the plaintive cry of the morning lark.

"Listen! The distant song of the lark. Do you hear it? The lark is risen."

She smiled faintly and nodded although she could not hear the music of the morning, only the gentle murmur of the lifting breeze. She thought she could hear the crow of the cockerel in a neighbouring farm but the song of the lark had eluded her. She did not want to disappoint him so she did not contradict his statement. She reached up to the hazel branch above her and plucked off two dark green perfectly shaped leaves that curved in a broad arc to a fine point. The hazel nuts were not yet ripe and so she refrained from picking them. She dipped the leaves into the water and caressed her face with them in a curious and childlike manner and then she placed them both in the water. The current slowly parted the leaves and one veered into the bank and got tangled up with the debris that lay there, whilst the other slipped away into the deep centre of the current and finally was swept away, disappearing out of all sight and sound. She felt her heart jump for no apparent reason.

She had been born and raised in the parish, had attended the village school where she had eventually learned to read and write under the supervision of the patient and long suffering spinster assistant teacher, and had endured the wrath of the Headmaster if she or any of the other children had stepped out of line. The school itself, a cold, grey, stone building with two classrooms, was always full to overflowing with the children of the neighbourhood. She had not been very happy there and had failed to make any lasting friendships. The lessons, such as they were, were beyond her most of the time and the mountain stream in her thoughts meandered so easily out of the big window and over the green hills.

When the Headmaster had spoken of great men from history, names like Wellington, Mr. Gladstone, Nelson and Julius Caesar, she had no inkling as to their fame and had made the class laugh out loud when, in her innocence, she had enquired whether the Master had known Mr. Caesar. Her sense of red faced shame and humiliation condemned her to never speaking out or asking a question again.

Now she was employed, like so many of her contemporaries, as a maid in the big house on the hill. Life was marginally better; she had a clean bed to herself, albeit in a cramped little room at the top of the stairs, and there was always plenty of food. She would not starve. She said very little, behaved herself, was always obedient and polite, followed the instructions given her by the governess, to wash, scrub, and peel potatoes, sew and stitch, serve at the table and do any other chore that was necessary, and accepted her lot in life. She could count, write her name and that was all that was needed. She was the youngest of five children, all of whom had left home almost before she was born and she had been christened Victoria Maud.

He strode slowly and deliberately out of the water and as he passed her, still sitting dreamily on the boulder, he brushed her shoulder with his hand. He sat on the bank and quietly lit a pipe whilst his feet dried in the pale morning sun. She was fascinated by the way he was meticulous in his action, precise, clear and assertive. She watched as he got up slowly, tapped the contents of the pipe on to the bark of a silver birch and finished dressing, adjusting the collar of his shirt to accommodate a thin brown and white spotted tie. It seemed to her that they were the only people left on earth in the particular, holy silence of the morning. It was like an empty church. She saw him extract an old gold timepiece from his waistcoat and with deft movements wind it. It was a slow and calculated ritual. She noticed too, how his hands lovingly caressed the smooth casing of the watch as he returned it to his pocket. These were the same hands that had explored her body and loved her for so long. He was looking hard at her as if measuring her with his eye. She blushed slightly, averting his gaze as if he had been reading her mind. He smiled slowly and spoke.

"We must go directly. I dare not miss the train."

He had been born in a nearby parish some ten miles or so away, but such was the scattered but close community that people knew each other and often shared the same festivals and country pursuits. He was the only child of a widowed mother and he had left school with the barest of education but had been quick to learn and now as a young man of eighteen summers was an avid reader. He was a ploughman, noted for his prowess throughout the county and had won prizes in local agricultural shows. He had a way with horses and was well regarded by his employer, Colonel Wendover, who owned and farmed a big estate at the top of the valley. His own father had been killed in an accident during the harvest one year when a pitchfork had pierced his heart when he had accidently stumbled over some loose stones. The Colonel, anxious to keep the peace and maintain his position in the community, had generously allowed the widow and her young child to continue to live, rent free, in one of the little cottages on the estate.

They had named the boy Aubrey John and he was merely two years old when his father was laid to rest in the churchyard. Aubrey was well liked, good to his mother, honest as the day is long, a steadfast worker and to top it all had a beautiful singing tenor voice. When he had sung "Come into the garden Maud" in the Reading Room one dark November night, the young girl, sitting quietly at the back of the audience, with the far-away look in her eyes had been convinced that he was singing it to her. She was correct in her assumption and not long afterwards he gave her a little token of his affection in the shape of a handmade love spoon carved from the sycamore tree. She had accepted his gift with a shy smile, and the little symbol of his love, with its intricate and delicate carving, was placed under the pillow of her bed.

He finished dressing and she sat buttoning and lacing the little shoes that were neat and tiny on her feet. She carried no belongings whilst he placed a brown bowler hat rather obliquely on his thick dark hair and picked up the dark russet-coloured small suitcase that carried his meagre possessions. She had not seen its contents and did not want to now as she got up, brushed her dress and touched her hair. They began to walk slowly from the intimate and private spot by the river and followed the flow downstream along the well-worn path. The dew was still heavy on the ground and soon his boots were glistening in the early sun, with wild yellow flowers clinging to his heels. She held his arm, silently pleading with him to change his mind and reconsider. They saw the ancient little Parish Church on the hill, the grave-stones bending one way and then another as if avoiding a strong wind, surrounded by the yews, and she sighed audibly, gripping his arm just a little bit harder. Had she not imagined, perhaps a little foolishly, walking down the aisle in the little church to meet him at the altar?

They emerged from the river side into the grounds of the Healing Wells where the pungent smell of sulphur filled the air. She made a face and smiled up at him. He raised his eyebrows and continued to stare straight ahead, his jaw as determined as his resolve. The Hotel that accommodated and welcomed the visitors who came year after year to drink from the healing waters was slowly awakening, and already there was wood smoke emerging from the old tall chimneys. The familiar and comforting smell of smoke soon obliterated the gun-powder-like aroma that had infiltrated their senses. Maud was again suddenly reminded that she would soon be missed at the big house but she immediately dis-missed the thought from her mind and accepted the fact she would have to face the music later.

The grounds of the Hotel were impressive: a small boating lake, a bowling green, a tennis court and a band-stand. As they ventured past the adjoining stables and outhouses, they heard the deep snorting of the animals and the clump of iron shoes on the floor. There were various small carriages littered around the vicinity but it was still early and no sign of the paying guests. They continued to walk, although her heart was heavy and her small body ached with weariness. At the kissing gates which creaked and clanged when opened, he kissed her tenderly on the lips as she closed her eyes and lifted her face to meet his. He gently removed a piece of straw that had lodged itself in her summer dress and the touch of his fingers brought the blood rushing once more to her face.

Maud had barely been able to contain her excitement when she received a letter from him, smuggled to her by the trustworthy man who delivered the post and who was always given a glass of milk from the big house whilst his cob was given a pail of water. The postman had slipped the envelope to her discreetly when no one else was looking and she was grateful for his kindness. The note was written in bold upright letters using black lead pencil and informed her that presently he would have some important news for her as he was going to speak to both the Vicar and the Colonel. She was intrigued but blissfully happy and she pondered over what news he was going to tell her. She wistfully considered the possibility of living with Aubrey in a little cottage on the estate as his wife. Could this really happen? After all, he had declared his love for her, had given her a love spoon which she had accepted, and now she looked forward to Sunday night after the church service where they would meet.

The Vicar had been very fair minded and patient when Aubrey had sought his advice. There had been no trace of self-importance or condescension and that had warmed the young man's heart. The two men had sat in one of the many rooms in the draughty and dusty Vicarage. The walls were lined with books of contrasting shape and size and the clergyman's desk was littered with papers and writing utensils. Aubrey gazed with great interest at the library and the Vicar pointed out the various names of the writers. They sat around the empty hearth and the Vicar seemed very concerned at the young man's dilemma. The quiet, reserved man had suggested that each individual had to search his own conscience, ask himself the questions and make up his own mind about the conundrum. These were indeed troubled times and despite the public clamour, the increasing propaganda, the wave of patriotism that had swept across the land like a sudden tide, the decision would have to be entirely his own.

The Vicar had gently reminded Aubrey of the responsibility he carried for his widowed mother, but had not at any stage in the conversation tried to persuade or dissuade. He had also discussed the future and the immediate plans. It was evident that the older man was enjoying the company of his visitor and they began to discuss one or two of the books on show. Some of the writers were unknown to Aubrey and he was touched when the Vicar suddenly reached for a volume from the shelf and, wiping the cover with the sleeve of his coat, handed it to the young man.

"Read it at your leisure and return it when it's completed."

Aubrey began to protest but the Vicar merely held up a hand and shook his head. It was a copy of "A Tale of Two Cities" and although Aubrey had heard of the great writer, he had not yet had the opportunity of reading the novel. At the door they shook hands and the kindly vicar simply stated:

"You must also speak to your young lady. Maud, isn't it?"

He could of course not speak to Maud about anything until he had first consulted with his employer, who had reluctantly agreed to meet him the next morning. Aubrey was used to the back door of the great Georgian house and was bemused when one of the giggling girl servants led him into the deep recess of the echoing house and knocked on a door.

There was a log fire in the drawing room when Aubrey entered, despite the fact it was a warm early summer's day outside. Two ancient Labradors were stretched on the rug before the fire and they each opened an eye, saw there was no forthcoming food and went back to their dreaming. Each man took a seat either side of the fire. Despite his apprehension, and firmly knowing his place, he spoke in a measured voice both candidly and openly to the Colonel who in turn stroked his moustache and listened impassively. The Colonel, a white haired man in his late sixties, back as straight as a crowbar, realised within minutes of their conversation that the young man was sincere and serious about his ambition and resolve. The Colonel was quick to assert that the job of ploughman and general farm worker would be kept open for him until his return, and the Colonel gave a firm assurance that the cottage would be retained for the young man's widowed mother.

The old soldier pointed out the various hardships that lay ahead, the importance of self sacrifice and a rigid sense of discipline that was necessary. He was generous in his praise for his employee and was impressed with his hard work. The Colonel even insisted on arranging his travel and would give him a letter of introduction to the commanding officer in Shrewsbury. Aubrey was taken aback by the Colonel's generosity and merely nodded his agreement. The Colonel was in his element and looking at the young man that now stood to attention before him was filled with pride and a certain amount of envy.

"If only I were twenty years younger. I'd have a crack at the Hun, show the blighter a thing or two. Good luck young man!"

When they finally were able to meet on the Sunday night after Evensong, Maud was full of excitement and apprehension but tried to contain herself until they had both dismounted from his horse and the animal was tethered to a sapling by the river's edge. They retired to a secluded and private spot where they had done their courting over the last few months and she waited for his news. Aubrey, on the other hand, had been rehearsing his speech over the last few days but now when the words were to be uttered he was almost tongue-tied.

Maud had quite plausibly associated the Vicar, the Colonel and Aubrey with plans for the couple's future and when she was told of Aubrey's decision her heart fell at her feet. She tried not to display her feelings, had learned very early in life that if you were too open with your emotions you were set up for ridicule, but her face was like a torn piece of fine clothing and she bit her lip to stop herself from crying. He had mentioned in his rambling monologue, words and names of places that she had never heard, adding to her confusion and feeling that she was not worthy of him. What in the world was the Yeomanry Brigade? What did he mean when he spoke of mobilisation and armaments? Who was this man they called the Kaiser and what had he to do with Aubrey?

She recalled that she had been to Shrewsbury once on the train with her mother, had remembered a castle, a big bridge over a wide river, and a tea room where she had eaten scones and jam. Perhaps France was near the old Shropshire town and he would soon come back when he tired of his new adventure. The saddest thing for Maud was that he was going away to do something that she could not comprehend and was leaving her behind. She felt redundant and unwanted. A broken toy that is quietly discarded and forgotten.

They lay in silence that evening, a channel of cold confusion between them, and she did not return his kisses as she had so eagerly done so many times before. When he took her home that night, she left without a departing kiss or a reassuring word. She stole silently up the creaking stairs to her attic room and it seemed there was a dark shadow across the moon that had risen above the trees on the hill. She quietly prised open the little window and the cool night air entered but the aura of sadness and despair would not disappear.

Presently they left the wooded area and arrived on to the road that led into the small town. The empty school was silent now, eerie and unreal. She could imagine the sounds of children laughing with ribbons and swirling skirts, playing their childish games. A hullaballoo of hoops and handkerchiefs. The wonderful smell of baking bread met them at the top end of the street, and she suddenly felt the gnawing pangs of hunger. She had not eaten a thing since leaving the big house to meet Aubrey who was leaving on the morning train. They passed a row of little houses, some with flowers around the door, then a few shops that had not yet opened their doors to the new day.

The dark double doors of the Smithy with its new wagon wheels proudly standing outside along with a sprinkling of farm implements, was open, and already the blacksmith was at work lighting the fire for his forge. Aubrey stopped and stared into the interior of the shop. The wiry little man emerged and they exchanged words and warmly shook hands. The man nodded and smiled at Maud and disappeared into the shop. Maud could see two dead rabbits hanging on one door, their lifeless eyes staring at nothing. She shuddered as they continued their slow trek towards the station.

The Drapery shop was as quiet and still as the fine clothes that were arranged in the window and she noticed also that, in some of the larger houses in the long street, faces were staring behind the stirring curtains. They walked in silence, although she gripped his arm with an iron hand. He noticed The White Horse with its doors still open from the night before and the aroma of stale beer and tobacco emanating from its murky interior. There were empty barrels and crates of lifeless flagons in the yard and one or two traps waiting for their ponies. A wisp of blue smoke writhed slowly from an ivy-covered chimney. He wondered when he would once again share a beer with friends in the old ale house and join in with the singing of the old well-loved songs.

He glanced at Maud and it seemed her eyes were red from crying and lack of sleep. He sighed but continued their journey past the Ironmonger, the Butcher's shop where soon the cold carcasses of meat would be displayed in the window and the shoemaker's where the little man with a mouthful of tacks would sit hunched amongst a sea of footwear.

There were a few people at the station and the fussy little porter with his whistle and flag walked briskly up and down the platform looking intently at his watch now and again. A horse and cart stood waiting for provisions to be collected and an unhappy looking youth with a flat cap pulled over the side of his head, stood holding the horse's bridle. Maud was conspicuously the only female in the group. The silence was heavy. A magpie flashed by and landed on the slanting roof of the station building. She stood alone as Aubrey went into the Booking Office to finalise the arrangements of his journey. She could hear the muffled voices from within and she wished once again she were going with him.

"Who will take me to the November fair if you are not here?"

Aubrey did not reply but studiously checked the contents of his travel documents, including the letter of introduction from his benefactor, Colonel Wendover, and the book that the benign vicar had loaned him. He concluded that she would wait for his return but he had no inkling of when that would be. The ambiguity of silence prevailed.

At last the moment she had been dreading finally arrived with the distant sound of the approaching train. The porter began issuing instructions in a loud and assertive voice but nobody moved in response. The chugging of the engine got louder as the shiny, black, sweating, iron, animal snorted and hissed its way to a standstill in the little station. In the clamour of noise, soot and steam, a few men got off, doffed their hats to Maud and continued on their business. One or two men got on and the cart-horse flashed his tail and pawed the ground with his front feet.

He held her tightly for a second, said nothing in the way of farewell, and then in a matter of seconds he too was gone. The train pulled out of the station and slowly trundled its way northwards on the single line. She stared at its disappearing carriages, seeing the white puffs of smoke merge with the white clouds of the still and sad summer's morning.

When she passed through the little town on her way back to her place of work, she paused to drink from the pump on the square. The cold water revived her a little and she shuddered again at the thought of what awaited her. Whatever the consequences, now and in the future, she would accept without a murmur of dissent or contradiction. Half-way up the hill to the big house she turned and saw the little river glinting in the sun and heard the ring of the anvil in the Blacksmith's shop. Its steady, slow rhythm was like the sombre tolling of a bell.

Lightning Source UK Ltd.
Milton Keynes UK
18 November 2010

163034UK00001B/1/P